Internetworking With TCP/IP

Vol I:

Principles, Protocols, and Architecture

Fourth Edition

DOUGLAS E. COMER

Department of Computer Sciences
Purdue University
West Lafayette, IN 47907

PRENTICE HALL
Upper Saddle River, New Jersey 07458

Library of Congress Cataloging-in-Publication Data

Comer, Douglas
     Internetworking with TCP/IP / Douglas E. Comer. -- 4th ed.
        p. cm.
     Includes bibliographical references and index.
     ISBN 0-13-018380-6
     1. Principles, protocols, and architecture. 2. Client/server
     computing. 3. Internetworking (Telecommunications) I. Title

Publisher: *Alan Apt*
Project Manager: *Ana Arias Terry*
Editorial Assistant: *Toni Holm*
Vice-president and director of production and manufacturing, ESM: *David W. Riccardi*
Vice-president and editorial director of ECS: *Marcia Horton*
Executive Managing Editor: *Vince O'Brien*
Managing Editor: *David A. George*
Editorial/production supervision: *Irwin Zucker*
Art Director: *Heather Scott*
Assistant to Art Director: *John Christiana*
Manufacturing Buyer: *Pat Brown*
Marketing manager: *Danny Hoyt*

©2000, 1995 Prentice Hall
Prentice-Hall, Inc.
Upper Saddle River, New Jersey 07458

Prentice Hall books are widely used by corporations and government agencies for training, marketing, and resale. The publisher offers discounts on this book when ordered in bulk quantities.
For more information, contact Corporate Sales Department, Phone: 800-382-3419;
Fax: 201-236-7141; E-mail: corpsales@prenhall.com
Or write: Prentice Hall PTR, Corp. Sales Dept., One Lake Street, Upper Saddle River, NJ 07458.

UNIX is a registered trademark of UNIX System Laboratories, Incorporated
proNET-10 is a trademark of Proteon Corporation
LSI 11 is a trademark of Digital Equipment Corporation
Microsoft Windows is a trademark of Microsoft Corporation
EUI-64 is trademark of the Institute of Electrical and Electronics Engineers (IEEE)

Printed in the United States of America
10   9   8   7   6   5   4   3   2

ISBN 0-13-018380-6

Prentice-Hall International (UK) Limited, *London*
Prentice-Hall of Australia Pty. Limited, *Sydney*
Prentice-Hall Canada Inc., *Toronto*
Prentice-Hall Hispanoamericana, S.A., *Mexico*
Prentice-Hall of India Private Limited, *New Delhi*
Prentice-Hall of Japan, Inc., *Tokyo*
Pearson Education Asia Pte Ltd
Editora Prentice-Hall do Brasil, Ltda., *Rio de Janeiro*

To Chris

About The Author

Dr. Douglas Comer is an internationally recognized expert on TCP/IP protocols and the Internet. One of the researchers who contributed to the Internet as it was being formed in the late 1970s and 1980s, he was a member of the Internet Architecture Board, the group responsible for guiding the Internet's development. He was also chairman of the CSNET technical committee and a member of the CSNET executive committee.

Comer consults for companies on the design and implementation of networks, and gives professional seminars on TCP/IP and internetworking to both technical and nontechnical audiences around the world. His operating system, Xinu, and implementation of TCP/IP protocols are documented in his books, and used in commercial products.

Comer is a professor of computer science at Purdue University, where he teaches courses and does research on computer networking, internetworking, and operating systems. In addition to writing a series of best-selling technical books, he serves as the North American editor of the journal *Software — Practice and Experience.* Comer is a Fellow of the ACM.

Additional information can be found at:

www.cs.purdue.edu/people/comer

Contents

Chapter 5   Mapping Internet Addresses To Physical Addresses (ARP)   77

Chapter 6   Determining An Internet Address At Startup (RARP)   89

Chapter 7   Internet Protocol: Connectionless Datagram Delivery   95

Chapter 8   Internet Protocol: Routing IP Datagrams   115

Chapter 9   Internet Protocol: Error And Control Messages (ICMP)   129

Chapter 10   Classless And Subnet Address Extensions (CIDR)   147

Chapter 11   Protocol Layering   177

Chapter 12   User Datagram Protocol (UDP)   197

Chapter 13   Reliable Stream Transport Service (TCP)   209

Chapter 14 Routing: Cores, Peers, And Algorithms   253

Chapter 15 Routing: Exterior Gateway Protocols And Autonomous   269
Systems (BGP)

Chapter 16   Routing: In An Autonomous System (RIP, OSPF, HELLO)   293

Chapter 17   Internet Multicasting   319

Chapter 18   TCP/IP Over ATM Networks

353

Chapter 19   Mobile IP

377

Chapter 20   Private Network Interconnection (NAT, VPN)   389

Chapter 21   Client-Server Model Of Interaction   403

Chapter 22   The Socket Interface   413

Chapter 23   Bootstrap And Autoconfiguration (BOOTP, DHCP)   443

Chapter 26   Applications: File Transfer And Access (FTP, TFTP, NFS)   497

Chapter 27   Applications: Electronic Mail (SMTP, POP, IMAP, MIME)   511

Chapter 28   Applications: World Wide Web (HTTP)   527

Chapter 29   Applications: Voice And Video Over IP (RTP)   539

Chapter 30   Applications: Internet Management (SNMP)   553

Chapter 33   The Future Of TCP/IP (IPv6)   **599**

Appendix 1   A Guide To RFCs   **623**

Appendix 2   Glossary Of Internetworking Terms And Abbreviations   **673**

Bibliography   **721**

Index   **729**

Foreword

This is the fourth edition of a landmark book, the book that signaled the coming of age of the Internet. Development of the protocols for the Internet started around 1974, and they had been in limited but real use starting in the early 80's, but as of 1987, there was still no good introduction to how they worked or how to code them. The standards documents for TCP, IP and the other protocols existed, of course, but the true truth — the collection of knowledge and wisdom necessary to implement a protocol stack and actually expect it to work — that was a mystery, known only to a small band of the initiated. That was not a good thing, and the initiated knew it. But it takes a lot of effort to pull all the right stuff together and write it down. We waited, knowing that a good book explaining TCP/IP would be an important step towards the broad acceptance of our protocols.

And Doug wrote the book.

We told jokes, waiting for the book. We looked to see how many books there were in mature fields, and speculated that the number of books was a metric of success. I actually went and looked to see how many books there were on ''how to build a compiler'' (a post-mature field by now, perhaps — time to count the books again). The compiler community was well off, and even ''how to build a database'' was available. But nothing on ''how to build a TCP/IP.'' And then we got our book.

Of course, knowing that back then this was a landmark book is not enough to make you buy it. Collectors might want to find the first edition, but that gives the true truth as of 12 years ago, a long time in Internet years. And that is why this is the fourth edition. A lot has changed over that time. We have learned a lot more, the field has grown up, whole new protocols have emerged, and Doug has rewritten the book three times. That is a measure both of how much and how fast the field changes, and how much work must go into keeping this book current. It has all the new stuff, and our best current knowledge about all the old stuff.

Other things have changed in 12 years. Not only has the Internet grown up, but some of our heroes have grown old, and some have died. The foreword to the first edition was written by Jon Postel, one of the true Internet pioneers, who died in the fall of 1998. Below, we have reprinted the foreword he wrote for the first edition. Much is the same, but much has changed. This is still a very readable book both for details on TCP/IP and for an introduction to communications protocols in general. But in 1987, Jon wrote ''Computer communication systems and networks are currently separated and fragmented. The goal of interconnection and internetworking, to have a single powerful computer communication network, is fundamental to the design of TCP/IP.'' Only 12 years ago networks were fragmented; today the Internet unites the world. And TCP/IP is still the glue, at the core of the Internet, that makes all this work. And this is still the book to read to learn about it.

David Clark
Massachusetts Institute of Technology

December, 1999

Foreword To The First Edition
By The Late Jon Postel

In this book Professor Douglas Comer has provided a long sought overview and introduction to TCP/IP. There have been many requests for "the" article, report, or book to read to get started on understanding the TCP/IP protocols. At last, this book satisfies those requests. Writing an introduction to TCP/IP for the uninitiated is a very difficult task. While combining the explanation of the general principles of computer communication with the specific examples from the TCP/IP protocol suite, Doug Comer has provided a very readable book.

While this book is specifically about the TCP/IP protocol suite, it is a good book for learning about computer communications protocols in general. The principles of architecture, layering, multiplexing, encapsulation, addressing and address mapping, routing, and naming are quite similar in any protocol suite, though, of course, different in detail (See Chapters 3, 10, 17, and 18)†. Computer communication protocols do not do anything themselves. Like operating systems, they are in the service of applications processes. Processes are the active elements that request communication and are the ultimate senders and receivers of the data transmitted. The various layers of protocols are like the various layers in a computer operating system, especially the file system. Understanding protocol architecture is like understanding operating system architecture. In this book Doug Comer has taken the "bottom up" approach — starting with the physical networks and moving up in levels of abstraction to the applications.

Since application processes are the active elements using the communication supported by the protocols, TCP/IP is an "interprocess communication" (IPC) mechanism. While there are several experiments in progress with operating system style message passing and procedure call types of IPC based on IP, the focus in this book is on more traditional applications that use the UDP datagram or TCP logical connection forms of IPC (See Chapters 11, 12, 17, 18, and 19).

One of the key ideas inherent in TCP/IP and in the title of this book is "internetworking." The power of a communication system is directly related to the number of entities in that system. The telephone network is very useful because (nearly) all of the

---

†Editor's note: chapter numbers have changed since the first edition.

telephones are in (as it appears to the users) one network. Computer communication systems and networks are currently separated and fragmented. The goal of interconnection and internetworking, to have a single powerful computer communication network, is fundamental to the design of TCP/IP. Essential to internetworking is addressing (See Chapters 4, 5, and 6), and a universal protocol — the Internet Protocol (See Chapters 7, 8, and 9).

To have an internetwork the individual networks must be connected. The connecting devices are called gateways. Further, these gateways must have some procedures for forwarding data from one network to the next. The data is in the form of IP datagrams and the destination is specified by an IP address, but the gateway must make a routing decision based on the IP address and what it knows about the connectivity of the networks making up the Internet. The procedures for distributing the current connectivity information to the gateways are called routing algorithms, and these are currently the subject of much study and development (See Chapters 13, 14, 15, and 16).

Like all communication systems, the TCP/IP protocol suite is an unfinished system. It is evolving to meet changing requirements and new opportunities. Thus, this book is, in a sense, a snapshot of TCP/IP circa 1987. And, as Doug Comer points out, there are many loose ends (See Chapter 20).

Most chapters end with a few pointers to material "for further study." Many of these refer to memos of the RFC series of notes. This series of notes is the result of a policy of making the working ideas and the protocol specifications developed by the TCP/IP research and development community widely available. This availability of the basic and detailed information about these protocols, and the availability of the early implementations of them, has had much to do with their current widespread use. This commitment to public documentation at this level of detail is unusual for a research effort, and has had significant benefits for the development of computer communication (See Appendix 3).

This book brings together information about the various parts of the TCP/IP architecture and protocols and makes it accessible. Its publication is a very significant milestone in the evolution of computer communications.

Jon Postel,
Internet Protocol Designer and
Deputy Internet Architect

December, 1987

Preface

The explosive growth of the Internet continues. When the third edition of this book was written five years ago, the Internet connected 4.8 million computers, up from 5,000 when the first edition was published. The Internet now reaches over 56 million computers, meaning that the 1995 Internet was only about 8% of its current size. During the early 1990s, those of us who were involved with the Internet marveled at how large an obscure research project had become. Now, it pervades almost every aspect of society.

TCP/IP has accommodated change well. The basic technology has survived nearly two decades of exponential growth and the associated increases in traffic. The protocols have worked over new high-speed network technologies, and the design has handled applications that could not be imagined in the original design. Of course, the entire protocol suite has not remained static. New protocols have been deployed, and new techniques have been developed to adapt existing protocols to new network technologies.

This edition contains updated information throughout the text as well as new material that describes technical advances and changes. For example, because classless addressing has become widely deployed, the description of IP forwarding examines techniques for classless lookup. In addition, the chapters on IP describe the Differentiated Services (DiffServe) scheme for classes of service as well as path MTU discovery and anonymous networks. The chapter on TCP describes Random Early Drop (RED). The chapter on exterior routing has been updated to use BGP as the primary example. The descriptions of protocols such as RIP, IGMP, SNMP, and IPv6 have been revised to incorporate new versions and recent changes. Finally, the chapter on security discusses IPsec.

Four new chapters contain detailed information about significant developments. Chapter 19 describes mobile IP — a technology that allows a computer to move from one network to another without changing its IP address. Chapter 20 considers two technologies used to interconnect private intranets and the global Internet: Virtual Private Network (VPN) and Network Address Translation (NAT). Each solves a slightly different problem; both are widely deployed. Chapter 28 covers the HTML and HTTP protocols that form the basis for the most significant Internet application: the world wide web. Chapter 29 focuses on an exciting new area: sending real-time data such as voice and video over an IP network. The chapter examines the RTP protocol that allows a receiver to coordinate and play such data as well as the RSVP and COPS protocols that can be used to provide resource reservation, and describes the H.323 suite of protocols used for IP telephony.

The fourth edition retains the same general contents and overall organization as the third edition. The entire text focuses on the concept of internetworking in general and the TCP/IP internet technology in particular. Internetworking is a powerful abstraction that allows us to deal with the complexity of multiple underlying communication technologies. It hides the details of network hardware and provides a high level communication environment. The text reviews both the architecture of network interconnections and the principles underlying protocols that make such interconnected networks function as a single, unified communication system. It also shows how an internet communication system can be used for distributed computation.

After reading this book, you will understand how it is possible to interconnect multiple physical networks into a coordinated system, how internet protocols operate in that environment, and how application programs use the resulting system. As a specific example, you will learn the details of the global TCP/IP Internet, including the architecture of its router system and the application protocols it supports. In addition, you will understand some of the limitations of the internet approach.

Designed as both a college text and as a professional reference, the book is written at an advanced undergraduate or graduate level. For professionals, the book provides a comprehensive introduction to the TCP/IP technology and the architecture of the Internet. Although it is not intended to replace protocol standards, the book is an excellent starting point for learning about internetworking because it provides a uniform overview that emphasizes principles. Moreover, it gives the reader perspective that can be extremely difficult to obtain from individual protocol documents.

When used in the classroom, the text provides more than sufficient material for a single semester network course at either the undergraduate or graduate level. Such a course can be extended to a two-semester sequence if accompanied by programming projects and readings from the literature. For undergraduate courses, many of the details are unnecessary. Students should be expected to grasp the basic concepts described in the text, and they should be able to describe or use them. At the graduate level, students should be expected to use the material as a basis for further exploration. They should understand the details well enough to answer exercises or solve problems that require them to explore extensions and subtleties. Many of the exercises suggest such subtleties; solving them often requires students to read protocol standards and apply creative energy to comprehend consequences.

At all levels, hands-on experience sharpens the concepts and helps students gain intuition. Thus, I encourage instructors to invent projects that force students to use Internet services and protocols. The semester project in my graduate Internetworking course at Purdue requires students to build an IP router. We supply hardware and the source code for an operating system, including device drivers for network interfaces; students build a working router that interconnects three networks with different MTUs. The course is extremely rigorous, students work in teams, and the results have been impressive (many industries recruit graduates from the course). Although such experimentation is safest when the instructional laboratory network is isolated from production computing facilities, we have found that students exhibit the most enthusiasm, and benefit the most, when they have access to a functional TCP/IP internet.

The book is organized into four main parts. Chapters 1 and 2 form an introduction that provides an overview and discusses existing network technologies. In particular, Chapter 2 reviews physical network hardware. The intention is to provide basic intuition about what is possible, not to spend inordinate time on hardware details. Chapters 3-13 describe the TCP/IP Internet from the viewpoint of a single host, showing the protocols a host contains and how they operate. They cover the basics of Internet addressing and routing as well as the notion of protocol layering. Chapters 14-20 and 32 describe the architecture of an internet when viewed globally. They explore routing architecture and the protocols routers use to exchange routing information. Finally, Chapters 21-31 discuss application level services available in the Internet. They present the client-server model of interaction, and give several examples of client and server software.

The chapters have been organized bottom up. They begin with an overview of hardware and continue to build new functionality on top of it. This view will appeal to anyone who has developed Internet software because it follows the same pattern one uses in implementation. The concept of layering does not appear until Chapter 11. The discussion of layering emphasizes the distinction between conceptual layers of functionality and the reality of layered protocol software in which multiple objects appear at each layer.

A modest background is required to understand the material. The reader is expected to have a basic understanding of computer systems, and to be familiar with data structures like stacks, queues, and trees. Readers need basic intuition about the organization of computer software into an operating system that supports concurrent programming and application programs that users invoke to perform computation. Readers do not need sophisticated mathematics, nor do they need to know information theory or theorems from data communications; the book describes the physical network as a black box around which an internetwork can be built. It states design principles clearly, and discusses motivations and consequences.

I thank all the people who have contributed to versions of this book. Michael Evangelista provided extensive assistance with this edition, including classifying RFCs. Jeff Case provided the SNMPv3 example. John Lin and Dennis Totin commented on some of the new chapters. Jin Zhang, Kechiun He, and Sara Steinbrueck proofread parts of the text. Special thanks go to my wife and partner, Chris, whose careful editing made many improvements throughout.

Douglas E. Comer

January, 2000

What Others Have Said About The Fourth Edition Of Internetworking With TCP/IP

"This is the book I go to for clear explanantions of the basic principles and latest developments in TCP/IP technologies. It's a 'must have' reference for networking professionals."

Dr. Ralph Droms
Professor at Bucknell University

"When the Nobel committee turns its attention to the Internet, Doug gets the prize for literature. This is an updated classic that is the best way to master Internet technology."

Dr. Paul V. Mockapetris
Inventor of the Domain Name System

"The best-written TCP/IP book I have ever read. Dr. Comer explains complex ideas clearly, with excellent diagrams and explanations."

Dr. John Lin,
Bell Laboratories

"Comer continues to prove himself the Baedeker of the Internet Protocols with this fine 4th edition."

Dr. Vinton Cerf
Senior Vice president, MCI WorldCom

"There are many TCP/IP books on the shelves today, but Doug Comer's 'Internetworking with TCP/IP' is the one that comes *off* the shelf for accessible and authoritative answers to questions about Internet technology."

Dr. Lyman Chapin,
Chief Scientist, BBN Technologies

Other Books In the Internetworking Series
from Douglas Comer and Prentice Hall

Internetworking With TCP/IP Volume II: Design, Implementation, and Internals (with David Stevens), 3rd edition: 1999, ISBN 0-13-973843-6

Volume II continues the discussion of Volume I by using code from a running implementation of TCP/IP to illustrate all the details. The text shows, for example, how TCP's slow start algorithm interacts with the Partridge-Karn exponential retransmission backoff algorithm and how routing updates interact with datagram forwarding.

Internetworking With TCP/IP Volume III: Client-Server Programming and Applications (with David Stevens)

BSD Socket Version, 2nd edition: 1996, ISBN 0-13-260969-X
AT&T TLI Version: 1994, ISBN 0-13-474230-3
Windows Sockets Version: 1997, ISBN 0-13-848714-6

Volume III describes the fundamental concept of client-server computing used to build all distributed computing systems. The text discusses various server designs as well as the tools and techniques used to build clients and servers, including Remote Procedure Call (RPC). It contains examples of running programs that illustrate each of the designs and tools. Three versions of Volume III are available for the socket API (Unix), the TLI API (AT&T System V), and the Windows Sockets API (Microsoft).

Computer Networks And Internets (with a CD-ROM by Ralph Droms), 2nd edition: 1999, ISBN 0-13-083617-6

A broad introduction to data communication, networking, internetworking, and client-server applications, *Computer Networks And Internets* examines the hardware and software components that make up computer networks, from the lowest levels through applications. The text covers transmission and modems, LANs and LAN extensions, access technologies, WANs, protocols (including TCP/IP), and network applications. The CD-ROM features animations and data sets.

The Internet Book: Everything you need to know about computer networking and how the Internet works, 2nd edition: 1997, ISBN 0-13-890161-9, paperback

A gentle introduction to networking and the Internet, *The Internet Book* does not assume the reader has a technical background. It explains the Internet, how it works, and services available in general terms, without focusing on a particular computer or a particular brand of software. Ideal for someone who wants to become Internet and computer networking literate, *The Internet Book* explains the terminology as well as the concepts; an extensive glossary of terms and abbreviations is included.

To order, visit the Prentice Hall Web page at www.prenhall.com/
or contact your local bookstore or Prentice Hall representative.
In North America, call 1-515-284-6751, or send a FAX to 1-515-284-6719.

1

Introduction And Overview

1.1 The Motivation For Internetworking

Internet communication has become a fundamental part of life. The World Wide Web contains information about such diverse subjects as atmospheric conditions, crop production, stock prices, and airline traffic. Groups establish electronic mailing lists so they can share information of common interest. Professional colleagues exchange business correspondence electronically, and relatives exchange personal greetings.

Unfortunately, most network technologies are designed for a specific purpose. Each enterprise chooses hardware technology appropriate for specific communication needs and budget. More important, it is impossible to engineer a universal network from a single network technology because no single network suffices for all uses. Some groups need high-speed networks to connect computers in a single building. Low-cost technologies that fill the need cannot span large geographic distances. Other groups settle for a slower speed network that connects machines thousands of miles apart.

For over two decades, a new technology has evolved that makes it possible to interconnect many disparate physical networks and make them function as a coordinated unit. The technology, called *internetworking*, accommodates multiple, diverse underlying hardware technologies by providing a way to interconnect heterogeneous networks and a set of communication conventions that makes them interoperate. The internet technology hides the details of network hardware, and permits computers to communicate independent of their physical network connections.

The internet technology described in this book is an example of *open system interconnection*. It is called *open* because, unlike proprietary communication systems available from one specific vendor, the specifications are publicly available. Thus, anyone can build the software needed to communicate across an internet. More important, the entire technology has been designed to foster communication among machines with

1

diverse hardware architectures, to use almost any packet switched network hardware, to accommodate a wide variety of applications, and to accommodate multiple computer operating systems.

To appreciate internet technology, think of how it has changed business. In addition to high-speed communication among employees in the office environment, networking technologies provide instant feedback among the production side of the business, sales and marketing, and customers. As a result, the speed with which business can plan, implement, assess, and retool has increased; the change is dramatic.

1.2 The TCP/IP Internet

U.S. government agencies realized the importance and potential of internet technology many years ago, and have funded research that has made possible a global Internet. This book discusses principles and ideas underlying the internet technology that has resulted from research funded by the *Advanced Research Projects Agency (ARPA)*†. The ARPA technology includes a set of network standards that specify the details of how computers communicate, as well as a set of conventions for interconnecting networks and routing traffic. Officially named the TCP/IP Internet Protocol Suite and commonly referred to as *TCP/IP* (after the names of its two main standards), it can be used to communicate across any set of interconnected networks. For example, some corporations use TCP/IP to interconnect all networks within their corporation, even though the corporation has no connection to outside networks. Other groups use TCP/IP for communication among geographically distant sites.

Although the TCP/IP technology is noteworthy by itself, it is especially interesting because its viability has been demonstrated on a large scale. It forms the base technology for the global Internet that connects over 170 million individuals in homes, schools, corporations, and government labs in virtually all populated countries. In the U.S., The *National Science Foundation (NSF)*, the *Department of Energy (DOE)*, the *Department of Defense (DOD)*, the *Health and Human Services Agency (HHS)*, and the *National Aeronautics and Space Administration (NASA)* have all participated in funding the Internet, and use TCP/IP to connect many of their research sites. Known as the *ARPA/NSF Internet*, the *TCP/IP Internet*, the *global Internet*, or just the *Internet*‡, the resulting communication system allows subscribers to share information with anyone around the world as easily as they share it with someone in the next room. An outstanding success, the Internet demonstrates the viability of the TCP/IP technology and shows how it can accommodate a wide variety of underlying network technologies.

Most of the material in this book applies to any internet that uses TCP/IP, but some chapters refer specifically to the global Internet. Readers interested only in the technology should be careful to watch for the distinction between the Internet architecture as it exists and general TCP/IP internets as they might exist. It would be a mistake, however, to ignore all sections of the text that describe the global Internet — many corporate networks are already more complex than the global Internet of a dozen

---

†At various times, *ARPA* was called the *Defense Advanced Research Projects Agency (DARPA)*.

‡We will follow the usual convention of capitalizing *Internet* when referring specifically to the global Internet, and use lower case to refer to private internets that use TCP/IP technology.

years ago, and many of the problems they face have already been solved in the global Internet.

1.3 Internet Services

One cannot appreciate the technical details underlying TCP/IP without understanding the services it provides. This section reviews internet services briefly, highlighting the services most users access, and leaves to later chapters the discussion of how computers connect to a TCP/IP internet and how the functionality is implemented.

Much of our discussion of services will focus on standards called *protocols*. Protocols like TCP and IP provide the syntactic and semantic rules for communication. They contain the details of message formats, describe how a computer responds when a message arrives, and specify how a computer handles errors or other abnormal conditions. Most important, they allow us to discuss computer communication independent of any particular vendor's network hardware. In a sense, protocols are to communication what algorithms are to computation. An algorithm allows one to specify or understand a computation without knowing the details of a particular CPU instruction set. Similarly, a communication protocol allows one to specify or understand data communication without depending on detailed knowledge of a particular vendor's network hardware.

Hiding the low-level details of communication helps improve productivity in several ways. First, because programmers deal with higher-level protocol abstractions, they do not need to learn or remember as many details about a given hardware configuration. Thus, they can create new programs quickly. Second, because programs built using higher-level abstractions are not restricted to a particular computer architecture or a particular network hardware, they do not need to be changed when computers or networks are replaced or reconfigured. Third, because application programs built using higher-level protocols are independent of the underlying hardware, they can provide direct communication between an arbitrary pair of computers. Programmers do not need to build a special version of application software for each type of computer or each type of network. Instead, software built to use protocols is general-purpose; the same code can be compiled and run on an arbitrary computer.

We will see that the details of each service available on the Internet are given by a separate protocol. The next sections refer to protocols that specify some of the application-level services as well as those used to define network-level services. Later chapters explain each of these protocols in detail.

1.3.1 Application Level Internet Services

From the user's point of view, the Internet appears to consist of a set of application programs that use the underlying network to carry out useful communication tasks. We use the term *interoperability* to refer to the ability of diverse computing systems to cooperate in solving computational problems. Internet application programs exhibit a high degree of interoperability. Most users that access the Internet do so merely by running application programs without understanding the types of computers being accessed, the TCP/IP technology, the structure of the underlying internet, or even the path the data travels to its destination; they rely on the application programs and the underlying network software to handle such details. Only programmers who write network application programs need to view a TCP/IP internet as a network and need to understand some of the technology.

The most popular and widespread Internet application services include:

- *World Wide Web.* The Web allows users to view documents that contain text and graphics, and to follow hypermedia links from one document to another. The Web grew to become the largest source of traffic on the global Internet between 1994 and 1995, and continues to dominate. Some service providers estimate that the Web now accounts for 80% of their Internet traffic.

- *Electronic mail (e-mail).* Electronic mail allows a user to compose a memo and send a copy to individuals or groups. Another part of the mail application allows users to read memos that they have received. A recent innovation allows users to include ''attachments'' with a mail message that consist of arbitrary files. Electronic mail has been so successful that many Internet users depend on it for most correspondence. One reason for the popularity of Internet e-mail arises from a careful design: the protocol makes delivery reliable. Not only does the mail system on the sender's computer contact the mail system on the receiver's computer directly, but the protocol specifies that a message cannot be deleted by the sender until the receiver has successfully placed a copy on permanent storage.

- *File transfer.* The file transfer application allows users to send or receive a copy of a data file. File transfer is one of the oldest, and still among the most heavily used application services in the Internet. Although small files can now be attached to an e-mail message, the file transfer service is still needed to handle arbitrarily large files. The system provides a way to check for authorized users, or even to prevent all access. Like mail, file transfer across a TCP/IP internet is reliable because the two machines involved communicate directly, without relying on intermediate machines to make copies of the file along the way.

- *Remote login.* Remote login allows a user sitting at one computer to connect to a remote machine and establish an interactive login session. The remote login makes it appear that a window on the user's screen connects directly to the remote machine by sending each keystroke from the user's keyboard to the remote machine and displaying each character the remote computer prints in the user's window. When the remote login session terminates, the application returns the user to the local system.

We will return to these and other applications in later chapters to examine them in more detail. We will see exactly how they use the underlying TCP/IP protocols, and why having standards for application protocols has helped ensure that they are widespread.

1.3.2 Network-Level Internet Services

A programmer who creates application programs that use TCP/IP protocols has an entirely different view of an internet than a user who merely executes applications like electronic mail. At the network level, an internet provides two broad types of service that all application programs use. While it is unimportant at this time to understand the details of these services, they cannot be omitted from any overview of TCP/IP:

- *Connectionless Packet Delivery Service.* This service, explained in detail throughout the text, forms the basis for all other internet services. Connectionless delivery is an abstraction of the service that most packet-switching networks offer. It means simply that a TCP/IP internet routes small messages from one computer to another based on address information carried in the message. Because the connectionless service routes each packet separately, it does not guarantee reliable, in-order delivery. Because it usually maps directly onto the underlying hardware, the connectionless service is extremely efficient. More important, having connectionless packet delivery as the basis for all internet services makes the TCP/IP protocols adaptable to a wide range of network hardware.

- *Reliable Stream Transport Service.* Most applications need much more than packet delivery because they require the communication software to recover automatically from transmission errors, lost packets, or failures of intermediate switches along the path between sender and receiver. The reliable transport service handles such problems. It allows an application on one computer to establish a "connection" with an application on another computer, and then to send a large volume of data across the connection as if it were a permanent, direct hardware connection. Underneath, of course, the communication protocols divide the stream of data into small messages and send them, one at a time, waiting for the receiver to acknowledge reception.

Many networks provide basic services similar to those outlined above, so one might wonder what distinguishes TCP/IP services from others. The primary distinguishing features are:

- *Network Technology Independence.* Although TCP/IP is based on conventional packet switching technology, it is independent of any particular vendor's hardware. The global Internet includes a variety of network technologies ranging from networks designed to operate within a single building to those designed to span large distances. TCP/IP protocols define the unit of data transmission, called a *datagram*, and specify how to transmit datagrams on a particular network.

- *Universal Interconnection.* A TCP/IP internet allows any pair of computers to which it attaches to communicate. Each computer is assigned an *address* that is universally recognized throughout the internet. Every datagram carries the addresses of its source and destination. Intermediate switching computers use the destination address to make routing decisions.

- *End-to-End Acknowledgements.* The TCP/IP internet protocols provide acknowledgements between the original source and ultimate destination instead of between successive machines along the path, even if the source and destination do not connect to a common physical network.

- *Application Protocol Standards.* In addition to the basic transport-level services (like reliable stream connections), the TCP/IP protocols include standards for many common applications including electronic mail, file transfer, and remote login. Thus, when designing application programs that use TCP/IP, programmers often find that existing software provides the communication services they need.

Later chapters will discuss the details of the services provided to the programmer as well as many of the application protocol standards.

1.4 History And Scope Of The Internet

Part of what makes the TCP/IP technology so exciting is its universal adoption as well as the size and growth rate of the global Internet. ARPA began working toward an internet technology in the mid 1970s, with the architecture and protocols taking their current form around 1977-79. At that time, ARPA was known as the primary funding agency for packet-switched network research and had pioneered many ideas in packet-switching with its well-known *ARPANET*. The ARPANET used conventional point-to-point leased line interconnection, but ARPA had also funded exploration of packet-switching over radio networks and satellite communication channels. Indeed, the growing diversity of network hardware technologies helped force ARPA to study network interconnection, and pushed internetworking forward.

The availability of research funding from ARPA caught the attention and imagination of several research groups, especially those researchers who had previous experience using packet switching on the ARPANET. ARPA scheduled informal meetings of researchers to share ideas and discuss results of experiments. Informally, the group was known as the *Internet Research Group*. By 1979, so many researchers were involved in the TCP/IP effort that ARPA created an informal committee to coordinate and guide the design of the protocols and architecture of the emerging Internet. Called the Internet Control and Configuration Board (*ICCB*), the group met regularly until 1983, when it was reorganized.

The global Internet began around 1980 when ARPA started converting machines attached to its research networks to the new TCP/IP protocols. The ARPANET, already in place, quickly became the backbone of the new Internet and was used for many of the early experiments with TCP/IP. The transition to Internet technology became complete in January 1983 when the Office of the Secretary of Defense mandated that all computers connected to long-haul networks use TCP/IP. At the same time, the *Defense Communication Agency* (*DCA*) split the ARPANET into two separate networks, one for further research and one for military communication. The research part retained the name ARPANET; the military part, which was somewhat larger, became known as the *military network, MILNET*.

To encourage university researchers to adopt and use the new protocols, ARPA made an implementation available at low cost. At that time, most university computer science departments were running a version of the UNIX operating system available in the University of California's *Berkeley Software Distribution*, commonly called *Berkeley UNIX* or *BSD UNIX*. By funding Bolt Beranek and Newman, Incorporated (*BBN*) to implement its TCP/IP protocols for use with UNIX and funding Berkeley to integrate the protocols with its software distribution, ARPA was able to reach over 90% of university computer science departments. The new protocol software came at a particularly significant time because many departments were just acquiring second or third computers and connecting them together with local area networks. The departments needed communication protocols.

The Berkeley software distribution became popular because it offered more than basic TCP/IP protocols. In addition to standard TCP/IP application programs, Berkeley offered a set of utilities for network services that resembled the UNIX services used on a single machine. The chief advantage of the Berkeley utilities lies in their similarity to standard UNIX. For example, an experienced UNIX user can quickly learn how to use Berkeley's remote file copy utility (*rcp*) because it behaves exactly like the UNIX file copy utility except that it allows users to copy files to or from remote machines.

Besides a set of utility programs, Berkeley UNIX provided a new operating system abstraction known as a *socket* that allowed application programs to access communication protocols. A generalization of the UNIX mechanism for I/O, the socket has options for several types of network protocols in addition to TCP/IP. Its design has been debated since its introduction, and many operating systems researchers have proposed alternatives. Independent of its overall merits, however, the introduction of the socket abstraction was important because it allowed programmers to use TCP/IP protocols with little effort. Thus, it encouraged researchers to experiment with TCP/IP.

The success of the TCP/IP technology and the Internet among computer science researchers led other groups to adopt it. Realizing that network communication would soon be a crucial part of scientific research, the National Science Foundation (*NSF*) took an active role in expanding the TCP/IP Internet to reach as many scientists as possible. In the late 1970s, NSF funded a project known as the *Computer Science NETwork* (*CSNET*), which had as its goal connecting all computer scientists. Starting in 1985, NSF began a program to establish access networks centered around its six supercomputer centers. In 1986 it expanded networking efforts by funding a new wide area backbone network, called the *NSFNET*†, that eventually reached all its supercomputer centers and tied them to the ARPANET. Finally, in 1986 NSF provided seed money for many regional networks, each of which now connects major scientific research institutions in a given area. All the NSF-funded networks use TCP/IP protocols, and all are part of the global Internet.

Within seven years of its inception, the Internet had grown to span hundreds of individual networks located throughout the United States and Europe. It connected nearly 20,000 computers at universities, government, and corporate research laboratories. Both the size and the use of the Internet continued to grow much faster than anticipated. By

---

†The term *NSFNET* is sometimes used loosely to mean all NSF-funded networking activities, but we will use it to refer to the backbone. The next chapter gives more details about the technology.

late 1987, it was estimated that the growth had reached 15% per month. By 2000, the global Internet reached over 50 million computers in 209 countries.

Early adoption of TCP/IP protocols and growth of the Internet has not been limited to government-funded projects. Major computer corporations connected to the Internet as did many other large corporations including: oil companies, the auto industry, electronics firms, pharmaceutical companies, and telecommunications carriers. Medium and small companies began connecting in the 1990s. In addition, many companies have used the TCP/IP protocols on their internal corporate internets even though they choose not to be part of the global Internet.

Rapid expansion introduced problems of scale unanticipated in the original design and motivated researchers to find techniques for managing large, distributed resources. In the original design, for example, the names and addresses of all computers attached to the Internet were kept in a single file that was edited by hand and then distributed to every site on the Internet. By the mid 1980s, it became apparent that a central database would not suffice. First, because computers were being added to the Internet at an increasing rate, requests to update the file would soon exceed the personnel available to process them. Second, even if a correct central file existed, network capacity was insufficient to allow either frequent distribution to every site or on-line access by each site.

New protocols were developed and a naming system was put in place across the global Internet that allows any user to resolve the name of a remote machine automatically. Known as the *Domain Name System* (*DNS*), the mechanism relies on machines called *name servers* to answer queries about names. No single machine contains the entire domain name database. Instead, data is distributed among a set of machines that use TCP/IP protocols to communicate among themselves when answering a query.

1.5 The Internet Architecture Board

Because the TCP/IP internet protocol suite did not arise from a specific vendor or from a recognized professional society, it is natural to ask, "who sets the technical direction and decides when protocols become standard?" The answer is a group known as the *Internet Architecture Board* (*IAB*†). The IAB provides the focus and coordination for much of the research and development underlying the TCP/IP protocols, and guides the evolution of the Internet. It decides which protocols are a required part of the TCP/IP suite and sets official policies.

Formed in 1983 when ARPA reorganized the Internet Control and Configuration Board, the IAB inherited much of its charter from the earlier group. Its initial goals were to encourage the exchange of ideas among the principals involved in research related to TCP/IP and the Internet, and to keep researchers focused on common objectives. Through the first six years, the IAB evolved from an ARPA-specific research group into an autonomous organization. During these years, each member of the IAB chaired an *Internet Task Force* charged with investigating a problem or set of issues deemed to be important. The IAB consisted of approximately ten task forces, with charters ranging from one that investigated how the traffic load from various applica-

---

†IAB originally stood for *Internet Activities Board*.

tions affects the Internet to one that handled short term Internet engineering problems. The IAB met several times each year to hear status reports from each task force, review and revise technical directions, discuss policies, and exchange information with representatives from agencies like ARPA and NSF, who funded Internet operations and research.

The chairman of the IAB had the title *Internet Architect* and was responsible for suggesting technical directions and coordinating the activities of the various task forces. The IAB chairman established new task forces on the advice of the IAB and also represented the IAB to others.

Newcomers to TCP/IP are sometimes surprised to learn that the IAB did not manage a large budget; although it set direction, it did not fund most of the research and engineering it envisioned. Instead, volunteers performed much of the work. Members of the IAB were each responsible for recruiting volunteers to serve on their task forces, for calling and running task force meetings, and for reporting progress to the IAB. Usually, volunteers came from the research community or from commercial organizations that produced or used TCP/IP. Active researchers participated in Internet task force activities for two reasons. On one hand, serving on a task force provided opportunities to learn about new research problems. On the other hand, because new ideas and problem solutions designed and tested by task forces often became part of the TCP/IP Internet technology, members realized that their work had a direct, positive influence on the field.

1.6 The IAB Reorganization

By the summer of 1989, both the TCP/IP technology and the Internet had grown beyond the initial research project into production facilities on which thousands of people depended for daily business. It was no longer possible to introduce new ideas by changing a few installations overnight. To a large extent, the literally hundreds of commercial companies that offer TCP/IP products determined whether products would interoperate by deciding when to incorporate changes in their software. Researchers who drafted specifications and tested new ideas in laboratories could no longer expect instant acceptance and use of the ideas. It was ironic that the researchers who designed and watched TCP/IP develop found themselves overcome by the commercial success of their brainchild. In short, TCP/IP became a successful, production technology and the market place began to dominate its evolution.

To reflect the political and commercial realities of both TCP/IP and the Internet, the IAB was reorganized in the summer of 1989. The chairmanship changed. Researchers were moved from the IAB itself to a subsidiary group and a new IAB board was constituted to include representatives from the wider community.

Figure 1.1 illustrates the IAB organization and the relationship of subgroups.

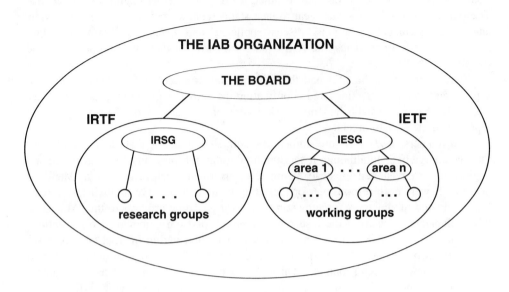

Figure 1.1 The structure of the IAB after the 1989 reorganization.

As Figure 1.1 shows, in addition to the board itself, the IAB organization contained two major groups: the *Internet Research Task Force* (*IRTF*) and the *Internet Engineering Task Force* (*IETF*).

As its name implies, the IETF concentrates on short-term or medium-term engineering problems. The IETF existed in the original IAB structure, and its success provided part of the motivation for reorganization. Unlike most IAB task forces, which were limited to a few individuals who focused on one specific issue, the IETF was large — before the reorganization, it had grown to include dozens of active members who worked on many problems concurrently. It was divided into over 20 *working groups*, each focusing on a specific problem. Working groups held individual meetings to formulate problem solutions. In addition, the entire IETF met regularly to hear reports from working groups and discuss proposed changes or additions to the TCP/IP technology. Usually held three times annually, full IETF meetings attracted hundreds of participants and spectators. The IETF had become too large for the chairman to manage.

Because the IETF was known throughout the Internet, and because its meetings were widely recognized and attended, the reorganized IAB structure retains the IETF, but splits it into approximately ten areas, each with its own manager. The IETF chairman and the area managers comprise the *Internet Engineering Steering Group* (*IESG*), the individuals responsible for coordinating the efforts of IETF working groups. The name ''IETF'' now refers to the entire body, including the chairman, area managers, and all members of working groups.

Created during the reorganization, the Internet Research Task Force is the research counterpart to the IETF. The IRTF coordinates research activities related to TCP/IP protocols or internet architecture in general. Like the IETF, the IRTF has a small group, called the *Internet Research Steering Group (IRSG)*, that sets priorities and coordinates research activities. Unlike the IETF, the IRTF is currently a much smaller and less active organization. In fact, most of the research is being done within the IETF.

1.7 The Internet Society

In 1992, as the Internet moved away from its U.S. government roots, a society was formed to encourage participation in the Internet. Called the *Internet Society (ISOC)*, the group is an international organization inspired by the National Geographic Society. The host for the IAB, the Internet Society continues to help people join and use the Internet around the world.

1.8 Internet Request For Comments

We have said that no vendor owns the TCP/IP technology nor does any professional society or standards body. Thus, the documentation of protocols, standards, and policies cannot be obtained from a vendor. Instead, the documentation is placed in on-line repositories and made available at no charge.

Documentation of work on the Internet, proposals for new or revised protocols, and TCP/IP protocol standards all appear in a series of technical reports called Internet *Requests For Comments*, or *RFC*s. RFCs can be short or long, can cover broad concepts or details, and can be standards or merely proposals for new protocols†. While RFCs are not refereed in the same way as academic research papers, they are edited. For many years, a single individual, Jon Postel‡, served as RFC editor. The task of editing RFCs now falls to area managers of the IETF; the IESG as a whole approves new RFCs.

Finally, a few reports pertinent to the Internet were published in an earlier, parallel series of reports called *Internet Engineering Notes*, or *IEN*s. Although the IEN series is no longer active, not all IENs appear in the RFC series. There are references to RFCs (and still a few to IENs) throughout the text.

The RFC series is numbered sequentially in the chronological order RFCs are written. Each new or revised RFC is assigned a new number, so readers must be careful to obtain the highest numbered version of a document; an RFC index is available to help identify the correct version.

To make document retrieval quicker, many sites around the world store copies of RFCs and make them available to the community. One can obtain RFCs by postal mail, by electronic mail, or directly across the Internet using a file transfer program. In addition, preliminary versions of RFC documents, which are known as *Internet drafts*,

---

†Appendix *1* contains an introduction to RFCs that examines the diversity of RFCs, including jokes that have appeared.

‡Jon passed away in the fall of 1998. He was one of the pioneers who made significant contributions to TCP/IP and the Internet. Those of us who knew him feel the loss deeply.

are also available. Ask a local network expert how to obtain RFCs or Internet drafts at your site, or refer to Appendix *1* for further instructions on how to retrieve them.

1.9 Internet Protocols And Standardization

Readers familiar with data communication networks realize that a myriad of communication protocol standards exist. Many of them precede the Internet, so the question arises, "Why did the Internet designers invent new protocols when so many international standards already existed?" The answer is complex, but follows a simple maxim:

> *Use existing protocol standards whenever such standards apply; invent new protocols only when existing standards are insufficient, and be prepared to use new standards when they become available and provide equivalent functionality.*

So, despite appearances to the contrary, the TCP/IP Internet Protocol Suite was not intended to ignore or avoid extant standards. It came about merely because none of the existing protocols satisfied the need for an interoperable internetworking communication system.

1.10 Future Growth And Technology

Both the TCP/IP technology and the Internet continue to evolve. New protocols are being proposed; old ones are being revised. NSF added considerable complexity to the system by introducing a backbone network, regional networks, and hundreds of campus networks. Other groups around the world continue to connect to the Internet as well. The most significant change comes not from added network connections, however, but from additional traffic. As new users connect to the Internet and new applications appear, traffic patterns change. When physicists, chemists, and biologists began to use the Internet, they exchanged files of data collected from experiments. Files of scientific data were large compared to electronic mail messages. As the Internet became popular and users began to browse information using services like the *World Wide Web*, traffic patterns increased again.

To accommodate growth in traffic, the capacity of the NSFNET backbone was increased three times. The final version, known as *ANSNET* after the company that supplied it, had a capacity approximately 840 times larger than the original. Since 1995, companies known as *Internet Service Providers* (*ISPs*) have each built their own backbone network, many of which have significantly more capacity than the last government-funded backbone. At the current time, it is difficult to foresee an end to the need for more capacity.

Growth in demands for networking is not unexpected. The computer industry has enjoyed a continual demand for increased processing power and larger data storage for many years. Users have only begun to understand how to use networks. In the future we can expect continual increases in the demand for communications. Soon, for example, TCP/IP technologies will be used for telephone and video services as well as data services. Thus, higher-capacity communication technologies will be needed to accommodate the growth.

Figure 1.2 summarizes expansion of the Internet and illustrates an important component of growth: much of the change in complexity has arisen because multiple groups now manage various parts of the whole. Because the technology was developed when a single person at ARPA had control of all aspects of the Internet, the designs of many subsystems depended on centralized management and control. As the Internet grew, responsibility and control were divided among multiple organizations. In particular, as the Internet became global, the operation and management needed to span multiple countries. Much of the effort since the early 1990s has been directed toward finding ways to extend the design to accommodate decentralized management.

	number of networks	number of computers	number of users	number of managers
1980	10	10^2	10^2	10^0
1990	10^3	10^5	10^6	10^1
2000	10^5	10^7	10^8	10^2

Figure 1.2 Growth of the connected Internet. In addition to traffic increases that result from increased size, the Internet faces complexity that results from decentralized management of both development and operations.

1.11 Organization Of The Text

The material on TCP/IP has been written in three volumes. This volume presents the TCP/IP technology, applications that use it, and the architecture of the global Internet in more detail. It discusses the fundamentals of protocols like TCP and IP, and shows how they fit together in an internet. In addition to giving details, the text highlights the general principles underlying network protocols, and explains why the TCP/IP protocols adapt easily to so many underlying physical network technologies. Volume II discusses in depth the internal details of the TCP/IP protocols and shows how they are implemented. It presents code from a working system to illustrate how the individual protocols work together, and contains details useful to people responsible for building a corporate internet. Volume III shows how distributed applications use TCP/IP for communication. It focuses on the client-server paradigm, the basis for all distributed programming. It discusses the interface between programs and protocols†, and shows how client and server programs are organized. In addition, Volume III describes the remote procedure concept, middleware, and shows how programmers use tools to build client and server software.

So far, we have talked about the TCP/IP technology and the Internet in general terms, summarizing the services provided and the history of their development. The next chapter provides a brief summary of the type of network hardware used throughout the Internet. Its purpose is not to illuminate nuances of a particular vendor's hardware, but to focus on the features of each technology that are of primary importance to an internet architect. Later chapters delve into the protocols and the Internet, fulfilling three purposes: they explore general concepts and review the Internet architectural model, they examine the details of TCP/IP protocols, and they look at standards for high-level services like electronic mail and electronic file transfer. Chapters *3* through *14* review fundamental principles and describe the network protocol software found in any machine that uses TCP/IP. Later chapters describe services that span multiple machines, including the propagation of routing information, name resolution, and applications like electronic mail.

Two appendices follow the main text. The first appendix contains a guide to RFCs. It expands on the description of RFCs found in this chapter, and gives examples of information that can be found in RFCs. It describes in detail how to obtain RFCs by electronic mail, postal mail, and file transfer. Finally, because the standard RFC index comes in chronological order, the appendix presents a list of RFCs organized by topic to make it easier for beginners to find RFCs pertinent to a given subject.

The second appendix contains an alphabetical list of terms and abbreviations used throughout the literature and the text. Because beginners often find the new terminology overwhelming and difficult to remember, they are encouraged to use the alphabetical list instead of scanning back through the text.

1.12 Summary

An internet consists of a set of connected networks that act as a coordinated whole. The chief advantage of an internet is that it provides universal interconnection while allowing individual groups to use whatever network hardware is best suited to their needs. We will examine principles underlying internet communication in general and the details of one internet protocol suite in particular. We will also discuss how internet protocols are used in an internet. Our example technology, called TCP/IP after its two main protocols, was developed by the Advanced Research Projects Agency. It provides the basis for the global Internet, a large, operational internet that connects universities, corporations, and government departments in many countries around the world. The global Internet is expanding rapidly.

---

†Volume III is available in three versions: one that uses the Unix *socket interface* interface in examples, a second that uses the *Transport Layer Interface* (*TLI*), and a third that uses the *Windows Sockets Interface* defined by Microsoft.

FOR FURTHER STUDY

Cerf's *A History Of The ARPANET* [1989] and *History of the Internet Activities Board* [RFC 1160] provide fascinating reading and point the reader to early research papers on TCP/IP and internetworking. Denning [Nov-Dec 1989] provides a different perspective on the history of the ARPANET. Jennings et. al. [1986] discusses the importance of computer networking for scientists. Denning [Sept-Oct 1989] also points out the importance of internetworking and gives one possible scenario for a world-wide Internet. The U.S. Federal Coordinating Committee for Science, Engineering and Technology [*FCCSET*] suggested networking should be a national priority.

The IETF (*ietf.org*) publishes minutes from its regular meetings. The Internet Society (*www.isoc.org*) produces newsletters that discuss the penetration of the Internet in countries around the world. The World Wide Web Consortium (*w3c.org*) produces protocols and standards for Web technologies. Finally, the reader is encouraged to remember that the TCP/IP protocol suite and the Internet continue to evolve; new information can be found in RFCs and at conferences such as the annual ACM SIGCOMM Symposium and NETWORLD+INTEROP events held around the world.

EXERCISES

1.1 Explore application programs at your site that use TCP/IP.

1.2 Plot the growth of TCP/IP technology and Internet access at your organization. How many computers, users, and networks were connected each year?

1.3 TCP/IP products account for several billion dollars per year in gross revenue. Read trade publications to find a list of vendors offering such products.

2

Review Of Underlying Network Technologies

2.1 Introduction

It is important to understand that the Internet is not a new kind of physical network. It is, instead, a method of interconnecting physical networks and a set of conventions for using networks that allow the computers they reach to interact. While network hardware plays only a minor role in the overall design, understanding the internet technology requires one to distinguish between the low-level mechanisms provided by the hardware itself and the higher-level facilities that the TCP/IP protocol software provides. It is also important to understand how the interfaces supplied by underlying packet-switched technology affect our choice of high-level abstractions.

This chapter introduces basic packet-switching concepts and terminology, and then reviews some of the underlying network hardware technologies that have been used in TCP/IP internets. Later chapters describe how these networks are interconnected and how the TCP/IP protocols accommodate vast differences in the hardware. While the list presented here is certainly not comprehensive, it clearly demonstrates the variety among physical networks over which TCP/IP operates. The reader can safely skip many of the technical details, but should try to grasp the idea of packet switching and try to imagine building a homogeneous communication system using such heterogeneous hardware. Most important, the reader should look closely at the details of the physical address schemes the various technologies use; later chapters will discuss in detail how high-level protocols use physical addresses.

2.2 Two Approaches To Network Communication

Whether they provide connections between one computer and another or between a terminal and a computer, communication networks can be divided into two basic types: *connection-oriented* (sometimes called *circuit-switched*) and *connectionless* (sometimes called *packet-switched†*). Connection-oriented networks operate by forming a dedicated *connection* or *circuit* between two points. The U.S. telephone system uses a connection-oriented technology — a telephone call establishes a connection from the originating phone through the local switching office, across trunk lines, to a remote switching office, and finally to the destination telephone. While a connection is in place, the phone equipment samples the microphone repeatedly, encodes the samples digitally, and transmits them across the connection to the receiver. The sender is guaranteed that the samples can be delivered and reproduced because the connection provides a guaranteed data path of 64 Kbps (thousand bits per second), the rate needed to send digitized voice. The advantage of connection-oriented networking lies in its guaranteed capacity: once a circuit is established, no other network activity will decrease the capacity of that circuit. One disadvantage of connection-oriented technology arises from cost: circuit costs are fixed, independent of use. For example, one pays a fixed rate for a phone call, even when the two parties do not talk.

Connectionless networks, the type often used to connect computers, take an entirely different approach. In a connectionless network, data to be transferred across a network is divided into small pieces called *packets* that are multiplexed onto high capacity intermachine connections. A packet, which usually contains only a few hundred bytes of data, carries identification that enables the network hardware to know how to send it to the specified destination. For example, a large file to be transmitted between two machines must be broken into many packets that are sent across the network one at a time. The network hardware delivers the packets to the specified destination, where software reassembles them into a single file again. The chief advantage of packet-switching is that multiple communications among computers can proceed concurrently, with intermachine connections shared by all pairs of computers that are communicating. The disadvantage, of course, is that as activity increases, a given pair of communicating computers receives less of the network capacity. That is, whenever a packet switched network becomes overloaded, computers using the network must wait before they can send additional packets.

Despite the potential drawback of not being able to guarantee network capacity, connectionless networks have become extremely popular. The motivations for adopting packet switching are cost and performance. Because multiple computers can share the network bandwidth, fewer connections are required and cost is kept low. Because engineers have been able to build high speed network hardware, capacity is not usually a problem. So many computer interconnections use connectionless networks that, throughout the remainder of this text, we will assume the term *network* refers to a connectionless network unless otherwise stated.

---

†In fact, it is possible to build hybrid hardware technologies; for our purposes, only the difference in functionality is important.

2.3 Wide Area And Local Area Networks

Data networks that span large geographical distances (e.g., the continental U.S.) are fundamentally different from those that span short distances (e.g., a single room). To help characterize the differences in capacity and intended use, packet switched technologies are often divided into two broad categories: *wide area networks* (*WANs*) and *Local Area Networks* (*LANs*). The two categories do not have formal definitions. Instead, vendors apply the terms loosely to help customers distinguish among technologies.

WAN technologies, sometimes called *long haul networks*, provide communication over long distances. Most WAN technologies do not limit the distance spanned; a WAN can allow the endpoints of a communication to be arbitrarily far apart. For example, a WAN can span a continent or can join computers across an ocean. Usually, WANs operate at slower speeds than LANs, and have much greater delay between connections. Typical speeds for a WAN range from 1.5 Mbps to 155 Mbps (million bits per second). Delays across a WAN can vary from a few milliseconds to several tenths of a second†.

LAN technologies provide the highest speed connections among computers, but sacrifice the ability to span long distances. For example, a typical LAN spans a small area like a single building or a small campus, and operates between 10 Mbps and 2 Gbps (billion bits per second). Because LAN technologies cover short distances, they offer lower delays than WANs. The delay across a LAN can be as short as a few tenths of a millisecond or as long as 10 milliseconds.

We have already stated the general tradeoff between speed and distance: technologies that provide higher speed communication operate over shorter distances. There are other differences among the technologies as well. In LAN technologies, each computer usually contains a device known as a *Network Interface Card* (*NIC*) that connects the machine directly to the network. The network itself need not contain much intelligence; it can depend on electronic interface devices in the attached computers to generate and receive the complex electrical signals. In WAN technologies, a network usually consists of a series of complex computers called *packet switches* interconnected by long-distance communication lines. The size of the network can be extended by adding a new switch and another communication line. Attaching a user's computer to a WAN means connecting it to one of the packet switches. Each switch along a path in the WAN introduces delay when it receives a packet and forwards it to the next switch. Thus, the larger the WAN becomes the longer it takes to route traffic across it.

This book discusses software that hides the technological differences among networks and makes interconnection independent of the underlying hardware. To appreciate design choices in the software, it is necessary to understand how it relates to network hardware. The next sections present examples of network technologies that have been used in the Internet, showing some of the differences among them. Later chapters show how the TCP/IP software isolates such differences and makes the communication system independent of the underlying hardware technology.

---

†Such long delays result from WANs that communicate by sending signals to a satellite orbiting the earth.

2.3.1 Network Hardware Addresses

Each network hardware technology defines an *addressing mechanism* that computers use to specify the destination for a packet. Every computer attached to a network is assigned a unique address, usually an integer. A packet sent across a network includes a *destination address field* that contains the address of the intended recipient. The destination address appears in the same location in all packets, making it possible for the network hardware to examine the destination address easily. A sender must know the address of the intended recipient, and must place the recipient's address in the destination address field of a packet before transmitting the packet.

Each hardware technology specifies how computers are assigned addresses. The hardware specifies, for example, the number of bits in the address as well as the location of the destination address field in a packet. Although some technologies use compatible addressing schemes, many do not. This chapter contains a few examples of hardware addressing schemes; later chapters explain how TCP/IP accommodates diverse hardware addressing schemes.

2.4 Ethernet Technology

Ethernet is the name given to a popular packet-switched LAN technology invented at Xerox PARC in the early 1970s. Xerox Corporation, Intel Corporation, and Digital Equipment Corporation standardized Ethernet in 1978; IEEE released a compatible version of the standard using the standard number *802.3*. Ethernet has become the most popular LAN technology; it now appears in virtually all corporate networks as well as many small installations. Because Ethernet is so popular, many variants exist. Although the original wiring scheme has been superceded, understanding the original design helps clarify the intent and some of the design decisions. Thus, we will discuss the original design first, and then cover variants.

Formally known as *10Base5*, the original Ethernet design uses a coaxial cable as Figure 2.1 illustrates.

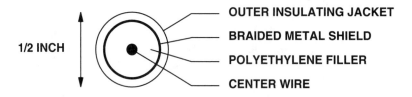

Figure 2.1 A cross-section of the coaxial cable used in the original Ethernet.

Called the *ether*, the cable itself is completely passive; all the active electronic components needed to make the network function are associated with the computers attached to the network. Each Ethernet cable is about 1/2 inch in diameter and up to 500 meters long. A resistor is added between the center wire and shield at each end to prevent reflection of electrical signals.

The connection between a computer and the original Ethernet coaxial cable requires a hardware device called a *transceiver*. Physically, the connection between a transceiver and the inner wire of an Ethernet cable enters through a small hole in the outer layers of the cable as Figure 2.2 illustrates. Technicians often use the term *tap* to describe such connections. Usually, small metal pins mounted in the transceiver go through the hole and provide electrical contacts to the center wire and the braided shield. Some manufacturers' connectors require that the cable be cut and a ''T'' inserted.

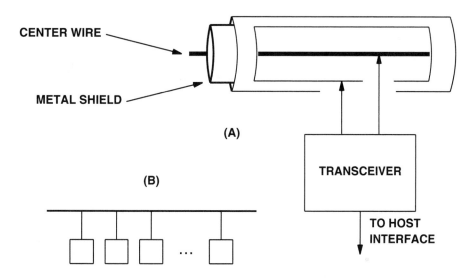

Figure 2.2 (a) A cutaway view of an Ethernet cable showing the details of electrical connections between a transceiver and the cable, and (b) the schematic diagram of an Ethernet with many computers connected.

Each connection to an original Ethernet uses two major electronic components. A *transceiver* connects to the center wire and braided shield on the cable, sensing and sending signals on the ether. A *host interface card* or *host adapter* plugs into the computer's bus (e.g., to a motherboard) and connects to the transceiver.

A transceiver is a small piece of hardware usually found physically adjacent to the ether. In addition to the analog hardware that senses and controls electrical signals on the ether, a transceiver contains digital circuitry that allows it to communicate with a digital computer. The transceiver senses when the ether is in use and translates analog electrical signals on the ether to (and from) digital form. A cable called the *Attachment Unit Interface* (*AUI*) cable connects the transceiver to an adapter board in a host computer. Informally called a *transceiver cable*, the AUI cable contains many wires. The wires carry the electrical power needed to operate the transceiver, the signals that control the transceiver operation, and the contents of the packets being sent or received. Figure 2.3 illustrates how the components form a connection between a bus in a computer system and an Ethernet cable.

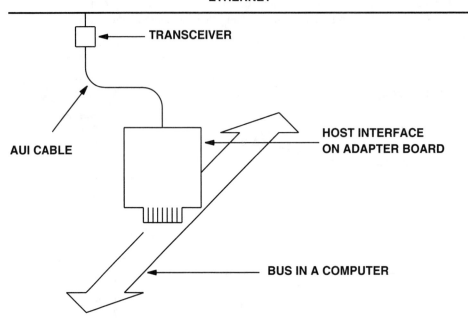

Figure 2.3 The two main electronic components that form a connection between a computer's bus and an Ethernet in the original scheme. The AUI cable that connects the host interface to the transceiver carry power and signals to control transceiver operation as well as packets being transmitted or received.

Each host interface controls the operation of one transceiver according to instructions it receives from the computer software. To the operating system software, the interface appears to be an input/output device that accepts basic data transfer instructions from the computer, controls the transceiver to carry them out, interrupts when the task has been completed, and reports status information. Although a transceiver is a simple hardware device, the host interface can be complex (e.g., some interfaces contain a microprocessor used to control transfers between the computer memory and the ether).

In practice, organizations that use the original Ethernet wiring in a conventional office environment run the Ethernet cable along the ceiling in each hall, and arrange for a connection from each office to attach to the cable. Figure 2.4 illustrates the resulting physical wiring scheme.

ETHERNET CABLE (USUALLY IN CEILING)

TRANSCEIVERS

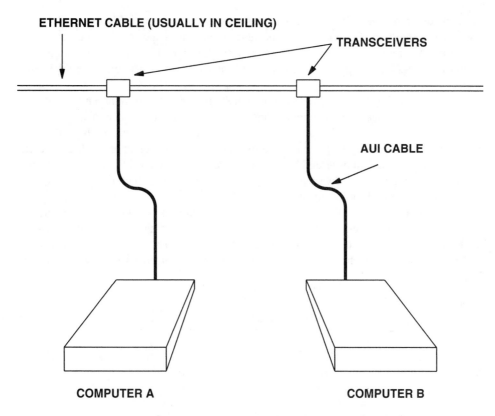

AUI CABLE

COMPUTER A   **COMPUTER B**

Figure 2.4 The physical connection of two computers to an Ethernet using the
original wiring scheme. In an office environment, the Ethernet
cable is usually placed in the hallway ceiling; each office has an
AUI cable that connects a computer in the office to a transceiver
attached to the Ethernet cable.

2.4.1 Thin-Wire Ethernet

Several components of the original Ethernet technology have undesirable properties. For example, because a transceiver contains electronic components, it has a nontrivial cost. Furthermore, because transceivers are located with the cable and not with
computers, locating or replacing them is difficult. The coaxial cable that forms the ether is difficult to install. In particular, to provide maximum protection against electrical
interference from devices like electric motors, the cable contains heavy shielding that
makes it difficult to bend. Finally, the AUI cable is also thick and difficult to bend.

To reduce costs for environments like offices that do not contain much electrical
interference, engineers developed an alternative Ethernet wiring scheme. Formally
known as *10Base2* and usually called *thin-wire Ethernet* or *thinnet*†, the alternative
coaxial cable is thinner, less expensive, and more flexible. However, thin-wire Ethernet

---

†To contrast it with thin-wire, the original Ethernet cable became known as *thick Ethernet*, or *thicknet*.

has some disadvantages. Because it does not provide as much protection from electrical interference, thin-wire Ethernet cannot be placed adjacent to powerful electrical equipment like that found in a factory. Furthermore, thin-wire Ethernet covers somewhat shorter distances and supports fewer computer connections per network than thick Ethernet.

When designing thin-wire Ethernet, engineers replaced costly transceiver hardware with special high-speed digital circuits, and provided a direct connection from a computer to the network. Thus, in a thin-wire scheme, a computer contains both the host interface and the circuitry that connects to the cable. Manufacturers of small computers and workstations find thin-wire Ethernet an especially attractive scheme because they can integrate Ethernet hardware into single board computers and mount connectors directly on the back of the computer.

Because a thin-wire Ethernet connects directly from one computer to another, the wiring scheme works well when many computers occupy a single room. The thin-wire cable runs directly from one computer to the next. To add a new computer, one only needs to link it into the chain. Figure 2.5 illustrates the connections used with thin-wire Ethernet.

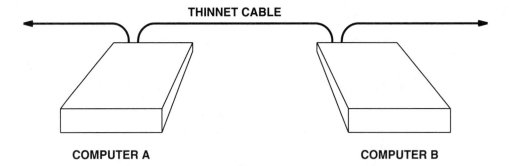

Figure 2.5 The physical connection of two computers using the thinnet wiring
scheme. The ether passes directly from one computer to another;
no external transceiver hardware is required.

Thin-wire Ethernets were designed to be easy to connect and disconnect. Thin-wire uses *BNC connectors*, which do not require tools to attach a computer to the cable. Thus, a user can connect a computer to a thin-wire Ethernet without the aid of a technician. Of course, allowing users to manipulate the ether has disadvantages: if a user disconnects the ether, it prevents all machines on the ether from communicating. In many situations, however, the advantages outweigh the disadvantages.

2.4.2 Twisted Pair Ethernet

Advances in technology have made it possible to build Ethernets that do not need the electrical shielding of a coaxial cable. Called *twisted pair Ethernet*, the technology allows a computer to access an Ethernet using conventional unshielded copper wires similar to the wires used to connect telephones†. The advantages of using twisted pair wiring are that it further reduces costs and protects other computers on the network from a user who disconnects a single computer. In some cases, a twisted pair technology can make it possible for an organization to use Ethernet over existing wiring; in others, the needed wiring (called *category 5 cable*) is cheaper and easier to install than coaxial cable.

Formally known as *10Base-T*, the first twisted pair Ethernet operated at 10 Mbps, exactly like thick or thin Ethernet. A set of eight wires (four pairs) is used to connect each computer to an Ethernet *hub* as Figure 2.6 shows.

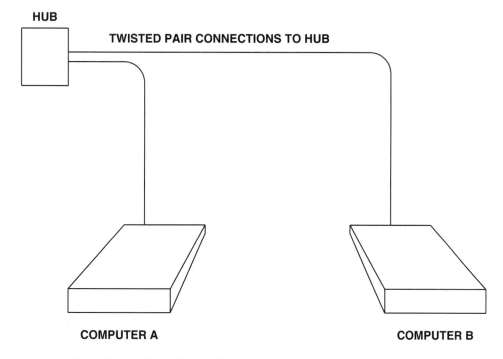

Figure 2.6 An illustration of Ethernet using twisted pair wiring. Each computer connects to a hub over four pairs of wire.

The hub is an electronic device that simulates the signals on an Ethernet cable. Physically, a hub consists of a small box that usually resides in a wiring closet; a connection between a hub and a computer must be less than 100 meters long. A hub requires power, and can allow authorized personnel to monitor and control its operation

---

†The term *twisted pair* arises because conventional telephone wiring uses the technique of twisting the wires to avoid interference.

over the network. To the host interface in a computer, a connection to a hub appears to operate the same way as a connection to a transceiver. That is, an Ethernet hub provides the same communication capability as a thick or thin Ethernet; hubs merely offer an alternative wiring scheme.

2.4.3 Ethernet Capacity

Although the wiring scheme evolved from the original thick cable to thin cable and finally to twisted pair, much of the original Ethernet design remained the same. In particular, the initial twisted pair Ethernet design operates at the same rate as the original thick Ethernet, which means that data can be transmitted at 10 million bits per second. Although a computer can generate data at Ethernet speed, raw network speed should not be thought of as the rate at which two computers can exchange data. Instead, network speed should be thought of as a measure of total traffic capacity. Think of a network as a highway connecting multiple cities, and think of packets as cars on the highway. High bandwidth makes it possible to carry heavy traffic loads, while low bandwidth means the highway cannot carry as much traffic. A 10 Mbps Ethernet, for example, can handle a few computers that generate heavy loads, or many computers that generate light loads.

In the late 1970s when Ethernet was standardized, a LAN operating at 10 Mbps had more than sufficient capacity for many computers because the available CPU speeds and network interface hardware prohibited a given computer from transmitting data rapidly. By the mid 1990s, however, CPU speeds had increased dramatically as had the use of networks. Consequently, an Ethernet operating at 10 Mbps did not have sufficient capacity to act as a central corporate backbone for even a moderate sized corporation — Ethernet had become a bottleneck.

2.4.4 Fast Ethernet

To overcome the throughput limitation of Ethernet, engineers designed a new version of Ethernet that operates an order of magnitude faster. Known formally as *100Base-T*, the technology is usually called *Fast Ethernet*. As the formal name implies, Fast Ethernet uses category 5 twisted pair wiring, the same wiring used for 10Base-T. However, through clever use of the wires, Fast Ethernet allows a station to transmit or receive data at 100 Mbps.

To understand the significance of the increase in capacity, it is important to understand two facts. First, although computers have become faster, few computer systems can transmit data at a sustained rate of 100 Mbps. Second, the 100Base-T standard did not change other parts of the Ethernet standard. In particular, the maximum packet size remains the same as for 10Base-T. These two facts imply that Fast Ethernet is not optimized to provide the highest possible throughput between a pair of computers. Instead, the design is optimized to allow more stations and more total traffic.

2.4.5 10/100 Ethernet

Soon after the invention of Fast Ethernet, manufacturers began to build devices that could accept either a 10 or 100 Mbps connection. The technology, which is known as *dual-speed Ethernet* or *10/100 Ethernet*, is available for computer interfaces as well as for hubs. In essence, all 100Base-T hardware interjects extra signals, making it possible for the hardware at one end of a cable to know which hardware type is connected to the other end. In fact, as long as all eight wires connect to the RJ-45 connector, the cabling and connectors used with 10Base-T are compatible with the cable and connectors used for 100Base-T.

Although 10/100 hardware is slightly more expensive than 10Base-T hardware, it has become extremely popular. Dual speed devices are especially helpful during a transition from 10 Mbps technology to 100 Mbps technology. For example, consider a computer that has a 10/100 interface card. If the computer is connected to a 10Base-T hub, the hardware in the card will automatically detect the speed and communicate at 10 Mbps. If the same computer is then unplugged from the 10Base-T hub and connected to a 100Base-T hub, the hardware will automatically detect the new speed and begin transmitting at 100 Mbps. The transition in speed is completely automatic: neither the software nor the hardware needs to be reconfigured.

2.4.6 Gigabit Ethernet

By the late 1990s, as the market share of 100Base-T Ethernet began to grow, it became obvious that there was a demand for even higher capacity Ethernet. Consequently, engineers extended the Ethernet technology to a bit rate of 1 Gbps (gigabits per second). Known as *1000Base-T*, the high throughput rate makes the technology extremely attractive for use in corporate backbone networks, where traffic from many computers passes through the network. The high data rate does have a slight disadvantage — it makes gigabit Ethernet more susceptible to electrical interference. Consequently, wiring that operates well with 10Base-T or even 100Base-T may not work well with 1000Base-T.

Like Fast Ethernet, the design of gigabit Ethernet was optimized for total throughput. The original packet format and maximum packet size were retained, making packets used on 10Base-T, 100Base-T and 1000Base-T networks interchangeable. Consequently, it is possible to collect traffic from ten 100Base-T Ethernets, each running at full speed, and pass the traffic across a single 1000Base-T network.

2.4.7 Properties of an Ethernet

Ethernet was designed to be a shared bus technology that supports broadcast, uses best-effort delivery semantics, and has distributed access control. The topology is called a *shared bus* because all stations connect to a single, shared communication channel; it is called a *broadcast technology* because all stations receive every transmission, making it possible to transmit a packet to all stations at the same time. The

method used to direct packets from one station to just one other station or a subset of
all stations will be discussed later. For now, it is enough to understand that the lowest
level hardware does not distinguish among transmissions — a hub passes all packets to
each host interface, which chooses packets the computer should receive and filters out
all others. Ethernet is called a *best-effort delivery* mechanism because the hardware
provides no information to the sender about whether the packet was delivered. For example, if the destination machine happens to be powered down, packets sent to it will
be lost, and the sender will not be notified. We will see later how the TCP/IP protocols
accommodate best-effort delivery hardware.

Ethernet access control is distributed because, unlike some network technologies,
Ethernet has no central authority to grant access. The Ethernet access scheme is called
Carrier Sense Multiple Access with *Collision Detect* (*CSMA/CD*). It is *CSMA* because
multiple machines can access an Ethernet simultaneously and each machine determines
whether the network is idle by sensing whether a carrier wave is present. When a host
interface has a packet to transmit, it listens to see if a message is being transmitted (i.e.,
performs carrier sensing). When no transmission is sensed, the host interface starts
transmitting. Each transmission is limited in duration because there is a maximum
packet size. Furthermore, the hardware must observe a minimum idle time between
transmissions, which means that no single pair of communicating machines can use the
network without giving other machines an opportunity for access.

2.4.8 Collision Detection And Recovery

When a station begins transmission, the signal does not reach all parts of the network simultaneously. Instead it travels along copper wires at approximately 70% of the
speed of light. Thus, it is possible for two transceivers to both sense that the network is
idle and begin transmission simultaneously. When the two electrical signals cross they
become scrambled, meaning that neither remains meaningful. Such incidents are called
collisions.

The Ethernet handles collisions in an ingenious fashion. Each station monitors the
cable while it is transmitting to see if a foreign signal interferes with its transmission.
Technically, the monitoring is called *collision detection* (*CD*), making the Ethernet a
CSMA/CD network. When a collision is detected, the host interface aborts transmission, waits for activity to subside, and tries again. Care must be taken or the network
could wind up with all stations busily attempting to transmit and every transmission
producing a collision. To help avoid such situations, Ethernet uses a binary exponential
backoff policy where a sender delays a random time after the first collision, doubles the
range if a second attempt to transmit also produces a collision, quadruples the range if a
third attempt results in a collision, and so on. The motivation for exponential backoff is
that in the unlikely event many stations attempt to transmit simultaneously, a severe
traffic jam could occur. In such a jam, there is a high probability two stations will
choose random backoffs that are close together. Thus, the probability of another collision is high. By doubling the range of the random delay, the exponential backoff strategy quickly spreads the stations' attempts to retransmit over a reasonably long period
of time, making the probability of further collisions extremely small.

2.4.9 Ethernet Hardware Addresses

Ethernet defines a 48-bit addressing scheme. Each computer attached to an Ethernet network is assigned a unique 48-bit number known as its *Ethernet address*. To assign an address, Ethernet hardware manufacturers purchase blocks of Ethernet addresses† and assign them in sequence as they manufacture Ethernet interface hardware. Thus, no two hardware interfaces have the same Ethernet address.

Usually, the Ethernet address is fixed in machine readable form on the host interface hardware. Because each Ethernet address belongs to a hardware device, they are sometimes called *hardware addresses*, *physical addresses*, *media access (MAC) addresses*, or *layer 2 addresses*. Note the following important property of Ethernet physical addresses:

> *Physical addresses are associated with the Ethernet interface hardware; moving the hardware interface to a new machine or replacing a hardware interface that has failed changes the machine's physical address.*

Knowing that Ethernet physical addresses can change will make it clear why higher levels of the network software are designed to accommodate such changes.

The host interface hardware examines packets and determines the packets that should be sent to the host. Recall that each interface receives a copy of every packet that passes through a hub — even those addressed to other machines. The host interface uses the destination address field in a packet as a filter. The interface ignores those packets that are addressed to other machines, and passes to the host only those packets addressed to it. The addressing mechanism and hardware filter are needed to prevent a computer from being overwhelmed with incoming data. Although the computer's central processor could perform the check, doing so in the host interface keeps traffic on the Ethernet from slowing down processing on all computers.

A 48-bit Ethernet address can do more than specify a single destination computer. An address can be one of three types:

- The physical address of one network interface (a *unicast address*)
- The network *broadcast address*
- A *multicast address*

By convention, the broadcast address (all 1s) is reserved for sending to all stations simultaneously. Multicast addresses provide a limited form of broadcast in which a subset of the computers on a network agree to listen to a given multicast address. The set of participating computers is called a *multicast group*. To join a multicast group, a computer must instruct its host interface to accept the group's multicast address. The advantage of multicasting lies in the ability to limit broadcasts: every computer in a multicast group can be reached with a single packet transmission, but computers that choose not to participate in a particular multicast group do not receive packets sent to the group.

---

†The Institute for Electrical and Electronic Engineers (IEEE) manages the Ethernet address space and assigns addresses as needed.

To accommodate broadcast and multicast addressing, Ethernet interface hardware must recognize more than its physical address. A computer interface usually accepts at least two kinds of packets: those addressed to the interface's physical (i.e., unicast) address and those addressed to the network broadcast address. Some interfaces can be programmed to recognize multicast addresses or even alternate physical addresses. When a computer boots, the operating system initializes the Ethernet interface hardware, giving it a set of addresses to recognize. The interface then examines the destination address field in each packet, passing on to the computer only those transmissions designated for one of the specified addresses.

2.4.10 Ethernet Frame Format

Ethernet should be thought of as a link-level connection among machines. Thus, it makes sense to view the data transmitted as a *frame*†. Ethernet frames are of variable length, with no frame smaller than 64 octets‡ or larger than 1518 octets (header, data, and CRC). As in all packet-switched networks, each Ethernet frame contains a field that contains the address of its destination. Figure 2.7 shows that the Ethernet frame format contains the physical source address as well as the destination address.

Preamble	Destination Address	Source Address	Frame Type	Frame Data	CRC
8 octets	6 octets	6 octets	2 octets	46–1500 octets	4 octets

Figure 2.7 The format of a frame (packet) as it travels across an Ethernet preceded by a preamble. Fields are not drawn to scale.

In addition to identifying the source and destination, each frame transmitted across the Ethernet contains a *preamble*, *type field*, *data field*, and *Cyclic Redundancy Check* (*CRC*). The preamble consists of 64 bits of alternating *0*s and *1*s to help receiving interfaces synchronize. The 32-bit CRC helps the interface detect transmission errors: the sender computes the CRC as a function of the data in the frame, and the receiver recomputes the CRC to verify that the packet has been received intact.

The frame type field contains a 16-bit integer that identifies the type of the data being carried in the frame. From the Internet point of view, the frame type field is essential because it means Ethernet frames are *self-identifying*. When a frame arrives at a given machine, the operating system uses the frame type to determine which protocol software module should process the frame. The chief advantages of self-identifying frames are that they allow multiple protocols to be used together on a single computer and they allow multiple protocols to be intermixed on the same physical network without interference. For example, one could have an application program on a computer using Internet protocols while another application on the same computer uses a local experimental protocol. The operating system examines the type field of each arriv-

---

†The term *frame* derives from communication over serial lines in which the sender ''frames'' the data by adding special characters before and after the transmitted data.

‡Technically, the term *byte* refers to a hardware-dependent character size; networking professionals use the term *octet*, because it refers to an 8-bit quantity on all computers.

ing frame to decide how to process the contents. We will see that the TCP/IP protocols use self-identifying Ethernet frames to distinguish among several protocols.

2.4.11 Extending An Ethernet With Repeaters

Although the original Ethernet cable had a maximum length, a network could be extended in two ways: using repeaters and bridges. An electronic device called a *repeater* operates on analog electrical signals. Like a hub in a twisted pair Ethernet, a repeater relays all electrical signals from one cable to another. Specifically, in the original thick Ethernet wiring scheme, a repeater can be placed between a pair of coaxial cables to double the total length. However, to preserve the CSMA/CD timing, the Ethernet standard restricts the use of repeaters — at most two repeaters can be placed between any two machines. Figure 2.8 shows a typical use of repeaters in an office building. A single cable runs vertically up the building, and a repeater attaches the backbone to an additional cable on each floor. Computers attach to the cables on each floor.

2.4.12 Extending An Ethernet With Bridges

Connecting two Ethernets with a bridge is superior to connecting them with a repeater or hub because bridges operate on packets rather than electrical signals. In particular, a bridge does not replicate noise, errors, or malformed frames; the bridge must receive a completely valid frame from one segment before the bridge will accept and transmit it on the other segment. Furthermore, each connection between a bridge and an Ethernet network follows the CSMA/CD rules, so collisions and propagation delays on one segment remain isolated from those on the other. As a result, an (almost) arbitrary number of Ethernets can be connected together with bridges. The important point is:

> *Bridges hide the details of interconnection: a set of bridged segments acts like a single Ethernet.*

Bridged networks are classified as *transparent* because a computer does not know how many bridges connect segments of the network. The computer uses exactly the same hardware, frame format, and procedures to communicate with a computer across a bridge as it uses to communicate with a computer on the local segment.

Most bridges do much more than replicate frames from one wire to another: they make intelligent decisions about which frames to forward. Such bridges are called *adaptive* or *learning* bridges. An adaptive bridge consists of a computer with two Ethernet interfaces. The software in an adaptive bridge keeps two address lists, one for each interface. When a frame arrives from Ethernet E_1, the adaptive bridge adds the 48-bit Ethernet *source* address to the list associated with E_1. Similarly, when a frame

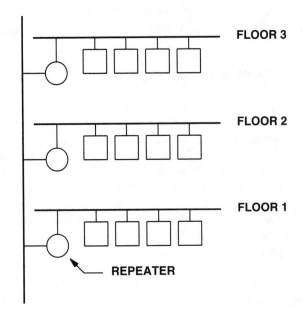

Figure 2.8 Repeaters used to join Ethernet cables in a building. At most two
repeaters can be placed between a pair of communicating
machines.

arrives from Ethernet E_2, the bridge adds the source address to the list associated with
E_2. Thus, over time the adaptive bridge will learn which machines lie on E_1 and which
lie on E_2.

After recording the source address of a frame, the adaptive bridge uses the destination address to determine whether to forward the frame. If the address list shows that
the destination lies on the Ethernet from which the frame arrived, the bridge does not
forward the frame. If the destination is not in the address list (i.e., the destination is a
broadcast or multicast address or the bridge has not yet learned the location of the destination), the bridge forwards the frame to the other Ethernet.

The advantages of adaptive bridges should be obvious. Because the bridge uses
addresses found in normal traffic, it is completely automatic — humans need not configure the bridge with specific addresses. Because it does not forward traffic unnecessarily, a bridge helps improve the performance of an overloaded network by isolating
traffic on specific segments. Bridges work exceptionally well if a network can be divided physically into two segments that each contain a set of computers that communicate
frequently (e.g., each segment contains a set of workstations along with a server, and
the workstations direct most of their traffic to the server). To summarize:

> *An adaptive Ethernet bridge connects two Ethernet segments, forwarding frames from one to the other. It uses source addresses to learn which machines lie on which Ethernet segment, and it combines information learned with destination addresses to eliminate forwarding when unnecessary.*

From the TCP/IP point of view, bridged Ethernets are merely another form of physical network connection. The important point is:

> *Because the connection among physical cables provided by bridges and repeaters is transparent to machines using the Ethernet, we think of multiple Ethernet segments connected by bridges and repeaters as a single physical network system.*

Most commercial bridges are much more sophisticated and robust than our description indicates. When first powered up, they check for other bridges and learn the topology of the network. They use a distributed spanning-tree algorithm to decide how to forward frames. In particular, the bridges decide how to propagate broadcast packets so only one copy of a broadcast frame is delivered to each wire. Without such an algorithm, Ethernets and bridges connected in a cycle would produce catastrophic results because they would forward broadcast packets in both directions simultaneously.

2.5 Fiber Distributed Data Interconnect (FDDI)

FDDI is another popular local area networking technology that provides a data rate of 100 Mbps (i.e., the same data rate as Fast Ethernet). Unlike Ethernet and other LAN technologies that use copper cables to carry electrical signals, FDDI is designed to use optical fiber. Data is encoded in pulses of light†.

Optical fiber has two advantages over copper wire. First, because electrical noise does not interfere with an optical connection, the fiber can lie adjacent to powerful electrical devices. Second, because optical fibers use light, the amount of data that can be sent per unit time is much higher than cables that carry electrical signals.

It might seem that glass fibers would be difficult to install and would break if bent. However, an optical cable is surprisingly flexible. The glass fiber itself has an extremely small diameter, and the cable includes a plastic jacket that protects the fiber from breaking. Such a cable cannot bend at a ninety degree angle, but it can bend in an arc with a diameter of a few inches. Thus, installation is not difficult.

---

†A related technology known as *Copper Distributed Data Interface* (*CDDI*) works like FDDI, but uses copper cables to carry signals.

2.5.1 Properties Of An FDDI Network

An FDDI network is a 100 Mbps shared token passing ring technology with a self-healing capability. An FDDI network is *shared* because multiple computers connect to a given network and take turns sending packets. FDDI is known as a *ring* because the network forms a cycle that starts at one computer, passes through all others computers, and ends back at the source. FDDI is a *token passing ring* (or simply a *token ring*) technology because it uses token passing to control transmission. When the network is idle, a special, reserved frame called a *token* circulates around the ring from station to station. When a station has a packet to send, it waits for the token to arrive, sends its packet, and then passes the token to the next station. The circulating token guarantees fairness: it ensures that all stations have an opportunity to send a packet before any station sends a second packet.

Perhaps the most interesting property of an FDDI lies in its ability to detect and correct problems. The network is called *self-healing* because the hardware can automatically accommodate a failure.

2.5.2 Dual Counter-Rotating Rings

To provide automatic recovery from failures, FDDI hardware uses two independent rings that both connect to each computer. Figure 2.9 illustrates the topology.

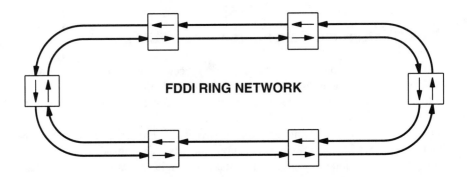

Figure 2.9 An FDDI network with optical fibers interconnecting six computers. Arrows show the direction of traffic on the fibers and through the attached computers.

FDDI rings are called *counter rotating* because traffic passes in the opposite direction on each ring. The reason for using a counter rotating scheme will become clear when we consider how FDDI handles failures.

Unless an error has occurred, an FDDI hardware does not need both rings. In fact, an FDDI interface behaves like any token passing network interface until an error occurs. The interface examines all packets that circulate around the ring, comparing the destination address in each packet to the computer's address. The interface keeps a copy of any packet destined for the local computer, but also forwards the packet around the ring.

When a computer needs to transmit a packet, it waits for the token to arrive, temporarily stops forwarding bits, and sends its packet. After sending one packet, the interface transmits the token, and begins forwarding bits again. Even if a station has more than one packet ready to be sent when it receives the token, the station only sends one packet before passing the token.

FDDI hardware becomes more interesting when a hardware error occurs. When an interface detects that it cannot communicate with the adjacent computer, the interface uses the backup ring to bypass the failure. For example, Figure 2.10 shows an FDDI ring in which an interface has failed, and the two adjacent interfaces have eliminated it from the ring.

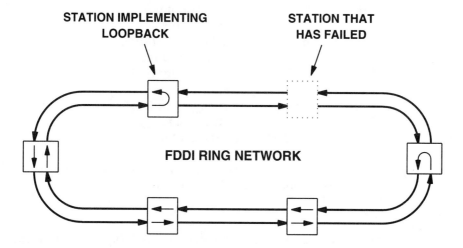

Figure 2.10 An FDDI ring after a failure. When FDDI hardware detects such a failure, it uses the second ring to bypass the failure and allows remaining stations to communicate.

The purpose of the second ring and the reason data flows in the opposite direction should now be clear: a failure can mean that the fiber has been disconnected (e.g., accidentally cut). If the fiber from both rings follows the same physical path, chances are high that the second fiber may have been disconnected as well. FDDI hardware automatically uses the counter rotating ring to form a closed loop in the direction that is still working. Doing so permits the other computers to continue communication despite the failure.

When FDDI hardware detects a failure on the network, it automatically loops data across the backup ring to permit communication among remaining stations.

2.5.3 FDDI Frame Format

FDDI standards specify the exact format of frames used on the network. The table in Figure 2.11 lists fields in an FDDI frame.

Field	Length in 4-bit units	Contents
PA	4 or more	Preamble
SD	2	Start Delimiter
FC	2	Frame Control
DA	4 or 12	Destination Address
SA	4 or 12	Source Address
RI	0 to 60	Routing Information
DATA	0 or more	Data
FCS	8	Frame Check Sequence
ED	1	End Delimiter
FS	3 or more	Frame Status

Figure 2.11 The format of frames used by FDDI, with fields measured in 4-bit units called *symbols*. The maximum frame length is 9000 symbols.

Like other technologies, each computer attached to an FDDI network is assigned an address, and each frame contains a destination address field. However, to make FDDI more flexible and to provide a standard way to interconnect two FDDI rings, the designers allowed more than one frame format. For example, the destination address field is either 4 or 12 symbols long, where a *symbol* is a 4-bit unit. The frame also includes a field used for routing. The sender can use the routing field to specify that a frame must be sent first to a connection point and then on to a destination on an attached ring.

One of the advantages of FDDI arises from its large frame size. Because a frame can contain 9000 4-bit symbols, the total frame can be 4500 octets long. Because header information occupies at most a few hundred octets, a single frame can carry 4K octets of user data. For applications that transfer large volumes of data (e.g., file transfer), the large frame size means less overhead and consequently high throughput.

2.6 Asynchronous Transfer Mode

Asynchronous Transfer Mode (ATM) is the name given to a connection-oriented networking technology that is intended for use in both local area and wide area networks. ATM is designed to permit extremely high speed data switching; the fastest ATM hardware can switch data at gigabit speeds†. Of course, such high speeds require complex, state-of-the-art hardware. As a result, ATM networks are more expensive than other technologies.

To achieve high transfer speeds, an ATM network uses special-purpose hardware and software techniques. First, an ATM network consists of one or more high-speed switches that each connect to computers and to other ATM switches. Second, ATM uses optical fibers for connections, including connections from a user's computer to an ATM switch. Optical fibers provide a higher transfer rate than copper wires; typically, the connection between a user's computer and an ATM switch operates at 155 Mbps. Third, the lowest layers of an ATM network use fixed-size frames called *cells*. Because each cell is exactly the same size, ATM switch hardware can process cells quickly.

2.6.1 ATM Cell Size

Surprisingly, each ATM cell is only 53 octets long. The cell contains 5 octets of header followed by 48 octets of data. Later chapters will show, however, that when using ATM to send IP traffic, the 53 octet size is irrelevant — an ATM network accepts and delivers much larger packets.

2.6.2 Connection-Oriented Networking

ATM differs from the packet-switching networks described earlier because it offers *connection-oriented* service. Before a computer connected to an ATM switch can send cells, a connection must be established manually or the host must first interact with the switch to specify a destination. The interaction is analogous to placing a telephone call‡. The requesting computer specifies the remote computer's address, and waits for the ATM switch to find a path through the network and establish a connection. If the remote computer rejects the request, does not respond, or the ATM switches between the sender and receiver cannot currently establish a path, the request to establish communication fails.

Once a connection succeeds, the local ATM switch chooses an identifier for the connection, and passes the connection identifier to the computer along with a message that informs the computer of success. The computer uses the connection identifier when sending or receiving cells.

When it finishes using a connection, the computer again communicates with the ATM switch to request that the connection be broken. The switch then disconnects the two computers. Disconnection is equivalent to hanging up a telephone at the end of a telephone call; after a disconnection, the computers cannot communicate until they es-

---

†Most computers cannot generate or absorb data at gigabit rates; ATM networks operate at gigabit speed to handle the traffic from many computers.

‡Because ATM was designed to carry voice as well as data, there is a strong relationship between an ATM network and a telephone system.

tablish a new connection. Furthermore, identifiers used for a connection can be recycled; once a disconnection occurs, the switch can reuse the connection identifier for a new connection.

2.7 WAN Technologies: ARPANET

We will see that wide area networks have important consequences for internet addressing and routing. The technologies discussed in the remainder of this chapter were selected because they figure prominently in both the history of the Internet and later examples in the text.

One of the oldest wide area technologies, the ARPANET, was funded by *ARPA*, the *Advanced Research Projects Agency*. ARPA awarded a contract for the development of the ARPANET to Bolt, Beranek and Newman of Cambridge, MA in the fall of 1968. By September 1969, the first pieces of the ARPANET were in place.

The ARPANET served as a testbed for much of the research in packet-switching. In addition to its use for network research, researchers in several universities, military bases, and government labs regularly used the ARPANET to exchange files and electronic mail and to provide remote login among their sites. In 1975, control of the network was transferred from ARPA to the U.S. Defense Communications Agency (DCA). The DCA made the ARPANET part of the Defense Data Network (DDN), a program that provides multiple networks as part of a world-wide communication system for the Department of Defense.

In 1983, the Department of Defense partitioned the ARPANET into two connected networks, leaving the ARPANET for experimental research and forming the *MILNET* for military use. MILNET was restricted to unclassified data because it was not considered secure. Although under normal circumstances, both ARPANET and MILNET agreed to pass traffic to each other, controls were established that allowed them to be disconnected†. Because the ARPANET and MILNET used the same hardware technology, our description of the technical details apply to both. In fact, the technology was also available commercially and was used by several corporations to establish private packet switching networks.

Because the ARPANET was already in place and used daily by many of the researchers who developed the Internet architecture, it had a profound effect on their work. They came to think of the ARPANET as a dependable wide area backbone around which the Internet could be built. The influence of a single, central wide area backbone is still painfully obvious in some of the Internet protocols that we will discuss later, and has prevented the Internet from accommodating additional backbone networks gracefully.

Physically, the ARPANET consisted of approximately 50 BBN Corporation C30 and C300 minicomputers, called *Packet Switching Nodes* or *PSNs*‡ scattered across the continental U.S. and western Europe; MILNET contained approximately 160 PSNs, including 34 in Europe and 18 in the Pacific and Far East. One PSN resided at each site participating in the network and was dedicated to the task of switching packets; it could

---

†Perhaps the best known example of disconnection occurred in November 1988 when a *worm* program attacked the Internet and replicated itself as quickly as possible.

‡PSNs were initially called *Interface Message Processors* or *IMPs*; some publications still use the term IMP as a synonym for packet switch.

not be used for general-purpose computation. Indeed, each PSN was considered to be part of the ARPANET, and was owned and controlled by the *Network Operations Center* (*NOC*) located at BBN in Cambridge, Massachusetts.

Point-to-point data circuits leased from common carriers connected the PSNs together to form a network. For example, leased data circuits connected the ARPANET PSN at Purdue University to the ARPANET PSNs at Carnegie Mellon and at the University of Wisconsin. Initially, most of the leased data circuits in the ARPANET operated at 56 Kbps, a speed considered fast in 1968 but extremely slow by current standards. Remember to think of the network speed as a measure of capacity rather than a measure of the time it takes to deliver packets. As more computers used the ARPANET, capacity was increased to accommodate the load. For example, during the final year the ARPANET existed, many of the cross-country links operated over megabit-speed channels.

The idea of having no single point of failure in a system is common in military applications because reliability is important. When building the ARPANET, ARPA decided to follow the military requirements for reliability, so they mandated that each PSN had to have at least two leased line connections to other PSNs, and the software had to automatically adapt to failures and choose alternate routes. As a result, the ARPANET continued to operate even if one of its data circuits failed.

In addition to connections for leased data circuits, each ARPANET PSN had up to 22 *ports* that connected it to user computers, called *hosts*. Originally, each computer that accessed the ARPANET connected directly to one of the ports on a PSN. Normally, host connections were formed with a special-purpose interface board that plugged into the computer's I/O bus.

The original PSN port hardware used a complex protocol for transferring data across the ARPANET. Known as 1822, after the number of a technical report that described it, the protocol permitted a host to send a packet across the ARPANET to a specified destination PSN and a specified port on that PSN. Performing the transfer was complicated, however, because 1822 offered reliable, flow-controlled delivery. To prevent a given host from saturating the net, 1822 limited the number of packets that could be in transit. To guarantee that each packet arrived at its destination, 1822 forced the sender to await a *Ready For Next Message* (*RFNM*) signal from the PSN before transmitting each packet. The RFNM acted as an acknowledgement. It included a buffer reservation scheme that required the sender to reserve a buffer at the destination PSN before sending a packet.

Although there are many aspects not discussed here, the key idea is that underneath all the detail, the ARPANET was merely a transfer mechanism. When a computer connected to one port sent a packet to another port, the data delivered was exactly the data sent. Because the ARPANET did not provide a network-specific frame header, packets sent across it did not have a fixed field to specify packet type. Thus, unlike some network technologies, the ARPANET did not deliver self-identifying packets. In summary:

Networks such as the ARPANET or an ATM network do not have self-identifying frames. The attached computers must agree on the format and contents of packets sent or received to a specific destination.

Unfortunately, 1822 was never an industry standard. Because few vendors manufactured 1822 interface boards, it became difficult to connect new machines to the ARPANET. To solve the problem, ARPA later revised the PSN interface to use the *X.25* standard†. The first version of an X.25 PSN implementation used only the data transfer part of the X.25 standard (known as HDLC/LAPB), but later versions made it possible to use all of X.25 when connecting to a PSN (i.e., ARPANET appeared to be an X.25 network).

Internally, of course, the ARPANET used its own set of protocols that were invisible to users. For example, there was a special protocol that allowed one PSN to request status from another, a protocol that PSNs used to send packets among themselves, and one that allowed PSNs to exchange information about link status and optimal routes.

Because the ARPANET was originally built as a single, independent network to be used for research, its protocols and addressing structure were designed without much thought given to expansion. By the mid 1970's, it became apparent no single network would solve all communication problems, and ARPA began to investigate satellite and packet radio network technologies. This experience with a variety of network technologies led to the concept of an internetwork.

2.7.1 ARPANET Addressing

While the details of ARPANET addressing are unimportant, they illustrate an alternative way in which wide area networks form physical addresses. Unlike the *flat address* schemes used by LAN technologies, wide area networks usually embed information in the address that helps the network route packets to their destination efficiently. In the ARPANET technology, each packet switch is assigned a unique integer, P, and each host port on the switch is numbered from 0 to $N-1$. Conceptually, a destination address consists of a pair of small integers, (P, N). In practice, the hardware uses a single, large integer address, with some bits of the address used to represent N and others used to represent P.

2.8 National Science Foundation Networking

Realizing that data communication would soon be crucial to scientific research, in 1987 the National Science Foundation established a *Division of Network and Communications Research and Infrastructure* to help ensure that requisite network communications will be available for U.S. scientists and engineers. Although the division funds basic research in networking, its emphasis so far has been concentrated on providing seed funds to build extensions to the Internet.

---

†X.25 was standardized by the *Consultative Committee on International Telephone and Telegraph (CCITT)*, which later became the *Telecommunication Section* of the *International Telecommunication Union (ITU)*.

NSF's Internet extensions introduced a three-level hierarchy consisting of a U.S. backbone, a set of ''mid-level'' or ''regional'' networks that each span a small geographic area, and a set of ''campus'' or ''access'' networks. In the NSF model, mid-level networks attach to the backbone and campus networks attach to the mid-level nets. Each researcher had a connection from their computer to the local campus network. They used that single connection to communicate with local researchers' computers across the local campus net, and with other researchers further away. The campus network routed traffic across local nets to one of the mid-level networks, which routed it across the backbone as needed.

2.8.1 The Original NSFNET Backbone

Of all the NSF-funded networks, the NSFNET backbone has the most interesting history and used the most interesting technology. The backbone evolved in four major steps; it increased in size and capacity at the time the ARPANET declined until it became the dominant backbone in the Internet. The first version was built quickly, as a temporary measure. One early justification for the backbone was to provide scientists with access to NSF supercomputers. As a result, the first backbone consisted of six Digital Equipment Corporation LSI-11 microcomputers located at the existing NSF supercomputer centers. Geographically, the backbone spanned the continental United States from Princeton, NJ to San Diego, CA, using 56 Kbps leased lines as Figure 2.12 shows.

At each site, the LSI-11 microcomputer ran software affectionately known as *fuzzball*† code. Developed by Dave Mills, each fuzzball accessed computers at the local supercomputer center using a conventional Ethernet interface; it accessed leased lines leading to fuzzballs at other supercomputer centers using conventional link-level protocols over leased serial lines. Fuzzballs contained tables with addresses of possible destinations and used those tables to direct each incoming packet toward its destination.

The primary connection between the original NSFNET backbone and the rest of the Internet was located at Carnegie Mellon, which had both an NSFNET backbone node and an ARPANET PSN. When a user, connected to NSFNET, sent traffic to a site on the ARPANET, the packets would travel across the NSFNET to CMU where the fuzzball would route them onto the ARPANET via a local Ethernet. Similarly, the fuzzball understood that packets destined for NSFNET sites should be accepted from the Ethernet and sent across the NSF backbone to the appropriate site.

---

†The exact origin of the term ''fuzzball'' is unclear.

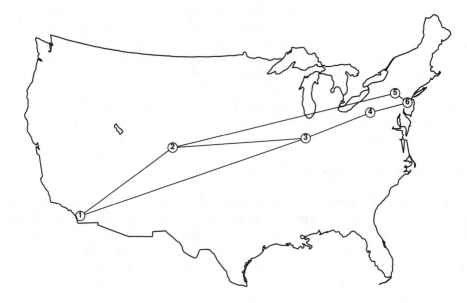

Figure 2.12 Circuits in the original NSFNET backbone with sites in (1) San
Diego, CA; (2) Boulder, CO; (3) Champaign, IL; (4) Pittsburgh,
PA; (5) Ithaca, NY; and (6) Princeton, NJ.

2.8.2 The Second NSFNET Backbone 1988-1989

Although users were excited about the possibilities of computer communication,
the transmission and switching capacities of the original backbone were too small to
provide adequate service. Within months after its inception, the backbone became overloaded and its inventor worked to engineer quick solutions for the most pressing problems, while NSF began the arduous process of planning for a second backbone.

In 1987, NSF issued a request for proposals from groups that were interested in establishing and operating a new, higher-speed backbone. Proposals were submitted in
August of 1987 and evaluated that fall. On November 24, 1987 NSF announced it had
selected a proposal submitted by a partnership of: MERIT Inc., the statewide computer
network run out of the University of Michigan in Ann Arbor; IBM Corporation; and
MCI Incorporated. The partners proposed to build a second backbone network, establish a network operation and control center in Ann Arbor, and have the system operational by the following summer. Because NSF had funded the creation of several new
mid-level networks, the proposed backbone was designed to serve more sites than the
original. Each additional site would provide a connection between the backbone and
one of the NSF mid-level networks.

The easiest way to envision the division of labor among the three groups is to assume that MERIT was in charge of planning, establishing, and operating the network center. IBM contributed machines and manpower from its research labs to help MERIT develop, configure, and test needed hardware and software. MCI, a long-distance carrier, provided the communication bandwidth using the optical fiber already in place for its voice network. Of course, in practice there was close cooperation between all groups, including joint study projects and representatives from IBM and MCI in the project management.

By the middle of the summer of 1988, the hardware was in place and NSFNET began to use the second backbone. Shortly thereafter, the original backbone was shut down and disconnected. Figure 2.13 shows the logical topology of the second backbone after it was installed in 1988.

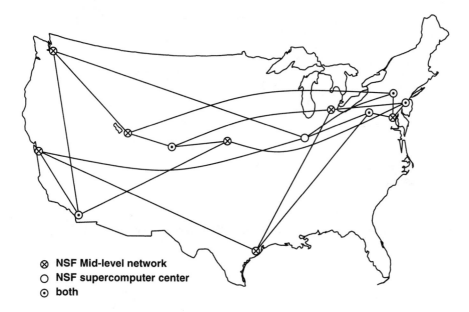

⊗ **NSF Mid-level network**
○ **NSF supercomputer center**
⊙ **both**

Figure 2.13 Logical circuits in the second NSFNET backbone from summer
1988 to summer 1989.

The technology chosen for the second NSFNET backbone was interesting. In essence, the backbone was a wide area network composed of packet routers interconnected by communication lines. As with the original backbone, the packet switch at each site connected to the site's local Ethernet as well as to communication lines leading to other sites.

2.8.3 NSFNET Backbone 1989-1990

After measuring traffic on the second NSFNET backbone for a year, the operations center reconfigured the network by adding some circuits and deleting others. In addition, they increased the speed of circuits to DS-1 (1.544 Mbps). Figure 2.14 shows the revised connection topology, which provided redundant connections to all sites.

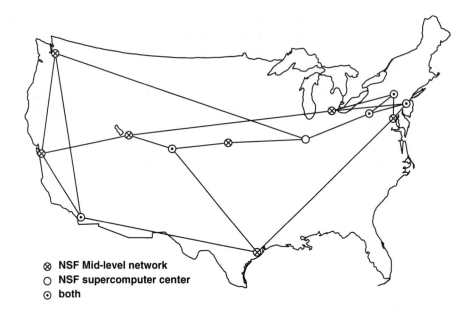

⊗ **NSF Mid-level network**
○ **NSF supercomputer center**
⊙ **both**

Figure 2.14 Circuits in the second NSFNET backbone from summer 1989 to 1990.

2.9 ANSNET

By 1991, NSF and other U.S. government agencies began to realize that the Internet was growing beyond its original academic and scientific domain. Companies around the world began to connect to the Internet, and nonresearch uses increased rapidly. Traffic on NSFNET had grown to almost one billion packets per day, and the 1.5 Mbps capacity was becoming insufficient for several of the circuits. A higher capacity backbone was needed. As a result, the U.S. government began a policy of commercialization and privatization. NSF decided to move the backbone to a private company and to charge institutions for connections.

Responding to the new government policy in December of 1991, IBM, MERIT, and MCI formed a not-for-profit company named *Advanced Networks and Services* (*ANS*). ANS proposed to build a new, higher speed Internet backbone. Unlike previous wide area networks used in the Internet which had all been owned by the U.S. government, ANS would own the new backbone. By 1993, ANS had installed a new network that replaced NSFNET. Called *ANSNET*, the backbone consisted of data circuits operating at 45 Mbps†, giving it approximately 30 times more capacity than the previous NSFNET backbone. Figure 2.15 shows major circuits in ANSNET and a few of the sites connected in 1994. Each point of presence represents a location to which many sites connect.

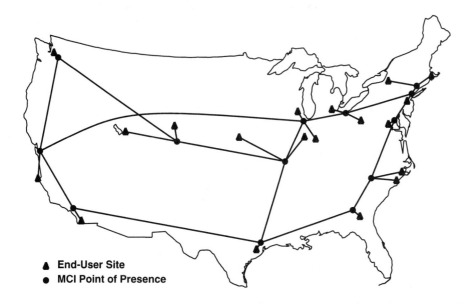

▲ **End-User Site**
● **MCI Point of Presence**

Figure 2.15 Circuits in ANSNET, the backbone of the U.S. Internet starting in 1993. Each circuit operates at 45 Mbps.

2.10 A Very High Speed Backbone (vBNS)

In 1995, NSF awarded MCI a contract to build a backbone operating at 155 Mbps (OC3 speed) to replace ANSNET. Called the *very high speed Backbone Network Service (vBNS)*, the new backbone offered a substantial increase in capacity, and required higher speed processors to route packets.

2.10.1 Commercial Internet Backbones

Since 1995, the Internet has become increasingly commercial, with the percentage of funding from the U.S. government steadily decreasing. Although vBNS still exists, it is now devoted to networking research. In its place, commercial companies have created large privately-funded backbones that carry Internet traffic. For example, public car-

---

†Telecommunication carriers use the term *DS3* to denote a circuit that operates at 45 Mbps; the term is often confused with *T3*, which denotes a specific encoding used over a circuit operating at DS3 speed.

riers like *AT&T* and *MCI* have each created large, high-capacity backbone networks used to carry Internet traffic from their customers. As discussed later, commercial backbones are interconnected through *peering arrangements*, making it possible for a customer of one company to send packets to a customer of another.

2.11 Other Technologies Over Which TCP/IP Has Been Used

One of the major strengths of TCP/IP lies in the variety of physical networking technologies over which it can be used. We have already discussed several widely used technologies, including local area and wide area networks. This section briefly reviews others that help illustrate an important principle:

> *Much of the success of the TCP/IP protocols lies in their ability to accommodate almost any underlying communication technology.*

2.11.1 X25NET And Tunnels

In 1980, NSF formed the *Computer Science NETwork* (*CSNET*) organization to help provide Internet services to industry and small schools. CSNET used several technologies to connect its subscribers to the Internet, including one called *X25NET*. Originally developed at Purdue University, X25NET ran TCP/IP protocols over *Public Data Networks* (*PDN*s). The motivation for building such a network arose from the economics of telecommunications: although leased serial lines were expensive, common carriers had begun to offer public packet-switched services. X25NET was designed to allow a site to use its connection to a public packet-switched service to send and receive Internet traffic.

Readers who know about public packet-switched networks may find X25NET strange because public services use the CCITT X.25 protocols exclusively while the Internet uses TCP/IP protocols. Unlike most packet switching hardware, X.25 protocols use a connection-oriented paradigm; like ATM, they were designed to provide connection-oriented service to individual applications. Thus, the use of X.25 to transport TCP/IP traffic foreshadowed the ways TCP/IP would later be transferred across ATM.

We have already stated that many underlying technologies can be used to carry Internet traffic, and X25NET illustrates how TCP/IP has been adapted to use high level facilities. The technique, sometimes called *tunneling*, simply means that TCP/IP treats a complex network system with its own protocols like any other hardware delivery system. To send TCP/IP traffic through an X.25 *tunnel*, a computer forms an X.25 connection and then sends TCP/IP packets as if they were data. The X.25 system carries the packets along its connection and delivers them to another X.25 endpoint, where they must be picked up and forwarded on to their ultimate destination. Because tunneling treats IP packets like data, the tunnel does not provide for self-identifying frames.

Thus, tunneling only works when both ends of the X.25 connection agree *a priori* that they will exchange IP packets (or agree on a format for encoding type information along with each packet).

Its connection-oriented interface makes X.25 even more unusual. Unlike connectionless networks, connection-oriented systems use a *virtual circuit* (*VC*) abstraction. Before data can be sent, switches in the network must set up a VC (i.e., a "path") between the sender and the receiver. We said that the Internet protocols were optimized to run over a connectionless packet delivery system, which means that extra effort is required to run them over a connection-oriented network.

In theory, a single connection suffices for a tunnel through a connection-oriented network — after a pair of computers has established a VC, that pair can exchange TCP/IP traffic. In practice, however, the design of the protocols used on the connection-oriented system can make a single connection inefficient. For example, because X.25 protocols limit the number of packets that can be sent on a connection before an acknowledgement is received, such networks exhibit substantially better throughput when data is sent across multiple connections simultaneously. Thus, instead of opening a single connection to a given destination, X25NET improved performance by arranging for a sender to open multiple VCs and distribute traffic among them. A receiver must accept packets arriving on all connections, and combine them together again.

Tunneling across a high-level network such as X.25 requires mapping between the addresses used by the internet and addresses used by the network. For example, consider the addressing scheme used by X.25 networks, which is given in a related standard known as *X.121*. Physical addresses each consist of a 14-digit number, with 10 digits assigned by the vendor that supplies the X.25 network service. Resembling telephone numbers, one popular vendor's assignment includes an area code based on geographic location. The addressing scheme is not surprising because it comes from an organization that determines international telephone standards. There is no mathematical relationship between such addresses and the addresses used by TCP/IP. Thus, a computer that tunnels TCP/IP data across an X.25 network must maintain a table of mappings between internet addresses and X.25 network addresses. Chapter 5 discusses the address mapping problem in detail and gives an alternative to using fixed tables. Chapter 18 shows that exactly the same problem arises for ATM networks, which use yet another alternative.

Because public X.25 networks operated independently of the Internet, a point of contact was needed between the two. Both ARPA and CSNET operated dedicated machines that provided the interconnection between X.25 and the ARPANET. The primary interconnection was known as the *VAN gateway*. The VAN agreed to accept X.25 connections and route each datagram that arrived over such a connection to its destination.

X25NET was significant because it illustrated the flexibility and adaptability of the TCP/IP protocols. In particular, it showed that tunneling makes it possible to use an extremely wide range of complex network technologies in an internet.

2.11.2 Point-To-Point Networks

We said that Wide Area Networks are usually composed of dedicated packet switches interconnected by data circuits leased from a telephone company. Phone companies originally designed such circuits to carry digitized voice calls; only later did their use in data networks become important. Consequently, the data rates of available circuits are not powers of ten. Instead, they have been chosen to carry multiples of 64 Kbps because a digitized voice call uses an encoding known as *Pulse Code Modulation* (*PCM*), which produces 8000 samples per second, where each sample is 8 bits.

The table in Figure 2.16 lists a few common data rates used in North America and Europe.

Name	Bit Rate	Voice Circuits	Location
–	0.064 Mbps	1	
T1	1.544 Mbps	24	North America
T2	6.312 Mbps	96	North America
T3	44.736 Mbps	672	North America
E1	2.048 Mbps	30	Europe
E2	8.448 Mbps	120	Europe
E3	34.368 Mbps	480	Europe

Figure 2.16 Example data rates available on digital circuits leased from a telephone company. The rates were chosen to encode multiple voice calls.

Higher rate digital circuits are also available. In addition to standards that specify the transmission of high data rates over copper, the phone companies have developed standards for transmission of the same rates over optical fiber. The table in Figure 2.17 contains examples. Of course, circuits that operate at such high data rates are considerably more expensive than circuits that operate at lower rates.

Standard Name	Optical Name	Bit Rate	Voice Circuits
STS-1	OC-1	51.840 Mbps	810
STS-3	OC-3	155.520 Mbps	2430
STS-12	OC-12	622.080 Mbps	9720
STS-24	OC-24	1,244.160 Mbps	19440
STS-48	OC-48	2,488.320 Mbps	38880

Figure 2.17 Example data rates of high-capacity circuits that can be leased from phone companies. Optical fiber is used to achieve such high rates over long distances.

From TCP/IP's point of view, any communication system that connects exactly two computers is known as a *point-to-point network*. Thus, a leased data circuit between two computers is an example of a point-to-point network. Of course, using the term "network" to describe a connection between two computers stretches the concept. However, we will learn that viewing a connection as a network helps maintain consistency. For now, we only need to note that a point-to-point network differs from conventional networks in one significant way: because only two computers attach, no hardware addresses are used. When we discuss internet address binding, the lack of hardware addresses will make point-to-point networks an exception.

2.11.3 Dial-up IP

Another interesting use of TCP/IP pioneered by CSNET involves running TCP/IP protocols over the dial-up voice network (i.e., the telephone system). CSNET member sites that used the Internet infrequently could not justify the cost of a leased line connection. For such sites, CSNET developed a dial-up IP system that worked as expected: whenever a connection was needed, software at the member's site used a modem to form a connection to the CSNET hub over the voice telephone network. A computer at the hub answered the phone call and, after obtaining valid authorization, began to forward traffic between the site and other computers on the Internet. Dialing introduced a delay after the first packet was sent. However, for automated services like electronic mail, the delay was unnoticeable.

Dialup internet access provides another example of a point-to-point network. From the TCP/IP view, dialing a telephone call is equivalent to running a wire. Once the call has been answered by a modem on the other end, there is a connection from one computer directly to another, and the connection stays in place as long as needed.

2.11.4 Other Token Ring Technologies

FDDI is not the first token ring network technology; token ring products have existed for nearly twenty years. For example, IBM produces a popular token ring LAN technology. Early versions of the IBM token ring operated at 4 Mbps; later versions operate at 16 Mbps. Like other token ring systems, an IBM token ring network consists of a loop that attaches to all computers. A station must wait for a token before transmitting, and sends the token along after transferring a packet.

An older token ring technology designed by Proteon Corporation employs a novel hardware addressing scheme that will be used in a later chapter to illustrate one of the ways TCP/IP uses hardware addresses. Called a *proNET* network, the technology permits customers to choose a hardware address for each computer. Unlike an Ethernet, in which each interface board contains a unique address assigned by the manufacturer, a proNET interface board contains eight switches that must be set before the interface is installed in a computer. The switches form a number in binary between 0 and 255, inclusive. A given proNET network could have at most 254 computers attached because address 255 was reserved for broadcast and address 0 was not used. When first installing a proNET network, a network administrator chose a unique address for each computer. Typically, addresses were assigned sequentially, starting with *1*.

A technology that permits customers to assign hardware addresses has advantages and disadvantages. The chief disadvantage arises from the potential for problems that occur if a network administrator accidentally assigns the same address to two computers. The chief advantage arises from ease of maintenance: if an interface board fails, it can be replaced without changing the computer's hardware address.

2.11.5 Wireless Network Technologies

One of the most interesting ARPA experiments in packet switching resulted in a *packet radio* technology that uses broadcast radio waves to carry packets. Designed for a military environment in which stations might be mobile, packet radio includes hardware and software that allow sites to find other sites, establish point-to-point communication, and then use the point-to-point communication to carry packets. Because sites change geographic location and may move out of communication range, the system must constantly monitor connectivity and recompute routes to reflect changes in topology. An operational packet radio system was built and used to demonstrate TCP/IP communication between a remote packet radio site and other sites on the Internet.

In recent years, a wide variety of wireless networking equipment has become available commercially. Wireless LANs use spread spectrum techniques such as direct sequencing or frequency hopping to provide data connections among a set of computers inside a building. The transmitters and antennas for such equipment are small and lightweight. The equipment can be attached to a portable notebook computer, making it convenient to move around an area such as an office building while remaining in communication.

Wireless broadband technology, originally developed as an alternative to cable television, is being used to transmit data. Known as *Multichannel Multipoint Distribution System (MMDS)*, the scheme has sufficient capacity to provide data rates as fast as those offered by the popular *Digital Subscriber Line (DSL)* technologies that deliver high data rates over copper telephone wires.

Cellular technology, which was originally designed for voice networks, has also been adapted to carry data. The chief advantage of a cellular system is the speed with which it allows users to move. Because the technology was designed to maintain voice communication even if a user travels by car, the underlying hardware can easily maintain contact with a mobile unit while transferring a stream of packets.

2.12 Summary And Conclusion

We have reviewed several network hardware technologies used by the TCP/IP protocols, ranging from inexpensive Local Area Network technologies like Ethernet and FDDI to expensive Wide Area Network technologies that use leased digital circuits to provide backbones. We have also seen that it is possible to run the TCP/IP protocols over other general-purpose network protocols using a technique called tunneling. While the details of specific network technologies are not important, a general idea has emerged:

The TCP/IP protocols are extremely flexible; almost any underlying technology can be used to transfer TCP/IP traffic.

FOR FURTHER STUDY

Early computer communication systems employed point-to-point interconnection, often using general-purpose serial line hardware that McNamara [1982] describes. Metcalf and Boggs [1976] introduces the Ethernet with a 3 Mbps prototype version. Digital *et. al.* [1980] specifies the original 10 Mbps Ethernet standard, with IEEE standard 802.3 reported in Nelson [1983]. Shoch, Dalal, and Redell [1982] provides an historical perspective of the Ethernet evolution. Related work on the ALOHA network is reported in Abramson [1970], with a survey of technologies given by Cotton [1979].

Token passing ring technology is proposed in Farmer and Newhall [1969]. Miller and Thompson [1982], as well as Andrews and Shultz [1982], provide summaries. Another alternative, the slotted ring network, is proposed by Pierce [1972]. For a comparison of technologies, see Rosenthal [1982].

For more information on the ARPANET see Cerf [1989] and BBN [1981]. The ideas behind X25NET are summarized in Comer and Korb [1983]; Lanzillo and Partridge [January 1989] describes dial-up IP. De Prycker [1993] describes Asynchronous Transfer Mode and its use for wide area services. Partridge [1994] surveys many gigabit technologies, including ATM, and describes the internal structure of high speed switches.

EXERCISES

2.1   Find out which network technologies your site uses.

2.2   What is the maximum size packet that can be sent on a high-speed network like Network System Corporation's Hyperchannel?

2.3   If your site uses Ethernet hub technology, find out how many connections can be attached to a single hub. If your site has multiple hubs (e.g., one on each floor of a building), find out how the hubs communicate.

2.4   What are the advantages and disadvantages of tunneling?

2.5   Read the Ethernet standard to find exact details of the inter-packet gap and preamble size. What is the maximum steady-state rate at which Ethernet can transport data?

2.6   What characteristic of a satellite communication channel is most desirable? Least desirable?

2.7   Find a lower bound on the time it takes to transfer a 5 megabyte file across a network that operates at: 28.8 Kbps, 1.54 Mbps, 10 Mbps, 100 Mbps, and 2.4 Gbps.

2.8   Does the processor, disk, and internal bus on your computer operate fast enough to send data from a disk file at 2 gigabits per second?

3

Internetworking Concept And Architectural Model

3.1 Introduction

So far we have looked at the low-level details of transmission across individual data networks, the foundation on which all computer communication is built. This chapter makes a giant conceptual leap by describing a scheme that allows us to collect the diverse network technologies into a coordinated whole. The primary goal is a system that hides the details of underlying network hardware while providing universal communication services. The primary result is a high-level abstraction that provides the framework for all design decisions. Succeeding chapters show how we use this abstraction to build the necessary layers of internet communication software and how the software hides the underlying physical transport mechanisms. Later chapters also show how applications use the resulting communication system.

3.2 Application-Level Interconnection

Designers have taken two different approaches to hiding network details, using application programs to handle heterogeneity or hiding details in the operating system. Early heterogeneous network interconnections provided uniformity through application-level programs called *application gateways*. In such systems, an application-level program, executing on each computer in the network, understands the details of the network connections for that computer, and interoperates across those connections with application programs on other computers. For example, some electronic mail systems consist of mail programs that are each configured to forward a memo to a mail program on the next computer. The path from source to destination may involve many different networks, but that does not matter as long as the mail systems on all the machines cooperate by forwarding each message.

Using application programs to hide network details may seem natural at first, but such an approach results in limited, cumbersome communication. Adding new functionality to the system means building a new application program for each computer. Adding new network hardware means modifying existing programs (or creating new programs) for each possible application. On a given computer, each application program must understand the network connections for the computer, resulting in duplication of code.

Users who are experienced with networking understand that once the interconnections grow to hundreds or thousands of networks, no one can possibly build all the necessary application programs. Furthermore, success of the step-at-a-time communication scheme requires correctness of all application programs executing along the path. When an intermediate program fails, the source and destination remain unable to detect or control the problem. Thus, systems that use intermediate applications programs cannot guarantee reliable communication.

3.3 Network-Level Interconnection

The alternative to providing interconnection with application-level programs is a system based on network-level interconnection. A network-level interconnection provides a mechanism that delivers small packets of data from their original source to their ultimate destination without using intermediate application programs. Switching small units of data instead of files or large messages has several advantages. First, the scheme maps directly onto the underlying network hardware, making it extremely efficient. Second, network-level interconnection separates data communication activities from application programs, permitting intermediate computers to handle network traffic without understanding the applications that are sending or receiving it. Third, using network connections keeps the entire system flexible, making it possible to build general purpose communication facilities. Fourth, the scheme allows network managers to add new network technologies by modifying or adding a single piece of new network level software, while application programs remain unchanged.

The key to designing universal network-level interconnection can be found in an abstract communication system concept known as *internetworking*. The internetwork, or *internet*, concept is an extremely powerful one. It detaches the notions of communication from the details of network technologies and hides low-level details from the user. More important, it drives all software design decisions and explains how to handle physical addresses and routes. After reviewing basic motivations for internetworking, we will consider the properties of an internet in more detail.

We begin with two fundamental observations about the design of communication systems:

  • No single network hardware technology can satisfy all constraints.
  • Users desire universal interconnection.

The first observation is an economic as well as technical one. Inexpensive Local Area Networks that provide high speed communication only cover short distances; wide area networks that span long distances cannot supply local communication cheaply. Because no single network technology satisfies all needs, we are forced to consider multiple underlying hardware technologies.

The second observation is self-evident. Ultimately, users would like to be able to communicate between any two points. In particular, we desire a communication system that is not constrained by the boundaries of physical networks.

The goal is to build a unified, cooperative interconnection of networks that supports a universal communication service. Within each network, computers will use underlying technology-dependent communication facilities like those described in Chapter 2. New software, inserted between the technology-dependent communication mechanisms and application programs, will hide the low-level details and make the collection of networks appear to be a single large network. Such an interconnection scheme is called an *internetwork* or *internet*.

The idea of building an internet follows a standard pattern of system design: researchers imagine a high-level computing facility and work from available computing technology, adding layers of software until they have a system that efficiently implements the imagined high-level facility. The next section shows the first step of the design process by defining the goal more precisely.

3.4 Properties Of The Internet

The notion of universal service is important, but it alone does not capture all the ideas we have in mind for a unified internet because there can be many implementations of universal services. In our design, we want to hide the underlying internet architecture from the user. That is, we do not want to require users or application programs to understand the details of hardware interconnections to use the internet. We also do not want to mandate a network interconnection topology. In particular, adding a new network to the internet should not mean connecting to a centralized switching point, nor should it mean adding direct physical connections between the new network and all existing networks. We want to be able to send data across intermediate networks even though they are not directly connected to the source or destination computers. We want all computers in the internet to share a universal set of machine identifiers (which can be thought of as *names* or *addresses*).

Our notion of a unified internet also includes the idea of network independence in the user interface. That is, we want the set of operations used to establish communication or to transfer data to remain independent of the underlying network technologies and the destination computer. Certainly, a user should not have to understand the network interconnection topology when creating or using application programs that communicate.

3.5 Internet Architecture

We have seen how computers connect to individual networks. The question arises, "How are networks interconnected to form an internetwork?" The answer has two parts. Physically, two networks can only be connected by a computer that attaches to both of them. A physical attachment does not provide the interconnection we have in mind, however, because such a connection does not guarantee that the computer will cooperate with other machines that wish to communicate. To have a viable internet, we need special computers that are willing to transfer packets from one network to another. Computers that interconnect two networks and pass packets from one to the other are called *internet gateways* or *internet routers*†.

Consider an example consisting of two physical networks shown in Figure 3.1. In the figure, router *R* connects to both network *1* and network *2*. For *R* to act as a router, it must capture packets on network *1* that are bound for machines on network *2* and transfer them. Similarly, *R* must capture packets on network *2* that are destined for machines on network *1* and transfer them.

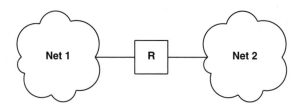

Figure 3.1 Two physical networks interconnected by *R*, a router (IP gateway).

In the figure, clouds are used to denote physical networks because the exact hardware is unimportant. Each network can be a LAN or a WAN, and each may have many computers attached or a few computers attached.

3.6 Interconnection Through IP Routers

Although it illustrates the basic connection strategy, Figure 3.1 is quite simplistic. In an actual internet that includes many networks and routers, each router needs to know about the topology of the internet beyond the networks to which it connects. For example, Figure 3.2 shows three networks interconnected by two routers.

---

†The original literature used the term *IP gateway*. However, vendors have adopted the term *IP router* — the two terms are used interchangeably throughout this text.

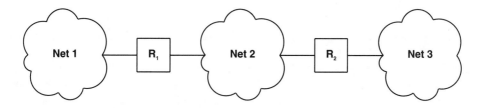

Figure 3.2 Three networks interconnected by two routers.

In this example, router R_1 must transfer from network *1* to network *2* all packets destined for computers on either network *2* or network *3*. For a large internet composed of many networks, the router's task of making decisions about where to send packets becomes more complex.

The idea of a router seems simple, but it is important because it provides a way to interconnect networks, not just computers. In fact, we have already discovered the principle of interconnection used throughout an internet:

> *In a TCP/IP internet, special computers called* IP routers *or* IP gateways *provide interconnections among physical networks.*

You might suspect that routers, which must each know how to forward packets toward their destination, are large machines with enough primary or secondary memory to hold information about every computer in the internet to which they attach. In fact, routers used with TCP/IP internets are usually small computers. They often have little disk storage and modest main memories. The trick to building a small internet router lies in the following concept:

> *Routers use the destination network, not the destination computer, when forwarding a packet.*

If packet forwarding is based on networks, the amount of information that a router needs to keep is proportional to the number of networks in the internet, not the number of computers.

Because routers play a key role in internet communication, we will return to them in later chapters and discuss the details of how they operate and how they learn about routes. For now, we will assume that it is possible and practical to have correct routes for all networks in each router in the internet. We will also assume that only routers provide connections between physical networks in an internet.

3.7 The User's View

Remember that TCP/IP is designed to provide a universal interconnection among computers independent of the particular networks to which they attach. Thus, we want a user to view an internet as a single, virtual network to which all machines connect despite their physical connections. Figure 3.3a shows how thinking of an internet instead of constituent networks simplifies the details and makes it easy for the user to conceptualize communication. In addition to routers that interconnect physical networks, software is needed on each computer to allow application programs to use an internet as if it were a single, physical network.

The advantage of providing interconnection at the network level now becomes clear. Because application programs that communicate over the internet do not know the details of underlying connections, they can be run without change on any computer. Because the details of each machine's physical network connections are hidden in the internet software, only the internet software needs to change when new physical connections are added or existing connections are removed. In fact, it is possible to optimize the internal structure of the internet by altering physical connections while application programs are executing.

A second advantage of having communication at the network level is more subtle: users do not have to understand, remember, or specify how networks connect or what traffic they carry. Application programs can be written that communicate independent of underlying physical connectivity. In fact, network managers are free to change interior parts of the underlying internet architecture without changing application software in most of the computers attached to the internet (of course, network software must be reconfigured when a computer moves to a new network).

As Figure 3.3b shows, routers do not provide direct connections among all pairs of networks. It may be necessary for traffic traveling from one computer to another to pass through several routers as the traffic crosses intermediate networks. Thus, networks participating in an internet are analogous to highways in the U.S. interstate system: each net agrees to handle transit traffic in exchange for the right to send traffic throughout the internet. Typical users are unaffected and unaware of extra traffic on their local network.

3.8 All Networks Are Equal

Chapter 2 reviewed examples of the network hardware used to build TCP/IP internets, and illustrated the great diversity of technologies. We have described an internet as a collection of cooperative, interconnected networks. It is now important to understand a fundamental concept: from the internet point of view, any communication system capable of transferring packets counts as a single network, independent of its delay and throughput characteristics, maximum packet size, or geographic scale. In particular, Figure 3.3b uses the same small cloud shape to depict each physical network because TCP/IP treats them equally despite their differences. The point is:

> *The TCP/IP internet protocols treat all networks equally. A Local Area Network like an Ethernet, a Wide Area Network used as a backbone, or a point-to-point link between two computers each count as one network.*

Readers unaccustomed to internet architecture may find it difficult to accept such a simplistic view of networks. In essence, TCP/IP defines an abstraction of "network" that hides the details of physical networks; we will learn that such abstractions help make TCP/IP extremely powerful.

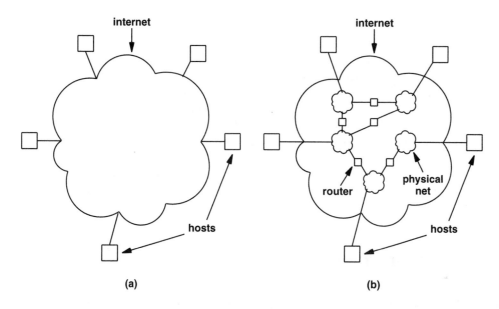

Figure 3.3 (a) The user's view of a TCP/IP internet in which each computer appears to attach to a single large network, and (b) the structure of physical networks and routers that provide interconnection.

3.9 The Unanswered Questions

Our sketch of internets leaves many unanswered questions. For example, you might wonder about the exact form of internet addresses assigned to computers or how such addresses relate to the Ethernet, FDDI, or ATM physical hardware addresses described in Chapter 2. The next three chapters confront these questions. They describe the format of IP addresses and illustrate how software on a computer maps between internet addresses and physical addresses. You might also want to know exactly what a packet looks like when it travels through an internet, or what happens when packets arrive too fast for some computer or router to handle. Chapter 7 answers these questions. Finally, you might wonder how multiple application programs executing concurrently on a single computer can send and receive packets to multiple destinations without becoming entangled in each other's transmissions or how internet routers learn about routes. All of these questions will be answered as well.

Although it may seem vague now, the direction we are following will let us learn about both the structure and use of internet protocol software. We will examine each part, looking at the concepts and principles as well as technical details. We began by describing the physical communication layer on which an internet is built. Each of the following chapters will explore one part of the internet software, until we understand how all the pieces fit together.

3.10 Summary

An internet is more than a collection of networks interconnected by computers. Internetworking implies that the interconnected systems agree to conventions that allow each computer to communicate with every other computer. In particular, an internet will allow two computers to communicate even if the communication path between them passes across a network to which neither connects directly. Such cooperation is only possible when computers agree on a set of universal identifiers and a set of procedures for moving data to its final destination.

In an internet, interconnections among networks are formed by computers called IP routers, or IP gateways, that attach to two or more networks. A router forwards packets between networks by receiving them from one network and sending them to another.

FOR FURTHER STUDY

Our model of an internetwork comes from Cerf and Cain [1983] and Cerf and Kahn [1974], which describe an internet as a set of networks interconnected by routers and sketch an internet protocol similar to that eventually developed for the TCP/IP protocol suite. More information on the connected Internet architecture can be found in Postel [1980]; Postel, Sunshine, and Chen [1981]; and in Hinden, Haverty, and Sheltzer [1983]. Shoch [1978] presents issues in internetwork naming and addressing. Boggs *et. al.* [1980] describes the internet developed at Xerox PARC, an alternative to the TCP/IP internet we will examine. Cheriton [1983] describes internetworking as it relates to the V-system.

EXERCISES

3.1 What processors have been used as routers in the connected Internet? Does the size and speed of early router hardware surprise you? Why?

3.2 Approximately how many networks comprise the internet at your site? Approximately how many routers?

3.3 Consider the internal structure of the example internet shown in Figure 3.3b. Which routers are most crucial? Why?

3.4 Changing the information in a router can be tricky because it is impossible to change all routers simultaneously. Investigate algorithms that guarantee to either install a change on a set of computers or install it on none.

3.5 In an internet, routers periodically exchange information from their routing tables, making it possible for a new router to appear and begin routing packets. Investigate the algorithms used to exchange routing information.

3.6 Compare the organization of a TCP/IP internet to the style of internet designed by Xerox Corporation.

4

Classful Internet Addresses

4.1 Introduction

The previous chapter defines a TCP/IP internet as a virtual network built by interconnecting physical networks with routers. This chapter discusses addressing, an essential ingredient that helps TCP/IP software hide physical network details and makes the resulting internet appear to be a single, uniform entity.

4.2 Universal Identifiers

A communication system is said to supply *universal communication service* if it allows any host computer to communicate with any other host. To make our communication system universal, it needs a globally accepted method of identifying each computer that attaches to it.

Often, host identifiers are classified as *names*, *addresses*, or *routes*. Shoch [1978] suggests that a name identifies *what* an object is, an address identifies *where* it is, and a route tells *how* to get there†. Although these definitions are intuitive, they can be misleading. Names, addresses, and routes really refer to successively lower level representations of host identifiers. In general, people usually prefer pronounceable names to identify machines, while software works more efficiently with compact representations of identifiers that we think of as addresses. Either could have been chosen as the TCP/IP universal host identifiers. The decision was made to standardize on compact, binary addresses that make computations such as the selection of a route efficient. For now, we will discuss only binary addresses, postponing until later the questions of how to map between binary addresses and pronounceable names, and how to use addresses for routing.

---

†An identifier that specifies where an object can be found is also called a *locator*.

63

4.3 The Original Classful Addressing Scheme

Think of an internet as a large network like any other physical network. The difference, of course, is that the internet is a virtual structure, imagined by its designers, and implemented entirely in software. Thus, the designers are free to choose packet formats and sizes, addresses, delivery techniques, and so on; nothing is dictated by hardware. For addresses, the designers of TCP/IP chose a scheme analogous to physical network addressing in which each host on the internet is assigned a 32-bit integer address called its *internet address* or *IP address*. The clever part of internet addressing is that the integers are carefully chosen to make routing efficient. Specifically, an IP address encodes the identification of the network to which a host attaches as well as the identification of a unique host on that network. We can summarize:

> *Each host on a TCP/IP internet is assigned a unique 32-bit internet address that is used in all communication with that host.*

The details of IP addresses help clarify the abstract ideas. For now, we give a simplified view and expand it later. In the simplest case, each host attached to an internet is assigned a 32-bit universal identifier as its internet address. A prefix of an IP address identifies a network. That is, the IP addresses in all hosts on a given network share a common prefix.

Conceptually, each address is a pair (*netid*, *hostid*), where *netid* identifies a network, and *hostid* identifies a host on that network. In practice, however, the partition into prefix and suffix is not uniform throughout the entire internet because the designers did not specify a single boundary. In the original addressing scheme, which is known as *classful*, each IP address had one of the first three forms shown in Figure 4.1†.

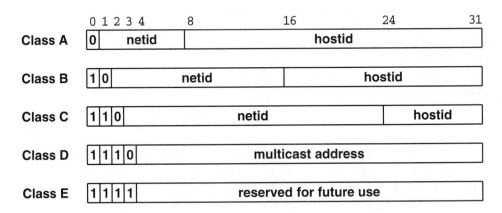

Figure 4.1 The five forms of Internet (IP) addresses used with the original classful addressing scheme. The three primary classes, *A*, *B* and *C*, can be distinguished by the first three bits.

---

†The fourth form, reserved for internet multicasting, will be described later; for now, we will restrict our comments to the forms that specify addresses of individual objects.

In the classful addressing scheme, each address is said to be *self-identifying* because the boundary between prefix and suffix can be computed from the address alone, without reference to external information. In particular, the class of an address can be determined from the three high-order bits, with two bits being sufficient to distinguish among the three primary classes. Class *A* addresses, used for the handful of networks that have more than 2^{16} (i.e., 65,536) hosts, devote 7 bits to netid and 24 bits to hostid. Class *B* addresses, used for intermediate size networks that have between 2^8 (i.e., 256) and 2^{16} hosts, allocate 14 bits to the netid and 16 bits to the hostid. Finally, class *C* addresses, used for networks that have less than 2^8 hosts, allocate 21 bits to the netid and only 8 bits to the hostid. Note that the IP address was originally defined in such a way that it was possible to extract the hostid or netid portions quickly. Efficiency was especially important for routers, which use the netid portion of an address when deciding where to send a packet. We will return to the discussion of efficient route lookup after examining recent changes and extensions to the addressing scheme.

4.4 Addresses Specify Network Connections

To simplify the discussion, we said that an internet address identifies a host, but that is not strictly accurate. Consider a router that attaches to two physical networks. How can we assign a single IP address if the address encodes a network identifier as well as a host identifier? In fact, we cannot. When conventional computers have two or more physical connections they are called *multi-homed hosts*. Multi-homed hosts and routers require multiple IP addresses. Each address corresponds to one of the machine's network connections. Looking at multi-homed hosts leads to the following important idea:

> *Because IP addresses encode both a network and a host on that network, they do not specify an individual computer, but a connection to a network.*

Thus, a router connecting *n* networks has *n* distinct IP addresses, one for each network connection.

4.5 Network And Directed Broadcast Addresses

We have already cited the major advantage of encoding network information in internet addresses: it makes efficient routing possible. Another advantage is that internet addresses can refer to networks as well as hosts. By convention, hostid *0* is never assigned to an individual host. Instead, an IP address with hostid portion equal to zero is used to refer to the network itself. In summary:

Internet addresses can be used to refer to networks as well as individual hosts. By convention, an address that has all bits of the hostid equal to 0 is reserved to refer to the network.

Another significant advantage of the internet addressing scheme is that it includes a *directed broadcast address* that refers to all hosts on the network. According to the standard, any address with the hostid consisting of all *1s* is reserved for directed broadcast†. When a packet is sent to such an address, a single copy of the packet is transferred across the internet from the source. Routers along the path use the netid portion of the address when choosing a path; they do not look at the host portion. Once the packet reaches a router attached to the final network, that router examines the host portion of the address to determine how to deliver the packet. If it finds all *1s*, the router broadcasts the packet to all hosts on the network.

On many network technologies (e.g., Ethernet), broadcasting is as efficient as unicast transmission; on others, broadcasting is supported by the network software, but requires substantially more delay than single transmission. Some network hardware does not support broadcast at all. Thus, having an IP directed broadcast address does not guarantee the availability or efficiency of broadcast delivery. In summary,

IP addresses can be used to specify a directed broadcast in which a packet is sent to all computers on a network; such addresses map to hardware broadcast, if available. By convention, a directed broadcast address has a valid netid and has a hostid with all bits set to 1.

4.6 Limited Broadcast

The broadcast address we just described is known as *directed* because it contains both a valid network ID and the broadcast hostid. A directed broadcast address can be interpreted unambiguously at any point in an internet because it uniquely identifies the target network in addition to specifying broadcast on that network. Directed broadcast addresses provide a powerful (and somewhat dangerous) mechanism that allows a remote system to send a single packet that will be broadcast on the specified network.

From an addressing point of view, the chief disadvantage of directed broadcast is that it requires knowledge of the network address. Another form of broadcast address, called a *limited broadcast address* or *local network broadcast address*, provides a broadcast address for the local network independent of the assigned IP address. The local broadcast address consists of thirty-two *1s* (hence, it is sometimes called the "all *1s*" broadcast address). A host may use the limited broadcast address as part of a startup procedure before it learns its IP address or the IP address prefix for the local network. Once the host learns the correct IP address for the local network, however, it should use directed broadcast.

---

†Unfortunately, an early release of TCP/IP code that accompanied Berkeley UNIX incorrectly used all zeroes for broadcast. Because the error still survives, TCP/IP software often includes an option that allows a site to use all zeroes for directed broadcast.

As a general rule, TCP/IP protocols restrict broadcasting to the smallest possible set of machines. We will see how this rule affects multiple networks that share addresses in the chapter on subnet addressing.

4.7 Interpreting Zero To Mean "This"

We have seen that a field consisting of *1*s can be interpreted to mean "all," as in "all hosts" on a network. In general, internet software interprets fields consisting of *0*s to mean "this." The interpretation appears throughout the literature. Thus, an IP address with hostid *0* refers to "this" host, and an internet address with network ID *0* refers to "this" network. Of course, it is only meaningful to use such an address in a context where it can be interpreted unambiguously. For example, if a machine receives a packet in which the netid portion of the destination address is *0* and the hostid portion of the destination address matches its address, the receiver interprets the netid field to mean "this" network (i.e., the network over which the packet arrived).

Using netid *0* is especially important in those cases where a host wants to communicate over a network but does not yet know the network IP address. The host uses network ID *0* temporarily, and other hosts on the network interpret the address as meaning "this" network. In most cases, replies will have the network address fully specified, allowing the original sender to record it for future use. Chapters 9 and 23 will discuss in detail mechanisms a host can use to determine the network ID of the local network.

4.8 Subnet And Supernet Extensions

The addressing scheme described so far requires a unique network prefix for each physical network. Although that was, indeed, the original plan, it did not last long. In the 1980s as Local Area Network technologies became increasingly popular, it became apparent that requiring a unique prefix for each physical network would exhaust the address space quickly. Consequently, an addressing extension was developed to conserve network prefixes. Known as *subnet addressing*, the scheme allows multiple physical networks to share a prefix.

In the 1990s, a second extension was devised that ignored the classful hierarchy and allowed the division between prefix and suffix to occur at an arbitrary point. Called *classless addressing* or *supernetting*, the scheme allows more complete utilization of the address space.

Chapter 10 will consider details of the subnet and supernet addressing extensions. For now, it is only important to know that the addressing scheme has been extended, and that the original classful scheme described in this chapter is no longer the most widely used.

4.9 IP Multicast Addresses

In addition to *unicast delivery*, in which a packet is delivered to a single computer, and *broadcast delivery*, in which a packet is delivered to all computers on a given network, the IP addressing scheme supports a special form of multipoint delivery known as *multicasting*, in which a packet is delivered to a specific subset of hosts. IP multicasting is especially useful for networks where the hardware technology supports multicast delivery. Chapter 17 discusses multicast addressing and delivery in detail. For now, it is sufficient to understand that Class *D* addresses are reserved for multicasting.

4.10 Weaknesses In Internet Addressing

Encoding network information in an internet address does have some disadvantages. The most obvious disadvantage is that addresses refer to network connections, not to the host computer:

> *If a host computer moves from one network to another, its IP address must change.*

To understand the consequences, consider a traveler who wishes to disconnect his or her personal computer, carry it along on a trip, and reconnect it to the Internet after reaching the destination. The personal computer cannot be assigned a permanent IP address because an IP address identifies the network to which the machine attaches. Chapter 19 shows how the IP addressing scheme makes *mobility* a complex problem.

Another weakness of the classful addressing scheme is that when any class *C* network grows to more than 255 hosts, it must have its address changed to a class *B* address. While this may seem like a minor problem, changing network addresses can be incredibly time-consuming and difficult to debug. Because most software is not designed to handle multiple addresses for the same physical network, administrators cannot plan a smooth transition in which they introduce new addresses slowly. Instead, they must abruptly stop using one network address, change the addresses of all machines, and then resume communication using the new network address.

The most important flaw in the internet addressing scheme will not become fully apparent until we examine routing. However, its importance warrants a brief introduction here. We have suggested that routing will be based on internet addresses, with the netid portion of an address used to make routing decisions. Consider a host with two connections to the internet. We know that such a host must have more than one IP address. The following is true:

> *Because routing uses the network portion of the IP address, the path taken by packets traveling to a host with multiple IP addresses depends on the address used.*

The implications are surprising. Humans think of each host as a single entity and want to use a single name. They are often surprised to find that they must learn more than one name and even more surprised to find that packets sent using multiple names can behave differently.

Another surprising consequence of the internet addressing scheme is that merely knowing one IP address for a destination may not be sufficient; it may be impossible to reach the destination using that address. Consider the example internet shown in Figure 4.2. In the figure, two hosts, *A* and *B*, both attach to network *1*, and usually communicate directly using that network. Thus, users on host *A* should normally refer to host *B* using IP address I_3. An alternate path from *A* to *B* exists through router *R*, and is used whenever *A* sends packets to IP address I_5 (B's address on network *2*). Now suppose *B*'s connection to network *1* fails, but the machine itself remains running (e.g., a wire breaks between *B* and network *1*). Users on *A* who specify IP address I_3 cannot reach *B*, although users who specify address I_5 can. These problems with naming and addressing will arise again in later chapters when we consider routing and name binding.

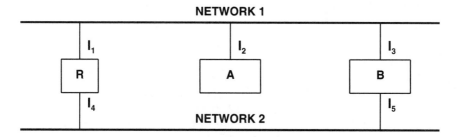

Figure 4.2 An example internet with a multi-homed host, *B*, that demonstrates a disadvantage of the IP addressing scheme. If interface I_3 becomes disconnected, *A* must use address I_5 to reach *B*, sending packets through router *R*.

4.11 Dotted Decimal Notation

When communicated to humans, either in technical documents or through application programs, IP addresses are written as four decimal integers separated by decimal points, where each integer gives the value of one octet of the IP address†. Thus, the 32-bit internet address

10000000   00001010   00000010   00011110

is written

128.10.2.30

---

†Dotted decimal notation is sometimes called *dotted quad notation*.

We will use dotted decimal notation when expressing IP addresses throughout the remainder of this text. Indeed, most TCP/IP software that displays or requires a human to enter an IP address uses dotted decimal notation. For example, the UNIX *netstat* command, which displays information about routes and connections, and application programs such as *telnet* and *ftp* all use dotted decimal notation when accepting or displaying IP addresses. Thus, when classful addressing is used, it is helpful to understand the relationship between IP address classes and dotted decimal numbers. The table in Figure 4.3 summarizes the range of values for each class.

Class	Lowest Address	Highest Address
A	1.0.0.0	126.0.0.0
B	128.1.0.0	191.255.0.0
C	192.0.1.0	223.255.255.0
D	224.0.0.0	239.255.255.255
E	240.0.0.0	255.255.255.254

Figure 4.3 The range of dotted decimal values that correspond to each IP address class. Some values are reserved for special purposes.

4.12 Loopback Address

The table in Figure 4.3 shows that not all possible addresses have been assigned to classes. In particular, the network prefix 127.0.0.0, a value from the class A range, is reserved for *loopback*, and is intended for use in testing TCP/IP and for inter-process communication on the local computer. When any program uses the loopback address as a destination, the protocol software in the computer processes the data without sending traffic across any network. The literature explicitly states that a packet sent to a network 127 address should never appear on any network. Furthermore, a host or router should never propagate routing or reachability information for network number *127*; it is not a network address.

4.13 Summary Of Special Address Conventions

In practice, IP uses only a few combinations of *0*s (''this'') or *1*s (''all''). Figure 4.4 lists the possibilities.

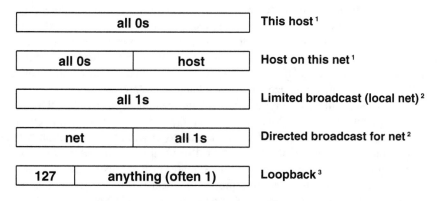

Notes: [1] Allowed only at system startup and is
never a valid destination address.
[2] Never a valid source address.
[3] Should never appear on a network.

Figure 4.4 Special forms of IP addresses, including valid combinations of *0*s ("this"), *1*s ("all"). The length of the net portion of a directed broadcast depends on the network address class.

As the notes in the figure mention, using all *0*s for the network is only allowed during the bootstrap procedure. Doing so allows a machine to communicate temporarily. Once the machine learns its correct network and IP address, it must not use network prefix *0*.

4.14 Internet Addressing Authority

Each network address prefix used within a given TCP/IP internet must be unique. An organization that uses TCP/IP technology to build a completely private internet (i.e., one that is not connected to the global Internet) can assign address prefixes without considering the assignments made by other organizations. However, an organization that connects to the global Internet must not use address prefixes assigned to another organization. To ensure that the network portion of an address is unique in the global internet, all Internet addresses are assigned by a central authority. Originally, the *Internet Assigned Number Authority* (*IANA*) had control over numbers assigned, and set the policy. From the time the Internet began until the fall of 1998, a single individual, Jon Postel, ran the IANA and assigned addresses. In late 1998, after Jon's untimely death, a new organization was created to handle address assignment. Named the *Internet Corporation For Assigned Names and Numbers* (*ICANN*), the organization sets policy and assigns values for names and other constants used in protocols as well as addresses.

In the original classful scheme, the Internet authority chose an address appropriate to the size of the network. A class C number was assigned to a network with a small number of attached computers (less than 255); class B numbers were reserved for larger networks. Finally, a network needed to have more than 65,535 hosts before it could obtain a class A number. The address space was skewed because most networks are small, fewer are of medium size, and only a handful are gigantic.

Most organizations never interact with the central authority directly. Instead, to connect its networks to the global Internet, an organization usually contracts with a local *Internet Service Provider* (*ISP*). In addition to providing a connection between the organization and the rest of the Internet, an ISP obtains a valid address prefix for each of the customer's networks. Many local ISPs are, in fact, customers of larger ISPs — when a customer requests an address prefix, the local ISP merely obtains a prefix from a larger ISP. Thus, only the largest ISPs need to contact ICANN.

Note that the central authority only assigns the network portion of an address; once an organization obtains a prefix for a network, the organization can choose how to assign a unique suffix to each host on the network without contacting the central authority. Furthermore, remember that it is only essential for the central authority to assign IP addresses for networks that are (or will be) attached to the global Internet.

4.15 Reserved Address Prefixes

We said that as long as it never connects to the outside world, an individual corporation has responsibility for assigning unique network addresses within its TCP/IP internet. Indeed, many corporate groups that use TCP/IP protocols do assign internet addresses on their own. For example, the network address 9.0.0.0 has been assigned to IBM Corporation, and address 12.0.0.0 has been assigned to AT&T. If an organization decides to use TCP/IP protocols on two of their networks with no connections to the global Internet, the organization can choose to assign addresses 9.0.0.0 and 12.0.0.0 to their local networks.

Experience has shown, however, that it is unwise to create a private internet using the same network addresses as the global Internet because most sites eventually connect to the Internet and doing so may cause problems when trying to exchange software with other sites. To avoid addressing conflicts between addresses used on private internets and addresses used on the global Internet, the IETF reserved several address prefixes, and recommends using them on private internets. Because the set of reserved prefixes includes both classful and classless values, they are described in Chapter 10.

4.16 An Example

To clarify the IP addressing scheme, consider an example of two networks in the Computer Science Department at Purdue University as they were connected to the Internet in the mid-1980s. Figure 4.5 shows the network addresses, and illustrates how routers interconnect the networks.

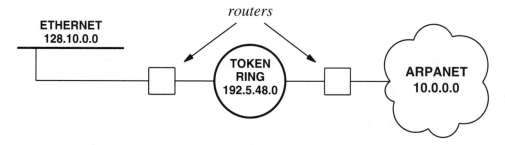

Figure 4.5 The logical connection of two networks to the Internet backbone.
Each network has been assigned an IP address.

The example shows three networks and the network numbers they have been assigned: the ARPANET (10.0.0.0), an Ethernet (128.10.0.0), and a token ring network (192.5.48.0). According to the table in Figure 4.3, the addresses have classes A, B, and C, respectively.

Figure 4.6 shows the same networks with host computers attached and Internet addresses assigned to each network connection.

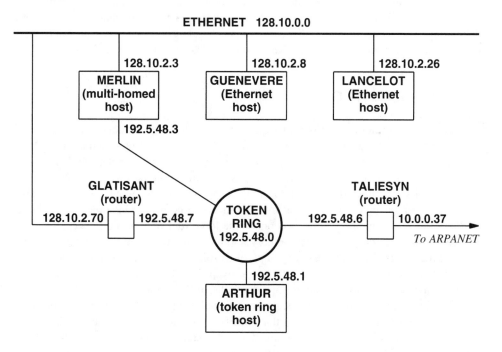

Figure 4.6 Example IP address assignment for routers and hosts attached to
the three networks in the previous figure.

In the figure, four hosts labeled *Arthur*, *Merlin*, *Guenevere*, and *Lancelot*, attach to the networks, *Taliesyn* is a router that connects the ARPANET and the token ring network, and *Glatisant* is a router that connects the token ring network to the Ethernet. Host *Merlin* has connections to both the Ethernet and the token ring network, so it can reach destinations on either network directly. Although a multi-homed host like *Merlin* can be configured to route packets between the two nets, most sites use dedicated computers as routers to avoid overloading conventional computer systems with the processing required for routing. In the figure, a dedicated router, *Glatisant*, performs the task of routing traffic between the Ethernet and token ring networks. (Note: actual traffic between these two networks was higher than this configuration suggests because the figure only shows a few of the computers attached to the nets.)

As Figure 4.5 shows, an IP address must be assigned to each network connection. *Lancelot*, which connects only to the Ethernet, has been assigned 128.10.2.26 as its only IP address. *Merlin* has address 128.10.2.3 for its connection to the Ethernet and 192.5.48.3 for its connection to the token ring network. Whoever made the address assignment chose the same value for the low-order byte of each address. The addresses assigned to routers *Glatisant* and *Taliesyn* do not follow the convention. For example, *Taliesyn's* addresses, 10.0.0.37 and 192.5.48.6, are two completely unrelated strings of digits. IP does not care whether any of the bytes in the dotted decimal form of a computer's addresses are the same or different. However, network technicians, managers, and administrators may need to use addresses for maintenance, testing, and debugging. Choosing to make all of a computer's addresses end with the same octet makes it easier for humans to remember or guess the address of a particular interface.

4.17 Network Byte Order

To create an internet that is independent of any particular vendor's machine architecture or network hardware, the software must define a standard representation for data. Consider what happens, for example, when software on one computer sends a 32-bit binary integer to another computer. The physical transport hardware moves the sequence of bits from the first machine to the second without changing the order. However, not all architectures store 32-bit integers in the same way. On some (called *Little Endian*), the lowest memory address contains the low-order byte of the integer. On others (called *Big Endian*), the lowest memory address holds the high-order byte of the integer. Still others store integers in groups of 16-bit words, with the lowest addresses holding the low-order word, but with bytes swapped. Thus, direct copying of bytes from one machine to another may change the value of the number.

Standardizing byte-order for integers is especially important in an internet because internet packets carry binary numbers that specify information like destination addresses and packet lengths. Such quantities must be understood by both the senders and receivers. The TCP/IP protocols solve the byte-order problem by defining a *network standard byte order* that all machines must use for binary fields in internet packets. Each host or router converts binary items from the local representation to network standard byte order before sending a packet, and converts from network byte order to the host-specific order when a packet arrives. Naturally, the user data field in a packet is exempt from this standard because the TCP/IP protocols do not know what data is being carried — application programmers are free to format their own data representation and translation. When sending integer values, many application programmers do choose to follow the TCP/IP byte-order standards. Of course, users who merely invoke application programs never need to deal with the byte order problem directly.

The internet standard for byte order specifies that integers are sent with the most significant byte first (i.e., *Big Endian* style). If one considers the successive bytes in a packet as it travels from one machine to another, a binary integer in that packet has its most significant byte nearest the beginning of the packet and its least significant byte nearest the end of the packet. Many arguments have been offered about which data representation should be used, and the internet standard still comes under attack from time to time. In particular, proponents of change argue that although most computers were big endian when the standard was defined, most are now little endian. However, everyone agrees that having a standard is crucial, and the exact form of the standard is far less important.

4.18 Summary

TCP/IP uses 32-bit binary addresses as universal machine identifiers. Called Internet Protocol addresses or IP addresses, the identifiers are partitioned into two parts: a prefix identifies the network to which the computer attaches and the suffix provides a unique identifier for the computer on that network. The original IP addressing scheme is known as classful, with each prefix assigned to one of three primary classes. Leading bits define the class of an address; the classes are of unequal size. The classful scheme provides for 127 networks with over a million hosts each, thousands of networks with thousands of hosts each, and over a million networks with up to 254 hosts each. To make such addresses easier for humans to understand, they are written in dotted decimal notation, with the values of the four octets written in decimal, separated by decimal points.

Because the IP address encodes network identification as well as the identification of a specific host on that network, routing is efficient. An important property of IP addresses is that they refer to network connections. Hosts with multiple connections have multiple addresses. One advantage of the internet addressing scheme is that the form includes an address for a specific host, a network, or all hosts on a network (broadcast). The biggest disadvantage of the IP addressing scheme is that if a machine has multiple addresses, knowing one address may not be sufficient to reach it when no path exists to the specified interface (e.g., because a particular network is unavailable).

To permit the exchange of binary data among machines, TCP/IP protocols enforce a standard byte ordering for integers within protocol fields. A host must convert all binary data from its internal form to network standard byte order before sending a packet, and it must convert from network byte order to internal order upon receipt.

FOR FURTHER STUDY

The internet addressing scheme presented here can be found in Reynolds and Postel [RFC 1700]; further information can be found in Stahl, Romano, and Recker [RFC 1117].

Several important additions have been made to the Internet addressing scheme over the years; later chapters cover them in more detail. Chapter 10 discusses an important extension called *classless addressing* that permits the division between prefix and suffix to occur at an arbitrary bit position. In addition, Chapter 10 examines an essential part of the Internet address standard called *subnet addressing*. Subnet addressing allows a single network address to be used with multiple physical networks. Chapter 17 continues the exploration of IP addresses by describing how class D addresses are assigned for internet *multicast*.

Cohen [1981] explains bit and byte ordering, and introduces the terms ''Big Endian'' and ''Little Endian.''

EXERCISES

4.1   Exactly how many class A, B, and C networks can exist? Exactly how many hosts can a network in each class have? Be careful to allow for broadcast as well as class D and E addresses.

4.2   A machine readable list of assigned addresses is sometimes called an internet *host table*. If your site has a host table, find out how many class A, B, and C network numbers have been assigned.

4.3   How many hosts are attached to each of the local area networks at your site? Does your site have any local area networks for which a class C address is insufficient?

4.4   What is the chief difference between the IP addressing scheme and the U.S. telephone numbering scheme?

4.5   A single central authority cannot manage to assign Internet addresses fast enough to accommodate the demand. Can you invent a scheme that allows the central authority to divide its task among several groups but still ensure that each assigned address is unique?

4.6   Does network standard byte order differ from your local machine's byte order?

4.7   How many IP addresses would be needed to assign a unique IP address to every house in your country? the world? Is the IP address space sufficient?

5

Mapping Internet Addresses
To Physical Addresses
(ARP)

5.1 Introduction

We described the TCP/IP address scheme in which each host is assigned a 32-bit address, and said that an internet behaves like a virtual network, using only the assigned addresses when sending and receiving packets. We also reviewed several network hardware technologies, and noted that two machines on a given physical network can communicate *only if they know each other's physical network address*. What we have not mentioned is how a host or a router maps an IP address to the correct physical address when it needs to send a packet across a physical net. This chapter considers that mapping, showing how it is implemented for the two most common physical network address schemes.

5.2 The Address Resolution Problem

Consider two machines A and B that connect to the same physical network. Each has an assigned IP address I_A and I_B and a physical address P_A and P_B. The goal is to devise low-level software that hides physical addresses and allows higher-level programs to work only with internet addresses. Ultimately, however, communication must be carried out by physical networks using whatever physical address scheme the underlying network hardware supplies. Suppose machine A wants to send a packet to machine B across a physical network to which they both attach, but A has only B's internet address I_B. The question arises: how does A map that address to B's physical address, P_B?

Address mapping must be performed at each step along a path from the original source to the ultimate destination. In particular, two cases arise. First, at the last step of delivering a packet, the packet must be sent across one physical network to its final destination. The computer sending the packet must map the final destination's Internet address to the destination's physical address. Second, at any point along the path from the source to the destination other than the final step, the packet must be sent to an intermediate router. Thus, the sender must map the intermediate router's Internet address to a physical address.

The problem of mapping high-level addresses to physical addresses is known as the *address resolution problem* and has been solved in several ways. Some protocol suites keep tables in each machine that contain pairs of high-level and physical addresses. Others solve the problem by encoding hardware addresses in high-level addresses. Using either approach exclusively makes high-level addressing awkward at best. This chapter discusses two techniques for address resolution used by TCP/IP protocols and shows when each is appropriate.

5.3 Two Types Of Physical Addresses

There are two basic types of physical addresses, exemplified by the Ethernet, which has large, fixed physical addresses, and proNET, which has small, easily configured physical addresses. Address resolution is difficult for Ethernet-like networks, but easy for networks like proNET. We will consider the easy case first.

5.4 Resolution Through Direct Mapping

Consider a proNET token ring network. Recall from Chapter 2 that proNET uses small integers for physical addresses and allows the user to choose a hardware address when installing an interface board in a computer. The key to making address resolution easy with such network hardware lies in observing that as long as one has the freedom to choose both IP and physical addresses, they can be selected such that parts of them are the same. Typically, one assigns IP addresses with the hostid portion equal to 1, 2, 3, and so on, and then, when installing network interface hardware, selects a physical address that corresponds to the IP address. For example, the system administrator would select physical address 3 for a computer with the IP address 192.5.48.3 because 192.5.48.3 is a class C address with the host portion equal to 3.

For networks like proNET, computing a physical address from an IP address is trivial. The computation consists of extracting the host portion of the IP address. Extraction is computationally efficient on most architectures because it requires only a few machine instructions. The mapping is easy to maintain because it can be performed without reference to external data. Finally, new computers can be added to the network without changing existing assignments or recompiling code.

Conceptually, choosing a numbering scheme that makes address resolution efficient means selecting a function f that maps IP addresses to physical addresses. The designer may be able to select a physical address numbering scheme as well, depending on the hardware. Resolving IP address I_A means computing

$$P_A = f(I_A)$$

We want the computation of f to be efficient. If the set of physical addresses is constrained, it may be possible to arrange efficient mappings other than the one given in the example above. For instance, when using IP over a connection-oriented network such as ATM, one cannot choose physical addresses. On such networks, one or more computers (servers) store pairs of addresses, where each pair contains an Internet address and the corresponding physical address. Typically, such servers store the pairs in a table in memory to speed searching. To guarantee efficient address resolution in such cases, software can use a conventional hash function to search the table. Exercise 5.1 suggests a related alternative.

5.5 Resolution Through Dynamic Binding

To understand why address resolution is difficult for some networks, consider Ethernet technology. Recall from Chapter 2 that each Ethernet interface is assigned a 48-bit physical address when the device is manufactured. As a consequence, when hardware fails and requires that an Ethernet interface be replaced, the machine's physical address changes. Furthermore, because the Ethernet address is 48 bits long, there is no hope it can be encoded in a 32-bit IP address†.

Designers of TCP/IP protocols found a creative solution to the address resolution problem for networks like the Ethernet that have broadcast capability. The solution allows new hosts or routers to be added to the network without recompiling code, and does not require maintenance of a centralized database. To avoid maintaining a table of mappings, the designers chose to use a low-level protocol to bind addresses dynamically. Termed the *Address Resolution Protocol* (*ARP*), the protocol provides a mechanism that is both reasonably efficient and easy to maintain.

As Figure 5.1 shows, the idea behind dynamic resolution with ARP is simple: when host A wants to resolve IP address I_B, it broadcasts a special packet that asks the host with IP address I_B to respond with its physical address, P_B. All hosts, including B, receive the request, but only host B recognizes its IP address and sends a reply that contains its physical address. When A receives the reply, it uses the physical address to send the internet packet directly to B. We can summarize:

---

†Because direct mapping is more convenient and efficient than dynamic binding, the next generation of IP is being designed to allow 48-bit hardware addresses to be encoded in IP addresses.

The Address Resolution Protocol, ARP, allows a host to find the physical address of a target host on the same physical network, given only the target's IP address.

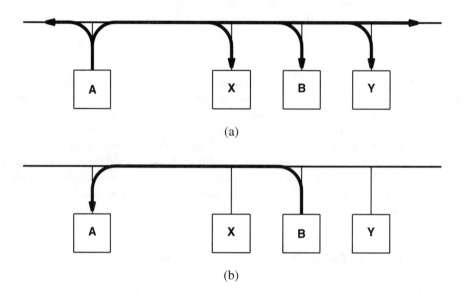

(a)

(b)

Figure 5.1 The ARP protocol. To determine P_B, B's physical address, from I_B, its IP address, (a) host A broadcasts an ARP request containing I_B to all machines on the net, and (b) host B responds with an ARP reply that contains the pair (I_B, P_B).

5.6 The Address Resolution Cache

It may seem silly that for A to send a packet to B it first sends a broadcast that reaches B. Or it may seem even sillier that A broadcasts the question, "how can I reach you?" instead of just broadcasting the packet it wants to deliver. But there is an important reason for the exchange. Broadcasting is far too expensive to be used every time one machine needs to transmit a packet to another because every machine on the network must receive and process the broadcast packet.

5.7 ARP Cache Timeout

To reduce communication costs, computers that use ARP maintain a cache of recently acquired IP-to-physical address bindings. That is, whenever a computer sends an ARP request and receives an ARP reply, it saves the IP address and corresponding hardware address information in its cache for successive lookups. When transmitting a packet, a computer always looks in its cache for a binding before sending an ARP request. If it finds the desired binding in its ARP cache, the computer need not broadcast on the network. Thus, when two computers on a network communicate, they begin with an ARP request and response, and then repeatedly transfer packets without using ARP for each one. Experience shows that because most network communication involves more than one packet transfer, even a small cache is worthwhile.

The ARP cache provides an example of *soft state*, a technique commonly used in network protocols. The name describes a situation in which information can become ''stale'' without warning. In the case of ARP, consider two computers, A and B, both connected to an Ethernet. Assume A has sent an ARP request, and B has replied. Further assume that after the exchange B crashes. Computer A will not receive any notification of the crash. Moreover, because it already has address binding information for B in its ARP cache, computer A will continue to send packets to B. The Ethernet hardware provides no indication that B is not on-line because Ethernet does not have guaranteed delivery. Thus, A has no way of knowing when information in its ARP cache has become incorrect.

To accommodate soft state, responsibility for correctness lies with the owner of the information. Typically, protocols that implement soft state use timers, with the state information being deleted when the timer expires. For example, whenever address binding information is placed in an ARP cache, the protocol requires a timer to be set, with a typical timeout being 20 minutes. When the timer expires, the information must be removed. After removal there are two possibilities. If no further packets are sent to the destination, nothing occurs. If a packet must be sent to the destination and there is no binding present in the cache, the computer follows the normal procedure of broadcasting an ARP request and obtaining the binding. If the destination is still reachable, the binding will again be placed in the ARP cache. If not, the sender will discover that the destination is off-line.

The use of soft state in ARP has advantages and disadvantages. The chief advantage arises from autonomy. First, a computer can determine when information in its ARP cache should be revalidated independent of other computers. Second, a sender does not need successful communication with the receiver or a third party to determine that a binding has become invalid; if a target does not respond to an ARP request, the sender will declare the target to be down. Third, the scheme does not rely on network hardware to provide reliable transfer. The chief disadvantage of soft state arises from delay — if the timer interval is N seconds, a sender may not detect that a receiver has crashed until N seconds elapse.

5.8 ARP Refinements

Several refinements of ARP have been included in the protocol. First, observe that if host *A* is about to use ARP because it needs to send to *B*, there is a high probability that host *B* will need to send to *A* in the near future. To anticipate *B*'s need and avoid extra network traffic, *A* includes its IP-to-physical address binding when sending *B* a request. *B* extracts *A*'s binding from the request, saves the binding in its ARP cache, and then sends a reply to *A*. Second, notice that because *A* broadcasts its initial request, all machines on the network receive it and can extract and update *A*'s IP-to-physical address binding in their cache. Third, when a computer has its host interface replaced, (e.g., because the hardware has failed) its physical address changes. Other computers on the net that have stored a binding in their ARP cache need to be informed so they can change the entry. The computer can notify others of a new address by sending an ARP broadcast when it boots.

The following rule summarizes refinements:

> *The sender's IP-to-physical address binding is included in every ARP broadcast; receivers update the IP-to-physical address binding information in their cache before processing an ARP packet.*

5.9 Relationship Of ARP To Other Protocols

ARP provides one possible mechanism to map from IP addresses to physical addresses; we have already seen that some network technologies do not need it. The point is that ARP would be completely unnecessary if we could make all network hardware recognize IP addresses. Thus, ARP merely imposes a new address scheme on top of whatever low-level address mechanism the hardware uses. The idea can be summarized:

> *ARP is a low-level protocol that hides the underlying network physical addressing, permitting one to assign an arbitrary IP address to every machine. We think of ARP as part of the physical network system, and not as part of the internet protocols.*

5.10 ARP Implementation

Functionally, ARP is divided into two parts. The first part maps an IP address to a physical address when sending a packet, and the second part answers requests from other machines. Address resolution for outgoing packets seems straightforward, but small details complicate an implementation. Given a destination IP address the software consults its ARP cache to see if it knows the mapping from IP address to physical address.

If it does, the software extracts the physical address, places the data in a frame using that address, and sends the frame. If it does not know the mapping, the software must broadcast an ARP request and wait for a reply.

Broadcasting an ARP request to find an address mapping can become complex. The target machine can be down or just too busy to accept the request. If so, the sender may not receive a reply or the reply may be delayed. Because the Ethernet is a best-effort delivery system, the initial ARP broadcast request can also be lost (in which case the sender should retransmit, at least once). Meanwhile, the host must store the original outgoing packet so it can be sent once the address has been resolved†. In fact, the host must decide whether to allow other application programs to proceed while it processes an ARP request (most do). If so, the software must handle the case where an application generates additional ARP requests for the same address without broadcasting multiple requests for a given target.

Finally, consider the case where machine A has obtained a binding for machine B, but then B's hardware fails and is replaced. Although B's address has changed, A's cached binding has not, so A uses a nonexistent hardware address, making successful reception impossible. This case shows why it is important to have ARP software treat its table of bindings as a cache and remove entries after a fixed period. Of course, the timer for an entry in the cache must be reset whenever an ARP broadcast arrives containing the binding (but it is not reset when the entry is used to send a packet).

The second part of the ARP code handles ARP packets that arrive from the network. When an ARP packet arrives, the software first extracts the sender's IP address and hardware address pair, and examines the local cache to see if it already has an entry for the sender. If a cache entry exists for the given IP address, the handler updates that entry by overwriting the physical address with the physical address obtained from the packet. The receiver then processes the rest of the ARP packet.

A receiver must handle two types of incoming ARP packets. If an ARP request arrives, the receiving machine must see if it is the target of the request (i.e., some other machine has broadcast a request for the receiver's physical address). If so, the ARP software forms a reply by supplying its physical hardware address, and sends the reply directly back to the requester. The receiver also adds the sender's address pair to its cache if the pair is not already present. If the IP address mentioned in the ARP request does not match the local IP address, the packet is requesting a mapping for some other machine on the network and can be ignored.

The other interesting case occurs when an ARP reply arrives. Depending on the implementation, the handler may need to create a cache entry, or the entry may have been created when the request was generated. In any case, once the cache has been updated, the receiver tries to match the reply with a previously issued request. Usually, replies arrive in response to a request, which was generated because the machine has a packet to deliver. Between the time a machine broadcasts its ARP request and receives the reply, application programs or higher-level protocols may generate additional requests for the same address; the software must remember that it has already sent a request and not send more. Usually, ARP software places the additional packets on a queue. Once the reply arrives and the address binding is known, the ARP software re-

---

†If the delay is significant, the host may choose to discard the outgoing packet(s).

moves packets from the queue, places each packet in a frame, and uses the address binding to fill in the physical destination address. If it did not previously issue a request for the IP address in the reply, the machine updates the sender's entry in its cache, and then simply stops processing the packet.

5.11 ARP Encapsulation And Identification

When ARP messages travel from one machine to another, they must be carried in physical frames. Figure 5.2 shows that the ARP message is carried in the data portion of a frame.

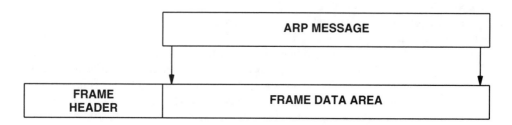

Figure 5.2 An ARP message encapsulated in a physical network frame.

To identify the frame as carrying an ARP message, the sender assigns a special value to the type field in the frame header, and places the ARP message in the frame's data field. When a frame arrives at a computer, the network software uses the frame type to determine its contents. In most technologies, a single type value is used for all frames that carry an ARP message — network software in the receiver must further examine the ARP message to distinguish between ARP requests and ARP replies. For example, on an Ethernet, frames carrying ARP messages have a type field of 0806_{16}. This is a standard value assigned by the authority for Ethernet; other network hardware technologies use other values.

5.12 ARP Protocol Format

Unlike most protocols, the data in ARP packets does not have a fixed-format header. Instead, to make ARP useful for a variety of network technologies, the length of fields that contain addresses depend on the type of network. However, to make it possible to interpret an arbitrary ARP message, the header includes fixed fields near the beginning that specify the lengths of the addresses found in succeeding fields. In fact, the ARP message format is general enough to allow it to be used with arbitrary physical addresses and arbitrary protocol addresses. The example in Figure 5.3 shows the 28-octet ARP message format used on Ethernet hardware (where physical addresses are

48-bits or 6 octets long), when resolving IP protocol addresses (which are 4 octets long).

Figure 5.3 shows an ARP message with 4 octets per line, a format that is standard throughout this text. Unfortunately, unlike most of the remaining protocols, the variable-length fields in ARP packets do not align neatly on 32-bit boundaries, making the diagram difficult to read. For example, the sender's hardware address, labeled *SENDER HA*, occupies 6 contiguous octets, so it spans two lines in the diagram.

0	8	16	24	31
HARDWARE TYPE		PROTOCOL TYPE		
HLEN	PLEN	OPERATION		
SENDER HA (octets 0-3)				
SENDER HA (octets 4-5)		SENDER IP (octets 0-1)		
SENDER IP (octets 2-3)		TARGET HA (octets 0-1)		
TARGET HA (octets 2-5)				
TARGET IP (octets 0-3)				

Figure 5.3 An example of the ARP/RARP message format when used for IP-to-Ethernet address resolution. The length of fields depends on the hardware and protocol address lengths, which are 6 octets for an Ethernet address and 4 octets for an IP address.

Field *HARDWARE TYPE* specifies a hardware interface type for which the sender seeks an answer; it contains the value *1* for Ethernet. Similarly, field *PROTOCOL TYPE* specifies the type of high-level protocol address the sender has supplied; it contains 0800_{16} for IP addresses. Field *OPERATION* specifies an ARP request (*1*), ARP response (*2*), RARP† request (*3*), or RARP response (*4*). Fields *HLEN* and *PLEN* allow ARP to be used with arbitrary networks because they specify the length of the hardware address and the length of the high-level protocol address. The sender supplies its hardware address and IP address, if known, in fields *SENDER HA* and *SENDER IP*.

When making a request, the sender also supplies the target hardware address (RARP) or target IP address (ARP), using fields *TARGET HA* or *TARGET IP*. Before the target machine responds, it fills in the missing addresses, swaps the target and sender pairs, and changes the operation to a reply. Thus, a reply carries the IP and hardware addresses of the original requester, as well as the IP and hardware addresses of the machine for which a binding was sought.

---

†The next chapter describes RARP, another protocol that uses the same message format.

5.13 Summary

IP addresses are assigned independent of a machine's physical hardware address. To send an internet packet across a physical net from one computer to another, the network software must map the IP address into a physical hardware address and use the hardware address to transmit the frame. If hardware addresses are smaller than IP addresses, a direct mapping can be established by having the machine's physical address encoded in its IP address. Otherwise, the mapping must be performed dynamically. The Address Resolution Protocol (ARP) performs dynamic address resolution, using only the low-level network communication system. ARP permits machines to resolve addresses without keeping a permanent record of bindings.

A machine uses ARP to find the hardware address of another machine by broadcasting an ARP request. The request contains the IP address of the machine for which a hardware address is needed. All machines on a network receive an ARP request. If the request matches a machine's IP address, the machine responds by sending a reply that contains the needed hardware address. Replies are directed to one machine; they are not broadcast.

To make ARP efficient, each machine caches IP-to-physical address bindings. Because internet traffic tends to consist of a sequence of interactions between pairs of machines, the cache eliminates most ARP broadcast requests.

FOR FURTHER STUDY

The address resolution protocol used here is given by Plummer [RFC 826] and has become a TCP/IP internet protocol standard. Dalal and Printis [1981] describes the relationship between Ethernet and IP addresses, and Clark [RFC 814] discusses addresses and bindings in general. Parr [RFC 1029] discusses fault tolerant address resolution. Kirkpatrick and Recker [RFC 1166] specifies values used to identify network frames in the Internet Numbers document. Volume 2 of this text presents an example ARP implementation, and discusses the caching policy.

EXERCISES

5.1 Given a small set of physical addresses (positive integers), can you find a function f and an assignment of IP addresses such that f maps the IP addresses 1-to-1 onto the physical addresses and computing f is efficient? (Hint: look at the literature on perfect hashing).

5.2 In what special cases does a host connected to an Ethernet not need to use ARP or an ARP cache before transmitting an IP datagram?

5.3   One common algorithm for managing the ARP cache replaces the least recently used entry when adding a new one. Under what circumstances can this algorithm produce unnecessary network traffic?

5.4   Read the standard carefully. Should ARP update the cache if an old entry already exists for a given IP address? Why or why not?

5.5   Should ARP software modify the cache even when it receives information without specifically requesting it? Why or why not?

5.6   Any implementation of ARP that uses a fixed-size cache can fail when used on a network that has many hosts and much ARP traffic. Explain how.

5.7   ARP is often cited as a security weakness. Explain why.

5.8   Suppose an (incorrect) ARP implementation does not remove cache entries if they are frequently used. Explain what can happen if the hardware address field in an ARP response becomes corrupted during transmission.

5.9   Suppose machine C receives an ARP request sent from A looking for target B, and suppose C has the binding from I_B to P_B in its cache. Should C answer the request? Explain.

5.10 How can a workstation use ARP when it boots to find out if any other machine on the network is impersonating it? What are the disadvantages of the scheme?

5.11 Explain how sending IP packets to nonexistent addresses on a remote Ethernet can generate excess broadcast traffic on that network.

6

Determining An Internet Address At Startup (RARP)

6.1 Introduction

We now know that physical network addresses are both low-level and hardware dependent, and we understand that each machine using TCP/IP is assigned one or more 32-bit IP addresses that are independent of the machine's hardware addresses. Application programs always use the IP address when specifying a destination. Because hosts and routers must use a physical address to transmit a datagram across an underlying hardware network; they rely on address resolution schemes like ARP to map between an IP address and an equivalent hardware address.

Usually, a computer's IP address is kept on its secondary storage, where the operating system finds it at startup. The question arises, "How does a machine without a permanently attached disk determine its IP address?" The problem is critical for workstations that store files on a remote server or for small embedded systems because such machines need an IP address before they can use standard TCP/IP file transfer protocols to obtain their initial boot image. This chapter explores the question of how to obtain an IP address, and describes a low-level protocol that such machines can use before they boot from a remote file server. Chapter 23 extends the discussion of bootstrapping, and considers popular alternatives to the protocol presented here.

Because an operating system image that has a specific IP address bound into the code cannot be used on multiple computers, designers usually try to avoid compiling a machine's IP address in the operating system code or support software. In particular, the bootstrap code often found in Read Only Memory (ROM) is usually built so the same image can run on many machines. When such code starts execution, it uses the network to contact a server and obtain the computer's IP address.

The bootstrap procedure sounds paradoxical: a machine communicates with a remote server to obtain an address needed for communication. The paradox is only imagined, however, because the machine *does* know how to communicate. It can use its physical address to communicate over a single network. Thus, the machine must resort to physical network addressing temporarily in the same way that operating systems use physical memory addressing to set up page tables for virtual addressing. Once a machine knows its IP address, it can communicate across an internet.

The idea behind finding an IP address is simple: a machine that needs to know its address sends a request to a *server†* on another machine, and waits until the server sends a response. We assume the server has access to a disk where it keeps a database of internet addresses. In the request, the machine that needs to know its internet address must uniquely identify itself, so the server can look up the correct internet address and send a reply. Both the machine that issues the request and the server that responds use physical network addresses during their brief communication. How does the requester know the physical address of a server? Usually, it does not — it simply broadcasts the request to all machines on the local network. One or more servers respond.

Whenever a machine broadcasts a request for an address, it must uniquely identify itself. What information can be included in its request that will uniquely identify the machine? Any unique hardware identification suffices (e.g., the CPU serial number). However, the identification should be something that an executing program can obtain easily. Unfortunately, the length or format of CPU-specific information may vary among processor models, and we would like to devise a server that accepts requests from all machines on the physical network using a single format. Furthermore, engineers who design bootstrap code attempt to create a single software image that can execute on an arbitrary processor, and each processor model may have a slightly different set of instructions for obtaining a serial number.

6.2 Reverse Address Resolution Protocol (RARP)

The designers of TCP/IP protocols realized that there is another piece of uniquely identifying information readily available, namely, the machine's physical network address. Using the physical address as a unique identification has two advantages. Because a host obtains its physical addresses from the network interface hardware, such addresses are always available and do not have to be bound into the bootstrap code. Because the identifying information depends on the network and not on the CPU vendor or model, all machines on a given network will supply uniform, unique identifiers. Thus, the problem becomes the reverse of address resolution: given a physical network address, devise a scheme that will allow a server to map it into an internet address.

The TCP/IP protocol that allows a computer to obtain its IP address from a server is known as the *Reverse Address Resolution Protocol* (*RARP*). RARP is adapted from the ARP protocol of the previous chapter and uses the same message format shown in Figure 5.3. In practice, the RARP message sent to request an internet address is a little more general than what we have outlined above: it allows a machine to request the IP

---

†Chapter 21 discusses servers in detail.

address of a third party as easily as its own. It also allows for multiple physical network types.

Like an ARP message, a RARP message is sent from one machine to another encapsulated in the data portion of a network frame. For example, an Ethernet frame carrying a RARP request has the usual preamble, Ethernet source and destination addresses, and packet type fields in front of the frame. The frame type contains the value
8035_{16} to identify the contents of the frame as a RARP message. The data portion of
the frame contains the 28-octet RARP message.

Figure 6.1 illustrates how a host uses RARP. The sender broadcasts a RARP request that specifies itself as both the sender and target machine, and supplies its physical network address in the target hardware address field. All computers on the network
receive the request, but only those authorized to supply the RARP service process the
request and send a reply; such computers are known informally as *RARP servers*. For
RARP to succeed, the network must contain at least one RARP server.

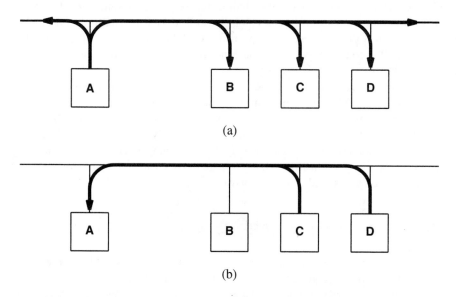

Figure 6.1 Example exchange using the RARP protocol. (a) Machine *A*
broadcasts a RARP request specifying itself as a target, and (b)
those machines authorized to supply the RARP service (*C* and *D*)
reply directly to *A*.

Servers answer requests by filling in the target protocol address field, changing the
message type from *request* to *reply*, and sending the reply back directly to the machine
making the request. The original machine receives replies from all RARP servers, even
though only the first is needed.

Keep in mind that all communication between the computer seeking its IP address and the server supplying it must be carried out using only the physical network. Furthermore, the protocol allows a host to ask about an arbitrary target. Thus, the sender supplies its hardware address separate from the target hardware address, and the server is careful to send the reply to the sender's hardware address. On an Ethernet, having a field for the sender's hardware address may seem redundant because the information is also contained in the Ethernet frame header. However, not all Ethernet hardware provides the operating system with access to the physical frame header.

6.3 Timing RARP Transactions

Like any communication on a best-effort delivery network, RARP requests and responses are susceptible to loss (including discard by the network interface if the CRC indicates that the frame was corrupted). Because RARP uses the physical network directly, no other protocol software will time the response or retransmit the request; RARP software must handle these tasks. In general, RARP is used only on local area networks like the Ethernet, where the probability of failure is low. If a network has only one RARP server, however, that machine may not be able to handle the load, so packets may be dropped.

Some computers that rely on RARP to boot, choose to retry indefinitely until they receive a response. Other implementations announce failure after only a few tries to avoid flooding the network with unnecessary broadcast traffic (e.g., in case the server is unavailable). On an Ethernet, network failure is less likely than server overload. Making RARP software retransmit quickly may have the unwanted effect of flooding a congested server with more traffic. Using a large delay ensures that servers have ample time to satisfy the request and return an answer.

6.4 Primary And Backup RARP Servers

The chief advantage of having several computers function as RARP servers is that it makes the system more reliable. If one server is down or too heavily loaded to respond, another answers the request. Thus, it is highly likely that the service will be available. The chief disadvantage of using many servers is that when a machine broadcasts a RARP request, the network becomes overloaded because all servers attempt to respond. On an Ethernet, for example, using multiple RARP servers makes the probability of collision high.

How can the RARP service be arranged to keep it available and reliable without incurring the cost of multiple, simultaneous replies? There are at least two possibilities, and they both involve delaying responses. In the first solution, each machine that makes RARP requests is assigned a *primary server*. Under normal circumstances, only the machine's primary server responds to its RARP request. All nonprimary servers receive the request but merely record its arrival time. If the primary server is unavailable, the original machine will timeout waiting for a response and then rebroadcast the request. Whenever a nonprimary server receives a second copy of a RARP request within a short time of the first, it responds.

The second solution uses a similar scheme but attempts to avoid having all nonprimary servers transmit responses simultaneously. Each nonprimary machine that receives a request computes a random delay and then sends a response. Under normal circumstances, the primary server responds immediately and successive responses are delayed, so there is low probability that several responses arrive at the same time. When the primary server is unavailable, the requesting machine experiences a small delay before receiving a reply. By choosing delays carefully, the designer can ensure that requesting machines do not rebroadcast before they receive an answer.

6.5 Summary

At system startup, a computer that does not have permanent storage must contact a server to find its IP address before it can communicate using TCP/IP. This chapter examined the RARP protocol that uses physical network addressing to obtain the machine's internet address. The RARP mechanism supplies the target machine's physical hardware address to uniquely identify the processor and broadcasts the RARP request. Servers on the network receive the message, look up the mapping in a table (presumably from secondary storage), and reply to the sender. Once a machine obtains its IP address, it stores the address in memory and does not use RARP again until it reboots.

FOR FURTHER STUDY

The details of RARP are given in Finlayson, *et. al.* [RFC 903]. Finlayson [RFC 906] describes workstation bootstrapping using the TFTP protocol. Bradley and Brown [RFC 1293] specifies a related protocol, *Inverse ARP*. Inverse ARP permits a computer to query the machine at the opposite end of a hardware connection to determine its IP address, and was intended for computers on a connection-oriented network such as Frame Relay or ATM. Volume 2 of this text describes an example implementation of RARP.

Chapter 23 considers alternatives to RARP known as BOOTP and DHCP. Unlike the low-level address determination scheme RARP supplies, BOOTP and DHCP build on higher level protocols like IP and UDP. Chapter 23 compares the two approaches, discussing the strengths and weaknesses of each.

EXERCISES

6.1   A RARP server can broadcast RARP replies to all machines or transmit each reply directly to the machine that makes the request. Characterize a network technology in which broadcasting replies to all machines is beneficial.

6.2   RARP is a narrowly focused protocol in the sense that replies only contain one piece of information (i.e., the requested IP address). When a computer boots, it usually needs to know its name in addition to its Internet address. Extend RARP to supply the additional information.

6.3   How much larger will Ethernet frames become when information is added to RARP as described in the previous exercise?

6.4   Adding a second RARP server to a network increases reliability. Does it ever make sense to add a third? How about a fourth? Why or Why not?

6.5   The diskless workstations from one vendor use RARP to obtain their IP addresses, but always assume the response comes from the workstation's file server. The diskless machine then tries to obtain a boot image from that server. If it does not receive a response, the workstation enters an infinite loop broadcasting boot requests. Explain how adding a backup RARP server to such a configuration can cause the network to become congested with broadcasts. Hint: think of power failures.

6.6   Monitor a local network while you reboot various computers. Which use RARP?

6.7   The backup RARP servers discussed in the text use the arrival of a second request in a short period of time to trigger a reply. Consider the RARP server scheme that has all servers answer the first request, but avoids congestion by having each server delay a random time before answering. Under what circumstances could such a design yield better results than the design described in the text?

7

Internet Protocol: Connectionless Datagram Delivery

7.1 Introduction

Previous chapters review pieces of network hardware and software that make internet communication possible, explaining the underlying network technologies and address resolution. This chapter explains the fundamental principle of connectionless delivery and discusses how it is provided by the *Internet Protocol* (*IP*), which is one of the two major protocols used in internetworking (TCP being the other). We will study the format of IP datagrams and see how they form the basis for all internet communication. The next two chapters continue our examination of the Internet Protocol by discussing datagram routing and error handling.

7.2 A Virtual Network

Chapter 3 discusses an internet architecture in which routers connect multiple physical networks. Looking at the architecture may be misleading, because the focus should be on the interface that an internet provides to users, not on the interconnection technology.

> *A user thinks of an internet as a single virtual network that intercon-*
> *nects all hosts, and through which communication is possible; its*
> *underlying architecture is both hidden and irrelevant.*

In a sense, an internet is an abstraction of physical networks because, at the lowest level, it provides the same functionality: accepting packets and delivering them. Higher
levels of internet software add most of the rich functionality users perceive.

7.3 Internet Architecture And Philosophy

Conceptually, a TCP/IP internet provides three sets of services as shown in Figure
7.1; their arrangement in the figure suggests dependencies among them. At the lowest
level, a connectionless delivery service provides a foundation on which everything rests.
At the next level, a reliable transport service provides a higher level platform on which
applications depend. We will soon explore each of these services, understand what they
provide, and see the protocols associated with them.

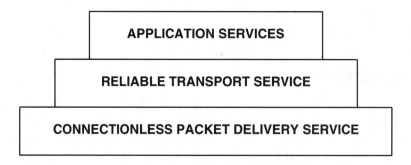

Figure 7.1 The three conceptual layers of internet services.

7.4 The Conceptual Service Organization

Although we can associate protocol software with each of the services in Figure
7.1, the reason for identifying them as conceptual parts of the internet is that they clearly point out the philosophical underpinnings of the design. The point is:

> *Internet software is designed around three conceptual networking ser-*
> *vices arranged in a hierarchy; much of its success has resulted be-*
> *cause this architecture is surprisingly robust and adaptable.*

One of the most significant advantages of this conceptual separation is that it becomes possible to replace one service without disturbing others. Thus, research and development can proceed concurrently on all three.

7.5 Connectionless Delivery System

The most fundamental internet service consists of a packet delivery system. Technically, the service is defined as an unreliable, best-effort, connectionless packet delivery system, analogous to the service provided by network hardware that operates on a best-effort delivery paradigm. The service is called *unreliable* because delivery is not guaranteed. The packet may be lost, duplicated, delayed, or delivered out of order, but the service will not detect such conditions, nor will it inform the sender or receiver. The service is called *connectionless* because each packet is treated independently from all others. A sequence of packets sent from one computer to another may travel over different paths, or some may be lost while others are delivered. Finally, the service is said to use *best-effort delivery* because the internet software makes an earnest attempt to deliver packets. That is, the internet does not discard packets capriciously; unreliability arises only when resources are exhausted or underlying networks fail.

7.6 Purpose Of The Internet Protocol

The protocol that defines the unreliable, connectionless delivery mechanism is called the *Internet Protocol* and is usually referred to by its initials, *IP†*. IP provides three important definitions. First, the IP protocol defines the basic unit of data transfer used throughout a TCP/IP internet. Thus, it specifies the exact format of all data as it passes across the internet. Second, IP software performs the *routing* function, choosing a path over which data will be sent. Third, in addition to the precise, formal specification of data formats and routing, IP includes a set of rules that embody the idea of unreliable packet delivery. The rules characterize how hosts and routers should process packets, how and when error messages should be generated, and the conditions under which packets can be discarded. IP is such a fundamental part of the design that a TCP/IP internet is sometimes called an *IP-based technology*.

We begin our consideration of IP in this chapter by looking at the packet format it specifies. We leave until later chapters the topics of routing and error handling.

7.7 The Internet Datagram

The analogy between a physical network and a TCP/IP internet is strong. On a physical network, the unit of transfer is a frame that contains a header and data, where the header gives information such as the (physical) source and destination addresses. The internet calls its basic transfer unit an *Internet datagram*, sometimes referred to as

---

†The abbreviation IP gives rise to the term ''IP address.''

an *IP datagram* or merely a *datagram*. Like a typical physical network frame, a datagram is divided into header and data areas. Also like a frame, the datagram header contains the source and destination addresses and a type field that identifies the contents of the datagram. The difference, of course, is that the datagram header contains IP addresses whereas the frame header contains physical addresses. Figure 7.2 shows the general form of a datagram:

DATAGRAM HEADER	DATAGRAM DATA AREA

Figure 7.2 General form of an IP datagram, the TCP/IP analogy to a network frame. IP specifies the header format including the source and destination IP addresses. IP does not specify the format of the data area; it can be used to transport arbitrary data.

7.7.1 Datagram Format

Now that we have described the general layout of an IP datagram, we can look at the contents in more detail. Figure 7.3 shows the arrangement of fields in a datagram:

0	4	8	16	19	24	31
VERS	HLEN	SERVICE TYPE	TOTAL LENGTH			
IDENTIFICATION			FLAGS	FRAGMENT OFFSET		
TIME TO LIVE		PROTOCOL	HEADER CHECKSUM			
SOURCE IP ADDRESS						
DESTINATION IP ADDRESS						
IP OPTIONS (IF ANY)					PADDING	
DATA						
. . .						

Figure 7.3 Format of an Internet datagram, the basic unit of transfer in a TCP/IP internet.

Because datagram processing occurs in software, the contents and format are not constrained by any hardware. For example, the first 4-bit field in a datagram (*VERS*) contains the version of the IP protocol that was used to create the datagram. It is used to verify that the sender, receiver, and any routers in between them agree on the format of the datagram. All IP software is required to check the version field before processing a datagram to ensure it matches the format the software expects. If standards change, machines will reject datagrams with protocol versions that differ from theirs, preventing them from misinterpreting datagram contents according to an outdated format. The current IP protocol version is *4*. Consequently, the term *IPv4* is often used to denote the current protocol.

The header length field (*HLEN*), also 4 bits, gives the datagram header length measured in 32-bit words. As we will see, all fields in the header have fixed length except for the *IP OPTIONS* and corresponding *PADDING* fields. The most common header, which contains no options and no padding, measures 20 octets and has a header length field equal to *5*.

The *TOTAL LENGTH* field gives the length of the IP datagram measured in octets, including octets in the header and data. The size of the data area can be computed by subtracting the length of the header (*HLEN*) from the *TOTAL LENGTH*. Because the *TOTAL LENGTH* field is 16 bits long, the maximum possible size of an IP datagram is 2^{16} or 65,535 octets. In most applications this is not a severe limitation. It may become more important in the future if higher speed networks can carry data packets larger than 65,535 octets.

7.7.2 Datagram Type Of Service And Differentiated Services

Informally called *Type Of Service* (*TOS*), the 8-bit *SERVICE TYPE* field specifies how the datagram should be handled. The field was originally divided into five subfields as shown in Figure 7.4:

0	1	2	3	4	5	6	7
PRECEDENCE			D	T	R	UNUSED	

Figure 7.4 The original five subfields that comprise the 8-bit *SERVICE TYPE* field.

Three *PRECEDENCE* bits specify datagram precedence, with values ranging from 0 (normal precedence) through 7 (network control), allowing senders to indicate the importance of each datagram. Although some routers ignore type of service, it is an important concept because it provides a mechanism that can allow control information to have precedence over data. For example, many routers use a precedence value of 6 or 7 for routing traffic to make it possible for the routers to exchange routing information even when networks are congested.

Bits *D*, *T*, and *R* specify the type of transport desired for the datagram. When set, the *D* bit requests low delay, the *T* bit requests high throughput, and the *R* bit requests high reliability. Of course, it may not be possible for an internet to guarantee the type of transport requested (i.e., it could be that no path to the destination has the requested property). Thus, we think of the transport request as a hint to the routing algorithms, not as a demand. If a router does know more than one possible route to a given destination, it can use the type of transport field to select one with characteristics closest to those desired. For example, suppose a router can select between a low capacity leased line or a high bandwidth (but high delay) satellite connection. Datagrams carrying keystrokes from a user to a remote computer could have the *D* bit set requesting that they be delivered as quickly as possible, while datagrams carrying a bulk file transfer could have the *T* bit set requesting that they travel across the high capacity satellite path.

In the late 1990s, the IETF redefined the meaning of the 8-bit *SERVICE TYPE* field to accommodate a set of *differentiated services* (*DS*). Figure 7.5 illustrates the resulting definition.

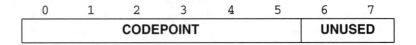

Figure 7.5 The differentiated services (DS) interpretation of the *SERVICE TYPE* field in an IP datagram.

Under the differentiated services interpretation, the first six bits comprise a *codepoint*, which is sometimes abbreviated *DSCP*, and the last two bits are left unused. A codepoint value maps to an underlying service definition, typically through an array of pointers. Although it is possible to define 64 separate services, the designers suggest that a given router will only have a few services, and multiple codepoints will map to each service. Moreover, to maintain backward compatibility with the original definition, the standard distinguishes between the first three bits of the codepoint (the bits that were formerly used for precedence) and the last three bits. When the last three bits contain zero, the precedence bits define eight broad classes of service that adhere to the same guidelines as the original definition: datagrams with a higher number in their precedence field are given preferential treatment over datagrams with a lower number. That is, the eight ordered classes are defined by codepoint values of the form:

xxx000

where x denotes either a zero or a one.

The differentiated services design also accommodates another existing practice — the widespread use of precedence 6 or 7 for routing traffic. The standard includes a special case to handle these precedence values. A router is required to implement at least two priority schemes: one for normal traffic and one for high-priority traffic. When the last three bits of the *CODEPOINT* field are zero, the router must map a codepoint with precedence 6 or 7 into the higher priority class and other codepoint values into the lower priority class. Thus, if a datagram arrives that was sent using the original TOS scheme, a router using the differentiated services scheme will honor precedence 6 and 7 as the datagram sender expects.

The 64 codepoint values are divided into three administrative groups as Figure 7.6 illustrates.

Pool	Codepoint	Assigned By
1	xxxxx0	Standards organization
2	xxxx11	Local or experimental
3	xxxx01	Local or experimental for now

Figure 7.6 The three administrative pools of codepoint values.

As the figure indicates, half of the values (i.e., the 32 values in pool *1*) must be assigned interpretations by the IETF. Currently, all values in pools *2* and *3* are available for experimental or local use. However, if the standards bodies exhaust all values in pool *1*, they may also choose to assign values in pool *3*.

The division into pools may seem unusual because it relies on the low-order bits of the value to distinguish pools. Thus, rather than a contiguous set of values, pool *1* contains every other codepoint value (i.e., the even numbers between 2 and 64). The division was chosen to keep the eight codepoints corresponding to values xxx000 in the same pool.

Whether the original TOS interpretation or the revised differentiated services interpretation is used, it is important to realize that routing software must choose from among the underlying physical network technologies at hand and must adhere to local policies. Thus, specifying a level of service in a datagram does not guarantee that routers along the path will agree to honor the request. To summarize:

> *We regard the service type specification as a hint to the routing algorithm that helps it choose among various paths to a destination based on local policies and its knowledge of the hardware technologies available on those paths. An internet does not guarantee to provide any particular type of service.*

7.7.3 Datagram Encapsulation

Before we can understand the next fields in a datagram, it is important to consider how datagrams relate to physical network frames. We start with a question: "How large can a datagram be?" Unlike physical network frames that must be recognized by hardware, datagrams are handled by software. They can be of any length the protocol designers choose. We have seen that the IPv4 datagram format allots 16 bits to the total length field, limiting the datagram to at most 65,535 octets.

More fundamental limits on datagram size arise in practice. We know that as datagrams move from one machine to another, they must always be transported by the underlying physical network. To make internet transportation efficient, we would like to guarantee that each datagram travels in a distinct physical frame. That is, we want our abstraction of a physical network packet to map directly onto a real packet if possible.

The idea of carrying one datagram in one network frame is called *encapsulation*. To the underlying network, a datagram is like any other message sent from one machine to another. The hardware does not recognize the datagram format, nor does it understand the IP destination address. Thus, as Figure 7.7 shows, when one machine sends an IP datagram to another, the entire datagram travels in the data portion of the network frame†.

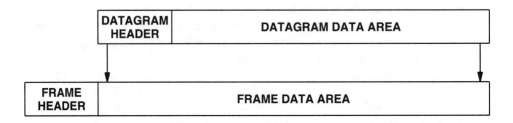

Figure 7.7 The encapsulation of an IP datagram in a frame. The physical network treats the entire datagram, including the header, as data.

7.7.4 Datagram Size, Network MTU, and Fragmentation

In the ideal case, the entire IP datagram fits into one physical frame, making transmission across the physical net efficient. To achieve such efficiency, the designers of IP might have selected a maximum datagram size such that a datagram would always fit into one frame. But which frame size should be chosen? After all, a datagram may travel across many types of physical networks as it moves across an internet to its final destination.

To understand the problem, we need a fact about network hardware: each packet-switching technology places a fixed upper bound on the amount of data that can be transferred in one physical frame. For example, Ethernet limits transfers to 1500‡ octets of data, while FDDI permits approximately 4470 octets of data per frame. We refer to these limits as the network's *maximum transfer unit* or *MTU*. MTU sizes can be quite small: some hardware technologies limit transfers to 128 octets or less. Limiting datagrams to fit the smallest possible MTU in the internet makes transfers inefficient when datagrams pass across a network that can carry larger size frames. However, allowing datagrams to be larger than the minimum network MTU in an internet means that a datagram may not always fit into a single network frame.

---

†A field in the frame header usually identifies the data being carried; Ethernet uses the type value 0800_{16} to specify that the data area contains an encapsulated IP datagram.

‡The limit of 1500 comes from the Ethernet specification; when used with a SNAP header the IEEE 802.3 standard limits data to 1492 octets. Some vendors' implementations allow slightly larger transfers.

The choice should be obvious: the point of the internet design is to hide underlying network technologies and make communication convenient for the user. Thus, instead of designing datagrams that adhere to the constraints of physical networks, TCP/IP software chooses a convenient initial datagram size and arranges a way to divide large datagrams into smaller pieces when the datagram needs to traverse a network that has a small MTU. The small pieces into which a datagram is divided are called *fragments*, and the process of dividing a datagram is known as *fragmentation*.

As Figure 7.8 illustrates, fragmentation usually occurs at a router somewhere along the path between the datagram source and its ultimate destination. The router receives a datagram from a network with a large MTU and must send it over a network for which the MTU is smaller than the datagram size.

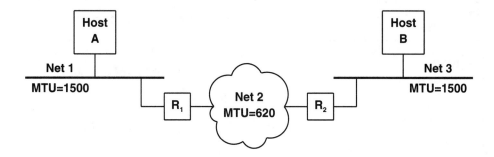

Figure 7.8 An illustration of where fragmentation occurs. Router R_1 fragments large datagrams sent from A to B; R_2 fragments large datagrams sent from B to A.

In the figure, both hosts attach directly to Ethernets which have an MTU of 1500 octets. Thus, both hosts can generate and send datagrams up to 1500 octets long. The path between them, however, includes a network with an MTU of 620. If host A sends host B a datagram larger than 620 octets, router R_1 will fragment the datagram. Similarly, if B sends a large datagram to A, router R_2 will fragment the datagram.

Fragment size is chosen so each fragment can be shipped across the underlying network in a single frame. In addition, because IP represents the offset of the data in multiples of eight octets, the fragment size must be chosen to be a multiple of eight. Of course, choosing the multiple of eight octets nearest to the network MTU does not usually divide the datagram into equal size pieces; the last piece is often shorter than the others. Fragments must be *reassembled* to produce a complete copy of the original datagram before it can be processed at the destination.

The IP protocol does not limit datagrams to a small size, nor does it guarantee that large datagrams will be delivered without fragmentation. The source can choose any datagram size it thinks appropriate; fragmentation and reassembly occur automatically, without the source taking special action. The IP specification states that routers must accept datagrams up to the maximum of the MTUs of networks to which they attach.

In addition, a router must always handle datagrams of up to 576 octets. (Hosts are also required to accept, and reassemble if necessary, datagrams of at least 576 octets.)

Fragmenting a datagram means dividing it into several pieces. It may surprise you to learn that each piece has the same format as the original datagram. Figure 7.9 illustrates the result of fragmentation.

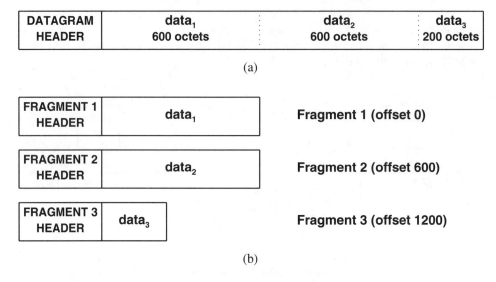

(a)

(b)

Figure 7.9 (a) An original datagram carrying 1400 octets of data and (b) the three fragments for network MTU of 620. Headers 1 and 2 have the *more fragments* bit set. Offsets shown are decimal octets; they must be divided by 8 to get the value stored in the fragment headers.

Each fragment contains a datagram header that duplicates most of the original datagram header (except for a bit in the *FLAGS* field that shows it is a fragment), followed by as much data as can be carried in the fragment while keeping the total length smaller than the MTU of the network over which it must travel.

7.7.5 Reassembly Of Fragments

Should a datagram be reassembled after passing across one network, or should the fragments be carried to the final host before reassembly? In a TCP/IP internet, once a datagram has been fragmented, the fragments travel as separate datagrams all the way to the ultimate destination where they must be reassembled. Preserving fragments all the way to the ultimate destination has two disadvantages. First, because datagrams are not reassembled immediately after passing across a network with small MTU, the small fragments must be carried from the point of fragmentation to the ultimate destination.

Reassembling datagrams at the ultimate destination can lead to inefficiency: even if some of the physical networks encountered after the point of fragmentation have large MTU capability, only small fragments traverse them. Second, if any fragments are lost, the datagram cannot be reassembled. The receiving machine starts a *reassembly timer* when it receives an initial fragment. If the timer expires before all fragments arrive, the receiving machine discards the surviving pieces without processing the datagram. Thus, the probability of datagram loss increases when fragmentation occurs because the loss of a single fragment results in loss of the entire datagram.

Despite the minor disadvantages, performing reassembly at the ultimate destination works well. It allows each fragment to be routed independently, and does not require intermediate routers to store or reassemble fragments.

7.7.6 Fragmentation Control

Three fields in the datagram header, *IDENTIFICATION*, *FLAGS*, and *FRAGMENT OFFSET*, control fragmentation and reassembly of datagrams. Field *IDENTIFICATION* contains a unique integer that identifies the datagram. Recall that when a router fragments a datagram, it copies most of the fields in the datagram header into each fragment. Thus, the *IDENTIFICATION* field must be copied. Its primary purpose is to allow the destination to know which arriving fragments belong to which datagrams. As a fragment arrives, the destination uses the *IDENTIFICATION* field along with the datagram source address to identify the datagram. Computers sending IP datagrams must generate a unique value for the *IDENTIFICATION* field for each datagram†. One technique used by IP software keeps a global counter in memory, increments it each time a new datagram is created, and assigns the result as the datagram's *IDENTIFICATION* field.

Recall that each fragment has exactly the same format as a complete datagram. For a fragment, field *FRAGMENT OFFSET* specifies the offset in the original datagram of the data being carried in the fragment, measured in units of 8 octets‡, starting at offset zero. To reassemble the datagram, the destination must obtain all fragments starting with the fragment that has offset *0* through the fragment with highest offset. Fragments do not necessarily arrive in order, and there is no communication between the router that fragmented the datagram and the destination trying to reassemble it.

The low-order two bits of the 3-bit *FLAGS* field control fragmentation. Usually, application software using TCP/IP does not care about fragmentation because both fragmentation and reassembly are automatic procedures that occur at a low level in the operating system, invisible to end users. However, to test internet software or debug operational problems, it may be important to test sizes of datagrams for which fragmentation occurs. The first control bit aids in such testing by specifying whether the datagram may be fragmented. It is called the *do not fragment* bit because setting it to *1* specifies that the datagram should not be fragmented. An application may choose to disallow fragmentation when only the entire datagram is useful. For example, consider a bootstrap sequence in which a small embedded system executes a program in ROM that sends a request over the internet to which another machine responds by sending

---

†In theory, retransmissions of a packet can carry the same *IDENTIFICATION* field as the original; in practice, higher-level protocols perform retransmission, resulting in a new datagram with its own *IDENTIFICATION*.

‡To save space in the header, offsets are specified in multiples of 8 octets.

back a memory image. If the embedded system has been designed so it needs the entire image or none of it, the datagram should have the *do not fragment* bit set. Whenever a router needs to fragment a datagram that has the *do not fragment* bit set, the router discards the datagram and sends an error message back to the source.

The low order bit in the *FLAGS* field specifies whether the fragment contains data from the middle of the original datagram or from the end. It is called the *more fragments* bit. To see why such a bit is needed, consider the IP software at the ultimate destination attempting to reassemble a datagram. It will receive fragments (possibly out of order) and needs to know when it has received all fragments for a datagram. When a fragment arrives, the *TOTAL LENGTH* field in the header refers to the size of the fragment and not to the size of the original datagram, so the destination cannot use the *TOTAL LENGTH* field to tell whether it has collected all fragments. The *more fragments* bit solves the problem easily: once the destination receives a fragment with the *more fragments* bit turned off, it knows this fragment carries data from the tail of the original datagram. From the *FRAGMENT OFFSET* and *TOTAL LENGTH* fields, it can compute the length of the original datagram. By examining the *FRAGMENT OFFSET* and *TOTAL LENGTH* of all fragments that have arrived, a receiver can tell whether the fragments on hand contain all pieces needed to reassemble the original datagram.

7.7.7 Time to Live (TTL)

In principle, field *TIME TO LIVE* specifies how long, in seconds, the datagram is allowed to remain in the internet system. The idea is both simple and important: whenever a computer injects a datagram into the internet, it sets a maximum time that the datagram should survive. Routers and hosts that process datagrams must decrement the *TIME TO LIVE* field as time passes and remove the datagram from the internet when its time expires.

Estimating exact times is difficult because routers do not usually know the transit time for physical networks. A few rules simplify processing and make it easy to handle datagrams without synchronized clocks. First, each router along the path from source to destination is required to decrement the *TIME TO LIVE* field by *1* when it processes the datagram header. Furthermore, to handle cases of overloaded routers that introduce long delays, each router records the local time when the datagram arrives, and decrements the *TIME TO LIVE* by the number of seconds the datagram remained inside the router waiting for service†.

Whenever a *TIME TO LIVE* field reaches zero, the router discards the datagram and sends an error message back to the source. The idea of keeping a timer for datagrams is interesting because it guarantees that datagrams cannot travel around an internet forever, even if routing tables become corrupt and routers route datagrams in a circle.

Although once important, the notion of a router delaying a datagram for many seconds is now outdated — current routers and networks are designed to forward each datagram within a reasonable time. If the delay becomes excessive, the router simply discards the datagram. Thus, in practice, the *TIME TO LIVE* acts as a ''hop limit'' rather than an estimate of delay. Each router only decrements the value by 1.

---

†In practice, modern routers do not hold datagrams for multiple seconds.

7.7.8 Other Datagram Header Fields

Field *PROTOCOL* is analogous to the type field in a network frame; the value specifies which high-level protocol was used to create the message carried in the *DATA* area of the datagram. In essence, the value of *PROTOCOL* specifies the format of the *DATA* area. The mapping between a high level protocol and the integer value used in the *PROTOCOL* field must be administered by a central authority to guarantee agreement across the entire Internet.

Field *HEADER CHECKSUM* ensures integrity of header values. The IP checksum is formed by treating the header as a sequence of 16-bit integers (in network byte order), adding them together using one's complement arithmetic, and then taking the one's complement of the result. For purposes of computing the checksum, field *HEADER CHECKSUM* is assumed to contain zero.

It is important to note that the checksum only applies to values in the IP header and not to the data. Separating the checksum for headers and data has advantages and disadvantages. Because the header usually occupies fewer octets than the data, having a separate checksum reduces processing time at routers which only need to compute header checksums. The separation also allows higher level protocols to choose their own checksum scheme for the data. The chief disadvantage is that higher level protocols are forced to add their own checksum or risk having corrupted data go undetected.

Fields *SOURCE IP ADDRESS* and *DESTINATION IP ADDRESS* contain the 32-bit IP addresses of the datagram's sender and intended recipient. Although the datagram may be routed through many intermediate routers, the source and destination fields never change; they specify the IP addresses of the original source and ultimate destination†.

The field labeled *DATA* in Figure 7.3 shows the beginning of the data area of the datagram. Its length depends, of course, on what is being sent in the datagram. The *IP OPTIONS* field, discussed below, is variable length. The field labeled *PADDING*, depends on the options selected. It represents bits containing zero that may be needed to ensure the datagram header extends to an exact multiple of 32 bits (recall that the header length field is specified in units of 32-bit words).

7.8 Internet Datagram Options

The *IP OPTIONS* field following the destination address is not required in every datagram; options are included primarily for network testing or debugging. Options processing is an integral part of the IP protocol, however, so all standard implementations must include it.

The length of the *IP OPTIONS* field varies depending on which options are selected. Some options are one octet long; they consist of a single octet *option code*. Other options are variable length. When options are present in a datagram, they appear contiguously, with no special separators between them. Each option consists of a single octet option code, which may be followed by a single octet length and a set of data octets for that option. The option code octet is divided into three fields as Figure 7.10 shows.

---

†An exception is made when the datagram includes the source route options listed below.

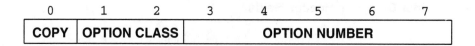

Figure 7.10 The division of the option code octet into three fields of length 1, 2, and 5 bits.

The fields of the *OPTION CODE* consist of a 1-bit *COPY* flag, a 2-bit *OPTION CLASS*, and the 5-bit *OPTION NUMBER*. The *COPY* flag controls how routers treat options during fragmentation. When the *COPY* bit is set to *1*, it specifies that the option should be copied into all fragments. When set to *0*, the *COPY* bit means that the option should only be copied into the first fragment and not into all fragments.

The *OPTION CLASS* and *OPTION NUMBER* bits specify the general class of the option and a specific option in that class. The table in Figure 7.11 shows how option classes are assigned.

Option Class	Meaning
0	Datagram or network control
1	Reserved for future use
2	Debugging and measurement
3	Reserved for future use

Figure 7.11 Classes of IP options as encoded in the *OPTION CLASS* bits of an option code octet.

The table in Figure 7.12 lists examples of options that can accompany an IP datagram and gives their *OPTION CLASS* and *OPTION NUMBER* values. As the list shows, most options are used for control purposes.

Option Class	Option Number	Length	Description
0	0	-	End of option list. Used if options do not end at end of header (see header padding field for explanation).
0	1	-	No operation. Used to align octets in a list of options.
0	2	11	Security and handling restrictions (for military applications).
0	3	var	Loose source route. Used to request routing that includes the specified routers.
0	7	var	Record route. Used to trace a route.
0	8	4	Stream identifier. Used to carry a SATNET stream identifier (obsolete).
0	9	var	Strict source route. Used to specify a exact path through the internet.
0	11	4	MTU Probe. Used for path MTU discovery.
0	12	4	MTU Reply. Used for path MTU discovery.
0	20	4	Router Alert. Router should examine this datagram even if not an addressee.
2	4	var	Internet timestamp. Used to record timestamps along the route.
2	18	var	Traceroute. Used by traceroute program to find routers along a path.

Figure 7.12 Examples of IP options with their numeric class and number codes. The value *var* in the length column stands for *variable*.

7.8.1 Record Route Option

The routing and timestamp options are the most interesting because they provide a way to monitor or control how internet routers route datagrams. The *record route* option allows the source to create an empty list of IP addresses and arrange for each router that handles the datagram to add its IP address to the list. Figure 7.13 shows the format of the record route option.

As described above, the *CODE* field contains the option class and option number (*0* and *7* for record route). The *LENGTH* field specifies the total length of the option as it appears in the IP datagram, including the first three octets. The fields starting with the one labeled *FIRST IP ADDRESS* comprise the area reserved for recording internet addresses. The *POINTER* field specifies the offset within the option of the next available slot.

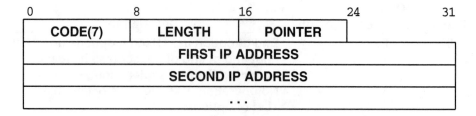

Figure 7.13 The format of the record route option in an IP datagram. The option begins with three octets immediately followed by a list of addresses. Although the diagram shows addresses in 32 bit units, they are not aligned on any octet boundary in a datagram.

Whenever a machine handles a datagram that has the record route option set, the machine adds its address to the record route list (enough space must be allocated in the option by the original source to hold all entries that will be needed). To add itself to the list, a machine first compares the pointer and length fields. If the pointer is greater than the length, the list is full, so the machine forwards the datagram without inserting its entry. If the list is not full, the machine inserts its 4-octet IP address at the position specified by the *POINTER*, and increments the *POINTER* by four.

When the datagram arrives, the destination machine can extract and process the list of IP addresses. Usually, a computer that receives a datagram ignores the recorded route. Using the record route option requires two machines that agree to cooperate; a computer will not automatically receive recorded routes in incoming datagrams after it turns on the record route option in outgoing datagrams. The source must agree to enable the record route option and the destination must agree to process the resultant list.

7.8.2 Source Route Options

Another idea that network builders find interesting is the *source route* option. The idea behind source routing is that it provides a way for the sender to dictate a path through the internet. For example, to test the throughput over a particular physical network, *N*, system administrators can use source routing to force IP datagrams to traverse network *N* even if routers would normally choose a path that did not include it. The ability to make such tests is especially important in a production environment, because it gives the network manager freedom to route users' datagrams over networks that are known to operate correctly while simultaneously testing other networks. Of course, source routing is only useful to people who understand the network topology; the average user has no need to know or use it.

IP supports two forms of source routing. One form, called *strict source routing*, specifies a routing path by including a sequence of IP addresses in the option as Figure 7.14 shows.

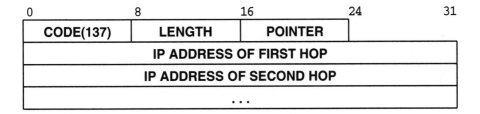

Figure 7.14 The strict source route option specifies an exact route by giving a list of IP addresses the datagram must follow.

Strict source routing means that the addresses specify the exact path the datagram must follow to reach its destination. The path between two successive addresses in the list must consist of a single physical network; an error results if a router cannot follow a strict source route. The other form, called *loose source routing*, also includes a sequence of IP addresses. It specifies that the datagram must follow the sequence of IP addresses, but allows multiple network hops between successive addresses on the list.

Both source route options require routers along the path to overwrite items in the address list with their local network addresses. Thus, when the datagram arrives at its destination, it contains a list of all addresses visited, exactly like the list produced by the record route option.

The format of a source route option resembles that of the record route option shown above. Each router examines the *POINTER* and *LENGTH* fields to see if the list has been exhausted. If it has, the pointer is greater than the length, and the router routes the datagram to its destination as usual. If the list is not exhausted, the router follows the pointer, picks up the IP address, replaces it with the router's address†, and routes the datagram using the address obtained from the list.

7.8.3 Timestamp Option

The *timestamp option* works like the record route option in that the timestamp option contains an initially empty list, and each router along the path from source to destination fills in one item in the list. Each entry in the list contains two 32-bit items: the IP address of the router that supplied the entry and a 32-bit integer timestamp. Figure 7.15 shows the format of the timestamp option.

---

†A router has one address for each interface; it records the address that corresponds to the network over which it routes the datagram.

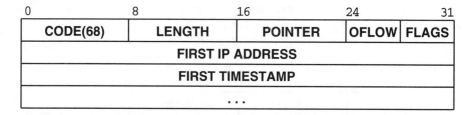

Figure 7.15 The format of the timestamp option. Bits in the FLAGS field control the exact format and rules routers use to process this option.

In the figure, the *LENGTH* and *POINTER* fields are used to specify the length of the space reserved for the option and the location of the next unused slot (exactly as in the record route option). The 4-bit *OFLOW* field contains an integer count of routers that could not supply a timestamp because the option was too small.

The value in the 4-bit *FLAGS* field controls the exact format of the option and tells how routers should supply timestamps. The values are:

Flags value	Meaning
0	Record timestamps only; omit IP addresses.
1	Precede each timestamp by an IP address (this is the format shown in Figure 7.15).
3	IP addresses are specified by sender; a router only records a timestamp if the next IP address in the list matches the router's IP address.

Figure 7.16 The interpretation of values in the FLAGS field of a timestamp option.

Timestamps give the time and date at which a router handles the datagram, expressed as milliseconds since midnight, Universal Time†. If the standard representation for time is unavailable, the router can use any representation of local time provided it turns on the high-order bit in the timestamp field. Of course, timestamps issued by independent computers are not always consistent even if represented in universal time; each machine reports time according to its local clock, and clocks may differ. Thus, timestamp entries should always be treated as estimates, independent of the representation.

It may seem odd that the timestamp option includes a mechanism to have routers record their IP addresses along with timestamps because the record route option already provides that capability. However, recording IP addresses with timestamps eliminates

---

† Universal Time was formerly called Greenwich Mean Time; it is the time of day at the prime meridian.

ambiguity. Having an address recorded along with each timestamp is also useful because it allows the receiver to know exactly which path the datagram followed.

7.8.4 Processing Options During Fragmentation

The idea behind the *COPY* bit in the option *CODE* field should now be clear. When fragmenting a datagram, a router replicates some IP options in all fragments while it places others in only one fragment. For example, consider the option used to record the datagram route. We said that each fragment will be handled as an independent datagram, so there is no guarantee that all fragments follow the same path to the destination. If all fragments contained the record route option, the destination might receive a different list of routes from each fragment. It could not produce a single, meaningful list of routes for the reassembled datagram. Therefore, the IP standard specifies that the record route option should only be copied into one of the fragments.

Not all IP options can be restricted to one fragment. Consider the source route option, for example, that specifies how a datagram should travel through the internet. Source routing information must be replicated in all fragment headers, or fragments will not follow the specified route. Thus, the code field for source route specifies that the option must be copied into all fragments.

7.9 Summary

The fundamental service provided by TCP/IP internet software is a connectionless, unreliable, best-effort packet delivery system. The Internet Protocol (IP) formally specifies the format of internet packets, called *datagrams*, and informally embodies the ideas of connectionless delivery. This chapter concentrated on datagram formats; later chapters will discuss IP routing and error handling.

Analogous to a physical frame, the IP datagram is divided into header and data areas. Among other information, the datagram header contains the source and destination IP addresses, fragmentation control, precedence, and a checksum used to catch transmission errors. Besides fixed-length fields, each datagram header can contain an options field. The options field is variable length, depending on the number and type of options used as well as the size of the data area allocated for each option. Intended to help monitor and control an internet, options allow one to specify or record routing information, or to gather timestamps as the datagram traverses an internet.

FOR FURTHER STUDY

Postel [1980] discusses possible ways to approach internet protocols, addressing, and routing. In later publications, Postel [RFC 791] gives the standard for the Internet Protocol. Braden [RFC 1122] further refines the standard. Hornig [RFC 894] specifies the standard for the transmission of IP datagrams across an Ethernet. Clark [RFC 815] describes efficient reassembly of fragments; Kent and Mogul [1987] discusses the disadvantages of fragmentation.

Nichols et. al. [RFC 2474] specifies the differentiated service interpretation of the service type bits in datagram headers, and Blake et. al. [RFC 2475] discusses an architecture for differentiated services. In addition to the packet format, many constants needed in the network protocols are also standardized; the values can be found in the Official Internet Protocols RFC, which is issued periodically.

An alternative internet protocol suite known as *XNS*, is given in Xerox [1981]. Boggs *et. al.* [1980] describes the PARC Universal Packet (PUP) protocol, an abstraction from *XNS* closely related to the IP datagram.

EXERCISES

7.1   What is the single greatest advantage of having the IP checksum cover only the datagram header and not the data? What is the disadvantage?

7.2   Is it ever necessary to use an IP checksum when sending packets over an Ethernet? Why or why not?

7.3   What is the MTU size for a Frame Relay network? Hyperchannel? an ATM network?

7.4   Do you expect a high-speed local area network to have larger or smaller MTU size than a wide area network?

7.5   Argue that fragments should have small, nonstandard headers.

7.6   Find out when the IP protocol version last changed. Is having a protocol version number useful?

7.7   Extend the previous exercise by arguing that if the IP version changes, it makes more sense to assign a new frame type than to encode the version number in the datagram.

7.8   Can you imagine why a one's complement checksum was chosen for IP instead of a cyclic redundancy check?

7.9   What are the advantages of doing reassembly at the ultimate destination instead of doing it after the datagram travels across one network?

7.10 What is the minimum network MTU required to send an IP datagram that contains at least one octet of data?

7.11 Suppose you are hired to implement IP datagram processing in hardware. Is there any rearrangement of fields in the header that would have made your hardware more efficient? Easier to build?

7.12 If you have access to an implementation of IP, revise it and test your locally available implementations of IP to see if they reject IP datagrams with an out-of-date version number.

7.13 When a minimum-size IP datagram travels across an Ethernet, how large is the frame?

7.14 The differentiated services interpretation of the *SERVICE TYPE* field allows up to 64 separate service levels. Argue that fewer levels are needed (i.e., make a list of all possible services that a user might access).

7.15 The differentiated service definition was chosen to make it backward compatible with the original type-of-service priority bits. Will the backward compatibility force implementations to be less efficient than an alternative scheme? Explain.

8

Internet Protocol: Routing IP Datagrams

8.1 Introduction

We have seen that all internet services use an underlying, connectionless packet delivery system, and that the basic unit of transfer in a TCP/IP internet is the IP datagram. This chapter adds to the description of connectionless service by describing how routers forward IP datagrams and deliver them to their final destinations. We think of the datagram format from Chapter 7 as characterizing the static aspects of the Internet Protocol. The description of routing in this chapter characterizes the operational aspects. The next chapter completes our basic presentation of IP by describing how errors are handled. Chapter 10 then describes extensions for classless and subnet addressing, and later chapters show how other protocols use IP to provide higher-level services.

8.2 Routing In An Internet

In a packet switching system, *routing* refers to the process of choosing a path over which to send packets, and *router* refers to a computer making the choice. Routing occurs at several levels. For example, within a wide area network that has multiple physical connections between packet switches, the network itself is responsible for routing packets from the time they enter until they leave. Such internal routing is completely self-contained inside the wide area network. Machines on the outside cannot participate in decisions; they merely view the network as an entity that delivers packets.

Remember that the goal of IP is to provide a virtual network that encompasses multiple physical networks and offers a connectionless datagram delivery service. Thus, we will focus on *IP forwarding*, which is also called *internet routing* or *IP routing*†. The information used to make routing decisions is known as *IP routing information*. Like routing within a single physical network, IP routing chooses a path over which a datagram should be sent. Unlike routing within a single network, the IP routing algorithm must choose how to send a datagram across multiple physical networks.

Routing in an internet can be difficult, especially among computers that have multiple physical network connections. Ideally, the routing software would examine network load, datagram length, or the type of service specified in the datagram header when selecting the best path. Most internet routing software is much less sophisticated, however, and selects routes based on fixed assumptions about shortest paths.

To understand IP routing completely, we must review the architecture of a TCP/IP internet. First, recall that an internet is composed of multiple physical networks interconnected by computers called *routers*. Each router has direct connections to two or more networks. By contrast, a host computer usually connects directly to one physical network. We know that it is possible, however, to have a multi-homed host connected directly to multiple networks.

Both hosts and routers participate in routing an IP datagram to its destination. When an application program on a host attempts to communicate, the TCP/IP protocols eventually generate one or more IP datagrams. The host must make an initial routing decision when it chooses where to send the datagrams. As Figure 8.1 shows, hosts must make routing decisions even if they have only one network connection.

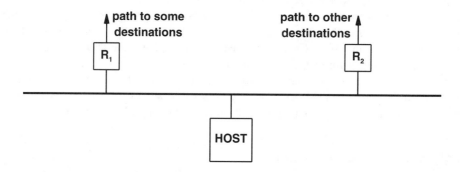

Figure 8.1 An example of a singly-homed host that must route datagrams. The host must choose to send a datagram either to router R_1 or to router R_2, because each router provides the best path to some destinations.

The primary purpose of routers is to make IP routing decisions. What about multi-homed hosts? Any computer with multiple network connections can act as a router, and as we will see, multi-homed hosts running TCP/IP have all the software

---

†Chapter 18 describes a related topic known as *layer 3 switching* or *IP switching*.

needed for routing. Furthermore, sites that cannot afford separate routers sometimes use general-purpose timesharing machines as both hosts and routers. However, the TCP/IP standards draw a sharp distinction between the functions of a host and those of a router, and sites that try to mix host and router functions on a single machine sometimes find that their multi-homed hosts engage in unexpected interactions. For now, we will distinguish hosts from routers, and assume that hosts do not perform the router's function of transferring packets from one network to another.

8.3 Direct And Indirect Delivery

Loosely speaking, we can divide routing into two forms: *direct delivery* and *indirect delivery*. Direct delivery, the transmission of a datagram from one machine across a single physical network directly to another, is the basis on which all internet communication rests. Two machines can engage in direct delivery only if they both attach directly to the same underlying physical transmission system (e.g., a single Ethernet). *Indirect delivery* occurs when the destination is not on a directly attached network, forcing the sender to pass the datagram to a router for delivery.

8.3.1 Datagram Delivery Over A Single Network

We know that one machine on a given physical network can send a physical frame directly to another machine on the same network. To transfer an IP datagram, the sender encapsulates the datagram in a physical frame, maps the destination IP address into a physical address, and uses the network hardware to deliver it. Chapter 5 presented two possible mechanisms for address resolution, including using the ARP protocol for dynamic address binding on Ethernet-like networks. Chapter 7 discussed datagram encapsulation. Thus, we have reviewed all the pieces needed to understand direct delivery. To summarize:

> *Transmission of an IP datagram between two machines on a single physical network does not involve routers. The sender encapsulates the datagram in a physical frame, binds the destination IP address to a physical hardware address, and sends the resulting frame directly to the destination.*

How does the sender know whether the destination lies on a directly connected network? The test is straightforward. We know that IP addresses are divided into a network-specific prefix and a host-specific suffix. To see if a destination lies on one of the directly connected networks, the sender extracts the network portion of the destination IP address and compares it to the network portion of its own IP address(es). A match means the datagram can be sent directly. Here we see one of the advantages of the Internet address scheme, namely:

> *Because the internet addresses of all machines on a single network in-
> clude a common network prefix and extracting that prefix requires
> only a few machine instructions, testing whether a machine can be
> reached directly is extremely efficient.*

From an internet perspective, it is easiest to think of direct delivery as the final
step in any datagram transmission, even if the datagram traverses many networks and
intermediate routers. The final router along the path between the datagram source and
its destination will connect directly to the same physical network as the destination.
Thus, the final router will deliver the datagram using direct delivery. We can think of
direct delivery between the source and destination as a special case of general purpose
routing – in a direct route the datagram does not happen to pass through any intervening
routers.

8.3.2 Indirect Delivery

Indirect delivery is more difficult than direct delivery because the sender must
identify a router to which the datagram can be sent. The router must then forward the
datagram on toward its destination network.

To visualize how indirect routing works, imagine a large internet with many networks interconnected by routers but with only two hosts at the far ends. When one host
wants to send to the other, it encapsulates the datagram and sends it to the nearest
router. We know that the host can reach a router because all physical networks are interconnected, so there must be a router attached to each network. Thus, the originating
host can reach a router using a single physical network. Once the frame reaches the
router, software extracts the encapsulated datagram, and the IP software selects the next
router along the path towards the destination. The datagram is again placed in a frame
and sent over the next physical network to a second router, and so on, until it can be
delivered directly. These ideas can be summarized:

> *Routers in a TCP/IP internet form a cooperative, interconnected
> structure. Datagrams pass from router to router until they reach a
> router that can deliver the datagram directly.*

How can a router know where to send each datagram? How can a host know
which router to use for a given destination? The two questions are related because they
both involve IP routing. We will answer them in two stages, considering the basic
table-driven routing algorithm in this chapter and postponing a discussion of how
routers learn new routes until later.

8.4 Table-Driven IP Routing

The usual IP routing algorithm employs an *Internet routing table* (sometimes called an *IP routing table*) on each machine that stores information about possible destinations and how to reach them. Because both hosts and routers route datagrams, both have IP routing tables. Whenever the IP routing software in a host or router needs to transmit a datagram, it consults the routing table to decide where to send the datagram.

What information should be kept in routing tables? If every routing table contained information about every possible destination address, it would be impossible to keep the tables current. Furthermore, because the number of possible destinations is large, machines would have insufficient space to store the information.

Conceptually, we would like to use the principle of information hiding and allow machines to make routing decisions with minimal information. For example, we would like to isolate information about specific hosts to the local environment in which they exist and arrange for machines that are far away to route packets to them without knowing such details. Fortunately, the IP address scheme helps achieve this goal. Recall that IP addresses are assigned to make all machines connected to a given physical network share a common prefix (the network portion of the address). We have already seen that such an assignment makes the test for direct delivery efficient. It also means that routing tables only need to contain network prefixes and not full IP addresses.

8.5 Next-Hop Routing

Using the network portion of a destination address instead of the complete host address makes routing efficient and keeps routing tables small. More important, it helps hide information, keeping the details of specific hosts confined to the local environment in which those hosts operate. Typically, a routing table contains pairs (N, R), where N is the IP address of a destination *network*, and R is the IP address of the "next" router along the path to network N. Router R is called the *next hop*, and the idea of using a routing table to store a next hop for each destination is called *next-hop routing*. Thus, the routing table in a router R only specifies one step along the path from R to a destination network – the router does not know the complete path to a destination.

It is important to understand that each entry in a routing table points to a router that can be reached across a single network. That is, all routers listed in machine M's routing table must lie on networks to which M connects directly. When a datagram is ready to leave M, IP software locates the destination IP address and extracts the network portion. M then uses the network portion to make a routing decision, selecting a router that can be reached directly.

In practice, we apply the principle of information hiding to hosts as well. We insist that although hosts have IP routing tables, they must keep minimal information in their tables. The idea is to force hosts to rely on routers for most routing.

Figure 8.2 shows a concrete example that helps explain routing tables. The example internet consists of four networks connected by three routers. In the figure, the routing table gives the routes that router R uses. Because R connects directly to networks 20.0.0.0 and 30.0.0.0, it can use direct delivery to send to a host on either of those networks (possibly using ARP to find physical addresses). Given a datagram destined for a host on network 40.0.0.0, R routes it to the address of router S, 30.0.0.7. S will then deliver the datagram directly. R can reach address 30.0.0.7 because both R and S attach directly to network 30.0.0.0.

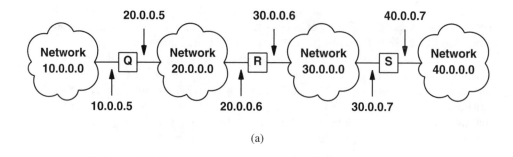

(a)

TO REACH HOSTS ON NETWORK	ROUTE TO THIS ADDRESS
20.0.0.0	DELIVER DIRECTLY
30.0.0.0	DELIVER DIRECTLY
10.0.0.0	20.0.0.5
40.0.0.0	30.0.0.7

(b)

Figure 8.2 (a) An example internet with 4 networks and 3 routers, and (b) the routing table in R.

As Figure 8.2 demonstrates, the size of the routing table depends on the number of networks in the internet; it only grows when new networks are added. However, the table size and contents are independent of the number of individual hosts connected to the networks. We can summarize the underlying principle:

To hide information, keep routing tables small, and make routing decisions efficient, IP routing software only keeps information about destination network addresses, not about individual host addresses.

Choosing routes based on the destination network ID alone has several consequences. First, in most implementations, it means that all traffic destined for a given
network takes the same path. As a result, even when multiple paths exist, they may not
be used concurrently. Also, all types of traffic follow the same path without regard to
the delay or throughput of physical networks. Second, because only the final router
along the path attempts to communicate with the destination host, only it can determine
if the host exists or is operational. Thus, we need to arrange a way for that router to
send reports of delivery problems back to the original source. Third, because each
router forwards traffic independently, datagrams traveling from host *A* to host *B* may
follow an entirely different path than datagrams traveling from host *B* back to host A.
We need to ensure that routers cooperate to guarantee that two-way communication is
always possible.

8.6 Default Routes

Another technique used to hide information and keep routing table sizes small con-
solidates multiple entries into a default case. The idea is to have the IP routing software
first look in the routing table for the destination network. If no route appears in the
table, the routing routines send the datagram to a *default router*.

Default routing is especially useful when a site has a small set of local addresses
and only one connection to the rest of the internet. For example, default routes work
well in host computers that attach to a single physical network and reach only one
router leading to the remainder of the internet. The routing decision consists of two
tests: one for the local net and a default that points to the only router. Even if the site
contains a few local networks, the routing is simple because it consists of a few tests for
the local networks plus a default for all other destinations.

8.7 Host-Specific Routes

Although we said that all routing is based on networks and not on individual hosts,
most IP routing software allows per-host routes to be specified as a special case. Having per-host routes gives the local network administrator more control over network use,
permits testing, and can also be used to control access for security purposes. When debugging network connections or routing tables, the ability to specify a special route to
one individual machine turns out to be especially useful.

8.8 The IP Routing Algorithm

Taking into account everything we have said, the IP algorithm used to forward datagrams becomes†:

---

†Chapter 10 discusses a slightly modified algorithm used with classless IP addresses.

Algorithm:

RouteDatagram (Datagram , RoutingTable)

Extract destination IP address, D, from the datagram
    and compute the network prefix, N;
if N matches any directly connected network address
    deliver datagram to destination D over that network
    (This involves resolving D to a physical address,
    encapsulating the datagram, and sending the frame.)
else if the table contains a host-specific route for D
    send datagram to next-hop specified in table
else if the table contains a route for network N
    send datagram to next-hop specified in table
else if the table contains a default route
    send datagram to the default router specified in table
else declare a routing error;

Figure 8.3 The algorithm IP uses to forward a datagram. Given an IP datagram and a routing table, this algorithm selects the next hop to
which the datagram should be sent. All routes must specify a
next hop that lies on a directly connected network.

8.9 Routing With IP Addresses

It is important to understand that except for decrementing the time to live and
recomputing the checksum, IP routing does not alter the original datagram. In particular, the datagram source and destination addresses remain unaltered; they always specify
the IP address of the original source and the IP address of the ultimate destination†.
When IP executes the routing algorithm, it selects a new IP address, the IP address of
the machine to which the datagram should be sent next. The new address is most likely
the address of a router. However, if the datagram can be delivered directly, the new address is the same as the address of the ultimate destination.

We said that the IP address selected by the IP routing algorithm is known as the
next hop address because it tells where the datagram must be sent next. Where does IP
store the next hop address? Not in the datagram; no place is reserved for it. In fact, IP
does not ''store'' the next hop address at all. After executing the routing algorithm, IP
passes the datagram and the next hop address to the network interface software responsible for the physical network over which the datagram must be sent. The network in-

---
†The only exception occurs when the datagram contains a source route option.

terface software binds the next hop address to a physical address, forms a frame using that physical address, places the datagram in the data portion of the frame, and sends the result. After using the next hop address to find a physical address, the network interface software discards the next hop address.

It may seem odd that routing tables store the IP address of a next hop for each destination network when those addresses must be translated into corresponding physical addresses before the datagram can be sent. If we imagine a host sending a sequence of datagrams to the same destination address, the use of IP addresses will appear incredibly inefficient. IP dutifully extracts the destination address in each datagram and uses the routing table to produce a next hop address. It then passes the datagram and next hop address to the network interface, which recomputes the binding to a physical address. If the routing table used physical addresses, the binding between the next hop's IP address and physical address could be performed once, saving unneeded computation.

Why does IP software avoid using physical addresses when storing and computing routes? As Figure 8.4 illustrates, there are two important reasons.

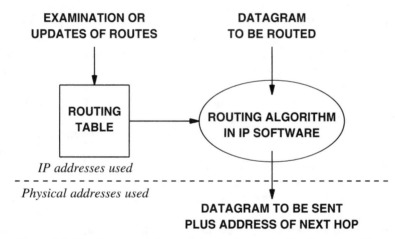

Figure 8.4 IP software and the routing table it uses reside above the address
boundary. Using only IP addresses makes routes easy to examine
or change and hides the details of physical addresses.

First, the routing table provides an especially clean interface between IP software that routes datagrams and high-level software that manipulates routes. To debug routing problems, network managers often need to examine the routing tables. Using only IP addresses in the routing table makes it easy for managers to understand and to determine whether software has updated the routes correctly. Second, the whole point of the Internet Protocol is to build an abstraction that hides the details of underlying networks.

Figure 8.4 shows the *address boundary*, the important conceptual division between low-level software that understands physical addresses and internet software that only uses high-level addresses. Above this boundary, all software can be written to communicate using internet addresses; knowledge of physical addresses is relegated to a few small, low-level routines. We will see that observing the boundary also helps keep the implementation of remaining TCP/IP protocols easy to understand, test, and modify.

8.10 Handling Incoming Datagrams

So far, we have discussed IP routing by describing how forwarding decisions are made about outgoing packets. It should be clear, however, that IP software must process incoming datagrams as well.

When an IP datagram arrives at a host, the network interface software delivers it to the IP module for processing. If the datagram's destination address matches the host's IP address, IP software on the host accepts the datagram and passes it to the appropriate higher-level protocol software for further processing. If the destination IP address does not match, a host is required to discard the datagram (i.e., hosts are forbidden from attempting to forward datagrams that are accidentally routed to the wrong machine).

Unlike hosts, routers perform forwarding. When an IP datagram arrives at a router, it is delivered to the IP software. Again, two cases arise: the datagram could have reached its final destination, or it may need to travel further. As with hosts, if the datagram destination IP address matches the router's own IP address, the IP software passes the datagram to higher-level protocol software for processing†. If the datagram has not reached its final destination, IP routes the datagram using the standard algorithm and the information in the local routing table.

Determining whether an IP datagram has reached its final destination is not quite as trivial as it seems. Remember that even a host may have multiple physical connections, each with its own IP address. When an IP datagram arrives, the machine must compare the destination internet address to the IP address for each of its network connections. If any match, it keeps the datagram and processes it. A machine must also accept datagrams that were broadcast on the physical network if their destination IP address is the limited IP broadcast address or the directed IP broadcast address for that network. As we will see in Chapters 10 and 17, classless, subnet, and multicast addresses make address recognition even more complex. In any case, if the address does not match any of the local machine's addresses, IP decrements the time-to-live field in the datagram header, discarding the datagram if the count reaches zero, or computing a new checksum and routing the datagram if the count remains positive.

Should every machine forward the IP datagrams it receives? Obviously, a router must forward incoming datagrams because that is its main function. We have also said that some multi-homed hosts act as routers even though they are really general purpose computing systems. While using a host as a router is not usually a good idea, if one chooses to use that arrangement, the host must be configured to route datagrams just as a router does. But what about other hosts, those that are not intended to be routers?

---

†Usually, the only datagrams destined for a router are those used to test connectivity or those that carry router management commands, but a router must also keep a copy of datagrams that are broadcast on the network.

The answer is that hosts not designated to be routers should *not* route datagrams that they receive; they should discard them.

There are four reasons why a host not designated to serve as a router should refrain from performing any router functions. First, when such a host receives a datagram intended for some other machine, something has gone wrong with internet addressing, routing, or delivery. The problem may not be revealed if the host takes corrective action by routing the datagram. Second, routing will cause unnecessary network traffic (and may steal CPU time from legitimate uses of the host). Third, simple errors can cause chaos. Suppose that every host routes traffic, and imagine what happens if one machine accidentally broadcasts a datagram that is destined for some host, *H*. Because it has been broadcast, every host on the network receives a copy of the datagram. Every host forwards its copy to *H*, which will be bombarded with many copies. Fourth, as later chapters show, routers do more than merely route traffic. As the next chapter explains, routers use a special protocol to report errors, while hosts do not (again, to avoid having multiple error reports bombard a source). Routers also propagate routing information to ensure that their routing tables are consistent. If hosts route datagrams without participating fully in all router functions, unexpected anomalies can arise.

8.11 Establishing Routing Tables

We have discussed how IP routes datagrams based on the contents of routing tables, without saying how systems initialize their routing tables or update them as the network changes. Later chapters deal with these questions and discuss protocols that allow routers to keep routes consistent. For now, it is only important to understand that IP software uses the routing table whenever it decides how to forward a datagram, so changing routing tables will change the paths datagrams follow.

8.12 Summary

IP uses routing information to forward datagrams; the computation consists of deciding where to send a datagram based on its destination IP address. Direct delivery is possible if the destination machine lies on a network to which the sending machine attaches; we think of this as the final step in datagram transmission. If the sender cannot reach the destination directly, the sender must forward the datagram to a router. The general paradigm is that hosts send indirectly routed datagrams to the nearest router; the datagrams travel through the internet from router to router until they can be delivered directly across one physical network.

When IP software looks up a route, the algorithm produces the IP address of the next machine (i.e., the address of the next hop) to which the datagram should be sent; IP passes the datagram and next hop address to network interface software. Transmission of a datagram from one machine to the next always involves encapsulating the datagram in a physical frame, mapping the next hop internet address to a physical address, and sending the frame using the underlying hardware.

The internet routing algorithm is table driven and uses only IP addresses. Although it is possible for a routing table to contain a host-specific destination address, most routing tables contain only network addresses, keeping routing tables small. Using a default route can also help keep a routing table small, especially for hosts that can access only one router.

FOR FURTHER STUDY

Routing is an important topic. Frank and Chou [1971] and Schwartz and Stern [1980] discuss routing in general; Postel [1980] discusses internet routing. Braden and Postel [RFC 1009] provides a summary of how Internet routers handle IP datagrams. Narten [1989] contains a survey of Internet routing. Fultz and Kleinrock [1971] analyzes adaptive routing schemes; and McQuillan, Richer, and Rosen [1980] describes the ARPANET adaptive routing algorithm.

The idea of using policy statements to formulate rules about routing has been considered often. Leiner [RFC 1124] considers policies for interconnected networks. Braun [RFC 1104] discusses models of policy routing for internets, Rekhter [RFC 1092] relates policy routing to the second NSFNET backbone, and Clark [RFC 1102] describes using policy routing with IP.

EXERCISES

8.1   Complete routing tables for all routers in Figure 8.2. Which routers will benefit most from using a default route?

8.2   Examine the routing algorithm used on your local system. Are all the cases mentioned in the chapter covered? Does the algorithm allow anything not mentioned?

8.3   What does a router do with the *time to live* value in an IP header?

8.4   Consider a machine with two physical network connections and two IP addresses I_1 and I_2. Is it possible for that machine to receive a datagram destined for I_2 over the network with address I_1? Explain.

8.5   Consider two hosts, A and B, that both attach to a common physical network, N. Is it ever possible, when using our routing algorithm, for A to receive a datagram destined for B? Explain.

8.6   Modify the routing algorithm to accommodate the IP source route options discussed in Chapter 7.

8.7   An IP router must perform a computation that takes time proportional to the length of the datagram header each time it processes a datagram. Explain.

8.8   A network administrator argues that to make monitoring and debugging his local network easier, he wants to rewrite the routing algorithm so it tests host-specific routes *before* it tests for direct delivery. How can he use the revised algorithm to build a network monitor?

8.9 Is it possible to address a datagram to a router's IP address? Does it make sense to do so?

8.10 Consider a modified routing algorithm that examines host-specific routes before testing for delivery on directly connected networks. Under what circumstances might such an algorithm be desirable? undesirable?

8.11 Play detective: after monitoring IP traffic on a local area network for 10 minutes one evening, someone notices that all frames destined for machine *A* carry IP datagrams that have destination equal to *A*'s IP address, while all frames destined for machine *B* carry IP datagrams with destination *not* equal to *B*'s IP address. Users report that both *A* and *B* can communicate. Explain.

8.12 How could you change the IP datagram format to support high-speed packet switching at routers? Hint: a router must recompute a header checksum after decrementing the time-to-live field.

8.13 Compare CLNP, the ISO connectionless delivery protocol (ISO standard 8473) with IP. How well will the ISO protocol support high-speed switching? Hint: variable length fields are expensive.

9

Internet Protocol: Error And Control Messages (ICMP)

9.1 Introduction

The previous chapter shows how the Internet Protocol software provides an unreliable, connectionless datagram delivery service by arranging for each router to forward datagrams. A datagram travels from router to router until it reaches one that can deliver the datagram directly to its final destination. If a router cannot route or deliver a datagram, or if the router detects an unusual condition that affects its ability to forward the datagram (e.g., network congestion), the router needs to inform the original source to take action to avoid or correct the problem. This chapter discusses a mechanism that internet routers and hosts use to communicate such control or error information. We will see that routers use the mechanism to report problems and hosts use it to test whether destinations are reachable.

9.2 The Internet Control Message Protocol

In the connectionless system we have described so far, each router operates autonomously, routing or delivering datagrams that arrive without coordinating with the original sender. The system works well if all machines operate correctly and agree on routes. Unfortunately, no large communication system works correctly all the time. Besides failures of communication lines and processors, IP fails to deliver datagrams when the destination machine is temporarily or permanently disconnected from the network, when the time-to-live counter expires, or when intermediate routers become so congested that they cannot process the incoming traffic. The important difference between having a single network implemented with dedicated hardware and an internet implemented with software is that in the former, the designer can add special hardware to inform attached hosts when problems arise. In an internet, which has no such hardware mechanism, a sender cannot tell whether a delivery failure resulted from a local malfunction or a remote one. Debugging becomes extremely difficult. The IP protocol itself contains nothing to help the sender test connectivity or learn about such failures.

To allow routers in an internet to report errors or provide information about unexpected circumstances, the designers added a special-purpose message mechanism to the TCP/IP protocols. The mechanism, known as the *Internet Control Message Protocol* (*ICMP*), is considered a required part of IP and must be included in every IP implementation.

Like all other traffic, ICMP messages travel across the internet in the data portion of IP datagrams. The ultimate destination of an ICMP message is not an application program or user on the destination machine, however, but the Internet Protocol software on that machine. That is, when an ICMP error message arrives, the ICMP software module handles it. Of course, if ICMP determines that a particular higher-level protocol or application program has caused a problem, it will inform the appropriate module. We can summarize:

> *The Internet Control Message Protocol allows routers to send error or control messages to other routers or hosts; ICMP provides communication between the Internet Protocol software on one machine and the Internet Protocol software on another.*

Initially designed to allow routers to report the cause of delivery errors to hosts, ICMP is not restricted to routers. Although guidelines restrict the use of some ICMP messages, an arbitrary machine can send an ICMP message to any other machine. Thus, a host can use ICMP to correspond with a router or another host. The chief advantage of allowing hosts to use ICMP is that it provides a single mechanism used for all control and information messages.

9.3 Error Reporting vs. Error Correction

Technically, ICMP is an *error reporting mechanism*. It provides a way for routers that encounter an error to report the error to the original source. Although the protocol specification outlines intended uses of ICMP and suggests possible actions to take in response to error reports, ICMP does not fully specify the action to be taken for each possible error. In short,

When a datagram causes an error, ICMP can only report the error condition back to the original source of the datagram; the source must relate the error to an individual application program or take other action to correct the problem.

Most errors stem from the original source, but others do not. Because ICMP reports problems to the original source, however, it cannot be used to inform intermediate routers about problems. For example, suppose a datagram follows a path through a sequence of routers, R_1, R_2, ..., R_k. If R_k has incorrect routing information and mistakenly routes the datagram to router R_E, R_E cannot use ICMP to report the error back to router R_k; ICMP can only send a report back to the original source. Unfortunately, the original source has no responsibility for the problem or control over the misbehaving router. In fact, the source may not be able to determine which router caused the problem.

Why restrict ICMP to communication with the original source? The answer should be clear from our discussion of datagram formats and routing in the previous chapters. A datagram only contains fields that specify the original source and the ultimate destination; it does not contain a complete record of its trip through the internet (except for unusual cases where the record route option is used). Furthermore, because routers can establish and change their own routing tables, there is no global knowledge of routes. Thus, when a datagram reaches a given router, it is impossible to know the path it has taken to arrive there. If the router detects a problem, it cannot know the set of intermediate machines that processed the datagram, so it cannot inform them of the problem. Instead of silently discarding the datagram, the router uses ICMP to inform the original source that a problem has occurred, and trusts that host administrators will cooperate with network administrators to locate and repair the problem.

9.4 ICMP Message Delivery

ICMP messages require two levels of encapsulation as Figure 9.1 shows. Each ICMP message travels across the internet in the data portion of an IP datagram, which itself travels across each physical network in the data portion of a frame. Datagrams carrying ICMP messages are routed exactly like datagrams carrying information for users; there is no additional reliability or priority. Thus, error messages themselves may be lost or discarded. Furthermore, in an already congested network, the error message may cause additional congestion. An exception is made to the error handling procedures if an IP datagram carrying an ICMP message causes an error. The exception, established to avoid the problem of having error messages about error messages, specifies that ICMP messages are not generated for errors that result from datagrams carrying ICMP error messages.

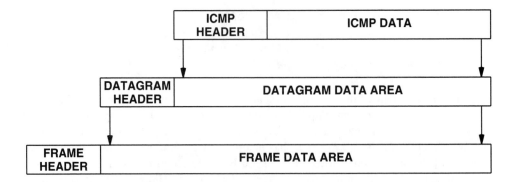

Figure 9.1 Two levels of ICMP encapsulation. The ICMP message is encapsulated in an IP datagram, which is further encapsulated in a
frame for transmission. To identify ICMP, the datagram protocol
field contains the value *1*.

It is important to keep in mind that even though ICMP messages are encapsulated
and sent using IP, ICMP is not considered a higher level protocol — it is a required part
of IP. The reason for using IP to deliver ICMP messages is that they may need to travel across several physical networks to reach their final destination. Thus, they cannot
be delivered by the physical transport alone.

9.5 ICMP Message Format

Although each ICMP message has its own format, they all begin with the same
three fields: an 8-bit integer message *TYPE* field that identifies the message, an 8-bit
CODE field that provides further information about the message type, and a 16-bit
CHECKSUM field (ICMP uses the same additive checksum algorithm as IP, but the
ICMP checksum only covers the ICMP message). In addition, ICMP messages that report errors always include the header and first 64 data bits of the datagram causing the
problem.

The reason for returning more than the datagram header alone is to allow the receiver to determine more precisely which protocol(s) and which application program
were responsible for the datagram. As we will see later, higher-level protocols in the
TCP/IP suite are designed so that crucial information is encoded in the first 64 bits.

The ICMP *TYPE* field defines the meaning of the message as well as its format.
The types include:

Type Field	ICMP Message Type
0	Echo Reply
3	Destination Unreachable
4	Source Quench
5	Redirect (change a route)
8	Echo Request
9	Router Advertisement
10	Router Solicitation
11	Time Exceeded for a Datagram
12	Parameter Problem on a Datagram
13	Timestamp Request
14	Timestamp Reply
15	Information Request (obsolete)
16	Information Reply (obsolete)
17	Address Mask Request
18	Address Mask Reply

The next sections describe each of these messages, giving details of the message format and its meaning.

9.6 Testing Destination Reachability And Status (Ping)

TCP/IP protocols provide facilities to help network managers or users identify network problems. One of the most frequently used debugging tools invokes the ICMP *echo request* and *echo reply* messages. A host or router sends an ICMP echo request message to a specified destination. Any machine that receives an echo request formulates an echo reply and returns it to the original sender. The request contains an optional data area; the reply contains a copy of the data sent in the request. The echo request and associated reply can be used to test whether a destination is reachable and responding. Because both the request and reply travel in IP datagrams, successful receipt of a reply verifies that major pieces of the transport system work. First, IP software on the source computer must route the datagram. Second, intermediate routers between the source and destination must be operating and must route the datagram correctly. Third, the destination machine must be running (at least it must respond to interrupts), and both ICMP and IP software must be working. Finally, all routers along the return path must have correct routes.

On many systems, the command users invoke to send ICMP echo requests is named *ping*†. Sophisticated versions of ping send a series of ICMP echo requests, capture responses, and provide statistics about datagram loss. They allow the user to specify the length of the data being sent and the interval between requests. Less sophisticated versions merely send one ICMP echo request and await a reply.

---

†Dave Mills once suggested that *PING* is an acronym for *Packet InterNet Groper*.

9.7 Echo Request And Reply Message Format

Figure 9.2 shows the format of echo request and reply messages.

0	8	16	31
TYPE (8 or 0)	CODE (0)	CHECKSUM	
IDENTIFIER		SEQUENCE NUMBER	
OPTIONAL DATA			
. . .			

Figure 9.2 ICMP echo request or reply message format.

The field listed as *OPTIONAL DATA* is a variable length field that contains data to be returned to the sender. An echo reply always returns exactly the same data as was received in the request. Fields *IDENTIFIER* and *SEQUENCE NUMBER* are used by the sender to match replies to requests. The value of the *TYPE* field specifies whether the message is a request (*8*) or a reply (*0*).

9.8 Reports Of Unreachable Destinations

When a router cannot forward or deliver an IP datagram, it sends a *destination un-reachable* message back to the original source, using the format shown in Figure 9.3.

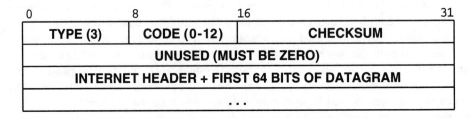

0	8	16	31
TYPE (3)	CODE (0-12)	CHECKSUM	
UNUSED (MUST BE ZERO)			
INTERNET HEADER + FIRST 64 BITS OF DATAGRAM			
. . .			

Figure 9.3 ICMP destination unreachable message format.

The *CODE* field in a destination unreachable message contains an integer that further describes the problem. Possible values are:

Code Value	Meaning
0	Network unreachable
1	Host unreachable
2	Protocol unreachable
3	Port unreachable
4	Fragmentation needed and DF set
5	Source route failed
6	Destination network unknown
7	Destination host unknown
8	Source host isolated
9	Communication with destination network administratively prohibited
10	Communication with destination host administratively prohibited
11	Network unreachable for type of service
12	Host unreachable for type of service

Although IP is a best-effort delivery mechanism, discarding datagrams should not be taken lightly. Whenever an error prevents a router from routing or delivering a datagram, the router sends a destination unreachable message back to the source and then *drops* (i.e., discards) the datagram. Network unreachable errors usually imply routing failures; host unreachable errors imply delivery failures†. Because the ICMP error message contains a short prefix of the datagram that caused the problem, the source will know exactly which address is unreachable.

Destinations may be unreachable because hardware is temporarily out of service, because the sender specified a nonexistent destination address, or (in rare circumstances) because the router does not have a route to the destination network. Note that although routers report failures they encounter, they may not know of all delivery failures. For example, if the destination machine connects to an Ethernet network, the network hardware does not provide acknowledgements. Therefore, a router can continue to send packets to a destination after the destination is powered down without receiving any indication that the packets are not being delivered. To summarize:

> *Although a router sends a destination unreachable message when it encounters a datagram that cannot be forwarded or delivered, a router cannot detect all such errors.*

The meaning of protocol and port unreachable messages will become clear when we study how higher level protocols use abstract destination points called *ports*. Most of the remaining messages are self explanatory. If the datagram contains the source route option with an incorrect route, it may trigger a *source route* failure message. If a router needs to fragment a datagram but the "don't fragment" bit is set, the router sends a *fragmentation needed* message back to the source.

---

†An exception occurs for routers using the subnet addressing scheme of Chapter 10. They report a subnet routing failure with an ICMP host unreachable message.

9.9 Congestion And Datagram Flow Control

Because IP is connectionless, a router cannot reserve memory or communication resources in advance of receiving datagrams. As a result, routers can be overrun with traffic, a condition known as *congestion*. It is important to understand that congestion can arise for two entirely different reasons. First, a high-speed computer may be able to generate traffic faster than a network can transfer it. For example, imagine a supercomputer generating internet traffic. The datagrams may eventually need to cross a slower-speed wide area network (WAN) even though the supercomputer itself attaches to a high-speed local area net. Congestion will occur in the router that attaches the LAN to the WAN because datagrams arrive faster than they can be sent. Second, if many computers simultaneously need to send datagrams through a single router, the router can experience congestion, even though no single source causes the problem.

When datagrams arrive too quickly for a host or router to process, it enqueues them in memory temporarily. If the datagrams are part of a small burst, such buffering solves the problem. If the traffic continues, the host or router eventually exhausts memory and must discard additional datagrams that arrive. A machine uses ICMP *source quench* messages to report congestion to the original source. A source quench message is a request for the source to reduce its current rate of datagram transmission. Usually, congested routers send one source quench message for every datagram that they discard. Routers may also use more sophisticated congestion control techniques. Some monitor incoming traffic and quench sources that have the highest datagram transmission rates. Others attempt to avoid congestion altogether by arranging to send quench requests as their queues start to become long, but before they overflow.

There is no ICMP message to reverse the effect of a source quench. Instead, a host that receives source quench messages for a destination, D, lowers the rate at which it sends datagrams to D until it stops receiving source quench messages; it then gradually increases the rate as long as no further source quench requests are received.

9.10 Source Quench Format

In addition to the usual ICMP *TYPE, CODE, CHECKSUM* fields, and an unused 32-bit field, source quench messages have a field that contains a datagram prefix. Figure 9.4 illustrates the format. As with most ICMP messages that report an error, the datagram prefix field contains a prefix of the datagram that triggered the source quench request.

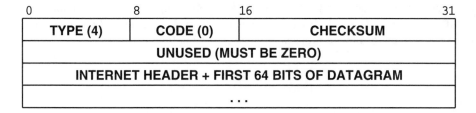

Figure 9.4 ICMP source quench message format. A congested router sends
one source quench message each time it discards a datagram; the
datagram prefix identifies the datagram that was dropped.

9.11 Route Change Requests From Routers

Internet routing tables usually remain static over long periods of time. Hosts initialize them from a configuration file at system startup, and system administrators seldom make routing changes during normal operations. If the network topology changes, routing tables in a router or host may become incorrect. A change can be temporary (e.g., when hardware needs to be repaired) or permanent (e.g., when a new network is added to the internet). As we will see in later chapters, routers exchange routing information periodically to accommodate network changes and keep their routes up-to-date. Thus, as a general rule:

> *Routers are assumed to know correct routes; hosts begin with minimal
> routing information and learn new routes from routers.*

To help follow this rule and to avoid duplicating routing information in the configuration file on each host, the initial host route configuration specifies the minimum possible routing information needed to communicate (e.g., the address of a single router). Thus, the host begins with minimal information and relies on routers to update its routing table. In one special case, when a router detects a host using a nonoptimal route, it sends the host an ICMP message, called a *redirect*, requesting that the host change its route. The router also forwards the original datagram on to its destination.

The advantage of the ICMP redirect scheme is simplicity: it allows a host to boot knowing the address of only one router on the local network. The initial router returns ICMP redirect messages whenever a host sends a datagram for which there is a better route. The host routing table remains small but still contains optimal routes for all destinations in use.

Redirect messages do not solve the problem of propagating routes in a general way, however, because they are limited to interactions between a router and a host on a directly connected network. Figure 9.5 illustrates the limitation. In the figure, assume source S sends a datagram to destination D. Assume that router R_1 incorrectly routes the datagram through router R_2 instead of through router R_4 (i.e., R_1 incorrectly chooses a longer path than necessary). When router R_5 receives the datagram, it cannot send an ICMP redirect message to R_1 because it does not know R_1's address. Later chapters explore the problem of how to propagate routes across multiple networks.

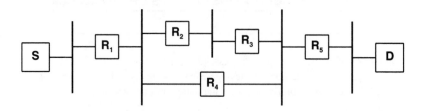

Figure 9.5 ICMP redirect messages do not provide routing changes among routers. In this example, router R_5 cannot redirect R_1 to use the shorter path for datagrams from S to D.

In addition to the requisite *TYPE, CODE,* and *CHECKSUM* fields, each redirect message contains a 32-bit *ROUTER INTERNET ADDRESS* field and an *INTERNET HEADER* field, as Figure 9.6 shows.

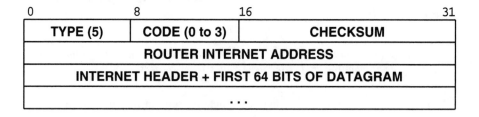

Figure 9.6 ICMP redirect message format.

The *ROUTER INTERNET ADDRESS* field contains the address of a router that the host is to use to reach the destination mentioned in the datagram header. The *INTERNET HEADER* field contains the IP header plus the next 64 bits of the datagram that triggered the message. Thus, a host receiving an ICMP redirect examines the datagram prefix to determine the datagram's destination address. The *CODE* field of an ICMP redirect message further specifies how to interpret the destination address, based on values assigned as follows:

Code Value	Meaning
0	Redirect datagrams for the Net (now obsolete)
1	Redirect datagrams for the Host
2	Redirect datagrams for the Type of Service† and Net
3	Redirect datagrams for the Type of Service and Host

As a general rule, routers only send ICMP redirect requests to hosts and not to other routers. We will see in later chapters that routers use other protocols to exchange routing information.

9.12 Detecting Circular Or Excessively Long Routes

Because internet routers compute a next hop using local tables, errors in routing tables can produce a *routing cycle* for some destination, *D*. A routing cycle can consist of two routers that each route a datagram for destination *D* to the other, or it can consist of several routers. When several routers form a cycle, they each route a datagram for destination *D* to the next router in the cycle. If a datagram enters a routing cycle, it will pass around the cycle endlessly. As mentioned previously, to prevent datagrams from circling forever in a TCP/IP internet, each IP datagram contains a time-to-live counter, sometimes called a *hop count*. A router decrements the time-to-live counter whenever it processes the datagram and discards the datagram when the count reaches zero.

Whenever a router discards a datagram because its hop count has reached zero or because a timeout occurred while waiting for fragments of a datagram, it sends an ICMP *time exceeded* message back to the datagram's source, using the format shown in Figure 9.7.

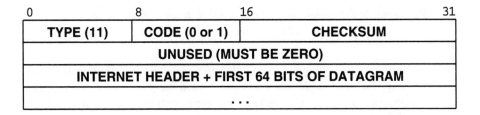

Figure 9.7 ICMP time exceeded message format. A router sends this message whenever a datagram is discarded because the time-to-live field in the datagram header has reached zero or because its reassembly timer expired while waiting for fragments.

ICMP uses the *CODE* field in each time exceeded message (value zero or one) to explain the nature of the timeout being reported:

---

†Recall that each IP header specifies a type of service used for routing.

Code Value	Meaning
0	Time-to-live count exceeded
1	Fragment reassembly time exceeded

Fragment reassembly refers to the task of collecting all the fragments from a datagram. When the first fragment of a datagram arrives, the receiving host starts a timer and considers it an error if the timer expires before all the pieces of the datagram arrive. Code value *1* is used to report such errors to the sender; one message is sent for each such error.

9.13 Reporting Other Problems

When a router or host finds problems with a datagram not covered by previous ICMP error messages (e.g., an incorrect datagram header), it sends a *parameter problem* message to the original source. One possible cause of such problems occurs when arguments to an option are incorrect. The message, formatted as shown in Figure 9.8, is only sent when the problem is so severe that the datagram must be discarded.

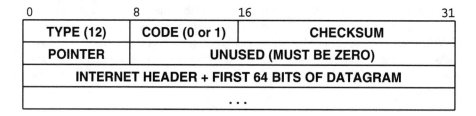

Figure 9.8 ICMP parameter problem message format. Such messages are only sent when the problem causes the datagram to be dropped.

To make the message unambiguous, the sender uses the *POINTER* field in the message header to identify the octet in the datagram that caused the problem. Code *1* is used to report that a required option is missing (e.g., a security option in the military community); the *POINTER* field is not used for code *1*.

9.14 Clock Synchronization And Transit Time Estimation

Although machines on an internet can communicate, they usually operate independently, with each machine maintaining its own notion of the current time. Clocks that differ widely can confuse users of distributed systems software. The TCP/IP protocol suite includes several protocols that can be used to synchronize clocks. One of the simplest techniques uses an ICMP message to obtain the time from another machine. A requesting machine sends an ICMP *timestamp request* message to another machine, asking that the second machine return its current value for the time of day. The receiving machine returns a *timestamp reply* back to the machine making the request. Figure 9.9 shows the format of timestamp request and reply messages.

0	8	16	31
TYPE (13 or 14)	CODE (0)	CHECKSUM	
IDENTIFIER		SEQUENCE NUMBER	
ORIGINATE TIMESTAMP			
RECEIVE TIMESTAMP			
TRANSMIT TIMESTAMP			

Figure 9.9 ICMP timestamp request or reply message format.

The *TYPE* field identifies the message as a request (*13*) or a reply (*14*); the *IDENTIFIER* and *SEQUENCE NUMBER* fields are used by the source to associate replies with requests. Remaining fields specify times, given in milliseconds since midnight, Universal Time†. The *ORIGINATE TIMESTAMP* field is filled in by the original sender just before the packet is transmitted, the *RECEIVE TIMESTAMP* field is filled immediately upon receipt of a request, and the *TRANSMIT TIMESTAMP* field is filled immediately before the reply is transmitted.

Hosts use the three timestamp fields to compute estimates of the delay time between them and to synchronize their clocks. Because the reply includes the *ORIGINATE TIMESTAMP* field, a host can compute the total time required for a request to travel to a destination, be transformed into a reply, and return. Because the reply carries both the time at which the request entered the remote machine, as well as the time at which the reply left, the host can compute the network transit time, and from that, estimate the differences in remote and local clocks.

In practice, accurate estimation of round-trip delay can be difficult and substantially restricts the utility of ICMP timestamp messages. Of course, to obtain an accurate estimate of round trip delay, one must take many measurements and average them. However, the round-trip delay between a pair of machines that connect to a large internet can vary dramatically, even over short periods of time. Furthermore, recall that because IP is a best-effort technology, datagrams can be dropped, delayed, or delivered out of order. Thus, merely taking many measurements may not guarantee consistency; sophisticated statistical analysis is needed to produce precise estimates.

---

† Universal Time was formerly called Greenwich Mean Time; it is the time of day at the prime meridian.

9.15 Information Request And Reply Messages

The ICMP *information request* and *information reply* messages (types *15* and *16*) are now considered obsolete and should not be used. They were originally intended to allow hosts to discover their internet address at system startup. The current protocols for address determination are RARP, described in Chapter 6, and BOOTP, described in Chapter 23.

9.16 Obtaining A Subnet Mask

Chapter 10 discusses the motivation for subnet addressing as well as the details of how subnets operate. For now, it is only important to understand that when hosts use subnet addressing, some bits in the hostid portion of their IP address identify a physical network. To participate in subnet addressing, a host needs to know which bits of the 32-bit internet address correspond to the physical network and which correspond to host identifiers. The information needed to interpret the address is represented in a 32-bit quantity called the *subnet mask.*

To learn the subnet mask used for the local network, a machine can send an *address mask request* message to a router and receive an *address mask reply*. The machine making the request can either send the message directly, if it knows the router's address, or broadcast the message if it does not. Figure 9.10 shows the format of address mask messages.

0	8	16	31
TYPE (17 or 18)	CODE (0)	CHECKSUM	
IDENTIFIER		SEQUENCE NUMBER	
ADDRESS MASK			

Figure 9.10 ICMP address mask request or reply message format. Usually, hosts broadcast a request without knowing which specific router will respond.

The *TYPE* field in an address mask message specifies whether the message is a request (*17*) or a reply (*18*). A reply contains the network's subnet address mask in the *ADDRESS MASK* field. As usual, the *IDENTIFIER* and *SEQUENCE NUMBER* fields allow a machine to associate replies with requests.

9.17 Router Discovery

After a host boots, it must learn the address of at least one router on the local network before it can send datagrams to destinations on other networks. ICMP supports a *router discovery* scheme that allows a host to discover a router address.

ICMP router discovery is not the only mechanism a host can use to find a router address. The BOOTP and DHCP protocols described in Chapter 23 provide the main alternative — each of the protocols provides a way for a host to obtain the address of a default router along with other bootstrap information. However, BOOTP and DHCP have a serious deficiency: the information they return comes from a database that network administrators configure manually. Thus, the information cannot change quickly.

Of course, static router configuration does work well in some situations. For example, consider a network that has only a single router connecting it to the rest of the Internet. There is no need for a host on such a network to dynamically discover routers or change routes. However, if a network has multiple routers connecting it to the rest of the Internet, a host that obtains a default route at startup can lose connectivity if a single router crashes. More important, the host cannot detect the crash.

The ICMP router discovery scheme helps in two ways. First, instead of providing a statically configured router address via a bootstrap protocol, the scheme allows a host to obtain information directly from the router itself. Second, the mechanism uses a *soft state* technique with timers to prevent hosts from retaining a route after a router crashes — routers advertise their information periodically, and a host discards a route if the timer for a route expires.

Figure 9.11 illustrates the format of the advertisement message a router sends.

0	8	16	31
TYPE (9)	**CODE (0)**	**CHECKSUM**	
NUM ADDRS	**ADDR SIZE (1)**	**LIFETIME**	
ROUTER ADDRESS 1			
PREFERENCE LEVEL 1			
ROUTER ADDRESS 2			
PREFERENCE LEVEL 2			
⋮			

Figure 9.11 ICMP router advertisement message format used with IPv4. Routers send these messages periodically.

Besides the *TYPE*, *CODE*, and *CHECKSUM* fields, the message contains a field labeled *NUM ADDRS* that specifies the number of address entries which follow (often 1), an *ADDR SIZE* field that specifies the size of an address in 32-bit units (1 for IPv4 addresses), and a *LIFETIME* field that specifies the time in seconds a host may use the advertised address(es). The default value for *LIFETIME* is 30 minutes, and the default value for periodic retransmission is 10 minutes, which means that a host will not discard a route if the host misses a single advertisement message.

The remainder of the message consists of *NUM ADDRS* pairs of fields, where each pair contains a *ROUTER ADDRESS* and an integer *PRECEDENCE LEVEL* for the route. The precedence value is a two's complement integer; a host chooses the route with highest precedence.

If the router and the network support multicast as described in Chapter 17, a router multicasts ICMP router advertisement messages to the all-systems multicast address (i.e., 224.0.0.1). If not, the router sends the messages to the limited broadcast address (i.e., the all 1's address). Of course, a host must never send a router advertisement message.

9.18 Router Solicitation

Although the designers provided a range of values to be used as the delay between successive router advertisements, they chose the default of 10 minutes. The value was selected as a compromise between rapid failure detection and low overhead. A smaller value would allow more rapid detection of router failure, but would increase network traffic; a larger value would decrease traffic, but would delay failure detection. One of the issues the designers considered was how to accommodate a large number of routers on the same network.

From the point of view of a host, the default delay has a severe disadvantage: a host cannot afford to wait many minutes for an advertisement when it first boots. To avoid such delays, the designers included an *ICMP router solicitation message* that allows a host to request an immediate advertisement. Figure 9.12 illustrates the message format.

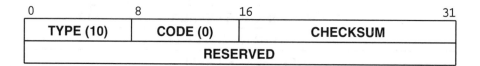

Figure 9.12 ICMP router solicitation message. A host sends a solicitation after booting to request that routers on the local net immediately respond with an ICMP router advertisement.

If a host supports multicasting, the host sends the solicitation to the all-routers multicast address (i.e., 224.0.0.2); otherwise the host sends the solicitation to the limited broadcast address (i.e., the all 1's address). The arrival of a solicitation message causes a router to send a normal router advertisement. As the figure shows, the solicitation does not need to carry information beyond the *TYPE*, *CODE*, and *CHECKSUM* fields.

9.19 Summary

Normal communication across an internet involves sending messages from an application on one host to an application on another host. Routers may need to communicate directly with the network software on a particular host to report abnormal conditions or to send the host new routing information.

The Internet Control Message Protocol provides for extranormal communication among routers and hosts; it is an integral, required part of IP. ICMP includes *source quench* messages that retard the rate of transmission, *redirect* messages that request a host to change its routing table, *echo request/reply* messages that hosts can use to determine whether a destination can be reached, and *router solicitation* and *advertisement* messages that hosts use to dynamically maintain a default route. An ICMP message travels in the data area of an IP datagram and has three fixed-length fields at the beginning of the message: an ICMP message *type* field, a *code* field, and an ICMP *checksum* field. The message type determines the format of the rest of the message as well as its meaning.

FOR FURTHER STUDY

Both Tanenbaum [1981] and Stallings [1985] discuss control messages in general and relate them to various network protocols. The central issue is not how to send control messages but when. Grange and Gien [1979], as well as Driver, Hopewell, and Iaquinto [1979], concentrate on a problem for which control messages are essential, namely, flow control. Gerla and Kleinrock [1980] compares flow control strategies analytically. For a discussion of clock synchronization protocols see Mills [RFCs 956, 957, and 1305].

The Internet Control Message Protocol described here is a TCP/IP standard defined by Postel [RFC 792] and updated by Braden [RFC [1122]. Nagle [RFC 896] discusses ICMP source quench messages and shows how routers should use them to handle congestion control. Prue and Postel [RFC 1016] discusses a more recent technique routers use in response to source quench. Nagle [1987] argues that congestion is always a concern in packet switched networks. Mogul and Postel [RFC 950] discusses subnet mask request and reply messages, and Deering [RFC 1256] discusses the solicitation and advertisement messages used in router discovery. Jain, Ramakrishnan and Chiu [1987] considers how routers and transport protocols could cooperate to avoid congestion.

EXERCISES

9.1   Devise an experiment to record how many of each ICMP message type appear on your lo-
        cal network during a day.

9.2   Experiment to see if you can send packets through a router fast enough to trigger an ICMP
        source quench message.

9.3   Devise an algorithm that synchronizes clocks using ICMP timestamp messages.

9.4   See if your local computer system contains a *ping* command. How does the program inter-
        face with protocols in the operating system? In particular, does the mechanism allow an ar-
        bitrary user to create a *ping* program, or does such a program require special privilege?
        Explain.

9.5   Assume that all routers send ICMP time-exceeded messages, and that your local TCP/IP
        software will return such messages to an application program. Use the facility to build a
        traceroute command that reports the list of routers between the source and a particular des-
        tination.

9.6   If you connect to the global Internet, try to ping host 128.10.2.1 (a machine at Purdue).

9.7   Should a router give ICMP messages priority over normal traffic? Why or why not?

9.8   Consider an Ethernet that has one conventional host, *H*, and 12 routers connected to it.
        Find a single (slightly illegal) frame carrying an IP packet that, when sent by host *H*,
        causes *H* to receive exactly 24 packets.

9.9   Compare ICMP source quench packets with Jain's 1-bit scheme used in DECNET. Which
        is a more effective strategy for dealing with congestion? Why?

9.10   There is no ICMP message that allows a machine to inform the source that transmission er-
        rors are causing datagrams to arrive corrupted. Explain why.

9.11   In the previous question, under what circumstances might such a message be useful?

9.12   Should ICMP error messages contain a timestamp that specifies when they are sent? Why
        or why not?

9.13   If routers at your site participate in ICMP router discovery, find out how many addresses
        each router advertises on each interface.

9.14   Try to reach a server on a nonexistent host on your local network. Also try to communi-
        cate with a nonexistent host on a remote network. In which case do you receive an error
        message? Why?

9.15   Try using *ping* with a network broadcast address. How many computers answer? Read the
        protocol documents to determine whether answering a broadcast request is required, recom-
        mended, not recommended, or prohibited.

10

Classless And Subnet Address Extensions (CIDR)

10.1 Introduction

Chapter 4 discusses the original Internet addressing scheme and presents the three primary forms of IP addresses. This chapter examines five extensions of the IP address scheme all designed to conserve network prefixes. The chapter considers the motivation for each extension and describes the basic mechanisms used. In particular, it presents the details of the address subnet scheme that is now part of the TCP/IP standards, and the classless address scheme that is an elective standard.

10.2 Review Of Relevant Facts

Chapter 4 discusses addressing in internetworks and presents the fundamentals of the IP address scheme. We said that the 32-bit addresses are carefully assigned to make the IP addresses of all hosts on a given physical network share a common prefix. In the original IP address scheme, designers thought of the common prefix as defining the network portion of an internet address and the remainder as a host portion. The consequence of importance to us is:

> In the original IP addressing scheme, each physical network is as-signed a unique network address; each host on a network has the net-work address as a prefix of the host's individual address.

The chief advantage of dividing an IP address into two parts arises from the size of the routing tables required in routers. Instead of keeping one routing entry per destination host, a router can keep one routing entry per network, and examine only the network portion of a destination address when making routing decisions.

Recall that the original IP addressing scheme accommodated diverse network sizes by dividing host addresses into three primary classes. Networks assigned class *A* addresses partition the 32 bits into an 8-bit network portion and a 24-bit host portion. Class *B* addresses partition the 32 bits into 16-bit network and host portions, while class *C* partitions the address into a 24-bit network portion and an 8-bit host portion.

To understand some of the address extensions in this chapter, it will be important to realize that individual sites have the freedom to modify addresses and routes as long as the modifications remain invisible to other sites. That is, a site can choose to assign and use IP addresses in unusual ways internally as long as:

- All hosts and routers at the site agree to honor the site's addressing scheme.
- Other sites on the Internet can treat addresses as a network prefix and a host suffix.

10.3 Minimizing Network Numbers

The original classful IP addressing scheme seems to handle all possibilities, but it has a minor weakness. How did the weakness arise? What did the designers fail to envision? The answer is simple: growth. Because they worked in a world of expensive mainframe computers, the designers envisioned an internet with hundreds of networks and thousands of hosts. They did not foresee tens of thousands of small networks of personal computers that would suddenly appear in the decade after TCP/IP was designed.

Growth has been most apparent in the connected Internet, where the size has been doubling every nine to fifteen months. The large population of networks with trivial size stresses the entire Internet design because it means (1) immense administrative overhead is required merely to manage network addresses, (2) the routing tables in routers are extremely large, and (3) the address space will eventually be exhausted†. The second problem is important because it means that when routers exchange information from their routing tables, the load on the Internet is high, as is the computational effort required in participating routers. The third problem is crucial because the original address scheme could not accommodate the number of networks currently in the global Internet. In particular, insufficient class B prefixes exist to cover all the medium-size networks in the Internet. So the question is, "How can one minimize the number of assigned network addresses, especially class B, without abandoning the 32-bit addressing scheme?"

To minimize the number of addresses used, we must avoid assigning network prefixes whenever possible, and the same IP network prefix must be shared by multiple physical networks. To minimize the use of class B addresses, class C addresses must be used instead. Of course, the routing procedures must be modified, and all machines that connect to the affected networks must understand the conventions used.

---

†Although there were many predictions that the IPv4 address space would be exhausted before the year 2000, it now appears that with careful allocation and the techniques described in this chapter, IPv4 addresses will suffice until around the year 2019.

The idea of sharing one network address among multiple physical networks is not new and has taken several forms. We will examine three: transparent routers, proxy ARP, and standard IP subnets. In addition, we will explore anonymous point-to-point networks, a special case in which no network prefix needs to be assigned. Finally, we will consider classless addressing, which abandons the rigid class system and allows the address space to be divided in arbitrary ways.

10.4 Transparent Routers

The *transparent router* scheme is based on the observation that a network assigned a class *A* IP address can be extended through a simple trick illustrated in Figure 10.1.

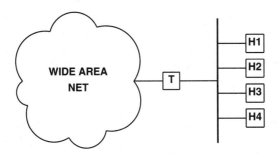

Figure 10.1 Transparent router *T* extending a wide area network to multiple hosts at a site. Each host appears to have an IP address on the WAN.

The trick consists of arranging for a physical network, usually a WAN, to multiplex several host connections through a single host port. As Figure 10.1 shows, a special purpose router, *T*, connects the single host port from the wide area net to a local area network. *T* is called a *transparent router* because other hosts and routers on the WAN do not know it exists.

The local area network does not have its own IP prefix; hosts attached to it are assigned addresses as if they connected directly to the WAN. The transparent router demultiplexes datagrams that arrive from the WAN by sending them to the appropriate host (e.g., by using a table of addresses). The transparent router also accepts datagrams from hosts on the local area network and routes them across the WAN toward their destination.

To make demultiplexing efficient, transparent routers often divide the IP address into multiple parts and encode information in unused parts. For example, the ARPANET was assigned class *A* network address *10.0.0.0*. Each packet switch node (PSN) on the ARPANET had a unique integer address. Internally, the ARPANET treated any 4-octet IP address of the form *10.p.u.i* as four separate octets that specify a network (*10*), a specific port on the destination PSN (*p*), and a destination PSN (*i*). Octet *u* remained uninterpreted. Thus, the ARPANET addresses *10.2.5.37* and *10.2.9.37* both refer to host *2* on PSN *37*. A transparent router connected to PSN *37* on port *2* can use octet *u* to decide which real host should receive a datagram. The WAN itself need not be aware of the multiple hosts that lie beyond the PSN.

Transparent routers have advantages and disadvantages when compared to conventional routers. The chief advantage is that they require fewer network addresses because the local area network does not need a separate IP prefix. Another is that they can support load balancing. That is, if two transparent routers connect to the same local area network, traffic to hosts on that network can be split between them. By comparison, conventional routers can only advertise one route to a given network.

One disadvantage of transparent routers is that they only work with networks that have a large address space from which to choose host addresses. Thus, they work best with class *A* networks, and they do not work well with class *C* networks. Another disadvantage is that because they are not conventional routers, transparent routers do not provide all the same services as standard routers. In particular, transparent routers may not participate fully in ICMP or network management protocols like SNMP. Therefore, they do not return ICMP echo requests (i.e., one cannot easily ''ping'' a transparent router to determine if it is operating).

10.5 Proxy ARP

The terms *proxy ARP*, *promiscuous ARP*, and *the ARP hack* refer to a second technique used to map a single IP network prefix into two physical addresses. The technique, which only applies to networks that use ARP to bind internet addresses to physical addresses, can best be explained with an example. Figure 10.2 illustrates the situation.

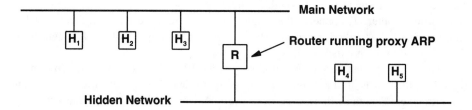

Figure 10.2 Proxy ARP technique (the ARP hack) allows one network address to be shared between two physical nets. Router *R* answers ARP requests on each network for hosts on the other network, giving its hardware address and then routing datagrams correctly when they arrive. In essence, *R* lies about IP-to-physical address bindings.

In the figure, two networks share a single IP network address. Imagine that the network labeled *Main Network* was the original network, and that the second, labeled *Hidden Network*, was added later. The router connecting the two networks, R, knows which hosts lie on which physical network and uses ARP to maintain the illusion that only one network exists. To make the illusion work, R keeps the location of hosts completely hidden, allowing all other machines on the network to communicate as if directly connected. In our example, when host H_1 needs to communicate with host H_4, it first invokes ARP to map H_4's IP address into a physical address. Once it has a physical address, H_1 can send the datagram directly to that physical address.

Because R runs proxy ARP software, it captures the broadcast ARP request from H_1, decides that the machine in question lies on the other physical network, and responds to the ARP request by sending its own physical address. H_1 receives the ARP response, installs the mapping in its ARP table, and then uses the mapping to send datagrams destined for H_4 to R. When R receives a datagram, it searches a special routing table to determine how to route the datagram. R must forward datagrams destined for H_4 over the hidden network. To allow hosts on the hidden network to reach hosts on the main network, R performs the proxy ARP service on that network as well.

Routers using the proxy ARP technique are taking advantage of an important feature of the ARP protocol, namely, trust. ARP is based on the idea that all machines cooperate and that any response is legitimate. Most hosts install mappings obtained through ARP without checking their validity and without maintaining consistency. Thus, it may happen that the ARP table maps several IP addresses to the same physical address, but that does not violate the protocol specification.

Some implementations of ARP are not as lax as others. In particular, ARP implementations designed to alert managers to possible security violations will inform them whenever two distinct IP addresses map to the same physical hardware address. The purpose of alerting the manager is to warn about *spoofing*, a situation in which one machine claims to be another in order to intercept packets. Host implementations of ARP that warn managers of possible spoofing cannot be used on networks that have proxy ARP routers because the software will generate messages frequently.

The chief advantage of proxy ARP is that it can be added to a single router on a network without disturbing the routing tables in other hosts or routers on that network. Thus, proxy ARP completely hides the details of physical connections.

The chief disadvantage of proxy ARP is that it does not work for networks unless they use ARP for address resolution. Furthermore, it does not generalize to more complex network topology (e.g., multiple routers interconnecting two physical networks), nor does it support a reasonable form of routing. In fact, most implementations of proxy ARP rely on managers to maintain tables of machines and addresses manually, making it both time consuming and prone to errors.

10.6 Subnet Addressing

The third technique used to allow a single network address to span multiple physical networks is called *subnet addressing*, *subnet routing*, or *subnetting*. Subnetting is the most widely used of the three techniques because it is the most general and because it has been standardized. In fact, subnetting is a required part of IP addressing.

The easiest way to understand subnet addressing is to imagine that a site has a single class *B* IP network address assigned to it, but it has two or more physical networks. Only local routers know that there are multiple physical nets and how to route traffic among them; routers in other autonomous systems route all traffic as if there were a single physical network. Figure 10.3 shows an example.

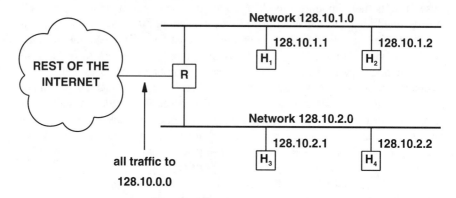

Figure 10.3 A site with two physical networks using subnet addressing to label them with a single class *B* network address. Router *R* accepts all traffic for net 128.10.0.0 and chooses a physical network based on the third octet of the address.

In the example, the site is using the single class *B* network address *128.10.0.0* for two networks. Except for router *R*, all routers in the internet route as if there were a single physical net. Once a packet reaches *R*, it must be sent across the correct physical network to its destination. To make the choice of physical network efficient, the local site has chosen to use the third octet of the address to distinguish between the two networks. The manager assigns machines on one physical net addresses of the form *128.10.1. X*, and machines on the other physical net addresses of the form *128.10.2. X*, where *X*, the final octet of the address, contains a small integer used to identify a specific host. To choose a physical network, *R* examines the third octet of the destination address and routes datagrams with value *1* to the network labeled *128.10.1.0* and those with value *2* to the network labeled *128.10.2.0*.

Conceptually, adding subnets only changes the interpretation of IP addresses slightly. Instead of dividing the 32-bit IP address into a network prefix and a host suffix, subnetting divides the address into a *network portion* and a *local portion*. The interpretation of the network portion remains the same as for networks that do not use subnet-ting. As before, reachability to the network must be advertised to outside autonomous systems; all traffic destined for the network will follow the advertised route. The in-terpretation of the local portion of an address is left up to the site (within the constraints of the formal standard for subnet addressing). To summarize:

> *We think of a 32-bit IP address as having an internet portion and a local portion, where the internet portion identifies a site, possibly with multiple physical networks, and the local portion identifies a physical network and host at that site.*

The example of Figure 10.3 showed subnet addressing with a class *B* address that had a 2-octet internet portion and a 2-octet local portion. To make routing among the physical networks efficient, the site administrator in our example chose to use one octet of the local portion to identify a physical network, and the other octet of the local por-tion to identify a host on that network, as Figure 10.4 shows.

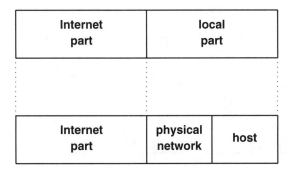

Figure 10.4 (a) Conceptual interpretation of a 32-bit IP address in the original IP address scheme, and (b) conceptual interpretation of ad-dresses using the subnet scheme shown in Figure 10.3. The lo-cal portion is divided into two parts that identify a physical net-work and a host on that network.

The result is a form of *hierarchical addressing* that leads to corresponding *hierarchical routing*. The top level of the routing hierarchy (i.e., other autonomous sys-tems in the internet) uses the first two octets when routing, and the next level (i.e., the local site) uses an additional octet. Finally, the lowest level (i.e., delivery across one physical network) uses the entire address.

Hierarchical addressing is not new; many systems have used it before. The best example is the U.S. telephone system, where a 10-digit phone number is divided into a 3-digit area code, 3-digit exchange, and 4-digit connection. The advantage of using hierarchical addressing is that it accommodates large growth because it means a given router does not need to know as much detail about distant destinations as it does about local ones. One disadvantage is that choosing a hierarchical structure is difficult, and it often becomes difficult to change a hierarchy once it has been established.

10.7 Flexibility In Subnet Address Assignment

The TCP/IP standard for subnet addressing recognizes that not every site will have the same needs for an address hierarchy; it allows sites flexibility in choosing how to assign them. To understand why such flexibility is desirable, imagine a site with five networks interconnected, as Figure 10.5 shows. Suppose the site has a single class *B* network address that it wants to use for all physical networks. How should the local part be divided to make routing efficient?

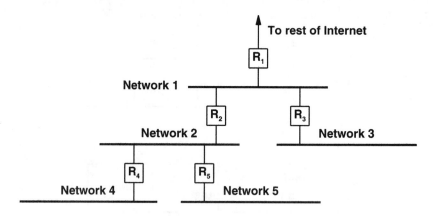

Figure 10.5 A site with five physical networks arranged in three "levels." The simplistic division of addresses into physical net and host parts may not be optimal for such cases.

In our example, the site will choose a partition of the local part of the IP address based on how it expects to grow. Dividing the 16-bit local part into an 8-bit network identifier and an 8-bit host identifier as shown in Figure 10.4 allows up to 256 networks, with up to 256 hosts per network†. Figure 10.6 illustrates the possible choices if a site uses the *fixed-length subnetting* scheme described above and avoids the all 0s and all 1s subnet and host addresses.

---

†In practice, the limit is 254 subnets of 254 hosts per subnet because the all 1s and all 0s host addresses are reserved for broadcast, and the all 1s or all 0s subnet is not recommended.

Subnet Bits	Number of Subnets	Hosts per Subnet
0	1	65534
2	2	16382
3	6	8190
4	14	4094
5	30	2046
6	62	1022
7	126	510
8	254	254
9	510	126
10	1022	62
11	2046	30
12	4094	14
13	8190	6
14	16382	2

Figure 10.6 The possible fixed-length subnets sizes for a class B number, with 8 subnet bits being the most popular choice; an organization must choose one line in the table.

As the figure shows, an organization that adopts fixed-length subnetting must choose a compromise. If the organization has a large number of physical networks, the networks cannot contain many hosts; if the number of hosts on a network is large, the number of physical networks must be small. For example, allocating 3 bits to identify a physical network results in up to 6 networks that each support up to 8190 hosts. Allocating 12 bits results in up to 4094 networks, but restricts the size of each to 62 hosts.

10.8 Variable-Length Subnets

We have implied that choosing a subnet addressing scheme is synonymous with choosing how to partition the local portion of an IP address into physical net and host parts. Indeed, most sites that implement subnetting use a fixed-length assignment. It should be clear that the designers did not choose a specific division for subnetting because no single partition of the local part of the address works for all organizations — some need many networks with few hosts per network, while others need a few networks with many hosts attached to each. The designers realized that the same problem can exist within a single organization. To allow maximum autonomy, the TCP/IP subnet standard provides even more flexibility than indicated above. An organization may select a subnet partition on a per-network basis. Although the technique is known as *variable-length subnetting*, the name is slightly misleading because the value does not "vary" over time — once a partition has been selected for a particular network, the partition never changes. All hosts and routers attached to that network must follow the decision; if they do not, datagrams can be lost or misrouted. We can summarize:

> *To allow maximum flexibility in choosing how to partition subnet ad-*
> *dresses, the TCP/IP subnet standard permits variable-length subnet-*
> *ting in which the partition can be chosen independently for each phy-*
> *sical network. Once a subnet partition has been selected, all*
> *machines on that network must honor it.*

The chief advantage of variable-length subnetting is flexibility: an organization can have a mixture of large and small networks, and can achieve higher utilization of the address space. However, variable-length subnetting has serious disadvantages. Most important, values for subnets must be assigned carefully to avoid *address ambiguity*, a situation in which an address is interpreted differently depending on the physical network. For example, an address can appear to match two different subnets. As a result, invalid variable-length subnets may make it impossible for all pairs of hosts to communicate. Routers cannot resolve such ambiguity, which means that an invalid assignment can only be repaired by renumbering. Thus, network managers are discouraged from using variable-length subnetting.

10.9 Implementation Of Subnets With Masks

The subnet technology makes configuration of either fixed or variable length easy. The standard specifies that a 32-bit mask is used to specify the division. Thus, a site using subnet addressing must choose a 32-bit *subnet mask* for each network. Bits in the subnet mask are set to *1* if machines on the network treat the corresponding bit in the IP address as part of the subnet prefix, and *0* if they treat the bit as part of the host identifier. For example, the 32-bit subnet mask:

11111111   11111111   11111111   00000000

specifies that the first three octets identify the network and the fourth octet identifies a host on that network. A subnet mask should have *1*s for all bits that correspond to the network portion of the address (e.g., the subnet mask for a class *B* network will have *1*s for the first two octets plus one or more bits in the last two octets).

The interesting twist in subnet addressing arises because the standard does not restrict subnet masks to select contiguous bits of the address. For example, a network might be assigned the mask:

11111111   11111111   00011000   01000000

which selects the first two octets, two bits from the third octet, and one bit from the fourth. Although such flexibility makes it possible to arrange interesting assignments of addresses to machines, doing so makes assigning host addresses and understanding routing tables tricky. Thus, it is recommended that sites use contiguous subnet masks and that they use the same mask throughout an entire set of physical nets that share an IP address.

10.10 Subnet Mask Representation

Specifying subnet masks in binary is both awkward and prone to errors. Therefore, most software allows alternative representations. Sometimes, the representation follows whatever conventions the local operating system uses for representation of binary quantities, (e.g., hexadecimal notation).

Most IP software uses dotted decimal representation for subnet masks; it works best when sites choose to align subnetting on octet boundaries. For example, many sites choose to subnet class B addresses by using the third octet to identify the physical net and the fourth octet to identify hosts as on the previous page. In such cases, the subnet mask has dotted decimal representation *255.255.255.0*, making it easy to write and understand.

The literature also contains examples of subnet addresses and subnet masks represented in braces as a 3-tuple:

{ <network number> , <subnet number> , <host number> }

In this representation, the value *-1* means ''all ones.'' For example, if the subnet mask for a class B network is *255.255.255.0*, it can be written *{-1, -1, 0}*.

The chief disadvantage of the 3-tuple representation is that it does not accurately specify how many bits are used for each part of the address; the advantage is that it abstracts away from the details of bit fields and emphasizes the values of the three parts of the address. To see why address values are sometimes more important than bit fields, consider the 3-tuple:

{ 128.10 , -1, 0 }

which denotes an address with a network number *128.10*, all ones in the subnet field, and all zeroes in the host field. Expressing the same address value using other representations requires a 32-bit subnet mask as well as a 32-bit IP address, and forces readers to decode bit fields before they can deduce the values of individual fields. Furthermore, the 3-tuple representation is independent of the IP address class or the size of the subnet field. Thus, the 3-tuple can be used to represent sets of addresses or abstract ideas. For example, the 3-tuple:

{ <network number>, -1, -1 }

denotes ''addresses with a valid network number, a subnet field containing all ones, and a host field containing all ones.'' We will see additional examples later in this chapter.

10.11 Routing In The Presence Of Subnets

The standard IP routing algorithm must be modified to work with subnet addresses. All hosts and routers attached to a network that uses subnet addressing must use the modified algorithm, which is called *subnet routing*. What may not be obvious is that unless restrictions are added to the use of subnetting, other hosts and routers at the site may also need to use subnet routing. To see how a problem arises without restrictions, consider the example set of networks shown in Figure 10.7.

In the figure, physical networks *2* and *3* have been (illegally) assigned subnet addresses of a single IP network address, *N*. Although host *H* does not directly attach to a network that has a subnet address, it must use subnet routing to decide whether to send datagrams destined for network *N* to router R_1 or router R_2. It could be argued that *H* can send to either router and let them handle the problem, but that solution means not all traffic will follow a shortest path. In larger examples, the difference between an optimal and nonoptimal path can be significant.

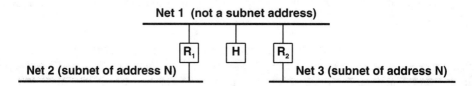

Figure 10.7 An example (illegal) topology with three networks where Nets *2* and *3* are subnets of a single IP network address, *N*. If such topologies were allowed, host *H* would need to use subnet routing even though Net *1* does not have a subnet address.

In theory, a simple rule determines when machines need to use subnet routing. The subnet rule is:

> *To achieve optimal routing, a machine* M *must use subnet routing for an IP network address* N, *unless there is a single path* P *such that* P *is a shortest path between* M *and every physical network that is a subnet of* N.

Unfortunately, understanding the theoretical restriction does not help in assigning subnets. First, shortest paths can change if hardware fails or if routing algorithms redirect traffic around congestion. Such dynamic changes make it difficult to use the subnet rule except in trivial cases. Second, the subnet rule fails to consider the boundaries of sites or the difficulties involved in propagating subnet masks. It is impossible to propagate subnet routes beyond the boundary of a given organization because the routing protocols discussed later do not provide for it. Realistically, it becomes extremely difficult to propagate subnet information beyond a given physical network. Therefore, the designers recommend that if a site uses subnet addressing, that site should keep subnetting as simple as possible. In particular, network administrators should adhere to the following guidelines:

> *All subnets of a given network IP address must be contiguous, the subnet masks should be uniform across all networks, and all machines should participate in subnet routing.*

The guidelines pose special difficulty for a large corporation that has multiple sites each connected to the Internet, but not connected directly to one another. Such a corporation cannot use subnets of a single address for all its sites because the physical networks are not contiguous.

10.12 The Subnet Routing Algorithm

Like the standard IP routing algorithm, the algorithm used with subnets searches a table of routes. Recall that in the standard algorithm, per-host routes and default routes are special cases that must be checked explicitly; table lookup is used for all others. A conventional routing table contains entries of the form:

(network address, next hop address)

where the *network address* field specifies the IP address of a destination network, N, and the *next hop address* field specifies the address of a router to which datagrams destined for N should be sent. The standard routing algorithm compares the network portion of a destination address to the *network address* field of each entry in the routing table until a match is found. Because the *next hop address* field is constrained to specify a machine that is reachable over a directly connected network, only one table lookup is ever needed.

The standard algorithm knows how an address is partitioned into network portion and local portion because the first three bits encode the address type and format (i.e., class A, B, C, or D). With subnets, it is not possible to decide which bits correspond to the network and which to the host from the address alone. Instead, the modified algorithm used with subnets maintains additional information in the routing table. Each table entry contains one additional field that specifies the subnet mask used with the network in that entry:

(subnet mask, network address, next hop address)

When choosing routes, the modified algorithm uses the *subnet mask* to extract bits of the destination address for comparison with the table entry. That is, it performs a bit-wise Boolean *and* of the full 32-bit destination IP address and the *subnet mask* field from an entry, and it then checks to see if the result equals the value in the *network address* field of that entry. If so, it routes the datagram to the address specified in the *next hop address* field† of the entry.

---

†As in the standard routing algorithm, the next hop router must be reachable by a directly connected network.

10.13 A Unified Routing Algorithm

Observant readers may have guessed that if we allow arbitrary masks, the subnet routing algorithm can subsume all the special cases of the standard algorithm. It can handle routes to individual hosts, a default route, and routes to directly connected networks using the same masking technique it uses for subnets. In addition, masks can handle routes to conventional classful addresses. The flexibility comes from the ability to combine arbitrary 32-bit values in a *subnet mask* field and arbitrary 32-bit addresses in a *network address* field. For example, to install a route for a single host, one uses a mask of all *1*s and a network address equal to the host's IP address. To install a default route, one uses a subnet mask of all *0*s and a network address of all *0*s (because any destination address *and* zero equals zero). To install a route to a (nonsubnetted) class *B* network, one specifies a mask with two octets of *1*s and two octets of *0*s. Because the table contains more information, the routing algorithm contains fewer special cases as Figure 10.8 shows.

Algorithm:

Route_IP_Datagram (datagram, routing_table)

Extract destination IP address, I_D, from datagram;
If prefix of I_D matches address of any directly connected
    network send datagram to destination over that network
    (This involves resolving I_D to a physical address,
    encapsulating the datagram, and sending the frame.)
else
    for each entry in routing table do
      Let N be the bitwise-and of I_D and the subnet mask
      If N equals the network address field of the entry then
        route the datagram to the specified next hop address
    endforloop
If no matches were found, declare a routing error;

Figure 10.8 The unified IP routing algorithm. Given an IP datagram and a routing table with masks, this algorithm selects a next hop router to which the datagram should be sent. The next hop must lie on a directly connected network.

In fact, most implementations eliminate the explicit test for destinations on directly connected networks. To do so, one must add a table entry for each directly connected network. Like other entries, each entry for a directly connected network contains a mask that specifies the number of bits in the prefix.

10.14 Maintenance Of Subnet Masks

How do subnet masks get assigned and propagated? Chapter *9* answered the second part of the question by showing that a host can obtain the subnet mask for a given network by sending an ICMP *subnet mask request* to a router on that network. The request can be broadcast if the host does not know the specific address of a router. Later chapters will complete the answer to the second part by explaining that some of the protocols routers use to exchange routing information pass subnet masks along with each network address.

The first part of the question is more difficult to answer. Each site is free to choose subnet masks for its networks. When making assignments, managers attempt to balance sizes of networks, numbers of physical networks, expected growth, and ease of maintenance. Difficulty arises because nonuniform masks give the most flexibility, but make possible assignments that lead to ambiguous routes. Or worse, they allow valid assignments that become invalid if more hosts are added to the networks. There are no easy rules, so most sites make conservative choices. Typically, a site selects contiguous bits from the local portion of an address to identify a network, and uses the same partition (i.e., the same mask) for all local physical networks at the site. For example, many sites simply use a single subnet octet when subnetting a class *B* address.

10.15 Broadcasting To Subnets

Broadcasting is more difficult in a subnet architecture. Recall that in the original IP addressing scheme, an address with a host portion of all *1*s denotes broadcast to all hosts on the specified network. From the viewpoint of an observer outside a subnetted site, broadcasting to the network address still makes sense†. That is, the address:

$$\{ \text{ network, -1, -1 } \}$$

means "deliver a copy to all machines that have *network* as their network addresses, even if they lie on separate physical networks." Operationally, broadcasting to such an address makes sense only if the routers that interconnect the subnets agree to propagate the datagram to all physical networks. Of course, care must be taken to avoid routing loops. In particular, a router cannot merely propagate a broadcast packet that arrives on one interface to all interfaces that share the subnet prefix. To prevent such loops, routers use *reverse path forwarding*. The router extracts the source of the broadcast datagram, and looks up the source in its routing table. The router then discards the da-

---

†Classless addressing, covered later in this chapter, has made broadcasting to all subnets obsolete.

tagram unless it arrived on the interface used to route to the source (i.e., arrived from the shortest path).

Within a set of subnetted networks, it becomes possible to broadcast to a specific subnet (i.e., to broadcast to all hosts on a physical network that has been assigned one of the subnet addresses). The subnet address standard uses a host field of all ones to denote subnet broadcast. That is, a subnet broadcast address becomes:

{ network, subnet, -1 }

Considering subnet broadcast addresses and subnet broadcasting clarifies the recommendation for using a consistent subnet mask across all networks that share a subnetted IP address. As long as the subnet and host fields are identical, subnet broadcast addresses are unambiguous. More complex subnet address assignments may or may not allow broadcasting to selected subsets of the physical networks that comprise a subnet.

10.16 Anonymous Point-To-Point Networks

In the original IP addressing scheme, each network was assigned a unique prefix. In particular, because IP views each point-to-point connection between a pair of machines as a ''network,'' the connection was assigned a network prefix and each computer was assigned a host suffix. When addresses became scarce, the use of a prefix for each point-to-point connection seemed absurd. The problem is especially severe for organizations that have many point-to-point connections. For example, an organization with multiple sites might use leased digital circuits (e.g., T1 lines) to form a backbone that interconnects a router at each site to routers at other sites.

To avoid assigning a prefix to each point-to-point connection, a simple technique was invented. Known as *anonymous networking*, the technique is often applied when a pair of routers is connected with a leased digital circuit. The technique simply avoids numbering the leased line, and does not assign a host address to the routers at each end. No hardware address is needed, so the interface software is configured to ignore the next hop address when sending datagrams. Consequently, an arbitrary value can be used as the next-hop address in the IP routing table.

When the anonymous networking technique is applied to a point-to-point connection, the connection is known as an *unnumbered network* or an *anonymous network*. The example in Figure 10.9 will help explain routing in unnumbered networks.

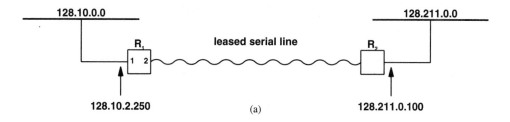

TO REACH HOSTS ON NETWORK	ROUTE TO THIS ADDRESS	USING THIS INTERFACE
128.10.0.0	DELIVER DIRECT	1
default	128.211.0.100	2

(b)

Figure 10.9 (a) An unnumbered point-to-point connection between two routers, and (b) the routing table in router R_1.

To understand why unnumbered networks are possible, one must remember that serial lines used for point-to-point connections do not operate like shared-media hardware. Because there is only one possible destination — the computer at the other end of the circuit — the underlying hardware does not use physical addresses when transmitting frames. Consequently, when IP hands a datagram to the network interface, any value can be specified as a next hop because the hardware will ignore it. Thus, the next-hop field of the IP routing table can contain an arbitrary value (e.g., zero).

The routing table in Figure 10.9b does not have a zero in the next hop field. Instead, the example demonstrates a technique often employed with unnumbered networks. Rather than leaving the next hop empty, it is filled with one of the IP addresses assigned to the next-hop router (i.e., an address assigned to another of the router's interfaces). In the example, the address of R_2's Ethernet connection has been used.

We said that the hardware ignores the next hop address, so it may seem odd that a value has been assigned. It may seem even more odd that the next-hop refers to a network not directly reachable from R_1. In fact, neither IP nor the network interface code uses the value in any way. The only reason for specifying a non-zero entry is to make it easier for humans to understand and remember the address of the router on the other end of the point-to-point connection. In the example, we chose the address assigned to R_2's Ethernet interface because R_2 does not have an address for the leased line interface.

10.17 Classless Addressing (Supernetting)

Subnet addressing was invented in the early 1980s to help conserve the IP address space; the unnumbered networking technique followed. By 1993, it became apparent that those techniques alone would not prevent Internet growth from eventually exhausting the address space. Work had begun on defining an entirely new version of IP with larger addresses. To accommodate growth until the new version of IP could be standardized and adopted, however, a temporary solution was found.

Called *classless addressing*, *supernet addressing*, or *supernetting*, the scheme takes an approach that is complementary to subnet addressing. Instead of using a single IP network prefix for multiple physical networks at a given organization, supernetting allows the addresses assigned to a single organization to span multiple classed prefixes.

To understand why classless addressing was adopted, one needs to know three facts. First, the classful scheme did not divide network addresses into classes equally. Although less than seventeen thousand class B numbers can be assigned, more than two million class C network numbers exist. Second, class C numbers were being requested slowly; only a small percentage of them had been assigned. Third, studies showed that at the rate class B numbers were being assigned, class B prefixes would be exhausted quickly. The situation became known as the *Running Out of ADdress Space* (*ROADS*) problem.

To understand how supernetting works, consider a medium-sized organization that joins the Internet. Such an organization would prefer to use a single class B address for two reasons: a class C address cannot accommodate more than 254 hosts and a class B address has sufficient bits to make subnetting convenient. To conserve class B numbers, the supernetting scheme assigns an organization a block of class C addresses instead of a single class B number. The block must be large enough to number all the networks the organization will eventually connect to the Internet. For example, suppose an organization requests a class B address and intends to subnet using the third octet as a subnet field. Instead of a single class B number, supernetting assigns the organization a block of 256 contiguous class C numbers that the organization can then assign to physical networks.

Although supernetting is easy to understand when viewed as a way to satisfy a single organization, the proposers intended it to be used in a broader context. They envisioned a hierarchical Internet in which commercial *Internet Service Providers* (*ISPs*) provide Internet connectivity. To connect its networks to the Internet, an organization contracts with an ISP; the service provider handles the details of assigning IP addresses to the organization as well as installing physical connections. The designers of supernetting propose that an Internet Service Provider be assigned a large part of the address space (i.e., a set of addresses that span many class C network numbers). The ISP can then allocate one or more addresses from the set to each of its subscribers.

10.18 The Effect Of Supernetting On Routing

Allocating many class C addresses in place of a single class B address conserves class B numbers and solves the immediate problem of address space exhaustion. However, it creates a new problem: the information that routers store and exchange increases dramatically. For example, assigning an organization 256 class C addresses instead of a class B address requires 256 routes instead of one.

A technique known as *Classless Inter-Domain Routing*† (*CIDR*) solves the problem. Conceptually, CIDR collapses a block of contiguous class C addresses into a single entry represented by a pair:

(network address , count)

where *network address* is the smallest address in the block, and *count* specifies the total number of network addresses in the block. For example, the pair:

(192.5.48.0 , 3)

is used to specify the three network addresses 192.5.48.0, 192.5.49.0, and 192.5.50.0.

If a few Internet Service Providers form the core of the Internet and each ISP owns a large block of contiguous IP network numbers, the benefit of supernetting becomes clear: routing tables are much smaller. Consider routing table entries in routers owned by service provider *P*. The table must have a correct route to each of *P*'s subscribers, but the table does not need to contain a route for other providers' subscribers. Instead, the table stores one entry for each other provider, where the entry identifies the block of addresses owned by the provider.

10.19 CIDR Address Blocks And Bit Masks

In practice, CIDR does not restrict network numbers to class C addresses nor does it use an integer count to specify a block size. Instead, CIDR requires the size of each block of addresses to be a power of two, and uses a bit mask to identify the size of the block. For example, suppose an organization is assigned a block of 2048 contiguous addresses starting at address 128.211.168.0. The table in Figure 10.10 shows the binary values of addresses in the range.

CIDR requires two items to specify the block of addresses in Figure 10.10: the 32-bit value of the lowest address in the block and a 32-bit mask. The mask operates like a standard subnet mask by delineating the end of the prefix‡. For the range shown, a CIDR mask has 21 bits set, which means that the division between prefix and suffix occurs after the 21st bit:

11111111   11111111   11111000   00000000

---

†The name is a slight misnomer because the scheme specifies addressing as well as routing.

‡Unlike a subnet mask, a CIDR mask must use contiguous bits.

	Dotted Decimal	32-bit Binary Equivalent
lowest	128.211.168.0	10000000 11010011 10101000 00000000
highest	128.211.175.255	10000000 11010011 10101111 11111111

Figure 10.10 An example CIDR block of 2048 addresses. The table shows the lowest and highest addresses in the range expressed as dotted decimal and binary values.

10.20 Address Blocks And CIDR Notation

Because identifying a CIDR block requires both an address and a mask, a shorthand notation was devised to express the two items. Called *CIDR notation* but known informally as *slash notation*, the shorthand represents the mask length in decimal and uses a slash to separate it from the address. Thus, in CIDR notation, the block of addresses in Figure 10.10 would be expressed as:

$$128.211.168.0 / 21$$

where */21* denotes 21 bits in a mask. The table in Figure 10.11 lists dotted decimal values for all possible CIDR masks. The */8*, */16*, and */24* prefixes correspond to traditional class *A*, *B*, and *C* divisions.

CIDR Notation	Dotted Decimal	CIDR Notation	Dotted Decimal
/1	128.0.0.0	/17	255.255.128.0
/2	192.0.0.0	/18	255.255.192.0
/3	224.0.0.0	/19	255.255.224.0
/4	240.0.0.0	/20	255.255.240.0
/5	248.0.0.0	/21	255.255.248.0
/6	252.0.0.0	/22	255.255.252.0
/7	254.0.0.0	/23	255.255.254.0
/8	255.0.0.0	/24	255.255.255.0
/9	255.128.0.0	/25	255.255.255.128
/10	255.192.0.0	/26	255.255.255.192
/11	255.224.0.0	/27	255.255.255.224
/12	255.240.0.0	/28	255.255.255.240
/13	255.248.0.0	/29	255.255.255.248
/14	255.252.0.0	/30	255.255.255.252
/15	255.254.0.0	/31	255.255.255.254
/16	255.255.0.0	/32	255.255.255.255

Figure 10.11 Dotted decimal mask values for all possible CIDR prefixes.

10.21 A Classless Addressing Example

The table in Figure 10.11 illustrates one of the chief advantages of classless addressing: complete flexibility in allocating blocks of various sizes. With CIDR, the ISP can choose to assign each customer a block of an appropriate size. If it owns a CIDR block of N bits, an ISP can choose to hand customers any piece of more than N bits. For example, if the ISP is assigned 128.211.0.0/16, the ISP may choose to give one of its customers the 2048 address in the /21 range that Figure 10.10 specifies. If the same ISP also has a small customer with only two computers, the ISP might choose to assign another block 128.211.176.212/29, which covers the address range that Figure 10.12 specifies.

	Dotted Decimal	**32-bit Binary Equivalent**
lowest	128.211.176.212	10000000 11010011 10110000 11010100
highest	128.211.176.215	10000000 11010011 10110000 11010111

Figure 10.12 An example of CIDR block 128.211.176.212/29. The use of an arbitrary bit mask allows more flexibility in assigning a block size than the classful addressing scheme.

One way to think about classless addresses is as if each customer of an ISP obtains a (variable-length) subnet of the ISP's CIDR block. Thus, a given block of addresses can be subdivided on an arbitrary bit boundary, and a separate route can be entered for each subdivision. As a result, although the group of computers on a given network will be assigned addresses in a contiguous range, the range does not need to correspond to a predefined class. Instead, the scheme makes subdivision flexible by allowing one to specify the exact number of bits that correspond to a prefix. To summarize:

Classless addressing, which is now used by ISPs, treats IP addresses as arbitrary integers, and allows a network administrator to assign addresses in contiguous blocks, where the number of addresses in a block is a power of two.

10.22 Data Structures And Algorithms For Classless Lookup

The fundamental criterion used to judge the algorithms and data structures used with routing tables is speed. There are two aspects: the primary consideration is the speed of finding a next hop for a given destination, while a secondary consideration is the speed of making changes to values in the table.

The introduction of classless addressing had a profound effect on routing because it changed a fundamental assumption: unlike a classful address, a CIDR address is not *self-identifying*. That is, a router cannot determine the division between prefix and suffix merely by looking at the address. The difference is important because it means that data structures and search algorithms used with classful addresses do not work when routing tables contain classless addresses. After a brief review of classful lookup, we will consider one of the data structures used for classless lookup.

10.22.1 Hashing And Classful Addresses

All route lookup algorithms are optimized for speed. When IP permitted only classful addresses, a single technique provided the necessary optimization: hashing. When a classful address is entered in a routing table, the router extracts the network portion, N, and uses it as a hash key. Similarly, given a destination address, the router also extracts the network portion, N, computes a hash function $h(N)$, and uses the result as an index into a bucket.

Hashing works well in a classful situation because addresses are self-identifying. Even if some entries in a table correspond to subnet routes, hashing is still efficient because the network portion of the address can be extracted and used as a key. If multiple routes hash to the same bucket in the table, entries within the bucket are arranged in decreasing order of specificity – subnet routes precede network routes. Thus, if a given destination matches both a network route and a subnet route, the algorithm will correctly find and use the subnet route.

In a classless world, however, where addresses are not self-identifying, hashing does not work well. Because it cannot compute the division between prefix and suffix, a router cannot find a hash key for an arbitrary address. Thus, an alternate scheme must be found.

10.22.2 Searching By Mask Length

The simplest lookup algorithm that accommodates classless addressing merely iterates over all possible divisions between prefix and suffix. That is, given a destination address, D, the algorithm first tries using 32 bits of D, then 31 bits, and so on down to 0 bits. For each possible size, M, the router extracts M bits from D, assumes the extracted bits comprise a network prefix, and looks up the prefix in the table. The algorithm chooses the longest prefix that corresponds to a route in the table (i.e., the search stops as soon as a match has been found).

The disadvantage of trying all possible lengths should be obvious: doing so is many times slower than a standard classful lookup because the algorithm must search the table for each possible prefix size until a match is found. The worst case occurs when no route exists; in which case, the algorithm searches the table 32 times. Even when it finds a route, a router using the iterative approach searches the table many times unnecessarily. For example, 16 lookups are required before a router can find a traditional class B network (i.e., /16) route. More important, the algorithm performs 31 unnecessary lookups before it succeeds in matching the default route (in many routing tables, the default route is heavily used).

10.22.3 Binary Trie Structures

To avoid inefficient searches, production software for classless routing lookup must avoid the iterative approach. Instead, classless routing tables are usually stored in a hierarchical data structure, and searching proceeds down the hierarchy. The most popular data structures are variants of a *binary trie* in which the value of successive bits in the address determine a path from the root downward.

A binary trie is a tree with paths determined by the data stored. To visualize a binary trie, imagine that a set of 32-bit addresses is written as binary strings and redundant suffixes are removed. What remains is a set of prefixes that uniquely identify each item. For example, Figure 10.13 shows a set of seven addresses written in binary and the corresponding unique prefixes.

As Figure 10.13 illustrates, the number of bits required to identify an address depends on the values in the set. For example, the first address in the figure can be uniquely identified by three bits because no other addresses begin with *001*. However, five bits are required to identify the last item in the table because the 4-bit prefix *1011* is shared by more than one item.

32-Bit Address	Unique Prefix
00110101 00000000 00000000 00000000	001
01000110 00000000 00000000 00000000	0100
01010110 00000000 00000000 00000000	0101
01100001 00000000 00000000 00000000	011
10101010 11110000 00000000 00000000	1010
10110000 00000010 00000000 00000000	10110
10111011 00001010 00000000 00000000	10111

Figure 10.13 A set of 32-bit binary addresses and the corresponding set of prefixes that uniquely identify each.

Once a set of unique prefixes has been computed, they can be used to define a binary trie. Figure 10.14 illustrates a trie for the seven prefixes in Figure 10.13.

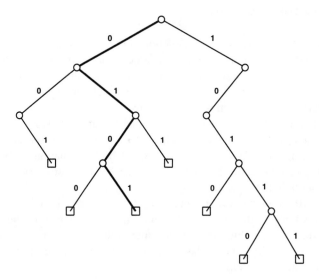

Figure 10.14 A binary trie for the seven binary prefixes listed in Figure 10.13. The path through the trie for prefix *0101* is shown darkened.

Each interior node in the trie (shown as a circle) corresponds to two or more prefixes, and each exterior node (shown as a square) corresponds to one unique prefix. The search algorithm stops when it reaches an exterior node or when no path exists for the specified prefix. For example, a search for address

10010010 11110000 00000000 00000001

fails because there is no branch with label *0* at the node corresponding to *10*.

> To make routing lookup efficient, routing software that handles classless routes must use data structures and algorithms that differ from those used for classful lookup. Many systems use a scheme based on a binary trie to accommodate classless lookup.

10.23 Longest-Match Routing And Mixtures Of Route Types

Our brief description of binary tries only gives a sketch of the data structure used in practice. For example, we said that a trie only needs to store a unique prefix for each route in the table, without stating that the prefix must cover the entire network portion of the route. To guarantee that a router does not forward datagrams unless the entire network prefix in the destination matches the route, each exterior node in the trie must contain a 32-bit address, *A*, and a 32-bit mask, *M*, that covers the entire network portion of *A*. When the search reaches an exterior node, the algorithm computes the logical *and* of *M* with the destination address, and compares the result to *A* in the same way that conventional lookup algorithms do. If the comparison fails, the datagram is rejected (also like conventional lookup algorithms). In other words, we can view the trie as a mechanism that quickly identifies items in the routing table that are potential candidates rather than a mechanism that finds an exact match.

Even if we consider the trie to be a mechanism that identifies potential matches, another important detail is missing from our description. We have assumed that each entry in a routing table has a unique binary prefix. In practice, however, the entries in most routing tables do not have unique prefixes because routing tables contain a mixture of general and specific routes for the same destination. For example, consider any routing table that contains a network-specific route and a different route for one particular subnet of the same network. Or consider a routing table that contains both a network-specific route and a special route for one host on that network. The binary prefix of the network route is also a prefix of the subnet or host-specific route. Figure 10.15 provides an example.

Prefix	Next Hop
128.10.0.0/16	10.0.0.2
128.10.2.0/24	10.0.0.4
128.10.3.0/24	10.1.0.5
128.10.4.0/24	10.0.0.6
128.10.4.3/32	10.0.0.3
128.10.5.0/24	10.0.0.6
128.10.5.1/32	10.0.0.3

Figure 10.15 An example set of routes without unique prefixes. The situation occurs frequently because many routing tables contain a mixture of general and specific routes for the same network.

To permit overlapping prefixes, the trie data structure described above must be modified to follow the *longest-match* paradigm when selecting a route. To do so, one must allow interior nodes to contain an address/mask pair, and modify the search algorithm to check for a match at each node. A match that occurs later in the search (i.e., a match that corresponds to a more specific route) must override any match that occurs earlier because a later match corresponds to a longer prefix.

10.23.1 PATRICIA And Level Compressed Tries

Our description of binary tries also omits details related to optimization of lookup. The most important involves ''skipping'' levels in the trie that do not distinguish among routes. For example, consider a binary trie for the set of routes in Figure 10.15. Because each route in the list begins with the same sixteen bits (i.e., the value

10000000 00001010), a binary trie for the routes will only have one node at each of the first sixteen levels below the root.

In this instance, it would be faster to examine all sixteen bits of a destination address at once rather than extracting bits one at a time and using them to move through the trie. Two modified versions of tries use the basic optimization. The first, a *PATRICIA tree*, allows each node to specify a value to test along with a number of bits to skip. The second, a *level compressed trie*, provides additional optimization by eliminating one or more levels in the trie that can be skipped along any path.

Of course, data structure optimizations represent a tradeoff. Although the optimizations improve search speed, they require more computation when creating or modifying a routing table. In most cases, however, such optimizations are justified because one expects a routing table to be modified much less frequently than it is searched.

10.24 CIDR Blocks Reserved For Private Networks

Chapter 4 stated that the IETF had designated a set of prefixes to be reserved for use with private networks. As a safeguard, reserved prefixes will never be assigned to networks in the global Internet. Collectively, the reserved prefixes are known as *private addresses* or *nonroutable addresses*. The latter term arises because routers in the global Internet understand that the addresses are reserved; if a datagram destined to one of the private addresses is accidentally routed onto the global Internet, a router in the Internet will be able to detect the problem.

In addition to blocks that correspond to classful addresses, the set of reserved IPv4 prefixes contains a CIDR block that spans multiple classes. Figure 10.16 lists the values in CIDR notation along with the dotted decimal value of the lowest and highest addresses in the block. The last address block listed, *169.254/16*, is unusual because it is used by systems that *autoconfigure* IP addresses.

Prefix	Lowest Address	Highest Address
10/8	10.0.0.0	10.255.255.255
172.16/12	172.16.0.0	172.31.255.255
192.168/16	192.168.0.0	192.168.255.255
169.254/16	169.254.0.0	169.254.255.255

Figure 10.16 The prefixes reserved for use with private internets not connected to the global Internet. If a datagram sent to one of these addresses accidentally reaches the Internet, an error will result.

10.25 Summary

The original IP address scheme assigns a unique prefix to each physical network. This chapter examined five techniques that have been invented to conserve IP addresses. The first technique uses transparent routers to extend the address space of a single network, usually a WAN, to include hosts on an attached local network. The second technique, called proxy ARP, arranges for a router to impersonate computers on another physical network by answering ARP requests on their behalf. Proxy ARP is useful only on networks that use ARP for address resolution, and only for ARP implementations that do not complain when multiple internet addresses map to the same hardware address. The third technique, a TCP/IP standard called subnet addressing, allows a site to share a single IP network address among multiple physical networks. All hosts and routers connected to networks using subnetting must use a modified routing scheme in which each routing table entry contains a subnet mask. The modified scheme can be viewed as a generalization of the original routing algorithm because it handles special cases like default routes or host-specific routes. The fourth technique allows a point-to-point link to remain unnumbered (i.e., have no IP prefix).

The fifth technique, known as classless addressing (CIDR), represents a major shift in IP technology. Instead of adhering to the original network classes, classless addressing allows the division between prefix and suffix to occur on an arbitrary bit boundary. CIDR allows the address space to be divided into blocks, where the size of each block is a power of two. One of the main motivations for CIDR arises from the desire to combine multiple class C prefixes into a single supernet block. Because classless addresses are not self-identifying like the original classful addresses, CIDR requires significant changes to the algorithms and data structures used by IP software on hosts and routers to store and look up routes. Many implementations use a scheme based on the binary trie data structure.

FOR FURTHER STUDY

The standard for subnet addressing comes from Mogul [RFC 950] with updates in Braden [RFC 1122]. Clark [RFC 932], Karels [RFC 936], Gads [RFC 940], and Mogul [RFC 917] all contain early proposals for subnet addressing schemes. Mogul [RFC 922] discusses broadcasting in the presence of subnets. Postel [RFC 925] considers the use of proxy ARP for subnets. Atallah and Comer [1998] presents a provably optimal algorithm for variable-length subnet assignment. Carl-Mitchell and Quarterman [RFC 1027] discusses using proxy ARP to implement transparent subnet routers. Rekhter and Li [RFC 1518] specifies classless IP address allocation. Fuller, Li, Yu, and Varadhan [RFC 1519] specifies CIDR routing and supernetting. Rekhter et. al. [RFC 1918] specifies address prefixes reserved for private networks. Knuth [1973] describes the PATRICIA data structure.

EXERCISES

10.1   If routers using proxy ARP use a table of host addresses to decide whether to answer ARP requests, the routing table must be changed whenever a new host is added to one of the networks. Explain how to assign IP addresses so hosts can be added without changing tables. Hint: think of subnets.

10.2   Although the standard allows all-0's to be assigned as a subnet number, some vendors' software does not operate correctly. Try to assign a zero subnet at your site and see if the route is propagated correctly.

10.3   Can transparent routers be used with local area networks like the Ethernet? Why or why not?

10.4   Show that proxy ARP can be used with three physical networks that are interconnected by two routers.

10.5   Consider a fixed subnet partition of a class *B* network number that will accommodate at least 76 networks. How many hosts can be on each network?

10.6   Does it ever make sense to subnet a class *C* network address? Why or why not?

10.7   A site that chose to subnet their class *B* address by using the third octet for the physical net was disappointed that they could not accommodate 255 or 256 networks. Explain.

10.8   Design a subnet address scheme for your organization assuming that you have one class *B* address to use.

10.9   Is it reasonable for a single router to use both proxy ARP and subnet addressing? If so, explain how. If not, explain why.

10.10 Argue that any network using proxy ARP is vulnerable to ''spoofing'' (i.e., an arbitrary machine can impersonate any other machine).

10.11 Can you devise a (nonstandard) implementation of ARP that supports normal use, but prohibits proxy ARP?

10.12 One vendor decided to add subnet addressing to its IP software by allocating a single subnet mask used for all IP network addresses. The vendor modified its standard IP routing software to make the subnet check a special case. Find a simple example in which this implementation cannot work correctly. (Hint: think of a multi-homed host.)

10.13 Characterize the (restricted) situations in which the subnet implementation discussed in the previous exercise will work correctly.

10.14 Read the standard to find out more about broadcasting in the presence of subnets. Can you characterize subnet address assignments that allow one to specify a broadcast address for all possible subnets?

10.15 The standard allows an arbitrary assignment of subnet masks for networks that comprise a subnetted IP address. Should the standard restrict subnet masks to cover contiguous bits in the address? Why or why not?

10.16 Find an example of variable length subnet assignments and host addresses that produces address ambiguity.

10.17 Carefully consider default routing in the presence of subnets. What can happen if a packet arrives destined for a nonexistent subnet?

10.18 Compare architectures that use subnet addressing and routers to interconnect multiple Ethernets to an architecture that uses bridges as described in Chapter 2. Under what circumstances is one architecture preferable to the other?

10.19 Consider a site that chooses to subnet a class *B* network address, but decides that some physical nets will use *6* bits of the local portion to identify the physical net while others will use *8*. Find an assignment of host addresses that makes destination addresses ambiguous.

10.20 The subnet routing algorithm in Figure 10.8 uses a sequential scan of entries in the routing table, allowing a manager to place host-specific routes before network-specific or subnet-specific routes. Invent a data structure that achieves the same flexibility but uses hashing to make the lookup efficient. [This exercise was suggested by Dave Mills.]

10.21 Although much effort has been expended on making routers operate quickly, software for classless route lookup still runs slower than the hashing schemes used with classful lookup. Investigate data structures and lookup algorithms that operate faster than a binary trie.

10.22 A binary trie uses one bit to select among two descendants at each node. Consider a trie that uses two bits to select among four descendants at each node. Under what conditions does such a trie make lookup faster? Slower?

10.23 If all Internet service providers use classless addressing and assign subscribers numbers from their block of addresses, what problem occurs when a subscriber changes from one provider to another?

11

Protocol Layering

11.1 Introduction

Previous chapters review the architectural foundations of internetworking, describe how hosts and routers forward Internet datagrams, and present mechanisms used to map IP addresses to physical network addresses. This chapter considers the structure of the software found in hosts and routers that carries out network communication. It presents the general principle of layering, shows how layering makes Internet Protocol software easier to understand and build, and traces the path of datagrams through the protocol software they encounter when traversing a TCP/IP internet.

11.2 The Need For Multiple Protocols

We have said that protocols allow one to specify or understand communication without knowing the details of a particular vendor's network hardware. They are to computer communication what programming languages are to computation. It should be apparent by now how closely the analogy fits. Like assembly language, some protocols describe communication across a physical network. For example, the details of the Ethernet frame format, network access policy, and frame error handling comprise a protocol that describes communication on an Ethernet. Similarly, like a high-level language, the Internet Protocol specifies higher-level abstractions (e.g., IP addressing, datagram format, and the concept of unreliable, connectionless delivery).

Complex data communication systems do not use a single protocol to handle all transmission tasks. Instead, they require a set of cooperative protocols, sometimes called a *protocol family* or *protocol suite*. To understand why, think of the problems that arise when machines communicate over a data network:

• *Hardware failure.* A host or router may fail either because the hardware fails or because the operating system crashes. A network transmission link may fail or accidentally be disconnected. The protocol software needs to detect such failures and recover from them if possible.

• *Network congestion.* Even when all hardware and software operates correctly, networks have finite capacity that can be exceeded. The protocol software needs to arrange ways that a congested machine can suppress further traffic.

• *Packet delay or loss.* Sometimes, packets experience extremely long delays or are lost. The protocol software needs to learn about failures or adapt to long delays.

• *Data corruption.* Electrical or magnetic interference or hardware failures can cause transmission errors that corrupt the contents of transmitted data. Protocol software needs to detect and recover from such errors.

• *Data duplication or inverted arrivals.* Networks that offer multiple routes may deliver data out of sequence or may deliver duplicates of packets. The protocol software needs to reorder packets and remove any duplicates.

Taken together, all the problems seem overwhelming. It is difficult to understand how to write a single protocol that will handle them all. From the analogy with programming languages, we can see how to conquer the complexity. Program translation has been partitioned into four conceptual subproblems identified with the software that handles each subproblem: compiler, assembler, link editor, and loader. The division makes it possible for the designer to concentrate on one subproblem at a time, and for the implementor to build and test each piece of software independently. We will see that protocol software is partitioned similarly.

Two final observations from our programming language analogy will help clarify the organization of protocols. First, it should be clear that pieces of translation software must agree on the exact format of data passed between them. For example, the data passed from a compiler to an assembler consists of a program defined by the assembly programming language. The translation process involves multiple representations. The analogy holds for communication software because multiple protocols define the representations of data passed among communication software modules. Second, the four parts of the translator form a linear sequence in which output from the compiler becomes input to the assembler, and so on. Protocol software also uses a linear sequence.

11.3 The Conceptual Layers Of Protocol Software

Think of the modules of protocol software on each machine as being stacked vertically into *layers*, as in Figure 11.1. Each layer takes responsibility for handling one part of the problem.

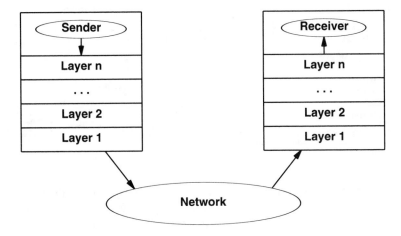

Figure 11.1 The conceptual organization of protocol software in layers.

Conceptually, sending a message from an application program on one machine to an application program on another means transferring the message down through successive layers of protocol software on the sender's machine, forwarding the message across the network, and transferring the message up through successive layers of protocol software on the receiver's machine.

In practice, the protocol software is much more complex than the simple model of Figure 11.1 indicates. Each layer makes decisions about the correctness of the message and chooses an appropriate action based on the message type or destination address. For example, one layer on the receiving machine must decide whether to keep the message or forward it to another machine. Another layer must decide which application program should receive the message.

To understand the difference between the conceptual organization of protocol software and the implementation details, consider the comparison shown in Figure 11.2. The conceptual diagram in Figure 11.2a shows an Internet layer between a high level protocol layer and a network interface layer. The realistic diagram in Figure 11.2b shows that the IP software may communicate with multiple high-level protocol modules and with multiple network interfaces.

Although a diagram of conceptual protocol layering does not show all details, it does help explain the general concept. For example, Figure 11.3 shows the layers of protocol software used by a message that traverses three networks. The diagram shows only the network interface and Internet Protocol layers in the routers because only those layers are needed to receive, route, and send datagrams. We understand that any machine attached to two networks must have two network interface modules, even though the conceptual layering diagram shows only a single network interface layer in each machine.

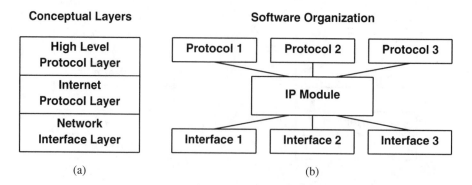

Figure 11.2 A comparison of (a) conceptual protocol layering and (b) a realistic view of software organization showing multiple network interfaces below IP and multiple protocols above it.

As Figure 11.3 shows, a sender on the original machine transmits a message which the IP layer places in a datagram and sends across network *1*. On intermediate routers, the datagram passes up to the IP layer which sends it back out again (on a different network). Only when it reaches the final destination machine, does IP extract the message and pass it up to higher layers of protocol software.

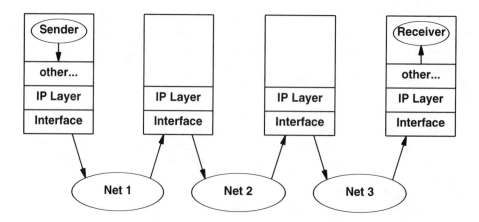

Figure 11.3 The path of a message traversing the Internet from the sender through two intermediate routers to the receiver. Intermediate routers only send the datagram to the IP software layer.

11.4 Functionality Of The Layers

Once the decision has been made to partition the communication problem and organize the protocol software into modules that each handle one subproblem, the question arises: "what functionality should reside in each module?" The question is not easy to answer for several reasons. First, given a set of goals and constraints governing a particular communication problem, it is possible to choose an organization that will optimize protocol software for that problem. Second, even when considering general network-level services such as reliable transport, it is possible to choose from among fundamentally distinct approaches to solving the problem. Third, the design of network (or internet) architecture and the organization of the protocol software are interrelated; one cannot be designed without the other.

11.4.1 ISO 7-Layer Reference Model

Two ideas about protocol layering dominate the field. The first, based on early work done by the International Organization for Standardization (ISO), is known as ISO's *Reference Model of Open System Interconnection*, often referred to as the *ISO model*. The ISO model contains 7 conceptual layers organized as Figure 11.4 shows.

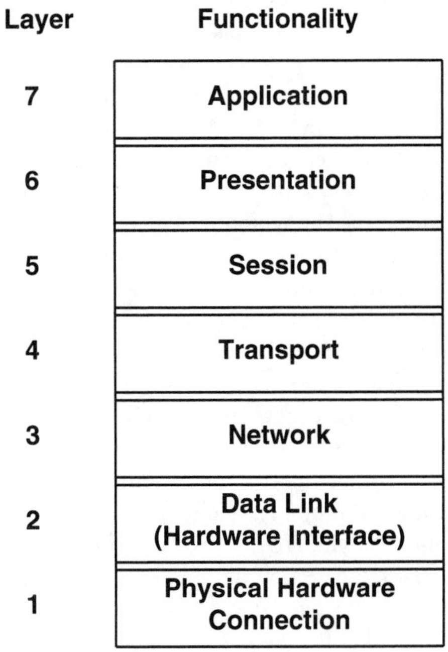

Layer	Functionality
7	Application
6	Presentation
5	Session
4	Transport
3	Network
2	Data Link (Hardware Interface)
1	Physical Hardware Connection

Figure 11.4 The ISO 7-layer reference model for protocol software.

The ISO model, built to describe protocols for a single network, does not contain a specific layer for internetwork routing in the same way TCP/IP protocols do.

11.5 X.25 And Its Relation To The ISO Model

Although it was designed to provide a conceptual model and not an implementation guide, the ISO layering scheme has been the basis for several protocol implementations. Among the protocols commonly associated with the ISO model, the suite of protocols known as X.25 is probably the best known and most widely used. X.25 was established as a recommendation of the *International Telecommunications Union (ITU)*, formerly the *CCITT*, an organization that recommends standards for international telephone services. X.25 has been adopted by public data networks, and became especially popular in Europe. Considering X.25 will help explain ISO layering.

In the X.25 view, a network operates much like a telephone system. An X.25 network is assumed to consist of complex packet switches that contain the intelligence needed to route packets. Hosts do not attach directly to communication wires of the network. Instead each host attaches to one of the packet switches using a serial communication line. In one sense, the connection between a host and an X.25 packet switch is a miniature network consisting of one serial link. The host must follow a complicated procedure to transfer packets onto the network.

• *Physical Layer.* X.25 specifies a standard for the physical interconnection between host computers and network packet switches, as well as the procedures used to transfer packets from one machine to another. In the reference model, layer *1* specifies the physical interconnection including electrical characteristics of voltage and current. A corresponding protocol, X.21, gives the details used by public data networks.

• *Data Link Layer.* The layer *2* portion of the X.25 protocol specifies how data travels between a host and the packet switch to which it connects. X.25 uses the term *frame* to refer to a unit of data as it passes between a host and a packet switch (it is important to understand that the X.25 definition of *frame* differs slightly from the way we have defined it). Because raw hardware delivers only a stream of bits, the layer *2* protocol must define the format of frames and specify how the two machines recognize frame boundaries. Because transmission errors can destroy data, the layer *2* protocol includes error detection (e.g., a frame checksum). Finally, because transmission is unreliable, the layer *2* protocol specifies an exchange of acknowledgements that allows the two machines to know when a frame has been transferred successfully.

One commonly used layer *2* protocol, named the *High Level Data Link Communication*, is best known by its acronym, *HDLC*. Several versions of HDLC exist, with the most recent known as *HDLC/LAPB*. It is important to remember that successful transfer at layer *2* means a frame has been passed to the network packet switch for delivery; it does not guarantee that the packet switch accepted the packet or was able to route it.

• *Network Layer.* The ISO reference model specifies that the third layer contains functionality that completes the definition of the interaction between host and network.

Called the *network* or *communication subnet* layer, this layer defines the basic unit of transfer across the network and includes the concepts of destination addressing and routing. Remember that in the X.25 world, communication between host and packet switch is conceptually isolated from the traffic that is being passed. Thus, the network might allow packets defined by layer 3 protocols to be larger than the size of frames that can be transferred at layer 2. The layer 3 software assembles a packet in the form the network expects and uses layer 2 to transfer it (possibly in pieces) to the packet switch. Layer 3 must also respond to network congestion problems.

    • *Transport Layer.* Layer 4 provides end-to-end reliability by having the destination host communicate with the source host. The idea here is that even though lower layers of protocols provide reliable checks at each transfer, the end-to-end layer double checks to make sure that no machine in the middle failed.

    • *Session Layer.* Higher layers of the ISO model describe how protocol software can be organized to handle all the functionality needed by application programs. The ISO committee considered the problem of remote terminal access so fundamental that they assigned layer 5 to handle it. In fact, the central service offered by early public data networks consisted of terminal to host interconnection. The carrier provides a special purpose host computer called a *Packet Assembler And Disassembler* (*PAD*) on the network with dialup access. Subscribers, often travelers who carry their own computer and modem, dial up the local PAD, make a network connection to the host with which they wish to communicate, and log in. Many carriers choose to make using the network for long distance communication less expensive than direct dialup.

    • *Presentation Layer.* ISO layer 6 is intended to include functions that many application programs need when using the network. Typical examples include standard routines that compress text or convert graphics images into bit streams for transmission across a network. For example an ISO standard known as *Abstract Syntax Notation 1* (*ASN.1*), provides a representation of data that application programs use. One of the TCP/IP protocols, SNMP, also uses ASN.1 to represent data.

    • *Application Layer.* Finally, ISO layer 7 includes application programs that use the network. Examples include electronic mail or file transfer programs. In particular, the ITU has devised a protocol for electronic mail known as the *X.400* standard. In fact, the ITU and ISO worked jointly on message handling systems; the ISO version is called *MOTIS*.

11.5.1 The TCP/IP 5-Layer Reference Model

The second major layering model did not arise from a standards committee, but came instead from research that led to the TCP/IP protocol suite. With a little work, the ISO model can be stretched to describe the TCP/IP layering scheme, but the underlying assumptions are different enough to warrant distinguishing the two.

Broadly speaking, TCP/IP software is organized into five conceptual layers — four software layers that build on a fifth layer of hardware. Figure 11.5 shows the conceptual layers as well as the form of data as it passes between them.

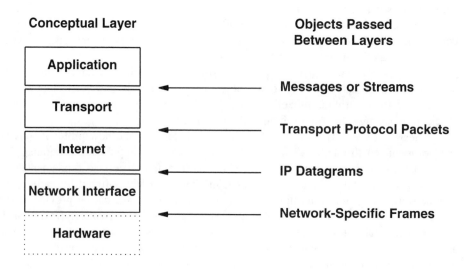

Figure 11.5 The 4 conceptual layers of TCP/IP software above the hardware layer, and the form of objects passed between layers. The layer labeled *network interface* is sometimes called the *data link* layer.

• *Application Layer.* At the highest layer, users invoke application programs that access services available across a TCP/IP internet. An application interacts with one of the transport layer protocols to send or receive data. Each application program chooses the style of transport needed, which can be either a sequence of individual messages or a continuous stream of bytes. The application program passes data in the required form to the transport layer for delivery.

• *Transport Layer.* The primary duty of the *transport layer* is to provide communication from one application program to another. Such communication is often called *end-to-end*. The transport layer may regulate flow of information. It may also provide reliable transport, ensuring that data arrives without error and in sequence. To do so, transport protocol software arranges to have the receiving side send back acknowledgements and the sending side retransmit lost packets. The transport software divides the stream of data being transmitted into small pieces (sometimes called *packets*) and passes each packet along with a destination address to the next layer for transmission.

Although Figure 11.5 uses a single block to represent the application layer, a general purpose computer can have multiple application programs accessing an internet at one time. The transport layer must accept data from several user programs and send it to the next lower layer. To do so, it adds additional information to each packet, including codes that identify which application program sent it and which application program should receive it, as well as a checksum. The receiving machine uses the checksum to verify that the packet arrived intact, and uses the destination code to identify the application program to which it should be delivered.

• *Internet Layer.* As we have already seen, the Internet layer handles communication from one machine to another. It accepts a request to send a packet from the transport layer along with an identification of the machine to which the packet should be sent. It encapsulates the packet in an IP datagram, fills in the datagram header, uses the routing algorithm to determine whether to deliver the datagram directly or send it to a router, and passes the datagram to the appropriate network interface for transmission. The Internet layer also handles incoming datagrams, checking their validity, and uses the routing algorithm to decide whether the datagram should be processed locally or forwarded. For datagrams addressed to the local machine, software in the internet layer deletes the datagram header, and chooses from among several transport protocols the one that will handle the packet. Finally, the Internet layer sends and receives ICMP error and control messages as needed.

• *Network Interface Layer.* The lowest layer TCP/IP software comprises a network interface layer, responsible for accepting IP datagrams and transmitting them over a specific network. A network interface may consist of a device driver (e.g., when the network is a local area network to which the machine attaches directly) or a complex subsystem that uses its own data link protocol (e.g., when the network consists of packet switches that communicate with hosts using HDLC).

11.6 Differences Between ISO And Internet Layering

There are two subtle and important differences between the TCP/IP layering scheme and the ISO/X.25 scheme. The first difference revolves around the focus of attention on reliability, while the second involves the location of intelligence in the overall system.

11.6.1 Link-Level vs. End-To-End Reliability

One major difference between the TCP/IP protocols and the X.25 protocols lies in their approaches to providing reliable data transfer services. In the X.25 model, protocol software detects and handles errors at all layers. At the link level, complex protocols guarantee that the transfer between a host and the packet switch to which it connects will be correct. Checksums accompany each piece of data transferred, and the receiver acknowledges each piece of data received. The link layer protocol includes timeout and retransmission algorithms that prevent data loss and provide automatic recovery after hardware fails and restarts.

Successive layers of X.25 provide reliability of their own. At layer *3*, X.25 also provides error detection and recovery for packets transferred onto the network, using checksums as well as timeout and retransmission techniques. Finally, layer *4* must provide end-to-end reliability, having the source correspond with the ultimate destination to verify delivery.

In contrast to such a scheme, TCP/IP bases its protocol layering on the idea that reliability is an end-to-end problem. The architectural philosophy is simple: construct the internet so it can handle the expected load, but allow individual links or machines to lose data or corrupt it without trying to repeatedly recover. In fact, there is little or no reliability in most TCP/IP network interface layer software. Instead, the transport layer handles most error detection and recovery problems.

The resulting freedom from interface layer verification makes TCP/IP software much easier to understand and implement correctly. Intermediate routers can discard datagrams that become corrupted because of transmission errors or that cannot be delivered. They can discard datagrams when the arrival rate exceeds machine capacity, and can reroute datagrams through paths with shorter or longer delay without informing the source or destination.

Having unreliable links means that some datagrams do not arrive. Detection and recovery of datagram loss is carried out between the source host and the ultimate destination and is, therefore, called *end-to-end* verification. The end-to-end software located in the TCP/IP transport layer uses checksums, acknowledgements, and timeouts to control transmission. Thus, unlike the connection-oriented X.25 protocol layering, the TCP/IP software focuses most of its reliability control in one layer.

11.6.2 Locus of Intelligence and Decision Making

Another difference between the X.25 model and the TCP/IP model emerges when one considers the locus of authority and control. As a general rule, networks using X.25 adhere to the idea that a network is a utility that provides a transport service. The vendor that offers the service controls network access and monitors traffic to keep records for accounting and billing. The network vendor also handles problems like routing, flow control, and acknowledgements internally, making transfers reliable. This view leaves little that the hosts can (or need to) do. In short, the network is a complex, independent system to which one can attach relatively simple host computers; the hosts themselves participate minimally in the network operation.

In contrast, TCP/IP requires hosts to participate in almost all of the network protocols. We have already mentioned that hosts actively implement end-to-end error detection and recovery. They also participate in routing because they must choose a router when sending datagrams, and they participate in network control because they must handle ICMP control messages. Thus, when compared to an X.25 network, a TCP/IP internet can be viewed as a relatively simple packet delivery system to which intelligent hosts attach.

11.7 The Protocol Layering Principle

Independent of the particular layering scheme used or the functions of the layers, the operation of layered protocols is based on a fundamental idea. The idea, called the *layering principle*, can be summarized succinctly:

> *Layered protocols are designed so that layer* n *at the destination receives exactly the same object sent by layer* n *at the source.*

The layering principle explains why layering is such a powerful idea. It allows the protocol designer to focus attention on one layer at a time, without worrying about how other layers perform. For example, when building a file transfer application, the designer considers only two copies of the application program executing on two computers, and concentrates on the messages they need to exchange for file transfer. The designer assumes that the application on one host receives exactly the data that the application on the other host sends.

Figure 11.6 illustrates how the layering principle works:

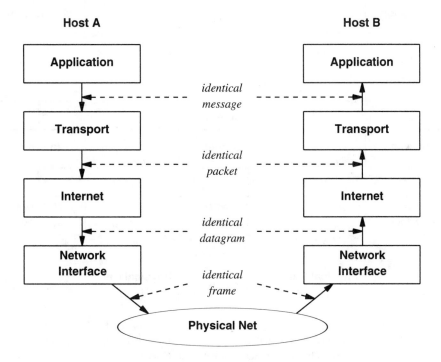

Figure 11.6 The path of a message as it passes from an application on one host to an application on another. Layer *n* on host *B* receives exactly the same object that layer *n* on host *A* sent.

11.7.1 Layering in a TCP/IP Internet Environment

Our statement of the layering principle is somewhat vague, and the illustration in Figure 11.6 skims over an important issue because it fails to distinguish between transfers from source to ultimate destination and transfers across multiple networks. Figure 11.7 illustrates the distinction, showing the path of a message sent from an application program on one host to an application on another through a router.

As the figure shows, message delivery uses two separate network frames, one for the transmission from host A to router R, and another from router R to host B. The network layering principle states that the frame delivered to R is identical to the frame sent by host A. By contrast, the application and transport layers deal with end-to-end issues and are designed so the software at the source communicates with its peer at the ultimate destination. Thus, the layering principle states that the packet received by the transport layer at the ultimate destination is identical to the packet sent by the transport layer at the original source.

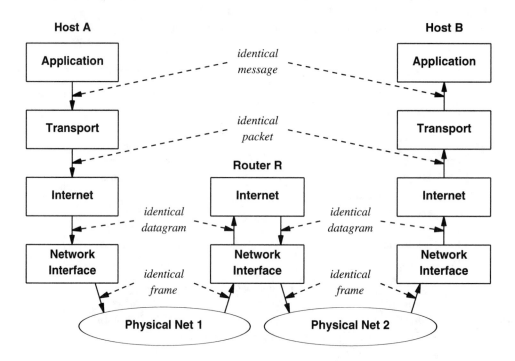

Figure 11.7 The layering principle when a router is used. The frame delivered to router R is exactly the frame sent from host A, but differs from the frame sent between R and B.

It is easy to understand that in higher layers, the layering principle applies across end-to-end transfers, and that at the lowest layer it applies to a single machine transfer. It is not as easy to see how the layering principle applies to the Internet layer. On one hand, we have said that hosts attached to an internet should view it as a large, virtual network, with the IP datagram taking the place of a network frame. In this view, datagrams travel from original source to ultimate destination, and the layering principle guarantees that the ultimate destination receives exactly the datagram that the original source sent. On the other hand, we know that the datagram header contains fields, like a *time to live* counter, that change each time the datagram passes through a router. Thus, the ultimate destination will not receive exactly the same datagram as the source sent. We conclude that although most of the datagram stays intact as it passes across an internet, the layering principle only applies to datagrams across single machine transfers. To be accurate, we should not view the Internet layer as providing end-to-end service.

11.8 Layering In The Presence Of Network Substructure

Recall from Chapter 2 that some wide area networks contain multiple packet switches. For example, a WAN can consist of routers that connect to a local network at each site as well as to other routers using leased serial lines. When a router receives a datagram, it either delivers the datagram to its destination on the local network, or transfers the datagram across a serial line to another router. The question arises: "How do the protocols used on serial lines fit into the TCP/IP layering scheme?" The answer depends on how the designer views the serial line interconnections.

From the perspective of IP, the set of point-to-point connections among routers can either function like a set of independent physical networks, or they can function collectively like a single physical network. In the first case, each physical link is treated exactly like any other network in the internet. The link is assigned a unique network number, and the two hosts that share the link each have a unique IP address assigned for their connection†. Routes are added to the IP routing table as they would be for any other network. A new software module is added at the network interface layer to control the new link hardware, but no substantial changes are made to the layering scheme. The main disadvantage of the independent network approach is that it proliferates network numbers (one for each connection between two machines) and causes routing tables to be larger than necessary. Both *Serial Line IP (SLIP)* and the *Point to Point Protocol (PPP)* treat each serial link as a separate network.

The second approach to accommodating point-to-point connections avoids assigning multiple IP addresses to the physical wires. Instead, it treats all the connections collectively as a single, independent IP network with its own frame format, hardware addressing scheme, and data link protocols. Routers that use the second approach need only one IP network number for all point-to-point connections.

Using the single network approach means extending the protocol layering scheme to add a new intranetwork routing layer between the network interface layer and the

---

†The only exception arises when using the anonymous network scheme described in Chapter 10; leaving the link unnumbered does not change the layering.

hardware devices. For machines with only one point-to-point connection, an additional layer seems unnecessary. To see why it is needed, consider a machine with several physical point-to-point connections, and recall from Figure 11.2 how the network interface layer is divided into multiple software modules that each control one network. We need to add one network interface for the new point-to-point network, but the new interface must control multiple hardware devices. Furthermore, given a datagram to send, the new interface must choose the correct link over which the datagram should be sent. Figure 11.8 shows the organization.

The Internet layer software passes to the network interface all datagrams that should be sent on any of the point-to-point connections. The network interface passes them to the intranet routing module that must further distinguish among multiple physical connections and route the datagram across the correct one.

The programmer who designs the intranet routing software determines exactly how the software chooses a physical link. Usually, the algorithm relies on an intranet routing table. The intranet routing table is analogous to the internet routing table in that it specifies a mapping of destination address to route. The table contains pairs of entries, (D, L), where D is a destination host address and L specifies the physical line used to reach that destination.

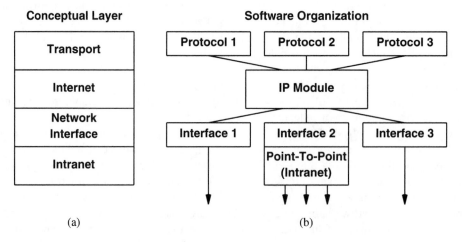

Figure 11.8 (a) Conceptual position of an intranet protocol for point-to-point
         connections when IP treats them as a single IP network, and (b)
         detailed diagram of corresponding software modules. Each arrow corresponds to one physical device.

The difference between an internet routing table and an intranet routing table is that intranet routing tables are quite small. They only contain routing information for hosts directly attached to the point-to-point network. The reason is simple: the Internet layer maps an arbitrary destination address to a specific router address before passing the datagram to a network interface. The intranet layer is asked only to distinguish among machines on a single point-to-point network.

11.9 Two Important Boundaries In The TCP/IP Model

The conceptual protocol layering includes two boundaries that may not be obvious: a protocol address boundary that separates high-level and low-level addressing, and an operating system boundary that separates the system from application programs.

11.9.1 High-Level Protocol Address Boundary

Now that we have seen the layering of TCP/IP software, we can be precise about an idea introduced in Chapter 8: a conceptual boundary partitions software that uses low-level (physical) addresses from software that uses high-level (IP) addresses. As Figure 11.9 shows, the boundary occurs between the network interface layer and the Internet layer. That is,

> *Application programs as well as all protocol software from the Internet layer upward use only IP addresses; the network interface layer handles physical addresses.*

Thus, protocols like ARP belong in the network interface layer. They are not part of IP.

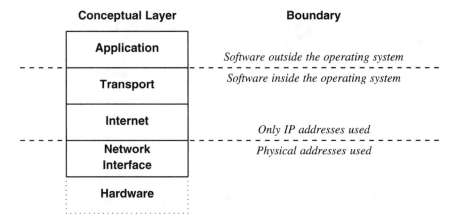

Figure 11.9 The relationship between conceptual layering and the boundaries for operating system and high-level protocol addresses.

11.9.2 Operating System Boundary

Figure 11.9 shows another important boundary as well, the division between software that is generally considered part of the operating system and software that is not. While each implementation of TCP/IP chooses how to make the distinction, many follow the scheme shown. Because they lie inside the operating system, passing data between lower layers of protocol software is much less expensive than passing it between an application program and a transport layer. Chapter 20 discusses the problem in more detail and describes an example of the interface an operating system might provide.

11.10 The Disadvantage Of Layering

We have said that layering is a fundamental idea that provides the basis for protocol design. It allows the designer to divide a complicated problem into subproblems and solve each one independently. Unfortunately, the software that results from strict layering can be extremely inefficient. As an example, consider the job of the transport layer. It must accept a stream of bytes from an application program, divide the stream into packets, and send each packet across the internet. To optimize transfer, the transport layer should choose the largest possible packet size that will allow one packet to travel in one network frame. In particular, if the destination machine attaches directly to one of the same networks as the source, only one physical net will be involved in the transfer, so the sender can optimize packet size for that network. If the software preserves strict layering, however, the transport layer cannot know how the Internet module will route traffic or which networks attach directly. Furthermore, the transport layer will not understand the datagram or frame formats nor will it be able to determine how many octets of header will be added to a packet. Thus, strict layering will prevent the transport layer from optimizing transfers.

Usually, implementors relax the strict layering scheme when building protocol software. They allow information like route selection and network MTU to propagate upward. When allocating buffers, they often leave space for headers that will be added by lower layer protocols and may retain headers on incoming frames when passing them to higher layer protocols. Such optimizations can make dramatic improvements in efficiency while retaining the basic layered structure.

11.11 The Basic Idea Behind Multiplexing And Demultiplexing

Communication protocols use techniques of *multiplexing* and *demultiplexing* throughout the layered hierarchy. When sending a message, the source computer includes extra bits that encode the message type, originating program, and protocols used.

Eventually, all messages are placed into network frames for transfer and combined into a stream of packets. At the receiving end, the destination machine uses the extra information to guide processing.

Consider an example of demultiplexing shown in Figure 11.10.

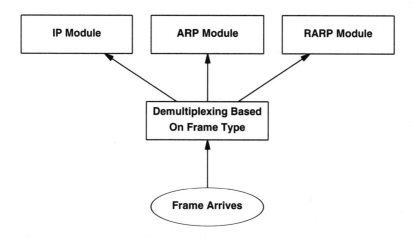

Figure 11.10 Demultiplexing of incoming frames based on the type field
found in the frame header.

The figure illustrates how software in the network interface layer uses the frame type to choose a procedure to handle the incoming frame. We say that the network interface *demultiplexes* the frame based on its type. To make such a choice possible, software in the source machine must set the frame type field before transmission. Thus, each software module that sends frames uses the type field to specify frame contents.

Multiplexing and demultiplexing occur at almost every protocol layer. For example, after the network interface demultiplexes frames and passes those frames that contain IP datagrams to the IP module, the IP software extracts the datagram and demultiplexes further based on the transport protocol. Figure 11.11 demonstrates demultiplexing at the Internet layer.

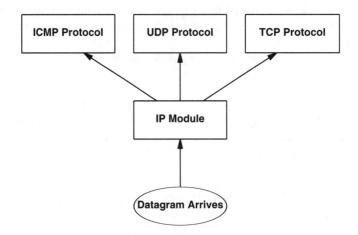

Figure 11.11 Demultiplexing at the Internet layer. IP software chooses an appropriate procedure to handle a datagram based on the protocol type field in the datagram header.

To decide how to handle a datagram, internet software examines the header of a datagram and selects a protocol handler based on the datagram type. In the example, the possible datagram types are: *ICMP*, which we have already examined, and *UDP*, and *TCP*, which we will examine in later chapters.

11.12 Summary

Protocols are the standards that specify how data is represented when being transferred from one machine to another. Protocols specify how the transfer occurs, how errors are detected, and how acknowledgements are passed. To simplify protocol design and implementation, communication problems are segregated into subproblems that can be solved independently. Each subproblem is assigned a separate protocol.

The idea of layering is fundamental because it provides a conceptual framework for protocol design. In a layered model, each layer handles one part of the communication problem and usually corresponds to one protocol. Protocols follow the layering principle, which states that the software implementing layer n on the destination machine receives exactly what the software implementing layer n on the source machine sends.

We examined the 5-layer Internet reference model as well as the older ISO 7-layer reference model. In both cases, the layering model provides only a conceptual framework for protocol software. The ITU X.25 protocols follow the ISO reference model and provide an example of reliable communication service offered by a commercial utility, while the TCP/IP protocols provide an example of a different layering scheme.

In practice, protocol software uses multiplexing and demultiplexing to distinguish among multiple protocols within a given layer, making protocol software more complex than the layering model suggests.

FOR FURTHER STUDY

Postel [RFC 791] provides a sketch of the Internet Protocol layering scheme, and Clark [RFC 817] discusses the effect of layering on implementations. Saltzer, Reed, and Clark [1984] argues that end-to-end verification is important. Chesson [1987] makes the controversial argument that layering produces intolerably bad network throughput. Volume 2 of this text examines layering in detail, and shows an example implementation that achieves efficiency by compromising strict layering and passing pointers between layers.

The ISO protocol documents [1987a] and [1987b] describe ASN.1 in detail. Sun [RFC 1014] describes XDR, an example of what might be called a TCP/IP presentation protocol. Clark [1985] discusses passing information upward through layers.

EXERCISES

11.1   Study the ISO layering model in more detail. How well does the model describe communication on a local area network like an Ethernet?

11.2   Build a case that TCP/IP is moving toward a six-layer protocol architecture that includes a presentation layer. (Hint: various programs use the XDR protocol, Courier-Dardi, ASN.1.)

11.3   Do you think any single presentation protocol will eventually emerge that replaces all others? Why or why not?

11.4   Compare and contrast the tagged data format used by the ASN.1 presentation scheme with the untagged format used by XDR. Characterize situations in which one is better than the other.

11.5   Find out how a UNIX system uses the *mbuf* structure to make layered protocol software efficient.

11.6   Read about the System V UNIX *streams* mechanism. How does it help make protocol implementation easier? What is its chief disadvantage?

12

User Datagram Protocol (UDP)

12.1 Introduction

Previous chapters describe a TCP/IP internet capable of transferring IP datagrams among host computers, where each datagram is routed through the internet based on the destination's IP address. At the Internet Protocol layer, a destination address identifies a host computer; no further distinction is made regarding which user or which application program will receive the datagram. This chapter extends the TCP/IP protocol suite by adding a mechanism that distinguishes among destinations within a given host, allowing multiple application programs executing on a given computer to send and receive datagrams independently.

12.2 Identifying The Ultimate Destination

The operating systems in most computers support multiprogramming, which means they permit multiple application programs to execute simultaneously. Using operating system jargon, we refer to each executing program as a *process*, *task*, *application program*, or a *user level process*; the systems are called multitasking systems. It may seem natural to say that a process is the ultimate destination for a message. However, specifying that a particular process on a particular machine is the ultimate destination for a datagram is somewhat misleading. First, because processes are created and destroyed dynamically, senders seldom know enough to identify a process on another machine. Second, we would like to be able to replace processes that receive datagrams without informing all senders (e.g., rebooting a machine can change all the processes, but senders should not be required to know about the new processes). Third, we need to identify destinations from the functions they implement without knowing the process that implements the function (e.g., to allow a sender to contact a file server without knowing which process on the destination machine implements the file server function). More important, in systems that allow a single process to handle two or more functions, it is essential that we arrange a way for a process to decide exactly which function the sender desires.

Instead of thinking of a process as the ultimate destination, we will imagine that each machine contains a set of abstract destination points called *protocol ports*. Each protocol port is identified by a positive integer. The local operating system provides an interface mechanism that processes use to specify a port or access it.

Most operating systems provide synchronous access to ports. From a particular process's point of view, synchronous access means the computation stops during a port access operation. For example, if a process attempts to extract data from a port before any data arrives, the operating system temporarily stops (blocks) the process until data arrives. Once the data arrives, the operating system passes the data to the process and restarts it. In general, ports are *buffered*, so data that arrives before a process is ready to accept it will not be lost. To achieve buffering, the protocol software located inside the operating system places packets that arrive for a particular protocol port in a (finite) queue until a process extracts them.

To communicate with a foreign port, a sender needs to know both the IP address of the destination machine and the protocol port number of the destination within that machine. Each message must carry the number of the *destination port* on the machine to which the message is sent, as well as the *source port* number on the source machine to which replies should be addressed. Thus, it is possible for any process that receives a message to reply to the sender.

12.3 The User Datagram Protocol

In the TCP/IP protocol suite, the *User Datagram Protocol* or *UDP* provides the primary mechanism that application programs use to send datagrams to other application programs. UDP provides protocol ports used to distinguish among multiple programs executing on a single machine. That is, in addition to the data sent, each UDP message contains both a destination port number and a source port number, making it possible for the UDP software at the destination to deliver the message to the correct recipient and for the recipient to send a reply.

UDP uses the underlying Internet Protocol to transport a message from one machine to another, and provides the same unreliable, connectionless datagram delivery semantics as IP. It does not use acknowledgements to make sure messages arrive, it does not order incoming messages, and it does not provide feedback to control the rate at which information flows between the machines. Thus, UDP messages can be lost, duplicated, or arrive out of order. Furthermore, packets can arrive faster than the recipient can process them. We can summarize:

The User Datagram Protocol (UDP) provides an unreliable connec-
tionless delivery service using IP to transport messages between
machines. It uses IP to carry messages, but adds the ability to distin-
guish among multiple destinations within a given host computer.

An application program that uses UDP accepts full responsibility for handling the
problem of reliability, including message loss, duplication, delay, out-of-order delivery,
and loss of connectivity. Unfortunately, application programmers often ignore these
problems when designing software. Furthermore, because programmers often test network software using highly reliable, low-delay local area networks, testing may not ex-
pose potential failures. Thus, many application programs that rely on UDP work well
in a local environment but fail in dramatic ways when used in a larger TCP/IP internet.

12.4 Format Of UDP Messages

Each UDP message is called a *user datagram*. Conceptually, a user datagram consists of two parts: a UDP header and a UDP data area. As Figure 12.1 shows, the
header is divided into four 16-bit fields that specify the port from which the message
was sent, the port to which the message is destined, the message length, and a UDP
checksum.

0	16	31
UDP SOURCE PORT	**UDP DESTINATION PORT**	
UDP MESSAGE LENGTH	**UDP CHECKSUM**	
DATA		
. . .		

Figure 12.1 The format of fields in a UDP datagram.

The *SOURCE PORT* and *DESTINATION PORT* fields contain the 16-bit UDP protocol port numbers used to demultiplex datagrams among the processes waiting to receive them. The *SOURCE PORT* is optional. When used, it specifies the port to which
replies should be sent; if not used, it should be zero.

The *LENGTH* field contains a count of octets in the UDP datagram, including the
UDP header and the user data. Thus, the minimum value for *LENGTH* is eight, the
length of the header alone.

The UDP checksum is optional and need not be used at all; a value of zero in the
CHECKSUM field means that the checksum has not been computed. The designers
chose to make the checksum optional to allow implementations to operate with little

computational overhead when using UDP across a highly reliable local area network. Recall, however, that IP does not compute a checksum on the data portion of an IP datagram. Thus, the UDP checksum provides the only way to guarantee that data has arrived intact and should be used.

Beginners often wonder what happens to UDP messages for which the computed checksum is zero. A computed value of zero is possible because UDP uses the same checksum algorithm as IP: it divides the data into 16-bit quantities and computes the one's complement of their one's complement sum. Surprisingly, zero is not a problem because one's complement arithmetic has two representations for zero: all bits set to zero or all bits set to one. When the computed checksum is zero, UDP uses the representation with all bits set to one.

12.5 UDP Pseudo-Header

The UDP checksum covers more information than is present in the UDP datagram alone. To compute the checksum, UDP prepends a *pseudo-header* to the UDP datagram, appends an octet of zeros to pad the datagram to an exact multiple of 16 bits, and computes the checksum over the entire object. The octet used for padding and the pseudo-header are *not* transmitted with the UDP datagram, nor are they included in the length. To compute a checksum, the software first stores zero in the *CHECKSUM* field, then accumulates a 16-bit one's complement sum of the entire object, including the pseudo-header, UDP header, and user data.

The purpose of using a pseudo-header is to verify that the UDP datagram has reached its correct destination. The key to understanding the pseudo-header lies in realizing that the correct destination consists of a specific machine and a specific protocol port within that machine. The UDP header itself specifies only the protocol port number. Thus, to verify the destination, UDP on the sending machine computes a checksum that covers the destination IP address as well as the UDP datagram. At the ultimate destination, UDP software verifies the checksum using the destination IP address obtained from the header of the IP datagram that carried the UDP message. If the checksums agree, then it must be true that the datagram has reached the intended destination host as well as the correct protocol port within that host.

The pseudo-header used in the UDP checksum computation consists of 12 octets of data arranged as Figure 12.2 shows. The fields of the pseudo-header labeled *SOURCE IP ADDRESS* and *DESTINATION IP ADDRESS* contain the source and destination IP addresses that will be used when sending the UDP message. Field *PROTO* contains the IP protocol type code (*17* for UDP), and the field labeled *UDP LENGTH* contains the length of the UDP datagram (not including the pseudo-header). To verify the checksum, the receiver must extract these fields from the IP header, assemble them into the pseudo-header format, and recompute the checksum.

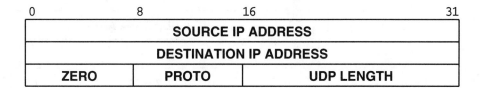

0	8	16	31
SOURCE IP ADDRESS			
DESTINATION IP ADDRESS			
ZERO	PROTO	UDP LENGTH	

Figure 12.2 The 12 octets of the pseudo-header used during UDP checksum
computation.

12.6 UDP Encapsulation And Protocol Layering

UDP provides our first example of a transport protocol. In the layering model of
Chapter 11, UDP lies in the layer above the Internet Protocol layer. Conceptually, application programs access UDP, which uses IP to send and receive datagrams as Figure
12.3 shows.

Conceptual Layering

Application
User Datagram (UDP)
Internet (IP)
Network Interface

Figure 12.3 The conceptual layering of UDP between application programs
and IP.

Layering UDP above IP means that a complete UDP message, including the UDP
header and data, is encapsulated in an IP datagram as it travels across an internet as Figure 12.4 shows.

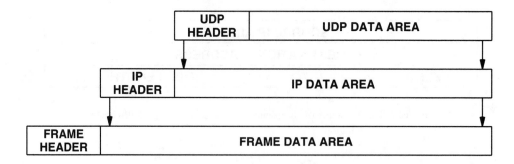

Figure 12.4 A UDP datagram encapsulated in an IP datagram for transmission across an internet. The datagram is further encapsulated in a frame each time it travels across a single network.

For the protocols we have examined, encapsulation means that UDP prepends a header to the data that a user sends and passes it to IP. The IP layer prepends a header to what it receives from UDP. Finally, the network interface layer embeds the datagram in a frame before sending it from one machine to another. The format of the frame depends on the underlying network technology. Usually, network frames include an additional header.

On input, a packet arrives at the lowest layer of network software and begins its ascent through successively higher layers. Each layer removes one header before passing the message on, so that by the time the highest level passes data to the receiving process, all headers have been removed. Thus, the outermost header corresponds to the lowest layer of protocol, while the innermost header corresponds to the highest protocol layer. When considering how headers are inserted and removed, it is important to keep in mind the layering principle. In particular, observe that the layering principle applies to UDP, so the UDP datagram received from IP on the destination machine is identical to the datagram that UDP passed to IP on the source machine. Also, the data that UDP delivers to a user process on the receiving machine will be exactly the data that a user process passed to UDP on the sending machine.

The division of duties among various protocol layers is rigid and clear:

> *The IP layer is responsible only for transferring data between a pair of hosts on an internet, while the UDP layer is responsible only for differentiating among multiple sources or destinations within one host.*

Thus, only the IP header identifies the source and destination hosts; only the UDP layer identifies the source or destination ports within a host.

12.7 Layering And The UDP Checksum Computation

Observant readers will have noticed a seeming contradiction between the layering rules and the UDP checksum computation. Recall that the UDP checksum includes a pseudo-header that has fields for the source and destination IP addresses. It can be argued that the destination IP address must be known to the user when sending a UDP datagram, and the user must pass it to the UDP layer. Thus, the UDP layer can obtain the destination IP address without interacting with the IP layer. However, the source IP address depends on the route IP chooses for the datagram, because the IP source address identifies the network interface over which the datagram is transmitted. Thus, UDP cannot know a source IP address unless it interacts with the IP layer.

We assume that UDP software asks the IP layer to compute the source and (possibly) destination IP addresses, uses them to construct a pseudo-header, computes the checksum, discards the pseudo-header, and then passes the UDP datagram to IP for transmission. An alternative approach that produces greater efficiency arranges to have the UDP layer encapsulate the UDP datagram in an IP datagram, obtain the source address from IP, store the source and destination addresses in the appropriate fields of the datagram header, compute the UDP checksum, and then pass the IP datagram to the IP layer, which only needs to fill in the remaining IP header fields.

Does the strong interaction between UDP and IP violate our basic premise that layering reflects separation of functionality? Yes. UDP has been tightly integrated with the IP protocol. It is clearly a compromise of the pure separation, made for entirely practical reasons. We are willing to overlook the layering violation because it is impossible to fully identify a destination application program without specifying the destination machine, and we want to make the mapping between addresses used by UDP and those used by IP efficient. One of the exercises examines this issue from a different point of view, asking the reader to consider whether UDP should be separated from IP.

12.8 UDP Multiplexing, Demultiplexing, And Ports

We have seen in Chapter 11 that software throughout the layers of a protocol hierarchy must multiplex or demultiplex among multiple objects at the next layer. UDP software provides another example of multiplexing and demultiplexing. It accepts UDP datagrams from many application programs and passes them to IP for transmission, and it accepts arriving UDP datagrams from IP and passes each to the appropriate application program.

Conceptually, all multiplexing and demultiplexing between UDP software and application programs occur through the port mechanism. In practice, each application program must negotiate with the operating system to obtain a protocol port and an associated port number before it can send a UDP datagram†. Once the port has been assigned, any datagram the application program sends through the port will have that port number in its UDP *SOURCE PORT* field.

---

†For now, we will describe ports abstractly; Chapter 22 provides an example of the operating system primitives used to create and use ports.

While processing input, UDP accepts incoming datagrams from the IP software and demultiplexes based on the UDP destination port, as Figure 12.5 shows.

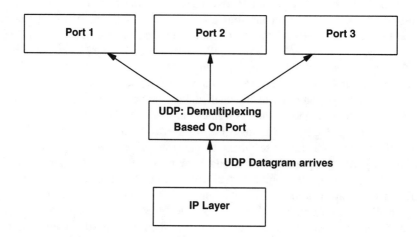

Figure 12.5 Example of demultiplexing one layer above IP. UDP uses the UDP destination port number to select an appropriate destination port for incoming datagrams.

The easiest way to think of a UDP port is as a queue. In most implementations, when an application program negotiates with the operating system to use a given port, the operating system creates an internal queue that can hold arriving messages. Often, the application can specify or change the queue size. When UDP receives a datagram, it checks to see that the destination port number matches one of the ports currently in use. If not, it sends an ICMP *port unreachable* error message and discards the datagram. If a match is found, UDP enqueues the new datagram at the port where an application program can access it. Of course, an error occurs if the port is full, and UDP discards the incoming datagram.

12.9 Reserved And Available UDP Port Numbers

How should protocol port numbers be assigned? The problem is important because two computers need to agree on port numbers before they can interoperate. For example, when computer *A* wants to obtain a file from computer *B*, it needs to know what port the file transfer program on computer *B* uses. There are two fundamental approaches to port assignment. The first approach uses a central authority. Everyone agrees to allow a central authority to assign port numbers as needed and to publish the list of all assignments. Then all software is built according to the list. This approach is sometimes called *universal assignment*, and the port assignments specified by the authority are called *well-known port assignments*.

The second approach to port assignment uses dynamic binding. In the dynamic binding approach, ports are not globally known. Instead, whenever a program needs a port, the network software assigns one. To learn about the current port assignment on another computer, it is necessary to send a request that asks about the current port assignment (e.g., What port is the file transfer service using?). The target machine replies by giving the correct port number to use.

The TCP/IP designers adopted a hybrid approach that assigns some port numbers a priori, but leaves many available for local sites or application programs. The assigned port numbers begin at low values and extend upward, leaving large integer values available for dynamic assignment. The table in Figure 12.6 lists some of the currently assigned UDP port numbers. The second column contains Internet standard assigned keywords, while the third contains keywords used on most UNIX systems.

Decimal	Keyword	UNIX Keyword	Description
0	-	-	Reserved
7	ECHO	echo	Echo
9	DISCARD	discard	Discard
11	USERS	systat	Active Users
13	DAYTIME	daytime	Daytime
15	-	netstat	Network status program
17	QUOTE	qotd	Quote of the Day
19	CHARGEN	chargen	Character Generator
37	TIME	time	Time
42	NAMESERVER	name	Host Name Server
43	NICNAME	whois	Who Is
53	DOMAIN	nameserver	Domain Name Server
67	BOOTPS	bootps	BOOTP or DHCP Server
68	BOOTPC	bootpc	BOOTP or DHCP Client
69	TFTP	tftp	Trivial File Transfer
88	KERBEROS	kerberos	Kerberos Security Service
111	SUNRPC	sunrpc	Sun Remote Procedure Call
123	NTP	ntp	Network Time Protocol
161	-	snmp	Simple Network Management Protocol
162	-	snmp-trap	SNMP traps
512	-	biff	UNIX comsat
513	-	who	UNIX rwho daemon
514	-	syslog	System log
525	-	timed	Time daemon

Figure 12.6 An illustrative sample of currently assigned UDP ports showing the standard keyword and the UNIX equivalent; the list is not exhaustive. To the extent possible, other transport protocols that offer identical services use the same port numbers as UDP.

12.10 Summary

Most computer systems permit multiple application programs to execute simultaneously. Using operating system jargon, we refer to each executing program as a *process*.
The User Datagram Protocol, UDP, distinguishes among multiple processes within a
given machine by allowing senders and receivers to add two 16-bit integers called protocol port numbers to each UDP message. The port numbers identify the source and
destination. Some UDP port numbers, called *well known*, are permanently assigned and
honored throughout the Internet (e.g., port *69* is reserved for use by the trivial file
transfer protocol *TFTP* described in Chapter 26). Other port numbers are available for
arbitrary application programs to use.

UDP is a thin protocol in the sense that it does not add significantly to the semantics of IP. It merely provides application programs with the ability to communicate using IP's unreliable connectionless packet delivery service. Thus, UDP messages can be
lost, duplicated, delayed, or delivered out of order; the application program using UDP
must handle these problems. Many programs that use UDP do not work correctly
across an internet because they fail to accommodate these conditions.

In the protocol layering scheme, UDP lies in the transport layer, above the Internet
Protocol layer and below the application layer. Conceptually, the transport layer is independent of the Internet layer, but in practice they interact strongly. The UDP checksum includes IP source and destination addresses, meaning that UDP software must interact with IP software to find addresses before sending datagrams.

FOR FURTHER STUDY

Tanenbaum [1981] contains a tutorial comparison of the datagram and virtual circuit models of communication. Ball *et. al.* [1979] describes message-based systems
without discussing the message protocol. The UDP protocol described here is a standard for TCP/IP and is defined by Postel [RFC 768].

EXERCISES

12.1   Try UDP in your local environment. Measure the average transfer speed with messages
        of 256, 512, 1024, 2048, 4096, and 8192 bytes. Can you explain the results (hint: what
        is your network MTU)?

12.2   Why is the UDP checksum separate from the IP checksum? Would you object to a pro-
        tocol that used a single checksum for the complete IP datagram including the UDP mes-
        sage?

12.3   Not using checksums can be dangerous. Explain how a single corrupted ARP packet
        broadcast by machine P can make it impossible to reach another machine, Q.

12.4   Should the notion of multiple destinations identified by protocol ports have been built into IP? Why, or why not?

12.5   *Name Registry.* Suppose you want to allow arbitrary pairs of application programs to establish communication with UDP, but you do not wish to assign them fixed UDP port numbers. Instead, you would like potential correspondents to be identified by a character string of 64 or fewer characters. Thus, a program on machine *A* might want to communicate with the "funny-special-long-id" program on machine *B* (you can assume that a process always knows the IP address of the host with which it wants to communicate). Meanwhile, a process on machine *C* wants to communicate with the "comer's-own-program-id" on machine *A*. Show that you only need to assign one UDP port to make such communication possible by designing software on each machine that allows (a) a local process to pick an unused UDP port ID over which it will communicate, (b) a local process to register the 64-character name to which it responds, and (c) a foreign process to use UDP to establish communication using only the 64-character name and destination internet address.

12.6   Implement name registry software from the previous exercise.

12.7   What is the chief advantage of using preassigned UDP port numbers? The chief disadvantage?

12.8   What is the chief advantage of using protocol ports instead of process identifiers to specify the destination within a machine?

12.9   UDP provides unreliable datagram communication because it does not guarantee delivery of the message. Devise a reliable datagram protocol that uses timeouts and acknowledgements to guarantee delivery. How much network overhead and delay does reliability introduce?

12.10   Send UDP datagrams across a wide area network and measure the percentage lost and the percentage reordered. Does the result depend on the time of day? The network load?

13

Reliable Stream Transport Service (TCP)

13.1 Introduction

Previous chapters explore the unreliable connectionless packet delivery service that forms the basis for all internet communication and the IP protocol that defines it. This chapter introduces the second most important and well-known network-level service, reliable stream delivery, and the *Transmission Control Protocol* (*TCP*) that defines it. We will see that TCP adds substantial functionality to the protocols already discussed, but that its implementation is also substantially more complex.

Although TCP is presented here as part of the TCP/IP Internet protocol suite, it is an independent, general purpose protocol that can be adapted for use with other delivery systems. For example, because TCP makes very few assumptions about the underlying network, it is possible to use it over a single network like an Ethernet, as well as over a complex internet. In fact, TCP has been so popular that one of the International Organization for Standardization's open systems protocols, TP-4, has been derived from it.

13.2 The Need For Stream Delivery

At the lowest level, computer communication networks provide unreliable packet delivery. Packets can be lost or destroyed when transmission errors interfere with data, when network hardware fails, or when networks become too heavily loaded to accommodate the load presented. Networks that route packets dynamically can deliver them out of order, deliver them after a substantial delay, or deliver duplicates. Furthermore, underlying network technologies may dictate an optimal packet size or pose other constraints needed to achieve efficient transfer rates.

At the highest level, application programs often need to send large volumes of data from one computer to another. Using an unreliable connectionless delivery system for large volume transfers becomes tedious and annoying, and it requires programmers to build error detection and recovery into each application program. Because it is difficult to design, understand, or modify software that correctly provides reliability, few application programmers have the necessary technical background. As a consequence, one goal of network protocol research has been to find general purpose solutions to the problems of providing reliable stream delivery, making it possible for experts to build a single instance of stream protocol software that all application programs use. Having a single general purpose protocol helps isolate application programs from the details of networking, and makes it possible to define a uniform interface for the stream transfer service.

13.3 Properties Of The Reliable Delivery Service

The interface between application programs and the TCP/IP reliable delivery service can be characterized by 5 features:

• *Stream Orientation*. When two application programs (user processes) transfer large volumes of data, we think of the data as a *stream* of bits, divided into 8-bit *octets*, which are informally called *bytes*. The stream delivery service on the destination machine passes to the receiver exactly the same sequence of octets that the sender passes to it on the source machine.

• *Virtual Circuit Connection*. Making a stream transfer is analogous to placing a telephone call. Before transfer can start, both the sending and receiving application programs interact with their respective operating systems, informing them of the desire for a stream transfer. Conceptually, one application places a "call" which must be accepted by the other. Protocol software modules in the two operating systems communicate by sending messages across an internet, verifying that the transfer is authorized, and that both sides are ready. Once all details have been settled, the protocol modules inform the application programs that a *connection* has been established and that transfer can begin. During transfer, protocol software on the two machines continue to communicate to verify that data is received correctly. If the communication fails for any reason (e.g., because network hardware along the path between the machines fails), both machines detect the failure and report it to the appropriate application programs. We use the term *virtual circuit* to describe such connections because although application programs view the connection as a dedicated hardware circuit, the reliability is an illusion provided by the stream delivery service.

• *Buffered Transfer*. Application programs send a data stream across the virtual circuit by repeatedly passing data octets to the protocol software. When transferring data, each application uses whatever size pieces it finds convenient, which can be as small as a single octet. At the receiving end, the protocol software delivers octets from the data stream in exactly the same order they were sent, making them available to the receiving application program as soon as they have been received and verified. The protocol software is free to divide the stream into packets independent of the pieces the application program transfers. To make transfer more efficient and to minimize network traffic, implementations usually collect enough data from a stream to fill a reasonably large datagram before transmitting it across an internet. Thus, even if the application program generates the stream one octet at a time, transfer across an internet may be quite efficient. Similarly, if the application program chooses to generate extremely large blocks of data, the protocol software can choose to divide each block into smaller pieces for transmission.

For those applications where data should be delivered even though it does not fill a buffer, the stream service provides a *push* mechanism that applications use to force a transfer. At the sending side, a push forces protocol software to transfer all data that has been generated without waiting to fill a buffer. When it reaches the receiving side, the push causes TCP to make the data available to the application without delay. The reader should note, however, that the push function only guarantees that all data will be transferred; it does not provide record boundaries. Thus, even when delivery is forced, the protocol software may choose to divide the stream in unexpected ways.

• *Unstructured Stream*. It is important to understand that the TCP/IP stream service does not honor structured data streams. For example, there is no way for a payroll application to have the stream service mark boundaries between employee records, or to identify the contents of the stream as being payroll data. Application programs using the stream service must understand stream content and agree on stream format before they initiate a connection.

• *Full Duplex Connection*. Connections provided by the TCP/IP stream service allow concurrent transfer in both directions. Such connections are called *full duplex*. From the point of view of an application process, a full duplex connection consists of two independent streams flowing in opposite directions, with no apparent interaction. The stream service allows an application process to terminate flow in one direction while data continues to flow in the other direction, making the connection *half duplex*. The advantage of a full duplex connection is that the underlying protocol software can send control information for one stream back to the source in datagrams carrying data in the opposite direction. Such *piggybacking* reduces network traffic.

13.4 Providing Reliability

We have said that the reliable stream delivery service guarantees to deliver a stream of data sent from one machine to another without duplication or data loss. The question arises: "How can protocol software provide reliable transfer if the underlying communication system offers only unreliable packet delivery?" The answer is complicated, but most reliable protocols use a single fundamental technique known as *positive acknowledgement with retransmission*. The technique requires a recipient to communicate with the source, sending back an *acknowledgement (ACK)* message as it receives data. The sender keeps a record of each packet it sends and waits for an acknowledgement before sending the next packet. The sender also starts a timer when it sends a packet and *retransmits* a packet if the timer expires before an acknowledgement arrives.

Figure 13.1 shows how the simplest positive acknowledgement protocol transfers data.

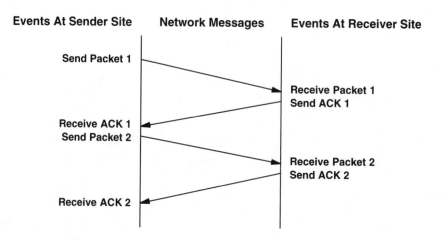

Figure 13.1 A protocol using positive acknowledgement with retransmission in which the sender awaits an acknowledgement for each packet sent. Vertical distance down the figure represents increasing time and diagonal lines across the middle represent network packet transmission.

In the figure, events at the sender and receiver are shown on the left and right. Each diagonal line crossing the middle shows the transfer of one message across the network.

Figure 13.2 uses the same format diagram as Figure 13.1 to show what happens when a packet is lost or corrupted. The sender starts a timer after transmitting a packet. When the timer expires, the sender assumes the packet was lost and retransmits it.

The final reliability problem arises when an underlying packet delivery system duplicates packets. Duplicates can also arise when networks experience high delays that cause premature retransmission. Solving duplication requires careful thought because both packets and acknowledgements can be duplicated. Usually, reliable protocols detect duplicate packets by assigning each packet a sequence number and requiring the receiver to remember which sequence numbers it has received. To avoid confusion caused by delayed or duplicated acknowledgements, positive acknowledgement protocols send sequence numbers back in acknowledgements, so the receiver can correctly associate acknowledgements with packets.

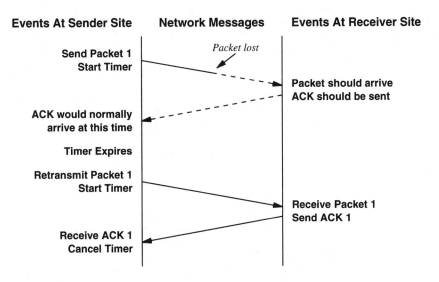

Figure 13.2 Timeout and retransmission that occurs when a packet is lost. The dotted lines show the time that would be taken by the transmission of a packet and its acknowledgement, if the packet was not lost.

13.5 The Idea Behind Sliding Windows

Before examining the TCP stream service, we need to explore an additional concept that underlies stream transmission. The concept, known as a *sliding window*, makes stream transmission efficient. To understand the motivation for sliding windows, recall the sequence of events that Figure 13.1 depicts. To achieve reliability, the sender transmits a packet and then waits for an acknowledgement before transmitting another. As Figure 13.1 shows, data only flows between the machines in one direction at any time, even if the network is capable of simultaneous communication in both directions. The network will be completely idle during times that machines delay responses (e.g., while machines compute routes or checksums). If we imagine a network with high transmission delays, the problem becomes clear:

> *A simple positive acknowledgement protocol wastes a substantial amount of network bandwidth because it must delay sending a new packet until it receives an acknowledgement for the previous packet.*

The sliding window technique is a more complex form of positive acknowledgement and retransmission than the simple method discussed above. Sliding window protocols use network bandwidth better because they allow the sender to transmit multiple packets before waiting for an acknowledgement. The easiest way to envision sliding window operation is to think of a sequence of packets to be transmitted as Figure 13.3 shows. The protocol places a small, fixed-size *window* on the sequence and transmits all packets that lie inside the window.

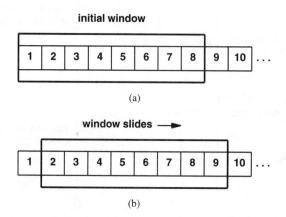

Figure 13.3 (a) A sliding window protocol with eight packets in the window, and (b) The window sliding so that packet *9* can be sent when an acknowledgement has been received for packet *1*. Only unacknowledged packets are retransmitted.

We say that a packet is *unacknowledged* if it has been transmitted but no acknowledgement has been received. Technically, the number of packets that can be unacknowledged at any given time is constrained by the *window size* and is limited to a small, fixed number. For example, in a sliding window protocol with window size *8*, the sender is permitted to transmit *8* packets before it receives an acknowledgement.

As Figure 13.3 shows, once the sender receives an acknowledgement for the first packet inside the window, it "slides" the window along and sends the next packet. The window continues to slide as long as acknowledgements are received.

The performance of sliding window protocols depends on the window size and the speed at which the network accepts packets. Figure 13.4 shows an example of the operation of a sliding window protocol when sending three packets. Note that the sender transmits all three packets before receiving any acknowledgements.

With a window size of *1*, a sliding window protocol is exactly the same as our simple positive acknowledgement protocol. By increasing the window size, it is possible to eliminate network idle time completely. That is, in the steady state, the sender can transmit packets as fast as the network can transfer them. The main point is:

> *Because a well tuned sliding window protocol keeps the network completely saturated with packets, it obtains substantially higher throughput than a simple positive acknowledgement protocol.*

Conceptually, a sliding window protocol always remembers which packets have been acknowledged and keeps a separate timer for each unacknowledged packet. If a packet is lost, the timer expires and the sender retransmits that packet. When the sender slides its window, it moves past all acknowledged packets. At the receiving end, the protocol software keeps an analogous window, accepting and acknowledging packets as they arrive. Thus, the window partitions the sequence of packets into three sets: those packets to the left of the window have been successfully transmitted, received, and acknowledged; those packets to the right have not yet been transmitted; and those packets that lie in the window are being transmitted. The lowest numbered packet in the window is the first packet in the sequence that has not been acknowledged.

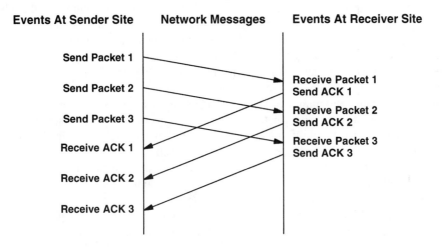

Figure 13.4 An example of three packets transmitted using a sliding window protocol. The key concept is that the sender can transmit all packets in the window without waiting for an acknowledgement.

13.6 The Transmission Control Protocol

Now that we understand the principle of sliding windows, we can examine the reliable stream service provided by the TCP/IP Internet protocol suite. The service is defined by the *Transmission Control Protocol*, or *TCP*. The reliable stream service is so important that the entire protocol suite is referred to as TCP/IP. It is important to understand that:

TCP is a communication protocol, not a piece of software.

The difference between a protocol and the software that implements it is analogous to the difference between the definition of a programming language and a compiler. As in the programming language world, the distinction between definition and implementation sometimes becomes blurred. People encounter TCP software much more frequently than they encounter the protocol specification, so it is natural to think of a particular implementation as the standard. Nevertheless, the reader should try to distinguish between the two.

Exactly what does TCP provide? TCP is complex, so there is no simple answer. The protocol specifies the format of the data and acknowledgements that two computers exchange to achieve a reliable transfer, as well as the procedures the computers use to ensure that the data arrives correctly. It specifies how TCP software distinguishes among multiple destinations on a given machine, and how communicating machines recover from errors like lost or duplicated packets. The protocol also specifies how two computers initiate a TCP stream transfer and how they agree when it is complete.

It is also important to understand what the protocol does not include. Although the TCP specification describes how application programs use TCP in general terms, it does not dictate the details of the interface between an application program and TCP. That is, the protocol documentation only discusses the operations TCP supplies; it does not specify the exact procedures application programs invoke to access these operations. The reason for leaving the application program interface unspecified is flexibility. In particular, because programmers usually implement TCP in the computer's operating system, they need to employ whatever interface the operating system supplies. Allowing the implementor flexibility makes it possible to have a single specification for TCP that can be used to build software for a variety of machines.

Because TCP assumes little about the underlying communication system, TCP can be used with a variety of packet delivery systems, including the IP datagram delivery service. For example, TCP can be implemented to use dialup telephone lines, a local area network, a high speed fiber optic network, or a lower speed long haul network. In fact, the large variety of delivery systems TCP can use is one of its strengths.

13.7 Ports, Connections, And Endpoints

Like the User Datagram Protocol (UDP) presented in Chapter 12, TCP resides above IP in the protocol layering scheme. Figure 13.5 shows the conceptual organization. TCP allows multiple application programs on a given machine to communicate concurrently, and it demultiplexes incoming TCP traffic among application programs. Like the User Datagram Protocol, TCP uses *protocol port* numbers to identify the ultimate destination within a machine. Each port is assigned a small integer used to identify it†.

---

†Although both TCP and UDP use integer port identifiers starting at *1* to identify ports, there is no confusion between them because an incoming IP datagram identifies the protocol being used as well as the port number.

Conceptual Layering

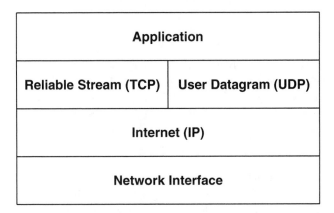

Figure 13.5 The conceptual layering of UDP and TCP above IP. TCP provides a reliable stream service, while UDP provides an unreliable datagram delivery service. Application programs use both.

When we discussed UDP ports, we said to think of each port as a queue into which protocol software places arriving datagrams. TCP ports are much more complex because a given port number does not correspond to a single object. Instead, TCP has been built on the *connection abstraction*, in which the objects to be identified are virtual circuit connections, not individual ports. Understanding that TCP uses the notion of connections is crucial because it helps explain the meaning and use of TCP port numbers:

> *TCP uses the connection, not the protocol port, as its fundamental abstraction; connections are identified by a pair of endpoints.*

Exactly what are the "endpoints" of a connection? We have said that a connection consists of a virtual circuit between two application programs, so it might be natural to assume that an application program serves as the connection "endpoint." It is not. Instead, TCP defines an *endpoint* to be a pair of integers (*host, port*), where *host* is the IP address for a host and *port* is a TCP port on that host. For example, the endpoint (*128.10.2.3, 25*) specifies TCP port *25* on the machine with IP address *128.10.2.3*.

Now that we have defined endpoints, it will be easy to understand connections. Recall that a connection is defined by its two endpoints. Thus, if there is a connection from machine (*18.26.0.36*) at MIT to machine (*128.10.2.3*) at Purdue University, it might be defined by the endpoints:

(*18.26.0.36, 1069*) and (*128.10.2.3, 25*).

Meanwhile, another connection might be in progress from machine (*128.9.0.32*) at the Information Sciences Institute to the same machine at Purdue, identified by its endpoints:

(*128.9.0.32*, *1184*) and (*128.10.2.3*, *53*).

So far, our examples of connections have been straightforward because the ports used at all endpoints have been unique. However, the connection abstraction allows multiple connections to share an endpoint. For example, we could add another connection to the two listed above from machine (*128.2.254.139*) at CMU to the machine at Purdue:

(*128.2.254.139*, *1184*) and (*128.10.2.3*, *53*).

It might seem strange that two connections can use the TCP port *53* on machine 128.10.2.3 simultaneously, but there is no ambiguity. Because TCP associates incoming messages with a connection instead of a protocol port, it uses both endpoints to identify the appropriate connection. The important idea to remember is:

> *Because TCP identifies a connection by a pair of endpoints, a given TCP port number can be shared by multiple connections on the same machine.*

From a programmer's point of view, the connection abstraction is significant. It means a programmer can devise a program that provides concurrent service to multiple connections simultaneously without needing unique local port numbers for each connection. For example, most systems provide concurrent access to their electronic mail service, allowing multiple computers to send them electronic mail concurrently. Because the program that accepts incoming mail uses TCP to communicate, it only needs to use one local TCP port even though it allows multiple connections to proceed concurrently.

13.8 Passive And Active Opens

Unlike UDP, TCP is a connection-oriented protocol that requires both endpoints to agree to participate. That is, before TCP traffic can pass across an internet, application programs at both ends of the connection must agree that the connection is desired. To do so, the application program on one end performs a *passive open* function by contacting its operating system and indicating that it will accept an incoming connection. At that time, the operating system assigns a TCP port number for its end of the connection. The application program at the other end must then contact its operating system using an *active open* request to establish a connection. The two TCP software modules communicate to establish and verify a connection. Once a connection has been created, application programs can begin to pass data; the TCP software modules at each end exchange messages that guarantee reliable delivery. We will return to the details of establishing connections after examining the TCP message format.

13.9 Segments, Streams, And Sequence Numbers

TCP views the data stream as a sequence of octets or bytes that it divides into *segments* for transmission. Usually, each segment travels across an internet in a single IP datagram.

TCP uses a specialized sliding window mechanism to solve two important problems: efficient transmission and flow control. Like the sliding window protocol described earlier, the TCP window mechanism makes it possible to send multiple segments before an acknowledgement arrives. Doing so increases total throughput because it keeps the network busy. The TCP form of a sliding window protocol also solves the end-to-end *flow control* problem, by allowing the receiver to restrict transmission until it has sufficient buffer space to accommodate more data.

The TCP sliding window mechanism operates at the octet level, not at the segment or packet level. Octets of the data stream are numbered sequentially, and a sender keeps three pointers associated with every connection. The pointers define a sliding window as Figure 13.6 illustrates. The first pointer marks the left of the sliding window, separating octets that have been sent and acknowledged from octets yet to be acknowledged. A second pointer marks the right of the sliding window and defines the highest octet in the sequence that can be sent before more acknowledgements are received. The third pointer marks the boundary inside the window that separates those octets that have already been sent from those octets that have not been sent. The protocol software sends all octets in the window without delay, so the boundary inside the window usually moves from left to right quickly.

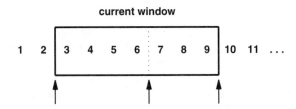

Figure 13.6 An example of the TCP sliding window. Octets through 2 have been sent and acknowledged, octets 3 through 6 have been sent but not acknowledged, octets 7 though 9 have not been sent but will be sent without delay, and octets 10 and higher cannot be sent until the window moves.

We have described how the sender's TCP window slides along and mentioned that the receiver must maintain a similar window to piece the stream together again. It is important to understand, however, that because TCP connections are full duplex, two transfers proceed simultaneously over each connection, one in each direction. We think of the transfers as completely independent because at any time data can flow across the connection in one direction, or in both directions. Thus, TCP software at each end maintains two windows per connection (for a total of four), one slides along the data stream being sent, while the other slides along as data is received.

13.10 Variable Window Size And Flow Control

One difference between the TCP sliding window protocol and the simplified sliding window protocol presented earlier occurs because TCP allows the window size to vary over time. Each acknowledgement, which specifies how many octets have been received, contains a *window advertisement* that specifies how many additional octets of data the receiver is prepared to accept. We think of the window advertisement as specifying the receiver's current buffer size. In response to an increased window advertisement, the sender increases the size of its sliding window and proceeds to send octets that have not been acknowledged. In response to a decreased window advertisement, the sender decreases the size of its window and stops sending octets beyond the boundary. TCP software should not contradict previous advertisements by shrinking the window past previously acceptable positions in the octet stream. Instead, smaller advertisements accompany acknowledgements, so the window size changes at the time it slides forward.

The advantage of using a variable size window is that it provides flow control as well as reliable transfer. To avoid receiving more data than it can store, the receiver sends smaller window advertisements as its buffer fills. In the extreme case, the receiver advertises a window size of zero to stop all transmissions. Later, when buffer space becomes available, the receiver advertises a nonzero window size to trigger the flow of data again†.

Having a mechanism for flow control is essential in an internet environment, where machines of various speeds and sizes communicate through networks and routers of various speeds and capacities. There are two independent flow problems. First, internet protocols need end-to-end flow control between the source and ultimate destination. For example, when a minicomputer communicates with a large mainframe, the minicomputer needs to regulate the influx of data, or protocol software would be overrun quickly. Thus, TCP must implement end-to-end flow control to guarantee reliable delivery. Second, internet protocols need a flow control mechanism that allows intermediate systems (i.e., routers) to control a source that sends more traffic than the machine can tolerate.

When intermediate machines become overloaded, the condition is called *congestion*, and mechanisms to solve the problem are called *congestion control* mechanisms. TCP uses its sliding window scheme to solve the end-to-end flow control problem; it does not have an explicit mechanism for congestion control. We will see later, however, that a carefully programmed TCP implementation can detect and recover from congestion while a poor implementation can make it worse. In particular, although a carefully chosen retransmission scheme can help avoid congestion, a poorly chosen scheme can exacerbate it.

---

†There are two exceptions to transmission when the window size is zero. First, a sender is allowed to transmit a segment with the urgent bit set to inform the receiver that urgent data is available. Second, to avoid a potential deadlock that can arise if a nonzero advertisement is lost after the window size reaches zero, the sender probes a zero-sized window periodically.

13.11 TCP Segment Format

The unit of transfer between the TCP software on two machines is called a *segment*. Segments are exchanged to establish connections, transfer data, send acknowledgements, advertise window sizes, and close connections. Because TCP uses piggybacking, an acknowledgement traveling from machine *A* to machine *B* may travel in the same segment as data traveling from machine *A* to machine *B*, even though the acknowledgement refers to data sent from *B* to *A*†. Figure 13.7 shows the TCP segment format.

0	4	10	16	24	31
SOURCE PORT			DESTINATION PORT		
SEQUENCE NUMBER					
ACKNOWLEDGEMENT NUMBER					
HLEN	RESERVED	CODE BITS	WINDOW		
CHECKSUM			URGENT POINTER		
OPTIONS (IF ANY)				PADDING	
DATA					
. . .					

Figure 13.7 The format of a TCP segment with a TCP header followed by data. Segments are used to establish connections as well as to carry data and acknowledgements.

Each segment is divided into two parts, a header followed by data. The header, known as the *TCP header*, carries the expected identification and control information. Fields *SOURCE PORT* and *DESTINATION PORT* contain the TCP port numbers that identify the application programs at the ends of the connection. The *SEQUENCE NUMBER* field identifies the position in the sender's byte stream of the data in the segment. The *ACKNOWLEDGEMENT NUMBER* field identifies the number of the octet that the source expects to receive next. Note that the sequence number refers to the stream flowing in the same direction as the segment, while the acknowledgement number refers to the stream flowing in the opposite direction from the segment.

The *HLEN*‡ field contains an integer that specifies the length of the segment header measured in 32-bit multiples. It is needed because the *OPTIONS* field varies in length, depending on which options have been included. Thus, the size of the TCP header varies depending on the options selected. The 6-bit field marked *RESERVED* is reserved for future use.

---

†In practice, piggybacking does not usually occur because most applications do not send data in both directions simultaneously.

‡The specification says the *HLEN* field is the *offset* of the data area within the segment.

Some segments carry only an acknowledgement while some carry data. Others carry requests to establish or close a connection. TCP software uses the 6-bit field labeled *CODE BITS* to determine the purpose and contents of the segment. The six bits tell how to interpret other fields in the header according to the table in Figure 13.8.

Bit (left to right)	Meaning if bit set to 1
URG	Urgent pointer field is valid
ACK	Acknowledgement field is valid
PSH	This segment requests a push
RST	Reset the connection
SYN	Synchronize sequence numbers
FIN	Sender has reached end of its byte stream

Figure 13.8 Bits of the CODE field in the TCP header.

TCP software advertises how much data it is willing to accept every time it sends a segment by specifying its buffer size in the *WINDOW* field. The field contains a 16-bit unsigned integer in network-standard byte order. Window advertisements provide another example of piggybacking because they accompany all segments, including those carrying data as well as those carrying only an acknowledgement.

13.12 Out Of Band Data

Although TCP is a stream-oriented protocol, it is sometimes important for the program at one end of a connection to send data *out of band*, without waiting for the program at the other end of the connection to consume octets already in the stream. For example, when TCP is used for a remote login session, the user may decide to send a keyboard sequence that *interrupts* or *aborts* the program at the other end. Such signals are most often needed when a program on the remote machine fails to operate correctly. The signals must be sent without waiting for the program to read octets already in the TCP stream (or one would not be able to abort programs that stop reading input).

To accommodate out of band signaling, TCP allows the sender to specify data as *urgent*, meaning that the receiving program should be notified of its arrival as quickly as possible, regardless of its position in the stream. The protocol specifies that when urgent data is found, the receiving TCP should notify whatever application program is associated with the connection to go into ''urgent mode.'' After all urgent data has been consumed, TCP tells the application program to return to normal operation.

The exact details of how TCP informs the application program about urgent data depend on the computer's operating system, of course. The mechanism used to mark urgent data when transmitting it in a segment consists of the URG code bit and the *URGENT POINTER* field. When the URG bit is set, the urgent pointer specifies the position in the segment where urgent data ends.

13.13 Maximum Segment Size Option

Not all segments sent across a connection will be of the same size. However, both ends need to agree on a maximum segment they will transfer. TCP software uses the *OPTIONS* field to negotiate with the TCP software at the other end of the connection; one of the options allows TCP software to specify the *maximum segment size* (*MSS*) that it is willing to receive. For example, when an embedded system that only has a few hundred bytes of buffer space connects to a large supercomputer, it can negotiate an MSS that restricts segments so they fit in the buffer. It is especially important for computers connected by high-speed local area networks to choose a maximum segment size that fills packets or they will not make good use of the bandwidth. Therefore, if the two endpoints lie on the same physical network, TCP usually computes a maximum segment size such that the resulting IP datagrams will match the network MTU. If the endpoints do not lie on the same physical network, they can attempt to discover the minimum MTU along the path between them, or choose a maximum segment size of *536* (the default size of an IP datagram, *576*, minus the standard size of IP and TCP headers).

In a general internet environment, choosing a good maximum segment size can be difficult because performance can be poor for either extremely large segment sizes or extremely small sizes. On one hand, when the segment size is small, network utilization remains low. To see why, recall that TCP segments travel encapsulated in IP datagrams which are encapsulated in physical network frames. Thus, each segment has at least 40 octets of TCP and IP headers in addition to the data. Therefore, datagrams carrying only one octet of data use at most 1/41 of the underlying network bandwidth for user data; in practice, minimum interpacket gaps and network hardware framing bits make the ratio even smaller.

On the other hand, extremely large segment sizes can also produce poor performance. Large segments result in large IP datagrams. When such datagrams travel across a network with small MTU, IP must fragment them. Unlike a TCP segment, a fragment cannot be acknowledged or retransmitted independently; all fragments must arrive or the entire datagram must be retransmitted. Because the probability of losing a given fragment is nonzero, increasing segment size above the fragmentation threshold decreases the probability the datagram will arrive, which decreases throughput.

In theory, the optimum segment size, *S*, occurs when the IP datagrams carrying the segments are as large as possible without requiring fragmentation anywhere along the path from the source to the destination. In practice, finding *S* is difficult for several reasons. First, most implementations of TCP do not include a mechanism for doing so†. Second, because routers in an internet can change routes dynamically, the path datagrams follow between a pair of communicating computers can change dynamically and so can the size at which datagrams must be fragmented. Third, the optimum size depends on lower-level protocol headers (e.g., the segment size must be reduced to accommodate IP options). Research on the problem of finding an optimal segment size continues.

---

†To discover the path MTU, a sender probes the path by sending datagrams with the IP *do not fragment* bit set. It then decreases the size if ICMP error messages report that fragmentation was required.

13.14 TCP Checksum Computation

The *CHECKSUM* field in the TCP header contains a 16-bit integer checksum used to verify the integrity of the data as well as the TCP header. To compute the checksum, TCP software on the sending machine follows a procedure like the one described in Chapter 12 for UDP. It prepends a *pseudo header* to the segment, appends enough zero bits to make the segment a multiple of 16 bits, and computes the 16-bit checksum over the entire result. TCP does not count the pseudo header or padding in the segment length, nor does it transmit them. Also, it assumes the checksum field itself is zero for purposes of the checksum computation. As with other checksums, TCP uses 16-bit arithmetic and takes the one's complement of the one's complement sum. At the receiving site, TCP software performs the same computation to verify that the segment arrived intact.

The purpose of using a pseudo header is exactly the same as in UDP. It allows the receiver to verify that the segment has reached its correct destination, which includes both a host IP address as well as a protocol port number. Both the source and destination IP addresses are important to TCP because it must use them to identify a connection to which the segment belongs. Therefore, whenever a datagram arrives carrying a TCP segment, IP must pass to TCP the source and destination IP addresses from the datagram as well as the segment itself. Figure 13.9 shows the format of the pseudo header used in the checksum computation.

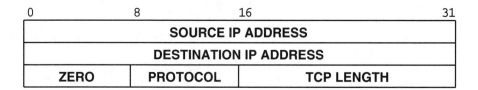

Figure 13.9 The format of the pseudo header used in TCP checksum computations. At the receiving site, this information is extracted from the IP datagram that carried the segment.

The sending TCP assigns field *PROTOCOL* the value that the underlying delivery system will use in its protocol type field. For IP datagrams carrying TCP, the value is 6. The *TCP LENGTH* field specifies the total length of the TCP segment including the TCP header. At the receiving end, information used in the pseudo header is extracted from the IP datagram that carried the segment and included in the checksum computation to verify that the segment arrived at the correct destination intact.

13.15 Acknowledgements And Retransmission

Because TCP sends data in variable length segments and because retransmitted segments can include more data than the original, acknowledgements cannot easily refer to datagrams or segments. Instead, they refer to a position in the stream using the stream sequence numbers. The receiver collects data octets from arriving segments and reconstructs an exact copy of the stream being sent. Because segments travel in IP datagrams, they can be lost or delivered out of order; the receiver uses the sequence numbers to reorder segments. At any time, the receiver will have reconstructed zero or more octets contiguously from the beginning of the stream, but may have additional pieces of the stream from datagrams that arrived out of order. The receiver always acknowledges the longest contiguous prefix of the stream that has been received correctly. Each acknowledgement specifies a sequence value one greater than the highest octet position in the contiguous prefix it received. Thus, the sender receives continuous feedback from the receiver as it progresses through the stream. We can summarize this important idea:

> *A TCP acknowledgement specifies the sequence number of the next octet that the receiver expects to receive.*

The TCP acknowledgement scheme is called *cumulative* because it reports how much of the stream has accumulated. Cumulative acknowledgements have both advantages and disadvantages. One advantage is that acknowledgements are both easy to generate and unambiguous. Another advantage is that lost acknowledgements do not necessarily force retransmission. A major disadvantage is that the sender does not receive information about all successful transmissions, but only about a single position in the stream that has been received.

To understand why lack of information about all successful transmissions makes cumulative acknowledgements less efficient, think of a window that spans *5000* octets starting at position *101* in the stream, and suppose the sender has transmitted all data in the window by sending five segments. Suppose further that the first segment is lost, but all others arrive intact. As each segment arrives, the receiver sends an acknowledgement, but each acknowledgement specifies octet *101*, the next highest contiguous octet it expects to receive. There is no way for the receiver to tell the sender that most of the data for the current window has arrived.

When a timeout occurs at the sender's side, the sender must choose between two potentially inefficient schemes. It may choose to retransmit one segment or all five segments. In this case retransmitting all five segments is inefficient. When the first segment arrives, the receiver will have all the data in the window, and will acknowledge *5101*. If the sender follows the accepted standard and retransmits only the first unacknowledged segment, it must wait for the acknowledgement before it can decide what and how much to send. Thus, it reverts to a simple positive acknowledgement protocol and may lose the advantages of having a large window.

13.16 Timeout And Retransmission

One of the most important and complex ideas in TCP is embedded in the way it handles timeout and retransmission. Like other reliable protocols, TCP expects the destination to send acknowledgements whenever it successfully receives new octets from the data stream. Every time it sends a segment, TCP starts a timer and waits for an acknowledgement. If the timer expires before data in the segment has been acknowledged, TCP assumes that the segment was lost or corrupted and retransmits it.

To understand why the TCP retransmission algorithm differs from the algorithm used in many network protocols, we need to remember that TCP is intended for use in an internet environment. In an internet, a segment traveling between a pair of machines may traverse a single, low-delay network (e.g., a high-speed LAN), or it may travel across multiple intermediate networks through multiple routers. Thus, it is impossible to know *a priori* how quickly acknowledgements will return to the source. Furthermore, the delay at each router depends on traffic, so the total time required for a segment to travel to the destination and an acknowledgement to return to the source varies dramatically from one instant to another. Figure 13.10, which shows measurements of round trip times across the global Internet for 100 consecutive packets, illustrates the problem. TCP software must accommodate both the vast differences in the time required to reach various destinations and the changes in time required to reach a given destination as traffic load varies.

TCP accommodates varying internet delays by using an *adaptive retransmission algorithm*. In essence, TCP monitors the performance of each connection and deduces reasonable values for timeouts. As the performance of a connection changes, TCP revises its timeout value (i.e., it adapts to the change).

To collect the data needed for an adaptive algorithm, TCP records the time at which each segment is sent and the time at which an acknowledgement arrives for the data in that segment. From the two times, TCP computes an elapsed time known as a *sample round trip time* or *round trip sample*. Whenever it obtains a new round trip sample, TCP adjusts its notion of the average round trip time for the connection. Usually, TCP software stores the estimated round trip time, *RTT*, as a weighted average and uses new round trip samples to change the average slowly. For example, when computing a new weighted average, one early averaging technique used a constant weighting factor, α, where $0 \le \alpha < 1$, to weight the old average against the latest round trip sample:

$$RTT = (\alpha * Old\_RTT) + ((1-\alpha) * New\_Round\_Trip\_Sample)$$

Choosing a value for α close to *1* makes the weighted average immune to changes that last a short time (e.g., a single segment that encounters long delay). Choosing a value for α close to *0* makes the weighted average respond to changes in delay very quickly.

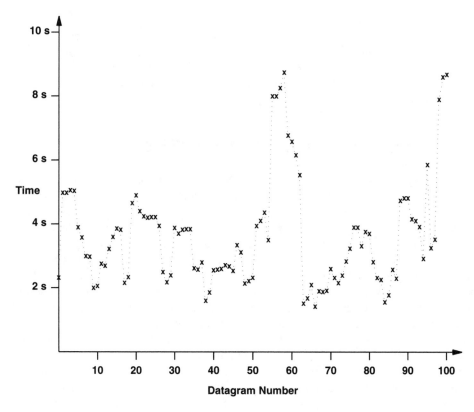

Figure 13.10 A plot of Internet round trip times as measured for 100 successive IP datagrams. Although the Internet now operates with
much lower delay, the delays still vary over time.

When it sends a packet, TCP computes a timeout value as a function of the current
round trip estimate. Early implementations of TCP used a constant weighting factor, β
($\beta > 1$), and made the timeout greater than the current round trip estimate:

$$\text{Timeout} = \beta * \text{RTT}$$

Choosing a value for β can be difficult. On one hand, to detect packet loss quickly, the
timeout value should be close to the current round trip time (i.e., β should be close to
1). Detecting packet loss quickly improves throughput because TCP will not wait an
unnecessarily long time before retransmitting. On the other hand, if $\beta = 1$, TCP is over-
ly eager — any small delay will cause an unnecessary retransmission, which wastes network bandwidth. The original specification recommended setting $\beta = 2$; more recent
work described below has produced better techniques for adjusting timeout.

We can summarize the ideas presented so far:

To accommodate the varying delays encountered in an internet en-vironment, TCP uses an adaptive retransmission algorithm that moni-tors delays on each connection and adjusts its timeout parameter ac-cordingly.

13.17 Accurate Measurement Of Round Trip Samples

In theory, measuring a round trip sample is trivial — it consists of subtracting the time at which the segment is sent from the time at which the acknowledgement arrives. However, complications arise because TCP uses a cumulative acknowledgement scheme in which an acknowledgement refers to data received, and not to the instance of a specific datagram that carried the data. Consider a retransmission. TCP forms a seg-ment, places it in a datagram and sends it, the timer expires, and TCP sends the seg-ment again in a second datagram. Because both datagrams carry exactly the same data, the sender has no way of knowing whether an acknowledgement corresponds to the ori-ginal or retransmitted datagram. This phenomenon has been called *acknowledgement ambiguity*, and TCP acknowledgements are said to be *ambiguous*.

Should TCP assume acknowledgements belong with the earliest (i.e., original) transmission or the latest (i.e., the most recent retransmission)? Surprisingly, neither as-sumption works. Associating the acknowledgement with the original transmission can make the estimated round trip time grow without bound in cases where an internet loses datagrams†. If an acknowledgement arrives after one or more retransmissions, TCP will measure the round trip sample from the original transmission, and compute a new RTT using the excessively long sample. Thus, RTT will grow slightly. The next time TCP sends a segment, the larger RTT will result in slightly longer timeouts, so if an acknowledgement arrives after one or more retransmissions, the next sample round trip time will be even larger, and so on.

Associating the acknowledgement with the most recent retransmission can also fail. Consider what happens when the end-to-end delay suddenly increases. When TCP sends a segment, it uses the old round trip estimate to compute a timeout, which is now too small. The segment arrives and an acknowledgement starts back, but the increase in delay means the timer expires before the acknowledgement arrives, and TCP retransmits the segment. Shortly after TCP retransmits, the first acknowledgement arrives and is associated with the retransmission. The round trip sample will be much too small and will result in a slight decrease of the estimated round trip time, RTT. Unfortunately, lowering the estimated round trip time guarantees that TCP will set the timeout too small for the next segment. Ultimately, the estimated round trip time can stabilize at a value, T, such that the correct round trip time is slightly longer than some multiple of T. Implementations of TCP that associate acknowledgements with the most recent re-transmission have been observed in a stable state with RTT slightly less than one-half of the correct value (i.e., TCP sends each segment exactly twice even though no loss occurs).

---

†The estimate can only grow arbitrarily large if every segment is lost at least once.

13.18 Karn's Algorithm And Timer Backoff

If the original transmission and the most recent transmission both fail to provide accurate round trip times, what should TCP do? The accepted answer is simple: TCP should not update the round trip estimate for retransmitted segments. This idea, known as *Karn's Algorithm*, avoids the problem of ambiguous acknowledgements altogether by only adjusting the estimated round trip for unambiguous acknowledgements (acknowledgements that arrive for segments that have only been transmitted once).

Of course, a simplistic implementation of Karn's algorithm, one that merely ignores times from retransmitted segments, can lead to failure as well. Consider what happens when TCP sends a segment after a sharp increase in delay. TCP computes a timeout using the existing round trip estimate. The timeout will be too small for the new delay and will force retransmission. If TCP ignores acknowledgements from retransmitted segments, it will never update the estimate and the cycle will continue.

To accommodate such failures, Karn's algorithm requires the sender to combine retransmission timeouts with a *timer backoff* strategy. The backoff technique computes an initial timeout using a formula like the one shown above. However, if the timer expires and causes a retransmission, TCP increases the timeout. In fact, each time it must retransmit a segment, TCP increases the timeout (to keep timeouts from becoming ridiculously long, most implementations limit increases to an upper bound that is larger than the delay along any path in the internet).

Implementations use a variety of techniques to compute backoff. Most choose a multiplicative factor, γ, and set the new value to:

$$new\_timeout = \gamma * timeout$$

Typically, γ is *2*. (It has been argued that values of γ less than 2 lead to instabilities.) Other implementations use a table of multiplicative factors, allowing arbitrary backoff at each step†.

Karn's algorithm combines the backoff technique with round trip estimation to solve the problem of never increasing round trip estimates:

> *Karn's algorithm: When computing the round trip estimate, ignore samples that correspond to retransmitted segments, but use a backoff strategy, and retain the timeout value from a retransmitted packet for subsequent packets until a valid sample is obtained.*

Generally speaking, when an internet misbehaves, Karn's algorithm separates computation of the timeout value from the current round trip estimate. It uses the round trip estimate to compute an initial timeout value, but then backs off the timeout on each retransmission until it can successfully transfer a segment. When it sends subsequent segments, it retains the timeout value that results from backoff. Finally, when an acknowledgement arrives corresponding to a segment that did not require retransmission,

---

†Berkeley UNIX is the most notable system that uses a table of factors, but current values in the table are equivalent to using $\gamma=2$.

TCP recomputes the round trip estimate and resets the timeout accordingly. Experience shows that Karn's algorithm works well even in networks with high packet loss†.

13.19 Responding To High Variance In Delay

Research into round trip estimation has shown that the computations described above do not adapt to a wide range of variation in delay. Queueing theory suggests that the variation in round trip time, σ, varies proportional to $1/(1-L)$, where L is the current network load, $0 \leq L \leq 1$. If an internet is running at 50% of capacity, we expect the round trip delay to vary by a factor of $\pm 2\sigma$, or 4. When the load reaches 80%, we expect a variation of 10. The original TCP standard specified the technique for estimating round trip time that we described earlier. Using that technique and limiting β to the suggested value of 2 means the round trip estimation can adapt to loads of at most 30%.

The 1989 specification for TCP requires implementations to estimate both the average round trip time and the variance, and to use the estimated variance in place of the constant β. As a result, new implementations of TCP can adapt to a wider range of variation in delay and yield substantially higher throughput. Fortunately, the approximations require little computation; extremely efficient programs can be derived from the following simple equations:

$$DIFF = SAMPLE - Old\_RTT$$

$$Smoothed\_RTT = Old\_RTT + \delta * DIFF$$

$$DEV = Old\_DEV + \rho \, (|DIFF| - Old\_DEV)$$

$$Timeout = Smoothed\_RTT + \eta * DEV$$

where DEV is the estimated mean deviation, δ is a fraction between 0 and 1 that controls how quickly the new sample affects the weighted average, ρ is a fraction between 0 and 1 that controls how quickly the new sample affects the mean deviation, and η is a factor that controls how much the deviation affects the round trip timeout. To make the computation efficient, TCP chooses δ and ρ to each be an inverse of a power of 2, scales the computation by 2^n for an appropriate n, and uses integer arithmetic. Research suggests values of $\delta = 1/2^3$, $\rho = 1/2^2$, and $n = 3$ will work well. The original value for η in 4.3BSD UNIX was 2; it was changed to 4 in 4.4 BSD UNIX.

Figure 13.11 uses a set of randomly generated values to illustrate how the computed timeout changes as the roundtrip time varies. Although the roundtrip times are artificial, they follow a pattern observed in practice: successive packets show small variations in delay as the overall average rises or falls.

---

†Phil Karn is an amateur radio enthusiast who developed this algorithm to allow TCP communication across a high-loss packet radio connection.

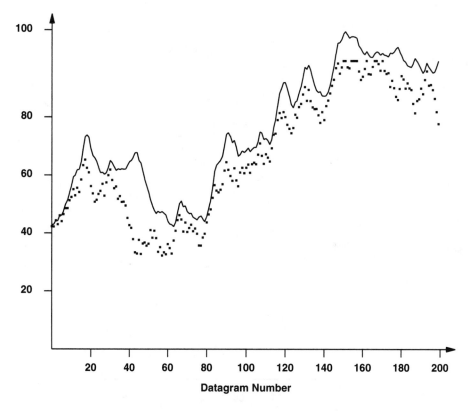

Figure 13.11 A set of 200 (randomly generated) roundtrip times shown as
dots, and the TCP retransmission timer shown as a solid line.
The timeout increases when delay varies.

Note that frequent change in the roundtrip time, including a cycle of increase and
decrease, can produce an increase in the retransmission timer. Furthermore, although
the timer tends to increase quickly when delay rises, it does not decrease as rapidly
when delay falls.

Figure 13.12 uses the data points from Figure 13.10 to show how TCP responds to
the extreme case of variance in delay. Recall that the goal is to have the retransmission
timer estimate the actual roundtrip time as closely as possible without underestimating.
The figure shows that although the timer responds quickly, it can underestimate. For
example, between the two successive datagrams marked with arrows, the delay doubles
from less than 4 seconds to more than 8. More important, the abrupt change follows a
period of relative stability in which the variation in delay is small, making it impossible
for any algorithm to anticipate the change. In the case of the TCP algorithm, because
the timeout (approximately 5) substantially underestimates the large delay, an unnecessary retransmission occurs. However, the estimate responds quickly to the increase in
delay, meaning that successive packets arrive without retransmission.

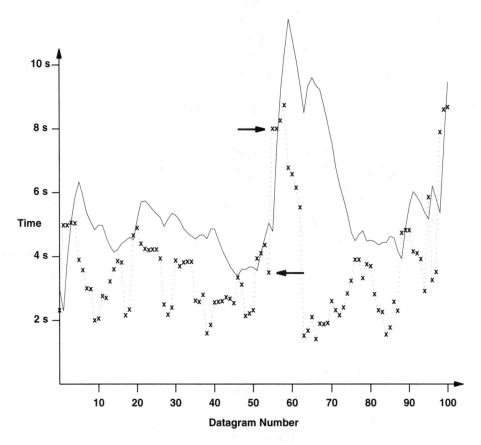

Figure 13.12 The TCP retransmission timer for the data from Figure 13.10.
Arrows mark two successive datagrams where the delay dou-
bles.

13.20 Response To Congestion

It may seem that TCP software could be designed by considering the interaction
between the two endpoints of a connection and the communication delays between
those endpoints. In practice, however, TCP must also react to *congestion* in the internet. Congestion is a condition of severe delay caused by an overload of datagrams at
one or more switching points (e.g., at routers). When congestion occurs, delays increase and the router begins to enqueue datagrams until it can route them. We must
remember that each router has finite storage capacity and that datagrams compete for
that storage (i.e., in a datagram based internet, there is no preallocation of resources to
individual TCP connections). In the worst case, the total number of datagrams arriving
at the congested router grows until the router reaches capacity and starts to drop datagrams.

Endpoints do not usually know the details of where congestion has occurred or why. To them, congestion simply means increased delay. Unfortunately, most transport protocols use timeout and retransmission, so they respond to increased delay by retransmitting datagrams. Retransmissions aggravate congestion instead of alleviating it. If unchecked, the increased traffic will produce increased delay, leading to increased traffic, and so on, until the network becomes useless. The condition is known as *congestion collapse.*

To avoid congestion collapse, TCP must reduce transmission rates when congestion occurs. Routers watch queue lengths and use techniques like ICMP source quench to inform hosts that congestion has occurred†, but transport protocols like TCP can help avoid congestion by reducing transmission rates automatically whenever delays occur. Of course, algorithms to avoid congestion must be constructed carefully because even under normal operating conditions an internet will exhibit wide variation in round trip delays.

To avoid congestion, the TCP standard now recommends using two techniques: *slow-start* and *multiplicative decrease.* They are related and can be implemented easily. We said that for each connection, TCP must remember the size of the receiver's window (i.e., the buffer size advertised in acknowledgements). To control congestion TCP maintains a second limit, called the *congestion window limit* or *congestion window*, that it uses to restrict data flow to less than the receiver's buffer size when congestion occurs. That is, at any time, TCP acts as if the window size is:

Allowed_window = min(receiver_advertisement, congestion_window)

In the steady state on a non-congested connection, the congestion window is the same size as the receiver's window. Reducing the congestion window reduces the traffic TCP will inject into the connection. To estimate congestion window size, TCP assumes that most datagram loss comes from congestion and uses the following strategy:

> *Multiplicative Decrease Congestion Avoidance: Upon loss of a segment, reduce the congestion window by half (down to a minimum of at least one segment). For those segments that remain in the allowed window, backoff the retransmission timer exponentially.*

Because TCP reduces the congestion window by half for *every* loss, it decreases the window exponentially if loss continues. In other words, if congestion is likely, TCP reduces the volume of traffic exponentially and the rate of retransmission exponentially. If loss continues, TCP eventually limits transmission to a single datagram and continues to double timeout values before retransmitting. The idea is to provide quick and significant traffic reduction to allow routers enough time to clear the datagrams already in their queues.

How can TCP recover when congestion ends? You might suspect that TCP should reverse the multiplicative decrease and double the congestion window when traffic begins to flow again. However, doing so produces an unstable system that oscillates wild-

---

†In a congested network, queue lengths grow exponentially for a significant time.

ly between no traffic and congestion. Instead, TCP uses a technique called *slow-start†* to scale up transmission:

> *Slow-Start (Additive) Recovery: Whenever starting traffic on a new connection or increasing traffic after a period of congestion, start the congestion window at the size of a single segment and increase the congestion window by one segment each time an acknowledgement arrives.*

Slow-start avoids swamping the internet with additional traffic immediately after congestion clears or when new connections suddenly start.

The term *slow-start* may be a misnomer because under ideal conditions, the start is not very slow. TCP initializes the congestion window to *1*, sends an initial segment, and waits. When the acknowledgement arrives, it increases the congestion window to *2*, sends two segments, and waits. When the two acknowledgements arrive they each increase the congestion window by *1*, so TCP can send *4* segments. Acknowledgements for those will increase the congestion window to *8*. Within four round-trip times, TCP can send *16* segments, often enough to reach the receiver's window limit. Even for extremely large windows, it takes only $\log_2 N$ round trips before TCP can send *N* segments.

To avoid increasing the window size too quickly and causing additional congestion, TCP adds one additional restriction. Once the congestion window reaches one half of its original size before congestion, TCP enters a *congestion avoidance* phase and slows down the rate of increment. During congestion avoidance, it increases the congestion window by *1* only if all segments in the window have been acknowledged.

Taken together, slow-start increase, multiplicative decrease, congestion avoidance, measurement of variation, and exponential timer backoff improve the performance of TCP dramatically without adding any significant computational overhead to the protocol software. Versions of TCP that use these techniques have improved the performance of previous versions by factors of *2* to *10*.

13.21 Congestion, Tail Drop, And TCP

We said that communication protocols are divided into layers to make it possible for designers to focus on a single problem at a time. The separation of functionality into layers is both necessary and useful — it means that one layer can be changed without affecting other layers, but it means that layers operate in isolation. For example, because it operates end-to-end, TCP remains unchanged when the path between the endpoints changes (e.g., routes change or additional networks routers are added). However, the isolation of layers restricts inter-layer communication. In particular, although TCP on the original source interacts with TCP on the ultimate destination, it cannot interact with lower layer elements along the path. Thus, neither the sending nor receiving

---

†The term *slow-start* is attributed to John Nagle; the technique was originally called *soft-start*.

TCP receives reports about conditions in the network, nor does either end inform lower layers along the path before transferring data.

Researchers have observed that the lack of communication between layers means that the choice of policy or implementation at one layer can have a dramatic effect on the performance of higher layers. In the case of TCP, policies that routers use to handle datagrams can have a significant effect on both the performance of a single TCP connection and the aggregate throughput of all connections. For example, if a router delays some datagrams more than others†, TCP will back off its retransmission timer. If the delay exceeds the retransmission timeout, TCP will assume congestion has occurred. Thus, although each layer is defined independently, researchers try to devise mechanisms and implementations that work well with protocols in other layers.

The most important interaction between IP implementation policies and TCP occurs when a router becomes overrun and drops datagrams. Because a router places each incoming datagram in a queue in memory until it can be processed, the policy focuses on queue management. When datagrams arrive faster than they can be forwarded, the queue grows; when datagrams arrive slower than they can be forwarded, the queue shrinks. However, because memory is finite, the queue cannot grow without bound. Early router software used a *tail-drop* policy to manage queue overflow:

> *Tail-Drop Policy For Routers: if the input queue is filled when a datagram arrives, discard the datagram.*

The name *tail-drop* arises from the effect of the policy on an arriving sequence of datagrams. Once the queue fills, the router begins discarding all additional datagrams. That is, the router discards the "tail" of the sequence.

Tail-drop has an interesting effect on TCP. In the simple case where datagrams traveling through a router carry segments from a single TCP connection, the loss causes TCP to enter slow-start, which reduces throughput until TCP begins receiving ACKs and increases the congestion window. A more severe problem can occur, however, when the datagrams traveling through a router carry segments from many TCP connections because tail-drop can cause global synchronization. To see why, observe that datagrams are typically multiplexed, with successive datagrams each coming from a different source. Thus, a tail-drop policy makes it likely that the router will discard one segment from N connections rather than N segments from one connection. The simultaneous loss causes all N instances of TCP to enter slow-start at the same time.

13.22 Random Early Discard (RED)

How can a router avoid global synchronization? The answer lies in a clever scheme that avoids tail-drop whenever possible. Known as *Random Early Discard*, *Random Early Drop*, or *Random Early Detection*, the scheme is more frequently referred to by its acronym, *RED*. A router that implements RED uses two threshold

---

†Technically, variance in delay is referred to as *jitter*.

values to mark positions in the queue: T_{min} and T_{max}. The general operation of RED can be described by three rules that determine the disposition of each arriving datagram:

- If the queue currently contains fewer than T_{min} datagrams, add the new datagram to the queue.
- If the queue contains more than T_{max} datagrams, discard the new datagram.
- If the queue contains between T_{min} and T_{max} datagrams, randomly discard the datagram according to a probability, p.

The randomness of RED means that instead of waiting until the queue overflows and then driving many TCP connections into slow-start, a router slowly and randomly drops datagrams as congestion increases. We can summarize:

> *RED Policy For Routers: if the input queue is full when a datagram arrives, discard the datagram; if the input queue is not full but the size exceeds a minimum threshold, avoid synchronization by discarding the datagram with probability* p.

The key to making RED work well lies in the choice of the thresholds T_{min} and T_{max}, and the discard probability p. T_{min} must be large enough to ensure that the output link has high utilization. Furthermore, because RED operates like tail-drop when the queue size exceeds T_{max}, the value must be greater than T_{min} by more than the typical increase in queue size during one TCP round trip time (e.g., set T_{max} at least twice as large as T_{min}). Otherwise, RED can cause the same global oscillations as tail-drop.

Computation of the discard probability, p, is the most complex aspect of RED. Instead of using a constant, a new value of p is computed for each datagram; the value depends on the relationship between the current queue size and the thresholds. To understand the scheme, observe that all RED processing can be viewed probabilistically. When the queue size is less than T_{min}, RED does not discard any datagrams, making the discard probability *0*. Similarly, when the queue size is greater than T_{max}, RED discards all datagrams, making the discard probability *1*. For intermediate values of queue size, (i.e., those between T_{min} and T_{max}), the probability can vary from *0* to *1* linearly.

Although the linear scheme forms the basis of RED's probability computation, a change must be made to avoid overreacting. The need for the change arises because network traffic is bursty, which results in rapid fluctuations of a router's queue. If RED used a simplistic linear scheme, later datagrams in each burst would be assigned high probability of being dropped (because they arrive when the queue has more entries). However, a router should not drop datagrams unnecessarily because doing so has a negative impact on TCP throughput. Thus, if a burst is short, it is unwise to drop datagrams because the queue will never overflow. Of course, RED cannot postpone discard indefinitely because a long-term burst will overflow the queue, resulting in a tail-drop policy which has the potential to cause global synchronization problems.

How can RED assign a higher discard probability as the queue fills without discarding datagrams from each burst? The answer lies in a technique borrowed from TCP: instead of using the actual queue size at any instant, RED computes a weighted average queue size, *avg*, and uses the average size to determine the probability. The value of *avg* is an exponential weighted average, updated each time a datagram arrives according to the equation:

$$avg = (1 - \gamma) * \text{Old\_avg} + \gamma * \text{Current\_queue\_size}$$

where γ denotes a value between *0* and *1*. If γ is small enough, the average will track long term trends, but will remain immune to short bursts†

In addition to equations that determine γ, RED contains other details that we have glossed over. For example, RED computations can be made extremely efficient by choosing constants as powers of two and using integer arithmetic. Another important detail concerns the measurement of queue size, which affects both the RED computation and its overall effect on TCP. In particular, because the time required to forward a datagram is proportional to its size, it makes sense to measure the queue in octets rather than in datagrams; doing so requires only minor changes to the equations for p and γ. Measuring queue size in octets affects the type of traffic dropped because it makes the discard probability proportional to the amount of data a sender puts in the stream rather than the number of segments. Small datagrams (e.g., those that carry remote login traffic or requests to servers) have lower probability of being dropped than large datagrams (e.g., those that carry file transfer traffic). One positive consequence of using size is that when acknowledgements travel over a congested path, they have a lower probability of being dropped. As a result, if a (large) data segment does arrive, the sending TCP will receive the ACK and will avoid unnecessary retransmission.

Both analysis and simulations show that RED works well. It handles congestion, avoids the synchronization that results from tail drop, and allows short bursts without dropping datagrams unnecessarily. The IETF now recommends that routers implement RED.

13.23 Establishing A TCP Connection

To establish a connection, TCP uses a *three-way handshake*. In the simplest case, the handshake proceeds as Figure 13.13 shows.

---

†An example value suggested for γ is .002.

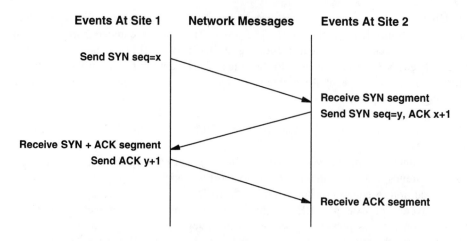

Figure 13.13 The sequence of messages in a three-way handshake. Time
proceeds down the page; diagonal lines represent segments sent
between sites. SYN segments carry initial sequence number
information.

The first segment of a handshake can be identified because it has the SYN† bit set in
the code field. The second message has both the SYN bit and ACK bits set, indicating
that it acknowledges the first SYN segment as well as continuing the handshake. The
final handshake message is only an acknowledgement and is merely used to inform the
destination that both sides agree that a connection has been established.

Usually, the TCP software on one machine waits passively for the handshake, and
the TCP software on another machine initiates it. However, the handshake is carefully
designed to work even if both machines attempt to initiate a connection simultaneously.
Thus, a connection can be established from either end or from both ends simultaneously. Once the connection has been established, data can flow in both directions equally
well. There is no master or slave.

The three-way handshake is both necessary and sufficient for correct synchronization between the two ends of the connection. To understand why, remember that TCP
builds on an unreliable packet delivery service, so messages can be lost, delayed, duplicated, or delivered out of order. Thus, the protocol must use a timeout mechanism and
retransmit lost requests. Trouble arises if retransmitted and original requests arrive
while the connection is being established, or if retransmitted requests are delayed until
after a connection has been established, used, and terminated. A three-way handshake
(plus the rule that TCP ignores additional requests for connection after a connection has
been established) solves these problems.

---

†SYN stands for *synchronization*; it is pronounced "sin."

13.24 Initial Sequence Numbers

The three-way handshake accomplishes two important functions. It guarantees that both sides are ready to transfer data (and that they know they are both ready), and it allows both sides to agree on initial sequence numbers. Sequence numbers are sent and acknowledged during the handshake. Each machine must choose an initial sequence number at random that it will use to identify bytes in the stream it is sending. Sequence numbers cannot always start at the same value. In particular, TCP cannot merely choose sequence *1* every time it creates a connection (one of the exercises examines problems that can arise if it does). Of course, it is important that both sides agree on an initial number, so octet numbers used in acknowledgements agree with those used in data segments.

To see how machines can agree on sequence numbers for two streams after only three messages, recall that each segment contains both a sequence number field and an acknowledgement field. The machine that initiates a handshake, call it *A*, passes its initial sequence number, *x*, in the sequence field of the first SYN segment in the three-way handshake. The second machine, *B*, receives the SYN, records the sequence number, and replies by sending its initial sequence number in the sequence field as well as an acknowledgement that specifies *B* expects octet *x+1*. In the final message of the handshake, *A* "acknowledges" receiving from *B* all octets through *y*. In all cases, acknowledgements follow the convention of using the number of the *next* octet expected.

We have described how TCP usually carries out the three-way handshake by exchanging segments that contain a minimum amount of information. Because of the protocol design, it is possible to send data along with the initial sequence numbers in the handshake segments. In such cases, the TCP software must hold the data until the handshake completes. Once a connection has been established, the TCP software can release data being held and deliver it to a waiting application program quickly. The reader is referred to the protocol specification for the details.

13.25 Closing a TCP Connection

Two programs that use TCP to communicate can terminate the conversation gracefully using the *close* operation. Internally, TCP uses a modified three-way handshake to close connections. Recall that TCP connections are full duplex and that we view them as containing two independent stream transfers, one going in each direction. When an application program tells TCP that it has no more data to send, TCP will close the connection *in one direction*. To close its half of a connection, the sending TCP finishes transmitting the remaining data, waits for the receiver to acknowledge it, and then sends a segment with the FIN bit set. The receiving TCP acknowledges the FIN segment and informs the application program on its end that no more data is available (e.g., using the operating system's end-of-file mechanism).

Once a connection has been closed in a given direction, TCP refuses to accept more data for that direction. Meanwhile, data can continue to flow in the opposite

direction until the sender closes it. Of course, acknowledgements continue to flow back
to the sender even after a connection has been closed. When both directions have been
closed, the TCP software at each endpoint deletes its record of the connection.

The details of closing a connection are even more subtle than suggested above because TCP uses a modified three-way handshake to close a connection. Figure 13.14 illustrates the procedure.

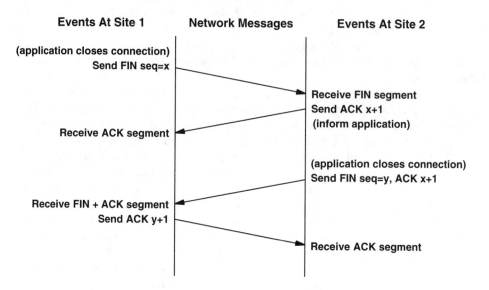

Figure 13.14 The modified three-way handshake used to close connections.
The site that receives the first FIN segment acknowledges it
immediately and then delays before sending the second FIN
segment.

The difference between three-way handshakes used to establish and break connections
occurs after a machine receives the initial FIN segment. Instead of generating a second
FIN segment immediately, TCP sends an acknowledgement and then informs the application of the request to shut down. Informing the application program of the request
and obtaining a response may take considerable time (e.g., it may involve human interaction). The acknowledgement prevents retransmission of the initial FIN segment
during the wait. Finally, when the application program instructs TCP to shut down the
connection completely, TCP sends the second FIN segment and the original site replies
with the third message, an ACK.

13.26 TCP Connection Reset

Normally, an application program uses the close operation to shut down a connection when it finishes using it. Thus, closing connections is considered a normal part of use, analogous to closing files. Sometimes abnormal conditions arise that force an application program or the network software to break a connection. TCP provides a reset facility for such abnormal disconnections.

To reset a connection, one side initiates termination by sending a segment with the RST bit in the *CODE* field set. The other side responds to a reset segment immediately by aborting the connection. TCP also informs the application program that a reset occurred. A reset is an instantaneous abort that means that transfer in both directions ceases immediately, and resources such as buffers are released.

13.27 TCP State Machine

Like most protocols, the operation of TCP can best be explained with a theoretical model called a *finite state machine*. Figure 13.15 shows the TCP finite state machine, with circles representing states and arrows representing transitions between them. The label on each transition shows what TCP receives to cause the transition and what it sends in response. For example, the TCP software at each endpoint begins in the *CLOSED* state. Application programs must issue either a *passive open* command (to wait for a connection from another machine), or an *active open* command (to initiate a connection). An active open command forces a transition from the *CLOSED* state to the *SYN SENT* state. When TCP follows the transition, it emits a SYN segment. When the other end returns a segment that contains a SYN plus ACK, TCP moves to the *ESTABLISHED* state and begins data transfer.

The *TIMED WAIT* state reveals how TCP handles some of the problems incurred with unreliable delivery. TCP keeps a notion of *maximum segment lifetime (MSL)*, the maximum time an old segment can remain alive in an internet. To avoid having segments from a previous connection interfere with a current one, TCP moves to the *TIMED WAIT* state after closing a connection. It remains in that state for twice the maximum segment lifetime before deleting its record of the connection. If any duplicate segments happen to arrive for the connection during the timeout interval, TCP will reject them. However, to handle cases where the last acknowledgement was lost, TCP acknowledges valid segments and restarts the timer. Because the timer allows TCP to distinguish old connections from new ones, it prevents TCP from responding with a *RST* (reset) if the other end retransmits a *FIN* request.

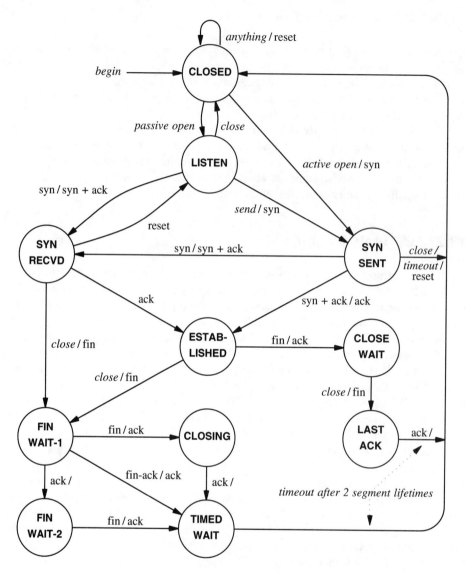

Figure 13.15 The TCP finite state machine. Each endpoint begins in the *closed* state. Labels on transitions show the input that caused the transition followed by the output if any.

13.28 Forcing Data Delivery

We have said that TCP is free to divide the stream of data into segments for transmission without regard to the size of transfer that application programs use. The chief advantage of allowing TCP to choose a division is efficiency. It can accumulate enough octets in a buffer to make segments reasonably long, reducing the high overhead that occurs when segments contain only a few data octets.

Although buffering improves network throughput, it can interfere with some applications. Consider using a TCP connection to pass characters from an interactive terminal to a remote machine. The user expects instant response to each keystroke. If the sending TCP buffers the data, response may be delayed, perhaps for hundreds of keystrokes. Similarly, because the receiving TCP may buffer data before making it available to the application program on its end, forcing the sender to transmit data may not be sufficient to guarantee delivery.

To accommodate interactive users, TCP provides a *push* operation that an application program can use to force delivery of octets currently in the stream without waiting for the buffer to fill. The push operation does more than force TCP to send a segment. It also requests TCP to set the *PSH* bit in the segment code field, so the data will be delivered to the application program on the receiving end. Thus, when sending data from an interactive terminal, the application uses the push function after each keystroke. Similarly, application programs can force output to be sent and displayed on the terminal promptly by calling the push function after writing a character or line.

13.29 Reserved TCP Port Numbers

Like UDP, TCP combines static and dynamic port binding, using a set of *well-known port assignments* for commonly invoked programs (e.g., electronic mail), but leaving most port numbers available for the operating system to allocate as programs need them. Although the standard originally reserved port numbers less than *256* for use as well-known ports, numbers over 1024 have now been assigned. Figure 13.16 lists some of the currently assigned TCP ports. It should be pointed out that although TCP and UDP port numbers are independent, the designers have chosen to use the same integer port numbers for any service that is accessible from both UDP and TCP. For example, a domain name server can be accessed either with TCP or with UDP. In either protocol, port number *53* has been reserved for servers in the domain name system.

13.30 TCP Performance

As we have seen, TCP is a complex protocol that handles communication over a wide variety of underlying network technologies. Many people assume that because TCP tackles a much more complex task than other transport protocols, the code must be cumbersome and inefficient. Surprisingly, the generality we discussed does not seem to hinder TCP performance. Experiments at Berkeley have shown that the same TCP that operates efficiently over the global Internet can deliver 8 Mbps of sustained throughput of user data between two workstations on a 10 Mbps Ethernet†. At Cray Research, Inc., researchers have demonstrated TCP throughput approaching a gigabit per second.

Decimal	Keyword	UNIX Keyword	Description
0			Reserved
1	TCPMUX	-	TCP Multiplexor
7	ECHO	echo	Echo
9	DISCARD	discard	Discard
11	USERS	systat	Active Users
13	DAYTIME	daytime	Daytime
15	-	netstat	Network status program
17	QUOTE	qotd	Quote of the Day
19	CHARGEN	chargen	Character Generator
20	FTP-DATA	ftp-data	File Transfer Protocol (data)
21	FTP	ftp	File Transfer Protocol
22	SSH	ssh	Secure Shell
23	TELNET	telnet	Terminal Connection
25	SMTP	smtp	Simple Mail Transport Protocol
37	TIME	time	Time
43	NICNAME	whois	Who Is
53	DOMAIN	nameserver	Domain Name Server
67	BOOTPS	bootps	BOOTP or DHCP Server
77	-	rje	any private RJE service
79	FINGER	finger	Finger
80	WWW	www	World Wide Web Server
88	KERBEROS	kerberos	Kerberos Security Service
95	SUPDUP	supdup	SUPDUP Protocol
101	HOSTNAME	hostnames	NIC Host Name Server
102	ISO-TSAP	iso-tsap	ISO-TSAP
103	X400	x400	X.400 Mail Service
104	X400-SND	x400-snd	X.400 Mail Sending
110	POP3	pop3	Post Office Protocol Vers. 3
111	SUNRPC	sunrpc	SUN Remote Procedure Call
113	AUTH	auth	Authentication Service
117	UUCP-PATH	uucp-path	UUCP Path Service
119	NNTP	nntp	USENET News Transfer Protocol
123	NTP	ntp	Network Time Protocol
139	NETBIOS-SSN	-	NETBIOS Session Service
161	SNMP	snmp	Simple Network Management Protocol

Figure 13.16 Examples of currently assigned TCP port numbers. To the extent possible, protocols like UDP use the same numbers.

---

†Ethernet, IP, and TCP headers and the required inter-packet gap account for the remaining bandwidth.

13.31 Silly Window Syndrome And Small Packets

Researchers who helped developed TCP observed a serious performance problem that can result when the sending and receiving applications operate at different speeds. To understand the problem, remember that TCP buffers incoming data, and consider what can happen if a receiving application chooses to read incoming data one octet at a time. When a connection is first established, the receiving TCP allocates a buffer of *K* bytes, and uses the *WINDOW* field in acknowledgement segments to advertise the available buffer size to the sender. If the sending application generates data quickly, the sending TCP will transmit segments with data for the entire window. Eventually, the sender will receive an acknowledgement that specifies the entire window has been filled, and no additional space remains in the receiver's buffer.

When the receiving application reads an octet of data from a full buffer, one octet of space becomes available. We said that when space becomes available in its buffer, TCP on the receiving machine generates an acknowledgement that uses the *WINDOW* field to inform the sender. In the example, the receiver will advertise a window of *1* octet. When it learns that space is available, the sending TCP responds by transmitting a segment that contains one octet of data.

Although single-octet window advertisements work correctly to keep the receiver's buffer filled, they result in a series of small data segments. The sending TCP must compose a segment that contains one octet of data, place the segment in an IP datagram, and transmit the result. When the receiving application reads another octet, TCP generates another acknowledgement, which causes the sender to transmit another segment that contains one octet of data. The resulting interaction can reach a steady state in which TCP sends a separate segment for each octet of data.

Transferring small segments consumes unnecessary network bandwidth and introduces unnecessary computational overhead. The transmission of small segments consumes unnecessary network bandwidth because each datagram carries only one octet of data; the ratio of header to data is large. Computational overhead arises because TCP on both the sending and receiving computers must process each segment. The sending TCP software must allocate buffer space, form a segment header, and compute a checksum for the segment. Similarly, IP software on the sending machine must encapsulate the segment in a datagram, compute a header checksum, route the datagram, and transfer it to the appropriate network interface. On the receiving machine, IP must verify the IP header checksum and pass the segment to TCP. TCP must verify the segment checksum, examine the sequence number, extract the data, and place it in a buffer.

Although we have described how small segments result when a receiver advertises a small available window, a sender can also cause each segment to contain a small amount of data. For example, imagine a TCP implementation that aggressively sends data whenever it is available, and consider what happens if a sending application generates data one octet at a time. After the application generates an octet of data, TCP creates and transmits a segment. TCP can also send a small segment if an application generates data in fixed-sized blocks of *B* octets, and the sending TCP extracts data from the buffer in maximum segment sized blocks, M, where $M \neq B$, because the last block in a buffer can be small.

Known as *silly window syndrome (SWS)*, the problem plagued early TCP implementations. To summarize,

> *Early TCP implementations exhibited a problem known as* silly window syndrome *in which each acknowledgement advertises a small amount of space available and each segment carries a small amount of data.*

13.32 Avoiding Silly Window Syndrome

TCP specifications now include heuristics that prevent silly window syndrome. A heuristic used on the sending machine avoids transmitting a small amount of data in each segment. Another heuristic used on the receiving machine avoids sending small increments in window advertisements that can trigger small data packets. Although the heuristics work well together, having both the sender and receiver avoid silly window helps ensure good performance in the case that one end of a connection fails to correctly implement silly window avoidance.

In practice, TCP software must contain both sender and receiver silly window avoidance code. To understand why, recall that a TCP connection is full duplex — data can flow in either direction. Thus, an implementation of TCP includes code to send data as well as code to receive it.

13.32.1 Receive-Side Silly Window Avoidance

The heuristic a receiver uses to avoid silly window is straightforward and easiest to understand. In general, a receiver maintains an internal record of the currently available window, but delays advertising an increase in window size to the sender until the window can advance a significant amount. The definition of "significant" depends on the receiver's buffer size and the maximum segment size. TCP defines it to be the minimum of one half of the receiver's buffer or the number of data octets in a maximum-sized segment.

Receive-side silly window prevents small window advertisements in the case where a receiving application extracts data octets slowly. For example, when a receiver's buffer fills completely, it sends an acknowledgement that contains a zero window advertisement. As the receiving application extracts octets from the buffer, the receiving TCP computes the newly available space in the buffer. Instead of sending a window advertisement immediately, however, the receiver waits until the available space reaches one half of the total buffer size or a maximum sized segment. Thus, the sender always receives large increments in the current window, allowing it to transfer large segments. The heuristic can be summarized as follows.

Receive-Side Silly Window Avoidance: Before sending an updated window advertisement after advertising a zero window, wait for space to become available that is either at least 50% of the total buffer size or equal to a maximum sized segment.

13.32.2 Delayed Acknowledgements

Two approaches have been taken to implement silly window avoidance on the receive side. In the first approach, TCP acknowledges each segment that arrives, but does not advertise an increase in its window until the window reaches the limits specified by the silly window avoidance heuristic. In the second approach, TCP delays sending an acknowledgement when silly window avoidance specifies that the window is not sufficiently large to advertise. The standards recommend delaying acknowledgements.

Delayed acknowledgements have both advantages and disadvantages. The chief advantage arises because delayed acknowledgements can decrease traffic and thereby increase throughput. For example, if additional data arrives during the delay period, a single acknowledgement will acknowledge all data received. If the receiving application generates a response immediately after data arrives (e.g., character echo in a remote login session), a short delay may permit the acknowledgement to piggyback on a data segment. Furthermore, TCP cannot move its window until the receiving application extracts data from the buffer. In cases where the receiving application reads data as soon as it arrives, a short delay allows TCP to send a single segment that acknowledges the data and advertises an updated window. Without delayed acknowledgements, TCP will acknowledge the arrival of data immediately, and later send an additional acknowledgement to update the window size.

The disadvantages of delayed acknowledgements should be clear. Most important, if a receiver delays acknowledgements too long, the sending TCP will retransmit the segment. Unnecessary retransmissions lower throughput because they waste network bandwidth. In addition, retransmissions require computational overhead on the sending and receiving machines. Furthermore, TCP uses the arrival of acknowledgements to estimate round trip times; delaying acknowledgements can confuse the estimate and make retransmission times too long.

To avoid potential problems, the TCP standards place a limit on the time TCP delays an acknowledgement. Implementations cannot delay an acknowledgement for more than 500 milliseconds. Furthermore, to guarantee that TCP receives a sufficient number of round trip estimates, the standard recommends that a receiver should acknowledge at least every other data segment.

13.32.3 Send-Side Silly Window Avoidance

The heuristic a sending TCP uses to avoid silly window syndrome is both surprising and elegant. Recall that the goal is to avoid sending small segments. Also recall that a sending application can generate data in arbitrarily small blocks (e.g., one octet at a time). Thus, to achieve the goal, a sending TCP must allow the sending application to make multiple calls to *write*, and must collect the data transferred in each call before transmitting it in a single, large segment. That is, a sending TCP must delay sending a segment until it can accumulate a reasonable amount of data. The technique is known as *clumping*.

The question arises, "How long should TCP wait before transmitting data?" On one hand, if TCP waits too long, the application experiences large delays. More important, TCP cannot know whether to wait because it cannot know whether the application will generate more data in the near future. On the other hand, if TCP does not wait long enough, segments will be small and throughput will be low.

Protocols designed prior to TCP confronted the same problem and used techniques to clump data into larger packets. For example, to achieve efficient transfer across a network, early remote terminal protocols delayed transmitting each keystroke for a few hundred milliseconds to determine whether the user would continue to press keys. Because TCP is designed to be general, however, it can be used by a diverse set of applications. Characters may travel across a TCP connection because a user is typing on a keyboard or because a program is transferring a file. A fixed delay is not optimal for all applications.

Like the algorithm TCP uses for retransmission and the slow-start algorithm used to avoid congestion, the technique a sending TCP uses to avoid sending small packets is adaptive — the delay depends on the current performance of the internet. Like slow-start, send-side silly window avoidance is called *self clocking* because it does not compute delays. Instead, TCP uses the arrival of an acknowledgement to trigger the transmission of additional packets. The heuristic can be summarized:

> *Send-Side Silly Window Avoidance: When a sending application generates additional data to be sent over a connection for which previous data has been transmitted but not acknowledged, place the new data in the output buffer as usual, but do not send additional segments until there is sufficient data to fill a maximum-sized segment. If still waiting to send when an acknowledgement arrives, send all data that has accumulated in the buffer. Apply the rule even when the user requests a push operation.*

If an application generates data one octet at a time, TCP will send the first octet immediately. However, until the ACK arrives, TCP will accumulate additional octets in its buffer. Thus, if the application is reasonably fast compared to the network (i.e., a file transfer), successive segments will each contain many octets. If the application is slow compared to the network (e.g., a user typing on a keyboard), small segments will be sent without long delay.

Known as the *Nagle algorithm* after its inventor, the technique is especially elegant because it requires little computational overhead. A host does not need to keep separate timers for each connection, nor does the host need to examine a clock when an application generates data. More important, although the technique adapts to arbitrary combinations of network delay, maximum segment size, and application speed, it does not lower throughput in conventional cases.

To understand why throughput remains high for conventional communication, observe that applications optimized for high throughput do not generate data one octet at a time (doing so would incur unnecessary operating system overhead). Instead, such applications write large blocks of data with each call. Thus, the outgoing TCP buffer begins with sufficient data for at least one maximum size segment. Furthermore, because the application produces data faster than TCP can transfer data, the sending buffer remains nearly full, and TCP does not delay transmission. As a result, TCP continues to send segments at whatever rate the internet can tolerate, while the application continues to fill the buffer. To summarize:

> *TCP now requires the sender and receiver to implement heuristics that avoid the silly window syndrome. A receiver avoids advertising a small window, and a sender uses an adaptive scheme to delay transmission so it can clump data into large segments.*

13.33 Summary

The Transmission Control Protocol, TCP, defines a key service provided by an internet, namely, reliable stream delivery. TCP provides a full duplex connection between two machines, allowing them to exchange large volumes of data efficiently.

Because it uses a sliding window protocol, TCP can make efficient use of a network. Because it makes few assumptions about the underlying delivery system, TCP is flexible enough to operate over a large variety of delivery systems. Because it provides flow control, TCP allows systems of widely varying speeds to communicate.

The basic unit of transfer used by TCP is a segment. Segments are used to pass data or control information (e.g., to allow TCP software on two machines to establish connections or break them). The segment format permits a machine to piggyback acknowledgements for data flowing in one direction by including them in the segment headers of data flowing in the opposite direction.

TCP implements flow control by having the receiver advertise the amount of data it is willing to accept. It also supports out-of-band messages using an urgent data facility and forces delivery using a push mechanism.

The current TCP standard specifies exponential backoff for retransmission timers and congestion avoidance algorithms like slow-start, multiplicative decrease, and additive increase. In addition, TCP uses heuristics to avoid transferring small packets. Finally, the IETF recommends that routers use RED instead of tail-drop because doing so avoids TCP synchronization and improves throughput.

FOR FURTHER STUDY

The standard for TCP can be found in Postel [RFC 793]; Braden [RFC 1122] contains an update that clarifies several points. Clark [RFC 813] describes TCP window management, Clark [RFC 816] describes fault isolation and recovery, and Postel [RFC 879] reports on TCP maximum segment sizes. Nagle [RFC 896] comments on congestion in TCP/IP networks and explains the effect of self clocking for send-side silly window avoidance. Karn and Partridge [1987] discusses estimation of round-trip times, and presents Karn's algorithm. Jacobson [1988] gives the congestion control algorithms that are now a required part of the standard. Floyd and Jacobson [1993] presents the RED scheme, and Clark and Fang [1998] discusses an allocation framework that uses RED. Tomlinson [1975] considers the three-way handshake in more detail. Mills [RFC 889] reports measurements of Internet round-trip delays. Jain [1986] describes timer-based congestion control in a sliding window environment. Borman [April 1989] summarizes experiments with high-speed TCP on Cray computers.

EXERCISES

13.1   TCP uses a finite field to contain stream sequence numbers. Study the protocol specification to find out how it allows an arbitrary length stream to pass from one machine to another.

13.2   The text notes that one of the TCP options permits a receiver to specify the maximum segment size it is willing to accept. Why does TCP support an option to specify maximum segment size when it also has a window advertisement mechanism?

13.3   Under what conditions of delay, bandwidth, load, and packet loss will TCP retransmit significant volumes of data unnecessarily?

13.4   Lost TCP acknowledgements do not necessarily force retransmissions. Explain why.

13.5   Experiment with local machines to determine how TCP handles machine restart. Establish a connection (e.g., a remote login) and leave it idle. Wait for the destination machine to crash and restart, and then force the local machine to send a TCP segment (e.g., by typing characters to the remote login).

13.6   Imagine an implementation of TCP that discards segments that arrive out of order, even if they fall in the current window. That is, the imagined version only accepts segments that extend the byte stream it has already received. Does it work? How does it compare to a standard TCP implementation?

13.7   Consider computation of a TCP checksum. Assume that although the checksum field in the segment has *not* been set to zero, the result of computing the checksum *is* zero. What can you conclude?

13.8   What are the arguments for and against automatically closing idle connections?

13.9   If two application programs use TCP to send data but only send one character per segment (e.g., by using the PUSH operation), what is the maximum percent of the network
bandwidth they will have for their data?

13.10   Suppose an implementation of TCP uses initial sequence number *1* when it creates a
connection. Explain how a system crash and restart can confuse a remote system into
believing that the old connection remained open.

13.11   Look at the round-trip time estimation algorithm suggested in the ISO TP-4 protocol
specification and compare it to the TCP algorithm discussed in this chapter. Which
would you prefer to use?

13.12   Find out how implementations of TCP must solve the *overlapping segment problem*.
The problem arises because the receiver must accept only one copy of all bytes from the
data stream even if the sender transmits two segments that partially overlap one another
(e.g., the first segment carries bytes 100 through 200 and the second carries bytes 150
through 250).

13.13   Trace the TCP finite state machine transitions for two sites that execute a passive and active open and step through the three-way handshake.

13.14   Read the TCP specification to find out the exact conditions under which TCP can make
the transition from *FIN WAIT-1* to *TIMED WAIT*.

13.15   Trace the TCP state transitions for two machines that agree to close a connection gracefully.

13.16   Assume TCP is sending segments using a maximum window size (64 Kbytes) on a channel that has infinite bandwidth and an average roundtrip time of 20 milliseconds. What
is the maximum throughput? How does throughput change if the roundtrip time increases to 40 milliseconds (while bandwidth remains infinite)?

13.17   As the previous exercise illustrates, higher throughput can be achieved with larger windows. One of the drawbacks of the TCP segment format is the size of the field devoted
to window advertisement. How can TCP be extended to allow larger windows without
changing the segment format?

13.18   Can you derive an equation that expresses the maximum possible TCP throughput as a
function of the network bandwidth, the network delay, and the time to process a segment
and generate an acknowledgement. Hint: consider the previous exercise.

13.19   Describe (abnormal) circumstances that can leave one end of a connection in state *FIN
WAIT-2* indefinitely (hint: think of datagram loss and system crashes).

13.20   Show that when a router implements RED, the probability a packet will be discarded
from a particular TCP connection is proportional to the percentage of traffic that the connection generates.

14

Routing: Cores, Peers, And Algorithms

14.1 Introduction

Previous chapters concentrate on the network level services TCP/IP offers and the details of the protocols in hosts and routers that provide those services. In the discussion, we assumed that routers always contain correct routes, and we observed that routers can ask directly connected hosts to change routes with the ICMP redirect mechanism.

This chapter considers two broad questions: "What values should routing tables contain?" and "How can those values be obtained?" To answer the first question, we will consider the relationship between internet architecture and routing. In particular, we will discuss internets structured around a backbone and those composed of multiple peer networks, and consider the consequences for routing. While many of our examples are drawn from the global Internet, the ideas apply equally well to smaller corporate internets. To answer the second question, we will consider the two basic types of route propagation algorithms and see how each supplies routing information automatically.

We begin by discussing routing in general. Later sections concentrate on internet architecture and describe the algorithms routers use to exchange routing information. Chapters 15 and 16 continue to expand our discussion of routing. They explore protocols that routers owned by two independent administrative groups use to exchange information, and protocols that a single group uses among all its routers.

14.2 The Origin Of Routing Tables

Recall from Chapter 3 that IP routers provide active interconnections among networks. Each router attaches to two or more physical networks and forwards IP datagrams among them, accepting datagrams that arrive over one network interface, and routing them out over another interface. Except for destinations on directly attached networks, hosts pass all IP traffic to routers which forward datagrams on toward their final destinations. A datagram travels from router to router until it reaches a router that attaches directly to the same network as the final destination. Thus, the router system forms the architectural basis of an internet and handles all traffic except for direct delivery from one host to another.

Chapter 8 describes the IP routing algorithm that hosts and routers follow to forward datagrams, and shows how the algorithm uses a table to make routing decisions. Each entry in the routing table specifies the network portion of a destination address and gives the address of the next machine along a path used to reach that network. Like hosts, routers directly deliver datagrams to destinations on networks to which the router attaches.

Although we have seen the basics of datagram forwarding, we have not said how hosts or routers obtain the information for their routing tables. The issue has two aspects: *what* values should be placed in the tables, and *how* routers obtain those values. Both choices depend on the architectural complexity and size of the internet as well as administrative policies.

In general, establishing routes involves initialization and update. Each router must establish an initial set of routes when it starts, and it must update the table as routes change (e.g., when a network interface fails). Initialization depends on the operating system. In some systems, the router reads an initial routing table from secondary storage at startup, keeping it resident in main memory. In others, the operating system begins with an empty table which must be filled in by executing explicit commands (e.g., commands found in a startup command script). Finally, some operating systems start by deducing an initial set of routes from the set of addresses for the local networks to which the machine attaches and contacting a neighboring machine to ask for additional routes.

Once an initial routing table has been built, a router must accommodate changes in routes. In small, slowly changing internets, managers can establish and modify routes by hand. In large, rapidly changing environments, however, manual update is impossibly slow and prone to human errors. Automated methods are needed.

Before we can understand the automatic routing table update protocols used in IP routers, we need to review several underlying ideas. The next sections do so, providing the necessary conceptual foundation for routing. Later sections discuss internet architecture and the protocols routers use to exchange routing information.

14.3 Routing With Partial Information

The principal difference between routers and typical hosts is that hosts usually know little about the structure of the internet to which they connect. Hosts do not have complete knowledge of all possible destination addresses, or even of all possible destination networks. In fact, many hosts have only two routes in their routing table: a route for the local network and a default route for a nearby router. The host sends all nonlocal datagrams to the local router for delivery. The point is that:

> *A host can route datagrams successfully even if it only has partial routing information because it can rely on a router.*

Can routers also route datagrams with only partial information? Yes, but only under certain circumstances. To understand the criteria, imagine an internet to be a foreign country crisscrossed with dirt roads that have directional signs posted at intersections. Imagine that you have no map, cannot ask directions because you cannot speak the local language, have no ideas about visible landmarks, but you need to travel to a village named *Sussex*. You leave on your journey, following the only road out of town and begin to look for directional signs. The first sign reads:

> Norfolk to the left; Hammond to the right; others straight ahead.†

Because the destination you seek is not listed explicitly, you continue straight ahead. In routing jargon, we say you follow a *default route*. After several more signs, you finally find one that reads:

> Essex to the left; Sussex to the right; others straight ahead.

You turn to the right, follow several more signs, and emerge on a road that leads to Sussex.

Our imagined travel is analogous to a datagram traversing an internet, and the road signs are analogous to routing tables in routers along the path. Without a map or other navigational aids, travel is completely dependent on road signs, just as datagram routing in an internet depends entirely on routing tables. Clearly, it is possible to navigate even though each road sign contains only partial information.

A central question concerns correctness. As a traveler, you might ask, "How can I be sure that following the signs will lead to my final destination?" You also might ask, "How can I be sure that following the signs will lead me to my destination along a shortest path?" These questions may seem especially troublesome if you pass many signs without finding your destination listed explicitly. Of course, the answers depend on the topology of the road system and the contents of the signs, but the fundamental idea is that when taken as a whole, the information on the signs should be both consistent and complete. Looking at this another way, we see that it is not necessary for each intersection to have a sign for every destination. The signs can list default paths as

---

†Fortunately, signs are printed in a language you can read.

long as all explicit signs point along a shortest path, and the turns for shortest paths to all destinations are marked. A few examples will explain some ways that consistency can be achieved.

At one extreme, consider a simple star-shaped topology of roads in which each village has exactly one road leading to it, and all those roads meet at a central point. To guarantee consistency, the sign at the central intersection must contain information about all possible destinations. At the other extreme, imagine an arbitrary set of roads with signs at all intersections listing all possible destinations. To guarantee consistency, it must be true that at any intersection if the sign for destination D points to road R, no road other than R leads to a shorter path to D.

Neither of these architectural extremes works well for an internet router system. On one hand, the central intersection approach fails because no machine is fast enough to serve as a central switch through which all traffic passes. On the other hand, having information about all possible destinations in all routers is impractical because it requires propagating large volumes of information whenever a change occurs or whenever administrators need to check consistency. Thus, we seek a solution that allows groups to manage local routers autonomously, adding new network interconnections and routes without changing distant routers.

To help explain some of the architecture described later, consider a third topology in which half the cities lie in the eastern part of the country and half lie in the western part. Suppose a single bridge spans the river that separates east from west. Assume that people living in the eastern part do not like westerners, so they are willing to allow road signs that list destinations in the east but none in the west. Assume that people living in the west do the opposite. Routing will be consistent if every road sign in the east lists all eastern destinations explicitly and points the default path to the bridge, while every road sign in the west lists all western destinations explicitly and points the default path to the bridge.

14.4 Original Internet Architecture And Cores

Much of our knowledge of routing and route propagation protocols has been derived from experience with the global Internet. When TCP/IP was first developed, participating research sites were connected to the ARPANET, which served as the Internet backbone. During initial experiments, each site managed routing tables and installed routes to other destinations by hand. As the fledgling Internet began to grow, it became apparent that manual maintenance of routes was impractical; automated mechanisms were needed.

The Internet designers selected a router architecture that consisted of a small, central set of routers that kept complete information about all possible destinations, and a larger set of outlying routers that kept partial information. In terms of our analogy, it is like designating a small set of centrally located intersections to have signs that list all destinations, and allowing the outlying intersections to list only local destinations. As long as the default route at each outlying intersection points to one of the central intersections, travelers will eventually reach their destination. The advantage of using partial information in outlying routers is that it permits local administrators to manage local structural changes without affecting other parts of the Internet. The disadvantage is that it introduces the potential for inconsistency. In the worst case, an error in an outlying router can make distant routes unreachable.

We can summarize these ideas:

> *The routing table in a given router contains partial information about possible destinations. Routing that uses partial information allows sites autonomy in making local routing changes, but introduces the possibility of inconsistencies that may make some destinations unreachable from some sources.*

Inconsistencies among routing tables usually arise from errors in the algorithms that compute routing tables, incorrect data supplied to those algorithms, or from errors that occur while transmitting the results to other routers. Protocol designers look for ways to limit the impact of errors, with the objective being to keep all routes consistent at all times. If routes become inconsistent for some reason, the routing protocols should be robust enough to detect and correct the errors quickly. Most important, the protocols should be designed to constrain the effect of errors.

14.5 Core Routers

Loosely speaking, early Internet routers could be partitioned into two groups, a small set of *core routers* controlled by the Internet Network Operations Center (INOC), and a larger set of *noncore routers*† controlled by individual groups. The core system was designed to provide reliable, consistent, authoritative routes for all possible destinations; it was the glue that held the Internet together and made universal interconnection possible. By fiat, each site assigned an Internet network address had to arrange to advertise that address to the core system. The core routers communicated among themselves, so they could guarantee that the information they shared was consistent. Because a central authority monitored and controlled the core routers, they were highly reliable.

To fully understand the core router system, it is necessary to recall that the Internet evolved with a wide-area network, the ARPANET, already in place. When the Internet experiments began, designers thought of the ARPANET as a main backbone on which to build. Thus, a large part of the motivation for the core router system came from the desire to connect local networks to the ARPANET. Figure 14.1 illustrates the idea.

---

†The terms *stub* and *nonrouting* have also been used in place of *noncore*.

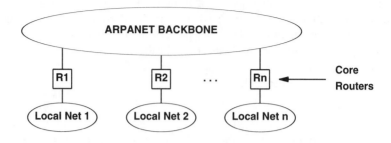

Figure 14.1 The early Internet core router system viewed as a set of routers that connect local area networks to the ARPANET. Hosts on the local networks pass all nonlocal traffic to the closest core router.

To understand why such an architecture does not lend itself to routing with partial information, suppose that a large internet consists entirely of local area networks, each attached to a backbone network through a router. Also imagine that some of the routers rely on default routes. Now consider the path a datagram follows. At the source site, the local router checks to see if it has an explicit route to the destination and, if not, sends the datagram along the path specified by its default route. All datagrams for which the router has no route follow the same default path regardless of their ultimate destination. The next router along the path diverts datagrams for which it has an explicit route, and sends the rest along its default route. To ensure global consistency, the chain of default routes must reach every router in a giant cycle as Figure 14.2 shows. Thus, the architecture requires all local sites to coordinate their default routes. In addition, depending on default routes can be inefficient even when it is consistent. As Figure 14.2 shows, in the worst case a datagram will pass through all *n* routers as it travels from source to destination instead of going directly across the backbone.

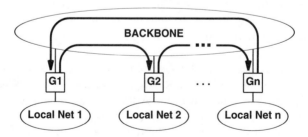

Figure 14.2 A set of routers connected to a backbone network with default routes shown. Routing is inefficient even though it is consistent.

To avoid the inefficiencies default routes cause, Internet designers arranged for all core routers to exchange routing information so that each would have complete information about optimal routes to all possible destinations. Because each core router knew routes to all possible destinations, it did not need a default route. If the destination address on a datagram was not in a core router's routing table, the router would generate an ICMP destination unreachable message and drop the datagram. In essence, the core design avoided inefficiency by eliminating default routes.

Figure 14.3 depicts the conceptual basis of a core routing architecture. The figure shows a central core system consisting of one or more core routers, and a set of outlying routers at local sites. Outlying routers keep information about local destinations and use a default route that sends datagrams destined for other sites to the core.

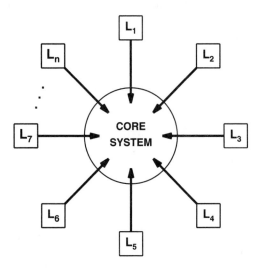

Figure 14.3 The routing architecture of a simplistic core system showing default routes. Core routers do not use default routes; outlying routers, labeled L_i, each have a default route that points to the core.

Although the simplistic core architecture illustrated in Figure 14.3 is easy to understand, it became impractical for three reasons. First, the Internet outgrew a single, centrally managed long-haul backbone. The topology became complex and the protocols needed to maintain consistency among core routers became nontrivial. Second, not every site could have a core router connected to the backbone, so additional routing structure and protocols were needed. Third, because core routers all interacted to ensure consistent routing information, the core architecture did not scale to arbitrary size. We will return to this last problem in Chapter 15 after we examine the protocols that the core system used to exchange routing information.

14.6 Beyond The Core Architecture To Peer Backbones

The introduction of the NSFNET backbone into the Internet added new complexity to the routing structure. From the core system point of view, the connection to NSFNET was initially no different than the connection to any other site. NSFNET attached to the ARPANET backbone through a single router in Pittsburgh. The core had explicit routes to all destinations in NSFNET. Routers inside NSFNET knew about local destinations and used a default route to send all non-NSFNET traffic to the core via the Pittsburgh router.

As NSFNET grew to become a major part of the Internet, it became apparent that the core routing architecture would not suffice. The most important conceptual change occurred when multiple connections were added between the ARPANET and NSFNET backbones. We say that the two became *peer backbone networks* or simply *peers*. Figure 14.4 illustrates the resulting peer topology.

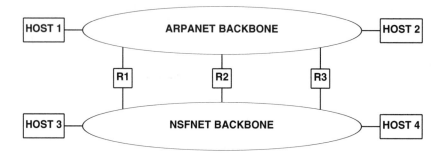

Figure 14.4 An example of peer backbones interconnected through multiple
routers. The diagram illustrates the architecture of the Internet
in 1989. In later generations, parallel backbones were each
owned by an ISP.

To understand the difficulties of IP routing among peer backbones, consider routes from host *3* to host *2* in Figure 14.4. Assume for the moment that the figure shows geographic orientation, so host *3* is on the West Coast attached to the NSFNET backbone while host *2* is on the East Coast attached to the ARPANET backbone. When establishing routes between hosts *3* and *2*, the managers must decide whether to (a) route the traffic from host *3* through the West Coast router, *R1*, and then across the ARPANET backbone, or (b) route the traffic from host *3* across the NSFNET backbone, through the Midwest router, *R2*, and then across the ARPANET backbone to host *2*, or (c) route the traffic across the NSFNET backbone, through the East Coast router, *R3*, and then to host *2*. A more circuitous route is possible as well: traffic could flow from host *3* through the West Coast router, across the ARPANET backbone to the Midwest router, back onto the NSFNET backbone to the East Coast router, and finally across the

ARPANET backbone to host *2*. Such a route may or may not be advisable, depending on the policies for network use and the capacity of various routers and backbones.

For most peer backbone configurations, traffic between a pair of geographically close hosts should take a shortest path, independent of the routes chosen for cross-country traffic. For example, traffic from host *3* to host *1* should flow through the West Coast router because it minimizes distance on both backbones.

All these statements sound simple enough, but they are complex to implement for two reasons. First, although the standard IP routing algorithm uses the network portion of an IP address to choose a route, optimal routing in a peer backbone architecture requires individual routes for individual hosts. For our example above, the routing table in host *3* needs different routes for host *1* and host *2*, even though both hosts *1* and *2* attach to the ARPANET backbone. Second, managers of the two backbones must agree to keep routes consistent among all routers or *routing loops* can develop (a routing loop occurs when routes in a set of routers point in a circle).

It is important to distinguish network topology from routing architecture. It is possible, for example, to have a single core system that spans multiple backbone networks. The core machines can be programmed to hide the underlying architectural details and to compute shortest routes among themselves. It is not possible, however, to partition the core system into subsets that each keep partial information without losing functionality. Figure 14.5 illustrates the problem.

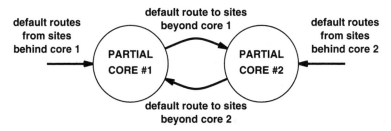

Figure 14.5 An attempt to partition a core routing architecture into two sets of routers that keep partial information and use default routes. Such an architecture results in a routing loop for datagrams that have an illegal (nonexistent) destination.

As the figure shows, outlying routers have default routes to one side of the partitioned core. Each side of the partition has information about destinations on its side of the world and a default route for information on the other side of the world. In such an architecture, any datagram sent to an illegal address will cycle between the two partitions in a routing loop until its time to live counter reaches zero.

We can summarize as follows:

A core routing architecture assumes a centralized set of routers serves as the repository of information about all possible destinations in an internet. Core systems work best for internets that have a single, centrally managed backbone. Expanding the topology to multiple backbones makes routing complex; attempting to partition the core architecture so that all routers use default routes introduces potential routing loops.

14.7 Automatic Route Propagation

We said that the original Internet core system avoided default routes because it propagated complete information about all possible destinations to every core router. Many corporate internets now use a similar scheme — routers in the corporation run programs that communicate routing information. The next sections discuss two basic types of algorithms that compute and propagate routing information, and use the original core routing protocol to illustrate one of the algorithms. A later section describes a protocol that uses the other type of algorithm.

It may seem that automatic route propagation mechanisms are not needed, especially on small internets. However, internets are not static. Connections fail and are later replaced. Networks can become overloaded at one moment and underutilized at the next. The purpose of routing propagation mechanisms is not merely to find a set of routes, but to continually update the information. Humans simply cannot respond to changes fast enough; computer programs must be used. Thus, when we think about route propagation, it is important to consider the dynamic behavior of protocols and algorithms.

14.8 Distance Vector (Bellman-Ford) Routing

The term *distance-vector*† refers to a class of algorithms routers use to propagate routing information. The idea behind distance-vector algorithms is quite simple. The router keeps a list of all known routes in a table. When it boots, a router initializes its routing table to contain an entry for each directly connected network. Each entry in the table identifies a destination network and gives the distance to that network, usually measured in hops (which will be defined more precisely later). For example, Figure 14.6 shows the initial contents of the table on a router that attaches to two networks.

---

†The terms *vector-distance, Ford-Fulkerson, Bellman-Ford,* and *Bellman* are synonymous with *distance-vector*; the last two are taken from the names of researchers who published the idea.

Destination	Distance	Route
Net 1	0	direct
Net 2	0	direct

Figure 14.6 An initial distance-vector routing table with an entry for each directly connected network. Each entry contains the IP address of a network and an integer distance to that network.

Periodically, each router sends a copy of its routing table to any other router it can reach directly. When a report arrives at router *K* from router *J*, *K* examines the set of destinations reported and the distance to each. If *J* knows a shorter way to reach a destination, or if *J* lists a destination that *K* does not have in its table, or if *K* currently routes to a destination through *J* and *J*'s distance to that destination changes, *K* replaces its table entry. For example, Figure 14.7 shows an existing table in a router, *K*, and an update message from another router, *J*.

Destination	Distance	Route		Destination	Distance
Net 1	0	direct		Net 1	2
Net 2	0	direct	➡	Net 4	3
Net 4	8	Router L		Net 17	6
Net 17	5	Router M	➡	Net 21	4
Net 24	6	Router J		Net 24	5
Net 30	2	Router Q		Net 30	10
Net 42	2	Router J	➡	Net 42	3

(a)   (b)

Figure 14.7 (a) An existing route table for a router *K*, and (b) an incoming routing update message from router *J*. The marked entries will be used to update existing entries or add new entries to *K*'s table.

Note that if *J* reports distance *N*, an updated entry in *K* will have distance *N+1* (the distance to reach the destination from *J* plus the distance to reach *J*). Of course, the routing table entries contain a third column that specifies a next hop. The next hop entry in each initial route is marked *direct delivery*. When router *K* adds or updates an entry in response to a message from router *J*, it assigns router *J* as the next hop for that entry.

The term *distance-vector* comes from the information sent in the periodic messages. A message contains a list of pairs *(V, D)*, where *V* identifies a destination (called the *vector*), and *D* is the distance to that destination. Note that distance-vector algorithms report routes in the first person (i.e., we think of a router advertising, "I can reach destination *V* at distance *D''*). In such a design, all routers must participate in the distance-vector exchange for the routes to be efficient and consistent.

Although distance-vector algorithms are easy to implement, they have disadvantages. In a completely static environment, distance-vector algorithms propagate routes to all destinations. When routes change rapidly, however, the computations may not stabilize. When a route changes (i.e, a new connection appears or an old one fails), the information propagates slowly from one router to another. Meanwhile, some routers may have incorrect routing information.

For now, we will examine a simple protocol that uses the distance-vector algorithm without discussing all the shortcomings. Chapter 16 completes the discussion by showing another distance-vector protocol, the problems that can arise, and the heuristics used to solve the most serious of them.

14.9 Gateway-To-Gateway Protocol (GGP)

The original core routers used a distance-vector protocol known as the *Gateway-to-Gateway Protocol†* *(GGP)* to exchange routing information. Although GGP only handled classful routes and is no longer part of the TCP/IP standards‡, it does provide a concrete example of distance-vector routing. GGP was designed to travel in IP datagrams similar to UDP datagrams or TCP segments. Each GGP message has a fixed format header that identifies the message type and the format of the remaining fields. Because only core routers participated in GGP, and because core routers were controlled by a central authority, other routers could not interfere with the exchange.

The original core system was arranged to permit new core routers to be added without modifying existing routers. When a new router was added to the core system, it was assigned one or more core *neighbors* with which it communicated. The neighbors, members of the core, already propagated routing information among themselves. Thus, the new router only needed to inform its neighbors about networks it could reach; they updated their routing tables and propagated this new information further.

GGP is a true distance-vector protocol. The information routers exchange with GGP consists of a set of pairs, *(N, D)*, where *N* is an IP network address, and *D* is a distance measured in *hops*. We say that a router using GGP *advertises* the networks it can reach and its cost for reaching them.

GGP measures distance in *router hops*, where a router is defined to be zero hops from directly connected networks, one hop from networks that are reachable through one other router, and so on. Thus, the *number of hops* or the *hop count* along a path from a given source to a given destination refers to the number of routers that a datagram encounters along that path. It should be obvious that using hop counts to calculate shortest paths does not always produce desirable results. For example, a path with hop count *3* that crosses three LANs may be substantially faster than a path with hop count *2* that crosses two slow speed serial lines. Many routers use artificially high hop counts for routes across slow networks.

---

†Recall that although vendors adopted the term *IP router*, scientists originally used the term *IP gateway*.

‡The IETF has declared GGP *historic*, which means that it is no longer recommended for use with TCP/IP.

14.10 Distance Factoring

Like most routing protocols, GGP uses multiple message *types*, each with its own format and purpose. A field in the message header contains a code that identifies the specific message type; a receiver uses the code to decide how to process the message. For example, before two routers can exchange routing information, they must establish communication, and some message types are used for that purpose. The most fundamental message type in GGP is also fundamental to any distance-vector protocol: a routing update which is used to exchange routing information.

Conceptually, a routing update contains a list of pairs, where each entry contains an IP network address and the distance to that network. In practice, however, many routing protocols rearrange the information to keep messages small. In particular, observe that few architectures consist of a linear arrangement of networks and routers. Instead, most are hierarchical, with multiple routers attached to each network. Consequently, most distance values in an update are small numbers, and the same values tend to be repeated frequently. To reduce message size, routing protocols often use a technique that was pioneered in GGP. Known as *distance factoring*, the technique avoids sending copies of the same distance number. Instead, the list of pairs is sorted by distance, each distance value is represented once, and the networks reachable at that distance follow. The next chapter shows how other routing protocols factor information.

14.11 Reliability And Routing Protocols

Most routing protocols use connectionless transport. For example, GGP encapsulates messages directly in IP datagrams; modern routing protocols usually encapsulate in UDP†. Both IP and UDP offer the same semantics: messages can be lost, delayed, duplicated, corrupted, or delivered out of order. Thus, a routing protocol that uses them must compensate for failures.

Routing protocols use several techniques to handle delivery problems. Checksums are used to handle corruption. Loss is either handled by *soft state‡* or through acknowledgement and retransmission. For example, GGP uses an extended acknowledgement scheme in which a receiver can return either a positive or negative acknowledgement.

To handle delivery out of order and the corresponding reply that occurs when an old message arrives, routing protocols often used *sequence numbers*. In GGP, for example, each side chooses an initial number to use for sequencing when communication begins. The other side must then acknowledge the sequence number. After the initial exchange, each message contains the next number in the sequence, which allows the receiver to know whether the message arrived in order. In a later chapter, we will see an example of a routing protocol that uses soft state information.

---

†There are exceptions — the next chapter discusses a protocol that uses TCP.

‡Recall that soft state relies on timeouts to remove old information rather than waiting for a message from the source.

14.12 Link-State (SPF) Routing

The main disadvantage of the distance-vector algorithm is that it does not scale well. Besides the problem of slow response to change mentioned earlier, the algorithm requires the exchange of large messages. Because each routing update contains an entry for every possible network, message size is proportional to the total number of networks in an internet. Furthermore, because a distance-vector protocol requires every router to participate, the volume of information exchanged can be enormous.

The primary alternative to distance-vector algorithms is a class of algorithms known as *link state*, *link status*, or *Shortest Path First*† (*SPF*). The SPF algorithm requires each participating router to have complete topology information. The easiest way to think of the topology information is to imagine that every router has a map that shows all other routers and the networks to which they connect. In abstract terms, the routers correspond to nodes in a graph and networks that connect routers correspond to edges. There is an edge (link) between two nodes if and only if the corresponding routers can communicate directly.

Instead of sending messages that contain lists of destinations, a router participating in an SPF algorithm performs two tasks. First, it actively tests the status of all neighbor routers. In terms of the graph, two routers are neighbors if they share a link; in network terms, two neighbors connect to a common network. Second, it periodically propagates the link status information to all other routers.

To test the status of a directly connected neighbor, a router periodically exchanges short messages that ask whether the neighbor is alive and reachable. If the neighbor replies, the link between them is said to be *up*. Otherwise, the link is said to be *down*‡. To inform all other routers, each router periodically broadcasts a message that lists the status (state) of each of its links. A status message does not specify routes — it simply reports whether communication is possible between pairs of routers. Protocol software in the routers arranges to deliver a copy of each link status message to all participating routers (if the underlying networks do not support broadcast, delivery is done by forwarding individual copies of the message point-to-point).

Whenever a link status message arrives, a router uses the information to update its map of the internet, by marking links up or down. Whenever link status changes, the router recomputes routes by applying the well-known *Dijkstra shortest path algorithm* to the resulting graph. Dijkstra's algorithm computes the shortest paths to all destinations from a single source.

One of the chief advantages of SPF algorithms is that each router computes routes independently using the same original status data; they do not depend on the computation of intermediate machines. Because link status messages propagate unchanged, it is easy to debug problems. Because routers perform the route computation locally, it is guaranteed to converge. Finally, because link status messages only carry information about the direct connections from a single router, the size does not depend on the number of networks in the internet. Thus, SPF algorithms scale better than distance-vector algorithms.

---

†The name "shortest path first" is a misnomer because all routing algorithms seek shortest paths.

‡In practice, to prevent oscillations between the up and down states, most protocols use a *k-out-of-n rule* to test liveness, meaning that the link remains up until a significant percentage of requests have no reply, and then it remains down until a significant percentage of messages receive a reply.

14.13 Summary

To ensure that all networks remain reachable with high reliability, an internet must provide globally consistent routing. Hosts and most routers contain only partial routing information; they depend on default routes to send datagrams to distant destinations. Originally, the global Internet solved the routing problem by using a core router architecture in which a set of core routers each contained complete information about all networks. Routers in the original Internet core system exchanged routing information periodically, meaning that once a single core router learned about a route, all core routers learned about it. To prevent routing loops, core routers were forbidden from using default routes.

A single, centrally managed core system works well for an internet architecture built on a single backbone network. However, a core architecture does not suffice for an internet that consists of a set of separately managed peer backbones that interconnect at multiple places.

When routers exchange routing information they use one of two basic algorithms, distance-vector or SPF. A distance-vector protocol, GGP, was originally used to propagate routing update information throughout the Internet core.

The chief disadvantage of distance-vector algorithms is that they perform a distributed shortest path computation that may not converge if the status of network connections changes continually. Another disadvantage is that routing update messages grow large as the number of networks increases.

The use of SPF routing predates the Internet. One of the earliest examples of an SPF protocol comes from the ARPANET, which used a routing protocol internally to establish and maintain routes among packet switches. The ARPANET algorithm was used for a decade.

FOR FURTHER STUDY

The definition of the core router system and GGP protocol in this chapter comes from Hinden and Sheltzer [RFC 823]. Braden and Postel [RFC 1812] contains further specifications for Internet routers. Almquist [RFC 1716] summarizes later discussions. Braun [RFC 1093] and Rekhter [RFC 1092] discuss routing in the NSFNET backbone. Clark [RFC 1102] and Braun [RFC 1104] both discuss policy-based routing. The next two chapters present protocols used for propagating routing information between separate sites and within a single site.

EXERCISES

14.1   Suppose a router discovers it is about to route an IP datagram back over the same network interface on which the datagram arrived. What should it do? Why?

14.2   After reading RFC 823 and RFC 1812, explain what an Internet core router (i.e., one
with complete routing information) should do in the situation described in the previous
question.

14.3   How can routers in a core system use default routes to send all illegal datagrams to a
specific machine?

14.4   Imagine students experimenting with a router that attaches a local area network to an internet that has a core routing system. The students want to advertise their network to a
core router, but if they accidentally advertise zero length routes to arbitrary networks,
traffic from the internet will be diverted to their router incorrectly. How can a core protect itself from illegal data while still accepting updates from such "untrusted" routers?

14.5   Which ICMP messages does a router generate?

14.6   Assume a router is using unreliable transport for delivery. How can the router determine
whether a designated neighbor is "up" or "down"? (Hint: consult RFC 823 to find out
how the original core system solved the problem.)

14.7   Suppose two routers each advertise the same cost, k, to reach a given network, N.
Describe the circumstances under which routing through one of them may take fewer total hops than routing through the other one.

14.8   How does a router know whether an incoming datagram carries a GGP message? An
OSPF message?

14.9   Consider the distance-vector update shown in Figure 14.7 carefully. For each item updated in the table, give the reason why the router will perform the update.

14.10 Consider the use of sequence numbers to ensure that two routers do not become confused when datagrams are duplicated, delayed, or delivered out of order. How should
initial sequence numbers be selected? Why?

15

Routing: Exterior Gateway Protocols And Autonomous Systems (BGP)

15.1 Introduction

The previous chapter introduces the idea of route propagation and examines one protocol routers use to exchange routing information. This chapter extends our understanding of internet routing architectures. It discusses the concept of autonomous systems, and shows a protocol that a group of networks and routers operating under one administrative authority uses to propagate routing information about its networks to other groups.

15.2 Adding Complexity To The Architectural Model

The original core routing system evolved at a time when the Internet had a single wide area backbone as the previous chapter describes. Consequently, part of the motivation for a core architecture was to provide connections between a network at each site and the backbone. If an internet consists of only a single backbone plus a set of attached local area networks, the core approach propagates all necessary routing information correctly. Because all routers attach to the wide area backbone network, they can exchange all necessary routing information directly. Each router knows the single local network to which it attaches, and propagates that information to the other routers. Each router learns about other destination networks from other routers.

It may seem that it would be possible to extend the core architecture to an arbitrary size internet merely by adding more sites, each with a router connecting to the backbone. Unfortunately, the scheme does not scale — having all routers participate in a single routing protocol only suffices for trivial size internets. There are three reasons. First, even if each site consists of a single network, the scheme cannot accommodate an arbitrary number of sites because each additional router generates routing traffic. If a large set of routers attempt to communicate, the total bandwidth becomes overwhelming. Second, the scheme cannot accommodate multiple routers and networks at a given site because only those routers that connect directly to the backbone network can communicate directly. Third, in a large internet, the networks and routers are not all managed by a single entity, nor are shortest paths always used. Instead, because networks are owned and managed by independent groups, the groups may choose policies that differ. A routing architecture must provide a way for each group to independently control routing and access.

The consequences of limiting router interaction are significant. The idea provides the motivation for much of the routing architecture used in the global Internet, and explains some of the mechanisms we will study. To summarize this important principle:

> *Although it is desirable for routers to exchange routing information, it is impractical for all routers in an arbitrarily large internet to participate in a single routing update protocol.*

15.3 Determining A Practical Limit On Group Size

The above statement leaves many questions open. For example, what size internet is considered ''large''? If only a limited set of routers can participate in an exchange of routing information, what happens to routers that are excluded? Do they function correctly? Can a router that is not participating ever forward a datagram to a router that is participating? Can a participating router forward a datagram to a non-participating router?

The answer to the question of size involves understanding the algorithm being used and the capacity of the network that connects the routers as well as the details of the routing protocol. There are two issues: delay and overhead. Delay is easy to understand. For example, consider the maximum delay until all routers are informed about a change when they use a distance-vector protocol. Each router must receive the new information, update its routing table, and then forward the information to its neighbors. In an internet with N routers arranged in a linear topology, N steps are required. Thus, N must be limited to guarantee rapid distribution of information.

The issue of overhead is also easy to understand. Because each router that participates in a routing protocol must send messages, a larger set of participating routers means more routing traffic. Furthermore, if routing messages contain a list of possible destinations, the size of each message grows as the number of routers and networks increase. To ensure that routing traffic remains a small percentage of the total traffic on the underlying networks, the size of routing messages must be limited.

In fact, most network managers do not have sufficient information required to perform detailed analysis of the delay or overhead. Instead, they follow a simple heuristic guideline:

> It is safe to allow up to a dozen routers to participate in a single routing information protocol across a wide area network; approximately five times as many can safely participate across a set of local area networks.

Of course, the rule only gives general advice and there are many exceptions. For example, if the underlying networks have especially low delay and high capacity, the number of participating routers can be larger. Similarly, if the underlying networks have unusually low capacity or a high amount of traffic, the number of participating routers must be smaller to avoid overloading the networks with routing traffic.

Because an internet is not static, it can be difficult to estimate how much traffic routing protocols will generate or what percentage of the underlying bandwidth the routing traffic will consume. For example, as the number of hosts on a network grows over time, increases in the traffic generated consume more of the network capacity. In addition, increased traffic can arise from new applications. Therefore, network managers cannot rely solely on the guideline above when choosing a routing architecture. Instead, they usually implement a *traffic monitoring* scheme. In essence, a traffic monitor listens passively to a network and records statistics about the traffic. In particular, a monitor can compute both the network utilization (i.e., percentage of the underlying bandwidth being used) and the percentage of packets carrying routing protocol messages. A manager can observe traffic trends by taking measurements over long periods (e.g., weeks or months), and can use the output to determine whether too many routers are participating in a single routing protocol.

15.4 A Fundamental Idea: Extra Hops

Although the number of routers that participate in a single routing protocol must be limited, doing so has an important consequence because it means that some routers will be outside the group. It might seem that an ''outsider'' could merely make a member of the group a default. In the early Internet, the core system did indeed function as a central routing mechanism to which noncore routers sent datagrams for delivery. However, researchers learned an important lesson: if a router outside of a group uses a member of the group as a default route, routing will be suboptimal. More important, one does not need a large number of routers or a wide area network — the problem can occur whenever a nonparticipating router uses a participating router for delivery. To see why, consider the example in Figure 15.1.

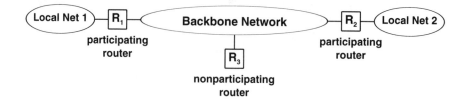

Figure 15.1 An architecture that can cause the extra hop problem. Nonoptimal routing occurs when a nonparticipating router connected to
the backbone has a default route to a participating router.

In the figure, routers R_1 and R_2 connect to local area networks *1* and *2*, respectively. Because they participate in a routing protocol, they both know how to reach both
networks. Suppose nonparticipating router R_3 chooses one of the participating routers,
say R_1, as a default. That is, R_3 sends R_1 all datagrams destined for networks to which it
has no direct connection. In particular, R_3 sends datagrams destined for network *2*
across the backbone to its chosen participating router, R_1, which must then forward
them back across the backbone to router R_2. The optimal route, of course, requires R_3
to transmit datagrams destined for network *2* directly to R_2. Notice that the choice of
participating router makes no difference. Only destinations that lie beyond the chosen
router have optimal routes; all paths that go through other backbone routers require the
datagram to make a second, unnecessary trip across the backbone network. Also notice
that the participating routers cannot use ICMP redirect messages to inform R_3 that it has
nonoptimal routes because ICMP redirect messages can only be sent to the original
source and not to intermediate routers.

We call the routing anomaly illustrated in Figure 15.1 the *extra hop problem*. The
problem is insidious because everything appears to work correctly — datagrams do
reach their destination. However, because routing is not optimal, the system is extremely inefficient. Each datagram that takes an extra hop consumes resources on the intermediate router as well as twice as much backbone bandwidth as it should. Solving the
problem requires us to change our view of architecture:

> *Treating a group of routers that participate in a routing update proto-*
> *col as a default delivery system can introduce an extra hop for da-*
> *tagram traffic; a mechanism is needed that allows nonparticipating*
> *routers to learn routes from participating routers so they can choose*
> *optimal routes.*

15.5 Hidden Networks

Before we examine mechanisms that allow a router outside a group to learn routes, we need to understand another aspect of routing: hidden networks (i.e. networks that are concealed from the view of routers in a group). Figure 15.2 shows an example that will illustrate the concept.

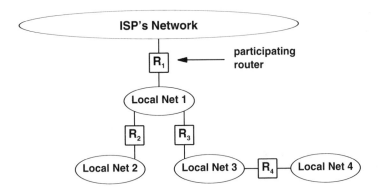

Figure 15.2 An example of multiple networks and routers with a single backbone connection. A mechanism is needed to pass reachability information about additional local networks into the core system.

In the figure, a site has multiple local area networks with multiple routers connecting them. Suppose the site has just installed local network *4* and has obtained an Internet address for it (for now, imagine that the site obtained the address from another ISP). Also assume that the routers R_2, R_3, and R_4 each have correct routes for all four of the site's local networks as well as a default route that passes other traffic to the ISP's router, R_1. Hosts directly attached to local network *4* can communicate with one another, and any computer on that network can route packets out to other Internet sites. However, because router R_1 attaches only to local network *1*, it does not know about local network *4*. We say that, from the viewpoint of the ISP's routing system, local network *4* is *hidden* behind local network *1*. The important point is:

> *Because an individual organization can have an arbitrarily complex set of networks interconnected by routers, no router from another organization can attach directly to all networks. A mechanism is needed that allows nonparticipating routers to inform the other group about hidden networks.*

We now understand a fundamental aspect of routing: information must flow in two directions. Routing information must flow from a group of participating routers to a nonparticipating router, and a nonparticipating router must pass information about hidden networks to the group. Ideally, a single mechanism should solve both problems. Building such a mechanism can be tricky. The subtle issues are responsibility and capability. Exactly where does responsibility for informing the group reside? If we decide that one of the nonparticipating routers should inform the group, which one is capable of doing it? Look again at the example. Router R_4 is the router most closely associated with local network *4*, but it lies *2* hops away from the nearest core router. Thus, R_4 must depend on router R_3 to route packets to network *4*. The point is that R_4 knows about local network *4* but cannot pass datagrams directly from R_1. Router R_3 lies one hop from the core and can guarantee to pass packets, but it does not directly attach to local network *4*. So, it seems incorrect to grant R_3 responsibility for advertising network *4*. Solving this dilemma will require us to introduce a new concept. The next sections discuss the concept and a protocol that implements it.

15.6 Autonomous System Concept

The puzzle over which router should communicate information to the group arises because we have only considered the mechanics of an internet routing architecture and not the administrative issues. Interconnections, like those in the example of Figure 15.2, that arise because an internet has a complex structure, should not be thought of as multiple independent networks connected to an internet. Instead, the architecture should be thought of as a single organization that has multiple networks under its control. Because the networks and routers fall under a single administrative authority, that authority can guarantee that internal routes remain consistent and viable. Furthermore, the administrative authority can choose one of its routers to serve as the machine that will apprise the outside world of networks within the organization. In the example from Figure 15.2, because routers R_2, R_3, and R_4 fall under control of one administrative authority, that authority can arrange to have R_3 advertise networks *2*, *3*, and *4* (R_1 already knows about network *1* because it has a direct connection to it).

For purposes of routing, a group of networks and routers controlled by a single administrative authority is called an *autonomous system (AS)*. Routers within an autonomous system are free to choose their own mechanisms for discovering, propagating, validating, and checking the consistency of routes. Note that, under this definition, the original Internet core routers formed an autonomous system. Each change in routing protocols within the core autonomous system was made without affecting the routers in other autonomous systems. In the previous chapter, we said that the original Internet core system used GGP to communicate, and a later generation used SPREAD. Eventually, ISPs evolved their own backbone networks that use more recent protocols. The next chapter reviews some of the protocols that autonomous systems use internally to propagate routing information.

15.7 From A Core To Independent Autonomous Systems

Conceptually, the autonomous system idea was a straightforward and natural generalization of the original Internet architecture, depicted by Figure 15.2, with autonomous systems replacing local area networks. Figure 15.3 illustrates the idea.

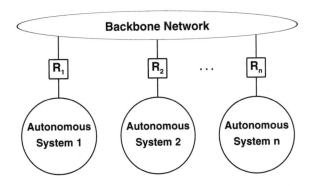

Figure 15.3 Architecture of an internet with autonomous systems at backbone sites. Each autonomous system consists of multiple networks and routers under a single administrative authority.

To make networks that are hidden inside autonomous systems reachable throughout the Internet, each autonomous system must advertise its networks to other autonomous systems. An advertisement can be sent to any autonomous system. In a centralized, core architecture, however, it is crucial that each autonomous system propagate information to one of the routers in the core autonomous system.

It may seem that our definition of an autonomous system is vague, but in practice the boundaries between autonomous systems must be precise to allow automated algorithms to make routing decisions. For example, an autonomous system owned by a corporation may choose not to route packets through an autonomous system owned by another even though they connect directly. To make it possible for automated routing algorithms to distinguish among autonomous systems, each is assigned an *autonomous system number* by the central authority that is charged with assigning all Internet network addresses. When routers in two autonomous systems exchange routing information, the protocol arranges for messages to carry the autonomous system number of the system each router represents.

We can summarize the ideas:

> *A large TCP/IP internet has additional structure to accommodate administrative boundaries: each collection of networks and routers managed by one administrative authority is considered to be a single autonomous system that is free to choose an internal routing architecture and protocols.*

We said that an autonomous system needs to collect information about all its networks and designate one or more routers to pass the information to other autonomous systems. The next sections presents the details of a protocol routers use to advertise network reachability. Later sections return to architectural questions to discuss an important restriction the autonomous system architecture imposes on routing.

15.8 An Exterior Gateway Protocol

Computer scientists use the term *Exterior Gateway Protocol* (*EGP*)† to denote any protocol used to pass routing information between two autonomous systems. Currently a single exterior protocol is used in most TCP/IP internets. Known as the *Border Gateway Protocol* (*BGP*), it has evolved through four (quite different) versions. Each version is numbered, which gives rise to the formal name of the current version: *BGP-4*. Throughout this text, the term *BGP* will refer to *BGP-4*.

When a pair of autonomous systems agree to exchange routing information, each must designate a router‡ that will speak BGP on its behalf; the two routers are said to become *BGP peers* of one another. Because a router speaking BGP must communicate with a peer in another autonomous system, it makes sense to select a machine that is near the "edge" of the autonomous system. Hence, BGP terminology calls the machine a *border gateway* or *border router*. Figure 15.4 illustrates the idea.

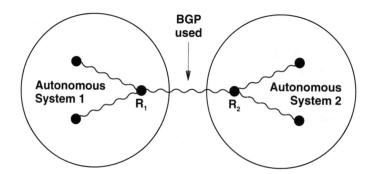

Figure 15.4 Conceptual illustration of two routers, R_1 and R_2, using BGP to advertise networks in their autonomous systems after collecting the information from other routers internally. An organization using BGP usually chooses a router that is close to the outer "edge" of the autonomous system.

In the figure, router R_1 gathers information about networks in autonomous system *1* and reports that information to router R_2 using BGP, while router R_2 reports information from autonomous system *2*.

---

†Originally, the term *EGP* referred to a specific protocol that was used for communication with the Internet core; the name was coined when the term *gateway* was used instead of *router*.

‡Although the protocol allows an arbitrary computer to be used, most autonomous systems run BGP on a router; all the examples in this text will assume BGP is running on a router.

15.9 BGP Characteristics

BGP is unusual in several ways. Most important, BGP is neither a pure distance-vector protocol nor a pure link state protocol. It can be characterized by the following:

Inter-Autonomous System Communication. Because BGP is designed as an exterior gateway protocol, its primary role is to allow one autonomous system to communicate with another.

Coordination Among Multiple BGP Speakers. If an autonomous system has multiple routers each communicating with a peer in an outside autonomous system, BGP can be used to coordinate among routers in the set to guarantee that they all propagate consistent information.

Propagation Of Reachability Information. BGP allows an autonomous system to advertise destinations that are reachable either in or through it, and to learn such information from another autonomous system.

Next-Hop Paradigm. Like distance-vector routing protocols, BGP supplies *next hop* information for each destination.

Policy Support. Unlike most distance-vector protocols that advertise exactly the routes in the local routing table, BGP can implement policies that the local administrator chooses. In particular, a router running BGP can be configured to distinguish between the set of destinations reachable by computers inside its autonomous system and the set of destinations advertised to other autonomous systems.

Reliable Transport. BGP is unusual among protocols that pass routing information because it assumes reliable transport. Thus, BGP uses TCP for all communication.

Path Information. In addition to specifying destinations that can be reached and a next hop for each, BGP advertisements include path information that allows a receiver to learn a series of autonomous systems along a path to the destination.

Incremental Updates. To conserve network bandwidth, BGP does not pass full information in each update message. Instead, full information is exchanged once, and then successive messages carry incremental changes called *deltas.*

Support For Classless Addressing. BGP supports CIDR addresses. That is, rather than expecting addresses to be self-identifying, the protocol provides a way to send a mask along with each address.

Route Aggregation. BGP conserves network bandwidth by allowing a sender to aggregate route information and send a single entry to represent multiple, related destinations.

Authentication. BGP allows a receiver to authenticate messages (i.e., verify the identity of a sender).

15.10 BGP Functionality And Message Types

BGP peers perform three basic functions. The first function consists of initial peer acquisition and authentication. The two peers establish a TCP connection and perform a message exchange that guarantees both sides have agreed to communicate. The second function forms the primary focus of the protocol — each side sends positive or negative reachability information. That is, a sender can advertise that one or more destinations are reachable by giving a next hop for each, or the sender can declare that one or more previously advertised destinations are no longer reachable. The third function provides ongoing verification that the peers and the network connections between them are functioning correctly.

To handle the three functions described above, BGP defines four basic message types. Figure 15.5 contains a summary.

Type Code	Message Type	Description
1	OPEN	Initialize communication
2	UPDATE	Advertise or withdraw routes
3	NOTIFICATION	Response to an incorrect message
4	KEEPALIVE	Actively test peer connectivity

Figure 15.5 The four basic message types in BGP-4.

15.11 BGP Message Header

Each BGP message begins with a fixed header that identifies the message type. Figure 15.6 illustrates the header format.

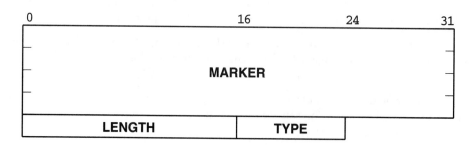

Figure 15.6 The format of the header that precedes every BGP message.

The 16-octet *MARKER* field contains a value that both sides agree to use to mark the beginning of a message. The 2-octet *LENGTH* field specifies the total message length measured in octets. The minimum message size is *19* octets (for a message type that has no data following the header), and the maximum allowable length is *4096* octets. Finally, the 1-octet *TYPE* field contains one of the four values for the message type listed in Figure 15.5.

The *MARKER* may seem unusual. In the initial message, the marker consists of all 1s; if the peers agree to use an authentication mechanism, the marker can contain authentication information. In any case, both sides must agree on the value so it can be used for *synchronization*. To understand why synchronization is necessary, recall that all BGP messages are exchanged across a stream transport (i.e., TCP), which does not identify the boundary between one message and the next. In such an environment, a simple error on either side can have dramatic consequences. In particular, if either the sender or receiver miscounts the octets in a message, a *synchronization error* will occur. More important, because the transport protocol does not specify message boundaries, the transport protocol will not alert the receiver to the error. Thus, to ensure that the sender and receiver remain synchronized, BGP places a well-known sequence at the beginning of each message, and requires a receiver to verify that the value is intact before processing the message.

15.12 BGP OPEN Message

As soon as two BGP peers establish a TCP connection, they each send an *OPEN* message to declare their autonomous system number and establish other operating parameters. In addition to the standard header, an *OPEN* message contains a value for a *hold timer* that is used to specify the maximum number of seconds which may elapse between the receipt of two successive messages. Figure 15.7 illustrates the format.

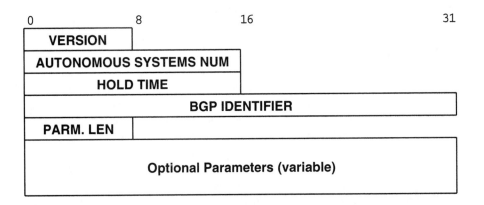

Figure 15.7 The format of the BGP OPEN message that is sent at startup. These octets follow the standard message header.

Most fields are straightforward. The *VERSION* field identifies the protocol version used (this format is for version 4). Recall that each autonomous system is assigned a unique number. Field *AUTONOMOUS SYSTEMS NUM* gives the autonomous system number of the sender's system. The *HOLD TIME* field specifies a maximum time that the receiver should wait for a message from the sender. The receiver is required to implement a timer using this value. The timer is reset each time a message arrives; if the timer expires, the receiver assumes the sender is no longer available (and stops forwarding datagrams along routes learned from the sender).

Field *BGP IDENTIFIER* contains a 32-bit integer value that uniquely identifies the sender. If a machine has multiple peers (e.g., perhaps in multiple autonomous systems), the machine must use the same identifier in all communication. The protocol specifies that the identifier is an IP address. Thus, a router must choose one of its IP addresses to use with all BGP peers.

The last field of an *OPEN* message is optional. If present, field *PARM. LEN* specifies the length measured in octets, and the field labeled *Optional Parameters* contains a list of parameters. It has been labeled *variable* to indicate that the size varies from message to message. When parameters are present, each parameter in the list is preceded by a 2-octet header, with the first octet specifying the type of the parameter, and the second octet specifying the length. If there are no parameters, the value of *PARM. LEN* is zero and the message ends with no further data.

Only one parameter type is defined in the original standard: type *1* is reserved for authentication. The authentication parameter begins with a header that identifies the type of authentication followed by data appropriate for the type. The motivation for making authentication a parameter arises from a desire to allow BGP peers to choose an authentication mechanism without making the choice part of the BGP standard.

When it accepts an incoming *OPEN* message, a machine speaking BGP responds by sending a *KEEPALIVE* message (discussed below). Each side must send an *OPEN* and receive a *KEEPALIVE* message before they can exchange routing information. Thus, a *KEEPALIVE* message functions as the acknowledgement for an *OPEN*.

15.13 BGP UPDATE Message

Once BGP peers have created a TCP connection, sent *OPEN* messages, and acknowledged them, the peers use *UPDATE* messages to advertise new destinations that are reachable or to withdraw previous advertisements when a destination has become unreachable. Figure 15.8 illustrates the format of *UPDATE* messages.

As the figure shows, each *UPDATE* message is divided into two parts: the first lists previously advertised destinations that are being withdrawn, and the second specifies new destinations being advertised. As usual, fields labeled *variable* do not have a fixed size; if the information is not needed for a particular *UPDATE*, the field can be omitted from the message. Field *WITHDRAWN LEN* is a 2-octet field that specifies the size of the *Withdrawn Destinations* field that follows. If no destinations are being withdrawn, *WITHDRAWN LEN* contains zero. Similarly, the *PATH LEN* field specifies the size of the *Path Attributes* that are associated with new destinations being advertised. If there are no new destinations, the *PATH LEN* field contains zero.

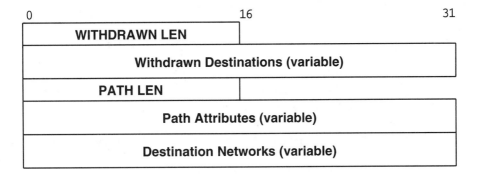

Figure 15.8 BGP UPDATE message format in which variable size areas of the message may be omitted. These octets follow the standard message header.

15.14 Compressed Mask-Address Pairs

Both the *Withdrawn Destinations* and the *Destination Networks* fields contain a list of IP network addresses. To accommodate classless addressing, BGP must send an address mask with each IP address. Instead of sending an address and a mask as separate 32-bit quantities, however, BGP uses a compressed representation to reduce message size. Figure 15.9 illustrates the format:

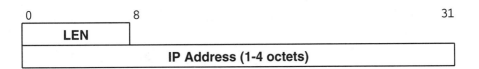

Figure 15.9 The compressed format BGP uses to store a destination address and the associated mask.

The figure shows that BGP does not actually send a bit mask. Instead, it encodes information about the mask into a single octet that precedes each address. The mask octet contains a binary integer that specifies the number of bits in the mask (mask bits are assumed to be contiguous). The address that follows the mask octet is also compressed — only those octets covered by the mask are included. Thus, only one address octet follows a mask value of *8* or less, two follow a mask value of *9* to *16*, three follow a mask value of *17* to *24*, and four follow a mask value of *25* to *32*. Interestingly, the standard also allows a mask octet to contain zero (in which case no address octets follow it). A zero length is useful because it corresponds to a default route.

15.15 BGP Path Attributes

We said that BGP is not a pure distance-vector protocol because it advertises more than a next hop. The additional information is contained in the *Path Attributes* field of an update message. A sender can use the path attributes to specify: a next hop for the advertised destinations, a list of autonomous systems along the path to the destinations, and whether the path information was learned from another autonomous system or derived from within the sender's autonomous system.

It is important to note that the path attributes are factored to reduce the size of the UPDATE message, meaning that the attributes apply to all destinations advertised in the message. Thus, if different attributes apply to some destinations, they must be advertised in a separate UPDATE message.

Path attributes are important in BGP for three reasons. First, path information allows a receiver to check for routing loops. The sender can specify an exact path through all autonomous systems to the destination. If any autonomous system appears more than once on the list, there must be a routing loop. Second, path information allows a receiver to implement policy constraints. For example, a receiver can examine paths to verify that they do not pass through untrusted autonomous systems (e.g., a competitor's autonomous system). Third, path information allows a receiver to know the source of all routes. In addition to allowing a sender to specify whether the information came from inside its autonomous system or from another system, the path attributes allow the sender to declare whether the information was collected with an exterior gateway protocol such as BGP or an interior gateway protocol†. Thus, each receiver can decide whether to accept or reject routes that originate in autonomous systems beyond the peer's.

Conceptually, the *Path Attributes* field contains a list of items, where each item consists of a triple:

$$(type, length, value)$$

Instead of fixed-size fields, the designers chose a flexible encoding scheme that minimizes the space each item occupies. As specified in Figure 15.10, the type information always requires two octets, but other fields vary in size.

---

†The next chapter describes interior gateway protocols.

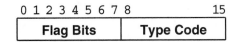

Flag Bits	Type Code

Flag Bits	Description
0	0 for required attribute, 1 if optional
1	1 for transitive, 0 for nontransitive
2	0 for complete, 1 for partial
3	0 if length field is one octet; 1 if two
5-7	unused (must be zero)

Figure 15.10 Bits of the 2-octet type field that appears before each BGP attribute path item and the meaning of each.

For each item in the *Path Attributes* list, a length field follows the 2-octet type field, and may be either one or two octets long. As the figure shows, flag bit *3* specifies the size of the length field. A receiver uses the type field to determine the size of the length field, and then uses the contents of the length field to determine the size of the value field.

Each item in the *Path attributes* field can have one of seven possible type codes. Figure 15.11 summarizes the possibilities.

Type Code	Meaning
1	Specify origin of the path information
2	List of autonomous systems on path to destination
3	Next hop to use for destination
4	Discriminator used for multiple AS exit points
5	Preference used within an autonomous system
6	Indication that routes have been aggregated
7	ID of autonomous system that aggregated routes

Figure 15.11 The BGP attribute type codes and the meaning of each.

15.16 BGP KEEPALIVE Message

Two BGP peers periodically exchange *KEEPALIVE* messages to test network connectivity and to verify that both peers continue to function. A *KEEPALIVE* message consists of the standard message header with no additional data. Thus, the total message size is *19* octets (the minimum BGP message size).

There are two reasons why BGP uses keepalive messages. First, periodic message exchange is needed because BGP uses TCP for transport, and TCP does not include a mechanism to continually test whether a connection endpoint is reachable. However,

TCP does report an error to an application if it cannot deliver data the application sends. Thus, as long as both sides periodically send a keepalive, they will know if the TCP connection fails. Second, keepalives conserve bandwidth compared to other messages. Many early routing protocols used periodic exchange of routing information to test connectivity. However, because routing information changes infrequently, the message content seldom changes. Furthermore, because routing messages are usually large, resending the same message wastes network bandwidth needlessly. To avoid the inefficiency, BGP separates the functionality of route update from connectivity testing, allowing BGP to send small *KEEPALIVE* messages frequently, and reserving larger *UPDATE* messages for situations when reachability information changes.

Recall that a BGP speaker specifies a *hold timer* when it opens a connection; the hold timer specifies a maximum time that BGP is to wait without receiving a message. As a special case, the hold timer can be zero to specify that no *KEEPALIVE* messages are used. If the hold timer is greater than zero, the standard recommends setting the *KEEPALIVE* interval to one third of the hold timer. In no case can a BGP speaker make the *KEEPALIVE* interval less than one second (which agrees with the requirement that a nonzero hold timer cannot be less than three seconds).

15.17 Information From The Receiver's Perspective

Unlike most protocols that propagate routing information, an Exterior Gateway Protocol does not merely report the set of destinations it can reach. Instead, exterior protocols must provide information that is correct from the outsider's perspective. There are two issues: policies and optimal routes. The policy issue is obvious: a router inside an autonomous system may be allowed to reach a given destination, while outsiders are prohibited from reaching the same destination. The routing issue means that a router must advertise a next hop that is optimal from the outsider's perspective. Figure 15.12 illustrates the idea.

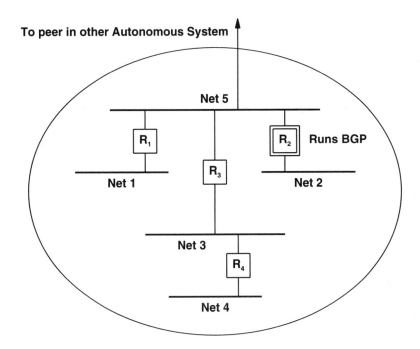

Figure 15.12 Example of an autonomous system. Router R_2 runs BGP and reports information from the outsider's perspective, not from its own routing table.

In the figure, router R_2 has been designated to speak BGP on behalf of the autonomous system. It must report reachability to networks *1* through *4*. However, when giving a next hop, it reports network *1* as reachable through router R_1, networks *3* and *4* as reachable through router R_3, and network *2* as reachable through R_2.

15.18 The Key Restriction Of Exterior Gateway Protocols

We have already seen that because exterior protocols follow policy restrictions, the networks they advertise may be a subset of the networks they can reach. However, there is a more fundamental limitation imposed on exterior routing:

> *An exterior gateway protocol does not communicate or interpret distance metrics, even if metrics are available.*

Protocols like BGP do allow a speaker to declare that a destination has become unreachable or to give a list of autonomous systems on the path to the destination, but they cannot transmit or compare the cost of two routes unless the routes come from within the same autonomous system. In essence, BGP can only specify whether a path exists to a given destination; it cannot transmit or compute the shorter of two paths.

We can see now why BGP is careful to label the origin of information it sends. The essential observation is this: when a router receives advertisements for a given destination from peers in two different autonomous systems, it cannot compare the costs. Thus, advertising reachability with BGP is equivalent to saying, "My autonomous system provides a path to this network." There is no way for the router to say, "My autonomous system provides a better path to this network than another autonomous system."

Looking at interpretation of distances allows us to realize that BGP cannot be used as a routing algorithm. In particular, even if a router learns about two paths to the same network, it cannot know which path is shorter because it cannot know the cost of routes across intermediate autonomous systems. For example, consider a router that uses BGP to communicate with two peers in autonomous systems p and f. If the peer in autonomous system p advertises a path to a given destination through autonomous systems p, q, and r, and the peer in f advertises a path to the same destination through autonomous systems f and g, the receiver has no way of comparing the lengths of the two paths. The path through three autonomous systems might involve one local area network in each system, while the path through two autonomous systems might require several hops in each. Because a receiver does not obtain full routing information, it cannot compare.

Because it does not include a distance metric, an autonomous system must be careful to advertise only routes that traffic should follow. Technically, we say that an Exterior Gateway Protocol is a *reachability protocol* rather than a routing protocol. We can summarize:

> *Because an Exterior Gateway Protocol like BGP only propagates reachability information, a receiver can implement policy constraints, but cannot choose a least cost route. A sender must only advertise paths that traffic should follow.*

The key point here is that any internet which uses BGP to provide exterior routing information must either rely on policies or assume that each autonomous system crossing is equally expensive. Although it may seem innocuous, the restriction has some surprising consequences:

1.   Although BGP can advertise multiple paths to a given network, it does not provide for the simultaneous use of multiple paths. That is, at any given instant, all traffic routed from a computer in one autonomous system to a network in another will traverse one path, even if multiple physical connections are present. Also note that an outside autonomous system will only use one return path even if the

source system divides outgoing traffic among two or more paths. As a result, delay and throughput between a pair of machines can be asymmetric, making an internet difficult to monitor or debug.

2. BGP does not support load sharing on routers between arbitrary autonomous systems. If two autonomous systems have multiple routers connecting them, one would like to balance the traffic equally among all routers. BGP allows autonomous systems to divide the load by network (e.g., to partition themselves into multiple subsets and have multiple routers advertise partitions), but it does not support more general load sharing.

3. As a special case of point 2, BGP alone is inadequate for optimal routing in an architecture that has two or more wide area networks interconnected at multiple points. Instead, managers must manually configure which networks are advertised by each exterior router.

4. To have rationalized routing, all autonomous systems in an internet must agree on a consistent scheme for advertising reachability. That is, BGP alone will not guarantee global consistency.

15.19 The Internet Routing Arbiter System

For an internet to operate correctly, routing information must be globally consistent. Individual protocols such as BGP that handle the exchange between a pair of routers, do not guarantee global consistency. Thus, a mechanism is needed to rationalize routing information globally. In the original Internet routing architecture, the core system guaranteed globally consistent routing information because at any time the core had exactly one path to each destination. When the core system was removed, a new mechanism was created to rationalize routing information.

Known as the *routing arbiter* (*RA*) system, the new mechanism consists of a replicated, authenticated database of reachability information. Updates to the database are *authenticated* to prevent an arbitrary router from advertising a path to a given destination. In general, only an autonomous system that owns a given network is allowed to advertise reachability. The need for such authentication became obvious in the early core system, which allowed any router to advertise reachability to any network. On several occasions, routing errors occurred when a router inadvertently advertised incorrect reachability information. The core accepted the information and changed routes, causing some networks to become unreachable.

To understand how other routers access the routing arbiter database, consider the current Internet architecture. We said that major ISPs interconnect at Network Access Points (NAPs). Thus, in terms of routing, a NAP represents the boundary between multiple autonomous systems. Although it would be possible to use BGP among each pair of ISPs at the NAP, doing so is both inefficient and prone to inconsistencies. Instead, each NAP has a computer called a *route server* (*RS*) that maintains a copy of the routing arbiter database and runs BGP. Each ISP designates one of its routers near a NAP to be a BGP border router. The designated border router maintains a connection to the route server over which it uses BGP. The ISP advertises reachability to its networks and the networks of its customers, and learns about networks in other ISPs.

One of the chief advantages of using BGP for route server access lies in its ability to carry negative information as well as positive information. When a destination becomes unreachable, the ISP informs the route server, which then makes the information available to other ISPs. Spreading negative information reduces unnecessary traffic because datagrams to unreachable destinations can be discarded before they transit from one ISP to another†.

15.20 BGP NOTIFICATION Message

In addition to the OPEN and UPDATE message types described above, BGP supports a *NOTIFICATION* message type used for control or when an error occurs. Errors are permanent — once it detects a problem, BGP sends a notification message and then closes the TCP connection. Figure 15.13 illustrates the message format.

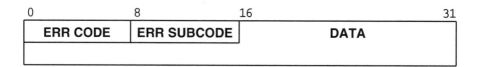

Figure 15.13 BGP NOTIFICATION message format. These octets follow the standard message header.

The 8-bit field labeled *ERR CODE* specifies one of the possible reasons listed in Figure 15.14.

ERR CODE	Meaning
1	Error in message header
2	Error in OPEN message
3	Error in UPDATE message
4	Hold timer expired
5	Finite state machine error
6	Cease (terminate connection)

Figure 15.14 The possible values of the *ERR CODE* field in a BGP NOTIFICATION message.

---

†Like the core system it replaced, the routing arbiter system does not include default routes. As a consequence, it is sometimes called a *default-free zone*.

For each possible *ERR CODE*, the *ERR SUBCODE* field contains a further explanation. Figure 15.15 lists the possible values.

```
┌─────────────────────────────────────────────┐
│      Subcodes For Message Header Errors       │
│                                               │
│      1    Connection not synchronized         │
│      2    Incorrect message length            │
│      3    Incorrect message type              │
├─────────────────────────────────────────────┤
│       Subcodes For OPEN Message Errors        │
│                                               │
│      1    Version number unsupported          │
│      2    Peer AS invalid                      │
│      3    BGP identifier invalid               │
│      4    Unsupported optional parameter       │
│      5    Authentication failure               │
│      6    Hold time unacceptable               │
├─────────────────────────────────────────────┤
│      Subcodes For UPDATE Message Errors       │
│                                               │
│      1    Attribute list malformed            │
│      2    Unrecognized attribute              │
│      3    Missing attribute                    │
│      4    Attribute flags error               │
│      5    Attribute length error              │
│      6    Invalid ORIGIN attribute            │
│      7    AS routing loop                      │
│      8    Next hop invalid                     │
│      9    Error in optional attribute         │
│     10    Invalid network field               │
│     11    Malformed AS path                    │
└─────────────────────────────────────────────┘
```

Figure 15.15 The meaning of the *ERR SUBCODE* field in a BGP NOTIFI-
CATION message.

15.21 Decentralization Of Internet Architecture

Two important architecture questions remain unanswered. The first focuses on centralization: how can the Internet architecture be modified to remove dependence on a (centralized) router system? The second concerns levels of trust: can an internet architecture be expanded to allow closer cooperation (trust) between some autonomous systems than among others?

Removing all dependence on a central system and adding trust are not easy. Although TCP/IP architectures continue to evolve, centralized roots are evident in many protocols. Without some centralization, each ISP would need to exchange reachability information with all ISPs to which it attached. Consequently, the volume of routing traffic would be significantly higher than with a routing arbiter scheme. Finally, centralization fills an important role in rationalizing routes and guaranteeing trust — in addition to storing the reachability database, the routing arbiter system guarantees global consistency and provides a trusted source of information.

15.22 Summary

Routers must be partitioned into groups or the volume of routing traffic would be intolerable. The connected Internet is composed of a set of autonomous systems, where each autonomous system consists of routers and networks under one administrative authority. An autonomous system uses an Exterior Gateway Protocol to advertise routes to other autonomous systems. Specifically, an autonomous system must advertise reachability of its networks to another system before its networks are reachable from sources within the other system.

The Border Gateway Protocol, BGP, is the most widely used Exterior Gateway Protocol. We saw that BGP contains three message types that are used to initiate communication (OPEN), send reachability information (UPDATE) and report an error condition (NOTIFICATION). Each message starts with a standard header that includes (optional) authentication information. BGP uses TCP for communication, but has a keepalive mechanism to ensure that peers remain in communication.

In the global Internet, each ISP is assigned to a separate autonomous system, and the main boundary among autonomous systems occurs at NAPs, where multiple ISPs interconnect. Instead of requiring pairs of ISPs to use BGP to exchange routing information, each NAP includes a route server. An ISP uses BGP to communicate with the route server, both to advertise reachability to its networks and its customers' networks as well as to learn about networks in other ISPs.

FOR FURTHER STUDY

Background on early Internet routing can be found in [RFCs 827, 888, 904, and 975]. Rekhter and Li [RFC 1771] describes version 4 of the Border Gateway Protocol *(BGP-4)*. BGP has been through three substantial revisions; earlier versions appear in [RFCs 1163, 1267, and 1654]. Traina [RFC 1773] reports experience with BGP-4, and Traina [RFC 1774] analyzes the volume of routing traffic generated. Finally, Villamizar et. al. {RFC 2439] considers the problem of route flapping.

EXERCISES

15.1   If your site runs an Exterior Gateway Protocol such as BGP, how many routes does NSFNET advertise?

15.2   Some implementations of BGP use a ''hold down'' mechanism that causes the protocol to delay accepting an *OPEN* from a peer for a fixed time following the receipt of a *cease request* message from that neighbor. Find out what problem a hold down helps solve.

15.3   For the networks in Figure 15.2, which router(s) should run BGP? Why?

15.4   The formal specification of BGP includes a finite state machine that explains how BGP operates. Draw a diagram of the state machine and label transitions.

15.5   What happens if a router in an autonomous system sends BGP routing update messages to a router in another autonomous system, claiming to have reachability for every possible internet destination?

15.6   Can two autonomous systems establish a routing loop by sending BGP update messages to one another? Why or why not?

15.7   Should a router that uses BGP to advertise routes treat the set of routes advertised differently than the set of routes in the local routing table? For example, should a router ever advertise reachability if it has not installed a route to that network in its routing table? Why or why not? Hint: read the RFC.

15.8   With regard to the previous question, examine the BGP-4 specification carefully. Is it legal to advertise reachability to a destination that is not listed in the local routing table?

15.9   If you work for a large corporation, find out whether it includes more than one autonomous system. If so, how do they exchange routing information?

15.10   What is the chief advantage of dividing a large, multi-national corporation into multiple autonomous systems? What is the chief disadvantage?

15.11   Corporations *A* and *B* use BGP to exchange routing information. To keep computers in *B* from reaching machines on one of its networks, *N*, the network administrator at corporation *A* configures BGP to omit *N* from advertisements sent to *B*. Is network *N* secure? Why or why not?

15.12   Because BGP uses a reliable transport protocol, KEEPALIVE messages cannot be lost. Does it make sense to specify a keepalive interval as one-third of the hold timer value? Why or why not?

15.13   Consult the RFCs for details of the *Path Attributes* field. What is the minimum size of a BGP UPDATE message?

16

Routing: In An Autonomous System (RIP, OSPF, HELLO)

16.1 Introduction

The previous chapter introduces the autonomous system concept and examines BGP, an Exterior Gateway Protocol that a router uses to advertise networks within its system to other autonomous systems. This chapter completes our overview of internet routing by examining how a router in an autonomous system learns about other networks within its autonomous system.

16.2 Static Vs. Dynamic Interior Routes

Two routers within an autonomous system are said to be *interior* to one another. For example, two routers on a university campus are considered interior to one another as long as machines on the campus are collected into a single autonomous system.

How can routers in an autonomous system learn about networks within the autonomous system? In small, slowly changing internets, managers can establish and modify routes by hand. The administrator keeps a table of networks and updates the table whenever a new network is added to, or deleted from, the autonomous system. For example, consider the small corporate internet shown in Figure 16.1.

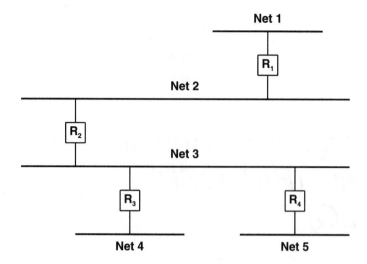

Figure 16.1 An example of a small internet consisting of 5 Ethernets and 4
routers at a single site. Only one possible route exists between
any two hosts in this internet.

Routing for the internet in the figure is trivial because only one path exists between
any two points. The manager can manually configure routes in all hosts and routers. If
the internet changes (e.g., a new network is added), the manager must reconfigure the
routes in all machines.

The disadvantages of a manual system are obvious: manual systems cannot accommodate rapid growth or rapid change. In large, rapidly changing environments like the
global Internet, humans simply cannot respond to changes fast enough to handle problems; automated methods must be used. Automated methods can also help improve reliability and response to failure in small internets that have alternate routes. To see
how, consider what happens if we add one additional router to the internet in Figure
16.1, producing the internet shown in Figure 16.2.

In internet architectures that have multiple physical paths, managers usually choose
one to be the primary path. If the routers along the primary path fail, routes must be
changed to send traffic along an alternate path. Changing routes manually is both time
consuming and error-prone. Thus, even in small internets, an automated system should
be used to change routes quickly and reliably.

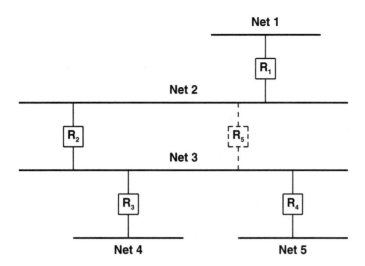

Figure 16.2 The addition of router R_5 introduces an alternate path between networks *2* and *3*. Routing software can quickly adapt to a failure and automatically switch routes to the alternate path.

To automate the task of keeping network reachability information accurate, interior routers usually communicate with one another, exchanging either network reachability data or network routing information from which reachability can be deduced. Once the reachability information for an entire autonomous system has been assembled, one of the routers in the system can advertise it to other autonomous systems using an Exterior Gateway Protocol.

Unlike exterior router communication, for which BGP provides a widely accepted standard, no single protocol has emerged for use within an autonomous system. Part of the reason for diversity comes from the varied topologies and technologies used in autonomous systems. Another part of the reason stems from the tradeoffs between simplicity and functionality — protocols that are easy to install and configure do not provide sophisticated functionality. As a result, a handful of protocols have become popular. Most small autonomous systems choose a single protocol, and use it exclusively to propagate routing information internally. Larger autonomous systems often choose a small set.

Because there is no single standard, we use the term *Interior Gateway Protocol* (*IGP*) as a generic description that refers to any algorithm that interior routers use when they exchange network reachability and routing information. For example, the last generation of core routers used a protocol named *SPREAD* as its Interior Gateway Protocol. Some autonomous systems use BGP as their IGP, although this seldom makes sense for small autonomous systems that span local area networks with broadcast capability.

Figure 16.3 illustrates two autonomous systems, each using an IGP to propagate routing information among its interior routers.

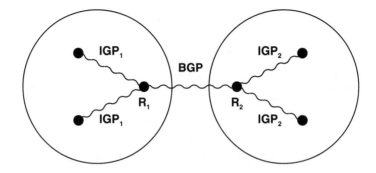

Figure 16.3 Conceptual view of two autonomous systems each using its own IGP internally, but using BGP to communicate between an exterior router and the other system.

In the figure, *IGP₁* refers to the interior router protocol used within autonomous system *1*, and *IGP₂* refers to the protocol used within autonomous system *2*. The figure also illustrates an important idea:

> *A single router may use two different routing protocols simultaneously, one for communication outside its autonomous system and another for communication within its autonomous system.*

In particular, routers that run BGP to advertise reachability usually also need to run an IGP to obtain information from within their autonomous system.

16.3 Routing Information Protocol (RIP)

16.3.1 History of RIP

One of the most widely used IGPs is the *Routing Information Protocol* (*RIP*), also known by the name of a program that implements it, *routed*†. The *routed* software was originally designed at the University of California at Berkeley to provide consistent routing and reachability information among machines on their local networks. It relies on physical network broadcast to make routing exchanges quickly. It was not designed to be used on large, wide area networks (although vendors now sell versions of RIP adapted for use on WANs).

Based on earlier internetworking research done at Xerox Corporation's Palo Alto Research Center (PARC), *routed* implements a protocol derived from the Xerox *NS Routing Information Protocol* (*RIP*), but generalizes it to cover multiple families of networks.

---

†The name comes from the UNIX convention of attaching ''d'' to the names of daemon processes; it is pronounced ''route-d''.

Despite minor improvements over its predecessors, the popularity of RIP as an IGP does not arise from its technical merits alone. Instead, it is the result of Berkeley distributing *routed* software along with their popular 4BSD UNIX systems. Thus, many TCP/IP sites adopted and installed *routed*, and started using RIP without even considering its technical merits or limitations. Once installed and running, it became the basis for local routing, and research groups adopted it for larger networks.

Perhaps the most startling fact about RIP is that it was built and widely adopted before a formal standard was written. Most implementations were derived from the Berkeley code, with interoperability among them limited by the programmer's understanding of undocumented details and subtleties. As new versions appeared, more problems arose. An RFC standard appeared in June 1988, and made it possible for vendors to ensure interoperability.

16.3.2 RIP Operation

The underlying RIP protocol is a straightforward implementation of distance-vector routing for local networks. It partitions participants into *active* and *passive* (i.e., *silent*) machines. Active participants advertise their routes to others; passive participants listen to RIP messages and use them to update their routing table, but do not advertise. Only a router can run RIP in active mode; a host must use passive mode.

A router running RIP in active mode broadcasts a routing update message every 30 seconds. The update contains information taken from the router's current routing database. Each update contains a set of pairs, where each pair contains an IP network address and an integer distance to that network. RIP uses a *hop count metric* to measure distances. In the RIP metric, a router is defined to be one hop from a directly connected network†, two hops from a network that is reachable through one other router, and so on. Thus, the *number of hops* or the *hop count* along a path from a given source to a given destination refers to the number of routers that a datagram encounters along that path. It should be obvious that using hop counts to calculate shortest paths does not always produce optimal results. For example, a path with hop count *3* that crosses three Ethernets may be substantially faster than a path with hop count *2* that crosses two satellite connections. To compensate for differences in technologies, many RIP implementations allow managers to configure artificially high hop counts when advertising connections to slow networks.

Both active and passive RIP participants listen to all broadcast messages, and update their tables according to the distance-vector algorithm described earlier. For example, in the internet of Figure 16.2, router R_1 will broadcast a message on network *2* that contains the pair *(1, 1)*, meaning that it can reach network *1* at cost *1*. Routers R_2 and R_5 will receive the broadcast and install a route to network *1* through R_1 (at cost *2*). Later, routers R_2 and R_5 will include the pair *(1, 2)* when they broadcast their RIP messages on network *3*. Eventually, all routers and hosts will install a route to network *1*.

RIP specifies a few rules to improve performance and reliability. For example, once a router learns a route from another router, it must apply *hysteresis*, meaning that it does not replace the route with an equal cost route. In our example, if routers R_2 and

---

†Other routing protocols define a direct connection to be zero hops.

R_5 both advertise network *1* at cost 2, routers R_3 and R_4 will install a route through the one that happens to advertise first. We can summarize:

> *To prevent oscillation among equal cost paths, RIP specifies that existing routes should be retained until a new route has strictly lower cost.*

What happens if the first router to advertise a route fails (e.g., if it crashes)? RIP specifies that all listeners must timeout routes they learn via RIP. When a router installs a route in its table, it starts a timer for that route. The timer must be restarted whenever the router receives another RIP message advertising the route. The route becomes invalid if 180 seconds pass without the route being advertised again.

RIP must handle three kinds of errors caused by the underlying algorithm. First, because the algorithm does not explicitly detect routing loops, RIP must either assume participants can be trusted or take precautions to prevent such loops. Second, to prevent instabilities RIP must use a low value for the maximum possible distance (RIP uses *16*). Thus, for internets in which legitimate hop counts approach *16*, managers must divide the internet into sections or use an alternative protocol. Third, the distance-vector algorithm used by RIP can create a *slow convergence* or *count to infinity* problem, in which inconsistencies arise because routing update messages propagate slowly across the network. Choosing a small infinity (*16*) helps limit slow convergence, but does not eliminate it.

Routing table inconsistency is not unique to RIP. It is a fundamental problem that occurs with any distance-vector protocol in which update messages carry only pairs of destination network and distance to that network. To understand the problem consider the set of routers shown in Figure 16.4. The figure depicts routes to network *1* for the internet shown in Figure 16.2.

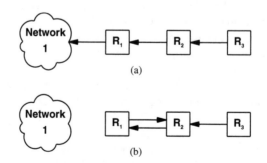

Figure 16.4 The slow convergence problem. In (a) three routers each have a route to network *1*. In (b) the connection to network *1* has vanished, but R_2 causes a loop by advertising it.

As Figure 16.4a shows, router R_1 has a direct connection to network *1*, so there is a route in its table with distance *1*, which will be included in its periodic broadcasts. Router R_2 has learned the route from R_1, installed the route in its routing table, and advertises the route at distance *2*. Finally, R_3 has learned the route from R_2 and advertises it at distance *3*.

Now suppose that R_1's connection to network *1* fails. R_1 will update its routing table immediately to make the distance *16* (infinity). In the next broadcast, R_1 will report the higher cost route. However, unless the protocol includes extra mechanisms to prevent it, some other router could broadcast its routes before R_1. In particular, suppose R_2 happens to advertise routes just after R_1's connection fails. If so, R_1 will receive R_2's message and follow the usual distance-vector algorithm: it notices that R_2 has advertised a route to network *1* at lower cost, calculates that it now takes *3* hops to reach network *1* (*2* for R_2 to reach network *1* plus *1* to reach R_2), *and installs a new route with R_2 list-ed as the next hop*. Figure 16.4b depicts the result. At this point, if either R_1 or R_2 receives a datagram destined for network *1*, they will route the datagram back and forth until the datagram's time-to-live counter expires.

Subsequent RIP broadcasts by the two routers do not solve the problem quickly. In the next round of routing exchanges, R_1 broadcasts its routing table entries. When it learns that R_1's route to network *1* has distance *3*, R_2 calculates a new distance for its route, making it *4*. In the third round, R_1 receives a report from R_2 which includes the increased distance, and then increases the distance in its table to *5*. The two routers continue counting to RIP infinity.

16.3.3 Solving The Slow Convergence Problem

For the example in Figure 16.4, it is possible to solve the slow convergence problem by using a technique known as *split horizon update*. When using split horizon, a router does not propagate information about a route back over the same interface from which the route arrived. In the example, split horizon prevents router R_2 from advertising a route to network *1* back to router R_1, so if R_1 loses connectivity to network *1*, it must stop advertising a route. With split horizon, no routing loop appears in the example network. Instead, after a few rounds of routing updates, all routers will agree that the network is unreachable. However, the split horizon heuristic does not prevent routing loops in all possible topologies as one of the exercises suggests.

Another way to think of the slow convergence problem is in terms of information flow. If a router advertises a short route to some network, all receiving routers respond quickly to install that route. If a router stops advertising a route, the protocol must depend on a timeout mechanism before it considers the route unreachable. Once the timeout occurs, the router finds an alternative route and starts propagating that information. Unfortunately, a router cannot know if the alternate route depended on the route that just disappeared. Thus, negative information does not always propagate quickly. A short epigram captures the idea and explains the phenomenon:

Good news travels quickly; bad news travels slowly.

Another technique used to solve the slow convergence problem employs *hold down*. Hold down forces a participating router to ignore information about a network for a fixed period of time following receipt of a message that claims the network is unreachable. Typically, the hold down period is set to 60 seconds. The idea is to wait long enough to ensure that all machines receive the bad news and not mistakenly accept a message that is out of date. It should be noted that all machines participating in a RIP exchange need to use identical notions of hold down, or routing loops can occur. The disadvantage of a hold down technique is that if routing loops occur, they will be preserved for the duration of the hold down period. More important, the hold down technique preserves all incorrect routes during the hold down period, even when alternatives exist.

A final technique for solving the slow convergence problem is called *poison reverse*. Once a connection disappears, the router advertising the connection retains the entry for several update periods, and includes an infinite cost in its broadcasts. To make poison reverse most effective, it must be combined with *triggered updates*. Triggered updates force a router to send an immediate broadcast when receiving bad news, instead of waiting for the next periodic broadcast. By sending an update immediately, a router minimizes the time it is vulnerable to believing good news.

Unfortunately, while triggered updates, poison reverse, hold down, and split horizon techniques all solve some problems, they introduce others. For example, consider what happens with triggered updates when many routers share a common network. A single broadcast may change all their routing tables, triggering a new round of broadcasts. If the second round of broadcasts changes tables, it will trigger even more broadcasts. A broadcast avalanche can result†.

The use of broadcast, potential for routing loops, and use of hold down to prevent slow convergence can make RIP extremely inefficient in a wide area network. Broadcasting always takes substantial bandwidth. Even if no avalanche problems occur, having all machines broadcast periodically means that the traffic increases as the number of routers increases. The potential for routing loops can also be deadly when line capacity is limited. Once lines become saturated by looping packets, it may be difficult or impossible for routers to exchange the routing messages needed to break the loops. Also, in a wide area network, hold down periods are so long that the timers used by higher level protocols can expire and lead to broken connections. Despite these well-known problems, many groups continue to use RIP as an IGP in wide area networks.

16.3.4 RIP1 Message Format

RIP messages can be broadly classified into two types: routing information messages and messages used to request information. Both use the same format which consists of a fixed header followed by an optional list of network and distance pairs. Figure 16.5 shows the message format used with version *1* of the protocol, which is known as *RIP1*:

---

†To help avoid collisions on the underlying network, RIP requires each router to wait a small random time before sending a triggered update.

0	8	16	24	31
COMMAND (1-5)	VERSION (1)	MUST BE ZERO		
FAMILY OF NET 1		MUST BE ZERO		
IP ADDRESS OF NET 1				
MUST BE ZERO				
MUST BE ZERO				
DISTANCE TO NET 1				
FAMILY OF NET 2		MUST BE ZERO		
IP ADDRESS OF NET 2				
MUST BE ZERO				
MUST BE ZERO				
DISTANCE TO NET 2				
. . .				

Figure 16.5 The format of a version 1 RIP message. After the 32-bit header, the message contains a sequence of pairs, where each pair consists of a network IP address and an integer distance to that network.

In the figure, field *COMMAND* specifies an operation according to the following table:

Command	Meaning
1	Request for partial or full routing information
2	Response containing network-distance pairs from sender's routing table
3	Turn on trace mode (obsolete)
4	Turn off trace mode (obsolete)
5	Reserved for Sun Microsystems internal use
9	Update Request (used with demand circuits)
10	Update Response (used with demand circuits)
11	Update Acknowledge (used with demand circuits)

A router or host can ask another router for routing information by sending a *request* command. Routers reply to requests using the *response* command. In most cases, however, routers broadcast unsolicited response messages periodically. Field *VERSION* contains the protocol version number (*1* in this case), and is used by the receiver to verify it will interpret the message correctly.

16.3.5 RIP1 Address Conventions

The generality of RIP is also evident in the way it transmits network addresses. The address format is not limited to use by TCP/IP; it can be used with multiple network protocol suites. As Figure 16.5 shows, each network address reported by RIP can have an address of up to 14 octets. Of course, IP addresses need only 4; RIP specifies that the remaining octets must be zero†. The field labeled *FAMILY OF NET i* identifies the protocol family under which the network address should be interpreted. RIP uses values assigned to address families under the 4BSD UNIX operating system (IP addresses are assigned value 2).

In addition to normal IP addresses, RIP uses the convention that address *0.0.0.0* denotes a *default route*. RIP attaches a distance metric to every route it advertises, including default routes. Thus, it is possible to arrange for two routers to advertise a default route (e.g., a route to the rest of the internet) at different metrics, making one of them a primary path and the other a backup.

The final field of each entry in a RIP message, *DISTANCE TO NET i*, contains an integer count of the distance to the specified network. Distances are measured in router hops, but values are limited to the range *1* through *16*, with distance *16* used to signify infinity (i.e., no route exists).

16.3.6 RIP1 Route Interpretation And Aggregation

Because RIP was originally designed to be used with classful addresses, version 1 did not include any provision for a subnet mask. When subnet addressing was added to IP, version 1 of RIP was extended to permit routers to exchange subnetted addresses. However, because RIP1 update messages do not contain explicit mask information, an important restriction was added: a router can include host-specific or subnet-specific addresses in routing updates as long as all receivers can unambiguously interpret the addresses. In particular, subnet routes can only be included in updates sent across a network that is part of the subnetted prefix, and only if the subnet mask used with the network is the same as the subnet mask used with the address. In essence, the restriction means that RIP1 cannot be used to propagate variable-length subnet address or classless addresses. We can summarize:

> *Because it does not include explicit subnet information, RIP1 only permits a router to send subnet routes if receivers can unambiguously interpret the addresses according to the subnet mask they have available locally. As a consequence, RIP1 can only be used with classful or fixed-length subnet addresses.*

What happens when a router running RIP1 connects to one or more networks that are subnets of a prefix N as well as to one or more networks that are not part of N? The router must prepare different update messages for the two types of interfaces. Updates sent over the interfaces that are subnets of N can include subnet routes, but updates sent

---

†The designers chose to locate an IP address in the third through sixth octets of the address field to ensure 32-bit alignment.

over other interfaces cannot. Instead, when sending over other interfaces the router is required to *aggregate* the subnet information and advertise a single route to network *N*.

16.3.7 RIP2 Extensions

The restriction on address interpretation means that version 1 of RIP cannot be used to propagate either variable-length subnet addresses or the classless addresses used with CIDR. When version 2 of RIP (*RIP2*) was defined, the protocol was extended to include an explicit subnet mask along with each address. In addition, RIP2 updates include explicit next-hop information, which prevents routing loops and slow convergence. As a result, RIP2 offers significantly increased functionality as well as improved resistance to errors.

16.3.8 RIP2 Message Format

The message format used with RIP2 is an extension of the RIP1 format, with additional information occupying unused octets of the address field. In particular, each address includes an explicit next hop as well as an explicit subnet mask as Figure 16.6 illustrates.

0	8	16	24	31
COMMAND (1-5)	VERSION (1)	MUST BE ZERO		
FAMILY OF NET 1		ROUTE TAG FOR NET 1		
IP ADDRESS OF NET 1				
SUBNET MASK FOR NET 1				
NEXT HOP FOR NET 1				
DISTANCE TO NET 1				
FAMILY OF NET 2		ROUTE TAG FOR NET 2		
IP ADDRESS OF NET 2				
SUBNET MASK FOR NET 2				
NEXT HOP FOR NET 2				
DISTANCE TO NET 2				
. . .				

Figure 16.6 The format of a RIP2 message. In addition to pairs of a network IP address and an integer distance to that network, the message contains a subnet mask for each address and explicit next-hop information.

RIP2 also attaches a 16-bit *ROUTE TAG* field to each entry. A router must send the same tag it receives when it transmits the route. Thus, the tag provides a way to propagate additional information such as the origin of the route. In particular, if RIP2 learns a route from another autonomous system, it can use the *ROUTE TAG* to propagate the autonomous system's number.

Because the version number in RIP2 occupies the same octet as in RIP1, both versions of the protocols can be used on a given router simultaneously without interference. Before processing an incoming message, RIP software examines the version number.

16.3.9 Transmitting RIP Messages

RIP messages do not contain an explicit length field or an explicit count of entries. Instead, RIP assumes that the underlying delivery mechanism will tell the receiver the length of an incoming message. In particular, when used with TCP/IP, RIP messages rely on UDP to tell the receiver the message length. RIP operates on UDP port *520*. Although a RIP request can originate at other UDP ports, the destination UDP port for requests is always *520*, as is the source port from which RIP broadcast messages originate.

16.3.10 The Disadvantage Of RIP Hop Counts

Using RIP as an interior router protocol limits routing in two ways. First, RIP restricts routing to a hop-count metric. Second, because it uses a small value of hop count for infinity, RIP restricts the size of any internet using it. In particular, RIP restricts the *span* of an internet (i.e., the maximum distance across) to 16. That is, an internet using RIP can have at most 15 routers between any two hosts.

Note that the limit on network span is neither a limit on the total number of routers nor a limit on density. In fact, most campus networks have a small span even if they have many routers because the topology is arranged as a *hierarchy*. Consider, for example, a typical corporate intranet. Most use a hierarchy that consists of a high-speed backbone network with multiple routers each connecting the backbone to a workgroup, where each workgroup occupies a single LAN. Although the corporation can include dozens of workgroups, the span of the entire intranet is only 2. Even if each workgroup is extended to include a router that connects one or more additional LANs, the maximum span only increases to 4. Similarly, extending the hierarchy one more level only increases the span to 6. Thus, the limit that RIP imposes affects large autonomous systems or autonomous systems that do not have a hierarchical organization.

Even in the best cases, however, hop counts provide only a crude measure of network capacity or responsiveness. Thus, using hop counts does not always yield routes with least delay or highest capacity. Furthermore, computing routes on the basis of minimum hop counts has the severe disadvantage that it makes routing relatively static because routes cannot respond to changes in network load. The next sections consider an alternative metric, and explain why hop count metrics remain popular despite their limitations.

16.4 The Hello Protocol

The HELLO protocol provides an example of an IGP that uses a routing metric other than hop count. Although HELLO is now obsolete, it was significant in the history of the Internet because it was the IGP used among the original NSFNET backbone ''fuzzball'' routers†. HELLO is significant to us because it provides an example of a protocol that uses a metric of delay.

HELLO provides two functions: it synchronizes the clocks among a set of machines, and it allows each machine to compute shortest delay paths to destinations. Thus, HELLO messages carry timestamp information as well as routing information. The basic idea behind HELLO is simple: each machine participating in the HELLO exchange maintains a table of its best estimate of the clocks in neighboring machines. Before transmitting a packet, a machine adds its timestamp by copying the current clock value into the packet. When a packet arrives, the receiver computes an estimate of the current delay on the link by subtracting the timestamp on the incoming packet from the local estimate for the current clock in the neighbor. Periodically, machines poll their neighbors to reestablish estimates for clocks.

HELLO messages also allow participating machines to compute new routes. The protocol uses a modified distance-vector scheme that uses a metric of delay instead of hop count. Thus, each machine periodically sends its neighbors a table of destinations it can reach and an estimated delay for each. When a message arrives from machine X, the receiver examines each entry in the message and changes the next hop to X if the route through X is less expensive than the current route (i.e., any route where the delay to X plus the delay from X to the destination is less than the current delay to the destination).

16.5 Delay Metrics And Oscillation

It may seem that using delay as a routing metric would produce better routes than using a hop count. In fact, HELLO worked well in the early Internet backbone. However, there is an important reasons why delay is not used as a metric in most protocols: instability.

Even if two paths have identical characteristics, any protocol that changes routes quickly can become unstable. Instability arises because delay, unlike hop counts, is not fixed. Minor variations in delay measurements occur because of hardware clock drift, CPU load during measurement, or bit delays caused by link-level synchronization. Thus, if a routing protocol reacts quickly to slight differences in delay, it can produce a two-stage oscillation effect in which traffic switches back and forth between the alternate paths. In the first stage, the router finds the delay on path *1* slightly less and abruptly switches traffic onto it. In the next round, the router finds that path *B* has slightly less delay and switches traffic back.

To help avoid oscillation, protocols that use delay implement several heuristics. First, they employ the *hold down* technique discussed previously to prevent routes from

---

†The term *fuzzball* referred to a noncommercial router that consisted of specially-crafted protocol software running on a PDP11 computer.

changing rapidly. Second, instead of measuring as accurately as possible and comparing the values directly, the protocols round measurements to large multiples or implement a minimum *threshold* by ignoring differences less than the threshold. Third, instead of comparing each individual delay measurement, they keep a running *average* of recent values or alternatively apply a *K-out-of-N* rule that requires at least *K* of the most recent *N* delay measurements be less than the current delay before the route can be changed.

Even with heuristics, protocols that use delay can become unstable when comparing delays on paths that do not have identical characteristics. To undersand why, it is necessary to know that traffic can have a dramatic effect on delay. With no traffic, the network delay is simply the time required for the hardware to transfer bits from one point to another. As the traffic load imposed on the network increases, however, delays begin to rise because routers in the system need to enqueue packets that are waiting for transmission. If the load is even slightly more than 100% of the network capacity, the queue becomes unbounded, meaning that the effective delay becomes infinite. To summarize:

> *The effective delay across a network depends on traffic; as the load increases to 100% of the network capacity, delay grows rapidly.*

Because delays are extremely sensitive to changes in load, protocols that use delay as a metric can easily fall into a *positive feedback cycle*. The cycle is triggered by a small external change in load (e.g., one computer injecting a burst of additional traffic). The increased traffic raises the delay, which causes the protocol to change routes. However, because a route change affects the load, it can produce an even larger change in delays, which means the protocol will again recompute routes. As a result, protocols that use delay must contain mechanisms to dampen oscillation.

We described heuristics that can solve simple cases of route oscillation when paths have identical throughput characteristics and the load is not excessive. The heuristics can become ineffective, however, when alternative paths have different delay and throughput characteristics. As an example consider the delay on two paths: one over a satellite and the other over a low capacity serial line (e.g., a 9600 baud serial line). In the first stage of the protocol when both paths are idle, the serial line will appear to have significantly lower delay than the satellite, and will be chosen for traffic. Because the serial line has low capacity, it will quickly become overloaded, and the delay will rise sharply. In the second stage, the delay on the serial line will be much greater than that of the satellite, so the protocol will switch traffic away from the overloaded path. Because the satellite path has large capacity, traffic which overloaded the serial line does not impose a significant load on the satellite, meaning that the delay on the satellite path does not change with traffic. In the next round, the delay on the unloaded serial line will once again appear to be much smaller than the delay on the satellite path. The protocol will reverse the routing, and the cycle will continue. Such oscillations do, in fact, occur in practice. As the example shows, they are difficult to manage because traffic which has little effect on one network can overload another.

16.6 Combining RIP, Hello, And BGP

We have already observed that a single router may use both an Interior Gateway Protocol to gather routing information within its autonomous system and an Exterior Gateway Protocol to advertise routes to other autonomous systems. In principle, it should be easy to construct a single piece of software that combines the two protocols, making it possible to gather routes and advertise them without human intervention. In practice, technical and political obstacles make doing so complex.

Technically, IGP protocols, like RIP and Hello, are routing protocols. A router uses such protocols to update its routing table based on information it acquires from other routers inside its autonomous system. Thus, *routed*, the UNIX program that implements RIP, advertises information from the local routing table and changes the local routing table when it receives updates. RIP trusts routers within the same autonomous system to pass correct data.

In contrast, exterior protocols such as BGP do not trust routers in other autonomous systems. Consequently, exterior protocols do not advertise all possible routes from the local routing table. Instead, such protocols keep a database of network reachability, and apply policy constraints when sending or receiving information. Ignoring such policy constraints can affect routing in a larger sense — some parts of the internet can be become unreachable. For example, if a router in an autonomous system that is running RIP happens to propagate a low-cost route to a network at Purdue University when it has no such route, other routers running RIP will accept and install the route. They will then pass Purdue traffic to the router that made the error. As a result, it may be impossible for hosts in that autonomous system to reach Purdue. The problem becomes more serious if Exterior Gateway Protocols do not implement policy constraints. For example, if a border router in the autonomous system uses BGP to propagate the illegal route to other autonomous systems, the network at Purdue may become unreachable from some parts of the internet.

16.7 Inter-Autonomous System Routing

We have seen that EGPs such as BGP allow one autonomous system to advertise reachability information to another. However, it would be useful to also provide *inter-autonomous system routing* in which routers choose least-cost paths. Doing so requires additional trust. Extending the notions of trust from a single autonomous system to multiple autonomous systems is complex. The simplest approach groups autonomous systems hierarchically. Imagine, for example, three autonomous systems in three separate academic departments on a large university campus. It is natural to group these three together because they share administrative ties. The motivation for hierarchical grouping comes primarily from the notion of trust. Routers within a group trust one another with a higher level of confidence than routers in separate groups.

Grouping autonomous systems requires extensions to routing protocols. When reporting distances, the values must be increased when passing across the boundary from one group to another. The technique, loosely called *metric transformation*, partitions distance values into three categories. For example, suppose routers within an autonomous system use distance values less than 128. We can make a rule that when passing distance information across an autonomous system boundary within a single group, the distances must be transformed into the range of 128 to 191. Finally, we can make a rule that when passing distance values across the boundary between two groups, the values must be transformed into the range of 192 to 254†. The effect of such transformations is obvious: for any given destination network, any path that lies entirely within the autonomous system is guaranteed to have lower cost than a path that strays outside the autonomous system. Furthermore, among all paths that stray outside the autonomous system, those that remain within the group have lower cost than those that cross group boundaries. The key advantage of metric transformations is that they allow each autonomous system to choose an IGP, yet make it possible for other systems to compare routing costs.

16.8 Gated: Inter-Autonomous System Communication

A mechanism has been created to provide an interface between autonomous systems. Known as *gated*‡, the mechanism understands multiple protocols (both IGPs and BGP), and ensures that policy constraints are honored. For example, *gated* can accept RIP messages and modify the local computer's routing table just like the *routed* program. It can also advertise routes from within its autonomous system using BGP. The rules gated follows allow a system administrator to specify exactly which networks *gated* may and may not advertise and how to report distances to those networks. Thus, although *gated* is not an IGP, it plays an important role in routing because it demonstrates that it is feasible to build an automated mechanism linking an IGP with BGP without sacrificing protection.

Gated performs another useful task by implementing metric transformations. Thus, it is possible and convenient to use gated between two autonomous systems as well as on the boundary between two groups of routers that each participate in an IGP.

16.9 The Open SPF Protocol (OSPF)

In Chapter 14, we said that a link state routing algorithm, which uses SPF to compute shortest paths, scales better than a distance-vector algorithm. To encourage the adoption of link state technology, a working group of the Internet Engineering Task Force has designed an interior gateway protocol that uses the link state algorithm. Called *Open SPF (OSPF)*, the new protocol tackles several ambitious goals.

• As the name implies, the specification is available in the published literature. Making it an open standard that anyone can implement without paying license fees has encouraged many vendors to support OSPF. Consequently, it has become a popular replacement for proprietary protocols.

---

†The term *autonomous confederation* has been used to describe a group of autonomous systems; boundaries of autonomous confederations correspond to transformations beyond 191.

‡The name *gated* is pronounced ''gate d'' from ''gate daemon.''

• OSPF includes *type of service routing*. Managers can install multiple routes to a given destination, one for each priority or type of service. When routing a datagram, a router running OSPF uses both the destination address and type of service field in an IP header to choose a route. OSPF is among the first TCP/IP protocols to offer type of service routing.

• OSPF provides *load balancing*. If a manager specifies multiple routes to a given destination at the same cost, OSPF distributes traffic over all routes equally. Again, OSPF is among the first open IGPs to offer load balancing; protocols like RIP compute a single route to each destination.

• To permit growth and make the networks at a site easier to manage, OSPF allows a site to partition its networks and routers into subsets called *areas*. Each area is self-contained; knowledge of an area's topology remains hidden from other areas. Thus, multiple groups within a given site can cooperate in the use of OSPF for routing even though each group retains the ability to change its internal network topology independently.

• The OSPF protocol specifies that all exchanges between routers can be *authenticated*. OSPF allows a variety of authentication schemes, and even allows one area to choose a different scheme than another area. The idea behind authentication is to guarantee that only trusted routers propagate routing information. To understand why this could be a problem, consider what can happen when using RIP1, which has no authentication. If a malicious person uses a personal computer to propagate RIP messages advertising low-cost routes, other routers and hosts running RIP will change their routes and start sending datagrams to the personal computer.

• OSPF includes support for host-specific, subnet-specific, and classless routes as well as classful network-specific routes. All types may be needed in a large internet.

• To accommodate multi-access networks like Ethernet, OSPF extends the SPF algorithm described in Chapter 14. We described the algorithm using a point-to-point graph and said that each router running SPF would periodically broadcast link status messages about each reachable neighbor. If K routers attach to an Ethernet, they will broadcast K^2 reachability messages. OSPF minimizes broadcasts by allowing a more complex graph topology in which each node represents either a router or a network. Consequently, OSPF allows every multi-access network to have a *designated gateway* (i.e., a *designated router*) that sends link status messages on behalf of all routers attached to the network; the messages report the status of all links from the network to routers attached to the network. OSPF also uses hardware broadcast capabilities, where they exist, to deliver link status messages.

• To permit maximum flexibility, OSPF allows managers to describe a virtual network topology that abstracts away from the details of physical connections. For example, a manager can configure a virtual link between two routers in the routing graph even if the physical connection between the two routers requires communication across a transit network.

• OSPF allows routers to exchange routing information learned from other (external) sites. Basically, one or more routers with connections to other sites learn information about those sites and include it when sending update messages. The message format distinguishes between information acquired from external sources and information acquired from routers interior to the site, so there is no ambiguity about the source or reliability of routes.

16.9.1 OSPF Message Format

Each OSPF message begins with a fixed, 24-octet header as Figure 16.7 shows:

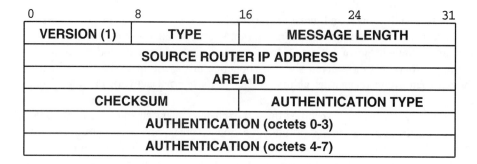

Figure 16.7 The fixed 24-octet OSPF message header.

Field *VERSION* specifies the version of the protocol. Field *TYPE* identifies the message type as one of:

Type	Meaning
1	Hello (used to test reachability)
2	Database description (topology)
3	Link status request
4	Link status update
5	Link status acknowledgement

The field labeled *SOURCE ROUTER IP ADDRESS* gives the address of the sender, and the field labeled *AREA ID* gives the 32-bit identification number for the area.

Because each message can include authentication, field *AUTHENTICATION TYPE* specifies which authentication scheme is used (currently, *0* means no authentication and *1* means a simple password is used).

16.9.2 OSPF Hello Message Format

OSPF sends *hello* messages on each link periodically to establish and test neighbor reachability. Figure 16.8 shows the format.

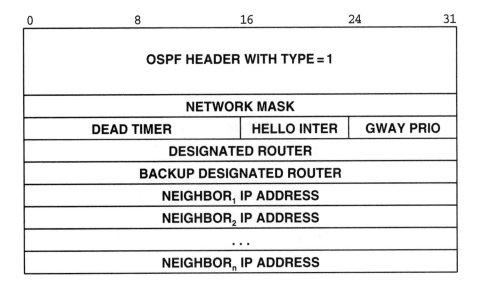

Figure 16.8 OSPF *hello* message format. A pair of neighbor routers exchanges these messages periodically to test reachability.

Field *NETWORK MASK* contains a mask for the network over which the message has been sent (see Chapter 10 for details about masks). Field *DEAD TIMER* gives a time in seconds after which a nonresponding neighbor is considered dead. Field *HELLO INTER* is the normal period, in seconds, between hello messages. Field *GWAY PRIO* is the integer priority of this router, and is used in selecting a backup designated router. The fields labeled *DESIGNATED ROUTER* and *BACKUP DESIGNATED ROUTER* contain IP addresses that give the sender's view of the designated router and backup designated router for the network over which the message is sent. Finally, fields labeled *NEIGHBOR$_i$ IP ADDRESS* give the IP addresses of all neighbors from which the sender has recently received hello messages.

16.9.3 OSPF Database Description Message Format

Routers exchange OSPF *database description* messages to initialize their network topology database. In the exchange, one router serves as a master, while the other is a slave. The slave acknowledges each database description message with a response. Figure 16.9 shows the format.

Because it can be large, the topology database may be divided into several messages using the *I* and *M* bits. Bit *I* is set to *1* in the initial message; bit *M* is set to *1* if additional messages follow. Bit *S* indicates whether a message was sent by a master (*1*) or by a slave (*0*). Field *DATABASE SEQUENCE NUMBER* numbers messages sequentially so the receiver can tell if one is missing. The initial message contains a random integer *R*; subsequent messages contain sequential integers starting at *R*.

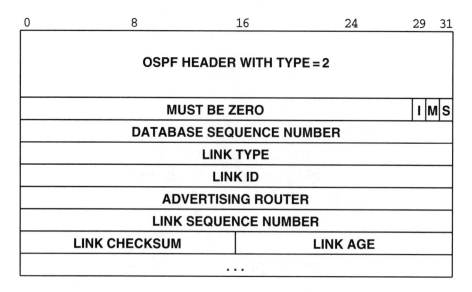

Figure 16.9 OSPF *database description* message format. The fields starting at *LINK TYPE* are repeated for each link being specified.

The fields from *LINK TYPE* through *LINK AGE* describe one link in the network topology; they are repeated for each link. The *LINK TYPE* describes a link according to the following table.

Link Type	Meaning
1	Router link
2	Network link
3	Summary link (IP network)
4	Summary link (link to border router)
5	External link (link to another site)

Field *LINK ID* gives an identification for the link (which can be the IP address of a router or a network, depending on the link type).

Field *ADVERTISING ROUTER* specifies the address of the router advertising this link, and *LINK SEQUENCE NUMBER* contains an integer generated by that router to ensure that messages are not missed or received out of order. Field *LINK CHECKSUM* provides further assurance that the link information has not been corrupted. Finally, field *LINK AGE* also helps order messages — it gives the time in seconds since the link was established.

16.9.4 OSPF Link Status Request Message Format

After exchanging database description messages with a neighbor, a router may discover that parts of its database are out of date. To request that the neighbor supply updated information, the router sends a *link status request* message. The message lists specific links as shown in Figure 16.10. The neighbor responds with the most current information it has about those links. The three fields shown are repeated for each link about which status is requested. More than one request message may be needed if the list of requests is long.

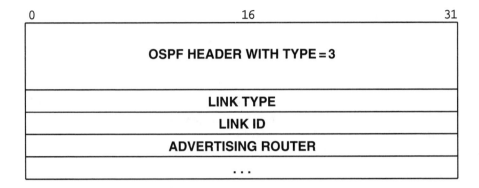

Figure 16.10 OSPF *link status request* message format. A router sends this message to a neighbor to request current information about a specific set of links.

16.9.5 OSPF Link Status Update Message Format

Routers broadcast the status of links with a *link status update* message. Each update consists of a list of advertisements, as Figure 16.11 shows.

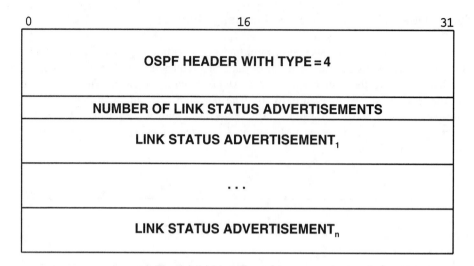

Figure 16.11 OSPF *link status update* message format. A router sends such a message to broadcast information about its directly connected links to all other routers.

Each link status advertisement has a header format as shown in Figure 16.12. The values used in each field are the same as in the database description message.

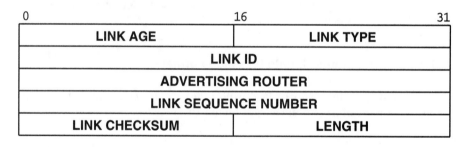

Figure 16.12 The format of the header used for all link status advertisements.

Following the link status header comes one of four possible formats to describe the links from a router to a given area, the links from a router to a specific network, the links from a router to the physical networks that comprise a single, subnetted IP network (see Chapter 10), or the links from a router to networks at other sites. In all cases, the *LINK TYPE* field in the link status header specifies which of the formats has been used. Thus, a router that receives a link status update message knows exactly which of the described destinations lie inside the site and which are external.

16.10 Routing With Partial Information

We began our discussion of internet router architecture and routing by discussing the concept of partial information. Hosts can route with only partial information because they rely on routers. It should be clear now that not all routers have complete information. Most autonomous systems have a single router that connects the autonomous system to other autonomous systems. For example, if the site connects to the global Internet, at least one router must have a connection that leads from the site to an ISP. Routers within the autonomous system know about destinations within that autonomous system, but they use a default route to send all other traffic to the ISP.

How to do routing with partial information becomes obvious if we examine a router's routing tables. Routers at the center of the Internet have a complete set of routes to all possible destinations that they learn from the routing arbiter system; such routers do not use default routing. In fact, if a destination network address does not appear in the routing arbiter database, only two possibilities exist: either the address is not a valid destination IP address, or the address is valid but currently unreachable (e.g., because routers or networks leading to that address have failed). Routers beyond those in ISPs at the center of the Internet do not usually have a complete set of routes; they rely on a default route to handle network addresses they do not understand.

Using default routes for most routers has two consequences. First, it means that local routing errors can go undetected. For example, if a machine in an autonomous system incorrectly routes a packet to an external autonomous system instead of to a local router, the external system will route it back (perhaps to a different entry point). Thus, connectivity may appear to be preserved even if routing is incorrect. The problem may not seem severe for small autonomous systems that have high speed local area networks, but in a wide area network, incorrect routes can be disastrous. Second, on the positive side, using default routes whenever possible means that the routing update messages exchanged by most routers will be much smaller than they would be if complete information had to be included.

16.11 Summary

Managers must choose how to pass routing information among the local routers within an autonomous system. Manual maintenance of routing information suffices only for small, slowly changing internets that have minimal interconnection; most require automated procedures that discover and update routes automatically. Two routers under the control of a single manager run an Interior Gateway Protocol, IGP, to exchange routing information.

An IGP implements either the distance-vector algorithm or the link state algorithm, which is known by the name Shortest Path First (SPF). We examined three specific IGPs: RIP, HELLO, and OSPF. RIP, a distance-vector protocol implemented by the UNIX program *routed*, is among the most popular. It uses split horizon, hold-down, and poison reverse techniques to help eliminate routing loops and the problem of counting to infinity. Although it is obsolete, Hello is interesting because it illustrates a distance-vector protocol that uses delay instead of hop counts as a distance metric. We discussed the disadvantages of delay as a routing metric, and pointed out that although heuristics can prevent instabilities from arising when paths have equal throughput characteristics, long-term instabilities arise when paths have different characteristics. Finally, OSPF is a protocol that implements the link status algorithm.

Also, we saw that the *gated* program provides an interface between an Interior Gateway Protocol like RIP and the Exterior Gateway Protocol, BGP, automating the process of gathering routes from within an autonomous system and advertising them to another autonomous system.

FOR FURTHER STUDY

Hedrick [RFC 1058] discusses algorithms for exchanging routing information in general and contains the standard specification for RIP1. Malkin [RFC 2453] gives the standard for RIP2. The HELLO protocol is documented in Mills [RFC 891]. Mills and Braun [1987] considers the problems of converting between delay and hop-count metrics. Moy [RFC 1583] contains the lengthy specification of OSPF as well as a discussion of the motivation behind it. Fedor [June 1988] describes *gated*.

EXERCISES

16.1   What network families does RIP support? Hint: read the networking section of the 4.3 BSD UNIX Programmer's Manual.

16.2   Consider a large autonomous system using an interior router protocol like HELLO that bases routes on delay. What difficulty does this autonomous system have if a subgroup decides to use RIP on its routers?

16.3   Within a RIP message, each IP address is aligned on a 32-bit boundary. Will such addresses be aligned on a 32-bit boundary if the IP datagram carrying the message starts on a 32-bit boundary?

16.4   An autonomous system can be as small as a single local area network or as large as multiple long haul networks. Why does the variation in size make it difficult to find a standard IGP?

16.5   Characterize the circumstances under which the split horizon technique will prevent slow convergence.

16.6   Consider an internet composed of many local area networks running RIP as an IGP. Find an example that shows how a routing loop can result even if the code uses ''hold down'' after receiving information that a network is unreachable.

16.7   Should a host ever run RIP in active mode? Why or why not?

16.8   Under what circumstances will a hop count metric produce better routes than a metric that uses delay?

16.9   Can you imagine a situation in which an autonomous system chooses *not* to advertise all its networks? Hint: think of a university.

16.10 In broad terms, we could say that RIP distributes the local routing table, while BGP distributes a table of networks and routers used to reach them (i.e., a router can send a BGP advertisement that does not exactly match items in its own routing table). What are the advantages of each approach?

16.11 Consider a function used to convert between delay and hop-count metrics. Can you find properties of such functions that are sufficient to prevent routing loops. Are your properties necessary as well? (Hint: look at Mills and Braun [1987].)

16.12 Are there circumstances under which an SPF protocol can form routing loops? Hint: think of best-effort delivery.

16.13 Build an application program that sends a request to a router running RIP and displays the routes returned.

16.14 Read the RIP specification carefully. Can routes reported in a response to a query differ from the routes reported by a routing update message? If so how?

16.15 Read the OSPF specification carefully. How can a manager use the virtual link facility?

16.16 OSPF allows managers to assign many of their own identifiers, possibly leading to duplication of values at multiple sites. Which identifier(s) may need to change if two sites running OSPF decide to merge?

16.17 Compare the version of OSPF available under 4BSD UNIX to the version of RIP for the same system. What are the differences in source code size? Object code size? Data storage size? What can you conclude?

16.18 Can you use ICMP redirect messages to pass routing information among *interior* routers? Why or why not?

16.19 Write a program that takes as input a description of your organization's internet, uses RIP queries to obtain routes from the routers, and reports any inconsistencies.

16.20 If your organization runs *gated*, obtain a copy of the configuration files and explain the meaning of each item.

17

Internet Multicasting

17.1 Introduction

Earlier chapters define the original IP classful addressing scheme and extensions such as subnetting and classless addressing. This chapter explores an additional feature of the IP addressing scheme that permits efficient multipoint delivery of datagrams. We begin with a brief review of the underlying hardware support. Later sections describe IP addressing for multipoint delivery and protocols that routers use to propagate the necessary routing information.

17.2 Hardware Broadcast

Many hardware technologies contain mechanisms to send packets to multiple destinations simultaneously (or nearly simultaneously). Chapter 2 reviews several technologies and discusses the most common form of multipoint delivery: *broadcasting*. Broadcast delivery means that the network delivers one copy of a packet to each destination. On bus technologies like Ethernet, broadcast delivery can be accomplished with a single packet transmission. On networks composed of switches with point-to-point connections, software must implement broadcasting by forwarding copies of the packet across individual connections until all switches have received a copy.

With most hardware technologies, a computer specifies broadcast delivery by sending a packet to a special, reserved destination address called the *broadcast address*. For example, Ethernet hardware addresses consist of 48-bit identifiers, with the all 1s address used to denote broadcast. Hardware on each machine recognizes the machine's hardware address as well as the broadcast address, and accepts incoming packets that have either address as their destination.

The chief disadvantage of broadcasting arises from its demand on resources — in addition to using network bandwidth, each broadcast consumes computational resources on all machines. For example, it would be possible to design an alternative internet protocol suite that used broadcast to deliver datagrams on a local network and relied on IP software to discard datagrams not intended for the local machine. However, such a scheme would be extremely inefficient because all computers on the network would receive and process every datagram, even though a machine would discard most of the datagrams that arrived. Thus, the designers of TCP/IP used unicast routing and address binding mechanisms like ARP to eliminate broadcast delivery.

17.3 Hardware Origins Of Multicast

Some hardware technologies support a second, less common form of multi-point delivery called *multicasting*. Unlike broadcasting, multicasting allows each system to choose whether it wants to participate in a given multicast. Typically, a hardware technology reserves a large set of addresses for use with multicast. When a group of machines want to communicate, they choose one particular *multicast address* to use for communication. After configuring their network interface hardware to recognize the selected multicast address, all machines in the group will receive a copy of any packet sent to that multicast address.

At a conceptual level, multicast addressing can be viewed as a generalization of all other address forms. For example, we can think of a conventional *unicast address* as a form of multicast addressing in which there is exactly one computer in the multicast group. Similarly, we can think of directed broadcast addressing as a form of multicasting in which all computers on a particular network are members of the multicast group. Other multicast addresses can correspond to arbitrary sets of machines.

Despite its apparent generality, multicasting cannot replace conventional forms because there is a fundamental difference in the underlying mechanisms that implement forwarding and delivery. Unicast and broadcast addresses identify a computer or a set of computers attached to one physical segment, so forwarding depends on the network topology. A multicast address identifies an arbitrary set of listeners, so the forwarding mechanism must propagate the packet to all segments. For example, consider two LAN segments connected by an adaptive bridge that has learned host addresses. If a host on segment *1* sends a unicast frame to another host on segment *1*, the bridge will not forward the frame to segment *2*. If a host uses a multicast address, however, the bridge will forward the frame. Thus, we can conclude:

> *Although it may help us to think of multicast addressing as a generalization that subsumes unicast and broadcast addresses, the underlying forwarding and delivery mechanisms can make multicast less efficient.*

17.4 Ethernet Multicast

Ethernet provides a good example of hardware multicasting. One-half of the Ethernet addresses are reserved for multicast — the low-order bit of the high-order octet distinguishes conventional unicast addresses (*0*) from multicast addresses (*1*). In dotted hexadecimal notation†, the multicast bit is given by:

$$01.00.00.00.00.00_{16}$$

When an Ethernet interface board is initialized, it begins accepting packets destined for either the computer's hardware address or the Ethernet broadcast address. However, device driver software can reconfigure the device to allow it to also recognize one or more multicast addresses. For example, suppose the driver configures the Ethernet multicast address:

$$01.5E.00.00.00.01_{16}$$

After the configuration, an interface will accept any packet sent to the computer's unicast address, the broadcast address, or that one multicast address (the hardware will continue to ignore packets sent to other multicast addresses). The next sections explain both how IP uses basic multicast hardware and the special meaning of the multicast address

17.5 IP Multicast

IP multicasting is the internet abstraction of hardware multicasting. It follows the paradigm of allowing transmission to a subset of host computers, but generalizes the concept to allow the subset to spread across arbitrary physical networks throughout the internet. In IP terminology, a given subset is known as a *multicast group*. IP multicasting has the following general characteristics:

- *Group address*. Each multicast group is a unique class *D* address. A few IP multicast addresses are permanently assigned by the Internet authority, and correspond to groups that always exist even if they have no current members. Other addresses are temporary, and are available for private use.

- *Number of groups*. IP provides addresses for up to 2^{28} simultaneous multicast groups. Thus, the number of groups is limited by practical constraints on routing table size rather than addressing.

- *Dynamic group membership*. A host can join or leave an IP multicast group at any time. Furthermore, a host may be a member of an arbitrary number of multicast groups.

---

†Dotted hexadecimal notation represents each octet as two hexadecimal digits with octets separated by periods; the subscript *16* can be omitted only when the context is unambiguous.

- *Use of hardware.* If the underlying network hardware supports multicast, IP uses hardware multicast to send IP multicast. If the hardware does not support multicast, IP uses broadcast or unicast to deliver IP multicast.

- *Inter-network forwarding.* Because members of an IP multicast group can attach to multiple physical networks, special *multicast routers* are required to forward IP multicast; the capability is usually added to conventional routers.

- *Delivery semantics.* IP multicast uses the same best-effort delivery semantics as other IP datagram delivery, meaning that multicast datagrams can be lost, delayed, duplicated, or delivered out of order.

- *Membership and transmission.* An arbitrary host may send datagrams to any multicast group; group membership is only used to determine whether the host receives datagrams sent to the group.

17.6 The Conceptual Pieces

Three conceptual pieces are required for a general purpose internet multicasting system:

1. A multicast addressing scheme
2. An effective notification and delivery mechanism
3. An efficient internetwork forwarding facility

Many goals, details, and constraints present challenges for an overall design. For example, in addition to providing sufficient addresses for many groups, the multicast *addressing scheme* must accommodate two conflicting goals: allow local autonomy in assigning addresses, while defining addresses that have meaning globally. Similarly, hosts need a *notification mechanism* to inform routers about multicast groups in which they are participating, and routers need a *delivery mechanism* to transfer multicast packets to hosts. Again there are two possibilities: we desire a system that makes effective use of hardware multicast when it is available, but also allows IP multicast delivery over networks that do not have hardware support for multicast. Finally a multicast *forwarding facility* presents the biggest design challenge of the three: our goal is a scheme that is both efficient and dynamic — it should route multicast packets along the shortest paths, should not send a copy of a datagram along a path if the path does not lead to a member of the group, and should allow hosts to join and leave groups at any time.

IP multicasting includes all three aspects. It defines IP multicast addressing, specifies how hosts send and receive multicast datagrams, and describes the protocol routers use to determine multicast group membership on a network. The remainder of the chapter considers each aspect in more detail, beginning with addressing.

17.7 IP Multicast Addresses

We said that IP multicast addresses are divided into two types: those that are permanently assigned, and those that are available for temporary use. Permanent addresses are called *well-known*; they are used for major services on the global Internet as well as for infrastructure maintenance (e.g., multicast routing protocols). Other multicast addresses correspond to *transient multicast groups* that are created when needed and discarded when the count of group members reaches zero.

Like hardware multicasting, IP multicasting uses the datagram's destination address to specify that a particular datagram must be delivered via multicast. IP reserves class *D* addresses for multicast; they have the form shown in Figure 17.1.

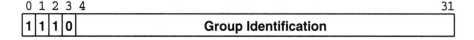

Figure 17.1 The format of class D IP addresses used for multicasting. Bits *4* through *31* identify a particular multicast group.

The first *4* bits contain *1110* and identify the address as a multicast. The remaining *28* bits specify a particular multicast group. There is no further structure in the group bits. In particular, the group field is not partitioned into bits that identify the origin or owner of the group, nor does it contain administrative information such as whether all members of the group are on one physical network.

When expressed in dotted decimal notation, multicast addresses range from

$$224.0.0.0 \quad \text{through} \quad 239.255.255.255$$

However, many parts of the address space have been assigned special meaning. For example, the lowest address, 224.0.0.0, is reserved; it cannot be assigned to any group. Furthermore, the remaining addresses up through 224.0.0.255 are devoted to multicast routing and group maintenance protocols; a router is prohibited from forwarding a datagram sent to any address in that range. Figure 17.2 shows a few examples of permanently assigned addresses.

Address	Meaning
224.0.0.0	Base Address (Reserved)
224.0.0.1	All Systems on this Subnet
224.0.0.2	All Routers on this Subnet
224.0.0.3	Unassigned
224.0.0.4	DVMRP Routers
224.0.0.5	OSPFIGP All Routers
224.0.0.6	OSPFIGP Designated Routers
224.0.0.7	ST Routers
224.0.0.8	ST Hosts
224.0.0.9	RIP2 Routers
224.0.0.10	IGRP Routers
224.0.0.11	Mobile-Agents
224.0.0.12	DHCP Server / Relay Agent
224.0.0.13	All PIM Routers
224.0.0.14	RSVP-Encapsulation
224.0.0.15	All-CBT-Routers
224.0.0.16	Designated-Sbm
224.0.0.17	All-Sbms
224.0.0.18	VRRP
224.0.0.19 through 224.0.0.255	Unassigned
224.0.1.21	DVMRP on MOSPF
224.0.1.84	Jini Announcement
224.0.1.85	Jini Request
239.192.0.0 through 239.251.255.255	Scope restricted to one organization
239.252.0.0 through 239.255.255.255	Scope restricted to one site

Figure 17.2 Examples of a few permanent IP multicast address assignments. Many other addresses have specific meanings.

We will see that two of the addresses in the figure are especially important to the multicast delivery mechanism. Address 224.0.0.1 is permanently assigned to the *all systems group*, and address 224.0.0.2 is permanently assigned to the *all routers group*. The *all systems* group includes all hosts and routers on a network that are participating in IP multicast, whereas the *all routers* group includes only the routers that are participating. In general, both of these groups are used for control protocols and not for the normal delivery of data. Furthermore, datagrams sent to these addresses only reach machines on the same local network as the sender; there are no IP multicast addresses that refer to all systems in the internet or all routers in the internet.

17.8 Multicast Address Semantics

IP treats multicast addresses differently than unicast addresses. For example, a multicast address can only be used as a destination address. Thus, a multicast address can never appear in the source address field of a datagram, nor can it appear in a source route or record route option. Furthermore, no ICMP error messages can be generated about multicast datagrams (e.g., destination unreachable, source quench, echo reply, or time exceeded). Thus, a ping sent to a multicast address will go unanswered.

The rule prohibiting ICMP errors is somewhat surprising because IP routers do honor the time-to-live field in the header of a multicast datagram. As usual, each router decrements the count, and discards the datagram (without sending an ICMP message) if the count reaches zero. We will see that some protocols use the time-to-live count as a way to limit datagram propagation.

17.9 Mapping IP Multicast To Ethernet Multicast

Although the IP multicast standard does not cover all types of network hardware, it does specify how to map an IP multicast address to an Ethernet multicast address. The mapping is efficient and easy to understand:

> *To map an IP multicast address to the corresponding Ethernet multicast address, place the low-order 23 bits of the IP multicast address into the low-order 23 bits of the special Ethernet multicast address $01.00.5E.00.00.00_{16}$.*

For example, IP multicast address 224.0.0.2 becomes Ethernet multicast address $01.00.5E.00.00.02_{16}$.

Interestingly, the mapping is not unique. Because IP multicast addresses have 28 significant bits that identify the multicast group, more than one multicast group may map onto the same Ethernet multicast address at the same time. The designers chose this scheme as a compromise. On one hand, using 23 of the 28 bits for a hardware address means most of the multicast address is included. The set of addresses is large enough so the chances of two groups choosing addresses with all low-order 23 bits identical is small. On the other hand, arranging for IP to use a fixed part of the Ethernet multicast address space makes debugging much easier and eliminates interference between IP and other protocols that share an Ethernet. The consequence of this design is that some multicast datagrams may be received at a host that are not destined for that host. Thus, the IP software must carefully check addresses on all incoming datagrams and discard any unwanted multicast datagrams.

17.10 Hosts And Multicast Delivery

We said that IP multicasting can be used on a single physical network or throughout an internet. In the former case, a host can send directly to a destination host merely by placing the datagram in a frame and using a hardware multicast address to which the receiver is listening. In the latter case, special *multicast routers* forward multicast datagrams among networks, so a host must send the datagram to a multicast router. Surprisingly, a host does not need to install a route to a multicast router, nor does the host's default route need to specify one. Instead, the technique a host uses to forward a multicast datagram to a router is unlike the routing lookup used for unicast and broadcast datagrams — the host merely uses the local network hardware's multicast capability to transmit the datagram. Multicast routers listen for all IP multicast transmissions; if a multicast router is present on the network, it will receive the datagram and forward it on to another network if necessary. Thus, the primary difference between local and nonlocal multicast lies in multicast routers, not in hosts.

17.11 Multicast Scope

The *scope* of a multicast group refers to the range of group members. If all members are on the same physical network, we say that the group's scope is restricted to one network. Similarly, if all members of a group lie within a single organization, we say that the group has a scope limited to one organization.

In addition to the group's scope, each multicast datagram has a scope which is defined to be the set of networks over which a given multicast datagram will be propagated. Informally, a datagram's scope is referred to as its *range*.

IP uses two techniques to control multicast scope. The first technique relies on the datagram's *time-to-live* (*TTL*) field to control its range. By setting the TTL to a small value, a host can limit the distance the datagram will be routed. For example, the standard specifies that control messages, which are used for communication between a host and a router on the same network, must have a TTL of 1. As a consequence, a router never forwards any datagram carrying control information because the TTL expires causing the router to discard the datagram. Similarly, if two applications running on a single host want to use IP multicast for interprocessor communication (e.g., for testing software), they can choose a TTL value of 0 to prevent the datagram from leaving the host. It is possible to use successively larger values of the TTL field to further extend the notion of scope. For example, some router vendors suggest configuring routers at a site to restrict multicast datagrams from leaving the site unless the datagram has a TTL greater than 15. We conclude that it is possible to use the TTL field in a datagram header to provide coarse-grain control over the datagram's scope.

Known as *administrative scoping*, the second technique used to control scoping consists of reserving parts of the address space for groups that are local to a given site or local to a given organization. According to the standard, routers in the Internet are forbidden from forwarding any datagram that has an address chosen from the restricted

space. Thus, to prevent multicast communication among group members from accidentally reaching outsiders, an organization can assign the group an address that has local
scope. Figure 17.2 shows examples of address ranges that correspond to administrative
scoping.

17.12 Extending Host Software To Handle Multicasting

A host participates in IP multicast at one of three levels as Figure 17.3 shows:

Level	Meaning
0	**Host can neither send nor receive IP multicast**
1	**Host can send but not receive IP multicast**
2	**Host can both send and receive IP multicast**

Figure 17.3 The three levels of participation in IP multicast.

Modifications that allow a host to send IP multicast are not difficult. The IP
software must allow an application program to specify a multicast address as a destination IP address, and the network interface software must be able to map an IP multicast
address into the corresponding hardware multicast address (or use broadcast if the
hardware does not support multicasting).

Extending host software to receive IP multicast datagrams is more complex. IP
software on the host must have an API that allows an application program to declare
that it wants to join or leave a particular multicast group. If multiple application programs join the same group, the IP software must remember to pass each of them a copy
of datagrams that arrive destined for that group. If all application programs leave a
group, the host must remember that it no longer participates in the group. Furthermore,
as we will see in the next section, the host must run a protocol that informs the local
multicast routers of its group membership status. Much of the complexity comes from
a basic idea:

Hosts join specific IP multicast groups on specific networks.

That is, a host with multiple network connections may join a particular multicast group
on one network and not on another. To understand the reason for keeping group
membership associated with networks, remember that it is possible to use IP multicasting among local sets of machines. The host may want to use a multicast application to
interact with machines on one physical net, but not with machines on another.

Because group membership is associated with particular networks, the software
must keep separate lists of multicast addresses for each network to which the machine
attaches. Furthermore, an application program must specify a particular network when
it asks to join or leave a multicast group.

17.13 Internet Group Management Protocol

To participate in IP multicast on a local network, a host must have software that allows it to send and receive multicast datagrams. To participate in a multicast that spans
multiple networks, the host must inform local multicast routers. The local routers contact other multicast routers, passing on the membership information and establishing
routes. We will see later that the concept is similar to conventional route propagation
among internet routers.

Before a multicast router can propagate multicast membership information, it must
determine that one or more hosts on the local network have decided to join a multicast
group. To do so, multicast routers and hosts that implement multicast must use the *Internet Group Management Protocol* (*IGMP*) to communicate group membership information. Because the current version is 2, the protocol described here is officially
known as *IGMPv2*.

IGMP is analogous to ICMP†. Like ICMP, it uses IP datagrams to carry messages. Also like ICMP, it provides a service used by IP. Therefore,

> *Although IGMP uses IP datagrams to carry messages, we think of it*
> *as an integral part of IP, not a separate protocol.*

Furthermore, IGMP is a standard for TCP/IP; it is required on all machines that receive
IP multicast (i.e., all hosts and routers that participate at level 2).

Conceptually, IGMP has two phases. Phase 1: When a host joins a new multicast
group, it sends an IGMP message to the group's multicast address declaring its
membership. Local multicast routers receive the message, and establish necessary routing by propagating the group membership information to other multicast routers
throughout the internet. Phase 2: Because membership is dynamic, local multicast
routers periodically poll hosts on the local network to determine whether any hosts still
remain members of each group. If any host responds for a given group, the router
keeps the group active. If no host reports membership in a group after several polls, the
multicast router assumes that none of the hosts on the network remain in the group, and
stops advertising group membership to other multicast routers.

17.14 IGMP Implementation

IGMP is carefully designed to avoid adding overhead that can congest networks.
In particular, because a given network can include multiple multicast routers as well as
hosts that all participate in multicasting, IGMP must avoid having all participants generate control traffic. There are several ways IGMP minimizes its effect on the network:

> First, all communication between hosts and multicast routers uses IP multi-
> cast. That is, when IGMP messages are encapsulated in an IP datagram for
> transmission, the IP destination address is a multicast address — routers

---

†Chapter 9 discusses ICMP, the Internet Control Message Protocol.

send general IGMP queries to the all hosts address, hosts send some IGMP messages to the all routers address, and both hosts and routers send IGMP messages that are specific to a group to the group's address. Thus, datagrams carrying IGMP messages are transmitted using hardware multicast if it is available. As a result, on networks that support hardware multicast, hosts not participating in IP multicast never receive IGMP messages.

Second, when polling to determine group membership, a multicast router sends a single query to request information about all groups instead of sending a separate message to each†. The default polling rate is 125 seconds, which means that IGMP does not generate much traffic.

Third, if multiple multicast routers attach to the same network, they quickly and efficiently choose a single router to poll host membership. Thus, the amount of IGMP traffic on a network does not increase as additional multicast routers are attached to the net.

Fourth, hosts do not respond to a router's IGMP query at the same time. Instead, each query contains a value, N, that specifies a maximum response time (the default is 10 seconds). When a query arrives, a host chooses a random delay between 0 and N which it waits before sending a response. In fact, if a given host is a member of multiple groups, the host chooses a different random number for each. Thus, a host's response to a router's query will be spaced randomly over 10 seconds.

Fifth, each host listens for responses from other hosts in the group, and suppresses unnecessary response traffic.

To understand why extra responses from group members can be suppressed, recall that a multicast router does not need to keep an exact record of group membership. Transmissions to the group are sent using hardware multicast. Thus, a router only needs to know whether at least one host on the network remains a member of the group. Because a query sent to the all systems address reaches every member of a group, each host computes a random delay and begins to wait. The host with smallest delay sends its response first. Because the response is sent to the group's multicast address, all other members receive a copy as does the multicast router. Other members cancel their timers and suppress transmission. Thus, in practice, only one host from each group responds to a request message.

17.15 Group Membership State Transitions

On a host, IGMP must remember the status of each multicast group to which the host belongs (i.e., a group from which the host accepts datagrams).‡. We think of a host as keeping a table in which it records group membership information. Initially, all entries in the table are unused. Whenever an application program on the host joins a

---

†The protocol does include a message type that allows a router to query a specific group, if necessary.
‡The *all systems group*, 224.0.0.1, is an exception — a host never reports membership in that group.

new group, IGMP software allocates an entry and fills in information about the group. Among the information, IGMP keeps a group reference counter which it initializes to *1*. Each time another application program joins the group, IGMP increments the reference counter in the entry. If one of the application programs terminates execution (or explicitly drops out of the group), IGMP decrements the group's reference counter. When the reference count reaches zero, the host informs multicast routers that it is leaving the multicast group.

The actions IGMP software takes in response to various events can best be explained by the state transition diagram in Figure 17.4.

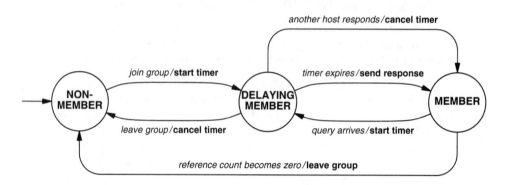

Figure 17.4 The three possible states of an entry in a host's multicast group table and transitions among them where each transition is labeled with an event and an action. The state transitions do not show messages sent when joining and leaving a group.

A host maintains an independent table entry for each group of which it is currently a member. As the figure shows, when a host first joins the group or when a query arrives from a multicast router, the host moves the entry to the *DELAYING MEMBER* state and chooses a random delay. If another host in the group responds to the router's query before the timer expires, the host cancels its timer and moves to the *MEMBER* state. If the timer expires, the host sends a response message before moving to the *MEMBER* state. Because a router only generates a query every 125 seconds, one expects the host to remain in the *MEMBER* state most of the time.

The diagram in Figure 17.4 omits a few details. For example, if a query arrives while the host is in the *DELAYING MEMBER* state, the protocol requires the host to reset its timer. More important, to maintain backward compatibility with IGMPv1, version *2* also handles version *1* messages, making it possible to use both IGMPv1 and IGMPv2 on the same network concurrently.

17.16 IGMP Message Format

As Figure 17.5 shows, IGMP messages used by hosts have a simple format.

0	8	16	31
TYPE	**RESP TIME**	**CHECKSUM**	
GROUP ADDRESS (ZERO IN QUERY)			

Figure 17.5 The format of the 8-octet IGMP message used for communication between hosts and routers.

Each IGMP message contains exactly eight octets. Field *TYPE* identifies the type of message, with the possible types listed in Figure 17.6. When a router polls for group membership, field labeled *RESP TIME* carries a maximum interval for the random delay that group members compute, measured in tenths of seconds. Each host in the group delays a random time between zero and the specified value before responding. As we said, the default is 10 seconds, which means all hosts in a group choose a random value between 0 and 10. IGMP allows routers set a maximum value in each query message to give managers control over IGMP traffic. If a network contains many hosts, a higher delay value further spreads out response times and, therefore, lowers the probability of having more than one host respond to the query. The *CHECKSUM* field contains a checksum for the message (IGMP checksums are computed over the IGMP message only, and use the same algorithm as TCP and IP). Finally, the *GROUP ADDRESS* field is either used to specify a particular group or contains zero to refer to all groups. When it sends a query to a specific group, a router fills in the *GROUP ADDRESS* field; hosts fill in the field when sending membership reports.

Type	Group Address	Meaning
0x11	unused (zero)	General membership query
0x11	used	Specific group membership query
0x16	used	Membership report
0x17	used	Leave group
0x12	used	Membership report (version 1)

Figure 17.6 IGMP message types used in version 2. The version 1 membership report message provides backward compatibility.

Note that IGMP does not provide a mechanism that allows a host to discover the IP address of a group — application software must know the group address before it can use IGMP to join the group. Some applications use permanently assigned addresses, some allow a manager to configure the address when the software is installed, and others obtain the address dynamically (e.g., from a server). In any case, IGMP provides no support for address lookup.

17.17 Multicast Forwarding And Routing Information

Although IGMP and the multicast addressing scheme described above specify how hosts interact with a local router and how multicast datagrams are transferred across a single network, they do not specify how routers exchange group membership information or how routers ensure that a copy of each datagram reaches all group members. More important, although multiple protocols have been proposed, no single standard has emerged for the propagation of multicast routing information. In fact, although much effort has been expended, there is no agreement on an overall plan — existing protocols differ in their goals and basic approach.

Why is multicast routing so difficult? Why not extend conventional routing schemes to handle multicast? The answer is that multicast routing differs from conventional routing in fundamental ways because multicast forwarding differs from conventional forwarding. To appreciate some of the differences, consider multicast forwarding over the architecture that Figure 17.7 depicts.

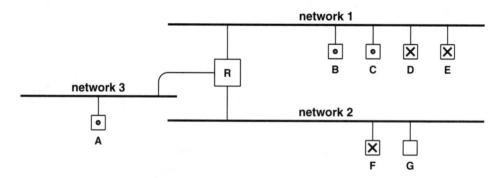

Figure 17.7 A simple internet with three networks connected by a router that illustrates multicast forwarding. Hosts marked with a dot participate in one multicast group while those marked with an ''x'' participate in another.

17.17.1 Need For Dynamic Routing

Even for the simple topology shown in the figure, multicast forwarding differs from unicast forwarding. For example, the figure shows two multicast groups: the group denoted by a dot has members A, B, and C, and the group denoted by a cross has members D, E, and F. The dotted group has no members on network 2. To avoid wasting bandwidth unnecessarily, the router should never send packets intended for the dotted group across network *2*. However, a host can join any group at any time — if the host is the first on its network to join the group, multicast routing must be changed to include the network. Thus, we come to an important difference between conventional routing and multicast routing:

> *Unlike unicast routing in which routes change only when the topology changes or equipment fails, multicast routes can change simply because an application program joins or leaves a multicast group.*

17.17.2 Insufficiency Of Destination Routing

The example in Figure 17.7 illustrates another aspect of multicast routing. If host *F* and host *E* each send a datagram to the cross group, router *R* will receive and forward them. Because both datagrams are directed at the same group, they have the same destination address. However, the correct forwarding actions differ: *R* sends the datagram from *E* to net *2*, and sends the datagram from *F* to net *1*. Interestingly, when it receives a datagram destinated for the cross group sent by host *A*, the router uses a third action: it forwards two copies, one to net *1* and the other to net *2*. Thus, we see the second major difference between conventional forwarding and multicast forwarding:

> *Multicast forwarding requires a router to examine more than the destination address.*

17.17.3 Arbitrary Senders

The final feature of multicast routing illustrated by Figure 17.7 arises because IP allows an arbitrary host, one that is not necessarily a member of the group, to send a datagram to the group. In the figure, for example, host *G* can send a datagram to the dotted group even though *G* is not a member of any group and there are no members of the dotted group on *G's* network. More important, as it travels through the internet, the datagram may pass across other networks that have no group members attached. Thus, we can summarize:

> *A multicast datagram may originate on a computer that is not part of the multicast group, and may be routed across networks that do not have any group members attached.*

17.18 Basic Multicast Routing Paradigms

We know from the example above that multicast routers use more than the destination address to forward datagrams, so the question arises: "exactly what information does a multicast router use when deciding how to forward a datagram?" The answer lies in understanding that because a multicast destination represents a set of computers, an optimal forwarding system will reach all members of the set without sending a datagram across a given network twice. Although a single multicast router such as the one in Figure 17.7 can simply avoid sending a datagram back over the interface on which it arrives, using the interface alone will not prevent a datagram from being forwarded among a set of routers that are arranged in a cycle. To avoid such routing loops, multicast routers rely on the datagram's source address.

One of the first ideas to emerge for multicast forwarding was a form of broadcasting described earlier. Known as *Reverse Path Forwarding (RPF)*,† the scheme uses a datagram's source address to prevent the datagram from traveling around a loop repeatedly. To use RPF, a multicast router must have a conventional routing table with shortest paths to all destinations. When a datagram arrives, the router extracts the source address, looks it up in the local routing table, and finds *I*, the interface that leads to the source. If the datagram arrived over interface *I*, the router forwards a copy to each of the other interfaces; otherwise, the router discards the copy.

Because it ensures that a copy of each multicast datagram is sent across every network in the internet, the basic RPF scheme guarantees that every host in a multicast group will receive a copy of each datagram sent to the group. However, RPF alone is not used for multicast routing because it wastes bandwidth by transmitting multicast datagrams over networks that neither have group members nor lead to group members.

To avoid propagating multicast datagrams where they are not needed, a modified form of RPF was invented. Known as *Truncated Reverse Path Forwarding (TRPF)* or *Truncated Reverse Path Broadcasting (TRPB)*, the scheme follows the RPF algorithm, but further restricts propagation by avoiding paths that do not lead to group members. To use TRPF, a multicast router needs two pieces of information: a conventional routing table and a list of multicast groups reachable through each network interface. When a multicast datagram arrives, the router first applies the RPF rule. If RPF specifies discarding the copy, the router does so. However, if RPF specifies transmitting the datagram over a particular interface, the router first makes an additional check to verify that one or more members of the group designated in the datagram's destination address are reachable over the interface. If no group members are reachable over the interface, the router skips that interface, and continues examining the next one. In fact, we can now understand the origin of the term *truncated* — a router truncates forwarding when no more group members lie along the path.

We can summarize:

> When making a forwarding decision, a multicast router uses both the datagram's source and destination addresses. The basic forwarding mechanism is known as Truncated Reverse Path Forwarding.

---

†Reverse path forwarding is sometimes called *Reverse Path Broadcasting (RPB)*.

17.19 Consequences Of TRPF

Although TRPF guarantees that each member of a multicast group receives a copy of each datagram sent to the group, it has two surprising consequences. First, because it relies on RPF to prevent loops, TRPF delivers an extra copy of datagrams to some networks just like conventional RPF. Figure 17.8 illustrates how duplicates arise.

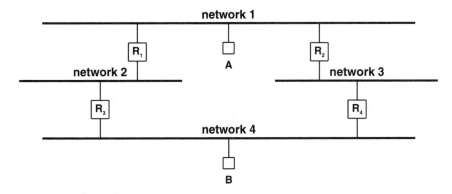

Figure 17.8 A topology that causes an RPF scheme to deliver multiple copies of a datagram to some destinations.

In the figure, when host A sends a datagram, routers R_1 and R_2 each receive a copy. Because the datagram arrives over the interface that lies along the shortest path to A, R_1 forwards a copy to network 2, and R_2 forwards a copy to network 3. When it receives a copy from network 2 (the shortest path to A), R_3 forwards the copy to network 4. Unfortunately, R_4 also forwards a copy to network 4. Thus, although RPF allows R_3 and R_4 to prevent a loop by discarding the copy that arrives over network 4, host B receives two copies of the datagram.

A second surprising consequence arises because TRPF uses both source and destination addresses when forwarding datagrams: delivery depends on a datagram's source. For example, Figure 17.9 shows how multicast routers forward datagrams from two different sources across a fixed topology.

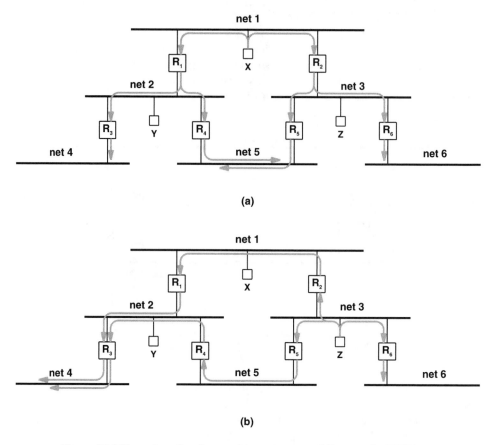

Figure 17.9 Examples of paths a multicast datagram follows under TRPF assuming the source is (a) host *X*, and (b) host *Z*, and the group has a member on each of the networks. The number of copies received depends on the source.

As the figure shows, the source affects both the path a datagram follows to reach a given network as well as the delivery details. For example, in part (a) of the figure, a transmission by host *X* causes TRPF to deliver two copies of the datagram to network *5*. In part (b), only one copy of a transmission by host *Z* reaches network *5*, but two copies reach networks *2* and *4*.

17.20 Multicast Trees

Researchers use graph theory terminology to describe the set of paths from a given source to all members of a multicast group: they say that the paths define a graph-theoretic *tree†*, which is sometimes called a *forwarding tree* or a *delivery tree*. Each multicast router corresponds to a *node* in the tree, and a network that connects two routers corresponds to an *edge* in the tree. The source of a datagram is the *root* or *root node* of the tree. Finally, the last router along each of the paths from the source is called a *leaf* router. The terminology is sometimes applied to networks as well — researchers call a network hanging off a leaf router a *leaf network*.

As an example of the terminology, consider Figure 17.9. Part *a* shows a tree with root *X*, and leaves R_3, R_4, R_5, and R_6. Technically, part *b* does not show a tree because router R_3 lies along two paths. Informally, researchers often overlook the details and refer to such graphs as trees.

The graph terminology allows us to express an important principle:

> *A multicast forwarding tree is defined as a set of paths through multi-cast routers from a source to all members of a multicast group. For a given multicast group, each possible source of datagrams can deter-mine a different forwarding tree.*

One of the immediate consequences of the principle concerns the size of tables used to forward multicast. Unlike conventional routing tables, each entry in a multicast table is identified by a pair:

(multicast group, source)

Conceptually, *source* identifies a single host that can send datagrams to the group (i.e., any host in the internet). In practice, keeping a separate entry for each host is unwise because the forwarding trees defined by all hosts on a single network are identical. Thus, to save space, routing protocol use a network prefix as a *source*. That is, each router defines one forwarding entry that is used for all hosts on the same physical network.

Aggregating entries by network prefix instead of by host address reduces the table size dramatically. However, multicast routing tables can grow much larger than conventional routing tables. Unlike a conventional table in which the size is proportional to the number of networks in the internet, a multicast table has size proportional to the product of the number of networks in the internet and the number of multicast groups.

---

†A graph is a tree if it does not contain any cycles (i.e., a router does not appear on more than one path).

17.21 The Essence Of Multicast Routing

Observant readers may have noticed an inconsistency between the features of IP multicasting and TRPF. We said that TRPF is used instead of conventional RPF to avoid unnecessary traffic: TRPF does not forward a datagram to a network unless that network leads to at least one member of the group. Consequently, a multicast router must have knowledge of group membership. We also said that IP allows any host to join or leave a multicast group at any time, which results in rapid membership changes. More important, membership does not follow local scope — a host that joins may be far from some router that is forwarding datagrams to the group. So, group membership information must be propagated across the internet.

The issue of membership is central to routing; all multicast routing schemes provide a mechanism for propagating membership information as well as a way to use the information when forwarding datagrams. In general, because membership can change rapidly, the information available at a given router is imperfect, so routing may lag changes. Therefore, a multicast design represents a tradeoff between routing traffic overhead and inefficient data transmission. On one hand, if group membership information is not propagated rapidly, multicast routers will not make optimal decisions (i.e., they either forward datagrams across some networks unnecessarily or fail to send datagrams to all group members). On the other hand, a multicast routing scheme that communicates every membership change to every router is doomed because the resulting traffic can overwhelm an internet. Each design chooses a compromise between the two extremes.

17.22 Reverse Path Multicasting

One of the earliest forms of multicast routing was derived from TRPF. Known as *Reverse Path Multicast (RPM)*, the scheme extends TRPF to make it more dynamic. Three assumptions underlie the design. First, it is more important to ensure that a multicast datagram reaches each member of the group to which it is sent than to eliminate unnecessary transmission. Second, multicast routers each contain a conventional routing table that has correct information. Third, multicast routing should improve efficiency when possible (i.e. eliminate needless transmission).

RPM uses a two step process. When it begins, RPM uses the RPF broadcast scheme to send a copy of each datagram across all networks in the internet. Doing so ensures that all group members receive a copy. Simultaneously, RPM proceeds to have multicast routers inform one another about paths that do not lead to group members. Once it learns that no group members lie along a given path, a router stops forwarding along that path.

How do routers learn about the location of group members? As in most multicast routing schemes, RPM propagates membership information bottom-up. The information starts with hosts that choose to join or leave groups. Hosts communicate membership information with their local router by using IGMP. Thus, although a multicast router does not know about distant group members, it does know about local members (i.e. members on each of its directly-attached networks). As a consequence, routers attached to leaf networks can decide whether to forward over the leaf network — if a leaf network contains no members for a given group, the router connecting that network to the rest of the internet does not forward on the network. In addition to taking local action, the leaf router informs the next router along the path back to the source. Once it learns that no group members lie beyond a given network interface, the next router stops forwarding datagrams for the group across the network. When a router finds that no group members lie beyond it, the router informs the next router along the path to the root.

Using graph-theoretic terminology, we say that when a router learns that a group has no members along a path and stops forwarding, it has *pruned* (i.e., removed) the path from the forwarding tree. In fact, RPM is called a *broadcast and prune* strategy because a router broadcasts (using RPF) until it receives information that allows it to prune a path. Researchers also use another term for the RPM algorithm: they say that the system is *data-driven* because a router does not send group membership information to any other routers until datagrams arrive for that group.

In the data-driven model, a router must also handle the case where a host decides to join a particular group after the router has pruned the path for that group. RPM handles joins bottom-up: when a host informs a local router that it has joined a group, the router consults its record of the group and obtains the address of the router to which it had previously sent a prune request. The router sends a new message that undoes the effect of the previous prune and causes datagrams to flow again. Such messages are known as *graft requests*, and the algorithm is said to graft the previously pruned branch back onto the tree.

17.23 Distance Vector Multicast Routing Protocol

One of the first multicast routing protocols is still in use in the global Internet. Known as the *Distance Vector Multicast Routing Protocol (DVMRP)*, the protocol allows multicast routers to pass group membership and routing information among themselves. DVMRP resembles the RIP protocol described in Chapter 16, but has been extended for multicast. In essence, the protocol passes information about current multicast group membership and the cost to transfer datagrams between routers. For each possible (group, source) pair, the routers impose a forwarding tree on top of the physical interconnections. When a router receives a datagram destined for an IP multicast group, it sends a copy of the datagram out over the network links that correspond to branches in the forwarding tree†.

Interestingly, DVMRP defines an extended form of IGMP used for communication between a pair of multicast routers. It specifies additional IGMP message types that allow routers to declare membership in a multicast group, leave a multicast group, and interrogate other routers. The extensions also provide messages that carry routing information, including cost metrics.

---

†DVMRP changed substantially between version *2* and *3* when it incorporated the RPM algorithm described above.

17.24 The Mrouted Program

Mrouted is a well-known program that implements DVMRP for UNIX systems. Like *routed†*, *mrouted* cooperates closely with the operating system kernel to install multicast routing information. Unlike *routed*, however, *mrouted* does not use the standard routing table. Instead, it can be used only with a special version of UNIX known as a *multicast kernel*. A UNIX multicast kernel contains a special multicast routing table as well as the code needed to forward multicast datagrams. *Mrouted* handles:

- *Route propagation.* *Mrouted* uses DVMRP to propagate multicast routing information from one router to another. A computer running *mrouted* interprets multicast routing information, and constructs a multicast routing table. As expected, each entry in the table specifies a (group, source) pair and a corresponding set of interfaces over which to forward datagrams that match the entry. *Mrouted* does not replace conventional route propagation protocols; a computer usually runs *mrouted* in addition to standard routing protocol software.

- *Multicast tunneling.* One of the chief problems with internet multicast arises because not all internet routers can forward multicast datagrams. *Mrouted* can arrange to *tunnel* a multicast datagram from one router to another through intermediate routers that do not participate in multicast routing.

Although a single *mrouted* program can perform both tasks, a given computer may not need both functions. To allow a manager to specify exactly how it should operate, *mrouted* uses a configuration file. The configuration file contains entries that specify which multicast groups *mrouted* is permitted to advertise on each interface, and how it should forward datagrams. Furthermore, the configuration file associates a metric and threshold with each route. The metric allows a manager to assign a cost to each path (e.g., to ensure that the cost assigned to a path over a local area network will be lower than the cost of a path across a slow serial link). The threshold gives the minimum IP *time to live (TTL)* that a datagram needs to complete the path. If a datagram does not have a sufficient TTL to reach its destination, a multicast kernel does not forward the datagram. Instead, it discards the datagram, which avoids wasting bandwidth.

Multicast tunneling is perhaps the most interesting capability of *mrouted*. A tunnel is needed when two or more hosts wish to participate in multicast applications, and one or more routers along the path between the participating hosts do not run multicast routing software. Figure 17.10 illustrates the concept.

---

†Recall that *routed* is the UNIX program that implements RIP.

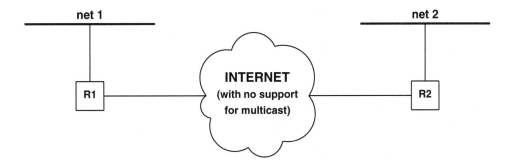

Figure 17.10 An example internet configuration that requires multicast tunneling for computers attached to networks *1* and *2* to participate in multicast communication. Routers in the internet that
separates the two networks do not propagate multicast routes,
and cannot forward datagrams sent to a multicast address.

To allow hosts on networks *1* and *2* to exchange multicast, managers of the two
routers configure an *mrouted tunnel*. The tunnel merely consists of an agreement
between the *mrouted* programs running on the two routers to exchange datagrams.
Each router listens on its local net for datagrams sent to the specified multicast destination for which the tunnel has been configured. When a multicast datagram arrives that
has a destination address equal to one of the configured tunnels, *mrouted* encapsulates
the datagram in a conventional unicast datagram and sends it across the internet to the
other router. When it receives a unicast datagram through one of its tunnels, *mrouted*
extracts the multicast datagram, and then forwards according to its multicast routing
table.

The encapsulation technique that *mrouted* uses to tunnel datagrams is known as
IP-in-IP. Figure 17.11 illustrates the concept.

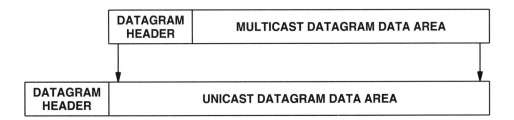

Figure 17.11 An illustration of IP-in-IP encapsulation in which one datagram
is placed in the data area of another. A pair of multicast
routers use the encapsulation to communicate when intermediate routers do not understand multicasting.

As the figure shows, IP-in-IP encapsulation preserves the original multicast datagram, including the header, by placing it in the data area of a conventional unicast datagram. On the receiving machine, the multicast kernel extracts and processes the multicast datagram as if it arrived over a local interface. In particular, once it extracts the multicast datagram, the receiving machine must decrement the time to live field in the header by one before forwarding. Thus, when it creates a tunnel, *mrouted* treats the internet connecting two multicast routers like a single, physical network. Note that the outer, unicast datagram has its own time to live counter, which operates independently from the time to live counter in the multicast datagram header. Thus, it is possible to limit the number of physical hops across a given tunnel independent of the number of logical hops a multicast datagram must visit on its journey from the original source to the ultimate destination.

Multicast tunnels form the basis of the Internet's *Multicast Backbone* (*MBONE*). Many Internet sites participate in the MBONE; the MBONE allows hosts at participating sites to send and receive multicast datagrams, which are then propagated to all other participating sites. The MBONE is often used to propagate audio and video (e.g., for teleconferences).

To participate in the MBONE, a site must have at least one multicast router connected to at least one local network. Another site must agree to tunnel traffic, and a tunnel is configured between routers at the two sites. When a host at the site sends a multicast datagram, the local router at the host's site receives a copy, consults its multicast routing table, and forwards the datagram over the tunnel using IP-in-IP. When it receives a multicast datagram over a tunnel, a multicast router removes the outer encapsulation, and then forwards the datagram according to the local multicast routing table.

The easiest way to understand the MBONE is to think of it as a virtual network built on top of the Internet (which is a virtual network). Conceptually, the MBONE consists of multicast routers that are interconnected by a set of point-to-point networks. Some of the conceptual point-to-point connections coincide with physical networks; others are achieved by tunneling. The details are hidden from the multicast routing software. Thus, when *mrouted* computes a multicast forwarding tree for a given (group, source), it thinks of a tunnel as a single link connecting two routers.

Tunneling has two consequences. First, because some tunnels are much more expensive than others, they cannot all be treated equally. *Mrouted* handles the problem by allowing a manager to assign a cost to each tunnel, and uses the costs when choosing routes. Typically, a manager assigns a cost that reflects the number of hops in the underlying internet. It is also possible to assign costs that reflect administrative boundaries (e.g., the cost assigned to a tunnel between two sites in the same company is assigned a much lower cost than a tunnel to another company). Second, because DVMRP forwarding depends on knowing the shortest path to each source, and because multicast tunnels are completely unknown to conventional routing protocols, DVMRP must compute its own version of unicast forwarding that includes the tunnels.

17.25 Alternative Protocols

Although DVMRP has been used in the MBONE for many years, as the Internet grew, the IETF became aware of its limitations. Like RIP, DVMRP uses a small value for *infinity*. More important, the amount of information DVMRP keeps is overwhelming — in addition to entries for each active (group, source), it must also store entries for previously active groups so it knows where to send a graft message when a host joins a group that was pruned. Finally, DVMRP uses a broadcast-and-prune paradigm that generates traffic on all networks until membership information can be propagated. Ironically, DVMRP also uses a distance-vector algorithm to propagate membership information, which makes propagation slow.

Taken together, the limitations of DVMRP mean that it cannot scale to handle a large number of routers, larger numbers of multicast groups, or rapid changes in membership. Thus, DVMRP is inappropriate as a general-purpose multicast routing protocol for the global Internet.

To overcome the limitations of DVMRP, the IETF has investigated other multicast protocols. Efforts have resulted in several designs, including *Core Based Trees* (*CBT*), *Protocol Independent Multicast* (*PIM*), and *Multicast extensions to OSPF* (*MOSPF*). Each is intended to handle the problems of scale, but does so in a slightly different way. Although all these protocols have been implemented and both PIM and MOSPF have been used in parts of the MBONE, none of them is a required standard.

17.26 Core Based Trees (CBT)

CBT avoids broadcasting and allows all sources to share the same forwarding tree whenever possible. To avoid broadcasting, CBT does not forward multicasts along a path until one or more hosts along that path join the multicast group. Thus, CBT reverses the fundamental scheme used by DVMRP — instead of forwarding datagrams until negative information has been propagated, CBT does not forward along a path until positive information has been received. We say that instead of using the data-driven paradigm, CBT uses a *demand-driven* paradigm.

The demand-driven paradigm in CBT means that when a host uses IGMP to join a particular group, the local router must then inform other routers before datagrams will be forwarded. Which router or routers should be informed? The question is critical in all demand-driven multicast routing schemes. Recall that in a data-driven scheme, a router uses the arrival of data traffic to know where to send routing messages (it propagates routing messages back over networks from which the traffic arrives). However, in a positive-information scheme, no traffic will arrive for a group until the membership information has been propagated.

CBT uses a combination of static and dynamic algorithms to build a multicast forwarding tree. To make the scheme scalable, CBT divides the internet into *regions*, where the size of a region is determined by network administrators. Within each region, one of the routers is designated as a *core router*; other routers in the region must either be configured to know the core for their region, or use a dynamic *discovery mechanism* to find it. In any case, core discovery only occurs when a router boots.

Knowledge of a core is important because it allows multicast routers in a region to form a *shared tree* for the region. As soon as a host joins a multicast group, the local router that receives the host request, *L*, generates a CBT *join request* which it sends to the core using conventional unicast routing. Each intermediate router along the path to the core examines the request. As soon as the request reaches a router *R* that is already part of the CBT shared tree, *R* returns an acknowledgement, passes the group membership information on to its parent, and begins forwarding traffic for the group. As the acknowledgement passes back to the leaf router, intermediate routers examine the message, and configure their multicast routing table to forward datagrams for the group. Thus, router *L* is linked into the forwarding tree at router *R*.

We can summarize:

> *Because CBT uses a demand-driven paradigm, it divides the internet into regions and designates a* core *router* for each region; other *routers in the region dynamically build a forwarding tree by sending* join requests *to the core.*

CBT includes a facility for tree maintenance that detects when a link between a pair of routers fails. To detect failure, each router periodically sends a CBT *echo request* to its parent in the tree (i.e., the next router along the path to the core). If the request is unacknowledged, CBT informs any routers that depend on it, and proceeds to rejoin the tree at another point.

17.27 Protocol Independent Multicast (PIM)

In reality, PIM consists of two independent protocols that share little beyond the name and basic message header formats: *PIM - Dense Mode* (*PIM-DM*) and *PIM - Sparse Mode* (*PIM-SM*). The distinction arises because no single protocol works well in all possible situations. In particular, PIM's dense mode is designed for a LAN environment in which all, or nearly all, networks have hosts listening to each multicast group; whereas, PIM's sparse mode is deigned to accommodate a wide area environment in which the members of a given multicast group occupy a small subset of all possible networks.

17.27.1 PIM Dense Mode (PIM-DM)

Because PIM's dense mode assumes low-delay networks that have plenty of bandwidth, the protocol has been optimized to guarantee delivery rather than to reduce overhead. Thus, PIM-DM uses a broadcast-and-prune approach similar to DVMRP — it begins by using RPF to broadcast each datagram to every group, and only stops sending when it receives explicit prune requests.

17.27.2 Protocol Independence

The greatest difference between DVMRP and PIM dense mode arises from the information PIM assumes is available. In particular, in order to use RPF, PIM-DM dense mode requires traditional unicast routing information — the shortest path to each destination must be known. Unlike DVMRP, however, PIM-DM does not contain facilities to propagate conventional routes. Instead, it assumes the router also uses a conventional routing protocol that computes the shortest path to each destination, installs the route in the routing table, and maintains the route over time. In fact, part of PIM-DM's *protocol independence* refers to its ability to co-exist with standard routing protocols. Thus, a router can use any of the routing protocols discussed (e.g., RIP, or OSPF) to maintain correct unicast routes, and PIM's dense mode can use routes produced by any of them. To summarize:

> *Although it assumes a correct unicast routing table exists, PIM dense mode does not propagate unicast routes. Instead, it assumes each router also runs a conventional routing protocol which maintains the unicast routes.*

17.27.3 PIM Sparse Mode (PIM-SM)

PIM's sparse mode can be viewed as an extension of basic concepts from CBT. Like CBT, PIM-SM is demand-driven. Also like CBT, PIM-SM needs a point to which join messages can be sent. Therefore, sparse mode designates a router called a *Rendezvous Point (RP)* that is the functional equivalent of a CBT core. When a host joins a multicast group, the local router unicasts a *join* request to the RP; routers along the path examine the message, and if any router is already part of the tree, the router intercepts the message and replies. Thus, PIM-SM builds a shared forwarding tree for each group like CBT, and the trees are rooted at the rendezvous point†.

The main conceptual difference between CBT and PIM-SM arises from sparse mode's ability to optimize connectivity through reconfiguration. For example, instead of a single RP, each sparse mode router maintains a set of potential RP routers, with one selected at any time. If the current RP becomes unreachable (e.g., because a network failure causes disconnection), PIM-SM selects another RP from the set and starts rebuilding the forwarding tree for each multicast group. The next section considers a more significant reconfiguration.

17.27.4 Switching From Shared To Shortest Path Trees

In addition to selecting an alternative RP, PIM-SM can switch from the shared tree to a *Shortest Path tree (SP tree)*. To understand the motivation, consider the network interconnection that Figure 17.12 illustrates.

---

†When an arbitrary host sends a datagram to a multicast group, the datagram is tunneled to the RP for the group, which then multicasts the datagram down the shared tree.

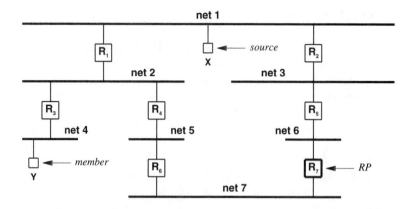

Figure 17.12 A set of networks with a rendezvous point and a multicast
group that contains two members. The demand-driven strategy
of building a shared tree to the rendezvous results in nonoptimal routing.

In the figure, router R_7 has been selected as the RP. Thus, routers join the shared
tree by sending along a path to R_7. For example, assume hosts X and Y have joined a
particular multicast group. The path to the shared tree from host X consists of routers
R_2, R_5, and R_7, and the path from host Y to the shared tree consists of routers R_3, R_4, R_6,
and R_7.

Although the shared tree approach forms shortest paths from each host to the RP, it
may not optimize routing. In particular, if group members are not close to the RP, the
inefficiency can be significant. For example, the figure shows that when host X sends a
datagram to the group, the datagram is routed from X to the RP and from the RP to Y.
Thus, the datagram must pass through six routers. However, the optimal (i.e., shortest)
path from X to Y only contains two routers (R_1 and R_3).

PIM sparse mode includes a facility to allow a router to choose between the shared
tree or a shortest path tree to the source (sometimes called a *source tree*). Although
switching trees is conceptually straightforward, many details complicate the protocol.
For example, most implementations use the receipt of traffic to trigger the change — if
the traffic from a particular source exceeds a preset threshold, the router begins to establish a shortest path†. Unfortunately, traffic can change rapidly, so routers must apply
hysteresis to prevent oscillations. Furthermore, the change requires routers along the
shortest path to cooperate; all routers must agree to forward datagrams for the group.
Interestingly, because the change affects only a single source, a router must continue its
connection to the shared tree so it can continue to receive from other sources. More important, it must keep sufficient routing information to avoid forwarding multiple copies
of each datagram from a (group, source) pair for which a shortest path tree has been established.

---

†The implementation from at least one vendor starts building a shortest path immediately (i.e., the traffic
threshold is zero).

17.28 Multicast Extensions To OSPF (MOSPF)

So far, we have seen that multicast routing protocols like PIM can use information from a unicast routing table to form delivery trees. Researchers have also investigated a broader question: ''how can multicast routing benefit from additional information that is gathered by conventional routing protocols?'' In particular, a link state protocol such as OSPF provides each router with a copy of the internet topology. More specifically, OSPF provides the router with the topology of its OSPF *area*.

When such information is available, multicast protocols can indeed use it to compute a forwarding tree. The idea has been demonstrated in a protocol known as *Multicast extensions to OSPF (MOSPF)*, which uses OSPF's topology database to form a forwarding tree for each source. MOSPF has the advantage of being *demand-driven*, meaning that the traffic for a particular group is not propagated until it is needed (i.e., because a host joins or leaves the group). The disadvantage of a demand-driven scheme arises from the cost of propagating routing information — all routers in an area must maintain membership about every group. Furthermore, the information must be synchronized to ensure that every router has exactly the same database. As a consequence, MOSPF sends less data traffic, but sends more routing information than data-driven protocols.

Although MOSPF's paradigm of sending all group information to all routers works within an area, it cannot scale to an arbitrary internet. Thus, MOSPF defines inter-area multicast routing in a slightly different way. OSPF designates one or more routers in an area to be an *Area Border Router (ABR)* which then propagates routing information to other areas. MOSPF further designates one or more of the area's ABRs to be a *Multicast Area Border Router MABR* which propagates group membership information to other areas. MABRs do not implement a symmetric transfer. Instead, MABRs use a core approach — they propagate membership information from their area to the backbone area, but do not propagate information from the backbone down.

An MABR can propagate multicast information to another area without acting as an active receiver for traffic. Instead, each area designates a router to receive multicast on behalf of the area. When an outside area sends in multicast traffic, traffic for all groups in the area is sent to the designated receiver, which is sometimes called a *multicast wildcard receiver*.

17.29 Reliable Multicast And ACK Implosions

The term *reliable multicast* refers to any system that uses multicast delivery, but also guarantees that all group members receive data in order without any loss, duplication, or corruption. In theory, reliable multicast combines the advantage of a forwarding scheme that is more efficient than broadcast with the advantage of having all data arrive intact. Thus, reliable multicast has great potential benefit and applicability (e.g., a stock exchange could use reliable multicast to deliver stock prices to many destinations).

In practice, reliable multicast is not as general or straightforward as it sounds. First, if a multicast group has multiple senders, the notion of delivering datagrams "in sequence" becomes meaningless. Second, we have seen that widely used multicast forwarding schemes such as RPF can produce duplication even on small internets. Third, in addition to guarantees that all data will eventually arrive, applications like audio or video expect reliable systems to bound the delay and jitter. Fourth, because reliability requires acknowledgements and a multicast group can have an arbitrary number of members, traditional reliable protocols require a sender to handle an arbitrary number of acknowledgements. Unfortunately, no computer has enough processing power to do so. We refer to the problem as an *ACK implosion*; it has become the main focus of much research.

To overcome the ACK implosion problem, reliable multicast protocols take a hierarchical approach in which multicasting is restricted to a single source†. Before data is sent, a forwarding tree is established from the source to all group members, and *acknowledgement points* must be identified.

An acknowledgement point, which is also known as an *acknowledgement aggregator* or *designated router* (*DR*), consists of a router in the forwarding tree that agrees to cache copies of the data and process acknowledgements from routers or hosts further down the tree. If a retransmission is required, the acknowledgement point obtains a copy from its cache.

Most reliable multicast schemes use negative rather than positive acknowledgements — the host does not respond unless a datagram is lost. To allow a host to detect loss, each datagram must be assigned a unique sequence number. When it detects loss, a host sends a *NACK* to request retransmission. The NACK propagates along the forwarding tree toward the source until it reaches an acknowledgement point. The acknowledgement point processes the NACK, and retransmits a copy of the lost datagram along the forwarding tree.

How does an acknowledgement point ensure that it has a copy of all datagrams in the sequence? It uses the same scheme as a host. When a datagram arrives, the acknowledgement point checks the sequence number, places a copy in its memory, and then proceeds to propagate the datagram down the forwarding tree. If it finds that a datagram is missing, the acknowledgement point sends a NACK up the tree toward the source. The NACK either reaches another acknowledgement point that has a copy of the datagram (in which case that acknowledgement point transmits a second copy), or the NACK reaches the source (which retransmits the missing datagram).

The choice of branching topology and acknowledgement points is crucial to the success of a reliable multicast scheme. Without sufficient acknowledgement points, a missing datagram can cause an ACK implosion. In particular, if a given router has many descendants, a lost datagram can cause that router to be overrun with retransmission requests. Unfortunately, automating selection of acknowledgement points has not turned out to be simple. Consequently, many reliable multicast protocols require manual configuration. Thus, multicast is best suited to: services that tend to persist over long periods of time, topologies that do not change rapidly, and situations where intermediate routers agree to serve as acknowledgement points.

---

†Note that a single source does not limit functionality because the source can agree to forward any message it receives via unicast. Thus, an arbitrary host can send a packet to the source, which then multicasts the packet to the group.

Is there an alternative approach to reliability? Some researchers are experimenting with protocols that incorporate redundant information to reduce or eliminate retransmission. One scheme sends redundant datagrams. Instead of sending a single copy of each datagram, the source sends *N* copies (typically *2* or *3*). Redundant datagrams work especially well when routers implement a *Random Early Discard* (*RED*) strategy because the probability of more than one copy being discarded is extremely small.

Another approach to redundancy involves *forward error-correcting codes*. Analogous to the error-correcting codes used with audio CDs, the scheme requires a sender to incorporate error-correction information into each datagram in a data stream. If one datagram is lost, the error correcting code contains sufficient redundant information to allow a receiver to reconstruct the missing datagram without requesting a retransmission.

17.30 Summary

IP multicasting is an abstraction of hardware multicasting. It allows delivery of a datagram to multiple destinations. IP uses class *D* addresses to specify multicast delivery; actual transmission uses hardware multicast, if it is available.

IP multicast groups are dynamic: a host can join or leave a group at any time. For local multicast, hosts only need the ability to send and receive multicast datagrams. However, IP multicasting is not limited to a single physical network – multicast routers propagate group membership information and arrange routing so that each member of a multicast group receives a copy of every datagram sent to that group.

Hosts communicate their group membership to multicast routers using IGMP. IGMP has been designed to be efficient and to avoid using network resources. In most cases, the only traffic IGMP introduces is a periodic message from a multicast router and a single reply for each multicast group to which hosts on that network belong.

A variety of protocols have been designed to propagate multicast routing information across an internet. The two basic approaches are data-driven and demand-driven. In either case, the amount of information in a multicast forwarding table is much larger than in a unicast routing table because multicasting requires entries for each (group, source) pair.

Not all routers in the global Internet propagate multicast routes or forward multicast traffic. Groups at two or more sites, separated by an internet that does not support multicast routing, can use an IP tunnel to transfer multicast datagrams. When using a tunnel, a program encapsulates a multicast datagram in a conventional unicast datagram. The receiver must extract and handle the multicast datagram.

Reliable multicast refers to a scheme that uses multicast forwarding but offers reliable delivery semantics. To avoid the ACK implosion problem, reliable multicast schemes either use a hierarchy of acknowledgement points or send redundant information.

FOR FURTHER STUDY

Deering [RFC 2236] specifies the standard for IP multicasting described in this chapter, which includes version 2 of IGMP. Waitzman, Partridge, and Deering [RFC 1075] describes DVMRP, Estrin et. al. [RFC 2362] describes PIM sparse mode, Ballardie [RFCs 2189 2201] describes CBT, and Moy [RFC 1585] describes MOSPF.

Eriksson [1994] explains the multicast backbone. Casner and Deering [July 1992] reports on the first multicast of an IETF meeting.

EXERCISES

17.1   The standard suggests using 23 bits of an IP multicast address to form a hardware multicast address. In such a scheme, how many IP multicast addresses map to a single hardware multicast address?

17.2   Argue that IP multicast addresses should use only 23 of the 28 possible bits. Hint: what are the practical limits on the number of groups to which a host can belong and the number of hosts on a single network?

17.3   IP must always check the destination addresses on incoming multicast datagrams and discard datagrams if the host is not in the specified multicast group. Explain how the host might receive a multicast destined for a group to which that host is not a member.

17.4   Multicast routers need to know whether a group has members on a given network. Is there any advantage to them knowing the exact set of hosts on a network that belong to a given multicast group?

17.5   Find three applications in your environment that can benefit from IP multicast.

17.6   The standard says that IP software must arrange to deliver a copy of any outgoing multicast datagram to application programs on the host that belong to the specified multicast group. Does this design make programming easier or more difficult? Explain.

17.7   When the underlying hardware does not support multicast, IP multicast uses hardware broadcast for delivery. How can doing so cause problems? Is there any advantage to using IP multicast over such networks?

17.8   DVMRP was derived from RIP. Read RFC 1075 on DVMRP and compare the two protocols. How much more complex is DVMRP than RIP?

17.9   IGMP does not include a strategy for acknowledgement or retransmission, even when used on networks that use best-effort delivery. What can happen if a query is lost? What can happen if a response is lost?

17.10 Explain why a multi-homed host may need to join a multicast group on one network, but not on another. (Hint: consider an audio teleconference.)

17.11 Estimate the size of the multicast forwarding table needed to handle multicast of audio from 100 radio stations, if each station has a total of ten million listeners at random locations around the world.

17.12 Argue that only two types of multicast are practical in the Internet: statically configured commercial services that multicast to large numbers of subscribers and dynamically configured services that include a few participants (e.g., family members in three households participating in a conference phone call).

17.13 Consider reliable multicast achieved through redundant transmission. If a given link has high probability of corruption, is it better to send redundant copies of a datagram or to send one copy that uses forward error-correcting codes? Explain.

17.14 The data-driven multicast routing paradigm works best on local networks that have low delay and excess capacity, while the demand-driven paradigm works best in a wide area environment that has limited capacity and higher delay. Does it make sense to devise a single protocol that combines the two schemes? Why or why not. (Hint: investigate MOSPF.)

17.15 Devise a quantitative measure that can be used to decide when PIM-SM should switch from a shared tree to a shortest path tree.

17.16 Read the protocol specification to find out the notion of ''sparse'' used in PIM-SM. Find an example of an internet in which the population of group members is sparse, but for which DVMRP is a better multicast routing protocol.

18

TCP/IP Over ATM Networks

18.1 Introduction

Previous chapters explain the fundamental parts of TCP/IP and show how the components operate over conventional LAN and WAN technologies. This chapter explores how TCP/IP, which was designed for connectionless networks, can be used over a connection-oriented technology†. We will see that TCP/IP is extremely flexible — a few of the address binding details must be modified for a connection-oriented environment, but most protocols remain unchanged.

The challenge arises when using TCP/IP over *Non-Broadcast Multiple-Access* (*NBMA*) networks (i.e., connection-oriented networks which allow multiple computers to attach, but do not support broadcast from one computer to all others). We will see that an NBMA environment requires modifications to IP protocols such as ARP that rely on broadcast.

To make the discussion concrete and relate it to available hardware, we will use *Asynchronous Transfer Mode* (*ATM*) in all examples. This chapter expands the brief description of ATM in Chapter 2, and covers additional details. The next sections describe the physical topology of an ATM network, the logical connectivity provided, ATM's connection paradigm, and the ATM adaptation protocol used to transfer data. Later sections discuss the relationship between ATM and TCP/IP. They explain ATM addressing, and show the relationship between a host's ATM address and its IP address. They also describe a modified form of the Address Resolution Protocol (ARP) used to resolve an IP address across a connection-oriented network, and a modified form of Inverse ARP that a server can use to obtain and manage addresses. Most important, we will see how IP datagrams travel across an ATM network without IP fragmentation.

---

†Some documents use the abbreviation *CL* for *connectionless* and *CO* for *connection-oriented*.

18.2 ATM Hardware

Like most connection-oriented technologies, ATM uses special-purpose electronic switches as the basic network building block. The switches in an ATM LAN usually provide connections for between 16 and 32 computers.† Although it is possible to use copper wiring between a host and an ATM switch, most installations use optical fiber to provide higher data rates. Figure 18.1 shows a diagram of an ATM switch with computers connected, and explains the connection.

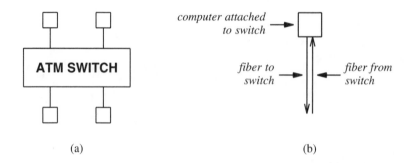

(a)   (b)

Figure 18.1 (a) The schematic diagram of a single ATM switch with four computers attached, and (b) the details of each connection. A pair of optical fibers carries data to and from the switch.

Physically, a host interface board plugs into a computer's bus. The interface hardware includes optical transmitters and receivers along with the circuitry needed to convert between electrical signals and the pulses of light that travel down the fiber to the switch. Because each fiber is used to carry light in only one direction, a connection that allows a computer to both send and receive data requires a pair of fibers.

18.3 Large ATM Networks

Although a single ATM switch has finite capacity, multiple switches can be interconnected to form a larger network. In particular, to connect computers at two sites to the same network, a switch can be installed at each site, and the two switches can then be connected. The connection between two switches differs slightly from the connection between a host computer and a switch. For example, interswitch connections usually operate at higher speeds, and use slightly modified protocols. Figure 18.2 illustrates the topology, and shows the conceptual difference between a *Network to Network Interface (NNI)* and a *User to Network Interface (UNI)*.

---

†Switches used in larger networks provide more connections; the point is that the number of computers attached to a given switch is limited.

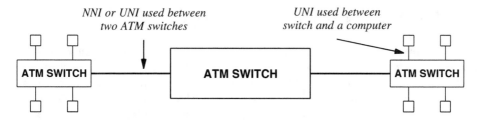

Figure 18.2 Three ATM switches combined to form a large network. Although an NNI interface is designed for use between switches, UNI connections can be used between ATM switches in a private network.

18.4 The Logical View Of An ATM Network

The goal of ATM is an end-to-end communication system. To a computer attached to an ATM network, an entire fabric of ATM switches appears to be a homogeneous network. Like the voice telephone system, a bridged Ethernet, or an IP internet, ATM hides the details of physical hardware and gives the appearance of a single, physical network with many computers attached. For example, Figure 18.3 illustrates how the ATM switching system in Figure 18.2 appears logically to the eight computers that are attached to it.

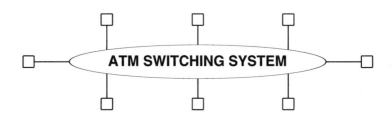

Figure 18.3 The logical view of the ATM switches in Figure 18.2. ATM gives the appearance of a uniform network; any computer can communicate with any other computer.

Thus, ATM provides the same general abstraction across homogeneous ATM hardware that TCP/IP provides for heterogeneous systems:

> *Despite a physical architecture that permits a switching fabric to contain multiple switches, ATM hardware provides attached computers with the appearance of a single, physical network. Any computer on an ATM network can communicate directly with any other; the computers remain unaware of the physical network structure.*

18.5 The Two ATM Connection Paradigms

ATM provides a connection-oriented interface to attached hosts. That is, before it can send data to a remote destination, a host must establish a *connection*, an abstraction analogous to a telephone call. Although there is only one type of underlying connection, ATM offers two ways to create a connection. The first is known as a *Permanent Virtual Circuit*† (*PVC*), and the second is known as a *Switched Virtual Circuit*† (*SVC*).

18.5.1 Permanent Virtual Circuits

In telephone jargon, a PVC is said to be a *provisioned service*. Provisioning simply means that a person is required to enter the necessary configuration manually into each switch along the path from the source to the destination (e.g., by typing into the console on each switch). Although the terms *PVC* and *provisioned service* may sound esoteric, the concept is not; even the most basic connection-oriented hardware supports PVCs.

On one hand, manual configuration has an obvious disadvantage: it cannot be changed rapidly or easily. Consequently, PVCs are only used for connections that stay in place for relatively long periods of time (weeks or years). On the other hand, manual configuration has advantages: a PVC does not require all switches to agree on a standard signaling mechanism. Thus, switches from two or more vendors may be able to interoperate when using PVCs, even if they cannot when using SVCs. Second, PVCs are often required for network management, maintenance, and debugging operations.

18.5.2 Switched Virtual Circuits

Unlike a PVC, an SVC is created automatically by software, and terminated when no longer needed. Software on a host initiates SVC creation; it passes a request to the local switch. The request includes the complete address of a remote host computer with which an SVC is needed and parameters that specify the quality of service required (e.g., the bandwidth and delay). The host then waits for the ATM network to create a circuit and respond. The ATM *signaling*‡ system establishes a path from the originating host across the ATM network (possibly through multiple switches) to the remote host computer.

During signaling, each ATM switch along the path and the remote computer must agree to establish the virtual circuit. When it agrees, a switch records information about the circuit, reserves the necessary resources, and sends the request to the next switch along the path. Once all the switches and the remote computer respond, signaling completes, and the switches at each end of the connection report to the hosts that the virtual circuit is in place.

Like all abstractions, connections must be identified. The UNI interface uses a 24-bit integer to identify each virtual circuit. When administrators create PVCs, they assign an identifier to each. When software on a host creates a new SVC, the local ATM switch assigns an identifier and informs the host. Unlike connectionless technolo-

---

†Although the ATM standard uses the term *virtual channel*, we will follow common practice and call it a *virtual circuit*.

‡The term *signaling* derives from telephone jargon.

gies, a connection-oriented system does not require each packet to carry either a source or destination address. Instead, a host places a circuit identifier in each outgoing packet, and the switch places a circuit identifier in each packet it delivers.

18.6 Paths, Circuits, And Identifiers

We said that a connection-oriented technology assigns a unique integer identifier to each circuit, and that a host uses the identifier when performing I/O operations or when closing the circuit. However, connection-oriented systems do not assign each circuit a globally unique identifier. Instead, the identifier is analogous to an I/O descriptor that is assigned to a program by the operating system. Like an I/O descriptor, a circuit identifier is a shorthand that a program uses in place of the full information that was used to create the circuit. Also like an I/O descriptor, a circuit identifier only remains valid while the circuit is open. Furthermore, a circuit identifier is meaningful only across a single hop — the circuit identifiers obtained by hosts at the two ends of a given virtual circuit usually differ. For example, the sender may be using identifier *17* while the receiver uses identifier *49*; each switch along the path translates the circuit identifier in a packet as the packet flows from one host to the other.

Technically, a circuit identifier used with the UNI interface consists of a 24-bit integer divided into two fields†. Figure 18.4 shows how ATM partitions the 24 bits into an 8-bit *virtual path identifier* (*VPI*) and a 16-bit *virtual circuit identifier* (*VCI*). Often, the entire identifier is referred to as a *VPI/VCI pair*.

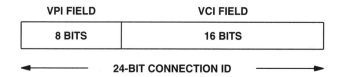

Figure 18.4 The 24-bit connection identifier used with UNI. The identifier is divided into virtual path and virtual circuit parts.

The motivation for dividing a connection identifier into VPI and VCI fields is similar to the reasons for dividing an IP address into network and host fields. If a set of virtual circuits follows the same path, an administrator can arrange for all circuits in the set to use the same VPI. ATM hardware can then use the VPI to route traffic efficiently. Commercial carriers can also use the VPI for accounting — a carrier can charge a customer for a virtual path, and then allow the customer to decide how to multiplex multiple virtual circuits over the path.

---

†The circuit identifier used with NNI has a slightly different format and a different length.

18.7 ATM Cell Transport

At the lowest level, an ATM network uses fixed-size frames called *cells* to carry data. ATM requires all cells to be the same size because doing so makes it possible to build faster switching hardware and to handle voice as well as data. Each ATM cell is 53 octets long, and consists of a 5-octet header followed by 48 octets of payload (i.e. data). Figure 18.5 shows the format of a cell header.

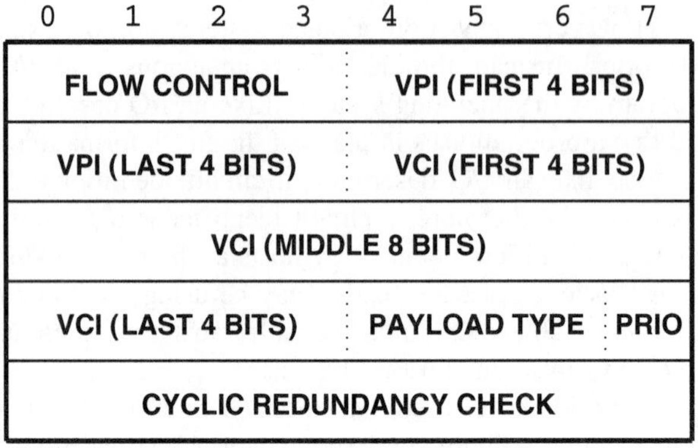

```
     0    1    2    3    4    5    6    7
   ┌─────────────────────┬─────────────────────┐
   │    FLOW CONTROL     │   VPI (FIRST 4 BITS) │
   ├─────────────────────┼─────────────────────┤
   │   VPI (LAST 4 BITS) │   VCI (FIRST 4 BITS) │
   ├─────────────────────┴─────────────────────┤
   │            VCI (MIDDLE 8 BITS)             │
   ├─────────────────────┬────────────────┬────┤
   │   VCI (LAST 4 BITS) │  PAYLOAD TYPE  │PRIO│
   ├─────────────────────┴────────────────┴────┤
   │          CYCLIC REDUNDANCY CHECK          │
   └───────────────────────────────────────────┘
```

Figure 18.5 The format of the five-octet UNI cell header used between a host and a switch. The diagram shows one octet per line; forty-eight octets of data follow the header.

18.8 ATM Adaptation Layers

Although ATM switches small cells at the lowest level, application programs that transfer data over ATM do not read or write cells. Instead, a computer interacts with ATM through an *ATM Adaptation Layer*, which is part of the ATM standard. The adaptation layer performs several functions, including detection and correction of errors such as lost or corrupted cells. Usually, firmware that implements an ATM adaptation layer is located on a host interface along with hardware and firmware that provide cell transmission and reception. Figure 18.6 illustrates the organization of a typical ATM interface, and shows how data passes from the computer's operating system through the interface board and into an ATM network.

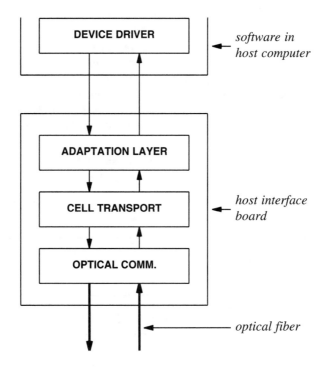

Figure 18.6 The conceptual organization of ATM interface hardware and the flow of data through it. Software on a host interacts with an adaptation layer protocol to send and receive data; the adaptation layer converts to and from cells.

When establishing a connection, a host must specify which adaptation layer protocol to use. Both ends of the connection must agree on the choice, and the adaptation layer cannot be changed once the connection has been established. To summarize:

> *Although ATM hardware uses small, fixed-size cells to transport data, a higher layer protocol called an ATM Adaptation Layer provides data transfer services for computers that use ATM. When a virtual circuit is created, both ends of the circuit must agree on which adaptation layer protocol will be used.*

18.9 ATM Adaptation Layer 5

Computers use *ATM Adaptation Layer 5* (*AAL5*) to send data across an ATM network. Interestingly, although ATM uses small fixed-size cells at the lowest level, AAL5 presents an interface that accepts and delivers large, variable-length packets. Thus, the interface computers use to send data makes ATM appear much like a connectionless technology. In particular, AAL5 allows each packet to contain between 1 and 65,535 octets of data. Figure 18.7 illustrates the packet format that AAL5 uses.

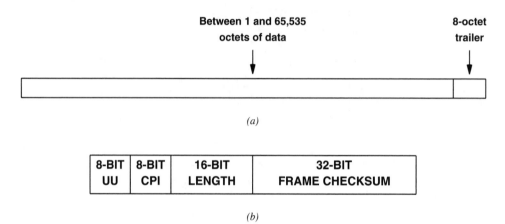

(a)

(b)

Figure 18.7 (a) The basic packet format that AAL5 accepts and delivers, and
(b) the fields in the 8-octet trailer that follows the data.

Unlike most network frames that place control information in a header, AAL5 places control information in an 8-octet trailer at the end of the packet. The AAL5 trailer contains a 16-bit length field, a 32-bit cyclic redundancy check (*CRC*) used as a frame checksum, and two 8-bit fields labeled *UU* and *CPI* that are currently unused†.

Each AAL5 packet must be divided into cells for transport across an ATM network, and then must be recombined to form a packet before being delivered to the receiving host. If the packet, including the 8-octet trailer, is an exact multiple of 48 octets, the division will produce completely full cells. If the packet is not an exact multiple of 48 octets, the final cell will not be full. To accommodate arbitrary length packets, AAL5 allows the final cell to contain between 0 and 40 octets of data, followed by zero padding, followed by the 8-octet trailer. In other words, AAL5 places the trailer in the last 8 octets of the final cell, where it can be found and extracted without knowing the length of the packet.

---

†Field *UU* can contain any value; field *CPI* must be set to zero.

18.10 AAL5 Convergence, Segmentation, And Reassembly

When an application sends data over an ATM connection using AAL5, the host delivers a block of data to the AAL5 interface. AAL5 generates a trailer, divides the information into 48-octet pieces, and transfers each piece across the ATM network in a single cell. On the receiving end of the connection, AAL5 reassembles incoming cells into a packet, checks the CRC to ensure that all pieces arrived correctly, and passes the resulting block of data to the host software. The process of dividing a block of data into cells and regrouping them is known as *ATM segmentation and reassembly*† (*SAR*).

By separating the functions of segmentation and reassembly from cell transport, AAL5 follows the layering principle. The ATM cell transfer layer is classified as *machine-to-machine* because the layering principle applies from one machine to the next (e.g., between a host and a switch or between two switches). The AAL5 layer is classified as *end-to-end* because the layering principle applies from the source to the destination — AAL5 presents the receiving software with data in exactly the same size blocks as the application passed to AAL5 on the sending end.

How does AAL5 on the receiving side know how many cells comprise a packet? The sending AAL5 uses the low-order bit of the *PAYLOAD TYPE* field of the ATM cell header to mark the final cell in a packet. One can think of it as an *end-of-packet bit*. Thus, the receiving AAL5 collects incoming cells until it finds one with the end-of-packet bit set. ATM standards use the term *convergence* to describe mechanisms that recognize the end of a packet. Although AAL5 uses a single bit in the cell header for convergence, other ATM adaptation layer protocols are free to use other convergence mechanisms.

To summarize:

> *A computer uses ATM Adaptation Layer 5 to transfer a large block of data over an ATM virtual circuit. On the sending host, AAL5 generates a trailer, segments the block of data into cells, and transmits each cell over the virtual circuit. On the receiving host, AAL5 reassembles the cells to reproduce the original block of data, strips off the trailer, and delivers the block of data to the receiving host software. A single bit in the cell header marks the final cell of a given data block.*

18.11 Datagram Encapsulation And IP MTU Size

We said that IP uses AAL5 to transfer datagrams across an ATM network. Before data can be sent, a virtual circuit (PVC or SVC) must be in place to the destination computer and both ends must agree to use AAL5 on the circuit. To transfer a datagram, the sender passes it to AAL5 along with the VPI/VCI identifying the circuit. AAL5 generates a trailer, divides the datagram into cells, and transfers the cells across the net-

---

†Use of the term *reassembly* suggests the strong similarity between AAL5 segmentation and IP fragmentation: both mechanisms divide a large block of data into smaller units for transfer.

work. At the receiving end, AAL5 reassembles the cells, checks the CRC to verify that no bits were lost or corrupted, extracts the datagram, and passes it to IP.

In reality, AAL5 uses a 16-bit length field, making it possible to send 64K octets in a single packet. Despite the capabilities of AAL5, TCP/IP restricts the size of datagrams that can be sent over ATM. The standards impose a default of 9180 octets† per datagram. As with any network interface, when an outgoing datagram is larger than the network MTU, IP fragments the datagram, and passes each fragment to AAL5. Thus, AAL5 accepts, transfers, and delivers datagrams of 9180 octets or less. To summarize:

> When TCP/IP sends data across an ATM network, it transfers an entire datagram using ATM Adaptation Layer 5. Although AAL5 can accept and transfer packets that contain up to 64K octets, the TCP/IP standards specify a default MTU of 9180 octets. IP must fragment any datagram larger than 9180 octets before passing it to AAL5.

18.12 Packet Type And Multiplexing

Observant readers will have noticed that the AAL5 trailer does not include a *type* field. Thus, an AAL5 frame is not self-identifying. As a result, the simplest form of encapsulation described above does not suffice if the two ends want to send more than one type of data across a single VC (e.g., packets other than IP). Two possibilities exist:

- The two computers at the ends of a virtual circuit agree *a priori* that the circuit will be used for a specific protocol (e.g., the circuit will only be used to send IP datagrams).
- The two computers at the ends of a virtual circuit agree *a priori* that some octets of the data area will be reserved for use as a type field.

The former scheme, in which the computers agree on the high-level protocol for a given circuit, has the advantage of not requiring additional information in a packet. For example, if the computers agree to transfer IP, a sender can pass each datagram directly to AAL5 to transfer; nothing needs to be sent besides the datagram and the AAL5 trailer. The chief disadvantage of such a scheme lies in duplication of virtual circuits: a computer must create a separate virtual circuit for each high-level protocol. Because most carriers charge for each virtual circuit, customers try to avoid using multiple circuits because it adds unnecessary cost.

The latter scheme, in which two computers use a single virtual circuit for multiple protocols, has the advantage of allowing all traffic to travel over the same circuit, but the disadvantage of requiring each packet to contain octets that identify the protocol type. The scheme also has the disadvantage that packets from all protocols travel with the same delay and priority.

---

†The size 9180 was chosen to make ATM compatible with an older technology called *Switched Multimegabit Data Service* (*SMDS*); a value other than 9180 can be used if both ends agree.

The TCP/IP standards specify that computers can choose between the two methods of using AAL5. Both the sender and receiver must agree on how the circuit will be used; the agreement may involve manual configuration. Furthermore, the standards suggest that when computers choose to include type information in the packet, they should use a standard IEEE 802.2 *Logical Link Control* (*LLC*) header followed by a *SubNetwork Attachment Point* (*SNAP*) header. Figure 18.8 illustrates the LLC/SNAP information prefixed to a datagram before it is sent over an ATM virtual circuit.

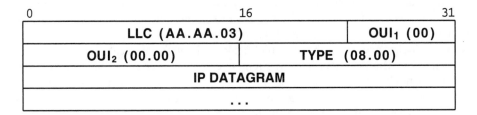

Figure 18.8 The packet format used to send a datagram over AAL5 when multiplexing multiple protocols on a single virtual circuit. The 8-octet LLC/SNAP header identifies the contents as an IP datagram.

As the figure shows, the LLC field consists of three octets that contain the hexadecimal values *AA.AA.03*†. The SNAP header consists of five octets: three that contain an *Organizationally Unique Identifier* (*OUI*) and two for a type‡. Field *OUI* identifies an organization that administers values in the *TYPE* field, and the *TYPE* field identifies the packet type. For an IP datagram, the *OUI* field contains *00.00.00* to identify the organization responsible for Ethernet standards, and the *TYPE* field contains *08.00*, the value used when encapsulating IP in an Ethernet frame. Software on the sending host must prefix the LLC/SNAP header to each packet before sending it to AAL5, and software on the receiving host must examine the header to determine how to handle the packet.

18.13 IP Address Binding In An ATM Network

We have seen that encapsulating a datagram for transmission across an ATM network is straightforward. By contrast, IP address binding in a Non-Broadcast Multiple-Access (*NBMA*) environment can be difficult. Like other network technologies, ATM assigns each attached computer a physical address that must be used when establishing a virtual circuit. On one hand, because an ATM physical address is larger than an IP address, an ATM physical address cannot be encoded within an IP address. Thus, IP cannot use static address binding for ATM networks. On the other hand, ATM

---

†The notation represents each octet as a hexadecimal value separated by decimal points.

‡To avoid unnecessary fragmentation, the eight octets of an LLC/SNAP header are ignored in the MTU computation (i.e., the effective MTU of an ATM connection that uses an LLC/SNAP header is 9188).

hardware does not support broadcast. Thus, IP cannot use conventional ARP to bind addresses on ATM networks.

ATM permanent virtual circuits further complicate address binding. Because a manager configures each permanent virtual circuit manually, a host only knows the circuit's VPI/VCI pair. Software on the host may not know the IP address nor the ATM hardware address of the remote endpoint. Thus, an IP address binding mechanism must provide for the identification of a remote computer connected over a PVC as well as the dynamic creation of SVCs to known destinations.

Switched connection-oriented technologies further complicate address binding because they require two levels of binding. First, when creating a virtual circuit over which datagrams will be sent, the IP address of the destination must be mapped to an ATM endpoint address. The endpoint address is used to create a virtual circuit. Second, when sending a datagram to a remote computer over an existing virtual circuit, the destination's IP address must be mapped to the VPI/VCI pair for the circuit. The second binding is used each time a datagram is sent over an ATM network; the first binding is necessary only when a host creates an SVC.

18.14 Logical IP Subnet Concept

Although no protocol has been proposed to solve the general case of address binding for NBMA networks like ATM, a protocol has been devised for a restricted form. The restricted form arises when a group of computers uses an ATM network in place of a single (usually local) physical network. The group forms a *Logical IP Subnet* (*LIS*). Multiple logical IP subnets can be defined among a set of computers that all attach to the same ATM hardware network. For example, Figure 18.9 illustrates eight computers attached to an ATM network divided into two LIS.

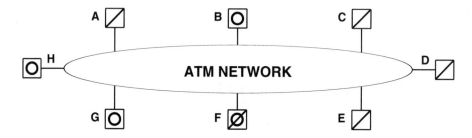

Figure 18.9 Eight computers attached to an ATM network participating in two Logical IP Subnets. Computers marked with a slash participate in one LIS, while computers marked with a circle participate in the other LIS.

As the figure shows, all computers attach to the same physical ATM network. Computers *A*, *C*, *D*, *E*, and *F* participate in one LIS, while computers *B*, *F*, *G*, and *H* participate in another. Each logical IP subnet functions like a separate LAN. The computers participating in an LIS establish virtual circuits among themselves to exchange datagrams†. Because each LIS forms a conceptually separate network, IP applies the standard rules for a physical network to each LIS. For example, all computers in an LIS share a single IP network prefix, and that prefix differs from the prefixes used by other logical subnets. Furthermore, although the computers in an LIS can choose a nonstandard MTU, all computers must use the same MTU on all virtual circuits that comprise the LIS. Finally, despite the ATM hardware that provides potential connectivity, a host in one LIS is forbidden from communicating directly with a host in another LIS. Instead, all communication between logical subnets must proceed through a router just as communication between two physical Ethernets proceeds through a router. In Figure 18.9, for example, machine *F* represents an IP router because it participates in both logical subnets.

To summarize:

> *TCP/IP allows a subset of computers attached to an ATM network to operate like an independent LAN. Such a group is called a* Logical IP Subnet *(LIS); computers in an LIS share a single IP network prefix. A computer in an LIS can communicate directly with any other computer in the same LIS, but is required to use a router when communicating with a computer in another LIS.*

18.15 Connection Management

Hosts must manage ATM virtual circuits carefully because creating a circuit takes time and, for commercial ATM services, can incur additional economic cost. Thus, the simplistic approach of creating a virtual circuit, sending one datagram, and then closing the circuit is too expensive. Instead, a host must maintain a record of open circuits so they can be reused.

Circuit management occurs in the network interface software below IP. When a host needs to send a datagram, it uses conventional IP routing to find the appropriate next-hop address, *N*‡, and passes it along with the datagram to the network interface. The network interface examines its table of open virtual circuits. If an open circuit exists to *N*, the host uses AAL5 to send the datagram. Otherwise, before the host can send the datagram, it must locate a computer with IP address *N*, create a circuit, and add the circuit to its table.

The concept of logical IP subnets constrains IP routing. In a properly configured routing table, the next-hop address for each destination must be a computer within the same logical subnet as the sender. To understand the constraint, remember that each LIS is designed to operate like a single LAN. The same constraint holds for a host at-

---

†The standard specifies the use of LLC/SNAP encapsulation within an LIS.
‡As usual, a next-hop address is an IP address.

tached to a LAN, namely, each next-hop address in the routing table must be a router attached to the LAN.

One of the reasons for dividing computers into logical subnets arises from hardware and software constraints. A host cannot maintain an arbitrarily large number of open virtual circuits at the same time because each circuit requires resources in the ATM hardware and in the operating system. Dividing computers into logical subnets limits the maximum number of simultaneously open circuits to the number of computers in the LIS.

18.16 Address Binding Within An LIS

When a host creates a virtual circuit to a computer in its LIS, the host must specify an ATM hardware address for the destination. How can a host map a next-hop address into an appropriate ATM hardware address? The host cannot broadcast a request to all computers in the LIS because ATM does not offer hardware broadcast. Instead, it contacts a server to obtain the mapping. Communication between the host and server uses *ATMARP*, a variant of the ARP protocol described in Chapter 5.

As with conventional ARP, a sender forms a request that includes the sender's IP and ATM hardware addresses as well as the IP address of a target for which the ATM hardware address is needed. The sender then transmits the request to the *ATMARP server* for the logical subnet. If the server knows the ATM hardware address, it sends an *ATMARP reply*. Otherwise, the server sends a *negative ATMARP reply*.

18.17 ATMARP Packet Format

Figure 18.10 illustrates the format of an ATMARP packet. As the figure shows, ATMARP modifies the ARP packet format slightly. The major change involves additional address length fields to accommodate ATM addresses. To appreciate the changes, one must understand that multiple address forms have been proposed for ATM, and that no single form appears to be the emerging standard. Telephone companies that offer public ATM networks use an 8-octet format where each address is an ISDN telephone number defined by ITU standard document *E.164*. By contrast, the ATM Forum† allows each computer attached to a private ATM network to be assigned a 20-octet *Network Service Access Point* (*NSAP*) address. Thus, a two-level hierarchical address may be needed that specifies an E.164 address for a remote site and an NSAP address of a host on a local switch at the site.

To accommodate multiple address formats and a two-level hierarchy, an ATMARP packet contains two length fields for each ATM address as well as a length field for each protocol address. As Figure 18.10 shows, an ATMARP packet begins with fixed-size fields that specify address lengths. The first two fields follow the same format as conventional ARP. The field labeled *HARDWARE TYPE* contains the hexadecimal

---

†The ATM Forum is a consortium of industrial members that recommends standards for private ATM networks.

value *0x0013* for ATM, and the field labeled *PROTOCOL TYPE* contains the hexadecimal value *0x0800* for IP.

Because the address format of the sender and target can differ, each ATM address requires a length field. Field *SEND HLEN* specifies the length of the sender's ATM address, and field *SEND HLEN2* specifies the length of the sender's ATM subaddress. Fields *TAR HLEN* and *TAR HLEN2* specify the lengths of the target's ATM address and subaddress. Finally, fields *SEND PLEN* and *TAR PLEN* specify the lengths of the sender's and target's protocol addresses.

Following the length fields in the header, an ATMARP packet contains six addresses. The first three address fields contain the sender's ATM address, ATM subaddress, and protocol address. The last three fields contain the target's ATM address, ATM subaddress, and protocol address. In the example in Figure 18.10, both the sender and target subaddress length fields contain zero, and the packet does not contain octets for subaddresses.

0	8	16	24	31
HARDWARE TYPE (0x0013)		PROTOCOL TYPE (0x0800)		
SEND HLEN (20)	SEND HLEN2 (0)	OPERATION		
SEND PLEN (4)	TAR HLEN (20)	TAR HLEN2 (0)		TAR PLEN (4)
SENDER'S ATM ADDRESS (octets 0-3)				
SENDER'S ATM ADDRESS (octets 4-7)				
SENDER'S ATM ADDRESS (octets 8-11)				
SENDER'S ATM ADDRESS (octets 12-15)				
SENDER'S ATM ADDRESS (octets 16-19)				
SENDER'S PROTOCOL ADDRESS				
TARGET'S ATM ADDRESS (octets 0-3)				
TARGET'S ATM ADDRESS (octets 4-7)				
TARGET'S ATM ADDRESS (octets 8-11)				
TARGET'S ATM ADDRESS (octets 12-15)				
TARGET'S ATM ADDRESS (octets 16-19)				
TARGET'S PROTOCOL ADDRESS				

Figure 18.10 The format of an ATMARP packet when used with 20-octet ATM addresses such as those recommended by the ATM Forum.

18.17.1 Format Of ATM Address Length Fields

Because ATMARP is designed for use with either E.164 addresses or 20-octet NSAP addresses, fields that contain an ATM address length include a bit that specifies the address format. Figure 18.11 illustrates how ATMARP encodes the address type and length in an 8-bit field.

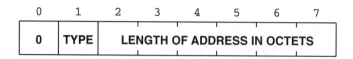

Figure 18.11 The encoding of ATM address type and length in an 8-bit field. Bit *1* distinguishes the two types of ATM addresses.

A single bit encodes the type of an ATM address because only two forms are available. If bit *1* contains zero, the address is in the NSAP format recommended by the ATM Forum. If bit *1* contains one, the address is in the E.164 format recommended by the ITU. Because each ATM address length field in an ATMARP packet has the form shown in Figure 18.11, a single packet can contain multiple types of ATM addresses.

18.17.2 Operation Codes Used With The ATMARP Protocol

The packet format shown in Figure 18.10 is used to request an address binding, reply to a request, or request an inverse address binding. When a computer sends an ATMARP packet, it must set the *OPERATION* field to specify the type of binding. The table in Figure 18.12 shows the values that can be used in the *OPERATION* field, and gives the meaning of each. The remainder of this section explains how the protocol works.

Code	Meaning
1	ATMARP Request
2	ATMARP Reply
8	Inverse ATMARP Request
9	Inverse ATMARP Reply
10	ATMARP Negative Ack

Figure 18.12 The values that can appear in the *OPERATION* field of an ATMARP packet and their meanings. When possible, values have been chosen to agree with the operation codes used in conventional ARP.

18.18 Using ATMARP Packets To Determine An Address

Performing address binding for connection-oriented hardware is slightly more complex than for connectionless hardware. Because ATM hardware supports two types of virtual circuits, two cases arise. First, we will consider the case of permanent virtual circuits. Second, we will consider the case of switched virtual circuits.

18.18.1 Permanent Virtual Circuits

To understand the problems PVCs introduce, recall how ATM hardware operates. A network administrator must configure each PVC; hosts themselves do not participate in PVC setup. In particular, a host begins operation with PVCs in place, and does not receive any information from the hardware about the address of the remote endpoint. Thus, unless address information has been configured into the hosts (e.g., stored on disk), the host does not know the IP address or ATM address of the computer to which a PVC connects.

The *Inverse ATMARP* protocol (*InATMARP*) solves the problem of finding addresses when using PVCs. To use the protocol, a computer must know each of the permanent virtual circuits that have been configured. To determine the IP and ATM addresses of the remote endpoint, a computer sends an Inverse ATMARP request packet with the *OPERATION* field set to *8*. Whenever such a request arrives over a PVC, the receiver generates an Inverse ATMARP reply with the *OPERATION* field set to *9*. Both the request and the reply contain the sender's IP address and ATM address. Thus, a computer at each end of the connection learns the binding for the computer at the other end. In summary,

> *Two computers that communicate over a permanent virtual circuit use Inverse ATMARP to discover each others' IP and ATM addresses. One computer sends an Inverse ATMARP request, to which the other sends a reply.*

18.18.2 Switched Virtual Circuits

Within an LIS, computers create switched virtual circuits on demand. When computer *A* needs to send a datagram to computer *B* and no circuit currently exists to *B*, *A* uses ATM signaling to create the necessary circuit. Thus, *A* begins with *B*'s IP address, which must be mapped to an equivalent ATM address. We said that each LIS has an ATMARP server, and all computers in an LIS must be configured so they know how to reach the server (e.g., a computer can have a PVC to the server or can have the server's ATM address stored on disk). A server does not form connections to other computers; the server merely waits for computers in the LIS to contact it. To map address *B* to an ATM address, computer *A* must have a virtual circuit open to the ATMARP server for the LIS. Computer *A* forms an ATMARP request packet and sends it over the connection to the server. The *OPERATION* field in the packet contains *1*, and the target's protocol address field contains *B*'s IP address.

An ATMARP server maintains a database of mappings from IP addresses to ATM addresses. If the server knows *B*'s ATM address, the ATMARP protocol operates similar to proxy ARP. The server forms an ATMARP reply by setting the *OPERATION* code to *2* and filling in the ATM address that corresponds to the target IP address. As in conventional ARP, the server exchanges sender and target entries before returning the reply to the computer that sent the request.

If the server does not know the ATM address that corresponds to the target IP address in a request, ATMARP's behavior differs from conventional ARP. Instead of ignoring the request, the server returns a negative acknowledgement (an ATMARP packet with an *OPERATION* field of *10*). A negative acknowledgement distinguishes between addresses for which a server does not have a binding and a malfunctioning server. Thus, when a host sends a request to an ATMARP server, it determines one of three outcomes unambiguously. The host can learn the ATM address of the target, that the target is not currently available in the LIS, or that the server is not currently responding.

18.19 Obtaining Entries For A Server Database

An ATMARP server builds and maintains its database of bindings automatically. To do so, it uses Inverse ATMARP. Whenever a host or router first opens a virtual circuit to an ATMARP server, the server immediately sends an Inverse ATMARP request packet†. The host or router must answer by sending an Inverse ATMARP reply packet. When it receives an Inverse ATMARP reply, the server extracts the sender's IP and ATM addresses, and stores the binding in its database. Thus, each computer in an LIS must establish a connection to the ATMARP server, even if the computer does not intend to look up bindings.

> *Each host or router in an LIS must register its IP address and corresponding ATM address with the ATMARP server for the LIS. Registration occurs automatically whenever a computer establishes a virtual circuit to an ATMARP server because the server sends an Inverse ATMARP to which the computer must respond.*

18.20 Timing Out ATMARP Information In A Server

Like the bindings in a conventional ARP cache, bindings obtained via ATMARP must be timed out and removed. How long should an entry persist in a server? Once a computer registers its binding with an ATMARP server, the server keeps the entry for a minimum of 20 minutes. After 20 minutes, the server examines the entry. If no circuit exists to the computer that sent the entry, the server deletes the entry‡. If the computer that sent the entry has maintained an open virtual circuit, the server attempts to revali-

---

†The circuit must use AAL5 with LLC/SNAP type identification.

‡A server does not automatically delete an entry when a circuit is closed; it waits for the timeout period.

date the entry. The server sends an Inverse ATMARP request and awaits a response. If the response verifies information in the entry, the server resets the timer and waits another 20 minutes. If the Inverse ATMARP response does not match the information in the entry, the server closes the circuit and deletes the entry.

To help reduce traffic, the ATMARP standard permits an optimization. It allows a host to use a single virtual circuit for all communication with an ATMARP server. When the host sends an ATMARP request, the request contains the host's binding in the *SENDER*'s field. The server can extract the binding and use it to revalidate its stored information. Thus, if a host sends more than one ATMARP request every 20 minutes, the server will not need to send the host an Inverse ATMARP request.

18.21 Timing Out ATMARP Information In A Host Or Router

A host or router must also use timers to invalidate information obtained from an ATMARP server. In particular, the standard specifies that a computer can keep a binding obtained from the ATMARP server for at most 15 minutes. When 15 minutes expire, the entry must be removed or revalidated. If an address binding expires and the host does not have an open virtual circuit to the destination, the host removes the entry from its ARP cache. If a host has an open virtual circuit to the destination, the host attempts to revalidate the address binding. Expiration of an address binding can delay traffic because:

> *A host or router must stop sending data to any destination for which the address binding has expired until the binding can be revalidated.*

The method a host uses to revalidate a binding depends on the type of virtual circuit being used. If the host can reach the destination over a PVC, the host sends an Inverse ATMARP request on the circuit and awaits a reply. If the host has an SVC open to the destination, the host sends an ATMARP request to the ATMARP server.

18.22 IP Switching Technologies

So far, we have described ATM as a connection-oriented network technology that IP uses to transfer datagrams. However, engineers have also investigated a more fundamental union of the two technologies. They began with the question: "can switching hardware be exploited to forward IP traffic at higher speeds?" The assumption underlying the effort is that hardware will be able to switch more packets per second than to route them. If the assumption is correct, the question makes sense because router vendors are constantly trying to find ways to increase router performance and scale.

Ipsilon Corporation was one of the first companies to produce products that combined IP and hardware switches; they used ATM, called their technology *IP switching*, and called the devices they produced *IP switches*. Since Ipsilon, other companies have produced a series of designs and names, including *tag switching*, *layer 3 switching*, and *label switching*. Several of the ideas have been folded into a standard endorsed by the IETF that is known as *Multi-Protocol Label Switching (MPLS)*†. Contributors to the open standard hope that it will allow products from multiple vendors to interoperate.

18.23 Switch Operation

How do IP switching technologies work? There are two general answers. Early technologies all assumed the presence of a conventional NBMA network (usually ATM). The goal was to optimize IP routing to send datagrams across the ATM fabric instead of other networks whenever possible. In addition to proposing ways to optimize routes, later efforts also proposed modifying the switching hardware to optimize it for IP traffic. In particular, two optimizations have been proposed. First, if switching hardware can be redesigned to either use large cells or to allow variable-length frames, header overhead will be reduced‡. Second, if hardware can be built to parse IP headers and extract needed fields, an incoming datagram can be forwarded faster.

Forwarding is at the heart of all label switching. There are three aspects. First, at the IP layer, a forwarding device must function as a conventional IP router to transfer datagrams between a local network and the switched fabric. Thus, the device must learn about remote destinations, and must map an IP destination address into a next-hop address. Second, at the network interface layer, a forwarding device must be able to create and manage connections through the switched fabric (i.e., by mapping IP addresses to underlying hardware addresses and creating SVCs as needed). Third, a forwarding device must optimize paths through the switched fabric.

18.24 Optimized IP Forwarding

Optimized forwarding involves high-speed classification and *shortcut paths*. To understand shortcut paths, imagine three switches, S_1, S_2, and S_3, and suppose that to reach a given destination the IP routing table in S_1 specifies forwarding to S_2, which forwards to S_3, which delivers to the destination. Further suppose that all three devices are connected to the same fabric. If S_1 observes that many datagrams are being sent to the destination, it can optimize routing by bypassing S_2 and setting up a shortcut path (i.e., a virtual circuit) directly to S_3. Of course, many details need to be handled. For example, although our example involves only three devices, a real network may have many. After it learns the path a datagram will travel to its destination, S_1 must find the last hop along the path that is reachable through the switched network, translate the IP address of that hop to an underlying hardware address, and form a connection. Recognizing whether a given hop on the path connects to the same switching fabric and translating addresses are not easy; complex protocols are needed to pass the necessary information. To give IP the illusion that datagrams are following the routes specified by IP, either S_1 or S_3 must agree to account for the bypassed router when decrementing the TTL field in

---

†Despite having ''multi-protocol'' in the name, MPLS is focused almost exclusively on finding ways to put IP over an NBMA switched hardware platform.

‡In the industry, ATM header overhead is known as the *cell tax*.

the datagram header. Furthermore, S_1 must continue to receive routing updates from S_2 so it can revert to the old path in case routes change.

18.25 Classification, Flows, And Higher Layer Switching

A *classification scheme* examines each incoming datagram and chooses a connection over which the datagram should travel. Building a classification scheme in hardware further enhances the technology by allowing a switch to make the selection at high speed. Most of the proposed classification schemes use a two-level hierarchy. First, the switch classifies a datagram into one of many possible *flows*, and then the flow is mapped onto a given connection. One can think of the mapping mathematically as a pair of functions:

$$f = c_1(\,datagram\,)$$

and

$$vc = c_2(f)$$

where f identifies a particular flow, and vc identifies a connection. We will see below that separating the two functions provides flexibility in the possible mappings.

In practice function c_1 does not examine the entire datagram. Instead, only header fields are used. Strict *layer 3 classification* restricts computation to fields in the IP header such as the source and destination IP addresses and type of service. Most vendors implement *layer 4 classification*†, and some offer *layer 5 classification*. In addition to examining fields in the IP header, layer 4 classification schemes also examine protocol port numbers in the TCP or UDP header. Layer 5 schemes look further into the datagram and consider the application.

The concept of flows is important in switching IP because it allows the switch to track activity. For example, imagine that as it processes datagrams, a switch makes a list of (source, destination) pairs and keeps a counter with each. It does not make sense for a switch to optimize all routes because some flows only contain a few packets (e.g., when someone pings a remote computer). The count of flow activity provides a measure — when the count reaches a threshold, the switch begins to look for an optimized route. Layer 4 classification helps optimize flows because it allows the switch to know the approximate duration of a connection and whether traffic is caused by multiple TCP connections or a single connection.

Flows are also an important tool to make switched schemes work well with TCP. If a switch begins using a shortcut on a path that TCP is using, the round-trip time changes and some segments arrive out of order, causing TCP to adjust its retransmission timer. Thus, a switch using layer 4 classification can map each TCP session to a different flow, and then choose whether to map a flow to the original path or the shortcut. Most switching technologies employ hysteresis by retaining the original path for existing TCP connections, but using a shortcut for new connections (i.e., moving existing

---

†Vendors use the term *layer 4 switching* to characterize products that implement layer 4 classification.

connections to the shortcut after a fixed amount of time has elapsed or if the connection is idle).

18.26 Applicability Of Switching Technology

Although many vendors are pushing products that incorporate switched IP, there are several reasons why the technology has not had more widespread acceptance. First, in many cases switching costs more than conventional routing, but does not offer much increase in performance. The difference is most significant in the local area environment where inexpensive LANs, like Ethernet, have sufficient capacity and inexpensive routers work. In fact, computer scientists continue to find ways to improve IP forwarding schemes, which means that traditional routers can process more datagrams per second without requiring an increase in hardware speed. Second, the availability of inexpensive higher-speed LANs, such as gigabit Ethernet, has made organizations unwilling to use more expensive connection-oriented technology for an entire organization. Third, although switching IP appears straightforward, the details make it complex. Consequently, the protocols are significantly more complex than other parts of IP, which makes them more difficult to build, install, configure, and manage. We conclude that although there may be advantages to switched IP, it will not replace all traditional routers.

18.27 Summary

IP can be used over connection-oriented technologies; we examined ATM as a specific example. ATM is a high-speed network technology in which a network consists of one or more switches interconnected to form a switching fabric. The resulting system is characterized as a Non-Broadcast Multiple-Access technology because it appears to operate as a single, large network that provides communication between any two attached computers, but does not allow a single packet to be broadcast to all of them.

Because ATM is connection-oriented, two computers must establish a virtual circuit through the network before they can transfer data; a host can choose between a switched or permanent type of virtual circuit. Switched circuits are created on demand; permanent circuits require manual configuration. In either case, ATM assigns each open circuit an integer identifier. Each frame a host sends and each frame the network delivers contains a circuit identifier; a frame does not contain a source or destination address.

Although the lowest levels of ATM use 53-octet cells to transfer information, IP always uses ATM Adaptation Layer 5 (AAL5). AAL5 accepts and delivers variable-size blocks of data, where each block can be up to 64K octets. To send an IP datagram across ATM, the sender must form a virtual circuit connection to the destination, specify using AAL5 on the circuit, and pass each datagram to AAL5 as a single block of data. AAL5 adds a trailer, divides the datagram and trailer into cells for transmission across the network, and then reassembles the datagram before passing it to the operating system on the destination computer. IP uses a default MTU of 9180, and AAL5 performs the segmentation into cells.

A Logical IP Subnet (LIS) consists of a set of computers that use ATM in place of a LAN; the computers form virtual circuits among themselves over which they exchange datagrams. Because ATM does not support broadcasting, computers in an LIS use a modified form of ARP known as ATMARP. An ATMARP server performs all address binding; each computer in the LIS must register with the server by supplying its IP address and ATM address. As with conventional ARP, a binding obtained from ATMARP is aged. After the aging period, the binding must be revalidated or discarded. A related protocol, Inverse ATMARP, is used to discover the ATM and IP addresses of a remote computer connected by a permanent virtual circuit.

Switching hardware technology can be used with IP. An IP switch acts as a router, but also classifies IP datagrams and sends them across the switched network when possible. Layer 3 classification uses only the datagram header; layer 4 classification also examines the TCP or UDP header. MPLS is a new standard for switching IP that is designed to allow systems from multiple vendors to interoperate.

FOR FURTHER STUDY

Newman et. al. [April 1998] describes IP switching. Laubach and Halpern [RFC 2225] introduces the concept of Logical IP Subnet, defines the ATMARP protocol, and specifies the default MTU. Grossman and Heinanen [RFC 2684] describes the use of LLC/SNAP headers when encapsulating IP in AAL5.

Partridge [1994] describes gigabit networking in general, and the importance of cell switching in particular. De Prycker [1993] considers many of the theoretical underpinnings of ATM and discusses its relationship to telephone networks.

EXERCISES

18.1 If your organization has an ATM switch or ATM service, find the technical and economic specifications, and then compare the cost of using ATM with the cost of another technology such as Ethernet.

18.2 A typical connection between a host and a private ATM switch operates at 155 Mbps. Consider the speed of the bus on your favorite computer. What percentage of the bus is required to keep an ATM interface busy?

18.3 Many operating systems choose TCP buffer sizes to be multiples of 8K octets. If IP fragments datagrams for an MTU of 9180 octets, what size fragments result from a datagram that carries a TCP segment of 16K octets? of 24K octets?

18.4   Look at the definition of IPv6 described in Chapter 33. What new mechanism relates directly to ATM?

18.5   ATM is a best-effort delivery system in which the hardware can discard cells if the network becomes congested. What is the probability of datagram loss if the probability of loss of a single cell is $1/P$ and the datagram is 576 octets long? 1500 octets? 4500 octets? 9180 octets?

18.6   A typical remote login session using TCP generates datagrams of 41 octets: 20 octets of IP header, 20 octets of TCP header, and 1 octet of data. How many ATM cells are required to send such a datagram using the default IP encapsulation over AAL5?

18.7   How many cells, octets, and bits can be present on a fiber that connects to an ATM switch if the fiber is 3 meters long? 100 meters? 3000 meters? To find out, consider an ATM switch transmitting data at 155 Mbps. Each bit is a pulse of light that lasts $1/(155 \times 10^6)$ second. Assume the pulse travels at the speed of light, calculate its length, and compare to the length of the fiber.

18.8   A host can specify a two-level ATM address when requesting an SVC. What ATM network topologies are appropriate for a two-level addressing scheme? Characterize situations for which additional levels of hierarchy are useful.

18.9   An ATM network guarantees to deliver cells in order, but may drop cells if it becomes congested. Is it possible to modify TCP to take advantage of cell ordering to reduce protocol overhead? Why or why not?

18.10 Read about the LANE and MPOA standards that allow ATM to emulate an Ethernet or other local area network. What is the chief advantage of using ATM to emulate LANs? The chief disadvantage?

18.11 A large organization that uses ATM to interconnect IP hosts must divide hosts into logical IP subnets. Two extremes exist: the organization can place all hosts in one large LIS, or the organization can have many LIS (e.g., each pair of hosts forms an LIS). Explain why neither extreme is desirable.

18.12 How many ATM cells are required to transfer a single ATMARP packet when each ATM address and subaddress is 20 octets and each protocol address is 4 octets?

18.13 ATM allows a host to establish multiple virtual circuits to a given destination. What is the major advantage of doing so?

18.14 Measure the throughput and delay of an ATM switch when using TCP. If your operating system permits, repeat the experiment with the TCP transmit buffer set to various sizes (if your system uses sockets, refer to the manual for details on how to set the buffer size). Do the results surprise you?

18.15 IP does not have a mechanism to associate datagrams traveling across an ATM network with a specific ATM virtual circuit. Under what circumstances would such a mechanism be useful?

18.16 A server does not immediately remove an entry from its cache when the host that sent the information closes its connection to the server. What is the chief advantage of such a design? What is the chief disadvantage?

18.17 Is IP switching worthwhile for applications you run? To find out, monitor the traffic from your computer and find the average duration of TCP connections, the number of simultaneous connections, and the number of IP destinations you contact in a week.

18.18 Read about MPLS. Should MPLS accommodate layer 2 forwarding (i.e., bridging) as well as optimized IP forwarding? Why or why not?

19

Mobile IP

19.1 Introduction

Previous chapters describe the original IP addressing and routing schemes used with stationary computers. This chapter considers a recent extension of IP designed to allow portable computers to move from one network to another.

19.2 Mobility, Routing, and Addressing

In the broadest sense, the term *mobile computing* refers to a system that allows computers to move from one location to another. Mobility is often associated with wireless technologies that allow movement across long distances at high speed. However, speed is not the central issue for IP. Instead, a challenge only arises when a host changes from one network to another. For example, a notebook computer attached to a wireless LAN can move around the range of the transmitter rapidly without affecting IP, but simply unplugging a desktop computer and plugging it into a different network requires reconfiguring IP.

The IP addressing scheme, which was designed and optimized for a stationary environment, makes mobility difficult. In particular, because a host's IP address includes a network prefix, moving the host to a new network means either:

- The host's address must change.
- Routers must propagate a host-specific route across the entire internet.

Neither alternative works well. On one hand, changing an address is time-consuming, usually requires rebooting the computer, and breaks all existing transport-layer connections. In addition, if the host contacts a server that uses addresses to authenticate, an additional change to DNS may be required. On the other hand, a host-specific routing approach cannot scale because it requires space in routing tables proportional to the number of hosts, and because transmitting routes consumes excessive bandwidth.

19.3 Mobile IP Characteristics

The IETF devised a solution to the mobility problem that overcomes some of the limitations of the original IP addressing scheme. Officially named *IP mobility support*, it is popularly called *mobile IP*. The general characteristics include the following.

Transparency. Mobility is transparent to applications and transport layer protocols as well as to routers not involved in the change. In particular, as long as they remain idle, all open TCP connections survive a change in network and are ready for further use.

Interoperability with IPv4. A host using mobile IP can interoperate with stationary hosts that run conventional IPv4 software as well as with other mobile hosts. Furthermore, no special addressing is required — the addresses assigned to mobile hosts do not differ from addresses assigned to fixed hosts.

Scalability. The solution scales to large internets. In particular, it permits mobility across the global Internet.

Security. Mobile IP provides security facilities that can be used to ensure all messages are authenticated (i.e., to prevent an arbitrary computer from impersonating a mobile host).

Macro mobility. Rather than attempting to handle rapid network transitions such as one encounters in a wireless cellular system, mobile IP focuses on the problem of long-duration moves. For example, mobile IP works well for a user who takes a portable computer on a business trip, and leaves it attached to the new location for a week.

19.4 Overview Of Mobile IP Operation

The biggest challenge for mobility lies in allowing a host to retain its address without requiring routers to learn host-specific routes. Mobile IP solves the problem by allowing a single computer to hold two addresses simultaneously. The first address, which can be thought of as the computer's *primary address*, is permanent and fixed. It is the address applications and transport protocols use. The second address, which can be thought of as a *secondary address*, is temporary — it changes as the computer moves, and is valid only while the computer visits a given location.

A mobile host obtains a primary address on its original, *home* network. After it moves to a *foreign* network and obtains a secondary address, the mobile must send the secondary address to an *agent* (usually a router) at home. The agent agrees to intercept datagrams sent to the mobile's primary address, and uses *IP-in-IP* encapsulation to *tunnel* each datagram to the secondary address†.

---

†Chapter 17 illustrates IP-in-IP encapsulation.

If the mobile moves again, it obtains a new secondary address, and informs the home agent of its new location. When the mobile returns home, it must contact the home agent to *deregister*, meaning that the agent will stop intercepting datagrams. Similarly, a mobile can choose to deregister at any time (e.g., when leaving a remote location).

We said that mobile IP is designed for macroscopic mobility rather than high-speed movement. The reason should be clear: overhead. In particular, after it moves, a mobile must detect that it has moved, communicate across the foreign network to obtain a secondary address, and then communicate across the internet to its agent at home to arrange forwarding. The point is:

> *Because it requires considerable overhead after each move, mobile IP is intended for situations in which a host moves infrequently and remains at a given location for a relatively long period of time.*

19.5 Mobile Addressing Details

A mobile's primary or *home address* is assigned and administered by the network administrator of the mobile's home network; there is no distinction between an address assigned to a stationary computer and a home address assigned to a mobile computer. Applications on a mobile computer always use the home address.

Whenever it connects to a network other than its home, a mobile must obtain a temporary address. Known as a *care of* address, the temporary address is never known or used by applications. Instead, only IP software on the mobile and agents on the home or foreign networks use the temporary address. A care-of address is administered like any other address on the foreign network, and a route to the care-of address is propagated using conventional routing protocols.

In practice, there are two types of care-of addresses; the type used by a mobile visiting a given network is determined by the network's administrator. The two types differ in the method by which the address is obtained and in the entity responsible for forwarding. The first form, which is known as a *co-located care-of address*, requires a mobile computer to handle all forwarding itself. In essence, a mobile that uses a co-located care-of address has software that uses two addresses simultaneously — applications use the home address, while lower layer software uses the care-of address to receive datagrams. The chief advantage of a co-located address lies in its ability to work with existing internet infrastructure. Routers on the foreign network do not know whether a computer is mobile; care-of addresses are allocated to mobile computers by the same mechanisms used to allocate addresses to fixed computers (e.g., the DHCP protocol discussed in Chapter 23). The chief disadvantage of the co-located form arises from the extra software required — the mobile must contain facilities to obtain an address and to communicate with the home agent.

The second form, which is known as a *foreign agent care-of address*, requires an active participant on the remote network. The active entity, also a router, is called a *foreign agent* to distinguish it from the *home agent* on the mobile's home network. When using a foreign agent care-of address, a mobile must first discover the identity of an agent, and then contact the agent to obtain a care-of address. Surprisingly, a foreign agent does not need to assign the mobile a unique address. Instead, we will see that the agent can supply one of its IP addresses, and agree to forward datagrams to the mobile. Although assigning a unique address makes communication slightly easier, using an existing address means that visiting mobiles do not consume IP addresses.

19.6 Foreign Agent Discovery

Known as *agent discovery*, the process of finding a foreign agent uses the ICMP *router discovery* mechanism. Recall from Chapter 9 that router discovery requires each router to periodically send an ICMP *router advertisement* message, and allows a host to send an ICMP *router solicitation* to prompt for an advertisement†. Agent discovery piggybacks additional information on router discovery messages to allow a foreign agent to advertise its presence or a mobile to solicit an advertisement. The additional information appended to each message is known as a *mobility agent extension‡*. Mobility extensions do not use a separate ICMP message type. Instead, a mobile host deduces that the extension is present when the datagram length specified in the IP header is greater than the length of the ICMP router discovery message. Figure 19.1 illustrates the extension format.

0	8	16	24	31
TYPE (16)	**LENGTH**		**SEQUENCE NUM**	
LIFETIME		**CODE**	**RESERVED**	
CARE-OF ADDRESSES				

Figure 19.1 The format of a Mobility Agent Advertisement Extension message. This extension is appended to an ICMP router advertisement.

Each message begins with a 1-octet *TYPE* field followed by a 1-octet *LENGTH* field. The *LENGTH* field specifies the size of the extension message in octets, excluding the *TYPE* and *LENGTH* octets. The *LIFETIME* field specifies the maximum amount of time in seconds that the agent is willing to accept registration requests, with all 1s indicating *infinity*. Field *SEQUENCE NUM* specifies a sequence number for the message to allow a recipient to determine when a message is lost. Each bit in the *CODE* field defines a specific feature of the agent as listed in Figure 19.2.

---

†A mobile that does not know an agent's IP address can multicast to the *all agents group* (*224.0.0.11*).

‡A mobility agent also appends a *prefix extension* to the message that specifies the IP prefix being used on the network; a mobile uses the prefix extension to determine when it has moved to a new network.

Bit	Meaning
0	Registration with an agent is required; co-located care-of addressing is not permitted
1	The agent is busy and is not accepting registrations
2	Agent functions as a home agent
3	Agent functions as a foreign agent
4	Agent uses minimal encapsulation
5	Agent uses GRE-style encapsulation†
6	Agent supports header compression when communicating with mobile
7	Unused (must be zero)

Figure 19.2 Bits of the CODE field of a mobility agent advertisement.

19.7 Agent Registration

Before it can receive datagrams at a foreign location, a mobile host must register. The *registration* procedure allows a host to:

- Register with an agent on the foreign network.

- Register directly with its home agent to request forwarding.

- Renew a registration that is due to expire.

- Deregister after returning home.

If it obtains a co-located care-of address, a mobile performs all necessary registration directly; the mobile can use the address to communicate with its home agent and register. If it obtains a care-of address from a foreign agent, however, a mobile cannot use the address to communicate directly with its home agent. Instead, the mobile must send registration requests to the foreign agent, which then contacts the mobile's home agent on its behalf. Similarly, the foreign agent must forward messages it receives that are destined for the mobile host.

19.8 Registration Message Format

All registration messages are sent via UDP. Agents listen to well-known port 434; requests may be sent from an arbitrary source port to destination port 434. An agent reverses the source and destination points, so a reply is sent from source port 434 to the port the requester used.

A registration message begins with a set of fixed-size fields followed by variable-length *extensions*. Each request is required to contain a *mobile-home authentication extension* that allows the home agent to verify the mobile's identity. Figure 19.3 illustrates the message format.

---

†*GRE*, which stands for *Generic Routing Encapsulation*, refers to a generalized encapsulation scheme that allows an arbitrary protocol to be encapsulated; IP-in-IP is one particular case.

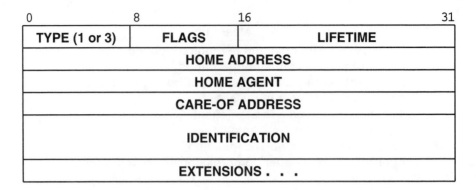

Figure 19.3 The format of a mobile IP registration message.

The *TYPE* field specifies whether the message is a registration request (*1*) or a registration reply (*3*). The *LIFETIME* field specifies the number of seconds the registration is valid (a zero requests immediate deregistration, and all 1s specifies an infinite lifetime). The *HOME ADDRESS*, *HOME AGENT*, and *CARE-OF ADDRESS* fields specify the two IP addresses of the mobile and the address of its home agent, and the *IDENTIFICATION* field contains a 64-bit number generated by the mobile that is used to match requests with incoming replies and to prevent the mobile from accepting old messages. Bits of the *FLAGS* field are used to specify forwarding details as listed in Figure 19.4.

Bit	Meaning
0	This is a simultaneous (additional) address rather than a replacement.
1	Mobile requests home agent to tunnel a copy of each broadcast datagram
2	Mobile is using a co-located care-of address and will decapsulate datagrams itself
3	Mobile requests agent to use minimal encapsulation
4	Mobile requests agent to use GRE encapsulation
5	Mobile requests header compression
6-7	Reserved (must be zero)

Figure 19.4 The meaning of *FLAGS* bits in a mobile registration request.

If it has a co-located care-of address, a mobile can send a registration request directly to its home agent. Otherwise, the mobile sends the request to a foreign agent, which then forwards the request to the home agent. In the latter case, both the foreign and home agents process the request, and both must approve. For example, either the home or foreign agents can limit the registration lifetime.

19.9 Communication With A Foreign Agent

We said that a foreign agent can assign one of its IP addresses for use as a care-of address. Doing so causes a problem because it means a mobile will not have a unique address on the foreign network. The question then becomes: how can a foreign agent and a mobile host communicate over a network if the mobile does not have a valid IP address on the network? Communication requires relaxing the rules for IP addressing and using an alternative scheme for address binding. In particular, when a mobile host sends to a foreign agent, the mobile is allowed to use its home address as an IP source address. Furthermore, when a foreign agent sends a datagram to a mobile, the agent is allowed to use the mobile's home address as an IP destination address.

Although the mobile's home address can be used, an agent is not allowed to ARP for the address (i.e., ARP is still restricted to IP addresses that are valid on the network). To perform address binding without ARP, an agent is required to record all information about a mobile when a registration request arrives and to keep the information during communication. In particular, an agent must record the mobile's hardware address. When it sends a datagram to the mobile, the agent consults its stored information to determine the appropriate hardware address. Thus, although ARP is not used, the agent can send datagrams to a mobile via hardware unicast. We can summarize:

> *If a mobile does not have a unique foreign address, a foreign agent must use the mobile's home address for communication. Instead of relying on ARP for address binding, the agent records the mobile's hardware address when a request arrives and uses the recorded information to supply the necessary binding.*

19.10 Datagram Transmission And Reception

Once it has registered, a mobile host on a foreign network can communicate with an arbitrary computer. To do so, the mobile creates a datagram that has the computer's address in the destination field and the mobile's home address in the source field†. The datagram follows the shortest path from the foreign network to the destination. However, a reply will not follow the shortest path directly to the mobile. Instead, the reply will travel to the mobile's home network. The home agent, which has learned the mobile's location from the registration, intercepts the datagram and uses *IP-in-IP* encapsulation to tunnel the datagram to the care-of address. If a mobile has a co-located care-of address, the encapsulated datagram passes directly to the mobile, which discareds the outer datagram and then processes the inner datagram. If a mobile is using a foreign agent for communication, the care-of address on the outer datagram specifies the foreign agent. When it receives a datagram from a home agent, a foreign agent decapsulates the datagram, consults its table of registered mobiles, and transmits the datagram across the local network to the appropriate mobile. To summarize:

---

†The foreign network and the ISP that connects it to the rest of the internet must agree to transmit datagrams with an arbitrary source address.

Because a mobile uses its home address as a source address when
communicating with an arbitrary destination, each reply is forwarded
to the mobile's home network, where an agent intercepts the da-
tagram, encapsulates it in another datagram, and forwards it either
directly to the mobile or to the foreign agent the mobile is using.

19.11 The Two-Crossing Problem

The description above highlights the major disadvantage of mobile IP: inefficient
routing. Because a mobile uses its home address, a datagram sent to the mobile will be
forwarded to the mobile's home network first and then to the mobile. The problem is
especially severe because computer communication often exhibits *spatial locality of*
reference, which means that a mobile visiting a foreign network will tend to communicate with computers on that network. To understand why mobile IP handles spatial locality poorly, consider Figure 19.5.

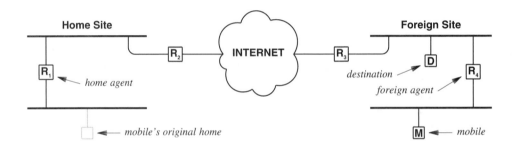

Figure 19.5 A topology in which mobile IP routing is inefficient. When
mobile *M* communicates with local destination *D*, datagrams
from *D* travel across the internet to the mobile's home agent and
then back to the mobile.

In the figure, mobile *M* has moved from it's original home to a foreign network.
We assume the mobile has registered with its home agent, router *R₁*, and the home
agent has agreed to forward datagrams. Now consider communication between the
mobile and destination *D*, which is located at the same site as the mobile. Datagrams
from *M* to *D* travel through router *R₄* and are then delivered to *D*. However, because
datagrams sent from *D* to *M* contain *M's* home address, they follow a path through *R₃*
and across the internet to the mobile's home network. When the datagrams reach *R₁*
(the mobile's home agent), they are tunneled back across the internet to the foreign site
(either directly to *M* or to a foreign agent). Because crossing an internet is much more
expensive than local delivery, the situation described above is known as the *two-*
crossing problem, and is sometimes called the *2X problem†*.

---

†If destination *D* is not close to the mobile, a slightly less severe version of the problem occurs which is
known as *triangle forwarding* or *dog-leg forwarding*.

Mobile IP does not guarantee to solve the 2X problem. However, some route optimization is possible. In particular, if a site expects a visiting mobile to interact heavily with local computers, the site can arrange to propagate a host-specific route for the mobile. To ensure correct routing, the host-specific route must be deleted when the mobile leaves. Of course, the problem remains whenever a mobile communicates with a destination outside the region where the host-specific route has been propagated. For example, suppose mobiles move frequently between two corporations in cities *A* and *B*. The network managers at the two sites can agree to propagate host-specific routes for all visiting mobiles, meaning that when a mobile communicates with other computers at the foreign site, traffic stays local to the site. However, because host-specific routes are limited to the two corporate sites, communication between the mobile and any other destination in the foreign city will result in replies being forwarded through the mobile's home agent. Thus, the 2X problem remains for any destination outside the corporation.

We can summarize:

> *Mobile IP introduces a routing inefficiency known as the 2X problem that occurs when a mobile visits a foreign network far from its home and then communicates with a computer near the foreign site. Each datagram sent to the mobile travels across the internet to the mobile's home agent which then forwards the datagram back to the foreign site. Eliminating the problem requires propagating host-specific routes; the problem remains for any destination that does not receive the host-specific route.*

19.12 Communication With Computers On the Home Network

We said that when a mobile is visiting a foreign network, the mobile's home agent must intercept all datagrams sent to the mobile. Normally, the home agent is the router that connects the mobile's home network to the rest of the internet. Thus, all datagrams that arrive for the host pass through the home agent. Before forwarding a datagram, the home agent examines its table of mobile hosts to determine whether the destination host is currently at home or visiting a foreign network.

Although a home agent can easily intercept all datagrams that arrive for a mobile host from outside, there is one additional case that the agent must handle: datagrams that originate locally. In particular, consider what happens when a host on the mobile's home network sends a datagram to a mobile. Because IP specifies direct delivery over the local network, the sender will not forward the datagram to a router. Instead, the sender will ARP for the mobile's hardware address, encapsulate the datagram, and transmit it.

If a mobile has moved to a foreign network, the home agent must intercept all datagrams, including those sent by local hosts. To guarantee that it can intercept datagrams from local hosts, the home agent uses *proxy ARP*. That is, a home agent must listen for ARP requests that specify the mobile as a target, and must answer the requests by supplying its own hardware address. Proxy ARP is completely transparent to local computers — any local system that ARPs for a mobile's address will receive a reply, and will forward the datagram as usual.

The use of proxy ARP also solves the problem of multiple connections. If a mobile's home network has multiple routers that connect to various parts of the internet, only one needs to function as a home agent for the mobile. The other routers remain unaware of mobility; they use ARP to resolve addresses as usual. Thus, because the home agent answers the ARP requests, other routers forward datagrams without distinguishing between mobile and nonmobile hosts.

19.13 Summary

Mobile IP allows a computer to move from one network to another without changing its IP address and without requiring all routers to propagate a host-specific route. When it moves from its original home network to a foreign network, a mobile computer must obtain an additional, temporary address known as a care-of address. Applications use the mobile's original, home address; the care-of address is only used by underlying network software to enable forwarding and delivery across the foreign network.

Once it detects that it has moved, a mobile either obtains a co-located care-of address or discovers a foreign mobility agent and requests the agent to assign a care-of address. After obtaining a care-of address, the mobile registers with its home agent (either directly or indirectly through the foreign agent), and requests the agent to forward datagrams.

Once registration is complete, a mobile can communicate with an arbitrary computer on the internet. Datagrams sent by the mobile are forwarded directly to the specified destination. However, each datagram sent back to the mobile follows a route to the mobile's home network where it is intercepted by the home agent, encapsulated in IP, and then tunneled to the mobile.

FOR FURTHER STUDY

Perkins [RFC 2002] describes IP Mobility Support and defines the details of messages; an Internet draft describes version 2 [draft-ietf-mobileip-v2-00.txt]. Perkins [RFC 2003], Perkins [RFC 2004], and Hanks et. al. {RFC 1701] describe the details of three IP-in-IP encapsulation schemes. Montenegro [RFC 2344] describes a reverse tunneling scheme for mobile IP. Finally, Perkins and Johnson [draft-ietf-mobileip-optim-07.txt] considers route optimization for mobile IP.

EXERCISES

19.1   Compare the encapsulation schemes in RFCs 2003 and 2004. What are the advantages and disadvantages of each?

19.2   Read the mobile IP specification carefully. How frequently must a router send a mobility agent advertisement? Why?

19.3   Consult the mobile IP specification. When a foreign agent forwards a registration request to a mobile's home agent, which protocol ports are used? Why?

19.4   The specification for mobile IP allows a single router to function as both a home agent for a network and a foreign agent that supports visitors on the network. What are the advantages and disadvantages of using a single router for both functions?

19.5   The mobile IP specification defines three conceptually separate forms of authentication: mobile to home agent, mobile to foreign agent, and foreign agent to home agent. What are the advantages of separating them? The disadvantages?

19.6   Read the mobile IP specification to determine how a mobile host joins a multicast group. How are multicast datagrams routed to the mobile? What is the optimal scheme?

20

Private Network
Interconnection (NAT, VPN)

20.1 Introduction

Previous chapters describe an internet as a single-level abstraction that consists of networks interconnected by routers. This chapter considers an alternative — a two-level internet architecture in which each organization has a private internet and a central internet interconnects them.

The chapter examines technologies used with a two-level architecture. One solves the pragmatic problem of limited address space, and the other offers increased functionality in the form of *privacy* that prevents outsiders from viewing the data.

20.2 Private And Hybrid Networks

One of the major drawbacks of a single-level internet architecture is the lack of privacy. If an organization comprises multiple sites, the contents of datagrams that travel across the Internet between the sites can be viewed by outsiders because they pass across networks owned by other organizations. A two-level architecture distinguishes between *internal* and *external* datagrams (i.e., datagrams sent between two computers within an organization and datagrams sent between a computer in the organization and a computer in another organization). The goal is to keep internal datagrams *private*, while still allowing external communication.

The easiest way to guarantee privacy among an organization's computers consists of building a completely isolated *private internet*, which is usually referred to as a *private network.* That is, an organization builds its own TCP/IP internet separate from the global Internet. A private network uses routers to interconnect networks at each site, and leased digital circuits to interconnect the sites. All data remains private because no outsiders have access to any part of a private network. Furthermore, because the private network is isolated from the global Internet, it can use arbitrary IP addresses.

Of course, complete isolation is not always desirable. Thus, many organizations choose a *hybrid network* architecture that combines the advantages of private networking with the advantages of global Internet connectivity. That is, the organization uses globally valid IP addresses and connects each site to the Internet. The advantage is that hosts in the organization can access the global Internet when needed, but can be assured of privacy when communicating internally. For example, consider the hybrid architecture illustrated by Figure 20.1 in which an organization has a private network that interconnects two sites and each site has a connection to the Internet.

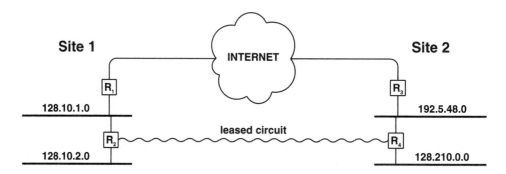

Figure 20.1 An example of a hybrid network. In addition to a leased circuit
that interconnects the two sites, each has a connection to the global Internet.

In the figure, a leased circuit between routers R_2 and R_4 provides privacy for intersite traffic. Thus, routing at each site is arranged to send traffic across the leased circuit rather than across the global Internet.

20.3 A Virtual Private Network (VPN)

The chief disadvantage of either a completely private network or a hybrid scheme arises from the high cost: each leased circuit (e.g., a T1 line) is expensive. Consequently, many organizations seek lower-cost alternatives. One way to reduce costs arises from the use of alternative circuit technologies. For example, a common carrier may change less for a Frame Relay or ATM PVC than for a T-series circuit that has equivalent capacity. Another way to lower costs involves using fewer circuits. Minimum circuit cost is achieved by eliminating all circuits and passing data across the global Internet.

Using the global Internet as an interconnection among sites appears to eliminate the privacy offered by a completely private network. The question becomes:

> *How can an organization that uses the global Internet to connect its sites keep its data private?*

The answer lies in a technology that allows an organization to configure a *Virtual Private Network (VPN)*†. A VPN is *private* in the same way as a private network — the technology guarantees that communication between any pair of computers in the VPN remains concealed from outsiders. A VPN is *virtual* because it does not use leased circuits to interconnect sites. Instead, a VPN uses the global Internet to pass traffic from one site to another.

Two basic techniques make a VPN possible: *tunneling* and *encryption*. We have already encountered tunneling in Chapters 17 and 19. VPNs use the same basic idea — they define a tunnel across the global Internet between a router at one site and a router at another, and use *IP-in-IP* encapsulation to forward datagrams across the tunnel.

Despite using the same basic concept, a VPN tunnel differs dramatically from the tunnels described previously. In particular, to guarantee privacy, a VPN encrypts each outgoing datagram before encapsulating it in another datagram for transmission‡. Figure 20.2 illustrates the concept.

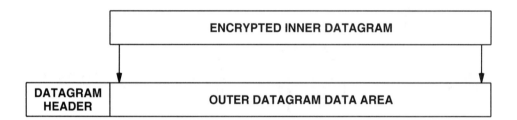

Figure 20.2 Illustration of IP-in-IP encapsulation used with a VPN. To ensure privacy, the inner datagram is encrypted before being sent.

As the figure shows, the entire inner datagram, including the header, is encrypted before being encapsulated. When a datagram arrives over a tunnel, the receiving router decrypts the data area to reproduce the inner datagram, which it then forwards. Although the outer datagram traverses arbitrary networks as it passes across the tunnel, outsiders cannot decode the contents because they do not have the encryption key. Furthermore, even the identity of the original source and destination are hidden because the header of the inner datagram is encrypted as well. Thus, only addresses in the outer datagram header are visible: the source address is the IP address of the router at one end of a tunnel, and the destination address is the IP address of the router at the other end of the tunnel.

---

†The name is a slight misnomer because the technology actually provides a virtual private internet.
‡Chapter 32 considers IP security, and discusses the encapsulation used with IPsec.

To summarize:

> *A Virtual Private Network sends data across the Internet, but encrypts intersite transmissions to guarantee privacy.*

20.4 VPN Addressing And Routing

The easiest way to understand VPN addressing and routing is to think of each VPN tunnel as a replacement for a leased circuit in a private network. As in the private network case, a router contains explicit routes for destinations within the organization. However, instead of routing data across a leased lined, a VPN routes the data through a tunnel. For example Figure 20.3 shows the VPN equivalent of the private network architecture from Figure 20.1 along with a routing table for a router that handles tunneling.

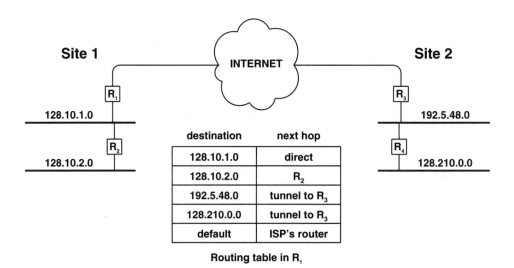

Figure 20.3 A VPN that spans two sites and R_1's routing table. The tunnel from R_1 to R_3 is configured like a point-to-point leased circuit.

As an example of forwarding in a VPN, consider a datagram sent from a computer on network *128.10.2.0* to a computer on network *128.210.0.0*. The sending host forwards the datagram to R_2, which forwards it to R_1. According to the routing table in R_1, the datagram must be sent across the tunnel to R_3. Therefore, R_1 encrypts the datagram, encapsulates it in the data area of an outer datagram with destination R_3. R_1 then forward the outer datagram through the local ISP and across the Internet. The datagram arrives at R_3, which recognizes it as tunneled from R_1. R_3 decrypts the data area to produce the original datagram, looks up the destination in its routing table, and forwards the datagram to R_4 for delivery.

20.5 A VPN With Private Addresses

A VPN offers an organization the same addressing options as a private network. If hosts in the VPN do not need general Internet connectivity, the VPN can be configured to use arbitrary IP addresses; if hosts need Internet access, a hybrid addressing scheme can be used. A minor difference is that when private addressing is used, one globally valid IP address is needed at each site for tunneling. Figure 20.4 illustrates the concept.

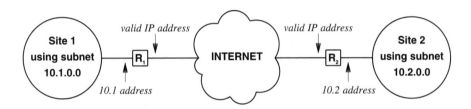

Figure 20.4 Illustration of addressing for a VPN that interconnects two completely private sites over the global Internet. Computers at each site use private addresses.

As the figure shows, site 1 uses subnet 10.1.0.0/16, while site 2 uses subnet 10.2.0.0/16. Only two globally valid addresses are needed. One is assigned to the connection from router R_1 to the Internet, and the other is assigned to the connection from R_2 to the Internet. Routing tables at the sites specify routes for private addresses; only the VPN tunneling software needs to know about or use the globally valid IP addresses.

VPNs use the same addressing structure as a private network. Hosts in a completely isolated VPN can use arbitrary addresses, but a hybrid architecture with valid IP addresses must be employed to provide hosts with access to the global Internet. The question remains: "How can a site provide access to the global Internet without assigning each host a valid IP address?" There are two general solutions.

Known as an *application gateway* approach, the first solution offers hosts access to Internet services without offering IP-level access. Each site has a multi-homed host connected to both the global Internet (with a globally valid IP address) and the internal network (using a private IP address). The multi-homed host runs a set of application programs, known as *application gateways*, that each handle one service. Hosts at the site do not send datagrams to the global Internet. Instead, they send each request to the appropriate application gateway on the multihomed host, which accesses the service on the Internet and then relays the information back across the internal network. For example, Chapter 27 describes an e-mail gateway that can relay e-mail messages between external hosts and internal hosts.

The chief advantage of the application gateway approach lies in its ability to work without changes to the underlying infrastructure or addressing. The chief disadvantage arises from the lack of generality, which can be summarized:

> *Each application gateway handles only one specific service; multiple gateways are required for multiple services.*

Consequently, although they are useful in special circumstances, application gateways do not solve the problem in a general way. Thus, a second solution was invented.

20.6 Network Address Translation (NAT)

A technology has been created that solves the general problem of providing IP-level access between hosts at a site and the rest of the Internet, without requiring each host at the site to have a globally valid IP address. Known as *Network Address Translation (NAT)*, the technology requires a site to have a single connection to the global Internet and at least one globally valid IP address, G. Address G is assigned to a computer (a multi-homed host or a router) that connects the site to the Internet and runs NAT software. Informally, we refer to a computer that runs NAT software as a *NAT box*; all datagrams pass through the NAT box as they travel from the site out to the Internet or from the Internet into the site.

NAT translates the addresses in both outgoing and incoming datagrams by replacing the source address in each outgoing datagram with G and replacing the destination address in each incoming datagram with the private address of the correct host. Thus, from the view of an external host, all datagrams come from the NAT box and all responses return to the NAT box. From the view of internal hosts, the NAT box appears to be a router that can reach the global Internet.

The chief advantage of NAT arises from its combination of generality and transparency. NAT is more general than application gateways because it allows an arbitrary internal host to access an arbitrary service on a computer in the global Internet. NAT is transparent because it allows an internal host to send and receive datagrams using a private (i.e., nonroutable) address.

To summarize:

> *Network Address Translation technology provides transparent IP-level access to the Internet from a host with a private address.*

20.7 NAT Translation Table Creation

Our overview of NAT omits an important detail because it does not specify how NAT knows which internal host should receive a datagram that arrives from the Internet. In fact, NAT maintains a translation table that it uses to perform the mapping. Each entry in the table specifies two items: the IP address of a host on the Internet and the internal IP address of a host at the site. When an incoming datagram arrives from the Internet, NAT looks up the datagram's destination address in the translation table, extracts the corresponding address of an internal host, replaces the datagram's destination address with the host's address, and forwards the datagram across the local network to the host†.

The NAT translation table must be in place before a datagram arrives from the Internet. Otherwise, NAT has no way to identify the correct internal host to which the datagram should be forwarded. How and when is the table initialized? There are several possibilities:

- *Manual initialization.* A manager configures the translation table manually before any communication occurs.

- *Outgoing datagrams.* The table is built as a side-effect of sending datagrams. When it receives a datagram from an internal host, NAT creates an entry in the translation table to record the address of the host and the address of the destination.

- *Incoming name lookups.* The table is built as a side-effect of handing domain name lookups. When a host on the Internet looks up the domain name of an internal host to find its IP address‡, the domain name software creates an entry in the NAT translation table, and then answers the request by sending address *G*. Thus, from outside the site, it appears that all host names at the site map to address *G*.

Each initialization technique has advantages and disadvantages. Manual initialization provides permanent mappings and allows IP datagrams to be sent in either direction at any time. Using an outgoing datagram to initialize the table has the advantage of being automatic, but does not allow communication to be initiated from the outside. Using incoming domain name lookups requires modifying domain name software. It accommodates communication initiated from outside the site, but only works if the sender performs a domain name lookup before sending datagrams.

Most implementations of NAT use outgoing datagrams to initialize the table; the strategy is especially popular among ISPs. To understand why, consider a small ISP that serves dialup customers. Figure 20.5 illustrates the architecture.

---

†Of course, whenever it replaces an address in a datagram header, NAT must recompute the header checksum.

‡Chapter 24 describes how the *Domain Name System (DNS)* operates.

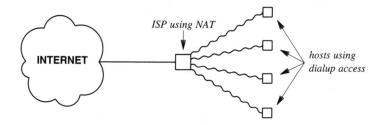

Figure 20.5 The use of NAT by a small ISP that serves dialup customers. NAT translation allows the ISP to assign a private address to each dialup customer.

The ISP must assign an IP address to a customer whenever the customer dials in. NAT permits the ISP to assign private addresses (e.g., the first customer is assigned *10.0.0.1*, the second *10.0.0.2*, and so on). When a customer sends a datagram to a destination on the Internet, NAT uses the outgoing datagram to initialize its translation table.

20.8 Multi-Address NAT

So far, we have described a simplistic implementation of NAT that performs a 1-to-1 address mapping between an external address and an internal address. That is, a 1-to-1 mapping permits at most one computer at the site to access a given machine on the global Internet at any time. In practice, more complex forms of NAT are used that allow multiple hosts at a site to access a given external address concurrently.

One variation of NAT permits concurrency by retaining the 1-to-1 mapping, but allowing the NAT box to hold multiple Internet addresses. Known as *multi-address NAT*, the scheme assigns the NAT box a set of K globally valid addresses, G_1, G_2,... G_k. When the first internal host accesses a given destination, the NAT box chooses address G_1, adds an entry to the translation table, and sends the datagram. If another host initiates contact with the same destination, the NAT box chooses address G_2, and so on. Thus, multi-address NAT allows up to K internal hosts to access a given destination concurrently.

20.9 Port-Mapped NAT

Another popular variant of NAT provides concurrency by translating TCP or UDP protocol port numbers as well as addresses. Sometimes called *Network Address Port Translation (NAPT)*, the scheme expands the NAT translation table to include additional fields. Besides a pair of source and destination IP addresses, the table contains a pair of source and destination protocol port numbers and a protocol port number used by the NAT box. Figure 20.6 illustrates the contents of the table.

Private Address	Private Port	External Address	External Port	NAT Port	Protocol Used
10.0.0.5	21023	128.10.19.20	80	14003	tcp
10.0.0.1	386	128.10.19.20	80	14010	tcp
10.0.2.6	26600	207.200.75.200	21	14012	tcp
10.0.0.3	1274	128.210.1.5	80	14007	tcp

Figure 20.6 An example of a translation table used by NAPT. The table includes port numbers as well as IP addresses.

The table in the figure has entries for four internal computers that are currently accessing destinations on the global Internet. All communication is using TCP. Interestingly, the table shows two internal hosts, *10.0.0.5* and *10.0.0.1*, both accessing protocol port *80* (a Web server) on computer *128.10.19.20*. In this case, it happens that the two source ports being used for the two connections differ. However, source port uniqueness cannot be guaranteed — it could turn out that two internal hosts happen to choose the same source port number. Thus, to avoid potential conflicts, NAT assigns a unique port number to each communication that is used on the Internet. Recall that TCP identifies each connection with a 4-tuple that represents the IP address and protocol port number of each endpoint. The first two items in the table correspond to TCP connections that the two internal hosts identify with the 4-tuples:

$$(\textit{10.0.0.5, 23023, 128.10.19.20, 80})$$
$$(\textit{10.0.0.1, 386, 128.10.19.20, 80})$$

However, the computer in the Internet that receives datagrams after NAPT performs the translation identifies the same two connections with the 4-tuples:

$$(\textit{G, 14003, 128.10.19.20, 80})$$
$$(\textit{G, 14010, 128.10.19.20, 80})$$

where *G* is the globally valid address of the NAT box.

The primary advantage of NAPT lies in the generality it achieves with a single globally valid IP address; the primary disadvantage arises because it restricts communication to TCP or UDP. As long as all communication uses TCP or UDP, NAPT allows an internal computer to access multiple external computers, and multiple internal computers to access the same external computer without interference. A port space of 16 bits allows up to 2^{16} pairs of applications to communicate at the same time. To summarize:

Several variants of NAT exist, including the popular NAPT form that translates protocol port numbers as well as IP addresses.

20.10 Interaction Between NAT And ICMP

Even straightforward changes to an IP address can cause unexpected side-effects in higher layer protocols. In particular, to maintain the illusion of transparency, NAT must handle ICMP. For example, suppose an internal host uses *ping* to test reachability of a destination on the Internet. The host expects to receive an ICMP *echo reply* for each ICMP *echo request* message it sends. Thus, NAT must forward incoming echo replies to the correct host. However, NAT does not forward all ICMP messages that arrive from the Internet. If routes in the NAT box are incorrect, for example, an ICMP *redirect* message must be processed locally. Thus, when an ICMP message arrives from the Internet, NAT must first determine whether the message should be handled locally or sent to an internal host. Before forwarding to an internal host, NAT translates the ICMP message.

To understand the need for ICMP translation, consider an ICMP *destination unreachable* message. The message contains the header from a datagram, *D*, that caused the error. Unfortunately, NAT translated addresses before sending *D*, so the source address is not the address the internal host used. Thus, before forwarding the message, NAT must open the ICMP message and translate the addresses in *D* so they appear in exactly the form that the internal host used. After making the change, NAT must recompute the checksum in *D*, the checksum in the ICMP header, and the checksum in the outer datagram header.

20.11 Interaction Between NAT And Applications

Although ICMP makes NAT complex, application protocols have a more serious effect. In general, NAT will not work with any application that sends IP addresses or protocol ports as data. For example, when two programs use the *File Transfer Protocol* (*FTP*) described in Chapter 26, they have a TCP connection between them. As part of the protocol, one program obtains a protocol port on the local machine, converts the number to ASCII, and sends the result across a TCP connection to another program. If the connection between the programs passes through NAPT from an internal host to a host on the Internet, the port number in the data stream must be changed to agree with the port number NAPT has selected instead of the port the internal host is using. In fact, if NAT fails to open the data stream and change the number, the protocol will fail. Implementations of NAT have been created that recognize popular protocols such as FTP and make the necessary change in the data stream. However, there exist applications that cannot use NAT. To summarize:

> *NAT affects ICMP and higher layer protocols; except for a few standard applications like FTP, an application protocol that passes IP addresses or protocol port numbers as data will not operate correctly across NAT.*

Changing items in a data stream increases the complexity of NAPT in two ways. First, it means that NAPT must have detailed knowledge of each application that transfers such information. Second, if the port numbers are represented in ASCII, as is the case with FTP, changing the value can change the number of octets transferred. Inserting even one additional octet into a TCP connection is difficult because each octet in the stream has a sequence number. Because a sender does not know that additional data has been inserted, it continues to assign sequence numbers without the additional data. When it receives additional data, the receiver will generate acknowledgements that account for the data. Thus, after it inserts additional data, NAT must translate the sequence numbers in each outgoing segment and each incoming acknowledgement.

20.12 Conceptual Address Domains

We have described NAT as a technology that can be used to connect a private network to the global Internet. In fact, NAT can be used to interconnect any two *address domains*. Thus, NAT can be used between two corporations that each have a private network using address 10.0.0.0. More important, NAT can be used at two levels: between a customer's private and an ISP's private address domains as well as between the ISP's address domain and the global Internet. Finally, NAT can be combined with VPN technology to form a hybrid architecture in which private addresses are used within the organization, and NAT is used to provide connectivity between each site and the global Internet.

As an example of multiple levels of NAT, consider an individual who works at home from several computers which are connected to a LAN. The individual can assign private addresses to the computers at home, and use NAT between the home network and the corporate intranet. The corporation can also assign private addresses and use NAT between its intranet and the global Internet.

20.13 Slirp And Masquerade

Two implementations of Network Address Translation have become especially popular; both were designed for the Unix operating system. The *slirp* program, derived from 4.4 BSD, comes with program source code. It was designed for use in a dialup architecture like the one shown in Figure 20.5. Slirp combines PPP and NAT into a single program. It runs on a computer that has: a valid IP address, a permanent Internet connection, and one or more dialup modems. The chief advantage of slirp is that it can use an ordinary user account on a Unix system for general-purpose Internet access. A computer that has a private address dials in and runs slirp. Once slirp begins, the dialup line switches from ASCII commands to PPP. The dialup computer starts PPP and obtains access to the Internet (e.g., to access a Web site).

Slirp implements NAPT — it uses protocol port numbers to demultiplex connections, and can rewrite protocol port numbers as well as IP addresses. It is possible to have multiple computers (e.g., computers on a LAN) accessing the Internet at the same time through a single occurrence of slirp running on a UNIX system.

Another popular implementation of NAT has been designed for the Linux operating system. Known as *masquerade*, the program implements NAPT. Unlike slirp, masquerade does not require computers to access it via dialup, nor does masquerade need a user to login to the UNIX system before starting it. Instead, masquerade offers many options; it can be configured to operate like a router between two networks, and it handles most of the NAT variations discussed in this chapter, including the use of multiple IP addresses.

20.14 Summary

Although a private network guarantees privacy, the cost can be high. Virtual Private Network (VPN) technology offers a lower cost alternative that allows an organization to use the global Internet to interconnect multiple sites and use encryption to guarantee that intersite traffic remains private. Like a traditional private network, a VPN can either be completely isolated (in which case hosts are assigned private addresses) or a hybrid architecture that allows hosts to communicate with destinations on the global Internet.

Two technologies exist that provide communication between hosts in different address domains: application gateways and Network Address Translation (NAT). An application gateway acts like a proxy by receiving a request from a host in one domain, sending the request to a destination in another, and then returning the result to the original host. A separate application gateway must be installed for each service.

Network Address Translation provides transparent IP-level access to the global Internet from a host that has a private address. NAT is especially popular among ISPs because it allows customers to access arbitrary Internet services while using a private IP address. Applications that pass address or port information in the data stream will not work with NAT until NAT has been programmed to recognize the application and make the necessary changes in the data; most implementations of NAT only recognize a few (standard) services.

FOR FURTHER STUDY

Many router and software vendors sell Virtual Private Network technologies, usually with a choice of encryption schemes and addressing architecture. Consult the vendors' literature for more information.

Several versions of NAT are also available commercially. The charter of the IETF working group on NAT can be found at:

http://www.ietf.org/html.charters/nat-charter.html

In addition, Srisuresh and Holdrege [RFC 2663] defines NAT terminology, and the Internet Draft repository at

http://www.ietf.org/ID.html

contains several Internet Drafts on NAT.

More details about the masquerade program can be found in the Linux documentation. A resource page can be found at URL:

http://ipmasq.cjb.net

More information on slirp can be found in the program documentation; a resource page for slirp can be found at:

http://blitzen.canberra.edu.au/slirp

EXERCISES

20.1   Under what circumstances will a VPN transfer substantially more packets than conventional IP when sending the same data across the Internet? Hint: think about encapsulation.

20.2   Read the slirp document to find out about *port redirection*. Why is it needed?

20.3   What are the potential problems when three address domains are connected by two NAT boxes?

20.4   In the previous question, how many times will a destination address be translated? A source address?

20.5   Consider an ICMP host unreachable message sent through two NAT boxes that interconnect three address domains. How many address translations will occur? How many translations of protocol port numbers will occur?

20.6   Imagine that we decide to create a new Internet parallel to the existing Internet that allocates addresses from the same address space. Can NAT technology be used to connect the two arbitrarily large Internets that use the same address space? If so, explain how. If not, explain why not.

20.7   Is NAT completely transparent to a host? To answer the question, try to find a sequence of packets that a host can transmit to determine whether it is located behind a NAT box.

20.8   What are the advantages of combining NAT technology with VPN technology? The disadvantages?

20.9   Obtain a copy of slirp and instrument it to measure performance. Does slirp processing overhead ever delay datagrams? Why or why not?

20.10 Obtain NAT and configure it on a Linux system between a private address domain and the Internet. Which well-known services work correctly and which do not?

20.11 Read about a variant of NAT called *twice NAT* that allows communication to be initiated from either side of the NAT box at any time. How does twice NAT ensure that translations are consistent? If two instances of twice NAT are used to interconnect three address domains, is the result completely transparent to all hosts?

21

Client-Server Model Of Interaction

21.1 Introduction

Early chapters present the details of TCP/IP technology, including the protocols that provide basic services and the router architecture that provides needed routing information. Now that we understand the basic technology, we can examine application programs that profit from the cooperative use of a TCP/IP internet. While the example applications are both practical and interesting, they do not comprise the main emphasis. Instead, focus rests on the patterns of interaction among the communicating application programs. The primary pattern of interaction among cooperating applications is known as the *client-server* paradigm†. Client-server interaction forms the basis of most network communication, and is fundamental because it helps us understand the foundation on which distributed algorithms are built. This chapter considers the relationship between client and server; later chapters illustrate the client-server pattern with further examples.

21.2 The Client-Server Model

The term *server* applies to any program that offers a service that can be reached over a network. A server accepts a request over the network, performs its service, and returns the result to the requester. For the simplest services, each request arrives in a single IP datagram and the server returns a response in another datagram.

---

†Marketing literature sometimes substitutes the term *application-server* for client-server; the underlying scientific principle is unchanged.

An executing program becomes a *client* when it sends a request to a server and waits for a response. Because the client-server model is a convenient and natural extension of interprocess communication on a single machine, it is easy to build programs that use the model to interact.

Servers can perform simple or complex tasks. For example, a *time-of-day server* merely returns the current time whenever a client sends the server a packet. A *web server* receives requests from a browser to fetch a copy of a Web page; the server obtains a copy of the file for the page and returns it to the browser.

Usually, servers are implemented as application programs†. The advantage of implementing servers as application programs is that they can execute on any computing system that supports TCP/IP communication. Thus, the server for a particular service can execute on a timesharing system along with other programs, or it can execute on a personal computer. Multiple servers can offer the same service, and can execute on the same machine or on multiple machines. In fact, managers commonly replicate copies of a given server onto physically independent machines to increase reliability or improve performance. If a computer's primary purpose is support of a particular server program, the term ''server'' may be applied to the computer as well as to the server program. Thus, one hears statements such as ''machine *A* is our file server.''

21.3 A Simple Example: UDP Echo Server

The simplest form of client-server interaction uses unreliable datagram delivery to convey messages from a client to a server and back. Consider, for example, a *UDP echo server*. The mechanics are straightforward as Figure 21.1 shows. At the server site, a UDP *echo server process* begins by negotiating with its operating system for permission to use the UDP port ID reserved for the *echo* service, the UDP *echo port*. Once it has obtained permission, the echo server process enters an infinite loop that has three steps: (1) wait for a datagram to arrive at the echo port, (2) reverse the source and destination addresses‡ (including source and destination IP addresses as well as UDP port ids), and (3) return the datagram to its original sender. At some other site, a program becomes a UDP *echo client* when it allocates an unused UDP protocol port, sends a UDP message to the UDP echo server, and awaits the reply. The client expects to receive back exactly the same data as it sent.

The UDP echo service illustrates two important points that are generally true about client-server interaction. The first concerns the difference between the lifetime of servers and clients:

> *A server starts execution before interaction begins and (usually) continues to accept requests and send responses without ever terminating. A client is any program that makes a request and awaits a response; it (usually) terminates after using a server a finite number of times.*

---

†Many operating systems refer to a running application program as a *process*, a *user process*, or a *task*.
‡One of the exercises suggests considering this step in more detail.

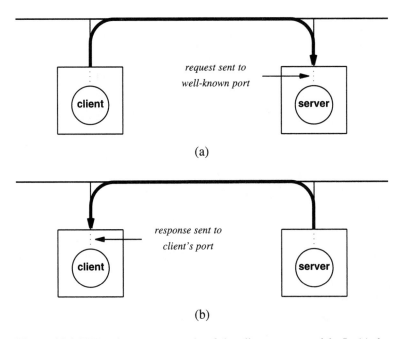

Figure 21.1 UDP echo as an example of the client-server model. In (a) the
client sends a request to the server at a known IP address and at
a well-known UDP port, and in (b) the server returns a response.
Clients use any UDP port that is available.

The second point, which is more technical, concerns the use of reserved and non-
reserved port identifiers:

> *A server waits for requests at a well-known port that has been
> reserved for the service it offers. A client allocates an arbitrary,
> unused, nonreserved port for its communication.*

In a client-server interaction, only one of the two ports needs to be reserved. Assigning
a unique port identifier to each service makes it easy to build both clients and servers.

Who would use an echo service? It is not a service that the average user finds interesting. However, programmers who design, implement, measure, or modify network
protocol software, or network managers who test routes and debug communication
problems, often use echo servers in testing. For example, an echo service can be used
to determine if it is possible to reach a remote machine.

21.4 Time And Date Service

The echo server is extremely simple, and little code is required to implement either the server or client side (provided that the operating system offers a reasonable way to access the underlying UDP/IP protocols). Our second example, a time server, shows that even simple client-server interaction can provide useful services. The problem a time server solves is that of setting a computer's time-of-day clock. The time of day clock is a hardware device that maintains the current date and time, making it available to programs. Once set, the time of day clock keeps time as accurately as a wristwatch.

Some systems solve the problem by asking a programmer to type in the time and date when the system boots. The system increments the clock periodically (e.g., every second). When an application program asks for the date or time, the system consults the internal clock and formats the time of day in human readable form. Client-server interaction can be used to set the system clock automatically when a machine boots. To do so, a manager configures one machine, typically the machine with the most accurate clock, to run a time-of-day server. When other machines boot, they contact the server to obtain the current time.

21.4.1 Representation for the Date and Time

How should an operating system maintain the date and time-of-day? One useful representation stores the time and date as the count of seconds since an epoch date. For example, the UNIX operating system uses the zeroth second of January 1, 1970 as its epoch date. The TCP/IP protocols also define an epoch date and report times as seconds past the epoch. For TCP/IP, the epoch is defined to be the zeroth second of January 1, 1900 and the time is kept in a 32-bit integer, a representation that accommodates all dates in the near future.

Keeping the date as the time in seconds since an epoch makes the representation compact and allows easy comparison. It ties together the date and time of day and makes it possible to measure time by incrementing a single binary integer.

21.4.2 Local and Universal Time

Given an epoch date and representation for the time, to what time zone does the count refer? When two systems communicate across large geographic distances, using the local time zone from one or the other becomes difficult; they must agree on a standard time zone to keep values for date and time comparable. Thus, in addition to defining a representation for the date and choosing an epoch, the TCP/IP time server standard specifies that all values are given with respect to a single time zone. Originally called Greenwich Mean Time, the time zone is now known as *universal coordinated time* or *universal time*.

The interaction between a client and a server that offers time service works much like an echo server. At the server side, the server application obtains permission to use the reserved port assigned to time servers, waits for a UDP message directed to that port, and responds by sending a UDP message that contains the current time in a 32-bit integer. We can summarize:

*Sending a datagram to a time server is equivalent to making a request
for the current time; the server responds by returning a UDP message
that contains the current time.*

21.5 The Complexity of Servers

In our examples so far, servers are fairly simple because they are sequential. That
is, the server processes one request at a time. After accepting a request, the server
forms a reply and sends it before going back to see if another request has arrived. We
implicitly assume that the operating system will queue requests that arrive for a server
while it is busy, and that the queue will not become too long because the server has
only a trivial amount of work to do.

In practice, servers are usually much more difficult to build than clients because
they need to accommodate multiple concurrent requests, even if a single request takes
considerable time to process. For example, consider a file transfer server responsible
for copying a file to another machine on request. Typically, servers have two parts: a
single master program that is responsible for accepting new requests, and a set of slaves
that are responsible for handling individual requests. The master server performs the
following five steps:

Open port
> The master opens the well-known port at which it can be
> reached.

Wait for client
> The master waits for a new client to send a request.

Choose port
> If necessary, the master allocates a new local protocol port for
> this request and informs the client (we will see that this step is
> unnecessary with TCP and most uses of UDP).

Start Slave
> The master starts an independent, concurrent slave to handle this
> request (e.g., in UNIX, it forks a copy of the server process).
> Note that the slave handles one request and then terminates —
> the slave does not wait for requests from other clients.

Continue
> The master returns to the *wait* step and continues accepting new
> requests while the newly created slave handles the previous re-
> quest concurrently.

Because the master starts a slave for each new request, processing proceeds concurrently. Thus, requests that require little time to complete can finish earlier than requests that take longer, independent of the order in which they are started. For example, suppose the first client that contacts a file server requests a large file transfer that

takes many minutes. If a second client contacts the server to request a transfer that takes only a few seconds, the second transfer can start and complete while the first transfer proceeds.

In addition to the complexity that results because servers handle concurrent requests, complexity also arises because servers must enforce authorization and protection rules. Server programs usually need to execute with highest privilege because they must read system files, keep logs, and access protected data. The operating system will not restrict a server program if it attempts to access users' files. Thus, servers cannot blindly honor requests from other sites. Instead, each server takes responsibility for enforcing the system access and protection policies.

Finally, servers must protect themselves against malformed requests or against requests that will cause the server program itself to abort. Often, it is difficult to foresee potential problems. For example, one project at Purdue University designed a file server that allowed student operating systems to access files on a UNIX timesharing system. Students discovered that requesting the server to open a file named */dev/tty* caused the server to abort because UNIX associates that name with the control terminal to which a program is attached. The server, created at system startup, had no such terminal. Once an abort occurred, no client could access files until a systems programmer restarted the server.

A more serious example of server vulnerability became known in the fall of 1988 when a student at Cornell University built a *worm* program that attacked computers on the global Internet. Once the worm started running on a machine, it searched the Internet for computers with servers that it knew how to exploit, and used the servers to create more copies of itself. In one of the attacks, the worm used a bug in the UNIX *fingerd* server. Because the server did not check incoming requests, the worm was able to send an illegal string of input that caused the server to overwrite parts of its internal data areas. The server, which executed with highest privilege, then misbehaved, allowing the worm to create copies of itself.

We can summarize our discussion of servers:

> *Servers are usually more difficult to build than clients because, although they can be implemented with application programs, servers must enforce all the access and protection policies of the computer system on which they run, and must protect themselves against all possible errors.*

21.6 RARP Server

So far, all our examples of client-server interaction require the client to know the complete server address. The RARP protocol from Chapter 6 provides an example of client-server interaction with a slightly different twist. Recall that a machine can use RARP to find its IP address at startup. Instead of having the client communicate directly with a server, RARP clients broadcast their requests. One or more machines executing RARP server processes respond, each returning a packet that answers the query.

There are two significant differences between a RARP server and a UDP echo or time server. First, RARP packets travel across the physical network directly in hardware frames, not in IP datagrams. Thus, unlike the UDP echo server which allows a client to contact a server anywhere on an internet, the RARP server requires the client to be on the same physical network. Second, RARP cannot be implemented by an application program. Echo and time servers can be built as application programs because they use UDP. By contrast, a RARP server needs access to raw hardware packets.

21.7 Alternatives To The Client-Server Model

What are the alternatives to client-server interaction, and when might they be attractive? This section gives an answer to these questions.

In the client-server model, programs usually act as clients when they need information, but it is sometimes important to minimize such interactions. The ARP protocol from Chapter 5 gives one example. It uses a modified form of client-server interaction to obtain physical address mappings. Machines that use ARP keep a cache of answers to improve the efficiency of later queries. Caching improves the performance of client-server interaction in cases where the recent history of queries is a good indicator of future use.

Although caching improves performance, it does not change the essence of client-server interaction. The essence lies in our assumption that processing must be driven by demand. We have assumed that a program executes until it needs information and then acts as a client to obtain the needed information. Taking a demand-driven view of the world is natural and arises from experience. Caching helps alleviate the cost of obtaining information by lowering the retrieval cost for all except the first process that makes a request.

How can we lower the cost of information retrieval for the first request? In a distributed system, it may be possible to have concurrent background activities that collect and propagate information *before* any particular program requests it, making retrieval costs low even for the initial request. More important, precollecting information can allow a given system to continue executing even though other machines or the networks connecting them fail.

Precollection is the basis for the 4BSD UNIX *ruptime* command. When invoked, *ruptime* reports the CPU load and time since system startup for each machine on the local network. A background program running on each machine uses UDP to broadcast information about the machine periodically. The same program also collects incoming information and places it in a file. Because machines propagate information continuously, each machine has a copy of the latest information on hand; a client seeking information never needs to access the network. Instead, it reads the information from secondary storage and prints it in a readable form.

The chief advantage of having information collected locally before the client needs it is speed. The *ruptime* command responds immediately when invoked without waiting for messages to traverse the network. A second benefit occurs because the client can find out something about machines that are no longer operating. In particular, if a machine stops broadcasting information, the client can report the time elapsed since the last broadcast (i.e., it can report how long the machine has been off-line).

Precollection has one major disadvantage: it uses processor time and network bandwidth even when no one cares about the data being collected. For example, the ruptime broadcast and collection continues running throughout the night, even if no one is logged in to read the information. If only a few machines connect to a given network, precollection cost is insignificant. It can be thought of as an innocuous background activity. For networks with many hosts, however, the large volume of broadcast traffic generated by precollection makes it too expensive. In particular, the cost of reading and processing broadcast messages becomes high. Thus, precollection is not among the most popular alternatives to client-server.

21.8 Summary

Distributed programs require network communication. Such programs often fall into a pattern of use known as client-server interaction. A server process awaits a request and performs action based on the request. The action usually includes sending a response. A client program formulates a request, sends it to a server, and then awaits a reply.

We have seen examples of clients and servers and found that some clients send requests directly, while others broadcast requests. Broadcast is especially useful on a local network when a machine does not know the address of a server.

We also noted that if servers use internet protocols like UDP, they can accept and respond to requests across an internet. If they communicate using physical frames and physical hardware addresses, they are restricted to a single physical network.

Finally, we considered an alternative to the client-server paradigm that uses precollection of information to avoid delays. An example of precollection came from a machine status service.

FOR FURTHER STUDY

UDP echo service is defined in Postel [RFC 862]. The *UNIX Programmer's Manual* describes the *ruptime* command (also see the related description of *rwho*). Feinler *et. al.* [1985] specifies many standard server protocols not discussed here, including discard, character generation, day and time, active users, and quote of the day. The next chapters consider others.

EXERCISES

21.1 Build a UDP echo client that sends a datagram to a specified echo server, awaits a reply, and compares it to the original message.

21.2 Carefully consider the manipulation of IP addresses in a UDP echo server. Under what conditions is it incorrect to create new IP addresses by reversing the source and destination IP addresses?

21.3 As we have seen, servers can be implemented by separate application programs or by building server code into the protocol software in an operating system. What are the advantages and disadvantages of having an application program (user process) per server?

21.4 Suppose you do not know the IP address of a local machine running a UDP echo server, but you know that it responds to requests sent to port 7. Is there an IP address you can use to reach it?

21.5 Build a client for the UDP time service.

21.6 Characterize situations in which a server can be located on a separate physical network from its client. Can a RARP server ever be located on a separate physical network from it clients? Why or why not?

21.7 What is the chief disadvantage of having all machines broadcast their status periodically?

21.8 Examine the format of data broadcast by the servers that implement the 4BSD UNIX *ruptime* command. What information is available to the client in addition to machine status?

21.9 What servers are running on computers at your site? If you do not have access to system configuration files that list the servers started for a given computer, see if your system has a command that prints a list of open TCP and UDP ports (e.g., the UNIX *netstat* command).

21.10 Some servers allow a manager to gracefully shut them down or restart them. What is the advantage of graceful shutdown?

22

The Socket Interface

22.1 Introduction

So far, we have concentrated on discussing the principles and concepts that underlie the TCP/IP protocols without specifying the interface between the application programs and the protocol software. This chapter reviews one example of an *Application Program Interface (API)*, the interface between application programs and TCP/IP protocols. There are two reasons for postponing the discussion of APIs. First, in principle we must distinguish between the interface and TCP/IP protocols because the standards do not specify exactly how application programs interact with protocol software. Thus, the interface architecture is not standardized; its design lies outside the scope of the protocol suite. Second, in practice, it is inappropriate to tie the protocols to a particular API because no single interface architecture works well on all systems. In particular, because protocol software resides in a computer's operating system, interface details depend on the operating system.

Despite the lack of a standard, reviewing an example will help us understand how programmers use TCP/IP. Although the example we have chosen is from the BSD UNIX operating system, it has become, de facto, a standard that is widely accepted and used in many systems. In particular, it forms the basis for Microsoft's *Windows Sockets*† interface. The reader should keep in mind that our goal is merely to give one concrete example, not to prescribe how APIs should be designed. The reader should also remember that the operations listed here are not part of the TCP/IP standards.

---

†Programmers often use the term *WINSOCK* as a replacement for Windows Sockets.

22.2 The UNIX I/O Paradigm And Network I/O

Developed in the late 1960s and early 1970s, UNIX was originally designed as a timesharing system for single processor computers. It is a process-oriented operating system in which each application program executes as a user level process. An application program interacts with the operating system by making *system calls*. From the programmer's point of view, system calls look and behave exactly like other procedure calls. They take arguments and return one or more results. Arguments can be values (e.g., an integer count) or pointers to objects in the application program (e.g., a buffer to be filled with characters).

Derived from those in Multics and earlier systems, the UNIX input and output (I/O) primitives follow a paradigm sometimes referred to as *open-read-write-close*. Before a user process can perform I/O operations, it calls *open* to specify the file or device to be used and obtains permission. The call to *open* returns a small integer *file descriptor*† that the process uses when performing I/O operations on the opened file or device. Once an object has been opened, the user process makes one or more calls to *read* or *write* to transfer data. *Read* transfers data into the user process; *write* transfers data from the user process to the file or device. Both *read* and *write* take three arguments that specify the file descriptor to use, the address of a buffer, and the number of bytes to transfer. After all transfer operations are complete, the user process calls *close* to inform the operating system that it has finished using the object (the operating system automatically closes all open descriptors if a process terminates without calling *close*).

22.3 Adding Network I/O to UNIX

Originally, UNIX designers cast all I/O operations in the open-read-write-close paradigm described above. The scheme included I/O for character-oriented devices like keyboards and block-oriented devices like disks and data files. An early implementation of TCP/IP under UNIX also used the open-read-write-close paradigm with a special file name, */dev/tcp*.

The group adding network protocols to BSD UNIX decided that because network protocols are more complex than conventional I/O devices, interaction between user processes and network protocols must be more complex than interactions between user processes and conventional I/O facilities. In particular, the protocol interface must allow programmers to create both server code that awaits connections passively as well as client code that forms connections actively. Furthermore, application programs sending datagrams may wish to specify the destination address along with each datagram instead of binding destinations at the time they call *open*. To handle all these cases, the designers chose to abandon the traditional UNIX open-read-write-close paradigm, and added several new operating system calls as well as new library routines. Adding network protocols to UNIX increased the complexity of the I/O interface substantially.

Further complexity arises in the UNIX protocol interface because designers attempted to build a general mechanism to accommodate many protocols. For example,

---

†The term ''file descriptor'' arises because in UNIX all devices are mapped into the file system name space. In most cases, I/O operations on files and devices are indistinguishable.

the generality makes it possible for the operating system to include software for other protocol suites as well as TCP/IP, and to allow an application program to use one or more of them at a time. As a consequence, the application program cannot merely supply a 32-bit address and expect the operating system to interpret it correctly. The application must explicitly specify that the 32-bit number represents an IP address.

22.4 The Socket Abstraction

The basis for network I/O in the socket API centers on an abstraction known as the *socket*†. We think of a socket as a generalization of the UNIX file access mechanism that provides an endpoint for communication. As with file access, application programs request the operating system to create a socket when one is needed. The system returns a small integer that the application program uses to reference the newly created socket. The chief difference between file descriptors and socket descriptors is that the operating system binds a file descriptor to a specific file or device when the application calls *open*, but it can create sockets without binding them to specific destination addresses. The application can choose to supply a destination address each time it uses the socket (e.g., when sending datagrams), or it can choose to bind the destination address to the socket and avoid specifying the destination repeatedly (e.g., when making a TCP connection).

Whenever it makes sense, sockets perform exactly like UNIX files or devices, so they can be used with traditional operations like *read* and *write*. For example, once an application program creates a socket and creates a TCP connection from the socket to a foreign destination, the program can use *write* to send a stream of data across the connection (the application program at the other end can use *read* to receive it). To make it possible to use primitives like *read* and *write* with both files and sockets, the operating system allocates socket descriptors and file descriptors from the same set of integers and makes sure that if a given integer has been allocated as a file descriptor, it will not also be allocated as a socket descriptor.

22.5 Creating A Socket

The *socket* function creates sockets on demand. It takes three integer arguments and returns an integer result:

$$result = socket(pf, type, protocol)$$

Argument *pf* specifies the protocol family to be used with the socket. That is, it specifies how to interpret addresses when they are supplied. Current families include the TCP/IP internet (PF_INET), Xerox Corporation PUP internet (PF_PUP), Apple Computer Incorporated AppleTalk network (PF_APPLETALK), and UNIX file system (PF_UNIX) as well as many others‡.

---

†For now, we will describe sockets as part of the operating system as they are implemented in UNIX; later sections describe how other operating systems use library routines to provide a socket API.

‡In UNIX, application programs contain symbolic names like *PF_INET*; system files contain the definitions that specify numeric values for each name.

Argument *type* specifies the type of communication desired. Possible types include reliable stream delivery service (SOCK_STREAM) and connectionless datagram delivery service (SOCK_DGRAM), as well as a raw type (SOCK_RAW) that allows privileged programs to access low-level protocols or network interfaces. Two additional types were planned, but not implemented.

Although the general approach of separating protocol families and types may seem sufficient to handle all cases easily, it does not. First, it may be that a given family of protocols does not support one or more of the possible service types. For example, the UNIX family has an interprocess communication mechanism called a *pipe* that uses a reliable stream delivery service, but has no mechanism for sequenced packet delivery. Thus, not all combinations of protocol family and service type make sense. Second, some protocol families have multiple protocols that support one type of service. For example, it may be that a single protocol family has two connectionless datagram delivery services. To accommodate multiple protocols within a family, the *socket* call has a third argument that can be used to select a specific protocol. To use the third argument, the programmer must understand the protocol family well enough to know the type of service each protocol supplies.

Because the designers tried to capture many of the conventional UNIX operations in their socket design, they needed a way to simulate the UNIX pipe mechanism. It is not necessary to understand the details of pipes; only one salient feature is important: pipes differ from standard network operations because the calling process creates both endpoints for the communication simultaneously. To accommodate pipes, the designers added a *socketpair* function that takes the form:

$$socketpair(pf, type, protocol, sarray)$$

Socketpair has one more argument than the *socket* procedure, *sarray*. The additional argument gives the address of a two-element integer array. *Socketpair* creates two sockets simultaneously and places the two socket descriptors in the two elements of *sarray*. Readers should understand that *socketpair* is not meaningful when applied to the TCP/IP protocol family (it has been included here merely to make our description of the interface complete).

22.6 Socket Inheritance And Termination

UNIX uses the *fork* and *exec* system calls to start new application programs. It is a two-step procedure. In the first step, *fork* creates a separate copy of the currently executing application program. In the second step, the new copy replaces itself with the desired application program. When a program calls *fork*, the newly created copy inherits access to all open sockets just as it inherits access to all open files. When a program calls *exec*, the new application retains access to all open sockets. We will see that master servers use socket inheritance when they create slave servers to handle a specific connection. Internally, the operating system keeps a reference count associated with each socket, so it knows how many application programs (processes) have access to it.

Both the old and new processes have the same access rights to existing sockets, and both can access the sockets. Thus, it is the responsibility of the programmer to ensure that the two processes use the shared socket meaningfully.

When a process finishes using a socket it calls *close*. *Close* has the form:

close(socket)

where argument *socket* specifies the descriptor of a socket to close. When a process terminates for any reason, the system closes all sockets that remain open. Internally, a call to *close* decrements the reference count for a socket and destroys the socket if the count reaches zero.

22.7 Specifying A Local Address

Initially, a socket is created without any association to local or destination addresses. For the TCP/IP protocols, this means no local protocol port number has been assigned and no destination port or IP address has been specified. In many cases, application programs do not care about the local address use and are willing to allow the protocol software to choose one for them. However, server processes that operate at a well-known port must be able to specify that port to the system. Once a socket has been created, a server uses the *bind* function to establish a local address for it. *Bind* has the following form:

bind(socket, localaddr, addrlen)

Argument *socket* is the integer descriptor of the socket to be bound. Argument *localaddr* is a structure that specifies the local address to which the socket should be bound, and argument *addrlen* is an integer that specifies the length of the address measured in bytes. Instead of giving the address merely as a sequence of bytes, the designers chose to use a structure for addresses as Figure 22.1 illustrates.

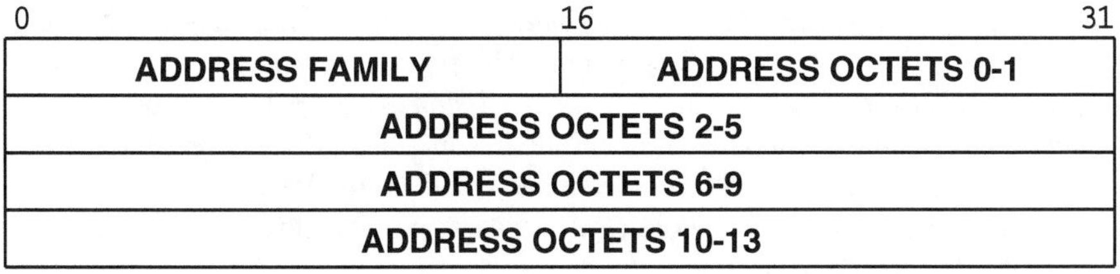

0	16	31
ADDRESS FAMILY	ADDRESS OCTETS 0-1	
ADDRESS OCTETS 2-5		
ADDRESS OCTETS 6-9		
ADDRESS OCTETS 10-13		

Figure 22.1 The *sockaddr* structure used when passing a TCP/IP address to the socket interface.

The structure, generically named *sockaddr*, begins with a 16-bit *ADDRESS FAMI-LY* field that identifies the protocol suite to which the address belongs. It is followed by an address of up to *14* octets. When declared in C, the socket address structure is a union of structures for all possible address families.

The value in the *ADDRESS FAMILY* field determines the format of the remaining address octets. For example, the value *2†* in the *ADDRESS FAMILY* field means the remaining address octets contain a TCP/IP address. Each protocol family defines how it will use octets in the address field. For TCP/IP addresses, the socket address is known as *sockaddr_in*. It includes both an IP address and a protocol port number (i.e., an internet socket address structure can contain both an IP address and a protocol port at that address). Figure 22.2 shows the exact format of a TCP/IP socket address.

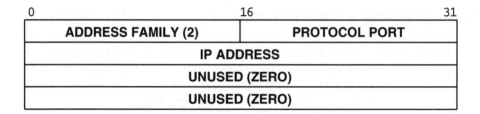

Figure 22.2 The format of a socket address structure (*sockaddr_in*) when used with a TCP/IP address. The structure includes both an IP address and a protocol port at that address.

Although it is possible to specify arbitrary values in the address structure when calling *bind*, not all possible bindings are valid. For example, the caller might request a local protocol port that is already in use by another program, or it might request an invalid IP address. In such cases, the *bind* call fails and returns an error code.

22.8 Connecting Sockets To Destination Addresses

Initially, a socket is created in the *unconnected state*, which means that the socket is not associated with any foreign destination. The function *connect* binds a permanent destination to a socket, placing it in the *connected state*. An application program must call *connect* to establish a connection before it can transfer data through a reliable stream socket. Sockets used with connectionless datagram services need not be connected before they are used, but doing so makes it possible to transfer data without specifying the destination each time.

The *connect* function has the form:

                    connect(socket, destaddr, addrlen)

---

†UNIX uses the symbolic name *PF_INET* to denote TCP/IP addresses.

Argument *socket* is the integer descriptor of the socket to connect. Argument *destaddr* is a socket address structure that specifies the destination address to which the socket should be bound. Argument *addrlen* specifies the length of the destination address measured in bytes.

The semantics of *connect* depend on the underlying protocols. Selecting the reliable stream delivery service in the PF_INET family means choosing TCP. In such cases, *connect* builds a TCP connection with the destination and returns an error if it cannot. In the case of connectionless service, *connect* does nothing more than store the destination address locally.

22.9 Sending Data Through A Socket

Once an application program has established a socket, it can use the socket to transmit data. There are five possible functions from which to choose: *send*, *sendto*, *sendmsg*, *write*, and *writev*. *Send*, *write*, and *writev* only work with connected sockets because they do not allow the caller to specify a destination address. The differences between the three are minor. *Write* takes three arguments:

write(socket, buffer, length)

Argument *socket* contains an integer socket descriptor (*write* can also be used with other types of descriptors). Argument *buffer* contains the address of the data to be sent, and argument *length* specifies the number of bytes to send. The call to *write* blocks until the data can be transferred (e.g., it blocks if internal system buffers for the socket are full). Like most system calls, *write* returns an error code to the application calling it, allowing the programmer to know if the operation succeeded.

The system call *writev* works like *write* except that it uses a ''gather write'' form, making it possible for the application program to write a message without copying the message into contiguous bytes of memory. *Writev* has the form:

writev(socket, iovector, vectorlen)

Argument *iovector* gives the address of an array of type *iovec* that contains a sequence of pointers to the blocks of bytes that form the message. As Figure 22.3 shows, a length accompanies each pointer. Argument *vectorlen* specifies the number of entries in *iovector*.

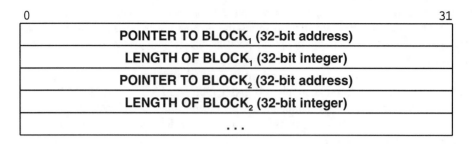

Figure 22.3 The format of an iovector of type *iovec* used with *writev* and
readv.

The *send* function has the form:

send(socket, message, length, flags)

where argument *socket* specifies the socket to use, argument *message* gives the address
of the data to be sent, argument *length* specifies the number of bytes to be sent, and argument *flags* controls the transmission. One value for *flags* allows the sender to specify
that the message should be sent out-of-band on sockets that support such a notion. For
example, recall from Chapter 13 that out-of-band messages correspond to TCP's notion
of urgent data. Another value for *flags* allows the caller to request that the message be
sent without using local routing tables. The intention is to allow the caller to take control of routing, making it possible to write network debugging software. Of course, not
all sockets support all requests from arbitrary programs. Some requests require the program to have special privileges; others are simply not supported on all sockets.

Functions *sendto* and *sendmsg* allow the caller to send a message through an unconnected socket because they both require the caller to specify a destination. *Sendto*,
which takes the destination address as an argument, has the form:

sendto(socket, message, length, flags, destaddr, addrlen)

The first four arguments are exactly the same as those used with the *send* function. The
final two arguments specify a destination address and give the length of that address.
Argument *destaddr* specifies the destination address using the *sockaddr_in* structure as
defined in Figure 22.2.

A programmer may choose to use function *sendmsg* in cases where the long list of
arguments required for *sendto* makes the program inefficient or difficult to read.
Sendmsg has the form:

sendmsg(socket, messagestruct, flags)

where argument *messagestruct* is a structure of the form illustrated in Figure 22.4. The
structure contains information about the message to be sent, its length, the destination

address, and the address length. This call is especially useful because there is a corresponding input operation (described below) that produces a message structure in exactly the same format.

0   31
POINTER TO SOCKETADDR
SIZE OF SOCKETADDR
POINTER TO IOVEC LIST
LENGTH OF IOVEC LIST
POINTER TO ACCESS RIGHTS LIST
LENGTH OF ACCESS RIGHTS LIST

Figure 22.4 The format of message structure *messagestruct* used by *sendmsg*.

22.10 Receiving Data Through A Socket

Analogous to the five different output operations, the socket API offers five functions that a process can use to receive data through a socket: *read, readv, recv, recvfrom,* and *recvmsg.* The conventional input operation, *read,* can only be used when the socket is connected. It has the form:

read(descriptor, buffer, length)

where *descriptor* gives the integer descriptor of a socket or file descriptor from which to read data, *buffer* specifies the address in memory at which to store the data, and *length* specifies the maximum number of bytes to read.

An alternative form, *readv,* allows the caller to use a "scatter read" style of interface that places the incoming data in noncontiguous locations. *Readv* has the form:

readv(descriptor, iovector, vectorlen)

Argument *iovector* gives the address of a structure of type *iovec* (see Figure 22.3) that contains a sequence of pointers to blocks of memory into which the incoming data should be stored. Argument *vectorlen* specifies the number of entries in *iovector.*

In addition to the conventional input operations, there are three additional functions for network message input. Processes call *recv* to receive data from a connected socket. It has the form:

recv(socket, buffer, length, flags)

Argument *socket* specifies a socket descriptor from which data should be received. Argument *buffer* specifies the address in memory into which the message should be placed, and argument *length* specifies the length of the buffer area. Finally, argument *flags* allows the caller to control the reception. Among the possible values for the *flags* argument is one that allows the caller to look ahead by extracting a copy of the next incoming message without removing the message from the socket.

The function *recvfrom* allows the caller to specify input from an unconnected socket. It includes additional arguments that allow the caller to specify where to record the sender's address. The form is:

recvfrom(socket, buffer, length, flags, fromaddr, addrlen)

The two additional arguments, *fromaddr* and *addrlen*, are pointers to a socket address structure and an integer. The operating system uses *fromaddr* to record the address of the message sender and uses *fromlen* to record the length of the sender's address. Notice that the output operation *sendto*, discussed above, takes an address in exactly the same form as *recvfrom* generates. Thus, sending replies is easy.

The final function used for input, *recvmsg*, is analogous to the *sendmsg* output operation. *Recvmsg* operates like *recvfrom*, but requires fewer arguments. Its form is:

recvmsg(socket, messagestruct, flags)

where argument *messagestruct* gives the address of a structure that holds the address for an incoming message as well as locations for the sender's address. The structure produced by *recvmsg* is exactly the same as the structure used by *sendmsg*, making them operate well as a pair.

22.11 Obtaining Local And Remote Socket Addresses

We said that newly created processes inherit the set of open sockets from the process that created them. Sometimes, a newly created process needs to determine the destination address to which a socket connects. A process may also wish to determine the local address of a socket. Two functions provide such information: *getpeername* and *getsockname* (despite their names, both deal with what we think of as ''addresses'').

A process calls *getpeername* to determine the address of the peer (i.e., the remote end) to which a socket connects. It has the form:

getpeername(socket, destaddr, addrlen)

Argument *socket* specifies the socket for which the address is desired. Argument *destaddr* is a pointer to a structure of type *sockaddr* (see Figure 22.1) that will receive the socket address. Finally, argument *addrlen* is a pointer to an integer that will receive the length of the address. *Getpeername* only works with connected sockets.

Function *getsockname* returns the local address associated with a socket. It has the form:

getsockname(socket, localaddr, addrlen)

As expected, argument *socket* specifies the socket for which the local address is desired. Argument *localaddr* is a pointer to a structure of type *sockaddr* that will contain the address, and argument *addrlen* is a pointer to an integer that will contain the length of the address.

22.12 Obtaining And Setting Socket Options

In addition to binding a socket to a local address or connecting it to a destination address, the need arises for a mechanism that permits application programs to control the socket. For example, when using protocols that use timeout and retransmission, the application program may want to obtain or set the timeout parameters. It may also want to control the allocation of buffer space, determine if the socket allows transmission of broadcast, or control processing of out-of-band data. Rather than add new functions for each new control operation, the designers decided to build a single mechanism. The mechanism has two operations: *getsockopt* and *setsockopt*.

Function *getsockopt* allows the application to request information about the socket. A caller specifies the socket, the option of interest, and a location at which to store the requested information. The operating system examines its internal data structures for the socket and passes the requested information to the caller. The call has the form:

getsockopt(socket, level, optionid, optionval, length)

Argument *socket* specifies the socket for which information is needed. Argument *level* identifies whether the operation applies to the socket itself or to the underlying protocols being used. Argument *optionid* specifies a single option to which the request applies. The pair of arguments *optionval* and *length* specify two pointers. The first gives the address of a buffer into which the system places the requested value, and the second gives the address of an integer into which the system places the length of the option value.

Function *setsockopt* allows an application program to set a socket option using the set of values obtained with *getsockopt*. The caller specifies a socket for which the option should be set, the option to be changed, and a value for the option. The call to *setsockopt* has the form:

setsockopt(socket, level, optionid, optionval, length)

where the arguments are like those for *getsockopt*, except that the *length* argument contains the length of the option being passed to the system. The caller must supply a legal value for the option as well as a correct length for that value. Of course, not all options apply to all sockets. The correctness and semantics of individual requests depend on the current state of the socket and the underlying protocols being used.

22.13 Specifying A Queue Length For A Server

One of the options that applies to sockets is used so frequently, a separate function has been dedicated to it. To understand how it arises, consider a server. The server creates a socket, binds it to a well-known protocol port, and waits for requests. If the server uses a reliable stream delivery, or if computing a response takes nontrivial amounts of time, it may happen that a new request arrives before the server finishes responding to an old request. To avoid having protocols reject or discard incoming requests, a server must tell the underlying protocol software that it wishes to have such requests enqueued until it has time to process them.

The function *listen* allows servers to prepare a socket for incoming connections. In terms of the underlying protocols, *listen* puts the socket in a passive mode ready to accept connections. When the server invokes *listen*, it also informs the operating system that the protocol software should enqueue multiple simultaneous requests that arrive at the socket. The form is:

listen(socket, qlength)

Argument *socket* gives the descriptor of a socket that should be prepared for use by a server, and argument *qlength* specifies the length of the request queue for that socket. After the call, the system will enqueue up to *qlength* requests for connections. If the queue is full when a request arrives, the operating system will refuse the connection by discarding the request. *Listen* applies only to sockets that have selected reliable stream delivery service.

22.14 How A Server Accepts Connections

As we have seen, a server process uses the functions *socket*, *bind*, and *listen* to create a socket, bind it to a well-known protocol port, and specify a queue length for connection requests. Note that the call to *bind* associates the socket with a well-known protocol port, but that the socket is not connected to a specific foreign destination. In fact, the foreign destination must specify a *wildcard*, allowing the socket to receive connection requests from an arbitrary client.

Once a socket has been established, the server needs to wait for a connection. To do so, it uses function *accept*. A call to *accept* blocks until a connection request arrives. It has the form:

newsock = accept(socket, addr, addrlen)

Argument *socket* specifies the descriptor of the socket on which to wait. Argument *addr* is a pointer to a structure of type *sockaddr*, and *addrlen* is a pointer to an integer. When a request arrives, the system fills in argument *addr* with the address of the client that has placed the request and sets *addrlen* to the length of the address. Finally, the system creates a new socket that has its destination connected to the requesting client, and returns the new socket descriptor to the caller. The original socket still has a wild-card foreign destination, and it still remains open. Thus, the master server can continue to accept additional requests at the original socket.

When a connection request arrives, the call to *accept* returns. The server can either handle requests iteratively or concurrently. In the iterative approach, the server handles the request itself, closes the new socket, and then calls *accept* to obtain the next connec-tion request. In the concurrent approach, after the call to *accept* returns, the master server creates a slave to handle the request (in UNIX terminology, it forks a child pro-cess to handle the request). The slave process inherits a copy of the new socket, so it can proceed to service the request. When it finishes, the slave closes the socket and ter-minates. The original (master) server process closes its copy of the new socket after starting the slave. It then calls *accept* to obtain the next connection request.

The concurrent design for servers may seem confusing because multiple processes will be using the same local protocol port number. The key to understanding the mechanism lies in the way underlying protocols treat protocol ports. Recall that in TCP a pair of endpoints define a connection. Thus, it does not matter how many processes use a given local protocol port number as long as they connect to different destinations. In the case of a concurrent server, there is one process per client and one additional pro-cess that accepts connections. The socket the master server process uses has a wildcard for the foreign destination, allowing it to connect with an arbitrary foreign site. Each remaining process has a specific foreign destination. When a TCP segment arrives, it will be sent to the socket connected to the segment's source. If no such socket exists, the segment will be sent to the socket that has a wildcard for its foreign destination. Furthermore, because the socket with a wildcard foreign destination does not have an open connection, it will only honor TCP segments that request a new connection.

22.15 Servers That Handle Multiple Services

The socket API provides another interesting possibility for server design because it allows a single process to wait for connections on multiple sockets. The system call that makes the design possible is called *select*, and it applies to I/O in general, not just to communication over sockets†. *Select* has the form:

nready = select(ndesc, indesc, outdesc, excdesc, timeout)

In general, a call to *select* blocks waiting for one of a set of file descriptors to be-come ready. Argument *ndesc* specifies how many descriptors should be examined (the descriptors checked are always 2 through *ndesc*-1). Argument *indesc* is a pointer to a

---

†The version of *select* in Windows Sockets applies only to socket descriptors.

bit mask that specifies the file descriptors to check for input, argument *outdesc* is a pointer to a bit mask that specifies the file descriptors to check for output, and argument *excdesc* is a pointer to a bit mask that specifies the file descriptors to check for exception conditions. Finally, if argument *timeout* is nonzero, it is the address of an integer that specifies how long to wait for a connection before returning to the caller. A zero value for timeout forces the call to block until a descriptor becomes ready. Because the *timeout* argument contains the address of the timeout integer and not the integer itself, a process can request zero delay by passing the address of an integer that contains zero (i.e., a process can poll to see if I/O is ready).

A call to *select* returns the number of descriptors from the specified set that are ready for I/O. It also changes the bit masks specified by *indesc*, *outdesc*, and *excdesc* to inform the application which of the selected file descriptors are ready. Thus, before calling *select*, the caller must turn on those bits that correspond to descriptors to be checked. Following the call, all bits that remain set to *1* correspond to a ready file descriptor.

To communicate over more than one socket at a time, a process first creates all the sockets it needs and then uses *select* to determine which of them becomes ready for I/O first. Once it finds a socket has become ready, the process uses the input or output procedures defined above to communicate.

22.16 Obtaining And Setting Host Names

Most operating systems maintain an internal host name. For machines on the Internet, the internal name is usually chosen to be the domain name for the machine's main network interface. The *gethostname* function allows user processes to access the host name, and the *sethostname* function allows privileged processes to set the host name. *Gethostname* has the form:

gethostname(name, length)

Argument *name* gives the address of an array of bytes where the name is to be stored, and argument *length* is an integer that specifies the length of the *name* array. To set the host name, a privileged process makes a call of the form:

sethostname(name, length)

Argument *name* gives the address of an array where the name is stored, and argument *length* is an integer that gives the length of the name array.

22.17 Obtaining And Setting The Internal Host Domain

The operating system maintains a string that specifies the name domain to which a machine belongs. When a site obtains authority for part of the domain name space, it invents a string that identifies its piece of the space and uses that string as the name of the domain. For example, machines in the domain

cs.purdue.edu

have names taken from the Arthurian legend. Thus, one finds machines named *merlin*, *arthur*, *guenevere*, and *lancelot*. The domain itself has been named *camelot*, so the operating system on each host in the group must be informed that it resides in the *camelot* domain. To do so, a privileged process uses function *setdomainname*, which has the form:

setdomainname(name, length)

Argument *name* gives the address of an array of bytes that contains the name of a domain, and argument *length* is an integer that gives the length of the name.

User processes call *getdomainname* to retrieve the name of the domain from the system. It has the form:

getdomainname(name, length)

where argument *name* specifies the address of an array where the name should be stored, and argument *length* is an integer that specifies the length of the array.

22.18 Socket Library Calls

In addition to the functions described above, the socket API offers a set of library routines that perform useful functions related to networking. Figure 22.5 illustrates the difference between system calls and library routines. System calls pass control to the computer's operating system, while library routines are like other procedures that the programmer binds into a program.

application program bound with library routines it calls

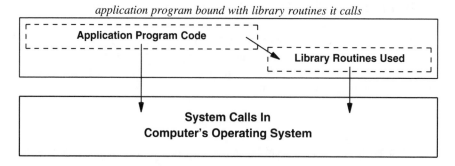

Figure 22.5 The difference between library routines, which are bound into an
application program, and system calls, which are part of the
operating system. A program can call either; library routines
can call other library routines or system calls.

Many of the socket library routines provide database services that allow a process
to determine the names of machines and network services, protocol port numbers, and
other related information. For example, one set of library routines provides access to
the database of network services. We think of entries in the services database as 3-
tuples, where each 3-tuple contains the (human readable) name of a network service, the
protocol that supports the service, and a protocol port number for the service. Library
routines exist that allow a process to obtain information from an entry given any piece.

The next sections examine groups of library routines, explaining their purposes and
providing information about how they can be used. As we will see, the sets of library
routines that provide access to a sequential database follow a pattern. Each set allows
the application to: establish a connection to the database, obtain entries one at a time,
and close the connection. The routines used for these three operations are named *setX-
ent*, *getXent*, and *endXent*, where *X* is the name of the database. For example, the library routines for the host database are named *sethostent*, *gethostent*, and *endhostent*.
The sections that describe these routines summarize the calls without repeating the details of their use.

22.19 Network Byte Order Conversion Routines

Recall that machines differ in the way they store integer quantities and that the
TCP/IP protocols define a machine independent standard for byte order. The socket
API provides four library functions that convert between the local machine byte order
and the network standard byte order. To make programs portable, they must be written
to call the conversion routines every time they copy an integer value from the local
machine to a network packet, or when they copy a value from a network packet to the
local machine.

All four conversion routines are functions that take a value as an argument and return a new value with the bytes rearranged. For example, to convert a short (2-byte) integer from network byte order to the local host byte order, a programmer calls *ntohs* (network to host short). The format is:

$$localshort = ntohs(netshort)$$

Argument *netshort* is a 2-byte (16-bit) integer in network standard byte order and the result, *localshort*, is in local host byte order.

The C programming language calls 4 byte (32 bit) integers *long*s. Function *ntohl* (network to host long) converts 4-byte longs from network standard byte order to local host byte order. Programs invoke *ntohl* as a function, supplying a long integer in network byte order as an argument:

$$locallong = ntohl(netlong)$$

Two analogous functions allow the programmer to convert from local host byte order to network byte order. Function *htons* converts a 2-byte (short) integer in the host's local byte order to a 2-byte integer in network standard byte order. Programs invoke *htons* as a function:

$$netshort = htons(localshort)$$

The final conversion routine, *htonl*, converts long integers to network standard byte order. Like the others, *htonl* is a function:

$$netlong = htonl(locallong)$$

It should be obvious that the conversion routines preserve the following mathematical relationships:

$$netshort = htons(\ ntohs(netshort)\ )$$

and

$$localshort = ntohs(\ htons(localshort)\ )$$

Similar relationships hold for the long integer conversion routines.

22.20 IP Address Manipulation Routines

Because many programs translate between 32-bit IP addresses and the corresponding dotted decimal notation, the socket library includes utility routines that perform the translation. Procedures *inet_addr* and *inet_network* both translate from dotted decimal format to a 32-bit IP address in network byte order. *Inet_addr* forms a 32-bit host IP address; *inet_network* forms the network address with zeroes for the host part. They have the form:

$$address = inet\_addr(string)$$

and

$$address = inet\_network(string)$$

where argument *string* gives the address of an ASCII string that contains the number expressed in dotted decimal format. The dotted decimal form can have 1 to 4 segments of digits separated by periods (dots). If all 4 appear, each corresponds to a single byte of the resulting 32-bit integer. If less than 4 appear, the last segment is expanded to fill remaining bytes.

Procedure *inet_ntoa* performs the inverse of *inet_addr* by mapping a 32-bit integer to an ASCII string in dotted decimal format. It has the form:

$$str = inet\_ntoa(internetaddr)$$

where argument *internetaddr* is a 32-bit IP address in network byte order, and *str* is the address of the resulting ASCII version.

Often programs that manipulate IP addresses must combine a network address with the local address of a host on that network. Procedure *inet_makeaddr* performs such a combination. It has the form:

$$internetaddr = inet\_makeaddr(net, local)$$

Argument *net* is a 32-bit network IP address in host byte order, and argument *local* is the integer representing a local host address on that network, also in local host byte order.

Procedures *inet_netof* and *inet_lnaof* provide the inverse of *inet_makeaddr* by separating the network and local portions of an IP address. They have the form:

$$net = inet\_netof(internetaddr)$$

and

$$local = inet\_lnaof(internetaddr)$$

where argument *internetaddr* is a 32-bit IP address in network byte order, and the results are returned in host byte order.

22.21 Accessing The Domain Name System†

A set of five library procedures comprise the interface to the TCP/IP domain name system. Application programs that call these routines become clients of one domain name system, sending one or more servers requests and receiving responses.

The general idea is that a program makes a query, sends it to a server, and awaits an answer. Because many options exist, the routines have only a few basic parameters and use a global structure, *res*, to hold others. For example, one field in *res* enables debugging messages while another controls whether the code uses UDP or TCP for queries. Most fields in *res* begin with reasonable defaults, so the routines can be used without changing *res*.

A program calls *res_init* before using other procedures. The call takes no arguments:

$$res\_init()$$

Res_init reads a file that contains information like the name of the machine that runs the domain name server and stores the results in global structure *res*.

Procedure *res_mkquery* forms a domain name query and places it in a buffer in memory. The form of the call is:

$$res\_mkquery(op, dname, class, type, data, datalen, newrr, buffer, buflen)$$

The first seven arguments correspond directly to the fields of a domain name query. Argument *op* specifies the requested operation, *dname* gives the address of a character array that contains a domain name, *class* is an integer that gives the class of the query, *type* is an integer that gives the type of the query, *data* gives the address of an array of data to be included in the query, and *datalen* is an integer that gives the length of the data. In addition to the library procedures, the socket API provides application programs with definitions of symbolic constants for important values. Thus, programmers can use the domain name system without understanding the details of the protocol. The last two arguments, *buffer* and *buflen*, specify the address of an area into which the query should be placed and the integer length of the buffer area, respectively. Finally, in the current implementation, argument *newrr* is unused.

Once a program has formed a query, it calls *res_send* to send it to a name server and obtain a response. The form is:

$$res\_send(buffer, buflen, answer, anslen)$$

Argument *buffer* is a pointer to memory that holds the message to be sent (presumably, the application called procedure *res_mkquery* to form the message). Argument *buflen* is an integer that specifies the length. Argument *answer* gives the address in memory into which a response should be written, and integer argument *anslen* specifies the length of the answer area.

---

†Chapter 24 considers the Domain Name System in detail.

In addition to routines that make and send queries, the socket library contains two routines that translate domain names between conventional ASCII and the compressed format used in queries. Procedure *dn_expand* expands a compressed domain name into a full ASCII version. It has the form:

dn_expand(msg, eom, compressed, full, fullen)

Argument *msg* gives the address of a domain name message that contains the name to be expanded, with *eom* specifying the end-of-message limit beyond which the expansion cannot go. Argument *compressed* is a pointer to the first byte of the compressed name. Argument *full* is a pointer to an array into which the expanded name should be written, and argument *fullen* is an integer that specifies the length of the array.

Generating a compressed name is more complex than expanding a compressed name because compression involves eliminating common suffixes. When compressing names, the client must keep a record of suffixes that have appeared previously. Procedure *dn_comp* compresses a full domain name by comparing suffixes to a list of previously used suffixes and eliminating the longest possible suffix. A call has the form:

dn_comp(full, compressed, cmprlen, prevptrs, lastptr)

Argument *full* gives the address of a full domain name. Argument *compressed* points to an array of bytes that will hold the compressed name, with argument *cmprlen* specifying the length of the array. The argument *prevptrs* is the address of an array of pointers to previously compressed suffixes, with *lastptr* pointing to the end of the array. Normally, *dn_comp* compresses the name and updates *prevptrs* if a new suffix has been used.

Procedure *dn_comp* can also be used to translate a domain name from ASCII to the internal form without compression (i.e., without removing suffixes). To do so, a process invokes *dn_comp* with the *prevptrs* argument set to *NULL* (i.e., zero).

22.22 Obtaining Information About Hosts

Library procedures exist that allow a process to retrieve information about a host given either its domain name or its IP address. When used on a machine that has access to a domain name server, the library procedures make the process a client of the domain name system by sending a request to a server and waiting for a response. When used on systems that do not have access to the domain name system (e.g., a host not on the Internet), the routines obtain the desired information from a database kept on secondary storage.

Function *gethostbyname* takes a domain name and returns a pointer to a structure of information for that host. A call takes the form:

ptr = gethostbyname(namestr)

Argument *namestr* is a pointer to a character string that contains a domain name for the host. The value returned, *ptr*, points to a structure that contains the following information: the official host name, a list of aliases that have been registered for the host, the host address type (i.e., whether the address is an IP address), the address length, and a list of one or more addresses for the host. More details can be found in the UNIX Programmer's Manual.

Function *gethostbyaddr* produces the same information as *gethostbyname*. The difference between the two is that *gethostbyaddr* accepts a host address as an argument:

$$ptr = gethostbyaddr(addr, len, type)$$

Argument *addr* is a pointer to a sequence of bytes that contain a host address. Argument *len* is an integer that gives the length of the address, and argument *type* is an integer that specifies the type of the address (e.g., that it is an IP address).

As mentioned earlier, procedures *sethostent*, *gethostent*, and *endhostent* provide sequential access to the host database.

22.23 Obtaining Information About Networks

Hosts either use the domain name system or keep a simple database of networks in their internet. The socket library routines include five routines that allow a process to access the network database. Procedure *getnetbyname* obtains and formats the contents of an entry from the database given the domain name of a network. A call has the form:

$$ptr = getnetbyname(name)$$

where argument *name* is a pointer to a string that contains the name of the network for which information is desired. The value returned is a pointer to a structure that contains fields for the official name of the network, a list of registered aliases, an integer address type, and a 32-bit network address (i.e., an IP address with the host portion set to zero).

A process calls library routine *getnetbyaddr* when it needs to search for information about a network given its address. The call has the form:

$$ptr = getnetbyaddr(netaddr, addrtype)$$

Argument *netaddr* is a 32-bit network address, and argument *addrtype* is an integer that specifies the type of *netaddr*. Procedures *setnetent*, *getnetent*, and *endnetent* provide sequential access to the network database.

22.24 Obtaining Information About Protocols

Five library routines provide access to the database of protocols available on a machine. Each protocol has an official name, registered aliases, and an official protocol number. Procedure *getprotobyname* allows a caller to obtain information about a protocol given its name:

$$ptr = getprotobyname(name)$$

Argument *name* is a pointer to an ASCII string that contains the name of the protocol for which information is desired. The function returns a pointer to a structure that has fields for the official protocol name, a list of aliases, and a unique integer value assigned to the protocol.

Procedure *getprotobynumber* allows a process to search for protocol information using the protocol number as a key:

$$ptr = getprotobynumber(number)$$

Finally, procedures *getprotoent*, *setprotoent*, and *endprotoent* provide sequential access to the protocol database.

22.25 Obtaining Information About Network Services

Recall from Chapters 12 and 13 that some UDP and TCP protocol port numbers are reserved for well-known services. For example, TCP port *43* is reserved for the *whois* service. *Whois* allows a client on one machine to contact a server on another and obtain information about a user that has an account on the server's machine. The entry for *whois* in the services database specifies the service name, *whois*, the protocol, *TCP*, and the protocol port number *43*. Five library routines exist that obtain information about services and the protocol ports they use.

Procedure *getservbyname* maps a named service onto a port number:

$$ptr = getservbyname(name, proto)$$

Argument *name* specifies the address of a string that contains the name of the desired service, and integer argument *proto* specifies the protocol with which the service is to be used. Typically, protocols are limited to TCP and UDP. The value returned is a pointer to a structure that contains fields for the name of the service, a list of aliases, an identification of the protocol with which the service is used, and an integer protocol port number assigned for that service.

Procedure *getservbyport* allows the caller to obtain an entry from the services database given the port number assigned to it. A call has the form:

$$ptr = getservbyport(port, proto)$$

Argument *port* is the integer protocol port number assigned to the service, and argument *proto* specifies the protocol for which the service is desired. As with other databases, a process can access the services database sequentially using *setservent*, *getservent*, and *endservent*.

22.26 An Example Client

The following example C program illustrates how a program uses the socket API to access TCP/IP protocols. It is a simple implementation of a *whois* client and server. As defined in RFC 954, the *whois* service allows a client on one machine to obtain information about a user on a remote system. In this implementation, the client is an application program that a user invokes with two arguments: the name of a remote machine and the name of a user on that machine about whom information is desired. The client calls *gethostbyname* to map the remote machine name into an IP address and calls *getservbyname* to find the well-known port for the *whois* service. Once it has mapped the host and service names, the client creates a socket, specifying that the socket will use reliable stream delivery (i.e., TCP). The client then binds the socket to the *whois* protocol port on the specified destination machine.

```
/* whoisclient.c - main */


#include <stdio.h>
#include <sys/types.h>
#include <sys/socket.h>
#include <netinet/in.h>
#include <netdb.h>


/*------------------------------------------------------------------------
 * Program:    whoisclient
 *
 * Purpose:    UNIX application program that becomes a client for the
 *             Internet "whois" service.
 *
 * Use:        whois hostname username
 *
 * Author:     Barry Shein, Boston University
 *
 * Date:       Long ago in a universe far, far away
 *
 *------------------------------------------------------------------------
 */
main(argc, argv)
int argc;                       /* standard UNIX argument declarations */
```

```
char *argv[];
{
    int s;                      /* socket descriptor                    */
    int len;                    /* length of received data              */
    struct sockaddr_in sa;      /* Internet socket addr. structure      */
    struct hostent *hp;         /* result of host name lookup           */
    struct servent *sp;         /* result of service lookup             */
    char buf[BUFSIZ+1];         /* buffer to read whois information      */
    char *myname;               /* pointer to name of this program      */
    char *host;                 /* pointer to remote host name          */
    char *user;                 /* pointer to remote user name          */

    myname = argv[0];
    /*
     * Check that there are two command line arguments
     */
    if(argc != 3) {
        fprintf(stderr, "Usage: %s host username\n", myname);
        exit(1);
    }
    host = argv[1];
    user = argv[2];
    /*
     * Look up the specified hostname
     */
    if((hp = gethostbyname(host)) == NULL) {
        fprintf(stderr,"%s: %s: no such host?\n", myname, host);
        exit(1);
    }
    /*
     * Put host's address and address type into socket structure
     */
    bcopy((char *)hp->h_addr, (char *)&sa.sin_addr, hp->h_length);
    sa.sin_family = hp->h_addrtype;
    /*
     * Look up the socket number for the WHOIS service
     */
    if((sp = getservbyname("whois","tcp")) == NULL) {
        fprintf(stderr,"%s: No whois service on this host\n", myname);
        exit(1);
    }
    /*
     * Put the whois socket number into the socket structure.
     */
```

```
  sa.sin_port = sp->s_port;
  /*
   * Allocate an open socket
   */
  if((s = socket(hp->h_addrtype, SOCK_STREAM, 0)) < 0) {
        perror("socket");
        exit(1);
  }
  /*
   * Connect to the remote server
   */
  if(connect(s, &sa, sizeof sa) < 0) {
        perror("connect");
        exit(1);
  }
  /*
   * Send the request
   */
  if(write(s, user, strlen(user)) != strlen(user)) {
        fprintf(stderr, "%s: write error\n", myname);
        exit(1);
  }
  /*
   * Read the reply and put to user's output
   */
  while( (len = read(s, buf, BUFSIZ)) > 0)
        write(1, buf, len);
  close(s);
  exit(0);
}
```

22.27 An Example Server

The example server is only slightly more complex than the client. The server listens on the well-known ''whois'' port and returns the requested information in response to a request from any client. The information is taken from the UNIX password file on the server's machine.

```
/* whoisserver.c - main */

#include <stdio.h>
#include <sys/types.h>
#include <sys/socket.h>
```

```
#include <netinet/in.h>
#include <netdb.h>
#include <pwd.h>


/*-------------------------------------------------------------------------
 * Program:      whoisserver
 *
 * Purpose:      UNIX application program that acts as a server for
 *               the "whois" service on the local machine.  It listens
 *               on well-known WHOIS port (43) and answers queries from
 *               clients.  This program requires super-user privilege to
 *               run.
 *
 * Use:          whois hostname username
 *
 * Author:       Barry Shein, Boston University
 *
 * Date:         Long ago in a universe far, far away
 *
 *-------------------------------------------------------------------------
 */

#define BACKLOG          5        /* # of requests we're willing to queue */
#define MAXHOSTNAME     32        /* maximum host name length we tolerate */

main(argc, argv)
int argc;                         /* standard UNIX argument declarations  */
char *argv[];
{
    int s, t;                     /* socket descriptors                   */
    int i;                        /* general purpose integer              */
    struct sockaddr_in sa, isa;   /* Internet socket address structure    */
    struct hostent *hp;           /* result of host name lookup           */
    char *myname;                 /* pointer to name of this program      */
    struct servent *sp;           /* result of service lookup             */
    char localhost[MAXHOSTNAME+1];/* local host name as character string  */

    myname = argv[0];
    /*
     * Look up the WHOIS service entry
     */
    if((sp = getservbyname("whois","tcp")) == NULL) {
        fprintf(stderr, "%s: No whois service on this host\n", myname);
        exit(1);
```

```
}
/*
 * Get our own host information
 */
gethostname(localhost, MAXHOSTNAME);
if((hp = gethostbyname(localhost)) == NULL) {
        fprintf(stderr, "%s: cannot get local host info?\n", myname);
        exit(1);
}
/*
 * Put the WHOIS socket number and our address info
 * into the socket structure
 */
sa.sin_port = sp->s_port;
bcopy((char *)hp->h_addr, (char *)&sa.sin_addr, hp->h_length);
sa.sin_family = hp->h_addrtype;
/*
 * Allocate an open socket for incoming connections
 */
if((s = socket(hp->h_addrtype, SOCK_STREAM, 0)) < 0) {
        perror("socket");
        exit(1);
}
/*
 * Bind the socket to the service port
 * so we hear incoming connections
 */
if(bind(s, &sa, sizeof sa) < 0) {
        perror("bind");
        exit(1);
}
/*
 * Set maximum connections we will fall behind
 */
listen(s, BACKLOG);
/*
 * Go into an infinite loop waiting for new connections
 */
while(1) {
        i = sizeof isa;
        /*
         * We hang in accept() while waiting for new customers
         */
        if((t = accept(s, &isa, &i)) < 0) {
```

```
                perror("accept");
                exit(1);
            }
            whois(t);              /* perform the actual WHOIS service */
            close(t);
    }
}
/*
 * Get the WHOIS request from remote host and format a reply.
 */
whois(sock)
int sock;
{
    struct passwd *p;
    char buf[BUFSIZ+1];
    int i;

    /*
     * Get one line request
     */
    if( (i = read(sock, buf, BUFSIZ)) <= 0)
            return;
    buf[i] = '\0';          /* Null terminate */
    /*
     * Look up the requested user and format reply
     */
    if((p = getpwnam(buf)) == NULL)
            strcpy(buf,"User not found\n");
    else
            sprintf(buf, "%s: %s\n", p->pw_name, p->pw_gecos);
    /*
     * Return reply
     */
    write(sock, buf, strlen(buf));
    return;
}
```

22.28 Summary

Because TCP/IP protocol software resides inside an operating system, the exact interface between an application program and TCP/IP protocols depends on the details of the operating system; it is not specified by the TCP/IP protocol standard. We examined the socket API, which was originally designed for BSD UNIX, but has become, de facto, a standard used by vendors such as Microsoft. We saw that sockets adopted the UNIX open-read-write-close paradigm. To use TCP, a program must create a socket, bind addresses to it, accept incoming connections, and then communicate using the *read* or *write* primitives. Finally, when finished using a socket, the program must close it. In addition to the socket abstraction and system calls that operate on sockets, BSD UNIX includes library routines that help programmers create and manipulate IP addresses, convert integers between the local machine format and network standard byte order, and search for information such as network addresses.

The socket interface has become popular and is widely supported by many vendors. Vendors who do not offer socket facilities in their operating systems often provide a socket library that makes it possible for programmers to write applications using socket calls even though the underlying operating system uses a different set of system calls.

FOR FURTHER STUDY

Detailed information on the socket functions can be found in the *UNIX Programmer's Manual*, where Section 2 contains a description of each UNIX system call and Section 3 contains a description of each library procedure. UNIX also supplies on-line copies of the manual pages via the *man* command. Leffler, McKusick, Karels, and Quarterman [1989] explores the UNIX system in more detail. Hall et. al. [1993] contains the original standard for Windows Sockets, and Hall et. al. [1996] describes version 2.

Operating system vendors often provide libraries of procedures that emulate sockets on their systems. Consult vendors' programming manuals for details. Gilligan [RFC 2133] considers socket extensions for IPv6.

Volume 3 of this text describes how client and server programs are structured and how they use the socket API. The BSD sockets version of Volume 3 contains example code for Unix; the Windows sockets version contains the same examples for Microsoft Windows. The TLI version of Volume 3 provides an introduction to the *Transport Layer Interface*, an alternative to sockets used in System V UNIX.

EXERCISES

22.1   Try running the sample *whois* client and server on your local system.

22.2   Build a simple server that accepts multiple concurrent connections (to test it, have the process that handles a connection print a short message, delay a random time, print another message, and exit).

22.3   When is the *listen* call important?

22.4   What procedures does your local system provide to access the domain name system?

22.5   Devise a server that uses a single UNIX process, but handles multiple concurrent TCP connections. Hint: think of *select* (*poll* in SYSTEM V).

22.6   Read about the AT&T System V Transport Library Interface (TLI) and compare it to the socket interface. What are the major conceptual differences?

22.7   Each operating system limits the number of sockets a given program can use at any time. How many sockets can a program create on your local system?

22.8   The socket/file descriptor mechanism and associated *read* and *write* operations can be considered a form of object-oriented design. Explain why.

22.9   Consider an alternative interface design that provides an interface for every layer of protocol software (e.g., the system allows an application program to send and receive raw packets without using IP, or to send and receive IP datagrams without using UDP or TCP). What are the advantages of having such an interface? The disadvantages?

22.10 A client and server can both run on the same computer and use a TCP socket to communicate. Explain how it is possible to build a client and server that can communicate on a single machine without learning the host's IP address.

22.11 Experiment with the sample server in this chapter to see if you can generate TCP connections sufficiently fast to exceed the backlog the server specifies. Do you expect incoming connection requests to exceed the backlog faster if the server operates on a computer that has *1* processor than on a computer that has *5* processors? Explain.

23

Bootstrap And Autoconfiguration (BOOTP, DHCP)

23.1 Introduction

This chapter shows how the client-server paradigm is used for bootstrapping. Each computer attached to a TCP/IP internet needs to know its IP address before it can send or receive datagrams. In addition, a computer needs other information such as the address of a router, the subnet mask to use, and the address of a name server. Chapter 6 describes how a computer can use the RARP protocol at system startup to determine its IP address. This chapter discusses an alternative: two closely-related bootstrap protocols that each allows a host to determine its IP address without using RARP. Surprisingly, the client and server communicate using UDP, the User Datagram Protocol described in Chapter 12.

What makes the bootstrapping procedure surprising is that UDP relies on IP to transfer messages, and it might seem impossible that a computer could use UDP to find an IP address to use when communicating. Examining the protocols will help us understand how a computer can use the special IP addresses mentioned in Chapter 4 and the flexibility of the UDP/IP transport mechanism. We will also see how a server assigns an IP address to a computer automatically. Such assignment is especially important in environments that permit temporary internet connections or where computers move from one network to another (e.g., an employee with a portable computer moves from one location in a company to another).

23.2 The Need For An Alternative To RARP

Chapter 6 presents the problem diskless computers face during system startup. Such machines usually contain a startup program in nonvolatile storage (e.g., in ROM). To minimize cost and keep parts interchangeable, a vendor uses exactly the same program in all machines. Because computers with different IP addresses run the same boot program, the code cannot contain an IP address. Thus, a diskless machine must obtain its IP address from another source. In fact, a diskless computer needs to know much more than its IP address. Usually, the ROM only contains a small startup program, so the diskless computer must also obtain an initial memory image to execute. In addition, each diskless machine must determine the address of a file server on which it can store and retrieve data, and the address of the nearest IP router.

The RARP protocol of Chapter 6 has three drawbacks. First, because RARP operates at a low level, using it requires direct access to the network hardware. Thus, it may be difficult or impossible for an application programmer to build a server. Second, although RARP requires a packet exchange between a client machine and a computer that answers its request, the reply contains only one small piece of information: the client's 4-octet IP address. This drawback is especially annoying on networks like an Ethernet that enforce a minimum packet size because additional information could be sent in the response at no additional cost. Third, because RARP uses a computer's hardware address to identify the machine, it cannot be used on networks that dynamically assign hardware addresses.

To overcome some of the drawbacks of RARP, researchers developed the *BOOTstrap Protocol* (*BOOTP*). Later, the *Dynamic Host Configuration Protocol* (*DHCP*) was developed as a successor to BOOTP. Because the two protocols are closely related, most of the description in this chapter applies to both. To simplify the text, we will describe BOOTP first, and then see how DHCP extends the functionality to provide dynamic address assignment.

Because it uses UDP and IP, BOOTP can be implemented with an application program. Like RARP, BOOTP operates in the client-server paradigm and requires only a single packet exchange. However, BOOTP is more efficient than RARP because a single BOOTP message specifies many items needed at startup, including a computer's IP address, the address of a router, and the address of a server. BOOTP also includes a vendor-specific field in the reply that allows hardware vendors to send additional information used only for their computers†.

23.3 Using IP To Determine An IP Address

We said that BOOTP uses UDP to carry messages and that UDP messages are encapsulated in IP datagrams for delivery. To understand how a computer can send BOOTP in an IP datagram before the computer learns its IP address, recall from Chapter 4 that there are several special-case IP addresses. In particular, when used as a destination address, the IP address consisting of all *1*s (255.255.255.255) specifies limit-

---

†As we will see, the term ''vendor-specific'' is a misnomer because the current specification also recommends using the vendor-specific area for general purpose information such as subnet masks; DHCP changes the name of the field to *options*.

ed broadcast. IP software can accept and broadcast datagrams that specify the limited broadcast address even before the software has discovered its local IP address information. The point is that:

> An application program can use the limited broadcast IP address to force IP to broadcast a datagram on the local network before IP has discovered the IP address of the local network or the machine's IP address.

Suppose client machine *A* wants to use BOOTP to find bootstrap information (including its IP address) and suppose *B* is the server on the same physical net that will answer the request. Because *A* does not know *B*'s IP address or the IP address of the network, it must broadcast its initial BOOTP request using the IP limited broadcast address. What about the reply? Can *B* send a directed reply? No, not usually. Although it may not be obvious, *B* may need to use the limited broadcast address for its reply, even though it knows *A*'s IP address. To see why, consider what happens if an application program on *B* attempts to send a datagram using *A*'s IP address. After routing the datagram, IP software on *B* will pass the datagram to the network interface software. The interface software must map the next hop IP address to a corresponding hardware address, presumably using ARP as described in Chapter 5. However, because *A* has not yet received the BOOTP reply, it does not recognize its IP address, so it cannot answer *B*'s ARP request. Therefore, *B* has only two alternatives: either broadcast the reply or use information from the request packet to manually add an entry to its ARP cache. On systems that do not allow application programs to modify the ARP cache, broadcasting is the only solution.

23.4 The BOOTP Retransmission Policy

BOOTP places all responsibility for reliable communication on the client. We know that because UDP uses IP for delivery, messages can be delayed, lost, delivered out of order, or duplicated. Furthermore, because IP does not provide a checksum for data, the UDP datagram could arrive with some bits corrupted. To guard against corruption, BOOTP requires that UDP use checksums. It also specifies that requests and replies should be sent with the *do not fragment* bit set to accommodate clients that have too little memory to reassemble datagrams. BOOTP is also constructed to allow multiple replies; it accepts and processes the first.

To handle datagram loss, BOOTP uses the conventional technique of *timeout and retransmission*. When the client transmits a request, it starts a timer. If no reply arrives before the timer expires, the client must retransmit the request. Of course, after a power failure all machines on a network will reboot simultaneously, possibly overrunning the BOOTP server(s) with requests. If all clients use exactly the same retransmission timeout, many or all of them will attempt to retransmit simultaneously. To avoid the resulting collisions, the BOOTP specification recommends using a random delay. In addition, the specification recommends starting with a random timeout value between *0* and *4* seconds, and doubling the timer after each retransmission. After the timer reaches a large value, *60* seconds, the client does not increase the timer, but continues to use randomization. Doubling the timeout after each retransmission keeps BOOTP from adding excessive traffic to a congested network; the randomization helps avoid simultaneous transmissions.

23.5 The BOOTP Message Format

To keep an implementation as simple as possible, BOOTP messages have fixed-length fields, and replies have the same format as requests. Although we said that clients and servers are programs, the BOOTP protocol uses the terms loosely, referring to the machine that sends a BOOTP request as the *client* and any machine that sends a reply as a *server*. Figure 23.1 shows the BOOTP message format.

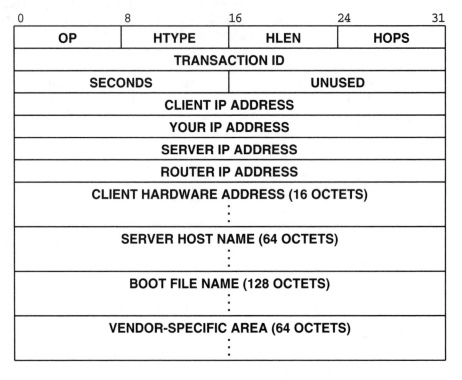

Figure 23.1 The format of a BOOTP message. To keep implementations small enough to fit in ROM, all fields have fixed length.

Field *OP* specifies whether the message is a request (*1*) or a reply (*2*). As in ARP, fields *HTYPE* and *HLEN* specify the network hardware type and length of the hardware address (e.g., Ethernet has type *1* and address length *6*)†. The client places *0* in the *HOPS* field. If it receives the request and decides to pass the request on to another machine (e.g., to allow bootstrapping across multiple routers), the BOOTP server increments the *HOPS* count. The *TRANSACTION ID* field contains an integer that diskless machines use to match responses with requests. The *SECONDS* field reports the number of seconds since the client started to boot.

The *CLIENT IP ADDRESS* field and all fields following it contain the most important information. To allow the greatest flexibility, clients fill in as much information as they know and leave remaining fields set to zero. For example, if a client knows the name or address of a specific server from which it wants information, it can fill in the *SERVER IP ADDRESS* or *SERVER HOST NAME* fields. If these fields are nonzero, only the server with matching name/address will answer the request; if they are zero, any server that receives the request will reply.

BOOTP can be used from a client that already knows its IP address (e.g., to obtain boot file information). A client that knows its IP address places it in the *CLIENT IP ADDRESS* field; other clients use zero. If the client's IP address is zero in the request, a server returns the client's IP address in the *YOUR IP ADDRESS* field.

23.6 The Two-Step Bootstrap Procedure

BOOTP uses a two-step bootstrap procedure. It does not provide clients with a memory image — it only provides the client with information needed to obtain an image. The client then uses a second protocol (e.g., TFTP from Chapter 26) to obtain the memory image. While the two-step procedure many seem unnecessary, it allows a clean separation of configuration and storage. A BOOTP server does not need to run on the same machine that stores memory images. In fact, the BOOTP server operates from a simple database that only knows the names of memory images.

Keeping configuration separate from storage is important because it allows administrators to configure sets of machines so they act identically or independently. The *BOOT FILE NAME* field of a BOOTP message illustrates the concept. Suppose an administrator has several workstations with different hardware architectures, and suppose that when users boot one of the workstations, they either choose to run UNIX or a local operating system. Because the set of workstations includes multiple hardware architectures, no single memory image will operate on all machines. To accommodate such diversity, BOOTP allows the *BOOT FILE NAME* field in a request to contain a generic name like "unix," which means, "I want to boot the UNIX operating system for this machine." The BOOTP server consults its configuration database to map the generic name into a specific file name that contains the UNIX memory image appropriate for the client hardware, and returns the specific (i.e., fully qualified) name in its reply. Of course, the configuration database also allows completely automatic bootstrapping in which the client places zeros in the *BOOT FILE NAME* field, and BOOTP selects a

---

†Values for the *HTYPE* field can be found in the latest Assigned Numbers RFC.

memory image for the machine. The advantage of the automatic approach is that it allows users to specify generic names that work on any machine; they do not need to remember specific file names or hardware architectures.

23.7 Vendor-Specific Field

The *VENDOR-SPECIFIC AREA* contains optional information to be passed from the server to the client. Although the syntax is intricate, it is not difficult. The first four octets of the field are called a *magic cookie* and define the format of remaining items; the standard format described here uses a magic cookie value of 99.130.83.99 (dotted decimal notation). A list of items follows the cookie, where each item contains a one-octet *type*, an optional one-octet *length*, and a multi-octet *value*†. The standard defines the following types that have predetermined, fixed length values:

Item Type	Item Code	Value Length	Contents of Value
Padding	0	-	Zero - used only for padding
Subnet Mask	1	4	Subnet mask for local net
Time of Day	2	4	Time of day in universal time
End	255	-	End of item list

Figure 23.2 Items in the vendor information. The length field must exist for types *1* and *2*; it must not exist for types *0* and *255*.

Although a computer can obtain subnet mask information with an ICMP request, the standard now recommends that BOOTP servers supply the subnet mask in each reply to eliminate unnecessary ICMP messages.

Additional items in the *VENDOR-SPECIFIC AREA* all use a TLV encoding — each item has a *type* octet, *length* octet, and a *value*. Figure 23.3 lists the possibilities.

23.8 The Need For Dynamic Configuration

BOOTP was designed for a relatively static environment in which each host has a permanent network connection. A manager creates a BOOTP configuration file that specifies a set of BOOTP parameters for each host. The file does not change frequently because the configuration usually remains stable. Typically, a configuration continues unchanged for weeks.

With the advent of wireless networking and portable computers such as laptops and notebooks, it has become possible to move a computer from one location to another quickly and easily. BOOTP does not adapt to such situations because configuration information cannot be changed quickly. BOOTP only provides a static mapping from a host identifier to parameters for the host. Furthermore, a manager must enter a set of

---

†The format is an example of *TLV* encoding, which stands for *Type Length Value*.

Item Type	Item Code	Length Octet	Contents of Value
Routers	3	N	IP addresses of N/4 routers
Time Server	4	N	IP addresses of N/4 time servers
IEN116 Server	5	N	IP addresses of N/4 IEN116 servers
Domain Server	6	N	IP addresses of N/4 DNS servers
Log Server	7	N	IP addresses of N/4 log servers
Quote Server	8	N	IP addresses of N/4 quote servers
Lpr Servers	9	N	IP addresses of N/4 lpr servers
Impress	10	N	IP addresses of N/4 Impress servers
RLP Server	11	N	IP addresses of N/4 RLP servers
Hostname	12	N	N bytes of client host name
Boot Size	13	2	2-octet integer size of boot file
RESERVED	128-254	-	Reserved for site specific use

Figure 23.3 Types and contents of items in the *VENDOR-SPECIFIC AREA* of a BOOTP reply that have variable lengths.

parameters for each host, and then store the information in a BOOTP server configuration file — BOOTP does not include a way to dynamically assign values to individual machines. In particular, a manager must assign each host an IP address, and must configure the server so it understands the mapping from host identifier to IP address.

Static parameter assignment works well if computers remain at fixed locations and a manager has sufficient IP addresses to assign each computer a unique IP address. However, in cases where computers move frequently or the number of physical computers exceeds the number of available IP host addresses, static assignment incurs excessive overhead.

To understand how the number of computers can exceed the number of available IP addresses, consider a LAN in a college laboratory that has been assigned a /24 address that allows up to 254 hosts. Assume that because the laboratory only has seats for 30 students, the college schedules labs at ten different times during the week to accommodate up to 300 students. Further assume that each student carries a personal notebook computer that they use in the lab. At any given time, the net has at most 30 active computers. However, because the network address can accommodate at most 254 hosts, a manager cannot assign a unique address to each computer. Thus, although resources such as physical connections limit the number of simultaneous connections, the number of potential computers that can use the facility is high. Clearly, a system is inadequate if it requires a manager to change the server's configuration file before a new computer can be added to the network and begin to communicate; an automated mechanism is needed.

23.9 Dynamic Host Configuration

To handle automated address assignment, the IETF has designed a new protocol. Known as the *Dynamic Host Configuration Protocol* (*DHCP*), the new protocol extends BOOTP in two ways. First, DHCP allows a computer to acquire all the configuration information it needs in a single message. For example, in addition to an IP address, a DHCP message can contain a subnet mask. Second, DHCP allows a computer to obtain an IP address quickly and dynamically. To use DHCP's dynamic address allocation mechanism, a manager must configure a DHCP server by supplying a set of IP addresses. Whenever a new computer connects to the network, the new computer contacts the server and requests an address. The server chooses one of the addresses the manager specified, and allocates that address to the computer.

To be completely general, DHCP allows three types of address assignment; a manager chooses how DHCP will respond for each network or for each host. Like BOOTP, DHCP allows *manual configuration* in which a manager can configure a specific address for a specific computer. DHCP also permits *automatic configuration* in which a manager allows a DHCP server to assign a permanent address when a computer first attaches to the network. Finally, DHCP permits completely *dynamic configuration* in which a server ''loans'' an address to a computer for a limited time.

Like BOOTP, DHCP uses the identity of the client to decide how to proceed. When a client contacts a DHCP server, the client sends an identifier, usually the client's hardware address. The server uses the client's identifier and the network to which the client has connected to determine how to assign the client and IP address. Thus, a manager has complete control over how addresses are assigned. A server can be configured to allocate addresses to specific computers statically (like BOOTP), while allowing other computers to obtain permanent or temporary addresses dynamically.

23.10 Dynamic IP Address Assignment

Dynamic address assignment is the most significant and novel aspect of DHCP. Unlike the static address assignment used in BOOTP, dynamic address assignment is not a one-to-one mapping, and the server does not need to know the identity of a client *a priori*. In particular, a DHCP server can be configured to permit an arbitrary computer to obtain an IP address and begin communicating. Thus, DHCP makes it possible to design systems that autoconfigure. After such a computer has been attached to a network, the computer uses DHCP to obtain an IP address, and then configures its TCP/IP software to use the address. Of course, autoconfiguration is subject to administrative restrictions — a manager decides whether each DHCP server allows autoconfiguration. To summarize:

> *Because it allows a host to obtain all the parameters needed for communication without manual intervention, DHCP permits autoconfiguration. Autoconfiguration is, of course, subject to administrative constraints.*

To make autoconfiguration possible, a DHCP server begins with a set of IP addresses that the network administrator gives the server to manage. The administrator specifies the rules by which the server operates. A DHCP client negotiates use of an address by exchanging messages with a server. In the exchange, the server provides an address for the client, and the client verifies that it accepts the address. Once a client has accepted an address, it can begin to use that address for communication.

Unlike static address assignment, which permanently allocates each IP address to a specific host, dynamic address assignment is temporary. We say that a DHCP server *leases* an address to a client for a finite period of time. The server specifies the lease period when it allocates the address. During the lease period, the server will not lease the same address to another client. At the end of the lease period, however, the client must renew the lease or stop using the address.

How long should a DHCP lease last? The optimal time for a lease depends on the particular network and the needs of a particular host. For example, to guarantee that addresses can be recycled quickly, computers on a network used by students in a university laboratory might have a short lease period (e.g., one hour). By contrast, a corporate network might use a lease period of one day or one week. To accommodate all possible environments, DHCP does not specify a fixed constant for the lease period. Instead, the protocol allows a client to request a specific lease period, and allows a server to inform the client of the lease period it grants. Thus, a manager can decide how long each server should allocate an address to a client. In the extreme, DHCP reserves a value for *infinity* to permit a lease to last arbitrarily long like the permanent address assignments used in BOOTP.

23.11 Obtaining Multiple Addresses

A multi-homed computer connects to more than one network. When such a computer boots, it may need to obtain configuration information for each of its interfaces. Like a BOOTP message, a DHCP message only provides information about one interface. A computer with multiple interfaces must handle each interface separately. Thus, although we will describe DHCP as if a computer needs only one address, the reader must remember that each interface of a multi-homed computer may be at a different point in the protocol.

Both BOOTP and DHCP use the notion of *relay agent* to permit a computer to contact a server on a nonlocal network. When a relay agent receives a broadcast request from a client, it forwards the request to a server and then returns the reply from the server to the host. Relay agents can complicate multi-homed configuration because a server may receive multiple requests from the same computer. However, although both BOOTP and DHCP use the term *client identifier*, we assume that a multihomed client sends a value that identifies a particular interface (e.g., a unique hardware address). Thus, a server will always be able to distinguish among requests from a multi-homed host, even when the server receives such requests via a relay agent.

23.12 Address Acquisition States

When it uses DHCP to obtain an IP address, a client is in one of six states. The state transition diagram in Figure 23.4 shows events and messages that cause a client to change state.

When a client first boots, it enters the *INITIALIZE* state. To start acquiring an IP address, the client first contacts all DHCP servers in the local net. To do so, the client broadcasts a *DHCPDISCOVER* message and moves to the state labeled *SELECT*. Because the protocol is an extension of BOOTP, the client sends the *DHCPDISCOVER* message in a UDP datagram with the destination port set to the BOOTP port (i.e., port *67*). All DHCP servers on the local net receive the message, and those servers that have been programmed to respond to the particular client send a *DHCPOFFER* message. Thus, a client may receive zero or more responses.

While in state *SELECT*, the client collects *DHCPOFFER* responses from DHCP servers. Each offer contains configuration information for the client along with an IP address that the server is offering to lease to the client. The client must choose one of the responses (e.g., the first to arrive), and negotiate with the server for a lease. To do so, the client sends the server a *DHCPREQUEST* message, and enters the *REQUEST* state. To acknowledge receipt of the request and start the lease, the server responds by sending a *DHCPACK*. Arrival of the acknowledgement causes the client to move to the *BOUND* state, where the client proceeds to use the address. To summarize:

> To use DHCP, a host becomes a client by broadcasting a message to all servers on the local network. The host then collects offers from servers, selects one of the offers, and verifies acceptance with the server.

23.13 Early Lease Termination

We think of the *BOUND* state as the normal state of operation; a client typically remains in the *BOUND* state while it uses the IP address it has acquired. If a client has secondary storage (e.g., a local disk), the client can store the IP address it was assigned, and request the same address when it restarts again. In some cases, however, a client in the *BOUND* state may discover it no longer needs an IP address. For example, suppose a user attaches a portable computer to a network, uses DHCP to acquire an IP address, and then uses TCP/IP to read electronic mail. The user may not know how long reading mail will require, or the portable computer may allow the server to choose a lease period. In any case, DHCP specifies a minimum lease period of one hour. If after obtaining an IP address, the user discovers that no e-mail messages are waiting to be read, the user may choose to shutdown the portable computer and move to another location.

When it no longer needs a lease, DHCP allows a client to terminate a lease without waiting for the lease to expire. Such termination is helpful in cases where neither the client nor the server can determine an appropriate lease duration at the time the lease is

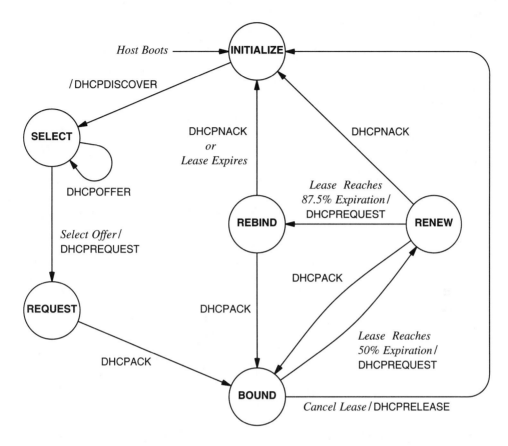

Figure 23.4 The six main states of a DHCP client and transitions among
them. Each label on a transition lists the incoming message or
event that causes the transmission, followed by a slash and the
message the client sends.

granted because it allows a server to choose a reasonably long lease period. Early termination is especially important if the number of IP addresses a server has available is
much smaller than the number of computers that attach to the network. If each client
terminates its lease as soon as the IP address is no longer needed, the server will be able
to assign the address to another client.

　　To terminate a lease early, a client sends a *DHCPRELEASE* message to the server.
Releasing an address is a final action that prevents the client from using the address
further. Thus, after transmitting the release message, the client must not send any other
datagrams that use the address. In terms of the state transition diagram of Figure 23.4,
a host that sends a *DHCPRELEASE* leaves the *BOUND* state, and must start at the *INI-
TIALIZE* state again before it can use IP.

23.14 Lease Renewal States

We said that when it acquires an address, a DHCP client moves to the *BOUND* state. Upon entering the *BOUND* state, the client sets three timers that control lease renewal, rebinding, and expiration. A DHCP server can specify explicit values for the timers when it allocates an address to the client; if the server does not specify timer values, the client uses defaults. The default value for the first timer is one-half of the total lease time. When the first timer expires, the client must attempt to renew its lease. To request a renewal, the client sends a *DHCPREQUEST* message to the server form which the lease was obtained. The client then moves to the *RENEW* state to await a response. The *DHCPREQUEST* contains the IP address the client is currently using, and asks the server to extend the lease on the address. As in the initial lease negotiation, a client can request a period for the extension, but the server ultimately controls the renewal. A server can respond to a client's renewal request in one of two ways: it can instruct the client to stop using the address or it can approve continued use. If it approves, the server sends a *DHCPACK*, which causes the client to return to the *BOUND* state and continue using the address. The *DHCPACK* can also contain new values for the client's timers. If a server disapproves of continued use, the server sends a *DHCPNACK* (negative acknowledgement), which causes the client to stop using the address immediately and return to the *INITIALIZE* state.

After sending a *DHCPREQUEST* message that requests an extension on its lease, a client remains in state *RENEW* awaiting a response. If no response arrives, the server that granted the lease is either down or unreachable. To handle the situation, DHCP relies on a second timer, which was set when the client entered the *BOUND* state. The second timer expires after *87.5%* of the lease period, and causes the client to move from state *RENEW* to state *REBIND*. When making the transition, the client assumes the old DHCP server is unavailable, and begins broadcasting a *DHCPREQUEST* message to any server on the local net. Any server configured to provide service to the client can respond positively (i.e., to extend the lease), or negatively (i.e. to deny further use of the IP address). If it receives a positive response, the client returns to the *BOUND* state, and resets the two timers. If it receives a negative response, the client must move to the *INITIALIZE* state, must immediately stop using the IP address, and must acquire a new IP address before it can continue to use IP.

After moving to the *REBIND* state, a client will have asked the original server plus all servers on the local net for a lease extension. In the rare case that a client does not receive a response from any server before its third timer expires, the lease expires. The client must stop using the IP address, must move back to the *INITIALIZE* state, and begin acquiring a new address.

23.15 DHCP Message Format

As Figure 23.5 illustrates, DHCP uses the BOOTP message format, but modifies the contents and meanings of some fields.

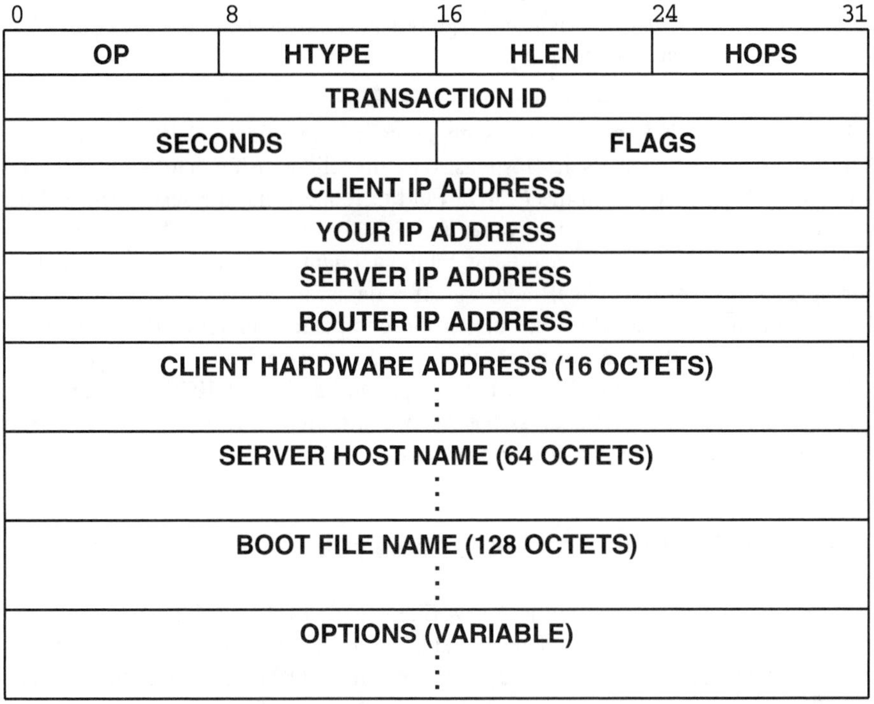

| 0 | 8 | 16 | 24 | 31 |

OP	HTYPE	HLEN	HOPS
TRANSACTION ID			
SECONDS		FLAGS	
CLIENT IP ADDRESS			
YOUR IP ADDRESS			
SERVER IP ADDRESS			
ROUTER IP ADDRESS			
CLIENT HARDWARE ADDRESS (16 OCTETS)			
SERVER HOST NAME (64 OCTETS)			
BOOT FILE NAME (128 OCTETS)			
OPTIONS (VARIABLE)			

Figure 23.5 The format of a DHCP message, which is an extension of a BOOTP message. The options field is variable length; a client must be prepared to accept at least 312 octets of options.

As the figure shows, most of the fields in a DHCP message are identical to fields in a BOOTP message. In fact, the two protocols are compatible; a DHCP server can be programmed to answer BOOTP requests. However, DHCP changes the meaning of two fields. First, DHCP interprets BOOTP's *UNUSED* field as a 16-bit *FLAGS* field. In fact, Figure 23.6 shows that only the high-order bit of the *FLAGS* field has been assigned a meaning.

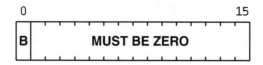

Figure 23.6 The format of the 16-bit *FLAGS* field in a DHCP message. The leftmost bit is interpreted as a broadcast request; all others bits must be set to zero.

Because the DHCP request message contains the client's hardware address, a DHCP server normally sends its responses to the client using hardware unicast. A client sets the high-order bit in the *FLAGS* field to request that the server respond using hardware broadcast instead of hardware unicast. To understand why a client might choose a broadcast response, recall that while a client communicates with a DHCP server, it does not yet have an IP address. If a datagram arrives via hardware unicast and the destination address does not match the computer's address, IP can discard the datagram. However, IP is required to accept and handle any datagram sent to the IP broadcast address. To ensure IP software accepts and delivers DHCP messages that arrive before the machine's IP address has been configured, a DHCP client can request that the server send responses using IP broadcast.

23.16 DHCP Options And Message Type

Surprisingly, DHCP does not add new fixed fields to the BOOTP message format, nor does it change the meaning of most fields. For example, the *OP* field in a DHCP message contains the same values as the *OP* field in a BOOTP message: the message is either a boot request (*1*) or a boot reply (*2*). To encode information such as the lease duration, DHCP uses *options*. In particular, Figure 23.7 illustrates the *DHCP message type* option used to specify which DHCP message is being sent.

The options field has the same format as the *VENDOR SPECIFIC AREA*, and DHCP honors all the vendor specific information items defined for BOOTP. As in BOOTP, each option consists of a 1-octet code field and a 1-octet length field followed by octets of data that comprise the option. As the figure shows, the option used to specify a DHCP message type consists of exactly three octets. The first octet contains the code *53*, the second contains the length *1*, and the third contains a value used to identify one of the possible DHCP messages.

```
0                    8                   16                  23
┌─────────────────┬─────────────────┬─────────────────┐
│   CODE (53)     │   LENGTH (1)    │   TYPE (1 - 7)  │
└─────────────────┴─────────────────┴─────────────────┘
```

TYPE FIELD	Corresponding DHCP Message Type
1	DHCPDISCOVER
2	DHCPOFFER
3	DHCPREQUEST
4	DHCPDECLINE
5	DHCPACK
6	DHCPNACK
7	DHCPRELEASE

Figure 23.7 The format of a DHCP message type option used to specify the DHCP message being sent. The table lists possible values of the third octet and their meaning.

23.17 Option Overload

Fields *SERVER HOST NAME* and *BOOT FILE NAME* in the DHCP message header each occupy many octets. If a given message does not contain information in either of those fields, the space is wasted. To allow a DHCP server to use the two fields for other options, DHCP defines an *Option Overload* option. When present, the overload option tells a receiver to ignore the usual meaning of the *SERVER HOST NAME* and *BOOT FILE NAME* fields, and look for options in the fields instead.

23.18 DHCP And Domain Names†

Although it can allocate an IP address to a computer on demand, DHCP does not completely automate all the procedures required to attach a permanent host to an internet. In particular, DHCP does not interact with the domain name system. Thus, the binding between a host name and the IP address DHCP assigns the host must be managed independently.

What name should a host receive when it obtains an IP address from DHCP? Conceptually, there are three possibilities. First, the host does not receive a name. Although it is possible to run client software on a host without a name, using an unnamed computer can be inconvenient. Second, the host is automatically assigned a name along with an IP address. This method is currently popular because names can be preallocated, and no change is required to the DNS. For example, a system administrator can configure the local domain name server to have a host name for each IP address DHCP manages. Once it has been installed in DNS, the name-to-address binding

---

†Chapter 24 considers the Domain Name System in detail.

remains static. The chief disadvantage of a static binding is that the host receives a new name whenever it receives a new address (e.g., if a host moves from one physical net to another). Third, the host can be assigned a permanent name that remains unchanged. Keeping a permanent host name is convenient because the computer can always be reached via one name, independent of the computer's current location.

Additional mechanisms are needed to support permanent host names. In particular, permanent host names require coordination between DHCP and DNS. A DNS server must change the name-to-address binding whenever a host receives an IP address, and must remove the binding when a lease expires. Although, an IETF working group is currently considering how DHCP should interact with the domain name system, there is currently no protocol for dynamic DNS update. Thus, until a dynamic update mechanism is developed, there is no protocol that maintains permanent host names while allowing DHCP to change IP addresses.

23.19 Summary

The BOOTstrap Protocol, BOOTP, provides an alternative to RARP for a computer that needs to determine its IP address. BOOTP is more general than RARP because it uses UDP, making it possible to extend bootstrapping across a router. BOOTP also allows a machine to determine a router address, a (file) server address, and the name of a program the computer should run. Finally, BOOTP allows administrators to establish a configuration database that maps a generic name, like ''unix,'' into the fully qualified file name that contains a memory image appropriate for the client hardware.

BOOTP is designed to be small and simple enough to reside in a bootstrap ROM. The client uses the limited broadcast address to communicate with the server, and takes responsibility for retransmitting requests if the server does not respond. Retransmission uses an exponential backoff policy similar to Ethernet to avoid congestion.

Designed as a successor to BOOTP, the Dynamic Host Configuration Protocol (DHCP) extends BOOTP in several ways. Most important, DHCP permits a server to allocate IP addresses automatically or dynamically. Dynamic allocation is necessary for environments such as a wireless network where computers can attach and detach quickly. To use DHCP, a computer becomes a client. The computer broadcasts a request for DHCP servers, selects one of the offers it receives, and exchanges messages with the server to obtain a lease on the advertised IP address.

When a client obtains an IP address, the client starts three timers. After the first timer expires, the client attempts to renew its lease. If a second timer expires before renewal completes, the client attempts to rebind its address from any server. If the final timer expires before a lease has been renewed, the client stops using the IP address and returns to the initial state to acquire a new address. A finite state machine explains lease acquisition and renewal.

FOR FURTHER STUDY

BOOTP is a standard protocol in the TCP/IP suite. Further details can be found in Croft and Gilmore [RFC 951], which compares BOOTP to RARP and serves as the official standard. Reynolds [RFC 1084] tells how to interpret the vendor-specific area, and Braden [RFC 1123] recommends using the vendor-specific area to pass the subnet mask.

Droms [RFC 2131] contains the specification for DHCP, including a detailed description of state transitions; another revision is expected soon. A related document, Alexander and Droms [RFC 2132], specifies the encoding of DHCP options and BOOTP vendor extensions. Finally, Droms [RFC 1534] discusses the interoperability of BOOTP and DHCP.

EXERCISES

23.1 BOOTP does not contain an explicit field for returning the time of day from the server to the client, but makes it part of the (optional) vendor-specific information. Should the time be included in the required fields? Why or why not?

23.2 Argue that separation of configuration and storage of memory images is *not* good. (See RFC 951 for hints.)

23.3 The BOOTP message format is inconsistent because it has two fields for client IP address and one for the name of the boot image. If the client leaves its IP address field empty, the server returns the client's IP address in the second field. If the client leaves the boot file name field empty, the server *replaces* it with an explicit name. Why?

23.4 Read the standard to find out how clients and servers use the *HOPS* field.

23.5 When a BOOTP client receives a reply via hardware broadcast, how does it know whether the reply is intended for another BOOTP client on the same physical net?

23.6 When a machine obtains its subnet mask with BOOTP instead of ICMP, it places less load on *other* host computers. Explain.

23.7 Read the standard to find out how a DHCP client and server can agree on a lease duration without having synchronized clocks.

23.8 Consider a host that has a disk and uses DHCP to obtain an IP address. If the host stores its address on disk along with the date the lease expires, and then reboots within the lease period, can it use the address? Why or why not?

23.9 DHCP mandates a minimum address lease of one hour. Can you imagine a situation in which DHCP's minimum lease causes inconvenience? Explain.

23.10 Read the RFC to find out how DHCP specifies renewal and rebinding timers. Should a server ever set one without the other? Why or why not?

23.11 The state transition diagram does not show retransmission. Read the standard to find out how many times a client should retransmit a request.

23.12   Can DHCP guarantee that a client is not ''spoofing'' (i.e., can DHCP guarantee that it will not send configuration information for host *A* to host *B*)? Does the answer differ for BOOTP? Why or why not?

23.13   DHCP specifies that a client must be prepared to handle at least *312* octets of options. How did the number *312* arise?

23.14   Can a computer that uses DHCP to obtain an IP address operate a server? If so, how does a client reach the server?

24

The Domain Name System (DNS)

24.1 Introduction

The protocols described in earlier chapters use 32-bit integers called Internet Protocol addresses (IP addresses) to identify machines. Although such addresses provide a convenient, compact representation for specifying the source and destination in packets sent across an internet, users prefer to assign machines pronounceable, easily remembered names.

This chapter considers a scheme for assigning meaningful high-level names to a large set of machines, and discusses a mechanism that maps between high-level machine names and IP addresses. It considers both the translation from high-level names to IP addresses and the translation from IP addresses to high-level machine names. The naming scheme is interesting for two reasons. First, it has been used to assign machine names throughout the global Internet. Second, because it uses a geographically distributed set of servers to map names to addresses, the implementation of the name mapping mechanism provides a large scale example of the client-server paradigm described in Chapter 21.

24.2 Names For Machines

The earliest computer systems forced users to understand numeric addresses for objects like system tables and peripheral devices. Timesharing systems advanced computing by allowing users to invent meaningful symbolic names for both physical objects (e.g., peripheral devices) and abstract objects (e.g., files). A similar pattern has emerged in computer networking. Early systems supported point-to-point connections between computers and used low-level hardware addresses to specify machines. Internetworking introduced universal addressing as well as protocol software to map universal addresses into low-level hardware addresses. Because most computing environments contain multiple machines, users need meaningful, symbolic names to identify them.

Early machine names reflected the small environment in which they were chosen. It was quite common for a site with a handful of machines to choose names based on the machines' purposes. For example, machines often had names like *research*, *production*, *accounting*, and *development*. Users find such names preferable to cumbersome hardware addresses.

Although the distinction between *address* and *name* is intuitively appealing, it is artificial. Any *name* is merely an identifier that consists of a sequence of characters chosen from a finite alphabet. Names are only useful if the system can efficiently map them to the object they denote. Thus, we think of an IP address as a *low-level name*, and we say that users prefer *high-level names* for machines.

The form of high-level names is important because it determines how names are translated to low-level names or bound to objects, as well as how name assignments are authorized. When only a few machines interconnect, choosing names is easy, and any form will suffice. On the Internet, to which approximately one hundred million machines connect, choosing symbolic names becomes difficult. For example, when its main departmental computer was connected to the Internet in 1980, the Computer Science Department at Purdue University chose the name *purdue* to identify the connected machine. The list of potential conflicts contained only a few dozen names. By mid 1986, the official list of hosts on the Internet contained 3100 officially registered names and 6500 official aliases†. Although the list was growing rapidly in the 1980s, most sites had additional machines (e.g., personal computers) that were not registered.

24.3 Flat Namespace

The original set of machine names used throughout the Internet formed a *flat namespace* in which each name consisted of a sequence of characters without any further structure. In the original scheme, a central site, the Network Information Center (*NIC*), administered the namespace and determined whether a new name was appropriate (i.e., it prohibited obscene names or new names that conflicted with existing names).

The chief advantage of a flat namespace is that names are convenient and short; the chief disadvantage is that a flat namespace cannot generalize to large sets of machines for both technical and administrative reasons. First, because names are drawn from a

---

†By 1990, more than 137,000 Internet hosts had names, and by 2000 the number exceeded 60 million.

single set of identifiers, the potential for conflict increases as the number of sites increases. Second, because authority for adding new names must rest at a single site, the administrative workload at that central site also increases with the number of sites. To understand the severity of the problem, imagine a rapidly growing internet with thousands of sites, each of which has hundreds of individual personal computers and workstations. Every time someone acquires and connects a new personal computer, its name must be approved by the central authority. Third, because the name-to-address bindings change frequently, the cost of maintaining correct copies of the entire list at each site is high and increases as the number of sites increases. Alternatively, if the name database resides at a single site, network traffic to that site increases with the number of sites.

24.4 Hierarchical Names

How can a naming system accommodate a large, rapidly expanding set of names without requiring a central site to administer it? The answer lies in decentralizing the naming mechanism by delegating authority for parts of the namespace and distributing responsibility for the mapping between names and addresses. TCP/IP internets use such a scheme. Before examining the details of the TCP/IP scheme, we will consider the motivation and intuition behind it.

The partitioning of a namespace must be defined in a way that supports efficient name mapping and guarantees autonomous control of name assignment. Optimizing only for efficient mapping can lead to solutions that retain a flat namespace and reduce traffic by dividing the names among multiple mapping machines. Optimizing only for administrative ease can lead to solutions that make delegation of authority easy but name mapping expensive or complex.

To understand how the namespace should be divided, consider the internal structure of large organizations. At the top, a chief executive has overall responsibility. Because the chief executive cannot oversee everything, the organization may be partitioned into divisions, with an executive in charge of each division. The chief executive grants each division autonomy within specified limits. More to the point, the executive in charge of a particular division can hire or fire employees, assign offices, and delegate authority, without obtaining direct permission from the chief executive.

Besides making it easy to delegate authority, the hierarchy of a large organization introduces autonomous operation. For example, when an office worker needs information like the telephone number of a new employee, he or she begins by asking local clerical workers (who may contact clerical workers in other divisions). The point is that although authority always passes down the corporate hierarchy, information can flow across the hierarchy from one office to another.

24.5 Delegation Of Authority For Names

A hierarchical naming scheme works like the management of a large organization. The namespace is *partitioned* at the top level, and authority for names in subdivisions is passed to designated agents. For example, one might choose to partition the namespace based on *site name* and to delegate to each site responsibility for maintaining names within its partition. The topmost level of the hierarchy divides the namespace and delegates authority for each division; it need not be bothered by changes within a division.

The syntax of hierarchically assigned names often reflects the hierarchical delegation of authority used to assign them. As an example, consider a namespace with names of the form:

local . site

where *site* is the site name authorized by the central authority, *local* is the part of a name controlled by the site, and the period† (".") is a delimiter used to separate them. When the topmost authority approves adding a new site, X, it adds X to the list of valid sites and delegates to site X authority for all names that end in "*.X*".

24.6 Subset Authority

In a hierarchical namespace, authority may be further subdivided at each level. In our example of partition by sites, the site itself may consist of several administrative groups, and the site authority may choose to subdivide its namespace among the groups. The idea is to keep subdividing the namespace until each subdivision is small enough to be manageable.

Syntactically, subdividing the namespace introduces another partition of the name. For example, adding a *group* subdivision to names already partitioned by site produces the following name syntax:

local . group . site

Because the topmost level delegates authority, group names do not have to agree among all sites. A university site might choose group names like *engineering*, *science*, and *arts*, while a corporate site might choose group names like *production*, *accounting*, and *personnel*.

The U.S. telephone system provides another example of a hierarchical naming syntax. The 10 digits of a phone number have been partitioned into a 3-digit *area code*, 3-digit *exchange*, and 4-digit *subscriber number* within the exchange. Each exchange has authority for assigning subscriber numbers within its piece of the namespace. Although it is possible to group arbitrary subscribers into exchanges and to group arbitrary exchanges into area codes, the assignment of telephone numbers is not capricious; they are carefully chosen to make it easy to route phone calls across the telephone network.

---

†In domain names, the period delimiter is pronounced "dot."

The telephone example is important because it illustrates a key distinction between the hierarchical naming scheme used in a TCP/IP internet and other hierarchies: partitioning the set of machines owned by an organization along lines of authority does not necessarily imply partitioning by physical location. For example, it could be that at some university, a single building houses the mathematics department as well as the computer science department. It might even turn out that although the machines from these two groups fall under completely separate administrative domains, they connect to the same physical network. It also may happen that a single group owns machines on several physical networks. For these reasons, the TCP/IP naming scheme allows arbitrary delegation of authority for the hierarchical namespace without regard to physical connections. The concept can be summarized:

> In a TCP/IP internet, hierarchical machine names are assigned according to the structure of organizations that obtain authority for parts of the namespace, not necessarily according to the structure of the physical network interconnections.

Of course, at many sites the organizational hierarchy corresponds with the structure of physical network interconnections. At a large university, for example, most departments have their own local area network. If the department is assigned part of the naming hierarchy, all machines that have names in its part of the hierarchy will also connect to a single physical network.

24.7 Internet Domain Names

The mechanism that implements a machine name hierarchy for TCP/IP internets is called the *Domain Name System (DNS)*. DNS has two, conceptually independent aspects. The first is abstract: it specifies the name syntax and rules for delegating authority over names. The second is concrete: it specifies the implementation of a distributed computing system that efficiently maps names to addresses. This section considers the name syntax, and later sections examine the implementation.

The domain name system uses a hierarchical naming scheme known as *domain names*. As in our earlier examples, a domain name consists of a sequence of subnames separated by a delimiter character, the period. In our examples we said that individual sections of the name might represent sites or groups, but the domain system simply calls each section a *label*. Thus, the domain name

cs.purdue.edu

contains three labels: *cs, purdue*, and *edu*. Any suffix of a label in a domain name is also called a *domain*. In the above example the lowest level domain is *cs.purdue.edu*, (the domain name for the Computer Science Department at Purdue University), the second level domain is *purdue.edu* (the domain name for Purdue University), and the top-level domain is *edu* (the domain name for educational institutions). As the example shows, domain names are written with the local label first and the top domain last. As we will see, writing them in this order makes it possible to compress messages that contain multiple domain names.

24.8 Official And Unofficial Internet Domain Names

In theory, the domain name standard specifies an abstract hierarchical namespace with arbitrary values for labels. Because the domain system dictates only the form of names and not their actual values, it is possible for any group that builds an instance of the domain system to choose labels for all parts of its hierarchy. For example, a private company can establish a domain hierarchy in which the top-level labels specify corporate subsidiaries, the next level labels specify corporate divisions, and the lowest level labels specify departments.

However, most users of the domain technology follow the hierarchical labels used by the official Internet domain system. There are two reasons. First, as we will see, the Internet scheme is both comprehensive and flexible. It can accommodate a wide variety of organizations, and allows each group to choose between geographical or organizational naming hierarchies. Second, most sites follow the Internet scheme so they can attach their TCP/IP installations to the global Internet without changing names. Because the Internet naming scheme dominates almost all uses of the domain name system, examples throughout the remainder of this chapter have labels taken from the Internet naming hierarchy. Readers should remember that, although they are most likely to encounter these particular labels, the domain name system technology can be used with other labels if desired.

The Internet authority has chosen to partition its top level into the domains listed in Figure 24.1†.

Domain Name	Meaning
COM	Commercial organizations
EDU	Educational institutions (4-year)
GOV	Government institutions
MIL	Military groups
NET	Major network support centers
ORG	Organizations other than those above
ARPA	Temporary ARPANET domain (obsolete)
INT	International organizations
country code	Each country (geographic scheme)

Figure 24.1 The top-level Internet domains and their meanings. Although labels are shown in upper case, domain name system comparisons are insensitive to case, so *EDU* is equivalent to *edu*.

---

†The following additional top-level domains have been proposed, but not formally adopted: *FIRM, STORE, WEB, ARTS, REC, INFO,* and *NOM*.

Conceptually, the top-level names permit two completely different naming hierarchies: geographic and organizational. The geographic scheme divides the universe of machines by country. Machines in the United States fall under the top-level domain *US*; when a foreign country wants to register machines in the domain name system, the central authority assigns the country a new top-level domain with the country's international standard 2-letter identifier as its label. The authority for the US domain has chosen to divide it into one second-level domain per state. For example, the domain for the state of Virginia is

$$va.us$$

As an alternative to the geographic hierarchy, the top-level domains also allow organizations to be grouped by organizational type. When an organization wants to participate in the domain naming system, it chooses how it wishes to be registered and requests approval. The central authority reviews the application and assigns the organization a subdomain† under one of the existing top-level domains. For example, it is possible for a university to register itself as a second-level domain under *EDU* (the usual practice), or to register itself under the state and country in which it is located. So far, few organizations have chosen the geographic hierarchy; most prefer to register under *COM*, *EDU*, *MIL*, or *GOV*. There are two reasons. First, geographic names are longer and therefore more difficult to type. Second, geographic names are much more difficult to discover or guess. For example, Purdue University is located in West Lafayette, Indiana. While a user could easily guess an organizational name, like *purdue.edu*, a geographic name is often difficult to guess because it is usually an abbreviation, like *laf.in.us*.

Another example may help clarify the relationship between the naming hierarchy and authority for names. A machine named *xinu* in the Computer Science Department at Purdue University has the official domain name

$$xinu.cs.purdue.edu$$

The machine name was approved and registered by the local network manager in the Computer Science Department. The department manager had previously obtained authority for the subdomain *cs.purdue.edu* from a university network authority, who had obtained permission to manage the subdomain *purdue.edu* from the Internet authority. The Internet authority retains control of the *edu* domain, so new universities can only be added with its permission. Similarly, the university network manager at Purdue University retains authority for the *purdue.edu* subdomain, so new third-level domains may only be added with the manager's permission.

Figure 24.2 illustrates a small part of the Internet domain name hierarchy. As the figure shows, Digital Equipment Corporation, a commercial organization, registered as *dec.com*, Purdue University registered as *purdue.edu*, and the National Science Foundation, a government agency, registered as *nsf.gov*. In contrast, the Corporation for National Research Initiatives chose to register under the geographic hierarchy as *cnri.reston.va.us*‡.

---

†The standard does not define the term "subdomain." We have chosen to use it because its analogy to "subset" helps clarify the relationship among domains.

‡Interestingly, CNRI also registered using the name *nri.reston.va.us*.

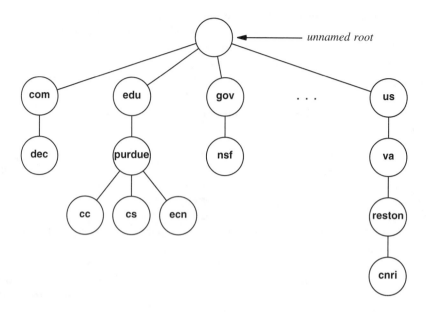

Figure 24.2 A small part of the Internet domain name hierarchy (tree). In practice, the tree is broad and flat; most host entries appear by the fifth level.

24.9 Named Items And Syntax Of Names

The domain name system is quite general because it allows multiple naming hierarchies to be embedded in one system. To allow clients to distinguish among multiple types of entries, each named item stored in the system is assigned a *type* that specifies whether it is the address of a machine, a mailbox, a user, and so on. When a client asks the domain system to resolve a name, it must specify the type of answer desired. For example, when an electronic mail application uses the domain system to resolve a name, it specifies that the answer should be the address of a *mail exchanger*. A remote login application specifies that it seeks a machine's IP address. It is important to understand the following:

> *A given name may map to more than one item in the domain system. The client specifies the type of object desired when resolving a name, and the server returns objects of that type.*

In addition to specifying the type of answer sought, the domain system allows the client to specify the protocol family to use. The domain system partitions the entire set of names by *class*, allowing a single database to store mappings for multiple protocol suites†.

---

†In practice, few domain servers use multiple protocol suites.

The syntax of a name does not determine what type of object it names or the class of protocol suite. In particular, the number of labels in a name does not determine whether the name refers to an individual object (machine) or a domain. Thus, in our example, it is possible to have a machine named

gwen.purdue.edu

even though

cs.purdue.edu

names a subdomain. We can summarize this important point:

> *One cannot distinguish the names of subdomains from the names of individual objects or the type of an object using only the domain name syntax.*

24.10 Mapping Domain Names To Addresses

In addition to the rules for name syntax and delegation of authority, the domain name scheme includes an efficient, reliable, general purpose, distributed system for mapping names to addresses. The system is distributed in the technical sense, meaning that a set of servers operating at multiple sites cooperatively solve the mapping problem. It is efficient in the sense that most names can be mapped locally; only a few require internet traffic. It is general purpose because it is not restricted to machine names (although we will use that example for now). Finally, it is reliable in that no single machine failure will prevent the system from operating correctly.

The domain mechanism for mapping names to addresses consists of independent, cooperative systems called *name servers*. A name server is a server program that supplies name-to-address translation, mapping from domain names to IP addresses. Often, server software executes on a dedicated processor, and the machine itself is called the name server. The client software, called a *name resolver*, uses one or more name servers when translating a name.

The easiest way to understand how domain servers work is to imagine them arranged in a tree structure that corresponds to the naming hierarchy, as Figure 24.3 illustrates. The root of the tree is a server that recognizes the top-level domains and knows which server resolves each domain. Given a name to resolve, the root can choose the correct server for that name. At the next level, a set of name servers each provide answers for one top-level domain (e.g., *edu*). A server at this level knows which servers can resolve each of the subdomains under its domain. At the third level of the tree, name servers provide answers for subdomains (e.g., *purdue* under *edu*). The conceptual tree continues with one server at each level for which a subdomain has been defined.

Links in the conceptual tree do not indicate physical network connections. Instead, they show which other name servers a given server knows and contacts. The servers themselves may be located at arbitrary locations on an internet. Thus, the tree of servers is an abstraction that uses an internet for communication.

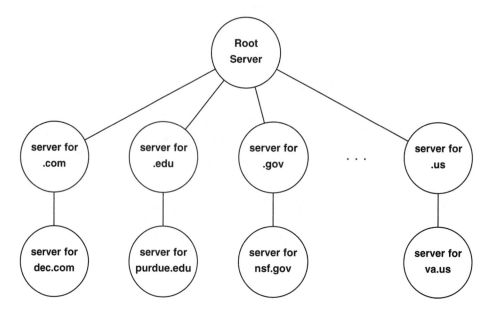

Figure 24.3 The conceptual arrangement of domain name servers in a tree that corresponds to the naming hierarchy. In theory, each server knows the addresses of all lower-level servers for all subdomains within the domain it handles.

If servers in the domain system worked exactly as our simplistic model suggests, the relationship between connectivity and authorization would be quite simple. When authority was granted for a subdomain, the organization requesting it would need to establish a domain name server for that subdomain and link it into the tree.

In practice, the relationship between the naming hierarchy and the tree of servers is not as simple as our model implies. The tree of servers has few levels because a single physical server can contain all of the information for large parts of the naming hierarchy. In particular, organizations often collect information from all of their subdomains into a single server. Figure 24.4 shows a more realistic organization of servers for the naming hierarchy of Figure 24.2.

A root server contains information about the root and top-level domains, and each organization uses a single server for its names. Because the tree of servers is shallow, at most two servers need to be contacted to resolve a name like *xinu.cs.purdue.edu*: the root server and the server for domain *purdue.edu* (i.e., the root server knows which server handles *purdue . edu*, and the entire domain information for Purdue resides in one server).

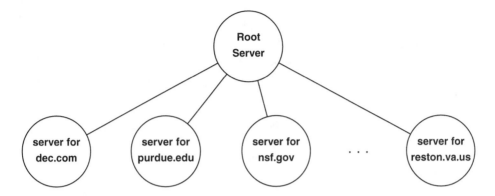

Figure 24.4 A realistic organization of servers for the naming hierarchy of Figure 24.2. Because the tree is broad and flat, few servers need to be contacted when resolving a name.

24.11 Domain Name Resolution

Although the conceptual tree makes understanding the relationship between servers easy, it hides several subtle details. Looking at the name resolution algorithm will help explain them. Conceptually, domain name resolution proceeds top-down, starting with the root name server and proceeding to servers located at the leaves of the tree. There are two ways to use the domain name system: by contacting name servers one at a time or asking the name server system to perform the complete translation. In either case, the client software forms a domain name query that contains the name to be resolved, a declaration of the class of the name, the type of answer desired, and a code that specifies whether the name server should translate the name completely. It sends the query to a name server for resolution.

When a domain name server receives a query, it checks to see if the name lies in the subdomain for which it is an authority. If so, it translates the name to an address according to its database, and appends an answer to the query before sending it back to the client. If the name server cannot resolve the name completely, it checks to see what type of interaction the client specified. If the client requested complete translation (*recursive resolution*, in domain name terminology), the server contacts a domain name server that can resolve the name and returns the answer to the client. If the client requested non-recursive resolution (*iterative resolution*), the name server cannot supply an answer. It generates a reply that specifies the name server the client should contact next to resolve the name.

How does a client find a name server at which to begin the search? How does a name server find other name servers that can answer questions when it cannot? The answers are simple. A client must know how to contact at least one name server. To ensure that a domain name server can reach others, the domain system requires that each server know the address of at least one root server†. In addition, a server may know the address of a server for the domain immediately above it (called the *parent*).

Domain name servers use a well-known protocol port for all communication, so clients know how to communicate with a server once they know the IP address of the machine in which the server executes. There is no standard way for hosts to locate a machine in the local environment on which a name server runs; that is left to whoever designs the client software‡.

In some systems, the address of the machine that supplies domain name service is bound into application programs at compile time, while in others, the address is configured into the operating system at startup. In others, the administrator places the address of a server in a file on secondary storage.

24.12 Efficient Translation

Although it may seem natural to resolve queries by working down the tree of name servers, it can lead to inefficiencies for three reasons. First, most name resolution refers to local names, those found within the same subdivision of the namespace as the machine from which the request originates. Tracing a path through the hierarchy to contact the local authority would be inefficient. Second, if each name resolution always started by contacting the topmost level of the hierarchy, the machine at that point would become overloaded. Third, failure of machines at the topmost levels of the hierarchy would prevent name resolution, even if the local authority could resolve the name. The telephone number hierarchy mentioned earlier helps explain. Although telephone numbers are assigned hierarchically, they are resolved in a bottom-up fashion. Because the majority of telephone calls are local, they can be resolved by the local exchange without searching the hierarchy. Furthermore, calls within a given area code can be resolved without contacting sites outside the area code. When applied to domain names, these ideas lead to a two-step name resolution mechanism that preserves the administrative hierarchy but permits efficient translation.

We have said that most queries to name servers refer to local names. In the two-step name resolution process, resolution begins with the local name server. If the local server cannot resolve a name, the query must then be sent to another server in the domain system.

---

†For reliability, there are multiple servers for each node in the domain server tree; the root server is further replicated to provide load balancing.

‡See BOOTP/DHCP in Chapter 23 for one possible approach.

24.13 Caching: The Key To Efficiency

The cost of lookup for nonlocal names can be extremely high if resolvers send each query to the root server. Even if queries could go directly to the server that has authority for the name, name lookup can present a heavy load to an internet. Thus, to improve the overall performance of a name server system, it is necessary to lower the cost of lookup for nonlocal names.

Internet name servers use *name caching* to optimize search costs. Each server maintains a cache of recently used names as well as a record of where the mapping information for that name was obtained. When a client asks the server to resolve a name, the server first checks to see if it has authority for the name according to the standard procedure. If not, the server checks its cache to see if the name has been resolved recently. Servers report cached information to clients, but mark it as a *nonauthoritative* binding, and give the domain name of the server, *S*, from which they obtained the binding. The local server also sends along additional information that tells the client the binding between *S* and an IP address. Therefore, clients receive answers quickly, but the information may be out-of-date. If efficiency is important, the client will choose to accept the nonauthoritative answer and proceed. If accuracy is important, the client will choose to contact the authority and verify that the binding between name and address is still valid.

Caching works well in the domain name system because name to address bindings change infrequently. However, they do change. If servers cached information the first time it was requested and never changed it, entries in the cache could become incorrect. To keep the cache correct, servers time each entry and dispose of entries that exceed a reasonable time. When the server is asked for the information after it has removed the entry from the cache, it must go back to the authoritative source and obtain the binding again. More important, servers do not apply a single fixed timeout to all entries, but allow the authority for an entry to configure its timeout. Whenever an authority responds to a request, it includes a *Time To Live* (TTL) value in the response that specifies how long it guarantees the binding to remain. Thus, authorities can reduce network overhead by specifying long timeouts for entries that they expect to remain unchanged, while improving correctness by specifying short timeouts for entries that they expect to change frequently.

Caching is important in hosts as well as in local domain name servers. Many timesharing systems run a complex form of resolver code that attempts to provide even more efficiency than the server system. The host downloads the complete database of names and addresses from a local domain name server at startup, maintains its own cache of recently used names, and uses the server only when names are not found. Naturally, a host that maintains a copy of the local server database must check with the server periodically to obtain new mappings, and the host must remove entries from its cache after they become invalid. However, most sites have little trouble maintaining consistency because domain names change so infrequently.

Keeping a copy of the local server's database in each host has several advantages. Obviously, it makes name resolution on local hosts extremely fast because it means the host can resolve names without any network activity. It also means that the local site has protection in case the local name server fails. Finally, it reduces the computational load on the name server, and makes it possible for a given server to supply names to more machines.

24.14 Domain Server Message Format

Looking at the details of messages exchanged between clients and domain name servers will help clarify how the system operates from the view of a typical application program. We assume that a user invokes an application program and supplies the name of a machine with which the application must communicate. Before it can use protocols like TCP or UDP to communicate with the specified machine, the application program must find the machine's IP address. It passes the domain name to a local resolver and requests an IP address. The local resolver checks its cache and returns the answer if one is present. If the local resolver does not have an answer, it formats a message and sends it to the server (i.e., it becomes a client). Although our example only involves one name, the message format allows a client to ask multiple questions in a single message. Each question consists of a domain name for which the client seeks an IP address, a specification of the query class (i.e., *internet*), and the type of object desired (e.g., *address*). The server responds by returning a similar message that contains answers to the questions for which the server has bindings. If the server cannot answer all questions, the response will contain information about other name servers that the client can contact to obtain the answers.

Responses also contain information about the servers that are authorities for the replies and the IP addresses of those servers. Figure 24.5 shows the message format. As the figure shows, each message begins with a fixed header. The header contains a unique *IDENTIFICATION* field that the client uses to match responses to queries, and a *PARAMETER* field that specifies the operation requested and a response code. Figure 24.6 gives the interpretation of bits in the *PARAMETER* field.

The fields labeled *NUMBER OF* each give a count of entries in the corresponding sections that occur later in the message. For example, the field labeled *NUMBER OF QUESTIONS* gives the count of entries that appear in the *QUESTION SECTION* of the message.

The *QUESTION SECTION* contains queries for which answers are desired. The client fills in only the question section; the server returns the questions and answers in its response. Each question consists of a *QUERY DOMAIN NAME* followed by *QUERY TYPE* and *QUERY CLASS* fields, as Figure 24.7 shows.

0	16	31
IDENTIFICATION		PARAMETER
NUMBER OF QUESTIONS		NUMBER OF ANSWERS
NUMBER OF AUTHORITY		NUMBER OF ADDITIONAL

QUESTION SECTION . . .
ANSWER SECTION . . .
AUTHORITY SECTION . . .
ADDITIONAL INFORMATION SECTION . . .

Figure 24.5 Domain name server message format. The question, answer, authority, and additional information sections are variable length.

Bit of PARAMETER field	Meaning
0	Operation:
	0 Query
	1 Response
1-4	Query Type:
	0 Standard
	1 Inverse
	2 Completion 1 (now obsolete)
	3 Completion 2 (now obsolete)
5	Set if answer authoritative
6	Set if message truncated
7	Set if recursion desired
8	Set if recursion available
9-11	Reserved
12-15	Response Type:
	0 No error
	1 Format error in query
	2 Server failure
	3 Name does not exist

Figure 24.6 The meaning of bits of the *PARAMETER* field in a domain name server message. Bits are numbered left to right starting at 0.

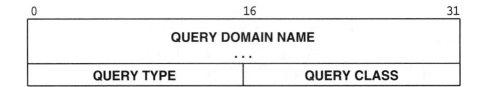

Figure 24.7 The format of entries in the *QUESTION SECTION* of a domain name server message. The domain name is variable length. Clients fill in the questions; servers return them along with answers.

Although the *QUERY DOMAIN NAME* field has variable length, we will see in the next section that the internal representation of domain names makes it possible for the receiver to know the exact length. The *QUERY TYPE* encodes the type of the question (e.g., whether the question refers to a machine name or a mail address). The *QUERY CLASS* field allows domain names to be used for arbitrary objects because official Internet names are only one possible class. It should be noted that, although the diagram in Figure 24.5 follows our convention of showing formats in 32-bit multiples, the *QUERY DOMAIN NAME* field may contain an arbitrary number of octets. No padding is used. Therefore, messages to or from domain name servers may contain an odd number of octets.

In a domain name server message, each of the *ANSWER SECTION*, *AUTHORITY SECTION*, and *ADDITIONAL INFORMATION SECTION* consists of a set of *resource records* that describe domain names and mappings. Each resource record describes one name. Figure 24.8 shows the format.

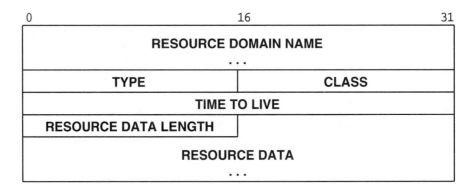

Figure 24.8 The format of resource records used in later sections of messages returned by domain name servers.

The *RESOURCE DOMAIN NAME* field contains the domain name to which this resource record refers. It may be an arbitrary length. The *TYPE* field specifies the type of the data included in the resource record; the *CLASS* field specifies the data's class. The *TIME TO LIVE* field contains a 32-bit integer that specifies the number of seconds information in this resource record can be cached. It is used by clients who have requested a name binding and may want to cache the results. The last two fields contain the results of the binding, with the *RESOURCE DATA LENGTH* field specifying the count of octets in the *RESOURCE DATA* field.

24.15 Compressed Name Format

When represented in a message, domain names are stored as a sequence of labels. Each label begins with an octet that specifies its length. Thus, the receiver reconstructs a domain name by repeatedly reading a 1-octet length, *n*, and then reading a label *n* octets long. A length octet containing zero marks the end of the name.

Domain name servers often return multiple answers to a query and, in many cases, suffixes of the domain overlap. To conserve space in the reply packet, the name servers compress names by storing only one copy of each domain name. When extracting a domain name from a message, the client software must check each segment of the name to see whether it consists of a literal string (in the format of a 1-octet count followed by the characters that make up the name) or a pointer to a literal string. When it encounters a pointer, the client must follow the pointer to a new place in the message to find the remainder of the name.

Pointers always occur at the beginning of segments and are encoded in the count byte. If the top two bits of the 8-bit segment count field are 1s, the client must take the next 14 bits as an integer pointer. If the top two bits are zero, the next 6 bits specify the number of characters in the label that follow the count octet.

24.16 Abbreviation Of Domain Names

The telephone number hierarchy illustrates another useful feature of local resolution, *name abbreviation*. Abbreviation provides a method of shortening names when the resolving process can supply part of the name automatically. Normally, a subscriber omits the area code when dialing a local telephone number. The resulting digits form an abbreviated name assumed to lie within the same area code as the subscriber's phone. Abbreviation also works well for machine names. Given a name like *xyz*, the resolving process can assume it lies in the same local authority as the machine on which it is being resolved. Thus, the resolver can supply missing parts of the name automatically. For example, within the Computer Science Department at Purdue, the abbreviated name

xinu

is equivalent to the full domain name

xinu.cs.purdue.edu

Most client software implements abbreviations with a *domain suffix list*. The local network manager configures a list of possible suffixes to be appended to names during lookup. When a resolver encounters a name, it steps through the list, appending each suffix and trying to look up the resulting name. For example, the suffix list for the Computer Science Department at Purdue includes:

```
.cs.purdue.edu
.cc.purdue.edu
.purdue.edu
null
```

Thus, local resolvers first append *cs.purdue.edu* onto the name *xinu*. If that lookup fails, they append *cc.purdue.edu* onto the name and look that up. The last suffix in the example list is the null string, meaning that if all other lookups fail, the resolver will attempt to look up the name with no suffix. Managers can use the suffix list to make abbreviation convenient or to restrict application programs to local names.

We said that the client takes responsibility for the expansion of such abbreviations, but it should be emphasized that such abbreviations are not part of the domain name system itself. The domain system only allows lookup of a fully specified domain name. As a consequence, programs that depend on abbreviations may not work correctly outside the environment in which they were built. We can summarize:

> *The domain name system only maps full domain names into addresses; abbreviations are not part of the domain name system itself, but are introduced by client software to make local names convenient for users.*

24.17 Inverse Mappings

We said that the domain name system can provide mappings other than machine name to IP address. *Inverse queries* allow the client to ask a server to map "backwards" by taking an answer and generating the question that would produce that answer. Of course, not all answers have a unique question. Even when they do, a server may not be able to provide it. Although inverse queries have been part of the domain system since it was first specified, they are generally not used because there is often no way to find the server that can resolve the query without searching the entire set of servers.

24.18 Pointer Queries

One form of inverse mapping is so obviously needed that the domain system supports a special domain and a special form of question called a *pointer query* to answer it. In a pointer query, the question presented to a domain name server specifies an IP address encoded as a printable string in the form of a domain name (i.e., a textual representation of digits separated by periods). A pointer query requests the name server to return the correct domain name for the machine with the specified IP address. Pointer queries are especially useful for diskless machines because they allow the system to obtain a high-level name given only an IP address. (We have already seen in Chapter 6 how a diskless machine can obtain its IP address.)

Pointer queries are not difficult to generate. If we think of an IP address written in dotted-decimal form, it has the following format:

$$aaa.bbb.ccc.ddd$$

To form a pointer query, the client rearranges the dotted decimal representation of the address into a string of the form:

$$ddd.ccc.bbb.aaa.in\text{-}addr.arpa$$

The new form is a name in the special *in-addr.arpa* domain†. Because the local name server may not be the authority for either the *arpa* domain or the *in-addr.arpa* domain, it may need to contact other name servers to complete the resolution. To make the resolution of pointer queries efficient, the Internet root domain servers maintain a database of valid IP addresses along with information about domain name servers that can resolve each address.

24.19 Object Types And Resource Record Contents

We have mentioned that the domain name system can be used for translating a domain name to a mail exchanger address as well as for translating a host name to an IP address. The domain system is quite general in that it can be used for arbitrary hierarchical names. For example, one might decide to store the names of available computational services along with a mapping from each name to the telephone number to call to find out about the corresponding service. Or one might store names of protocol products along with a mapping to the names and addresses of vendors that offer such products.

Recall that the system accommodates a variety of mappings by including a *type* in each resource record. When sending a request, a client must specify the type in its query‡; servers specify the data type in all resource records they return. The type determines the contents of the resource record according to the table in Figure 24.9

---

†The octets of the IP address must be reversed when forming a domain name because IP addresses have the most significant octets first while domain names have the least-significant octets first.

‡Queries can specify a few additional types (e.g., there is a query type that requests all resource records).

Type	Meaning	Contents
A	Host Address	32-bit IP address
CNAME	Canonical Name	Canonical domain name for an alias
HINFO	CPU & OS	Name of CPU and operating system
MINFO	Mailbox info	Information about a mailbox or mail list
MX	Mail Exchanger	16-bit preference and name of host that acts as mail exchanger for the domain
NS	Name Server	Name of authoritative server for domain
PTR	Pointer	Domain name (like a symbolic link)
SOA	Start of Authority	Multiple fields that specify which parts of the naming hierarchy a server implements
TXT	Arbitrary text	Uninterpreted string of ASCII text

Figure 24.9 Domain name system resource record types.

Most data is of type *A*, meaning that it consists of the name of a host attached to the Internet along with the host's IP address. The second most useful domain type, *MX*, is assigned to names used for electronic mail exchangers. It allows a site to specify multiple hosts that are each capable of accepting mail. When sending electronic mail, the user specifies an electronic mail address in the form *user@domain-part*. The mail system uses the domain name system to resolve *domain-part* with query type *MX*. The domain system returns a set of resource records that each contain a preference field and a host's domain name. The mail system steps through the set from highest preference to lowest (lower numbers mean higher preference). For each *MX* resource record, the mailer extracts the domain name and uses a type *A* query to resolve that name to an IP address. It then tries to contact the host and deliver mail. If the host is unavailable, the mailer will continue trying other hosts on the list.

To make lookup efficient, a server always returns additional bindings that it knows in the *ADDITIONAL INFORMATION SECTION* of a response. In the case of *MX* records, a domain server can use the *ADDITIONAL INFORMATION SECTION* to return type *A* resource records for domain names reported in the *ANSWER SECTION*. Doing so substantially reduces the number of queries a mailer sends to its domain server.

24.20 Obtaining Authority For A Subdomain

Before an institution is granted authority for an official second-level domain, it must agree to operate a domain name server that meets Internet standards. Of course, a domain name server must obey the protocol standards that specify message formats and the rules for responding to requests. The server must also know the addresses of servers that handle each subdomain (if any exist) as well as the address of at least one root server.

In practice, the domain system is much more complex than we have outlined. In most cases, a single physical server can handle more than one part of the naming hierarchy. For example, a single name server at Purdue University handles both the second-level domain *purdue.edu* as well as the geographic domain *laf.in.us*. A subtree of names managed by a given name server forms a *zone of authority*. Another practical complication arises because servers must be able to handle many requests, even though some requests take a long time to resolve. Usually, servers support concurrent activity, allowing work to proceed on later requests while earlier ones are being processed. Handling requests concurrently is especially important when the server receives a recursive request that forces it to send the request on to another server for resolution.

Server implementation is also complicated because the Internet authority requires that the information in every domain name server be replicated. Information must appear in at least two servers that do not operate on the same computer. In practice, the requirements are quite stringent: the servers must have no single common point of failure. Avoiding common points of failure means that the two name servers cannot both attach to the same network; they cannot even obtain electrical power from the same source. Thus, to meet the requirements, a site must find at least one other site that agrees to operate a backup name server. Of course, at any point in the tree of servers, a server must know how to locate both the primary and backup name servers for subdomains, and it must direct queries to a backup name server if the primary server is unavailable.

24.21 Summary

Hierarchical naming systems allow delegation of authority for names, making it possible to accommodate an arbitrarily large set of names without overwhelming a central site with administrative duties. Although name resolution is separate from delegation of authority, it is possible to create hierarchical naming systems in which resolution is an efficient process that starts at the local server even though delegation of authority always flows from the top of the hierarchy downward.

We examined the Internet domain name system (DNS) and saw that it offers a hierarchical naming scheme. DNS uses distributed lookup in which domain name servers map each domain name to an IP address or mail exchanger address. Clients begin by trying to resolve names locally. When the local server cannot resolve the name, the client must choose to work through the tree of name servers iteratively or request the local name server to do it recursively. Finally, we saw that the domain name system supports a variety of bindings including bindings from IP addresses to high-level names.

FOR FURTHER STUDY

Mockapetris [RFC 1034] discusses Internet domain naming in general, giving the overall philosophy, while Mockapetris [RFC 1035] provides a protocol standard for the domain name system. Mockapetris [RFC 1101] discusses using the domain name system to encode network names and proposes extensions useful for other mappings. Postel and Reynolds [RFC 920] states the requirements that an Internet domain name server must meet. Stahl [RFC 1032] gives administrative guidelines for establishing a domain, and Lottor [RFC 1033] provides guidelines for operating a domain name server. Eastlake [RFC 2535] presents security extensions. Partridge [RFC 974] relates domain naming to electronic mail addressing. Finally, Lottor [RFC 1296] provides an interesting summary of Internet growth obtained by walking the domain name tree.

EXERCISES

24.1 Machine names should not be bound into the operating system at compile time. Explain why.

24.2 Would you prefer to use a machine that obtained its name from a remote file or from a name server? Why?

24.3 Why should each name server know the IP address of its parent instead of the domain name of its parent?

24.4 Devise a naming scheme that tolerates changes to the naming hierarchy. As an example, consider two large companies that each have an independent naming hierarchy, and suppose the companies merge. Can you arrange to have all previous names still work correctly?

24.5 Read the standard and find out how the domain name system uses *SOA* records.

24.6 The Internet domain name system can also accommodate mailbox names. Find out how.

24.7 The standard suggests that when a program needs to find the domain name associated with an IP address, it should send an inverse query to the local server first and use domain *in-addr.arpa* only if that fails. Why?

24.8 How would you accommodate abbreviations in a domain naming scheme? As an example, show two sites that are both registered under *.edu* and a top level server. Explain how each site would treat each type of abbreviation.

24.9 Obtain the official description of the domain name system and build a client program. Look up the name *merlin.cs.purdue.edu*.

24.10 Extend the exercise above to include a pointer query. Try looking up the domain name for address *128.10.2.3* .

24.11 Find a copy of the program *nslookup*, and use it to look up the names in the two previous exercises.

24.12   If we extended the domain name syntax to include a dot after the top-level domain, names and abbreviations would be unambiguous. What are the advantages and disadvantages of the extension?

24.13   Read the RFCs on the domain name system. What are the maximum and minimum possible values a DNS server can store in the *TIME-TO-LIVE* field of a resource record?

24.14   Should the domain name system permit partial match queries (i.e. a wildcard as part of a name)? Why or why not?

24.15   The Computer Science Department at Purdue University chose to place the following type *A* resource record entry in its domain name server:

`localhost.cs.purdue.edu     127.0.0.1`

Explain what will happen if a remote site tries to *ping* a machine with domain name *localhost.cs.purdue.edu*.

25

Applications: Remote Login (TELNET, Rlogin)

25.1 Introduction

This chapter and the next five continue our exploration of internetworking by examining high-level internet services and the protocols that support them. These services form an integral part of TCP/IP. They determine how users perceive an internet and demonstrate the power of the technology.

We will learn that high-level services provide increased communication functionality, and allow users and programs to interact with automated services on remote machines and with remote users. We will see that high-level protocols are implemented with application programs, and will learn how they depend on the network level services described in previous chapters. This chapter begins by examining remote login.

25.2 Remote Interactive Computing

We have already seen how the client–server model can provide specific computational services like a time-of-day service to multiple machines. Reliable stream protocols like TCP make possible interactive use of remote machines as well. For example, imagine building a server that provides a remote text editing service. To implement an editing service, we need a server that accepts requests to edit a file and a client to make such requests. To invoke the remote editor service, a user executes the client program. The client establishes a TCP connection to the server, and then begins sending keystrokes to the server and reading output that the server sends back.

How can our imagined remote interactive editing service be generalized? The problem with using one server for each computational service is that machines quickly become swamped with server processes. We can eliminate most specialized servers and provide more generality by allowing the user to establish a login session on the remote machine and then execute commands. With a *remote login* facility, users have access to all the commands available on the remote system, and system designers need not provide specialized servers.

Of course, providing remote login may not be simple. Computer systems that are designed without considering networking expect login sessions only from a directly connected keyboard and display. On such a computer, adding a remote login server requires modifying the machine's operating system. Building interactive client software may also be difficult. Consider, for example, a system that assigns special meaning to some keystrokes. If the local system interprets Control–C to mean ''abort the currently executing command process,'' it may be impossible to pass Control–C to the remote machine. If the client does pass Control-C to the remote site, it may be impossible to abort the local client process.

Despite the technical difficulties, system programmers have managed to build remote login server software for most operating systems and to construct application programs that act as clients. Often, the client software overrides the local interpretation of all keys except one, allowing a user to interact with the remote machine exactly as one would from a locally connected terminal. The single key exception provides a way for a user to escape to the local environment and control the client (e.g., to abort the client). In addition, some remote login protocols recognize a set of *trusted hosts*, permitting remote login from such hosts without verifying passwords, and others achieve security by encrypting all transmissions.

25.3 TELNET Protocol

The TCP/IP protocol suite includes a simple remote terminal protocol called *TELNET* that allows a user to log into a computer across an internet. TELNET establishes a TCP connection, and then passes keystrokes from the user's keyboard directly to the remote computer as if they had been typed on a keyboard attached to the remote machine. TELNET also carries output from the remote machine back to the user's screen. The service is called *transparent* because it gives the appearance that the user's keyboard and display attach directly to the remote machine.

Although TELNET is not as sophisticated as some remote terminal protocols, it is widely available. Usually, TELNET client software allows the user to specify a remote machine either by giving its domain name or IP address. Because it accepts IP addresses, TELNET can be used with hosts even if a name-to-address binding cannot be established (e.g., when domain naming software is being debugged).

TELNET offers three basic services. First, it defines a *network virtual terminal* that provides a standard interface to remote systems. Client programs do not have to understand the details of all possible remote systems; they are built to use the standard interface. Second, TELNET includes a mechanism that allows the client and server to negotiate options, and it provides a set of standard options (e.g., one of the options controls whether data passed across the connection uses the standard 7-bit ASCII character set or an 8-bit character set). Finally, TELNET treats both ends of the connection symmetrically. In particular, TELNET does not force client input to come from a keyboard, nor does it force the client to display output on a screen. Thus, TELNET allows an arbitrary program to become a client. Furthermore, either end can negotiate options.

Figure 25.1 illustrates how application programs implement a TELNET client and server.

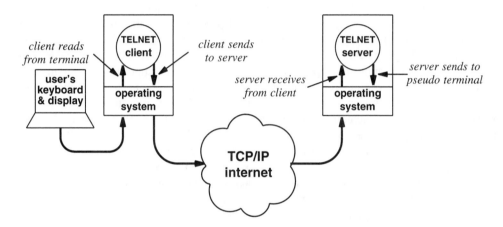

Figure 25.1 The path of data in a TELNET remote terminal session as it travels from the user's keyboard to the remote operating system. Adding a TELNET server to a timesharing system usually requires modifying the operating system.

As the figure shows, when a user invokes TELNET, an application program on the user's machine becomes the client. The client establishes a TCP connection to the server over which they will communicate. Once the connection has been established, the client accepts keystrokes from the user's keyboard and sends them to the server, while it concurrently accepts characters that the server sends back and displays them on the user's screen. The server must accept a TCP connection from the client, and then relay data between the TCP connection and the local operating system.

In practice, the server is more complex than the figure shows because it must handle multiple, concurrent connections. Usually, a master server process waits for new connections and creates a new slave to handle each connection. Thus, the 'TELNET server', shown in Figure 25.1, represents the slave that handles one particular connection. The figure does not show the master server that listens for new requests, nor does it show the slaves handling other connections.

We use the term *pseudo terminal*† to describe the operating system entry point that allows a running program like the TELNET server to transfer characters to the operating system as if they came from a keyboard. It is impossible to build a TELNET server unless the operating system supplies such a facility. If the system supports a pseudo terminal abstraction, the TELNET server can be implemented with application programs. Each slave server connects a TCP stream from one client to a particular pseudo terminal.

Arranging for the TELNET server to be an application level program has advantages and disadvantages. The most obvious advantage is that it makes modification and control of the server easier than if the code were embedded in the operating system. The obvious disadvantage is inefficiency. Each keystroke travels from the user's keyboard through the operating system to the client program, from the client program back through the operating system and across the internet to the server machine. After reaching the destination machine, the data must travel up through the server's operating system to the server application program, and from the server application program back into the server's operating system at a pseudo terminal entry point. Finally, the remote operating system delivers the character to the application program the user is running. Meanwhile, output (including remote character echo if that option has been selected) travels back from the server to the client over the same path.

Readers who understand operating systems will appreciate that for the implementation shown in Figure 25.1, every keystroke requires computers to switch process context several times. In most systems, an additional context switch is required because the operating system on the server's machine must pass characters from the pseudo terminal back to another application program (e.g., a command interpreter). Although context switching is expensive, the scheme is practical because users do not type at high speed.

25.4 Accommodating Heterogeneity

To make TELNET interoperate between as many systems as possible, it must accommodate the details of heterogeneous computers and operating systems. For example, some systems require lines of text to be terminated by the ASCII *carriage control* character (*CR*). Others require the ASCII *linefeed* (*LF*) character. Still others require the two-character sequence of CR-LF. In addition, most interactive systems provide a way for a user to enter a key that interrupts a running program. However, the specific keystroke used to interrupt a program varies from system to system (e.g., some systems use Control–C, while others use ESCAPE).

To accommodate heterogeneity, TELNET defines how data and command sequences are sent across the Internet. The definition is known as the *network virtual terminal* (*NVT*). As Figure 25.2 illustrates, the client software translates keystrokes and command sequences from the user's terminal into NVT format and sends them to the server. Server software translates incoming data and commands from NVT format into the format the remote system requires. For data returning, the remote server translates from the remote machine's format to NVT, and the local client translates from NVT to the local machine's format.

---

†UNIX calls the system entry point a *pseudo tty* because character-oriented devices are called *ttys*.

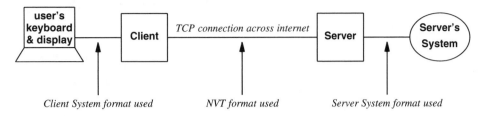

Figure 25.2 Use of the Network Virtual Terminal (NVT) format by TELNET.

The definition of NVT format is fairly straightforward. All communication involves 8-bit bytes. At startup, NVT uses the standard 7-bit USASCII representation for data and reserves bytes with the high order bit set for command sequences. The USASCII character set includes 95 characters that have "printable" graphics (e.g., letters, digits, and punctuation marks) as well as 33 "control" codes. All printable characters are assigned the same meaning as in the standard USASCII character set. The NVT standard defines interpretations for control characters as shown in Figure 25.3†.

ASCII Control Code	Decimal Value	Assigned Meaning
NUL	0	No operation (has no effect on output)
BEL	7	Sound audible/visible signal (no motion)
BS	8	Move left one character position
HT	9	Move right to the next horizontal tab stop
LF	10	Move down (vertically) to the next line
VT	11	Move down to the next vertical tab stop
FF	12	Move to the top of the next page
CR	13	Move to the left margin on the current line
other control	–	No operation (has no effect on output)

Figure 25.3 The TELNET NVT interpretation of USASCII control characters. TELNET does not specify the locations of tab stops.

In addition to the control character interpretation in Figure 25.3, NVT defines the standard line termination to be a two-character sequence *CR-LF*. When a user presses the key that corresponds to end-of-line on the local terminal (e.g., *ENTER* or *RETURN*), the TELNET client must map it into *CR-LF* for transmission. The TELNET server translates *CR-LF* into the appropriate end-of-line character sequence for the remote machine.

---

†The NVT interpretation of control characters follows the usual ASCII interpretation.

25.5 Passing Commands That Control The Remote Side

We said that most systems provide a mechanism that allows users to terminate a running program. Usually, the local operating system binds such mechanisms to a particular key or keystroke sequence. For example, unless the user specifies otherwise, many UNIX systems reserve the character generated by *CONTROL-C* as the interrupt key. Depressing *CONTROL-C* causes UNIX to terminate the executing program; the program does not receive *CONTROL-C* as input. The system may reserve other characters or character sequences for other control functions.

TELNET NVT accommodates control functions by defining how they are passed from the client to the server. Conceptually, we think of NVT as accepting input from a keyboard that can generate more than 128 possible characters. We assume the user's keyboard has virtual (imaginary) keys that correspond to the functions typically used to control processing. For example, NVT defines a conceptual ''interrupt'' key that requests program termination. Figure 25.4 lists the control functions that NVT allows.

Signal	Meaning
IP	Interrupt Process (terminate running program)
AO	Abort Output (discard any buffered output)
AYT	Are You There (test if server is responding)
EC	Erase Character (delete the previous character)
EL	Erase Line (delete the entire current line)
SYNCH	Synchronize (clear data path until TCP urgent data point, but do interpret commands)
BRK	Break (break key or attention signal)

Figure 25.4 The control functions TELNET NVT recognizes. Conceptually, the client receives these from a user in addition to normal data, and passes them to the server's system where they must be interpreted.

In practice, most keyboards do not provide extra keys for commands. Instead, individual operating systems or command interpreters have a variety of ways to generate them. We already mentioned the most common technique: binding an individual ASCII character to a control function so when the user presses the key, the operating system takes the appropriate action instead of accepting the character as input. The NVT designers chose to keep commands separate from the normal ASCII character set for two reasons. First, defining the control functions separately means TELNET has greater flexibility. It can transfer all possible ASCII character sequences between client and server as well as all possible control functions. Second, by separating signals from normal data, NVT allows the client to specify signals unambiguously — there is never confusion about whether an input character should be treated as data or as a control function.

To pass control functions across the TCP connection, TELNET encodes them using an *escape sequence*. An escape sequence uses a reserved octet to indicate that a control code octet follows. In TELNET, the reserved octet that starts an escape sequence is known as the *interpret as command (IAC)* octet. Figure 25.5 lists the possible commands and the decimal encoding used for each.

Command	Decimal Encoding	Meaning
IAC	255	Interpret next octet as command (when the IAC octet appears as data, the sender doubles it and sends the 2-octet sequence IAC-IAC)
DON'T	254	Denial of request to perform specified option
DO	253	Approval to allow specified option
WON'T	252	Refusal to perform specified option
WILL	251	Agreement to perform specified option
SB	250	Start of option subnegotiation
GA	249	The "go ahead" signal
EL	248	The "erase line" signal
EC	247	The "erase character" signal
AYT	246	The "are you there" signal
AO	245	The "abort output" signal
IP	244	The "interrupt process" signal
BRK	243	The "break" signal
DMARK	242	The data stream portion of a SYNCH (always accompanied by TCP Urgent notification)
NOP	241	No operation
SE	240	End of option subnegotiation
EOR	239	End of record

Figure 25.5 TELNET commands and encoding for each. The codes only have meaning if preceded by an *IAC* character. When *IAC* occurs in the data, it is sent twice.

As the figure shows, the signals generated by conceptual keys on an NVT keyboard each have a corresponding command. For example, to request that the server interrupt the executing program, the client must send the 2-octet sequence *IAC IP* (255 followed by 244). Additional commands allow the client and server to negotiate which options they will use and to synchronize communication.

25.6 Forcing The Server To Read A Control Function

Sending control functions along with normal data is not always sufficient to guarantee the desired results. To see why, consider the situation under which a user might send the *interrupt process* control function to the server. Usually, such control is only needed when the program executing on the remote machine is misbehaving and the user wants the server to terminate the program. For example, the program might be executing an endless loop without reading input or generating output. Unfortunately, if the application at the server's site stops reading input, operating system buffers will eventually fill and the server will be unable to write more data to the pseudo terminal. When this happens, the server must stop reading data from the TCP connection, causing its buffers to fill. Eventually, TCP on the server machine will begin advertising a zero window size, preventing data from flowing across the connection.

If the user generates an interrupt control function when buffers are filled, the control function will never reach the server. That is, the client can form the command sequence *IAC IP* and write it to the TCP connection, but because TCP has stopped sending to the server's machine, the server will not read the control sequence. The point is:

> *TELNET cannot rely on the conventional data stream alone to carry control sequences between client and server, because a misbehaving application that needs to be controlled might inadvertently block the data stream.*

To solve the problem, TELNET uses an *out of band* signal. TCP implements out of band signaling with the *urgent data* mechanism. Whenever it places a control function in the data stream, TELNET also sends a *SYNCH* command. TELNET then appends a reserved octet called the *data mark*, and causes TCP to signal the server by sending a segment with the URGENT DATA bit set. Segments carrying urgent data bypass flow control and reach the server immediately. In response to an urgent signal, the server reads and discards all data until it finds the data mark. The server returns to normal processing when it encounters the data mark.

25.7 TELNET Options

Our simple description of TELNET omits one of the most complex aspects: options. In TELNET, options are negotiable, making it possible for the client and server to reconfigure their connection. For example, we said that usually the data stream passes 7-bit data and uses octets with the eighth bit set to pass control information like the *Interrupt Process* command. However, TELNET also provides an option that allows the client and server to pass 8-bit data (when passing 8-bit data, the reserved octet *IAC* must still be doubled if it appears in the data). The client and server must negotiate, and both must agree to pass 8-bit data before such transfers are possible.

The range of TELNET options is wide: some extend the capabilities in major ways while others deal with minor details. For example, the original protocol was designed for a half-duplex environment where it was necessary to tell the other end to ''go ahead'' before it would send more data. One of the options controls whether TELNET operates in half- or full-duplex mode. Another option allows the server on a remote machine to determine the user's terminal type. The terminal type is important for software that generates cursor positioning sequences (e.g., a full screen editor executing on a remote machine).

Figure 25.6 lists several of the most commonly implemented TELNET options.

Name	Code	RFC	Meaning
Transmit Binary	0	856	Change transmission to 8-bit binary
Echo	1	857	Allow one side to echo data it receives
Suppress-GA	3	858	Suppress (no longer send) Go-ahead signal after data
Status	5	859	Request for status of a TELNET option from remote site
Timing-Mark	6	860	Request timing mark be inserted in return stream to synchronize two ends of a connection
Terminal-Type	24	884	Exchange information about the make and model of a terminal being used (allows programs to tailor output like cursor positioning sequences for the user's terminal)
End-of-Record	25	885	Terminate data sent with EOR code
Linemode	34	1116	Use local editing and send complete lines instead of individual characters

Figure 25.6 Commonly used TELNET options.

25.8 TELNET Option Negotiation

The way TELNET negotiates options is interesting. Because it sometimes makes sense for the server to initiate a particular option, the protocol is designed to allow either end to make a request. Thus, the protocol is said to be *symmetric* with respect to option processing. The receiving end either responds to a request with a positive acceptance or a rejection. In TELNET terminology, the request is *WILL X*, meaning *will you agree to let me use option X*; and the response is either *DO X* or *DON'T X*, meaning *I do agree to let you use option X* or *I don't agree to let you use option X*. The symmetry arises because *DO X* requests that the receiving party begin using option *X*, and *WILL X* or *WON'T X* means *I will start using option X* or *I won't start using it†*.

---

†To eliminate potential loops that arise when two sides each think the other's acknowledgement is a request, the protocol specifies that no acknowledgement be given to a request for an option that is already in use.

Another interesting negotiation concept arises because both ends are required to run an unenhanced NVT implementation (i.e., one without any options turned on). If one side tries to negotiate an option that the other does not understand, the side receiving the request can simply decline. Thus, it is possible to interoperate newer, more sophisticated versions of TELNET clients and servers (i.e., software that understands more options) with older, less sophisticated versions. If both the client and server understand the new options, they may be able to improve interaction. If not, they will revert to a less efficient, but workable style.

We can summarize:

> *TELNET uses a symmetric option negotiation mechanism to allow clients and servers to reconfigure the parameters controlling their interaction. Because all TELNET software understands a basic NVT protocol, clients and servers can interoperate even if one understands options another does not.*

25.9 Rlogin (BSD UNIX)

Operating systems derived from BSD UNIX include a remote login service, *rlogin*, that supports trusted hosts. It allows system administrators to choose a set of machines over which login names and file access protections are shared and to establish equivalences among user logins. Users can control access to their accounts by authorizing remote login based on remote host and remote user name. Thus, it is possible for a user to have login name X on one machine and Y on another, and still be able to remotely login from one of the machines to the other without typing a password each time.

Having automatic authorization makes remote login facilities useful for general purpose programs as well as human interaction. One variant of the *rlogin* command, *rsh*, invokes a command interpreter on the remote UNIX machine and passes the command line arguments to the command interpreter, skipping the login step completely. The format of a command invocation using *rsh* is:

`rsh` *machine command*

Thus, typing

`rsh merlin ps`

on any of the machines in the Computer Science Department at Purdue University executes the *ps* command on machine *merlin*, with UNIX's standard input and standard output connected across the network to the user's keyboard and display. The user sees the output as if he or she were logged into machine *merlin*. Because the user can arrange to have *rsh* invoke remote commands without prompting for a password, it can be used in programs as well as from the keyboard.

Because protocols like *rlogin* understand both the local and remote computing environments, they communicate better than general purpose remote login protocols like TELNET. For example, *rlogin* understands the UNIX notions of *standard input, standard output*, and *standard error*, and uses TCP to connect them to the remote machine. Thus, it is possible to type

```
rsh merlin ps > filename
```

and have output from the remote command redirected† into file *filename*. *Rlogin* also understands terminal control functions like flow control characters (typically Control–S and Control–Q). It arranges to stop output immediately without waiting for the delay required to send them across the network to the remote host. Finally, rlogin exports part of the user's environment to the remote machine, including information like the user's terminal type (i.e., the *TERM* variable). As a result, a remote login session appears to behave almost exactly like a local login session.

25.10 Summary

Much of the rich functionality associated with TCP/IP results from a variety of high-level services supplied by application programs. The high-level remote login protocols these programs use build on the basic services: unreliable datagram delivery and reliable stream transport. The services usually follow the client-server model in which servers operate at known protocol ports so clients know how to contact them.

We reviewed two remote login systems: TELNET, the TCP/IP internet standard, and rlogin, a popular protocol used with systems derived from BSD UNIX. TELNET provides a basic service. It allows the client to pass commands such as *interrupt process* as well as data to the server. It also permits a client and server to negotiate many options. In contrast to TELNET, *rlogin* allows system managers and users more flexibility in establishing the equivalence of accounts on multiple machines, but it is not as widely available as TELNET.

FOR FURTHER STUDY

Many high-level protocols have been proposed, but only a few are in common use. Edge [1979] compares end-to-end protocols with the hop-by-hop approach. Saltzer, Reed, and Clark [1984] argues for having the highest level protocols perform end-to-end acknowledgement and error detection.

Postel [RFC 854] contains the TELNET remote login protocol specification. It was preceded by over three dozen RFCs that discuss TELNET options, weaknesses, experiments, and proposed changes, including Postel [RFC 764] that contains an earlier standard. Postel and Reynolds [RFC 855] gives a specification for options and consid-

---

†The "greater than" symbol is the usual UNIX syntax for directing the output of a command into a file.

ers subnegotiation. A lengthy list of options can be found in RFCs 856, 857, 858, 859, 860, 861, 884, 885, 1041, 1091, 1096, 1097, 1184, 1372, 1416, and 1572. The program *tn3270* uses a TELNET-like mechanism to provide access to IBM computers running the VM/CMS operating system [RFCs 1576, 1646 and 1647]; Rekhter [RFC 1041] covers the TELNET option that permits communication with IBM 3270 displays.

EXERCISES

25.1 Experiment with both TELNET and *rlogin*. What are the noticeable differences?

25.2 Despite the large volume of notes written about TELNET, it can be argued that the protocol is still not well-defined. Experiment with TELNET: use it to reach a machine, *A*, and invoke TELNET on *A* to reach a second machine, *B*. Does the combination of two TELNET connections handle *line feed* and *carriage control* characters properly?

25.3 What is a remote procedure call?

25.4 Folklore says that operating systems come and go while protocols last forever. Test this axiom by surveying your local computing site to see whether operating systems or communication protocols have changed more frequently.

25.5 Build TELNET client software.

25.6 Use a TELNET client to connect your keyboard and display to the TCP protocol port for *echo* or *chargen* on your local system to see what happens.

25.7 Read the TELNET standard and find out how the SYNCH operation works.

25.8 TELNET uses TCP's *urgent data* mechanism to force the remote operating system to respond to control functions quickly. Read the standard to find out which commands the remote server honors while scanning the input stream.

25.9 How can the symmetric DO/DON'T — WILL/WON'T option negotiation produce an endless loop of responses if the other party *always* acknowledges a request?

25.10 RFC 854 (the TELNET protocol specification) contains exactly 854 lines of text. Do you think there is cosmic significance in this?

26

Applications: File Transfer And Access (FTP, TFTP, NFS)

26.1 Introduction

This chapter continues our exploration of application protocols. It examines the file access and transfer protocols that are part of the TCP/IP protocol suite. It describes their design and shows an example of a typical user interface. We will learn that the most widely used file transfer protocol builds on TCP, covered in Chapter 13, and TELNET, described in the previous chapter.

26.2 File Access And Transfer

Many network systems provide computers with the ability to access files on remote machines. Designers have explored a variety of approaches to remote access; each approach optimizes for a particular set of goals. For example, some designs use remote file access to lower overall cost. In such architectures, a single, centralized *file server* provides secondary storage for a set of inexpensive computers that have no local disk storage. For example, the diskless machines can be portable, hand-held devices used for chores such as inventory. Such machines communicate with a file server over a high-speed wireless network.

Some designs use remote storage to archive data. In such designs, users have conventional computers with local storage facilities and operate them as usual. Periodically the conventional computers send copies of files (or copies of entire disks) across a network to an archival facility, where they are stored in case of accidental loss.

Finally, some designs emphasize the ability to share data across multiple programs, multiple users, or multiple sites. For example, an organization might choose to have a single on-line database of outstanding orders shared by all groups in the organization.

26.3 On-line Shared Access

File sharing comes in two distinct forms: *on-line access* and *whole-file copying*. Shared on-line access means allowing multiple programs to access a single file concurrently. Changes to the file take effect immediately and are available to all programs that access the file. Whole-file copying means that whenever a program wants to access a file, it obtains a local copy. Copying is often used for read-only data, but if the file must be modified, the program makes changes to the local copy and transfers a copy of the modified file back to the original site.

Many users think that on-line data sharing can only be provided by a database system that operates as a server and allows users (clients) to contact it from remote sites. However, file sharing is usually more sophisticated and easier to use. For example, a file system that provides shared, on-line access for remote users does not necessarily require a user to invoke a special client program as a database system does. Instead, the operating system provides access to remote, shared files exactly the same way it provides access to local files. A user can execute any application program using a remote file as input or output. We say that the remote file is *integrated* with local files, and that the entire file system provides *transparent access* to shared files.

The advantage of transparent access should be obvious: remote file access occurs with no visible changes to application programs. Users can access both local and remote files, allowing them to perform arbitrary computations on shared data. The disadvantages are less obvious. Users may be surprised by the results. For example, consider an application program that uses both local and remote files. If the network or the remote machine is down, the application program may not work even though the user's machine is operating. Even if the remote machine is operating, it may be overloaded or the network may be congested, causing the application program to run slowly, or causing communication protocols to report timeout conditions that the user does not expect. The application program seems unreliable.

Despite its advantages, implementing integrated, transparent file access can be difficult. In a heterogeneous environment, file names available on one computer may be impossible to map into the file namespace of another. Similarly, a remote file access mechanism must handle notions of ownership, authorization, and access protection, which do not transcend computer system boundaries. Finally, because file representations and allowed operations vary from machine to machine, it may be difficult or impossible to implement all operations on all files.

26.4 Sharing By File Transfer

The alternative to integrated, transparent on-line access is *file transfer*. Accessing remote data with a transfer mechanism is a two-step process: the user first obtains a local copy of a file and then operates on the copy. Most transfer mechanisms operate outside the local file system (i.e., they are not integrated). A user must invoke a special-purpose client program to transfer files. When invoking the client, the user specifies a remote computer on which the desired file resides and, possibly, an authorization needed to obtain access (e.g., an account or password). The client contacts a server on the remote machine and requests a copy of the file. Once the transfer is complete, the user terminates the client and uses application programs on the local system to read or modify the local copy. One advantage of whole-file copying lies in the efficiency of operations — once a program has obtained a copy of a remote file, it can manipulate the copy efficiently. Thus, many computations run faster with whole-file copying than with remote file access.

As with on-line sharing, whole-file transfer between heterogeneous machines can be difficult. The client and server must agree on authorization, notions of file ownership and access protections, and data formats. The latter is especially important because it may make inverse translations impossible. To see why, consider copying between two machines, *A* and *B*, that use different representations for floating point numbers as well as different representations for text files. As most programmers realize, it may be impossible to convert from one machine's floating point format to another's without losing precision. The same can happen with text files. Suppose system *A* stores text files as variable-length lines and system *B* pads text lines to a fixed length. Transferring a file from *A* to *B* and back can add padding to every line, making the final copy different from the original. However, automatically removing padding from the ends of lines during the transfer back to *A* will also make the copy different from the original for any files that had padding on some lines.

The exact details of differences in representation and the techniques to handle them depend on the computer systems involved. Furthermore, we have seen that not all representational differences can be accommodated — information can be lost when data must be translated from one representation to another. While it is not essential to learn about all possible representational differences, remembering that TCP/IP is designed for a heterogeneous environment will help explain some of the features of the TCP/IP file transfer protocols.

26.5 FTP: The Major TCP/IP File Transfer Protocol

File transfer is among the most frequently used TCP/IP applications, and it accounts for much network traffic. Standard file transfer protocols existed for the ARPANET before TCP/IP became operational. These early versions of file transfer software evolved into a current standard known as the *File Transfer Protocol (FTP)*.

26.6 FTP Features

Given a reliable end-to-end transport protocol like TCP, file transfer might seem trivial. However, as the previous sections pointed out, the details of authorization, naming, and representation among heterogeneous machines make the protocol complex. In addition, FTP offers many facilities beyond the transfer function itself.

• *Interactive Access.* Although FTP is designed to be used by programs, most implementations provide an interactive interface that allows humans to easily interact with remote servers. For example, a user can ask for a listing of all files in a directory on a remote machine. Also, the client usually responds to the input ''help'' by showing the user information about possible commands that can be invoked.

• *Format (representation) Specification.* FTP allows the client to specify the type and format of stored data. For example, the user can specify whether a file contains text or binary integers and whether text files use the ASCII or EBCDIC character sets.

• *Authentication Control.* FTP requires clients to authorize themselves by sending a login name and password to the server before requesting file transfers. The server refuses access to clients that cannot supply a valid login and password.

26.7 FTP Process Model

Like other servers, most FTP server implementations allow concurrent access by multiple clients. Clients use TCP to connect to a server. As described in Chapter 21, a single master server process awaits connections and creates a slave process to handle each connection. Unlike most servers, however, the slave process does not perform all the necessary computation. Instead, the slave accepts and handles the *control connection* from the client, but uses an additional process or processes to handle a separate *data transfer connection*. The control connection carries commands that tell the server which file to transfer. The data transfer connection, which also uses TCP as the transport protocol, carries all data transfers.

Usually, both the client and server create a separate process to handle the data transfer. While the exact details of the process architecture depend on the operating systems used, Figure 26.1 illustrates the concept:

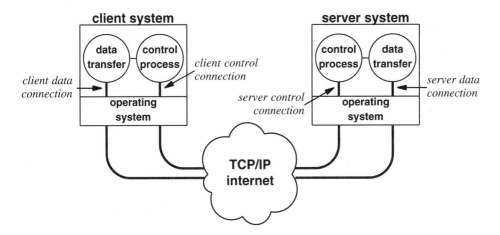

Figure 26.1 An FTP client and server with a TCP control connection between
them and a separate TCP connection between their associated
data transfer processes.

As the figure shows, the client control process connects to the server control process using one TCP connection, while the associated data transfer processes use their own TCP connection. In general, the control processes and the control connection remain alive as long as the user keeps the FTP session active. However, FTP establishes a new data transfer connection for each file transfer. In fact, many implementations create a new pair of data transfer processes, as well as a new TCP connection, whenever the server needs to send information to the client. The idea can be summarized:

> *Data transfer connections and the data transfer processes that use them can be created dynamically when needed, but the control connection persists throughout a session. Once the control connection disappears, the session is terminated and the software at both ends terminates all data transfer processes.*

Of course, client implementations that execute on a computer without operating system support for multiple processes may have a less complex structure. Such implementations often sacrifice generality by using a single application program to perform both the data transfer and control functions. However, the protocol requires that such clients still use multiple TCP connections, one for control and the other(s) for data transfer.

26.8 TCP Port Number Assignment

When a client forms an initial connection to a server, the client uses a random, locally assigned, protocol port number, but contacts the server at a well-known port (*21*). As Chapter 21 points out, a server that uses only one protocol port can accept connections from many clients because TCP uses both endpoints to identify a connection. The question arises, "When the control processes create a new TCP connection for a given data transfer, what protocol port numbers do they use?" Obviously, they cannot use the same pair of port numbers used in the control connection. Instead, the client obtains an unused port on its machine, which will be used for a TCP connection with the data transfer process on the server's machine. The data transfer process on the server machine uses the well-known port reserved for FTP data transfer (*20*). To ensure that a data transfer process on the server connects to the correct data transfer process on the client machine, the server side must not accept connections from an arbitrary process. Instead, when it issues the TCP active open request, a server specifies the port that will be used on the client machine as well as the local port.

We can see why the protocol uses two connections — the client control process obtains a local port to be used in the file transfer, creates a transfer process on the client machine to listen at that port, communicates the port number to the server over the control connection, and then waits for the server to establish a TCP connection to the port. In general:

> *In addition to passing user commands to the server, FTP uses the control connection to allow client and server control processes to coordinate their use of dynamically assigned TCP protocol ports and the creation of data transfer processes that use those ports.*

What format should FTP use for data passing across the control connection? Although they could have invented a new specification, the designers of FTP did not. Instead, they allow FTP to use the TELNET network virtual terminal protocol described in Chapter 25. Unlike the full TELNET protocol, FTP does not allow option negotiation; it uses only the basic NVT definition. Thus, management of an FTP control connection is much simpler than management of a standard TELNET connection. Despite its limitations, using the TELNET definition instead of inventing a new one helps simplify FTP considerably.

26.9 The User's View Of FTP

Users view FTP as an interactive system. Once invoked, the client performs the following operations repeatedly: read a line of input, parse the line to extract a command and its arguments, and execute the command with the specified arguments. For example, to initiate the version of FTP available under UNIX, the user invokes the *ftp* command:

% ftp

The local FTP client program begins and issues a prompt to the user. Following the prompt, the user can issue commands like *help*.

```
ftp> help
Commands may be abbreviated.    Commands are:

!                   cr              macdef          proxy           send
$                   delete          mdelete         sendport        status
account             debug           mdir            put             struct
append              dir             mget            pwd             sunique
ascii               disconnect      mkdir           quit            tenex
bell                form            mls             quote           trace
binary              get             mode            recv            type
bye                 glob            mput            remotehelp      user
case                hash            nmap            rename          verbose
cd                  help            ntrans          reset           ?
cdup                lcd             open            rmdir
close               ls              prompt          runique
```

To obtain more information about a given command the user types *help command* as in the following examples (output is shown in the format *ftp* produces):

```
ftp> help ls
ls                 list contents of remote directory
ftp> help cdup
cdup               change remote working directory to parent directory
ftp> help glob
glob               toggle metacharacter expansion of local file names
ftp> help bell
bell               beep when command completed
```

To execute a command, the user types the command name:

```
ftp> bell
Bell mode on.
```

26.10 An Example Anonymous FTP Session

While the access authorization facilities in FTP make it more secure, strict enforcement prohibits an arbitrary client from accessing any file until they obtain a login and
password for the computer on which the server operates. To provide access to public
files, many TCP/IP sites allow *anonymous FTP*. Anonymous FTP access means a
client does not need an account or password. Instead, the user specifies login name
anonymous and password *guest*. The server allows anonymous logins, but restricts access to only publicly available files†.

Usually, users execute only a few FTP commands to establish a connection and obtain a file; few users have ever tried most commands. For example, suppose someone
has placed an on-line copy of a text in file *tcpbook.tar* in the subdirectory *pub/comer* on
machine *ftp.cs.purdue.edu*. A user logged in at another site as *usera* could obtain a
copy of the file by executing the following:

```
% ftp ftp.cs.purdue.edu
Connected to lucan.cs.purdue.edu.
220 lucan.cs.purdue.edu FTP server (Version wu-2.4.2-VR16(1) ready.
Name (ftp.cs.purdue.edu:usera): anonymous
331 Guest login ok, send e-mail address as password.
Password: guest
230 Guest login ok, access restrictions apply.
ftp> get pub/comer/tcpbook.tar bookfile
200 PORT command okay.
150 Opening ASCII mode data connection for tcpbook.tar (9895469 bytes).
226 Transfer complete.
9895469 bytes received in 22.76 seconds (4.3e+02 Kbytes/s)
ftp> close
221 Goodbye.
ftp> quit
```

In this example, the user specifies machine *ftp.cs.purdue.edu* as an argument to the
FTP command, so the client automatically opens a connection and prompts for authorization. The user invokes anonymous FTP by specifying login *anonymous* and password
guest‡ (although our example shows the password that the user types, the ftp program
does not display it on the user's screen).

After typing a login and password, the user requests a copy of a file using the *get*
command. In the example, the *get* command is followed by two arguments that specify
the remote file name and a name for the local copy. The remote file name is
pub/comer/tcpbook.tar and the local copy will be placed in *bookfile*. Once the transfer
completes, the user types *close* to break the connection with the server, and types *quit* to
leave the client.

---

†In many UNIX systems, the server restricts anonymous FTP by changing the file system root to a small,
restricted directory (e.g., */usr/ftp*).

‡In practice, the server emits additional messages that request the user to use an e-mail address instead of
guest.

Intermingled with the commands the user types are informational messages. FTP messages always begin with a 3-digit number followed by text. Most come from the server; other output comes from the local client. For example, the message that begins *220* comes from the server and contains the domain name of the machine on which the server executes. The statistics that report the number of bytes received and the rate of transfer come from the client. In general:

> Control and error messages between the FTP client and server begin with a 3-digit number followed by text. The software interprets the number; the text is meant for humans.

The example session also illustrates a feature of FTP described earlier: the creation of new TCP connections for data transfer. Notice the *PORT* command in the output. The client *PORT* command reports that a new TCP port number has been obtained for use as a data connection. The client sends the port information to the server over the control connection; data transfer processes at both ends use the new port number when forming a connection. After the transfer completes, the data transfer processes at each end close the connection.

26.11 TFTP

Although FTP is the most general file transfer protocol in the TCP/IP suite, it is also the most complex and difficult to program. Many applications do not need the full functionality FTP offers, nor can they afford the complexity. For example, FTP requires clients and servers to manage multiple concurrent TCP connections, something that may be difficult or impossible on personal computers that do not have sophisticated operating systems.

The TCP/IP suite contains a second file transfer protocol that provides inexpensive, unsophisticated service. Known as the *Trivial File Transfer Protocol*, or (*TFTP*), it is intended for applications that do not need complex interactions between the client and server. TFTP restricts operations to simple file transfers and does not provide authentication. Because it is more restrictive, TFTP software is much smaller than FTP.

Small size is important in many applications. For example, manufacturers of diskless devices can encode TFTP in read-only memory (ROM) and use it to obtain an initial memory image when the machine is powered on. The program in ROM is called the system *bootstrap*†. The advantage of using TFTP is that it allows bootstrapping code to use the same underlying TCP/IP protocols that the operating system uses once it begins execution. Thus, it is possible for a computer to bootstrap from a server on another physical network.

Unlike FTP, TFTP does not need a reliable stream transport service. It runs on top of UDP or any other unreliable packet delivery system, using timeout and retransmission to ensure that data arrives. The sending side transmits a file in fixed size (*512* byte) blocks and awaits an acknowledgement for each block before sending the next. The receiver acknowledges each block upon receipt.

---

†Chapter 23 discusses the details of bootstrapping with DHCP.

The rules for TFTP are simple. The first packet sent requests a file transfer and establishes the interaction between client and server — the packet specifies a file name and whether the file will be read (transferred to the client) or written (transferred to the server). Blocks of the file are numbered consecutively starting at *1*. Each data packet contains a header that specifies the number of the block it carries, and each acknowledgement contains the number of the block being acknowledged. A block of less than *512* bytes signals the end of file. It is possible to send an error message either in the place of data or an acknowledgement; errors terminate the transfer.

Figure 26.2 shows the format of the five TFTP packet types. The initial packet must use operation codes *1* or *2*, specifying either a *read request* or a *write request*. The initial packet contains the name of the file as well as the access mode the client requests (*read* access or *write* access).

2-octet opcode	n octets	1 octet	n octets	1 octet
READ REQ. (1)	FILENAME	0	MODE	0

2-octet opcode	n octets	1 octet	n octets	1 octet
WRITE REQ. (2)	FILENAME	0	MODE	0

2-octet opcode	2 octets	up to 512 octets
DATA (3)	BLOCK #	DATA OCTETS...

2-octet opcode	2 octets
ACK (4)	BLOCK #

2-octet opcode	2 octets	n octets	1 octet
ERROR (5)	ERROR CODE	ERROR MESSAGE	0

Figure 26.2 The five TFTP message types. Fields are not shown to scale because some are variable length; an initial 2-octet operation code identifies the message format.

Once a *read* or *write* request has been made, the server uses the IP address and UDP protocol port number of the client to identify subsequent operations. Thus, neither *data* messages (the messages that carry blocks from the file) nor *ack* messages (the messages that acknowledge data blocks) need to specify the file name. The final message type illustrated in Figure 26.2 is used to report errors. Lost messages can be retransmitted after a timeout, but most other errors simply cause termination of the interaction.

TFTP retransmission is unusual because it is symmetric. Each side implements a timeout and retransmission. If the side sending data times out, it retransmits the last data block. If the side responsible for acknowledgements times out, it retransmits the last acknowledgement. Having both sides participate in retransmission helps ensure that transfer will not fail after a single packet loss.

While symmetric retransmission guarantees robustness, it can lead to excessive retransmissions. The problem, known as the *Sorcerer's Apprentice Bug*, arises when an acknowledgement for data packet k is delayed, but not lost. The sender retransmits the data packet, which the receiver acknowledges. Both acknowledgements eventually arrive, and each triggers a transmission of data packet $k+1$. The receiver will acknowledge both copies of data packet k+1, and the two acknowledgements will each cause the sender to transmit data packet $k+2$. The Sorcerer's Apprentice Bug can also start if the underlying internet duplicates packets. Once started, the cycle continues indefinitely with each data packet being transmitted exactly twice.

Although TFTP contains little except the minimum needed for transfer, it does support multiple file types. One interesting aspect of TFTP allows it to be integrated with electronic mail†. A client can specify to the server that it will send a file that should be treated as mail with the *FILENAME* field taken to be the name of a mailbox to which the server should deliver the message.

26.12 NFS

Initially developed by Sun Microsystems Incorporated, the *Network File System* (*NFS*) provides on-line shared file access that is transparent and integrated; many TCP/IP sites use NFS to interconnect their computers' file systems. From the user's perspective, NFS is almost invisible. A user can execute an arbitrary application program and use arbitrary files for input or output. The file names themselves do not show whether the files are local or remote.

26.13 NFS Implementation

Figure 26.3 illustrates how NFS is embedded in an operating system. When an application program executes, it calls the operating system to *open* a file, or to *store* and *retrieve* data in files. The file access mechanism accepts the request and automatically passes it to either the local file system software or to the NFS client, depending on whether the file is on the local disk or on a remote machine. When it receives a request, the client software uses the NFS protocol to contact the appropriate server on a remote machine and perform the requested operation. When the remote server replies, the client software returns the results to the application program.

---

†In practice, the use of TFTP as a mail transport is discouraged. Refer to Chapter 27 for details on electronic mail.

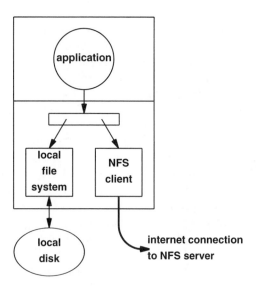

Figure 26.3 NFS code in an operating system. When an application program
requests a file operation, the operating system must pass the request to the local file system or to the NFS client software.

26.14 Remote Procedure Call (RPC)

Instead of defining the NFS protocol from scratch, the designers chose to build
three independent pieces: the NFS protocol itself, a general-purpose *Remote Procedure
Call (RPC)* mechanism, and a general-purpose *eXternal Data Representation (XDR)*.
Their intent was to separate the three to make it possible to use RPC and XDR in other
software, including application programs as well as other protocols.

From the programmer's point of view, NFS itself provides no new procedures that
a program can call. Instead, once a manager has configured NFS, programs access remote files using exactly the same operations as they use for local files. However, both
RPC and XDR provide mechanisms that programmers can use to build distributed programs. For example, a programmer can divide a program into a client side and a server
side that use RPC as the chief communication mechanism. On the client side, the programmer designates some procedures as *remote*, forcing the compiler to incorporate
RPC code into those procedures. On the server side, the programmer implements the
desired procedures and uses other RPC facilities to declare them to be part of a server.
When the executing client program calls one of the remote procedures, RPC automatically collects values for arguments, forms a message, sends the message to the remote
server, awaits a response, and stores returned values in the designated arguments. In
essence, communication with the remote server occurs automatically as a side-effect of
a remote procedure call. The RPC mechanism hides all the details of protocols, making
it possible for programmers who know little about the underlying communication protocols to write distributed programs.

A related tool, XDR, provides a way for programmers to pass data among heterogeneous machines without writing procedures to convert among the hardware data
representations. For example, not all computers represent 32-bit binary integers in the
same format. Some store the most significant byte at the highest memory address,
while others store the least significant byte at the highest address. Thus, if programmers use a network merely to move the bytes of an integer from one machine to another
without rearranging them, the value of the integer may change. XDR solves the problem by defining a machine-independent representation. At one end of a communication
channel, a program invokes XDR procedures to convert from the local hardware
representation to the machine-independent representation. Once the data has been
transferred to another machine, the receiving program invokes XDR routines to convert
from the machine-independent representation to the machine's local representation.

The chief advantage of XDR is that it automates much of the data conversion task.
Programmers do not need to type XDR procedure calls manually. Instead, they provide
the XDR compiler with the declaration statements from the program for which data
must be transformed, and the compiler automatically generates a program with the needed XDR library calls.

26.15 Summary

Access to data on remote files takes two forms: whole-file copying and shared on-
line access. The File Transfer Protocol, FTP, is the major file transfer protocol in the
TCP/IP suite. FTP uses whole-file copying and provides the ability for users to list
directories on the remote machine as well as transfer files in either direction. The Trivial File Transfer Protocol, TFTP, provides a small, simple alternative to FTP for applications that need only file transfer. Because it is small enough to be contained in ROM,
TFTP can be used for bootstrapping diskless machines.

The Network File System (NFS) designed by Sun Microsystems Incorporated provides on-line shared file access. It uses UDP for message transport and Sun's Remote
Procedure Call (RPC) and eXternal Data Representation (XDR) mechanisms. Because
RPC and XDR are defined separately from NFS, programmers can use them to build
distributed applications.

FOR FURTHER STUDY

Postel [RFC 959] contains the FTP protocol standard; Horowitz and Lunt [RFC
2228], Allman and Ostermann [RFC 2577], and Housley and Hoffman [RFC 2585] discuss security extensions. Over three dozen RFCs comment on FTP, propose modifications, or define new versions of the protocol. Among them, Lottor [RFC 913] describes
a Simple File Transfer Protocol. DeSchon and Braden [RFC 1068] shows how to use
FTP third-party transfer for background file transfer. Allman and Ostermann [RFC

2428] considers FTP with IPv6 and NATs. The Trivial File Transfer Protocol described in this chapter comes from Sollins [RFC 783]; Finlayson [RFC 906] describes TFTP's use in bootstrapping computer systems, and Malkin and Harkin [RFCs 2347 and 2348] discuss options.

Sun Microsystems has published three RFCs that define the Network File System and related protocols. RFC 1094 contains the standard for NFS, RFC 1057 defines RPC, and RFC 1014 specifies XDR. More details about RPC and NFS can be found in Volume 3 of this text.

EXERCISES

26.1 Why should file transport protocols compute a checksum on the file data they receive, even when using a reliable end-to-end stream transfer protocol like TCP?

26.2 Find out whether FTP computes a checksum for files it transfers.

26.3 What happens in FTP if the TCP connection being used for data transfer breaks, but the control connection does not?

26.4 What is the chief advantage of using separate TCP connections for control and data transfer? (Hint: think of abnormal conditions.)

26.5 Outline a method that uses TFTP to bootstrap a diskless machine. Be careful. Exactly what IP addresses does it use at each step?

26.6 Implement a TFTP client.

26.7 Experiment with FTP or an equivalent protocol to see how fast you can transfer a file between two reasonably large systems across a local area network. Try the experiment when the network is busy and when it is idle. Explain the result.

26.8 Try FTP from a machine to itself and then from the machine to another machine on the same local area network. Do the data transfer rates surprise you?

26.9 Compare the rates of transfer for FTP and NFS on a local area network. Can you explain the difference?

26.10 Examine the RPC definition. Does it handle datagram loss? duplication? delay? corruption?

26.11 Extend the previous question and consider NFS running over RPC. Will NFS work well across the global Internet? Why or why not?

26.12 Under what circumstances is the XDR scheme inefficient?

26.13 Consider translating floating point numbers from an internal form to an external form and back to an internal form. What are the tradeoffs in the choice of exponent and mantissa sizes in the external form?

26.14 FTP defaults to using *ASCII mode* (i.e. text mode) to transfer files. Is the default wise? Argue that the ascii mode default can be considered "harmful".

27

Applications: Electronic Mail (SMTP, POP, IMAP, MIME)

27.1 Introduction

This chapter continues our exploration of internetworking by considering electronic mail service and the protocols that support it. The chapter describes how a mail system is organized, explains alias expansion, and shows how mail system software uses the client-server paradigm to transfer each message.

27.2 Electronic Mail

An *electronic mail* (*e-mail*) facility allows users to send memos across an internet. E-mail is one of the most widely used application services. Indeed, some users rely on e-mail for normal business activities.

E-mail is also popular because it offers a fast, convenient method of transferring information. E-mail accommodates small notes or large voluminous memos with a single mechanism. It should not surprise you to learn that more users send files with electronic mail than with file transfer protocols.

Mail delivery is a new concept because it differs fundamentally from other uses of networks that we have discussed. In all our examples, network protocols send packets directly to destinations, using timeout and retransmission for individual segments if no acknowledgement returns. In the case of electronic mail, however, the system must provide for instances when the remote machine is temporarily unreachable (e.g., because a network connection has failed). A sender does not want to wait for the remote machine to respond before continuing work, nor does the user want the transfer to abort merely because the destination is temporarily unavailable.

To handle delayed delivery, mail systems use a technique known as *spooling*. When the user sends a mail message, the system places a copy in its private storage (spool†) area along with identification of the sender, recipient, destination machine, and time of deposit. The system then initiates the transfer to the remote machine as a background activity, allowing the sender to proceed with other computational activities. Figure 27.1 illustrates the concept.

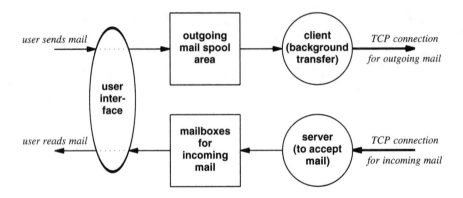

Figure 27.1 Conceptual components of an electronic mail system. The user invokes a user interface to deposit or retrieve mail; all transfers occur in the background.

The background mail transfer process becomes a client. It first uses the domain name system to map the destination machine name to an IP address, and then attempts to form a TCP connection to the mail server on the destination machine. If it succeeds, the transfer process passes a copy of the message to the remote server, which stores the copy in the remote system's spool area. Once the client and server agree that the copy has been accepted and stored, the client removes the local copy. If it cannot form a TCP connection or if the connection fails, the transfer process records the time delivery was attempted and terminates. The background transfer process sweeps through the spool area periodically, typically once every 30 minutes, checking for undelivered mail. Whenever it finds a message or whenever a user deposits new outgoing mail, the background process attempts delivery. If it finds that a mail message cannot be delivered after an extended time (e.g., 3 days), the mail software returns the message to the sender.

---

†A mail spool area is sometimes called a *mail queue* even though the term is technically inaccurate.

27.3 Mailbox Names And Aliases

There are three important ideas hidden in our simplistic description of mail delivery. First, users specify recipients by giving pairs of strings that identify the *mail destination machine name* and a *mailbox address* on that machine. Second, the names used in such specifications are independent of other names assigned to machines. Usually, a mailbox address is the same as a user's login id, and a destination machine name is the same as a machine's domain name, but that is not necessary. It is possible to assign a mailbox to a position of employment (e.g., the mailbox identifier *department-head* can refer to whoever currently chairs the department). Also, because the domain name system includes a separate query type for mail destinations, it is possible to decouple mail destination names from the usual domain names assigned to machines. Thus, mail sent to a user at *example.com* may go to a different machine than a telnet connection to the same name. Third, our simplistic diagram fails to account for *mail processing* and *mail forwarding*, which include mail sent from one user to another on the same machine, and mail that arrives on a machine but which should be forwarded to another machine.

27.4 Alias Expansion And Mail Forwarding

Most systems provide *mail forwarding* software that includes a *mail alias expansion* mechanism. A mail forwarder allows the local site to map identifiers used in mail addresses to a set of one or more new mail addresses. Usually, after a user composes a message and names a recipient, the mail interface program consults the local aliases to replace the recipient with the mapped version before passing the message to the delivery system. Recipients for which no mapping has been specified remain unchanged. Similarly, the underlying mail system uses the mail aliases to map incoming recipient addresses.

Aliases increase mail system functionality and convenience substantially. In mathematical terms, alias mappings can be many-one or one-many. For example, the alias system allows a single user to have multiple mail identifiers, including nicknames and positions, by mapping a set of identifiers to a single person. The system also allows a site to associate groups of recipients with a single identifier. Using aliases that map an identifier to a list of identifiers makes it possible to establish a *mail exploder* that accepts one incoming message and sends it to a large set of recipients. The set of recipients associated with an identifier is called an *electronic mailing list*. Not all the recipients on a list need to be local. Although it is uncommon, it is possible to have a mailing list at site, *Q*, with none of the recipients from the list located at *Q*. Expanding a mail alias into a large set of recipients is a popular technique used widely. Figure 27.2 illustrates the components of a mail system that supports mail aliases and list expansion.

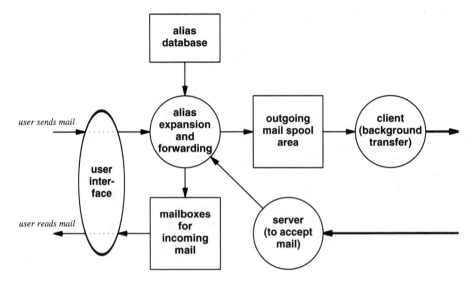

Figure 27.2 An extension of the mail system in Figure 27.1 that supports mail
aliases and forwarding. Both incoming and outgoing mail
passes through the alias expansion mechanism.

As Figure 27.2 shows, incoming and outgoing mail passes through the mail forwarder that expands aliases. Thus, if the alias database specifies that mail address x
maps to replacement y, alias expansion will rewrite destination address x, changing it to
y. The alias expansion program then determines whether y specifies a local or remote
address, so it knows whether to place the message in the incoming mail queue or outgoing mail queue.

Mail alias expansion can be dangerous. Suppose two sites establish conflicting
aliases. For example, assume site A maps mail address x into mail address y at site B,
while site B maps mail address y into address x at site A. A mail message sent to address x at site A could bounce forever between the two sites†. Similarly, if the manager
at site A accidentally maps a user's login name at that site to an address at another site,
the user will be unable to receive mail. The mail may go to another user or, if the alias
specifies an illegal address, senders will receive error messages.

27.5 The Relationship Of Internetworking And Mail

Commercial services exist that can forward electronic mail among computers
without using TCP/IP and without having the computers connected to the global Internet. How do such systems differ from the mail system described here? There are two
crucial differences. First, a TCP/IP internet makes possible universal delivery service.
Second, electronic mail systems built on TCP/IP are inherently more reliable than those

---

†In practice, most mail forwarders terminate messages after the number of exchanges reaches a predetermined threshold.

built from arbitrary networks. The first idea is easy to understand. TCP/IP makes possible universal mail delivery because it provides universal interconnection among machines. In essence, all machines attached to an internet behave as if attached to a single, vendor independent network. With the basic network services in place, devising a standard mail exchange protocol becomes easier.

The second claim, that using TCP/IP makes mail delivery more reliable than other mechanisms, needs explanation. The key idea is that TCP provides end-to-end connectivity. That is, mail software on the sending machine acts as a client, contacting a server on the ultimate destination. Only after the client successfully transfers a mail message to the server does it remove the message from the local machine. Thus, direct, end-to-end delivery enforces the following principle:

> *Mail systems that use end-to-end delivery can guarantee that each mail message remains in the sender's machine until it has been successfully copied to the recipient's machine.*

With such systems, the sender can always determine the exact status of a message by checking the local mail spool area.

The alternative form of electronic mail delivery uses the application gateway approach discussed in Chapter 20. The message is transferred through a series of *mail gateways*†, sometimes called *mail bridges*, *mail relays*, or *intermediate mail stops*. In such systems, the sender's machine does not contact the recipient's machine directly. Instead, a complete mail message is sent from the original sender to the first gateway. The message is then forwarded to the second gateway, and so on.

The main disadvantage of using mail gateways is that they introduce unreliability. Once it transfers a message to the first intermediate machine, the sender's computer discards the local copy. Thus, while the message is in transit, neither the sender nor the recipient have a copy. Failures at intermediate machines may result in message loss without either the sender or recipient being informed. Message loss can also result if the mail gateways route mail incorrectly. Another disadvantage of mail gateways is that they introduce delay. A mail gateway can hold messages for minutes, hours, or even days if it cannot forward them on to the next machine. Neither the sender nor receiver can determine where a message has been delayed, why it has not arrived, or how long the delay will last. The important point is that the sender and recipient must depend on computers over which they may have no control.

If mail gateways are less reliable than end-to-end delivery, why are they used? The chief advantage of mail gateways is interoperability. Mail gateways provide connections among standard TCP/IP mail systems and other mail systems, as well as between TCP/IP internets and networks that do not support Internet protocols. Suppose, for example, that company X has a large internal network and that employees use electronic mail, but that the network software does not support TCP/IP. Although it may be infeasible to make the company's network part of the global Internet, it might be easy to place a mail gateway between the company's private network and the Internet, and to devise software that accepts mail messages from the local network and forwards them to the Internet.

---

†Readers should not confuse the term *mail gateway* with the term *IP gateway*, discussed in Chapter 3.

While the idea of mail gateways may seem somewhat awkward, electronic mail has become such an important tool that users who do not have Internet access depend on the gateways. Thus, although gateways service is not as reliable or convenient as end-to-end delivery, it can still be useful.

27.6 TCP/IP Standards For Electronic Mail Service

Recall that the goal of the TCP/IP protocol effort is to provide for interoperability across the widest range of computer systems and networks. To extend the interoperability of electronic mail, TCP/IP divides its mail standards into two sets. One standard specifies the format for mail messages†. The other specifies the details of electronic mail exchange between two computers. Keeping the two standards for electronic mail separate makes it possible to build mail gateways that connect TCP/IP internets to some other vendor's mail delivery system, while still using the same message format for both.

As anyone who has used electronic mail knows, each memo is divided into two parts: a header and a body, separated by a blank line. The TCP/IP standard for mail messages specifies the exact format of mail headers as well as the semantic interpretation of each header field; it leaves the format of the body up to the sender. In particular, the standard specifies that headers contain readable text, divided into lines that consist of a keyword followed by a colon followed by a value. Some keywords are required, others are optional, and the rest are uninterpreted. For example, the header must contain a line that specifies the destination. The line begins *To:* and contains the electronic mail address of the intended recipient on the remainder of the line. A line that begins *From:* contains the electronic mail address of the sender. Optionally, the sender may specify an address to which replies should be sent (i.e., to allow the sender to specify that replies should be sent to an address other than the sender's mailbox). If present, a line that begins *Reply-to:* specifies the address for replies. If no such line exists, the recipient will use information on the *From:* line as the return address.

The mail message format is chosen to make it easy to process and transport across heterogeneous machines. Keeping the mail header format straightforward allows it to be used on a wide range of systems. Restricting messages to readable text avoids the problems of selecting a standard binary representation and translating between the standard representation and the local machine's representation.

27.7 Electronic Mail Addresses

A user familiar with electronic mail knows that mail address formats vary among e-mail systems. Thus, it can be difficult to determine a correct electronic mail address, or even to understand a sender's intentions. Within the global Internet, addresses have a simple, easy to remember form:

local-part @ domain-name

---

†Mail system experts refer to the mail message format as "822" because RFC 822 defines the standard.

where *domain-name* is the domain name of a mail destination† to which the mail should be delivered, and *local-part* is the address of a mailbox on that machine. For example, within the Internet, the author's electronic mail address is:

comer @ purdue.edu

However, mail gateways make addresses complex. Someone outside the Internet must either address the mail to the nearest mail gateway or have software that automatically does so. For example, when CSNET operated a mail gateway that connected between outside networks and the Internet, someone with access to the gateway might have used the following address to reach the author:

comer % purdue.edu @ relay.cs.net

Once the mail reached machine *relay.cs.net*, the mail gateway software extracted *local-part*, changed the percent sign (%) into an at sign (@), and used the result as a destination address to forward the mail.

The reason addresses become complex when they include non-Internet sites is that the mail address mapping function is local to each machine. Thus, some mail gateways require the local part to contain addresses of the form:

user % domain-name

while others require:

user : domain-name

and still others use completely different forms. More important, electronic mail systems do not usually agree on conventions for precedence or quoting, making it impossible for a user to guarantee how addresses will be interpreted. For example, consider the electronic mail address:

comer % purdue.edu @ relay.cs.net

mentioned earlier. A site using the TCP/IP standard for mail would interpret the address to mean, "send the message to mail exchanger *relay.cs.net* and let that mail exchanger decide how to interpret *comer % purdue.edu*" (the local part). In essence, the site acts as if the address were parenthesized:

(comer % purdue.edu) @ (relay.cs.net)

At a site that uses % to separate user names from destination machines, the same address might mean, "send the mail to user *comer* at the site given by the remainder of the address." That is, such sites act as if the address were parenthesized:

(comer) % (purdue.edu @ relay.cs.net)

---

†Technically, the domain name specifies a *mail exchanger*, not a machine name.

We can summarize the problem:

> *Because each mail gateway determines the exact details of how it in-*
> *terprets and maps electronic mail addresses, there is no standard for*
> *addresses that cross mail gateway boundaries to networks outside the*
> *Internet.*

27.8 Pseudo Domain Addresses

To help solve the problem of multiple mail systems, each with its own e-mail address format, a site can use domain-style names for all e-mail addresses, even if the site
does not use the domain name system. For example, a site that uses UUCP can implement a pseudo-domain, *uucp*, that allows users to specify mail addresses of the form:

uucp-style address @ uucp

or a related form:

user @ uucp-site . uucp

The local mail forwarding software recognizes the special addresses and translates them
to the address syntax required by the UUCP network software. From the user's perspective, the advantage is clear: all electronic addresses have the same general format
independent of the underlying communication network used to reach the recipient. Of
course, such addresses only work where local mailers have been instructed to map them
into appropriate forms and only when the appropriate transport mechanisms are available. Furthermore, even though pseudo-domain mail addresses have the same form as
domain names, they can only be used with electronic mail — one cannot use the
domain name system to resolve a pseudo address into an underlying IP address.

27.9 Simple Mail Transfer Protocol (SMTP)

In addition to message formats, the TCP/IP protocol suite specifies a standard for
the exchange of mail between machines. That is, the standard specifies the exact format
of messages a client on one machine uses to transfer mail to a server on another. The
standard transfer protocol is known as the *Simple Mail Transfer Protocol* (*SMTP*). As
you might guess, SMTP is simpler than the earlier *Mail Transfer Protocol*, (*MTP*). The
SMTP protocol focuses specifically on how the underlying mail delivery system passes
messages across an internet from one machine to another. It does not specify how the
mail system accepts mail from a user or how the user interface presents the user with
incoming mail. Also, SMTP does not specify how mail is stored or how frequently the
mail system attempts to send messages.

SMTP is surprisingly straightforward. Communication between a client and server consists of readable ASCII text. Although SMTP rigidly defines the command format, humans can easily read a transcript of interactions between a client and server. Initially, the client establishes a reliable stream connection to the server and waits for the server to send a *220 READY FOR MAIL* message. (If the server is overloaded, it may delay sending the *220* message temporarily.) Upon receipt of the *220* message, the client sends a *HELO*† command. The end of a line marks the end of a command. The server responds by identifying itself. Once communication has been established, the sender can transmit one or more mail messages, terminate the connection, or request the server to exchange the roles of sender and receiver so messages can flow in the opposite direction. The receiver must acknowledge each message. It can also abort the entire connection or abort the current message transfer.

Mail transactions begin with a *MAIL* command that gives the sender identification as well as a *FROM:* field that contains the address to which errors should be reported. A recipient prepares its data structures to receive a new mail message, and replies to a *MAIL* command by sending the response *250*. Response *250* means that all is well. The full response consists of the text *250 OK*. As with other application protocols, programs read the abbreviated commands and 3-digit numbers at the beginning of lines; the remaining text is intended to help humans debug mail software.

After a successful *MAIL* command, the sender issues a series of *RCPT* commands that identify recipients of the mail message. The receiver must acknowledge each *RCPT* command by sending *250 OK* or by sending the error message *550 No such user here*.

After all *RCPT* commands have been acknowledged, the sender issues a *DATA* command. In essence, a *DATA* command informs the receiver that the sender is ready to transfer a complete mail message. The receiver responds with message *354 Start mail input* and specifies the sequence of characters used to terminate the mail message. The termination sequence consists of 5 characters: carriage return, line feed, period, carriage return, and line feed‡.

An example will clarify the SMTP exchange. Suppose user *Smith* at host *Alpha.EDU* sends a message to users *Jones*, *Green*, and *Brown* at host *Beta.GOV*. The SMTP client software on host *Alpha.EDU* contacts the SMTP server software on host *Beta.GOV* and begins the exchange shown in Figure 27.3.

---

†*HELO* is an abbreviation for "hello."

‡SMTP uses *CR-LF* to terminate a line, and forbids the body of a mail message to have a period on a line by itself.

```
S: 220 Beta.GOV Simple Mail Transfer Service Ready
C: HELO Alpha.EDU
S: 250 Beta.GOV

C: MAIL FROM:<Smith@Alpha.EDU>
S: 250 OK

C: RCPT TO:<Jones@Beta.GOV>
S: 250 OK

C: RCPT TO:<Green@Beta.GOV>
S: 550 No such user here

C: RCPT TO:<Brown@Beta.GOV>
S: 250 OK

C: DATA
S: 354 Start mail input; end with <CR><LF>.<CR><LF>
C: ...sends body of mail message...
C: ...continues for as many lines as message contains
C: <CR><LF>.<CR><LF>
S: 250 OK

C: QUIT
S: 221 Beta.GOV Service closing transmission channel
```

Figure 27.3 Example of SMTP transfer from Alpha.EDU to Beta.GOV.
Lines that begin with ''C:'' are transmitted by the client (Alpha), while lines that begin with ''S:'' are transmitted by the server.
In the example, machine Beta.GOV does not recognize the intended recipient Green.

In the example, the server rejects recipient *Green* because it does not recognize the
name as a valid mail destination (i.e., it is neither a user nor a mailing list). The SMTP
protocol does not specify the details of how a client handles such errors — the client
must decide. Although clients can abort the delivery completely if an error occurs,
most clients do not. Instead, they continue delivery to all valid recipients and then report problems to the original sender. Usually, the client reports errors using electronic
mail. The error message contains a summary of the error as well as the header of the
mail message that caused the problem.

Once a client has finished sending all the mail messages it has for a particular destination, the client may issue the *TURN*† command to turn the connection around. If it
does, the receiver responds *250 OK* and assumes control of the connection. With the
roles reversed, the side that was originally a server sends back any waiting mail mes-

---

†In practice, few mail servers use the *TURN* command.

sages. Whichever side controls the interaction can choose to terminate the session; to do so, it issues a *QUIT* command. The other side responds with command *221*, which means it agrees to terminate. Both sides then close the TCP connection gracefully.

SMTP is much more complex than we have outlined here. For example, if a user has moved, the server may know the user's new mailbox address. SMTP allows the server to inform the client about the new address so the client can use it in the future. When informing the client about a new address, the server may choose to forward the mail that triggered the message, or it may request that the client take the responsibility for forwarding.

27.10 Mail Retrieval And Mailbox Manipulation Protocols

The SMTP transfer scheme described above implies that a server must remain ready to accept e-mail at all times; the client attempts to send a message as soon as a user enters it. The scenario works well if the server runs on a computer that has a permanent internet connection, but it does not work well for a computer that has intermittent connectivity. In particular, consider a user who only has dialup Internet access. It makes no sense for such a user to run a conventional e-mail server because the server will only be available while the user is dialed in — all other attempts to contact the server will fail, and e-mail sent to the user will remain undelivered. The question arises, "how can a user without a permanent connection receive e-mail?"

The answer to the question lies in a two-stage delivery process. In the first stage, each user is assigned a mailbox on a computer that has a permanent Internet connection. The computer runs a conventional SMTP server, which always remains ready to accept e-mail. In the second stage, the user forms a dialup connection, and then runs a protocol that retrieves messages from the permanent mailbox. The protocol transfers the messages to the user's computer where they can be read.

Two protocols exist that allow a remote user to retrieve mail from a permanent mailbox. The protocols have similar functionality: in addition to providing access, each protocol allows a user to manipulate the mailbox content (e.g., permanently delete a message). The next two sections describe the two protocols.

27.10.1 Post Office Protocol

The most popular protocol used to transfer e-mail messages from a permanent mailbox to a local computer is known as version 3 of the *Post Office Protocol* (*POP3*). The user invokes a POP3 client, which creates a TCP connection to a POP3 server on the mailbox computer. The user first sends a *login* and a *password* to authenticate the session. Once authentication has been accepted, the user client sends commands to retrieve a copy of one or more messages and to delete the message from the permanent mailbox. The messages are stored and transferred as text files in 822 standard format.

Note that the computer with the permanent mailbox must run two servers — an SMTP server accepts mail sent to a user and adds each incoming message to the user's permanent mailbox, and a POP3 server allows a user to extract messages from the mailbox and delete them. To ensure correct operation, the two servers must coordinate use of the mailbox so that if a message arrives via SMTP while a user is extracting messages via POP3, the mailbox is left in a valid state.

27.10.2 Internet Message Access Protocol

Version 4 of the *Internet Message Access Protocol* (*IMAP4*) is an alternative to POP3 that uses the same general paradigm. Like POP3, IMAP4 defines an abstraction known as a *mailbox*; mailboxes are located on the same computer as a server. Also like POP3, a user runs an IMAP4 client that contacts the server to retrieve messages. Unlike POP3, however, IMAP4 allows a user to dynamically create, delete, or rename mailboxes.

IMAP4 also provides extended functionality for message retrieval and processing. A user can obtain information about a message or examine header fields without retrieving the entire message. In addition, a user can search for a specified string and retrieve specified portions of a message. Partial retrieval is especially useful for slow-speed dialup connections because it means a user does not need to download useless information.

27.11 The MIME Extension For Non-ASCII Data

The *Multipurpose Internet Mail Extensions* (*MIME*) were defined to allow transmission of non-ASCII data through e-mail. MIME does not change SMTP or POP3, nor does MIME replace them. Instead, MIME allows arbitrary data to be encoded in ASCII and then transmitted in a standard e-mail message. To accommodate arbitrary data types and representations, each MIME message includes information that tells the recipient the type of the data and the encoding used. MIME information resides in the 822 mail header — the MIME header lines specify the version of MIME used, the type of the data being sent, and the encoding used to convert the data to ASCII. For example, Figure 27.4 illustrates a MIME message that contains a photograph in standard *GIF*† representation. The GIF image has been converted to a 7-bit ASCII representation using the *base64* encoding.

```
From: bill@acollege.edu
To: john@example.com
MIME-Version: 1.0
Content-Type: image/gif
Content-Transfer-Encoding: base64

...data for the image...
```

Figure 27.4 An example MIME message. Lines in the header identify the type of the data as well as the encoding used.

---

†GIF is the Graphics Interchange Format.

In the figure, the header line *MIME-Version:* declares that the message was composed using version *1.0* of the MIME protocol. The *Content-Type:* declaration specifies that the data is a GIF image, and the *Content-Transfer-Encoding:* header declares that *base64* encoding was used to convert the image to ASCII. To view the image, a receiver's mail system must first convert from *base64* encoding back to binary, and then run an application that displays a GIF image on the user's screen.

The MIME standard specifies that a *Content-Type* declaration must contain two identifiers, a *content type* and a *subtype*, separated by a slash. In the example, *image* is the content type, and *gif* is the subtype.

The standard defines seven basic content types, the valid subtypes for each, and transfer encodings. For example, although an *image* must be of subtype *jpeg* or *gif*, *text* cannot use either subtype. In addition to the standard types and subtypes, MIME permits a sender and receiver to define private content types†. Figure 27.5 lists the seven basic content types.

Content Type	Used When Data In the Message Is
text	Textual (e.g. a document).
image	A still photograph or computer-generated image
audio	A sound recording
video	A video recording that includes motion
application	Raw data for a program
multipart	Multiple messages that each have a separate content type and encoding
message	An entire e-mail message (e.g., a memo that has been forwarded) or an external reference to a message (e.g., an FTP server and file name)

Figure 27.5 The seven basic types that can appear in a MIME *Content-Type* declaration and their meanings.

27.12 MIME Multipart Messages

The MIME multipart content type is useful because it adds considerable flexibility. The standard defines four possible subtypes for a multipart message; each provides important functionality. Subtype *mixed* allows a single message to contain multiple, independent submessages that each can have an independent type and encoding. Mixed multipart messages make it possible to include text, graphics, and audio in a single message, or to send a memo with additional data segments attached, similar to *enclosures* included with a business letter. Subtype *alternative* allows a single message to include multiple representations of the same data. Alternative multipart messages are useful when sending a memo to many recipients who do not all use the same hardware and software system. For example, one can send a document as both plain ASCII text and in formatted form, allowing recipients who have computers with graphic capabilities to

---

†To avoid potential name conflicts, the standard requires that names chosen for private content types each begin with the string *X-* .

select the formatted form for viewing. Subtype *parallel* permits a single message to include subparts that should be viewed together (e.g., video and audio subparts that must
be played simultaneously). Finally, subtype *digest* permits a single message to contain
a set of other messages (e.g., a collection of the e-mail messages from a discussion).

Figure 27.6 illustrates one of the prime uses for multipart messages: an e-mail message can contain both a short text that explains the purpose of the message and other
parts that contain nontextual information. In the figure, a note in the first part of the
message explains that the second part contains a photographic image.

```
From: bill@acollege.edu
To: john@example.com
MIME-Version: 1.0
Content-Type: Multipart/Mixed; Boundary=StartOfNextPart

--StartOfNextPart
John,
    Here is the photo of our research lab that I promised
to send you.  You can see the equipment you donated.

Thanks again,
Bill

--StartOfNextPart
Content-Type: image/gif
Content-Transfer-Encoding: base64
      ...data for the image...
```

Figure 27.6 An example of a MIME mixed multipart message. Each part of
the message can have an independent content type.

The figure also illustrates a few details of MIME. For example, each header line
can contain parameters of the form $X = Y$ after basic declarations. The keyword *Boun-
dary=* following the multipart content type declaration in the header defines the string
used to separate parts of the message. In the example, the sender has selected the string
StartOfNextPart to serve as the boundary. Declarations of the content type and transfer
encoding for a submessage, if included, immediately follow the boundary line. In the
example, the second submessage is declared to be a GIF image.

27.13 Summary

Electronic mail is among the most widely available application services. Like
most TCP/IP services, it uses the client-server paradigm. The mail system buffers outgoing and incoming messages, allowing the transfer from client and server to occur in
background.

The TCP/IP protocol suite provides separate standards for mail message format and mail transfer. The mail message format, called *822*, uses a blank line to separate a message header and the body. The Simple Mail Transfer Protocol (SMTP) defines how a mail system on one machine transfers mail to a server on another. Version 3 of the Post Office Protocol (POP3) specifies how a user can retrieve the contents of a mailbox; it allows a user to have a permanent mailbox on a computer with continuous Internet connectivity and to access the contents from a computer with intermittent connectivity.

The Multipurpose Internet Mail Extensions (MIME) provides a mechanism that allows arbitrary data to be transferred using SMTP. MIME adds lines to the header of an e-mail message to define the type of the data and the encoding used. MIME's mixed multipart type permits a single message to contain multiple data types.

FOR FURTHER STUDY

The protocols described in this chapter are all specified in Internet RFCs. Postel [RFC 821] describes the Simple Mail Transfer Protocol and gives many examples. The exact format of mail messages is given by Crocker [RFC 822]; many RFCs specify additions and changes. Freed and Borenstein [RFCs 2045, 2046, 2047, 2048 and 2049] specify the standard for MIME, including the syntax of header declarations, the procedure for creating new content types, the interpretation of content types, and the *base64* encoding mentioned in this chapter. Partridge [RFC 974] discusses the relationship between mail routing and the domain name system. Horton [RFC 976] proposes a standard for the UNIX UUCP mail system.

EXERCISES

27.1   Some mail systems force the user to specify a sequence of machines through which the message should travel to reach its destination. The mail protocol in each machine merely passes the message on to the next machine. List three disadvantages of such a scheme.

27.2   Find out if your computing system allows you to invoke SMTP directly.

27.3   Build an SMTP client and use it to deliver a mail message.

27.4   See if you can send mail through a mail gateway and back to yourself.

27.5   Make a list of mail address forms that your site handles and write a set of rules for parsing them.

27.6   Find out how the UNIX *sendmail* program can be used to implement a mail gateway.

27.7   Find out how often your local mail system attempts delivery and how long it will continue before giving up.

27.8   Many mail systems allow users to direct incoming mail to a program instead of storing it in a mailbox. Build a program that accepts your incoming mail, places your mail in a file, and then sends a reply to tell the sender you are on vacation.

27.9   Read the SMTP standard carefully. Then use TELNET to connect to the SMTP port on a remote machine and ask the remote SMTP server to expand a mail alias.

27.10   A user receives mail in which the *To* field specifies the string *important-people*. The mail was sent from a computer on which the alias *important-people* includes no valid mailbox identifiers. Read the SMTP specification carefully to see how such a situation is possible.

27.11   POP3 separates message retrieval and deletion by allowing a user to retrieve and view a message without deleting it from the permanent mailbox. What are the advantages and disadvantages of such separation?

27.12   Read about POP3. How does the *TOP* command operate, and why is it useful?

27.13   Read the MIME standard carefully. What servers can be specified in a MIME external reference?

28

Applications: World Wide Web (HTTP)

28.1 Introduction

This chapter continues the discussion of applications that use TCP/IP technology by focusing on the application that has had the most impact: the *World Wide Web* (*WWW*). After a brief overview of concepts, the chapter examines the primary protocol used to transfer a Web page from a server to a Web browser. The discussion covers caching as well as the basic transfer mechanism.

28.2 Importance Of The Web

During the early history of the Internet, FTP data transfers accounted for approximately one third of Internet traffic, more than any other application. From its inception in the early 1990s, however, the Web had a much higher growth rate. By 1995, Web traffic overtook FTP to become the largest consumer of Internet backbone bandwidth, and has remained the leader ever since. By 2000, Web traffic completely overshadowed other applications.

Although traffic is easy to measure and cite, the impact of the Web cannot be understood from such statistics. More people know about and use the Web than any other Internet application. Most companies have Web sites and on-line catalogs; references to the Web appear in advertising. In fact, for many users, the Internet and the Web are indistinguishable.

28.3 Architectural Components

Conceptually, the Web consists of a large set of documents, called *Web pages*, that are accessible over the Internet. Each Web page is classified as a *hypermedia* document. The suffix *media* is used to indicate that a document can contain items other than text (e.g., graphics images); the prefix *hyper* is used because a document can contain *selectable links* that refer to other, related documents.

Two main building blocks are used to implement the Web on top of the global Internet. A *Web browser* consists of an application program that a user invokes to access and display a Web page. The browser becomes a client that contacts the appropriate *Web server* to obtain a copy of the specified page. Because a given server can manage more than one Web page, a browser must specify the exact page when making a request.

The data representation standard used for a Web page depends on its contents. For example, standard graphics representations such as *Graphics Interchange Format* (*GIF*) or *Joint Picture Encoding Group* (*JPEG*) can be used for a page that contains a single graphics image. Pages that contain a mixture of text and other items are represented using *HyperText Markup Language* (*HTML*). An HTML document consists of a file that contains text along with embedded commands, called *tags*, that give guidelines for display. A tag is enclosed in less-than and greater-than symbols; some tags come in pairs that apply to all items between the pair. For example, the two commands *<CENTER>* and *</CENTER>* cause items between them to be centered in the browser's window.

28.4 Uniform Resource Locators

Each Web page is assigned a unique name that is used to identify it. The name, which is called a *Uniform Resource Locator* (*URL*)†, begins with a specification of the *scheme* used to access the item. In effect, the scheme specifies the transfer protocol; the format of the remainder of the URL depends on the scheme. For example, a URL that follows the *http scheme* has the following form‡:

http: // *hostname [: port] / path [; parameters] [? query]*

where brackets denote an optional item. For now, it is sufficient to understand that the *hostname* string specifies the domain name or IP address of the computer on which the server for the item operates, *:port* is an optional protocol port number needed only in cases where the server does not use the well-known port (*80*), *path* is a string that identifies one particular document on the server, *;parameters* is an optional string that specifies additional parameters supplied by the client, and *?query* is an optional string used when the browser sends a question. A user is unlikely to ever see or use the optional parts directly. Instead, URLs that a user enters contain only a *hostname* and *path*. For example, the URL:

---

†A URL is a specific type of the more general *Uniform Resource Identifier* (*URI*).
‡Some of the literature refers to the initial string, *http:*, as a *pragma*.

http://www.cs.purdue.edu/people/comer/

specifies the author's Web page. The server operates on computer *www.cs.purdue.edu*, and the document is named */people/comer/*.

The protocol standards distinguish between the *absolute* form of a URL illustrated above, and a *relative* form. A relative URL, which is seldom seen by a user, is only meaningful when the server has already been determined. Relative URLs are useful once communication has been established with a specific server. For example, when communicating with server *www.cs.purdue.edu*, only the string */people/comer/* is needed to specify the document named by the absolute URL above. We can summarize.

> *Each Web page is assigned a unique identifier known as a Uniform Resource Locator (URL). The absolute form of a URL contains a full specification; a relative form that omits the address of the server is only useful when the server is implicitly known.*

28.5 An Example Document

In principle, Web access is straightforward. All access originates with a URL — a user either enters a URL via the keyboard or selects an item which provides the browser with a URL. The browser parses the URL, extracts the information, and uses it to obtain a copy of the requested page. Because the format of the URL depends on the scheme, the browser begins by extracting the scheme specification, and then uses the scheme to determine how to parse the rest of the URL.

An example will illustrate how a URL is produced from a *selectable link* in a document. In fact, a document contains a pair of values for each link: an item to be displayed on the screen and a URL to follow if the user selects the item. In HTML, the pair of tags *<A>* and *</A>* are known as an *anchor*. The anchor defines a link; a URL is added to the first tag, and items to be displayed are placed between the two tags. The browser stores the URL internally, and follows it when the user selects the link. For example, the following HTML document contains a selectable link:

```
<HTML>
    The author of this text is
    <A HREF="http://www.cs.purdue.edu/people/comer">
    Douglas Comer.</A>
</HTML>
```

When the document is displayed, a single line of text appears on the screen:

The author of this text is <u>Douglas Comer.</u>

The browser underlines the phrase *Douglas Comer* to indicate that it corresponds to a selectable link. Internally, of course, the browser stores the URL from the *<A>* tag, which it follows when the user selects the link.

28.6 Hypertext Transfer Protocol

The protocol used for communication between a browser and a Web server or between intermediate machines and Web servers is known as the *HyperText Transfer Protocol* (*HTTP*). HTTP has the following set of characteristics:

Application Level. HTTP operates at the application level. It assumes a reliable, connection-oriented transport protocol such as TCP, but does not provide reliability or retransmission itself.

Request/Response. Once a transport session has been established, one side (usually a browser) must send an HTTP request to which the other side responds.

Stateless. Each HTTP request is self-contained; the server does not keep a history of previous requests or previous sessions.

Bi-Directional Transfer. In most cases, a browser requests a Web page, and the server transfers a copy to the browser. HTTP also allows transfer from a browser to a server (e.g., when a user submits a so-called "form").

Capability Negotiation. HTTP allows browsers and servers to negotiate details such as the character set to be used during transfers. A sender can specify the capabilities it offers and a receiver can specify the capabilities it accepts.

Support For Caching. To improve response time, a browser caches a copy of each Web page it retrieves. If a user requests a page again, HTTP allows the browser to interrogate the server to determine whether the contents of the page has changed since the copy was cached.

Support For Intermediaries. HTTP allows a machine along the path between a browser and a server to act as a *proxy server* that caches Web pages and answers a browser's request from its cache.

28.7 HTTP GET Request

In the simplest case, a browser contacts a Web server directly to obtain a page. The browser begins with a URL, extracts the hostname section, uses DNS to map the name into an equivalent IP address, and uses the IP address to form a TCP connection to the server. Once the TCP connection is in place, the browser and Web server use HTTP to communicate; the browser sends a request to retrieve a specific page, and the server responds by sending a copy of the page.

A browser sends an HTTP *GET* command to request a Web page from a server†. The request consists of a single line of text that begins with the keyword *GET* and is followed by a URL and an HTTP version number. For example, to retrieve the Web page in the example above from server *www.cs.purdue.edu*, a browser can send the following request:

GET http://www.cs.purdue.edu/people/comer/ HTTP/1.1

Once a TCP connection is in place, there is no need to send an absolute URL — the following relative URL will retrieve the same page:

GET /people/comer/ HTTP/1.0

To summarize:

> *The Hypertext Transfer Protocol (HTTP) is used between a browser and a Web server. The browser sends a GET request to which a server responds by sending the requested item.*

28.8 Error Messages

How should a Web server respond when it receives an illegal request? In most cases, the request has been sent by a browser, and the browser will attempt to display whatever the server returns. Consequently, servers usually generate error messages in valid HTML. For example, one server generates the following error message:

```
<HTML>
  <HEAD> <TITLE>400 Bad Request</TITLE>
  </HEAD>
  <BODY>
    <H1>Bad Request</H1> Your browser sent a request
    that this server could not understand.
  </BODY>
</HTML>
```

The browser uses the "head" of the document (i.e., the items between <HEAD> and </HEAD>) internally, and only shows the "body" to the user. The pair of tags <H1> and </H1> causes the browser to display *Bad Request* as a heading (i.e., large and bold), resulting in two lines of output on the user's screen:

---

†The standard uses the object-oriented term *method* instead of *command*.

Bad Request

Your browser sent a request that this server could not understand.

28.9 Persistent Connections And Lengths

Early versions of HTTP follow the same paradigm as FTP by using a new TCP connection for each data transfer. That is, a client opens a TCP connection and sends a *GET* request. The server transmits a copy of the requested item, and then closes the TCP connection. Until it encounters an *end of file* condition, the client reads data from the TCP connection. Finally, the client closes its end of the connection.

Version 1.1, which appeared as an RFC in June of 1999, changed the basic HTTP paradigm in a fundamental way. Instead of using a TCP connection for each transfer, version 1.1 adopts a *persistent connection* approach as the default. That is, once a client opens a TCP connection to a particular server, the client leaves the connection in place during multiple requests and responses. When either a client or server is ready to close the connection, it informs the other side, and the connection is closed.

The chief advantage of persistent connections lies in reduced overhead — fewer TCP connections means lower response latency, less overhead on the underlying networks, less memory used for buffers, and less CPU time used. A browser using a persistent connection can further optimize by *pipelining* requests (i.e., send requests back-to-back without waiting for a response). Pipelining is especially attractive in situations where multiple images must be retrieved for a given page, and the underlying internet has both high throughput and long delay.

The chief disadvantage of using a persistent connection lies in the need to identify the beginning and end of each item sent over the connection. There are two possible techniques that handle the situation: either send a length followed by the item, or send a *sentinel value* after the item to mark the end. HTTP cannot reserve a sentinel value because the items transmitted include graphics images that can contain arbitrary sequences of octets. Thus, to avoid ambiguity between sentinel values and data, HTTP uses the approach of sending a length followed by an item of that size.

28.10 Data Length And Program Output

It may not be convenient or even possible for a server to know the length of an item before sending. To understand why, one must know that servers use the *Common Gateway Interface* (*CGI*) mechanism that allows a computer program running on the server machine to create a Web page dynamically. When a request arrives that corresponds to one of the CGI-generated pages, the server runs the appropriate CGI program, and sends the output from the program back to the client as a response. Dynamic Web page generation allows the creation of information that is current (e.g., a list of the current scores in sporting events), but means that the server may not know the exact data size in advance. Furthermore, saving the data to a file before sending it is undesirable for two reasons: it uses resources at the server and delays transmission. Thus, to provide for dynamic Web pages, the HTTP standard specifies that if the server does not know the length of an item *a priori*, the server can inform the browser that it will close the connection after transmitting the item. To summarize:

> *To allow a TCP connection to persist through multiple requests and responses, HTTP sends a length before each response. If it does not know the length, a server informs the client, sends the response, and then closes the connection.*

28.11 Length Encoding And Headers

What representation does a server use to send length information? Interestingly, HTTP borrows the basic format from e-mail, using 822 format and MIME Extensions†. Like a standard 822 message, each HTTP transmission contains a header, a blank line, and the item being sent. Furthermore, each line in the header contains a keyword, a colon, and information. Figure 28.2 lists a few of the possible headers and their meaning.

Header	Meaning
Content-Length	Size of item in octets
Content-Type	Type of the item
Content-Encoding	Encoding used for item
Content-Language	Language(s) used in item

Figure 28.1 Examples of items that can appear in the header sent before an item. The *Content-Type* and *Content-Encoding* are taken directly from MIME.

As an example, consider Figure 28.2 which shows a few of the headers that are used when a HTML document is transferred across a persistent TCP connection.

```
Content-Length:   34
Content-Language: en
Content-Encoding: ascii

<HTML> A trivial example. </HTML>
```

Figure 28.2 An illustration of an HTTP transfer with header lines used to specify attributes, a blank line, and the document itself. A *Content-Length* header is required if the connection is persistent.

---

†See Chapter 27 for a discussion of e-mail, 822 format, and MIME.

In addition to the examples shown in the figure, HTTP includes a wide variety of headers that allow a browser and server to exchange meta information. For example, we said that if a server does not know the length of an item, the server closes the connection after sending the item. However, the server does not act without warning — the server informs the browser to expect a close. To do so, the server includes a *Connection* header before the item in place of a *Content-Length* header:

Connection: close

When it receives a connection header, the browser knows that the server intends to close the connection after the transfer; the browser is forbidden from sending further requests. The next sections describe the purposes of other headers.

28.12 Negotiation

In addition to specifying details about an item being sent, HTTP uses headers to permit a client and server to *negotiate* capabilities. The set of negotiable capabilities includes a wide variety of characteristics about the connection (e.g., whether access is authenticated), representation (e.g., whether graphics images in jpeg format are acceptable or which types of compression can be used), content (e.g., whether text files must be in English), and control (e.g., the length of time a page remains valid).

There are two basic types of negotiation: *server-driven* and *agent-driven* (i.e., browser-driven). Server-driven negotiation begins with a request from a browser. The request specifies a list of preferences along with the URL of the desired item. The server selects, from among the available representations, one that satisfies the browser's preferences. If multiple items satisfy the preferences, the server makes a ''best guess.'' For example, if a document is stored in multiple languages and a request specifies a preference for English, the server will send the English version.

Agent-driven negotiation simply means that a browser uses a two-step process to perform the selection. First, the browser sends a request to the server to ask what is available. The server returns a list of possibilities. The browser selects one of the possibilities, and sends a second request to obtain the item. The disadvantage of agent-driven negotiation is that it requires two server interactions; the advantage is that a browser retains complete control over the choice.

A browser uses an HTTP *Accept* header to specify which media or representations are acceptable. The header lists names of formats with a preference value assigned to each. For example,

Accept: text/html, text/plain; q=0.5, text/x-dvi; q=0.8

specifies that the browser is willing to accept the *text/html* media type, but if that does not exist, the browser will accept *text/x-dvi*, and, if that does not exist, *text/plain*. The numeric values associated with the second and third entry can be thought of as a *prefer-*

ence level, where no value is equivalent to *q=1*, and a value of *q=0* means the type is unacceptable. For media types where ''quality'' is meaningful (e.g., audio), the value of *q* can be interpreted as a willingness to accept a given media type if it is the best available after other forms are reduced in quality by *q* percent.

A variety of *Accept* headers exist that correspond to the *Content* headers described earlier. For example, a browser can send any of the following:

```
Accept-Encoding:
Accept-Charset:
Accept-Language:
```

to specify which encodings, character sets, and languages the browser is willing to accept.

To summarize:

> *HTTP uses MIME-like headers to carry meta information. Both browsers and servers send headers that allow them to negotiate agreement on the document representation and encoding to be used.*

28.13 Conditional Requests

HTTP allows a sender to make a request *conditional*. That is, when a browser sends a request, it includes a header that qualifies conditions under which the request should be honored. If the specified condition is not met, the server does not return the requested item. Conditional requests allow a browser to optimize retrieval by avoiding unnecessary transfers. The *If-Modified-Since* request specifies one of the most straightforward conditionals — it allows a browser to avoid transferring an item unless the item has been updated since a specified date. For example, a browser can include the header:

If-Modified-Since: Sat, 01 Jan 2000 05:00:01 GMT

with a *GET* request to avoid a transfer if the item is older than January 1, 2000.

28.14 Support For Proxy Servers

Proxy servers are an important part of the Web architecture because they provide an optimization that decreases latency and reduces the load on servers. However, proxies are not transparent — a browser must be configured to contact a local proxy instead of the original source, and the proxy must be configured to cache copies of Web pages. For example, a corporation in which many employees use the Internet may choose to have a proxy server. The corporation configures all its browsers to send requests to the proxy. The first time a user in the corporation accesses a given Web page, the proxy must obtain a copy from the server that manages the page. The proxy places the copy in its cache, and returns the page as the response to the request. The next time a user accesses the same page, the proxy extracts the data from its cache without sending a request across the Internet. Consequently, traffic from the site to the Internet is significantly reduced.

To guarantee correctness, HTTP includes explicit support for proxy servers. The protocol specifies exactly how a proxy handles each request, how headers should be interpreted by proxies, how a browser negotiates with a proxy, and how a proxy negotiates with a server. Furthermore, several HTTP headers have been designed specifically for use by proxies. For example, one header allows a proxy to authenticate itself to a server, and another allows each proxy that handles an item to record its identity so the ultimate recipient receives a list of all intermediate proxies. Finally, HTTP allows a server to control how proxies handle each Web page. For example, a server can include the *Max-Forwards* header in a response to limit the number of proxies that handle an item before it is delivered to a browser. If the server specifies a count of one, as in:

Max-Forwards: 1

at most one proxy can handle the item along the path from the server to the browser. A count of zero prohibits any proxy from handling the item.

28.15 Caching

The goal of caching is improved efficiency: a cache reduces both latency and network traffic by eliminating unnecessary transfers. The most obvious aspect of caching is storage: when a Web page is initially accessed, a copy is stored on disk, either by the browser, an intermediate proxy, or both. Subsequent requests for the same page can short-circuit the lookup process and retrieve a copy of the page from the cache instead of the server.

The central question in all caching schemes concerns timing — how long should an item be kept in a cache? On one hand, keeping a cached copy too long results in the copy becoming *stale*, which means that changes to the original are not reflected in the cached copy. On the other hand, if the cached copy is not kept long enough, inefficiency results because the next request must go back to the server.

HTTP allows a server to control caching in two ways. First, when it answers a request for a page, a server can specify caching details, including whether the page can be cached at all, whether a proxy can cache the page, the community with which a cached copy can be shared, the time at which the cached copy must expire, and limits on transformations that can be applied to the copy. Second, HTTP allows a browser to force *revalidation* of a page. To do so, the browser sends a request for the page, and uses a header to specify that the maximum "age" (i.e., the time since a copy of the page was stored) cannot be greater than zero. No copy of the page in a cache can be used to satisfy the request because the copy will have a nonzero age. Thus, only the original server will answer the request. Intermediate proxies along the way will receive a fresh copy for their cache as will the browser that issued the request.

To summarize:

> *Caching is key to the efficient operation of the Web. HTTP allows servers to control whether and how a page can be cached as well as its lifetime; a browser can force a request for a page to bypass caches and obtain a fresh copy from the server that owns the page.*

28.16 Summary

The World Wide Web consists of hypermedia documents stored on a set of Web servers and accessed by browsers. Each document is assigned a URL that uniquely identifies it; the URL specifies the protocol used to retrieve the document, the location of the server, and the path to the document on that server.

The HyperText Markup Language, HTML, allows a document to contain text along with embedded commands that control formatting. HTML also allows a document to contain links to other documents.

A browser and server use the HyperText Transfer Protocol, HTTP, to communicate. HTTP is an application-level protocol with explicit support for negotiation, proxy servers, caching, and persistent connections.

FOR FURTHER STUDY

Berners-Lee, et. al. [RFC 1768] defines URLs. A variety of RFCs contain proposals for extensions. Daniel and Mealling [RFC 2168] considers how to store URLs in the Domain Name System.

Berners-Lee and Connolly [RFC 1866] contains the standard for version 2 of HTML. Nebel and Masinter [RFC 1867] specifies HTML form upload, and Raggett [RFC 1942] gives the standard for tables in HTML.

Fielding et. al. [RFC 2616] specifies version 1.1 of HTTP, which adds many features, including additional support for persistence and caching, to the previous version. Franks et. al. [RFC 2617] considers access authentication in HTTP.

EXERCISES

28.1   Read the standard for URLs. What does a pound sign (#) followed by a string mean at the end of a URL?

28.2   Extend the previous exercise. Is it legal to send the pound sign suffix on a URL to a Web server? Why or why not?

28.3   How does a browser distinguish between a document that contains HTML and a document that contains arbitrary text? To find out, experiment by using a browser to read from a file. Does the browser use the name of the file or the contents to decide how to interpret the file?

28.4   What is the purpose of an HTTP *TRACE* command?

28.5   What is the difference between an HTTP *PUT* command and an HTTP *POST* command? When is each useful?

28.6   When is an HTTP *Keep-Alive* header used?

28.7   Can an arbitrary Web server function as a proxy? To find out, choose an arbitrary Web server and configure your browser to use it as a proxy. Do the results surprise you?

28.8   Read about HTTP's *must-revalidate* cache control directive. Give an example of a Web page that would use such a directive.

28.9   If a browser does not send an HTTP *Content-Length* header before a request, how does a server respond?

29

Applications: Voice And Video Over IP (RTP)

29.1 Introduction

This chapter focuses on the transfer of real-time data such as voice and video over an IP network. In addition to discussing the protocols used to transport such data, the chapter considers two broader issues. First, it examines the question of how IP can be used to provide commercial telephone service. Second, it examines the question of how routers in an IP network can guarantee sufficient service to provide high-quality video and audio reproduction.

Although it was designed and optimized to transport data, IP has successfully carried audio and video since its inception. In fact, researchers began to experiment with audio transmission across the ARPANET before the Internet was in place. By the 1990s, commercial radio stations were sending audio across the Internet, and software was available that allowed an individual to send audio across the Internet or to the standard telephone network. Commercial telephone companies also began using IP technology internally to carry voice.

29.2 Audio Clips And Encoding Standards

The simplest way to transfer audio across an IP network consists of *digitizing* an analog audio signal to produce a data file, using a conventional protocol to transfer the file, and then decoding the digital file to reproduce the original analog signal. Of course, the technique does not work well for interactive exchange because placing encoded audio in a file and transferring the file introduces a long delay. Thus, file transfer is typically used to send short audio recordings, which are known as *audio clips*.

Special hardware is used to form high-quality digitized audio. Known as a *coder/decoder* (*codec*), the device can covert in either direction between an analog audio signal and an equivalent digital representation. The most common type of codec, a *waveform coder*, measures the amplitude of the input signal at regular intervals and converts each sample into a digital value (i.e., an integer)†. To decode, the codec takes a sequence of integers as input and recreates the continuous analog signal that matches the digital values.

Several digital encoding standards exist, with the main tradeoff being between quality of reproduction and the size of digital representation. For example, the conventional telephone system uses the *Pulse Code Modulation* (*PCM*) standard that specifies taking an 8-bit sample every 125 μ seconds (i.e., 8000 times per second). As a result, a digitized telephone call produces data at a rate of 64 Kbps. The PCM encoding produces a surprising amount of output — storing a 128 second audio clip requires one megabyte of memory.

There are three ways to reduce the amount of data generated by digital encoding: take fewer samples per second, use fewer bits to encode each sample, or use a digital compression scheme to reduce the size of the resulting output. Various systems exist that use one or more of the techniques, making it possible to find products that produce encoded audio at a rate of only 2.2 Kbps. However, each technique has disadvantages. The chief disadvantage of taking fewer samples or using fewer bits to encode a sample is lower quality audio — the system cannot reproduce as large a range of sounds. The chief disadvantage of compression is delay — digitized output must be held while it is compressed. Furthermore, because greater reduction in size requires more processing, the best compression either requires a fast CPU or introduces longer delay. Thus, compression is most useful when delay is unimportant (e.g., when the output from a codec is being stored in a file).

29.3 Audio And Video Transmission And Reproduction

Many audio and video applications are classified as *real-time* because they require timely transmission and delivery‡. For example, an interactive telephone call is a real-time exchange because audio must be delivered without significant delay or users find the system unsatisfactory. Timely transfer means more than low delay because the resulting signal is unintelligible unless it is presented in exactly the same order as the original, and with exactly the same timing. Thus, if a sender takes a sample every 125 μ seconds, the receiver must convert digital values to analog at exactly the same rate.

How can a network guarantee that the stream is delivered at exactly the same rate that the sender used? The conventional telephone system introduced one answer: an *isochronous* architecture. Isochronous design means that the entire system, including the digital circuits, must be engineered to deliver output with exactly the same timing as was used to generate input. Thus, an isochronous system that has multiple paths between any two points must be engineered so all paths have exactly the same delay.

---

†An alternative known as a *voice coder/decoder* (*vocodec*) recognizes and encodes human speech rather than general waveforms.

‡Timeliness is more important than reliability; missing data is merely skipped.

An IP internet is not isochronous. We have already seen that datagrams can be duplicated, delayed, or arrive out of order. Variance in delay is called *jitter*, and is especially pervasive in IP networks. To allow meaningful transmission and reproduction of
digitized signals across a network with IP semantics, additional protocol support is required. To handle datagram duplication and out-of-order delivery, each transmission
must contain a sequence number. To handle jitter, each transmission must contain a
timestamp that tells the receiver at which time the data in the packet should be played
back. Separating sequence and timing information allows a receiver to reconstruct the
signal accurately independent of how the packets arrive. Such timing information is
especially critical when a datagram is lost or if the sender stops encoding during periods
of silence; it allows the receiver to pause during playback the amount of time specified
by the timestamps. To summarize:

> *Because an IP internet is not isochronous, additional protocol support
> is required when sending digitized real-time data. In addition to
> basic sequence information that allows detection of duplicate or reor-
> dered packets, each packet must carry a separate timestamp that tells
> the receiver the exact time at which the data in the packet should be
> played.*

29.4 Jitter And Playback Delay

How can a receiver recreate a signal accurately if the network introduces jitter?
The receiver must implement a *playback buffer*† as Figure 29.1 illustrates.

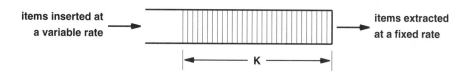

Figure 29.1 The conceptual organization of a playback buffer that compen-
sates for jitter. The buffer holds K time units of data.

When a session begins, the receiver delays playback and places incoming data in
the buffer. When data in the buffer reaches a predetermined threshold, known as the
playback point, output begins. The playback point, labeled K in the figure, is measured
in time units of data to be played. Thus, playback begins when a receiver has accumulated K time unit's worth of data.

As playback proceeds, datagrams continue to arrive. If there is no jitter, new data
will arrive at exactly the same rate old data is being extracted and played, meaning the
buffer will always contain exactly K time units of unplayed data. If a datagram experi-

---

†A playback buffer is also called a *jitter buffer*.

ences a small delay, playback is unaffected. The buffer size decreases steadily as data is extracted, and playback continues uninterrupted for K time units. When a delayed datagram arrives, the buffer is refilled.

Of course, a playback buffer cannot compensate for datagram loss. In such cases, playback eventually reaches an unfilled position in the buffer, and output pauses for a time period corresponding to the missing data. Furthermore, the choice of K is a compromise between loss and delay†. If K is too small, a small amount of jitter causes the system to exhaust the playback buffer before the needed data arrives. If K is too large, the system remains immune to jitter, but the extra delay, when added to the transmission delay in the underlying network, may be noticeable to users. Despite the disadvantages, most applications that send real-time data across an IP internet depend on playback buffering as the primary solution for jitter.

29.5 Real-Time Transport Protocol (RTP)

The protocol used to transmit digitized audio or video signals over an IP internet is known as the *Real-Time Transport Protocol* (*RTP*). Interestingly, RTP does not contain mechanisms that ensure timely delivery; such guarantees must be made by the underlying system. Instead, RTP provides two key facilities: a sequence number in each packet that allows a receiver to detect out-of-order delivery or loss, and a timestamp that allows a receiver to control playback.

Because RTP is designed to carry a wide variety of real-time data, including both audio and video, RTP does not enforce a uniform interpretation of semantics. Instead, each packet begins with a fixed header; fields in the header specify how to interpret remaining header fields and how to interpret the payload. Figure 29.2 illustrates the format of RTP's fixed header.

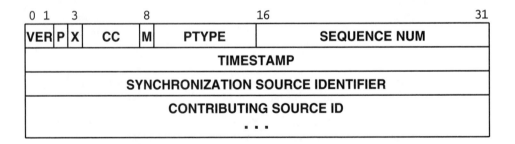

Figure 29.2 Illustration of the fixed header used with RTP. Each message begins with this header; the exact interpretation and additional header fields depend on the payload type, *PTYPE*.

---

†Although network delay and jitter can be used to determine a value for K dynamically, many playback buffering schemes use a constant.

As the figure shows, each packet begins with a two-bit RTP version number in field *VER*; the current version is *2*. The sixteen-bit *SEQUENCE NUM* field contains a sequence number for the packet. The first sequence number in a particular session is chosen at random. Some applications define an optional header extension to be placed between the fixed header and the payload. If the application type allows an extension, the *X* bit is used to specify whether the extension is present in the packet. The interpretation of most of the remaining fields in the header depends on the seven-bit *PTYPE* field that specifies the payload type. The *P* bit specifies whether zero padding follows the payload; it is used with encryption that requires data to be allocated in fixed-size blocks. Interpretation of the *M* ("marker") bit also depends on the application; it is used by applications that need to mark points in the data stream (e.g., the beginning of each frame when sending video).

The payload type also affects the interpretation of the *TIMESTAMP* field. A *timestamp* is a 32-bit value that gives the time at which the first octet of digitized data was sampled, with the initial timestamp for a session chosen at random. The standard specifies that the timestamp is incremented continuously, even during periods when no signal is detected and no values are sent, but it does not specify the exact granularity. Instead, the granularity is determined by the payload type, which means that each application can choose a clock granularity that allows a receiver to position items in the output with accuracy appropriate to the application. For example, if a stream of audio data is being transmitted over RTP, a logical timestamp granularity of one clock tick per sample is appropriate†. However, if video data is being transmitted, the timestamp granularity needs to be higher than one tick per frame to achieve smooth playback. In any case, the standard allows the timestamps in two packets to be identical, if the data in the two packets was sampled at the same time.

29.6 Streams, Mixing, And Multicasting

A key part of RTP is its support for *translation* (i.e., changing the encoding of a stream at an intermediate station) or *mixing* (i.e., receiving streams of data from multiple sources, combining them into a single stream, and sending the result). To understand the need for mixing, imagine that individuals at multiple sites participate in a conference call using IP. To minimize the number of RTP streams, the group can designate a *mixer*, and arrange for each site to establish an RTP session to the mixer. The mixer combines the audio streams (possibly by converting them back to analog and resampling the resulting signal), and sends the result as a single digital stream.

Fields in the RTP header identify the sender and indicate whether mixing occurred. The field labeled *SYNCHRONIZATION SOURCE IDENTIFIER* specifies the source of a stream. Each source must choose a unique 32-bit identifier; the protocol includes a mechanism for resolving conflicts if they arise. When a mixer combines multiple streams, the mixer becomes the synchronization source for the new stream. Information about the original sources is not lost, however, because the mixer uses the variable-size *CONTRIBUTING SOURCE ID* field to provide the synchronization IDs of streams that

---

†The *TIMESTAMP* is sometimes referred to as a *MEDIA TIMESTAMP* to emphasize that its granularity depends on the type of signal being measured.

were mixed together. The four-bit *CC* field gives a count of contributing sources; a maximum of 15 sources can be listed.

RTP is designed to work with IP multicasting, and mixing is especially attractive in a multicast environment. To understand why, imagine a teleconference that includes many participants. Unicasting requires a station to send a copy of each outgoing RTP packet to each participant. With multicasting, however, a station only needs to send one copy of the packet, which will be delivered to all participants. Furthermore, if mixing is used, all sources can unicast to a mixer, which combines them into a single stream before multicasting. Thus, the combination of mixing and multicast results in substantially fewer datagrams being delivered to each participating host.

29.7 RTP Encapsulation

Its name implies that RTP is a transport-level protocol. Indeed, if it functioned like a conventional transport protocol, RTP would require each message to be encapsulated directly in an IP datagram. In fact, RTP does not function like a transport protocol; although it is allowed, direct encapsulation in IP does not occur in practice. Instead, RTP runs over UDP, meaning that each RTP message is encapsulated in a UDP datagram. The chief advantage of using UDP is concurrency — a single computer can have multiple applications using RTP without interference.

Unlike many of the application protocols we have seen, RTP does not use a reserved UDP port number. Instead, a port is allocated for use with each session, and the remote application must be informed about the port number. By convention, RTP chooses an even numbered UDP port; the following section explains that a companion protocol, RTCP, uses the next port number.

29.8 RTP Control Protocol (RTCP)

So far, our description of real-time transmission has focused on the protocol mechanisms that allow a receiver to reproduce content. However, another aspect of real-time transmission is equally important: monitoring of the underlying network during the session and providing *out of band* communication between the endpoints. Such a mechanism is especially important in cases where adaptive schemes are used. For example, an application might choose a lower-bandwidth encoding when the underlying network becomes congested, or a receiver might vary the size of its playback buffer when network delay or jitter changes. Finally, an out-of-band mechanism can be used to send information in parallel with the real-time data (e.g., captions to accompany a video stream).

A companion protocol and integral part of RTP, known as the *RTP Control Protocol (RTCP)*, provides the needed control functionality. RTCP allows senders and receivers to transmit a series of reports to one another that contain additional information about the data being transferred and the performance of the network. RTCP messages are encapsulated in UDP for transmission†, and are sent using a protocol number one greater than the port number of the RTP stream to which they pertain.

29.9 RTCP Operation

RTCP uses five basic message types to allow senders and receivers to exchange information about a session. Figure 29.3 lists the types.

Type	Meaning
200	Sender report
201	Receiver report
202	Source description message
203	Bye message
204	Application specific message

Figure 29.3 The five RTCP message types. Each message begins with a fixed header that identifies the type.

The *bye* and *application specific* messages are the most straightforward. A sender transmits a bye message when shutting down a stream. The application specific message type provides an extension of the basic facility to allow the application to define a message type. For example, an application that sends a closed caption to accompany a video stream might choose to define an RTCP message that supports closed captioning.

Receivers periodically transmit *receiver report* messages that inform the source about conditions of reception. Receiver reports are important for two reasons. First, they allow all receivers participating in a session as well as a sender to learn about reception conditions of other receivers. Second, they allow receivers to adapt their rate of reporting to avoid using excessive bandwidth and overwhelming the sender. The adaptive scheme guarantees that the total control traffic will remain less than 5% of the real-time data traffic, and that receiver reports generate less than 75% of the control traffic. Each receiver report identifies one or more synchronization sources, and contains a separate section for each. A section specifies the highest sequence number packet received from the source, the cumulative and percentage packet loss experienced, time since the last RTCP report arrived from the source, and the interarrival jitter.

Senders periodically transmit a *sender report* message that provides an absolute timestamp. To understand the need for a timestamp, recall that RTP allows each stream to choose a granularity for its timestamp and that the first timestamp is chosen at random. The absolute timestamp in a sender report is essential because it provides the only mechanism a receiver has to *synchronize* multiple streams. In particular, because RTP requires a separate stream for each media type, the transmission of video and accompanying audio requires two streams. The absolute timestamp information allows a receiver to play the two streams simultaneously.

---

†Because some messages are short, the standard allows multiple RTCP messages to be combined into a single UDP datagram for transmission.

In addition to the periodic sender report messages, senders also transmit *source description* messages which provide general information about the user who owns or controls the source. Each message contains one section for each outgoing RTP stream; the contents are intended for humans to read. For example, the only required field consists of a *canonical name* for the stream owner, a character string in the form:

user @ host

where *host* is either the domain name of the computer or its IP address in dotted decimal form, and *user* is a login name. Optional fields in the source description contain further details such as the user's e-mail address (which may differ from the canonical name), telephone number, the geographic location of the site, the application program or tool used to create the stream, or other textual notes about the source.

29.10 IP Telephony And Signaling

One aspect of real-time transmission stands out as especially important: the use of IP as the foundation for telephone service. Known as *IP telephony* or *voice over IP*, the idea is endorsed by many telephone companies. The question arises, ''what additional technologies are needed before IP can be used in place of the existing isochronous telephone system?'' Although no simple answer exists, researchers are investigating three components. First, we have seen that a protocol like RTP is needed to transfer a digitized signal across an IP internet correctly. Second, a mechanism is needed to establish and terminate telephone calls. Third, researchers are exploring ways an IP internet can be made to function like an isochronous network.

The telephone industry uses the term *signaling* to refer to the process of establishing a telephone call. Specifically, the signaling mechanism used in the conventional *Public Switched Telephone Network (PSTN)* is *Signaling System 7 (SS7)*. SS7 performs call routing before any audio is sent. Given a phone number, it forms a circuit through the network, rings the designated telephone, and connects the circuit when the phone is answered. SS7 also handles details such as call forwarding and error conditions such as the destination phone being busy.

Before IP can be used to make phone calls, signaling functionality must be available. Furthermore, to enable adoption by the phone companies, IP telephony must be compatible with extant telephone standards — it must be possible for the IP telephony system to interoperate with the conventional phone system at all levels. Thus, it must be possible to translate between the signaling used with IP and SS7 just as it must be possible to translate between the voice encoding used with IP and standard PCM encoding. As a consequence, the two signaling mechanisms will have equivalent functionality.

The general approach to interoperability uses a *gateway* between the IP phone system and the conventional phone system. A call can be initiated on either side of the gateway. When a signaling request arrives, the gateway translates and forwards the request; the gateway must also translate and forward the response. Finally, after signaling is complete and a call has been established, the gateway must forward voice in both directions, translating from the encoding used on one side to the encoding used on the other.

Two groups have proposed standards for IP telephony. The ITU has defined a suite of protocols known as *H.323*, and the IETF has proposed a signaling protocol known as the *Session Initiation Protocol (SIP)*. The next sections summarize the two approaches.

29.10.1 H.323 Standards

The ITU originally created H.323 to allow the transmission of voice over local area network technologies. The standard has been extended to allow transmission of voice over IP internets, and telephone companies are expected to adopt it. H.323 is not a single protocol. Instead, it specifies how multiple protocols can be combined to form a functional IP telephony system. For example, in addition to gateways, H.323 defines devices known as *gatekeepers* that each provide a contact point for telephones using IP. To obtain permission to place outgoing calls and enable the phone system to correctly route incoming calls, each IP telephone must register with a gatekeeper; H.323 includes the necessary protocols.

In addition to specifying a protocol for the transmission of real-time voice and video, the H.323 framework allows participants to transfer data. Thus, a pair of users engaged in an audio-video conference can also share an on-screen whiteboard, send still images, or exchange copies of documents.

H.323 relies on the four major protocols listed in Figure 29.4.

Protocol	Purpose
H.225.0	Signaling used to establish a call
H.245	Control and feedback during the call
RTP	Real-time data transfer (sequence and timing)
T.120	Exchange of data associated with a call

Figure 29.4 The protocols used by H.323 for IP telephony.

Together, the suite of protocols covers all aspects of IP telephony, including phone registration, signaling, real-time data encoding and transfer (both voice and video), and control.

Figure 29.5 illustrates relationships among the protocols that comprise H.323. As the figure shows, the entire suite ultimately depends on UDP and TCP running over IP.

audio / video applications		signaling and control				data applications
video codec	audio codec	RTCP	H.225 Registr.	H.225 Signaling	H.245 Control	T.120 Data
RTP						
UDP				TCP		
IP						

Figure 29.5 Relationship among protocols that comprise the ITU's H.323 IP
telephony standard.

29.10.2 Session Initiation Protocol (SIP)

The IETF has proposed an alternative to H.323, called the *Session Initiation Proto-col* (*SIP*), that only covers signaling; it does not recommend specific codecs nor does it require the use of RTP for real-time transfer. Thus, SIP does not supply all of H.323 functionality.

SIP uses client-server interaction, with servers being divided into two types. A *user agent server* runs in a SIP telephone. It is assigned an identifier (e.g., *user @ site*), and can receive incoming calls. The second type of server is intermediate (i.e., between two SIP telephones) and handles tasks such as call set up and call forwarding. An inter-mediate server functions as a *proxy server* that can forward an incoming call request to the next proxy server along the path to the called phone, or as a *redirect server* that tells a caller how to reach the destination.

To provide information about a call, SIP relies on a companion protocol, the *Ses-sion Description Protocol* (*SDP*). SDP is especially important in a conference call, be-cause participants join and leave the call dynamically. SDP specifies details such as the media encoding, protocol port numbers, and multicast address.

29.11 Resource Reservation And Quality Of Service

The term *Quality Of Service* (*QoS*) refers to statistical performance guarantees that a network system can make regarding loss, delay, throughput, and jitter. An isochro-nous network that is engineered to meet strict performance bounds is said to provide QoS guarantees, while a packet switched network that uses best effort delivery is said to provide no QoS guarantee. Is guaranteed QoS needed for real-time transfer of voice and video over IP? If so, how should it be implemented? A major controversy sur-rounds the two questions. On one hand, engineers who designed the telephone system insist that toll-quality voice reproduction requires the underlying system to provide QoS guarantees about delay and loss for each phone call. On the other hand, engineers who designed IP insist that the Internet works reasonably well without QoS guarantees and that adding per-flow QoS is infeasible because routers will make the system both expensive and slow.

The QoS controversy has produced many proposals, implementations, and experiments. Although it operates without QoS, the Internet is already used to send audio. Technologies like ATM that were derived from the telephone system model provide QoS guarantees for each individual connection. Finally, in Chapter 7 we learned that the IETF adopted a conservative *differentiated services* approach that divides traffic into separate QoS classes. The differentiated services scheme sacrifices fine grain control for less complex forwarding.

29.12 QoS, Utilization, And Capacity

The debate over QoS is reminiscent of earlier debates on resource allocation such as those waged over operating system policies for memory allocation and processor scheduling. The central issue is utilization: when a network has sufficient resources for all traffic, QoS constraints are unnecessary; when traffic exceeds network capacity, no QoS system can satisfy all users' demands. That is, a network with 1% utilization does not need QoS, and a network with 101% utilization will fail under any QoS. In effect, proponents who argue for QoS mechanisms assert that complex QoS mechanisms achieve two goals. First, by dividing the existing resources among more users, they make the system more "fair". Second, by shaping the traffic from each user, they allow the network to run at higher utilization without danger of collapse.

One of the major arguments against complicated QoS mechanisms arises from improvements in the performance of underlying networks. Network capacity has increased dramatically. As long as rapid increases in capacity continue, QoS mechanisms merely represent unnecessary overhead. However, if demand rises more rapidly than capacity, QoS may become an economic issue — by associating higher prices with higher levels of service, ISPs can use cost to ration capacity.

29.13 RSVP

If QoS is needed, how can an IP network provide it? Before announcing the differentiated services solution, the IETF worked on a scheme that can be used to provide QoS in an IP environment. The work produced a pair of protocols: the *Resource Reservation Protocol* (*RSVP*) and the *Common Open Policy Services* (*COPS*) protocol.

QoS cannot be added to IP at the application layer. Instead, the basic infrastructure must change — routers must agree to reserve resources (e.g., bandwidth) for each flow between a pair of endpoints. There are two aspects. First, before data is sent, the endpoints must send a request that specifies the resources needed, and all routers along the path must agree to supply the resources; the procedure can be viewed as a form of signaling. Second, as datagrams traverse the flow, routers need to monitor and control traffic forwarding. Monitoring, sometimes called *traffic policing*, is needed to ensure

that the traffic sent on a flow does not exceed the specified bounds. Control of queueing and forwarding is needed for two reasons. The router must implement a queueing
policy that meets the guaranteed bounds on delay, and the router must smooth packet
bursts. The latter is sometimes referred to as *traffic shaping*, and is necessary because
network traffic is often *bursty*. For example, a flow that specifies an average
throughput of 1 Mbps may have 2 Mbps of traffic for a millisecond followed by no
traffic for a millisecond. A router can reshape the burst by temporarily queueing incoming datagrams and sending them at a steady rate of 1 Mbps.

RSVP handles reservation requests and replies. It is not a routing protocol, nor
does it enforce policies once a flow has been established. Instead, RSVP operates before any data is sent. To initiate an end-to-end flow, an endpoint first sends an RSVP
path message to determine the path to the destination; the datagram carrying the message uses the *router alert* option to guarantee that routers examine the message. After it
receives a reply to its path message, the endpoint sends a request message to reserve
resources for the flow. The request specifies QoS bounds desired; each router that forwards the request along to the destination must agree to reserve the resources the request specifies. If any router along the path denies the request, the router uses RSVP to
send a negative reply back to the source. If all systems along the path agree to honor
the request, RSVP returns a positive reply.

Each RSVP flow is *simplex* (i.e., unidirectional). If an application requires QoS
guarantees in two directions, each endpoint must use RSVP to request a flow. Because
RSVP uses existing routing, there is no guarantee that the two flows will pass through
the same routers, nor does approval of a flow in one direction imply approval in the
other. We can summarize:

> An endpoint uses RSVP to request a simplex flow through an IP inter-
> net with specified QoS bounds. If routers along the path agree to
> honor the request, they approve it; otherwise, they deny it. If an ap-
> plication needs QoS in two directions, each endpoint must use RSVP
> to request a separate flow.

29.14 COPS

When an RSVP request arrives, a router must evaluate two aspects: feasibility (i.e.,
whether the router has the resources necessary to satisfy the request) and policies (i.e.,
whether the request lies within policy constraints). Feasibility is a local decision — a
router can decide how to manage the bandwidth, memory, and processing power that is
available locally. However, policy enforcement requires global cooperation — all
routers must agree to the same set of policies.

To implement global policies, the IETF architecture uses a two-level model, with
client-server interaction between the levels. When a router receives a RSVP request, it
becomes a client that consults a server known as a *Policy Decision Point* (*PDP*) to
determine whether the request meets policy constraints. The PDP does not handle traff-

ic; it merely evaluates requests to see if they satisfy global policies. If a PDP approves a request, the router must operate as a *Policy Enforcement Point PEP* to ensure traffic does not exceed the approved policy.

The COPS protocol defines the client-server interaction between a router and a PDP (or between a router and a local PDP if the organization has multiple levels of policy servers). Although COPS defines its own message header, the underlying format shares many details with RSVP. In particular, COPS uses the same format as RSVP for individual items in a request message. Thus, when a router receives an RSVP request, it can extract items related to policy, place them in a COPS message, and send the result to a PDP.

29.15 Summary

Analog data such as audio can be encoded in digital form; the hardware to do so is known as a codec. The telephone standard for digital audio encoding, Pulse Code Modulation (PCM), produces digital values at 64 Kbps.

RTP is used to transfer real-time data across an IP network. Each RTP message contains two key pieces of information: a sequence number that a receiver uses to place messages in order and detect lost datagrams and a media timestamp that a receiver uses to determine when to play the encoded values. An associated control protocol, RTCP, is used to supply information about sources and to allow a mixer to combine several streams.

A debate continues over whether Quality of Service (QoS) guarantees are needed to provide real-time. Before announcing a differentiated services approach, the IETF designed a pair of protocols that can be used to provide per-flow QoS. Endpoints use RSVP to request a flow with specific QoS; intermediate routers either approve or deny the request. When an RSVP request arrives, a router uses the COPS protocol to contact a Policy Decision Point and verify that the request meets policy constraints.

FOR FURTHER STUDY

Schulzrinne et. al. [RFC 1889] gives the standard for RTP and RTCP. Perkins et. al. [RFC 2198] specifies the transmission of redundant audio data over RTP, and Schulzrinne [RFC 1890] specifies the use of RTP with an audio-video conference. Schulzrinne, Rao, and Lanphier [RFC 2326] describes a related protocol used for streaming of real-time traffic.

Zhang et. al. [RFC 2205] contains the specification for RSVP. Boyle et. al. [draft-rap-cops-06.txt] describes COPS.

EXERCISES

29.1   Read about the Real Time Streaming Protocol, RTSP. What are the major differences between RTSP and RTP?

29.2   Argue that although bandwidth is often cited as an example of the facilities a QoS mechanism can guarantee, delay is a more fundamental resource. (Hint: which constraint can be eased with sufficient money?)

29.3   If an RTP message arrives with a sequence number far greater than the sequence expected, what does the protocol do? Why?

29.4   Are sequence numbers necessary in RTP, or can a timestamp be used instead? Explain.

29.5   Would you prefer an internet where QoS was required for all traffic? Why or why not?

29.6   Measure the utilization on your connection to the Internet. If all traffic required QoS reservation, would service be better or worse? Explain.

30

Applications: Internet Management (SNMP)

30.1 Introduction

In addition to protocols that provide network level services and application programs that use those services, an internet needs software that allows managers to debug
problems, control routing, and find computers that violate protocol standards. We refer
to such activities as *internet management*. This chapter considers the ideas behind
TCP/IP internet management software, and describes an internet management protocol.

30.2 The Level Of Management Protocols

Originally, many wide area networks included management protocols as part of
their link level protocols. If a packet switch began misbehaving, the network manager
could instruct a neighboring packet switch to send it a special *control packet*. Control
packets caused the receiver to suspend normal operation and respond to commands from
the manager. The manager could interrogate the packet switch to identify problems, examine or change routes, test one of the communication interfaces, or reboot the switch.
Once managers repaired the problem, they could instruct the switch to resume normal
operations. Because management tools were part of the lowest level protocol, managers
were often able to control switches even if higher level protocols failed.

Unlike a homogeneous wide area network, a TCP/IP internet does not have a single link level protocol. Instead, the internet consists of multiple physical networks interconnected by IP routers. As a result, internet management differs from network

management. First, a single manager can control heterogeneous devices, including IP routers, bridges, modems, workstations, and printers. Second, the controlled entities may not share a common link level protocol. Third, the set of machines a manager controls may lie at arbitrary points in an internet. In particular, a manager may need to control one or more machines that do not attach to the same physical network as the manager's computer. Thus, it may not be possible for a manager to communicate with machines being controlled unless the management software uses protocols that provide end-to-end connectivity across an internet. As a consequence, the internet management protocol used with TCP/IP operates above the transport level:

> *In a TCP/IP internet, a manager needs to examine and control routers and other network devices. Because such devices attach to arbitrary networks, protocols for internet management operate at the application level and communicate using TCP/IP transport-level protocols.*

Designing internet management software to operate at the application level has several advantages. Because the protocols can be designed without regard to the underlying network hardware, one set of protocols can be used for all networks. Because the protocols can be designed without regard to the hardware on the managed machine, the same protocols can be used for all managed devices. From a manager's point of view, having a single set of management protocols means uniformity — all routers respond to exactly the same set of commands. Furthermore, because the management software uses IP for communication, a manager can control the routers across an entire TCP/IP internet without having direct attachment to every physical network or router.

Of course, building management software at the application level also has disadvantages. Unless the operating system, IP software, and transport protocol software work correctly, the manager may not be able to contact a router that needs managing. For example, if a router's routing table becomes damaged, it may be impossible to correct the table or reboot the machine from a remote site. If the operating system on a router crashes, it will be impossible to reach the application program that implements the internet management protocols even if the router can still field hardware interrupts and route packets.

30.3 Architectural Model

Despite the potential disadvantages, having TCP/IP management software operate at the application level has worked well in practice. The most significant advantage of placing network management protocols at a high level becomes apparent when one considers a large internet, where a manager's computer does not need to attach directly to all physical networks that contain managed entities. Figure 30.1 shows an example of the architecture.

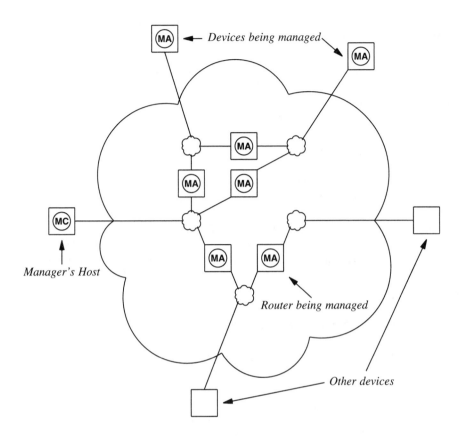

Figure 30.1 Example of network management. A manager invokes management client (MC) software that can contact management agent
(MA) software that runs on devices throughout the internet.

As the figure shows, client software usually runs on the manager's workstation.
Each participating router or host† runs a server program. Technically, the server
software is called a *management agent* or merely an *agent*. A manager invokes client
software on the local host computer and specifies an agent with which it communicates.
After the client contacts the agent, it sends queries to obtain information or it sends
commands to change conditions in the router. Of course, not all devices in a large internet fall under a single manager. Most managers only control devices at their local
sites; a large site may have multiple managers.

---

† Recall that the TCP/IP term *host* can refer to a device (e.g., a printer) or a conventional computer.

Internet management software uses an authentication mechanism to ensure only authorized managers can access or control a particular device. Some management protocols support multiple levels of authorization, allowing a manager specific privileges on each device. For example, a specific router could be configured to allow several managers to obtain information while only allowing a select subset of them to change information or control the router.

30.4 Protocol Framework

TCP/IP network management protocols† divide the management problem into two parts and specify separate standards for each part. The first part concerns communication of information. A protocol specifies how client software running on a manager's host communicates with an agent. The protocol defines the format and meaning of messages clients and servers exchange as well as the form of names and addresses. The second part concerns the data being managed. A protocol specifies which data items a managed device must keep as well as the name of each data item and the syntax used to express the name.

30.4.1 A Standard Network Management Protocol

The TCP/IP standard for network management is the *Simple Network Management Protocol* (*SNMP*). The protocol has evolved through three generations. Consequently, the current version is known as *SNMPv3*, and the predecessors are known as *SNMPv1* and *SNMPv2*. The changes have been minor — all three versions use the same general framework, and many features are backward compatible.

In addition to specifying details such as the message format and the use of transport protocols, the SNMP standard defines the set of operations and the meaning of each. We will see that the approach is minimalistic; a few operations provide all functionality.

30.4.2 A Standard For Managed Information

A device being managed must keep control and status information that the manager can access. For example, a router keeps statistics on the status of its network interfaces, incoming and outgoing packet traffic, dropped datagrams, and error messages generated; a modem keeps statistics about the number of characters sent and received, baud rate, and calls accepted. Although it allows a manager to access statistics, SNMP does not specify exactly which data can be accessed on which devices. Instead, a separate standard specifies the details for each type of device. Known as a *Management Information Base* (*MIB*), the standard specifies the data items a managed device must keep, the operations allowed on each, and the meanings. For example, the MIB for IP specifies that the software must keep a count of all octets that arrive over each network interface and that network management software can only read the count.

---

†Technically, there is a distinction between internet management protocols and network management protocols. Historically, however, TCP/IP internet management protocols are known as *network management* protocols; we will follow the accepted terminology.

The MIB for TCP/IP divides management information into many categories. The choice of categories is important because identifiers used to specify items include a code for the category. Figure 30.2 lists a few examples.

MIB category	Includes Information About
system	The host or router operating system
interfaces	Individual network interfaces
at	Address translation (e.g., ARP mappings)
ip	Internet Protocol software
icmp	Internet Control Message Protocol software
tcp	Transmission Control Protocol software
udp	User Datagram Protocol software
ospf	Open Shortest Path First software
bgp	Border Gateway Protocol software
rmon	Remote network monitoring
rip-2	Routing Information Protocol software
dns	Domain Name System software

Figure 30.2 Example categories of MIB information. The category is encoded in the identifier used to specify an object.

Keeping the MIB definition independent of the network management protocol has advantages for both vendors and users. A vendor can include SNMP agent software in a product such as a router, with the guarantee that the software will continue to adhere to the standard after new MIB items are defined. A customer can use the same network management client software to manage multiple devices that have slightly different versions of a MIB. Of course, a device that does not have new MIB items cannot provide the information in those items. However, because all managed devices use the same language for communication, they can all parse a query and either provide the requested information or send an error message explaining that they do not have the requested item.

30.5 Examples of MIB Variables

Versions 1 and 2 of SNMP each collected variables together in a single large MIB, with the entire set documented in a single RFC. After publication of the second generation, *MIB-II*, the IETF took a different approach by allowing the publication of many individual MIB documents that each specify the variables for a specific type of device. As a result, more than 100 separate MIBs have been defined as part of the standards process; they specify more than 10,000 individual variables. For example, separate RFCs now exist that specify the MIB variables associated with devices such as: a hardware bridge, an uninterruptible power supply, an ATM switch, and a dialup modem. In addition, many vendors have defined MIB variables for their specific hardware or software products.

Examining a few of the MIB data items associated with TCP/IP protocols will help clarify the contents. Figure 30.3 lists example MIB variables along with their categories.

MIB Variable	Category	Meaning
sysUpTime	system	Time since last reboot
ifNumber	interfaces	Number of network interfaces
ifMtu	interfaces	MTU for a particular interface
ipDefaultTTL	ip	Value IP uses in time-to-live field
ipInReceives	ip	Number of datagrams received
ipForwDatagrams	ip	Number of datagrams forwarded
ipOutNoRoutes	ip	Number of routing failures
ipReasmOKs	ip	Number of datagrams reassembled
ipFragOKs	ip	Number of datagrams fragmented
ipRoutingTable	ip	IP Routing table
icmpInEchos	icmp	Number of ICMP Echo Requests received
tcpRtoMin	tcp	Minimum retransmission time TCP allows
tcpMaxConn	tcp	Maximum TCP connections allowed
tcpInSegs	tcp	Number of segments TCP has received
udpInDatagrams	udp	Number of UDP datagrams received

Figure 30.3 Examples of MIB variables along with their categories.

Most of the items listed in Figure 30.3 are numeric — each value can be stored in a single integer. However, the MIB also defines more complex structures. For example, the MIB variable *ipRoutingTable* refers to an entire routing table. Additional MIB variables define the contents of a routing table entry, and allow the network management protocols to reference an individual entry in the table, including the prefix, address mask, and next hop fields. Of course, MIB variables present only a logical definition of each data item — the internal data structures a router uses may differ from the MIB definition. When a query arrives, software in the agent on the router is responsible for mapping between the MIB variable and the data structure the router uses to store the information.

30.6 The Structure Of Management Information

In addition to the standards that specify MIB variables and their meanings, a separate standard specifies a set of rules used to define and identify MIB variables. The rules are known as the *Structure of Management Information (SMI)* specification. To keep network management protocols simple, the SMI places restrictions on the types of variables allowed in the MIB, specifies the rules for naming those variables, and creates rules for defining variable types. For example, the SMI standard includes definitions of terms like *IpAddress* (defining it to be a 4-octet string) and *Counter* (defining it to be an integer in the range of 0 to $2^{32}-1$), and specifies that they are the terms used to define MIB variables. More important, the rules in the SMI describe how the MIB refers to tables of values (e.g., the IP routing table).

30.7 Formal Definitions Using ASN.1

The SMI standard specifies that all MIB variables must be defined and referenced using ISO's *Abstract Syntax Notation 1 (ASN.1†)*. ASN.1 is a formal language that has two main features: a notation used in documents that humans read and a compact encoded representation of the same information used in communication protocols. In both cases, the precise, formal notation removes any possible ambiguities from both the representation and meaning. For example, instead of saying that a variable contains an integer value, a protocol designer who uses ASN.1 must state the exact form and range of numeric values. Such precision is especially important when implementations include heterogeneous computers that do not all use the same representations for data items.

Besides keeping standards documents unambiguous, ASN.1 also helps simplify the implementation of network management protocols and guarantees interoperability. It defines precisely how to encode both names and data items in a message. Thus, once the documentation of a MIB has been expressed using ASN.1, the human readable form can be translated directly and mechanically into the encoded form used in messages. In summary:

> *The TCP/IP network management protocols use a formal notation called ASN.1 to define names and types for variables in the management information base. The precise notation makes the form and contents of variables unambiguous.*

30.8 Structure And Representation Of MIB Object Names

We said that ASN.1 specifies how to represent both data items and names. However, understanding the names used for MIB variables requires us to know about the underlying namespace. Names used for MIB variables are taken from the *object identifier* namespace administered by ISO and ITU. The key idea behind the object identifier namespace is that it provides a namespace in which all possible objects can be designated. The namespace is not restricted to variables used in network management — it includes names for arbitrary objects (e.g., each international protocol standard document has a name).

The object identifier namespace is *absolute* (*global*), meaning that names are structured to make them globally unique. Like most namespaces that are large and absolute, the object identifier namespace is hierarchical. Authority for parts of the namespace is subdivided at each level, allowing individual groups to obtain authority to assign some of the names without consulting a central authority for each assignment‡.

---

†ASN.1 is usually pronounced by reading the dot: ''A-S-N dot 1''.

‡Readers should recall from the Domain Name System discussion in Chapter 24 how authority for a hierarchical namespace is subdivided.

The root of the object identifier hierarchy is unnamed, but has three direct descendants managed by: ISO, ITU, and jointly by ISO and ITU. The descendants are assigned both short text strings and integers that identify them (the text strings are used by humans to understand object names; computer software uses the integers to form compact, encoded representations of the names). ISO has allocated one subtree for use by other national or international standards organizations (including U.S. standards organizations), and the U.S. National Institute for Standards and Technology† has allocated a subtree for the U.S. Department of Defense. Finally, the IAB has petitioned the Department of Defense to allocate it a subtree in the namespace. Figure 30.4 illustrates pertinent parts of the object identifier hierarchy and shows the position of the node used by TCP/IP network management protocols.

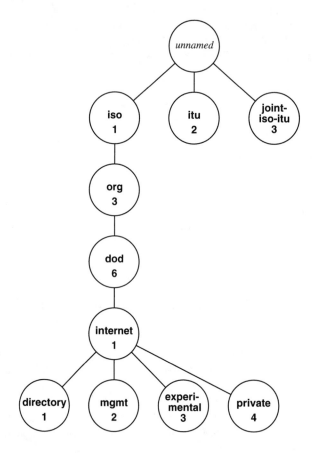

Figure 30.4 Part of the hierarchical object identifier namespace used to name MIB variables. An object's name consists of the numeric labels along a path from the root to the object.

---

†NIST was formerly the National Bureau of Standards.

The name of an object in the hierarchy is the sequence of numeric labels on the nodes along a path from the root to the object. The sequence is written with periods separating the individual components. For example, the name *1.3.6.1.2* denotes the node labeled *mgmt*, the *Internet management* subtree. The MIB has been assigned a node under the *mgmt* subtree with label *mib* and numeric value *1*. Because all MIB variables fall under that node, they all have names beginning with the prefix *1.3.6.1.2.1*.

Earlier we said that the MIB groups variables into categories. The exact meaning of the categories can now be explained: they are the subtrees of the *mib* node of the object identifier namespace. Figure 30.5 illustrates the idea by showing part of the naming subtree under the *mib* node.

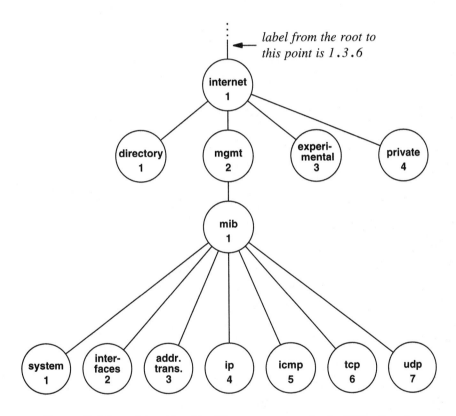

Figure 30.5 Part of the object identifier namespace under the IAB *mib* node. Each subtree corresponds to one of the categories of MIB variables.

Two examples will make the naming syntax clear. Figure 30.5 shows that the category labeled *ip* has been assigned the numeric value *4*. Thus, the names of all MIB variables corresponding to IP have an identifier that begins with the prefix *1.3.6.1.2.1.4*. If one wanted to write out the textual labels instead of the numeric representation, the name would be:

$$iso.org.dod.internet.mgmt.mib.ip$$

A MIB variable named *ipInReceives* has been assigned numeric identifier *3* under the *ip* node in the namespace, so its name is:

$$iso.org.dod.internet.mgmt.mib.ip.ipInReceives$$

and the corresponding numeric representation is:

$$1.3.6.1.2.1.4.3$$

When network management protocols use names of MIB variables in messages, each name has a suffix appended. For simple variables, the suffix *0* refers to the instance of the variable with that name. So, when it appears in a message sent to a router, the numeric representation of *ipInReceives* is:

$$1.3.6.1.2.1.4.3.0$$

which refers to the instance of *ipInReceives* on that router. Note that there is no way to guess the numeric value or suffix assigned to a variable. One must consult the published standards to find which numeric values have been assigned to each object type. Thus, programs that provide mappings between the textual form and underlying numeric values do so entirely by consulting tables of equivalences — there is no closed-form computation that performs the transformation.

As a second, more complex example, consider the MIB variable *ipAddrTable*, which contains a list of the IP addresses for each network interface. The variable exists in the namespace as a subtree under *ip*, and has been assigned the numeric value *20*. Therefore, a reference to it has the prefix:

$$iso.org.dod.internet.mgmt.mib.ip.ipAddrTable$$

with a numeric equivalent:

$$1.3.6.1.2.1.4.20$$

In programming language terms, we think of the IP address table as a one-dimensional array, where each element of the array consists of a structure (record) that contains five items: an IP address, the integer index of an interface corresponding to the entry, an IP subnet mask, an IP broadcast address, and an integer that specifies the maximum datagram size that the router will reassemble. Of course, it is unlikely that a router has such an array in memory. The router may keep this information in many variables or may need to follow pointers to find it. However, the MIB provides a name for the array as if it existed, and allows network management software on individual routers to map table references into appropriate internal variables. The point is:

> *Although they appear to specify details about data structures, MIB standards do not dictate the implementation. Instead, MIB definitions provide a uniform, virtual interface that managers use to access data; an agent must translate between the virtual items in a MIB and the internal implementation.*

Using ASN.1 style notation, we can define *ipAddrTable*:

ipAddrTable ::= SEQUENCE OF IpAddrEntry

where *SEQUENCE* and *OF* are keywords that define an ipAddrTable to be a one-dimensional array of *IpAddrEntry*s. Each entry in the array is defined to consist of five fields (the definition assumes that *IpAddress* has already been defined).

```
IpAddrEntry  ::=  SEQUENCE  {
    ipAdEntAddr
            IpAddress,
    ipAdEntIfIndex
            INTEGER,
    ipAdEntNetMask
            IpAddress,
    ipAdEntBcastAddr
            IpAddress,
    ipAdEntReasmMaxSize
            INTEGER (0..65535)
}
```

Further definitions must be given to assign numeric values to *ipAddrEntry* and to each item in the *IpAddrEntry* sequence. For example, the definition:

ipAddrEntry { ipAddrTable 1 }

specifies that *ipAddrEntry* falls under *ipAddrTable* and has numeric value *1*. Similarly, the definition:

ipAdEntNetMask { ipAddrEntry 3 }

assigns *ipAdEntNetMask* numeric value *3* under *ipAddrEntry*.

We said that *ipAddrTable* was like a one-dimensional array. However, there is a significant difference in the way programmers use arrays and the way network management software uses tables in the MIB. Programmers think of an array as a set of elements that have an index used to select a specific element. For example, the programmer might write *xyz[3]* to select the third element from array *xyz*. ASN.1 syntax does not use integer indices. Instead, MIB tables append a suffix onto the name to select a specific element in the table. For our example of an IP address table, the standard specifies that the suffix used to select an item consists of an IP address. Syntactically, the IP address (in dotted decimal notation) is concatenated onto the end of the object name to form the reference. Thus, to specify the network mask field in the IP address table entry corresponding to address 128.10.2.3, one uses the name:

iso.org.dod.internet.mgmt.mib.ip.ipAddrTable.ipAddrEntry.ipAdEntNetMask.128.10.2.3

which, in numeric form, becomes:

1.3.6.1.2.1.4.20.1.3.128.10.2.3

Although concatenating an index to the end of a name may seem awkward, it provides a powerful tool that allows clients to search tables without knowing the number of items or the type of data used as an index. The next section shows how network management protocols use this feature to step through a table one element at a time.

30.9 Simple Network Management Protocol

Network management protocols specify communication between the network management client program a manager invokes and a network management server program executing on a host or router. In addition to defining the form and meaning of messages exchanged and the representation of names and values in those messages, network management protocols also define administrative relationships among routers being managed. That is, they provide for authentication of managers.

One might expect network management protocols to contain a large number of commands. Some early protocols, for example, supported commands that allowed the manager to: *reboot* the system, *add* or *delete* routes, *disable* or *enable* a particular network interface, or *remove cached address bindings*. The main disadvantage of building management protocols around commands arises from the resulting complexity. The protocol requires a separate command for each operation on a data item. For example, the command to delete a routing table entry differs from the command to disable an interface. As a result, the protocol must change to accommodate new data items.

SNMP takes an interesting alternative approach to network management. Instead of defining a large set of commands, SNMP casts all operations in a *fetch-store paradigm*†. Conceptually, SNMP contains only two commands that allow a manager to fetch a value from a data item or store a value into a data item. All other operations are defined as side-effects of these two operations. For example, although SNMP does not

---

†The fetch-store paradigm comes from a management protocol system known as HEMS. See Partridge and Trewitt [RFCs 1021, 1022, 1023, and 1024] for details.

have an explicit *reboot* operation, an equivalent operation can be defined by declaring a data item that gives the time until the next reboot and allowing the manager to assign the item a value (including zero).

The chief advantages of using a fetch-store paradigm are stability, simplicity, and flexibility. SNMP is especially stable because its definition remains fixed, even though new data items are added to the MIB and new operations are defined as side-effects of storing into those items. SNMP is simple to implement, understand, and debug because it avoids the complexity of having special cases for each command. Finally, SNMP is especially flexible because it can accommodate arbitrary commands in an elegant framework.

From a manager's point of view, of course, SNMP remains hidden. The user interface to network management software can phrase operations as imperative commands (e.g., *reboot*). Thus, there is little visible difference between the way a manager uses SNMP and other network management protocols. In fact, vendors sell network management software that offers a graphical user interface. Such software displays diagrams of network connectivity, and uses a point-and-click style of interaction.

As Figure 30.6 shows, SNMP offers more than the two operations we have described.

Command	Meaning
get-request	Fetch a value from a specific variable
get-next-request	Fetch a value without knowing its exact name
get-bulk-request	Fetch a large volume of data (e.g., a table)
response	A response to any of the above requests
set-request	Store a value in a specific variable
inform-request	Reference to third-part data (e.g., for a proxy)
snmpv2-trap	Reply triggered by an event
report	Undefined at present

Figure 30.6 The set of possible SNMP operations. *Get-next-request* allows the manager to iterate through a table of items.

Operations *get-request* and *set-request* provide the basic fetch and store operations; *response* provides the reply. SNMP specifies that operations must be *atomic*, meaning that if a single SNMP message specifies operations on multiple variables, the server either performs all operations or none of them. In particular, no assignments will be made if any of them are in error. The *trap* operation allows managers to program servers to send information when an event occurs. For example, an SNMP server can be programmed to send a manager a *trap* message whenever one of the attached networks becomes unusable (i.e., an interface goes down).

30.9.1 Searching Tables Using Names

We said that ASN.1 does not provide mechanisms for declaring arrays or indexing them in the usual sense. However, it is possible to denote individual elements of a table by appending a suffix to the object identifier for the table. Unfortunately, a client program may wish to examine entries in a table for which it does not know all valid suffixes. The *get-next-request* operation allows a client to iterate through a table without knowing how many items the table contains. The rules are quite simple. When sending a *get-next-request*, the client supplies a prefix of a valid object identifier, *P*. The agent examines the set of object identifiers for all variables it controls, and sends a response for the variable that occurs next in lexicographic order. That is, the agent must know the ASN.1 names of all variables and be able to select the first variable with object identifier greater than *P*. Because the MIB uses suffixes to index a table, a client can send the prefix of an object identifier corresponding to a table and receive the first element in the table. The client can send the name of the first element in a table and receive the second, and so on.

Consider an example search. Recall that the *ipAddrTable* uses IP addresses to identify entries in the table. A client that does not know which IP addresses are in the table on a given router cannot form a complete object identifier. However, the client can still use the *get-next-request* operation to search the table by sending the prefix:

iso . org . dod . internet . mgmt . mib . ip . ipAddrTable . ipAddrEntry . ipAdEntNetMask

which, in numeric form, is:

$$1.3.6.1.2.1.4.20.1.3$$

The server returns the network mask field of the first entry in *ipAddrTable*. The client uses the full object identifier returned by the server to request the next item in the table.

30.10 SNMP Message Format

Unlike most TCP/IP protocols, SNMP messages do not have fixed fields. Instead, they use the standard ASN.1 encoding. Thus, a message can be difficult for humans to decode and understand. After examining the SNMP message definition in ASN.1 notation, we will review the ASN.1 encoding scheme briefly, and see an example of an encoded SNMP message.

Figure 30.7 shows how an SNMP message can be described with an ASN.1-style grammar. In general, each item in the grammar consists of a descriptive name followed by a declaration of the item's type. For example, an item such as

msgVersion INTEGER (0..2147483647)

declares the name *msgVersion* to be a nonnegative integer less than or equal to 2147483647.

```
SNMPv3Message  ::=
     SEQUENCE  {
          msgVersion  INTEGER  (0..2147483647),
               -- note: version number 3 is used for SNMPv3
          msgGlobalData  HeaderData,
          msgSecurityParameters  OCTET STRING,
          msgData  ScopedPduData
     }
```

Figure 30.7 The SNMP message format in ASN.1-style notation. Text following two consecutive dashes is a comment.

As the figure shows, each SNMP message consists of four main parts: an integer that identifies the protocol *version*, additional header data, a set of security parameters, and a data area that carries the payload. A precise definition must be supplied for each of the terms used. For example, Figure 30.8 illustrates how the contents of the *Header-Data* section can be specified.

```
HeaderData ::= SEQUENCE {
     msgID  INTEGER (0..2147483647),
          -- used to match responses with requests
     msgMaxSize  INTEGER (484..2147483647),
          -- maximum size reply the sender can accept
     msgFlags  OCTET STRING (SIZE(1)),
          -- Individual flag bits specify message characteristics
          -- bit 7 authorization used
          -- bit 6 privacy used
          -- bit 5 reportability (i.e., a response needed)
     msgSecurityModel  INTEGER (1..2147483647)
          -- determines exact format of security parameters that follow
     }
```

Figure 30.8 The definition of the *HeaderData* area in an SNMP message.

The data area in an SNMP message is divided into *protocol data units* (*PDUs*). Each PDU consists of a request (sent by client) or a response (sent by an agent). SNMPv3 allows each PDU to be sent as plain text or to be encrypted for privacy. Thus, the grammar specifies a *CHOICE*. In programming language terminology, the concept is known as a *discriminated union*.

```
ScopedPduData ::= CHOICE {
     plaintext  ScopedPDU,
     encryptedPDU  OCTET STRING  -- encrypted ScopedPDU value
     }
```

An encrypted PDU begins with an identifier of the *engine*† that produced it. The engine ID is followed by the name of the context and the octets of the encrypted message.

```
ScopedPDU ::= SEQUENCE {
    contextEngineID  OCTET STRING,
    contextName  OCTET STRING,
    data  ANY              -- e.g., a PDU as defined below
}
```

The item labeled *data* in the *ScopedPDU* definition has a type *ANY* because field *contextName* defines the exact details of the item. The SNMPv3 Message Processing Model (*v3MP*) specifies that the data must consist of one of the SNMP PDUs as Figure 30.9 illustrates:

```
PDU ::=
    CHOICE {
        get-request
            GetRequest-PDU,
        get-next-request
            GetNextRequest-PDU,
        get-bulk-request
            GetBulkRequest-PDU,
        response
            Response-PDU,
        set-request
            SetRequest-PDU,
        inform-request
            InformRequest-PDU,
        snmpV2-trap
            SNMPv2-Trap-PDU,
        report
            Report-PDU,
    }
```

Figure 30.9 The ASN.1 definitions of an SNMP PDU. The syntax for each request type must be specified further.

The definition specifies that each protocol data unit consists of one of eight types. To complete the definition of an SNMP message, we must further specify the syntax of the eight individual types. For example, Figure 30.10 shows the definition of a *get-request*.

---

†SNMPv3 distinguishes between an *application* that uses the service SNMP supplies and an *engine*, which is the underlying software that transmits requests and receives responses.

```
GetRequest-PDU  ::=  [0]
      IMPLICIT SEQUENCE  {
            request-id
                  Integer32,
            error-status
                  INTEGER (0..18),
            error-index
                  INTEGER (0..max-bindings),
            variable-bindings
                  VarBindList
      }
```

Figure 30.10 The ASN.1 definition of a *get-request* message. Formally, the
message is defined to be a *GetRequest-PDU*.

Further definitions in the standard specify the remaining undefined terms. Both
error-status and *error-index* are single octet integers which contain the value zero in a
request. If an error occurs, the values sent in a response identify the cause of the error.
Finally, *VarBindList* contains a list of object identifiers for which the client seeks
values. In ASN.1 terms, the definitions specify that *VarBindList* is a sequence of pairs
of object name and value. ASN.1 represents the pairs as a sequence of two items.
Thus, in the simplest possible request, *VarBindList* is a sequence of two items: a name
and a *null*.

30.11 Example Encoded SNMP Message

The encoded form of ASN.1 uses variable-length fields to represent items. In general, each field begins with a header that specifies the type of object and its length in
bytes. For example, each *SEQUENCE* begins with an octet containing 30 (hexadecimal); the next octet specifies the number of following octets that comprise the sequence.

Figure 30.11 contains an example SNMP message that illustrates how values are
encoded into octets. The message is a *get-request* that specifies data item *sysDescr*
(numeric object identifier *1.3.6.1.2.1.1.1.0*). Because the example shows an actual message, it includes many details. In particular, the message contains a *msgSecuri-
tyParameters* section which has not been discussed above. This particular message uses
the *UsmSecurityParameters* form of security parameters. It should be possible, however, to correlate other sections of the message with the definitions above.

```
   30        67        02        01        03
SEQUENCE len=103 INTEGER   len=1    vers=3
```

```
   30        0D        02        01        2A
SEQUENCE len=13 INTEGER   len=1    msgID=42
```

```
   02        02        08        00
INTEGER   len=2    maxmsgsize=2048
```

```
   04        01        04
 string   len=1   msgFlags=0x04 (bits mean noAuth, noPriv, reportable)
```

```
   02        01        03
INTEGER   len=1   used-based security
```

```
   04        25        30        23
 string   len=37 SEQUENCE len=35 UsmSecurityParameters
```

```
   04        0C        00        00        00        63        00        00        00
 string   len=12   msgAuthoritativeEngineID ...
   A1        C0        93        8E        23
engine is at IP address 192.147.142.35, port 161
```

```
   02        01        00
INTEGER   len=1   msgAuthoritativeEngineBoots=0
```

```
   02        01        00
INTEGER   len=1   msgAuthoritativeEngineTime=0
```

```
   04        09        43        6F        6D        65        72        42        6F
 string   len=9     -----msgUserName value is "ComerBook"-------------
   6F        6B
-------------
```

```
   04        00
 string   len=0   msgAuthenticationParameters (none)
```

```
   04        00
 string   len=0   msgPrivacyParameters (none)
```

```
   30        2C
SEQUENCE len=44  ScopedPDU
```

```
   04        0C        00        00        00        63        00        00
 string   len=12   -------------------contextEngineID-------
   00        A1        c0        93        8E        23
   --------------------------------------------
```

```
   04        00
 string   len=0   contextName = "" (default)
```

CONTEXT [0] IMPLICIT SEQUENCE

```
  A0          1A
getreq.  len=26


  02          02        4D        C6
INTEGER len=2    request-id = 19910


  02          01        00
INTEGER len=1 error-status = noError(0)


  02          01        00
INTEGER len=1 error-index=0


  30          0E
SEQUENCE   len=14 VarBindList


  30          0C
SEQUENCE   len=12 VarBind


  06          08
OBJECT IDENTIFIER name


  2B          06        01        02        01        01        01        00
  1.3    .    6    .    1    .    2    .    1    .    1    .    1    .    0  (sysDescr.0)


  05          00
null    len=0  (no value specified)
```

Figure 30.11 The encoded form of an SNMPv3 *get-request* for data item *sys-Descr* with octets shown in hexadecimal and a comment explaining their meaning below. Related octets have been grouped onto lines; they are contiguous in the message.

As Figure 30.11 shows, the message starts with a code for *SEQUENCE* which has a length of 103 octets†. The first item in the sequence is a 1-octet integer that specifies the protocol *version*; the value *3* indicates that this is an SNMPv3 message. Successive fields define a message ID and the maximum message size the sender can accept in a reply. Security information, including the name of the user (*ComerBook*) follows the message header.

The *GetRequest-PDU* occupies the tail of the message. The sequence labeled *ScopedPDU* specifies a context in which to interpret the remainder of the message. The octet *A0* specifies the operation as a *get-Request*. Because the high-order bit is turned on, the interpretation of the octet is *context specific*. That is, the hexadecimal value *A0* only specifies a *GetRequest-PDU* when used in context; it is not a universally reserved value. Following the request octet, the length octet specifies the request is *26* octets long. The request ID is *2* octets, but each of the error-status and error-index are one oc-

---

†Sequence items occur frequently in an SNMP message because SNMP uses *SEQUENCE* instead of conventional programming language constructs like *array* or *struct*.

tet. Finally, the sequence of pairs contains one binding, a single object identifier bound to a *null* value. The identifier is encoded as expected except that the first two numeric labels are combined into a single octet.

30.12 New Features In SNMPv3

We said that version 3 of SNMP represents an evolution that follows and extends the basic framework of earlier versions. The primary changes arise in the areas of security and administration. The goals are twofold. First, SNMPv3 is designed to have both general and flexible security policies, making it possible for the interactions between a manager and managed devices to adhere to the security policies an organization specifies. Second, the system is designed to make administration of security easy.

To achieve generality and flexibility, SNMPv3 includes facilities for several aspects of security, and allows each to be configured independently. For example, v3 supports *message authentication* to ensure that instructions originate from a valid manager, *privacy* to ensure that no one can read messages as they pass between a manager's station and a managed device, and *authorization* and *view-based access control* to ensure that only authorized managers access particular items. To make the security system easy to configure or change, v3 allows *remote configuration*, meaning that an authorized manager can change the configuration of security items listed above without being physically present at the device.

30.13 Summary

Network management protocols allow a manager to monitor and control routers and hosts. A network management client program executing on the manager's workstation contacts one or more servers, called agents, running on the devices to be controlled. Because an internet consists of heterogeneous machines and networks, TCP/IP management software executes as application programs and uses internet transport protocols (e.g., UDP) for communication between clients and servers.

The standard TCP/IP network management protocol is SNMP, the Simple Network Management Protocol. SNMP defines a low-level management protocol that provides two conceptual operations: fetch a value from a variable or store a value into a variable. In SNMP, other operations occur as side-effects of changing values in variables. SNMP defines the format of messages that travel between a manager's computer and a managed entity.

A set of companion standards to SNMP define the set of variables that a managed entity maintains. The set of variables comprise a Management Information Base (*MIB*). MIB variables are described using ASN.1, a formal language that provides a concise encoded form as well as a precise human-readable notation for names and objects. ASN.1 uses a hierarchical namespace to guarantee that all MIB names are globally unique while still allowing subgroups to assign parts of the namespace.

FOR FURTHER STUDY

Case et. al. [RFC 2570] presents an overview of SNMPv3, gives background and motivation, and discusses changes among the various versions. It also contains a summary of RFCs related to v3, and explains which v2 standards still apply. Many other RFCs discuss individual aspects of the protocol. For example, Wijnen et. al. [RFC 2575] presents the view-based access control model, and Case et. al. [RFC 2572] discusses message handling.

ISO [May 87a] and [May 87b] contain the standard for ASN.1 and specify the encoding. McCloghrie et. al. [RFCs 2578, 2579, 2580] define the language used for MIB modules and provide definitions of data types. Case et. al. [RFC 1907] defines version 2 of the MIB.

An older proposal for a network management protocol called HEMS can be found in Trewitt and Partridge [RFCs 1021, 1022, 1023, and 1024]. Davin, Case, Fedor, and Schoffstall [RFC 1028] specifies a predecessor to SNMP known as the Simple Gateway Monitoring Protocol (*SGMP*).

EXERCISES

30.1 Capture an SNMP packet with a network analyzer and decode the fields.

30.2 Read the standard to find out how ASN.1 encodes the first two numeric values from an object identifier in a single octet. Why does it do so?

30.3 Read the two standards and compare SNMPv2 to SNMPv3. Under what circumstances are the v2 security features valid? Invalid?

30.4 Suppose the MIB designers need to define a variable that corresponds to a two-dimensional array. How can ASN.1 notation accommodate references to such a variable?

30.5 What are the advantages and disadvantages of defining globally unique ASN.1 names for MIB variables?

30.6 Consult the standards and match each item in Figure 30.11 with a corresponding definition.

30.7 If you have SNMP client code available, try using it to read MIB variables in a local router. What is the advantage of allowing arbitrary managers to read variables in all routers? The disadvantage?

30.8 Read the MIB specification to find the definition of variable *ipRoutingTable* that corresponds to an IP routing table. Design a program that will use SNMP to contact multiple routers and see if any entries in their routing tables cause a routing loop. Exactly what ASN.1 names should such a program generate?

30.9 Consider the implementation of an SNMP agent. Does it make sense to arrange MIB variables in memory exactly the way SNMP describes them? Why or why not?

30.10 Argue that SNMP is a misnomer because SNMP is not ''simple.''

30.11 Read about the IPsec security standard described in Chapter 32. If an organization uses IPsec, is the security in SNMPv3 also necessary? Why or why not?

30.12 Does it make sense to use SNMP to manage all devices? Why or why not? (Hint: consider a simple hardware device such as a dialup modem.)

31

Summary Of Protocol Dependencies

31.1 Introduction

TCP/IP has spawned more applications than we can discuss in a single textbook. In general, each defines its own application protocol and relies on TCP or UDP for end-to-end transport. In fact, any programmer who builds a distributed application using TCP/IP defines an application-level protocol.

Although it is not important to understand the details of all protocols, it is important to know which protocols exist and how they can be used. This chapter provides a brief summary of the relationships among fundamental protocols, and shows which are available for use by applications.

31.2 Protocol Dependencies

The chart in Figure 31.1 shows dependencies among the major protocols we have discussed. Each enclosed polygon corresponds to one protocol, and resides directly above protocols that it uses. For example, the mail protocol, SMTP, depends on TCP, which depends on IP.

Users

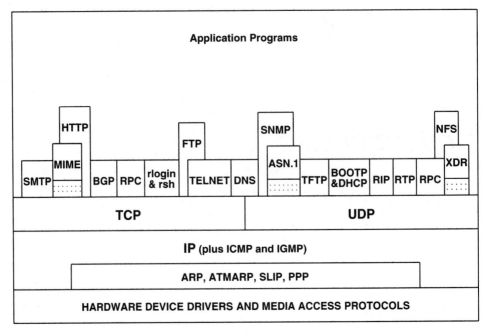

Figure 31.1 Dependencies among major, higher level TCP/IP protocols. A
protocol uses the protocols that lie directly below it. Application programs can use all protocols above IP.

Several parts of the diagram need further explanation. The bottom layer represents
all protocols that the hardware provides. This level includes all hardware control protocols (e.g., media access and logical link allocation). As we have throughout the text,
we will assume that any packet transfer system can be included in this layer as long as
IP can use it to transfer datagrams. Thus, if a system is configured to send datagrams
through a tunnel, the entry to the tunnel is treated like a hardware interface, despite its
software implementation.

The second layer from the bottom lists link layer and address resolution protocols
like SLIP, PPP, ARP, and ATMARP. Of course, not all networking technologies require such protocols. ARP is used on connectionless broadcast networks such as Ethernet; ATMARP is used on non-broadcast multiple access networks such as ATM; and
RARP is seldom used except for diskless machines. Other link layer or address binding
protocols can occur at the same level, but none is currently popular.

The third layer from the bottom contains IP. It includes the required error and control message protocol, ICMP, and the optional multicast group management protocol IGMP. Note that IP is the only protocol that spans an entire layer. All lower-level protocols deliver incoming information to IP, and all higher-level protocols must use IP to send outgoing datagrams. IP is shown with a direct dependency on the hardware layer because it needs to use the hardware link or access protocols to transmit datagrams after it uses ARP to bind addresses.

TCP and UDP comprise the transport layer. Of course, new transport protocols have been suggested, but none has been widely adopted yet.

The application layer illustrates the complex dependencies among the various application protocols. Recall, for example, that FTP uses the network virtual terminal definitions from TELNET to define communication on its control connection and TCP to form data connections. Also recall that HTTP uses syntax and content types from MIME. Thus, the diagram shows that FTP depends on both TELNET and TCP and that HTTP depends on both MIME and TCP. The domain name system (DNS) uses both UDP and TCP for communication, so the diagram shows both dependencies. Sun's NFS depends on the external data representation (XDR) and remote procedure call (RPC) protocols. RPC appears twice because, like the domain name system, it can use either UDP or TCP.

SNMP depends on *Abstract Syntax Notation* (ASN.1). Although SNMP can use either UDP or TCP, only dependence on UDP is shown because few implementations run over TCP. Because XDR, ASN.1, and MIME simply describe syntactic conventions and data representations, they do not use either TCP or UDP. Thus, although it shows that both SNMP and NFS depend on UDP, the diagram contains a dotted area below ASN.1 and XDR to show that neither of them depends on UDP. A few details have been omitted in our diagram. For example, it could be argued that IP depends on BOOTP/DHCP or that many protocols depend on DNS because software that implements such protocols requires name binding.

31.3 The Hourglass Model

Engineers describe Internet protocols as following an *hourglass model*. Because it lies at the heart of all communication, IP forms the center of the hourglass. Of all the protocols we discussed, IP is the only protocol common to all applications — ultimately all internet communication involves IP datagrams. Thus, universal interoperability is achieved by making IP run over all possible network technologies. Figure 31.2 illustrates the concept by showing the dependency among IP, applications, and underlying networks.

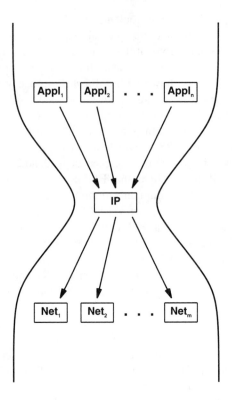

Figure 31.2 An illustration of the hourglass model. IP is at the center of the
hourglass because all applications depend on IP and IP runs over
all networks.

31.4 Application Program Access

Most systems restrict application programs from accessing lower-level protocols.
That is, most systems only allow an application program to access TCP or UDP or to
implement higher level protocols that use them (e.g., FTP). In fact, a system may
choose to restrict access to transport protocols by allowing only privileged applications
to open lower numbered TCP or UDP protocol ports.

Although direct access from an application to IP is unusual, a few systems do provide special purpose mechanisms that make it possible. For example, a mechanism
known as a *packet filter* allows privileged programs to control frame demultiplexing.
Using the packet filter primitives, an application program establishes the criteria used to
capture packets (e.g., the application program can specify that it wishes to capture all
packets with a given value in the *type* field of a frame). Once the operating system accepts the filter command, it places all packets that match the specified type on a queue.
The application program uses the packet filter mechanism to extract packets from the

queue. For such systems, the diagram in Figure 31.1 should be extended to show application access to lower layers.

31.5 Summary

Much of the rich functionality associated with the TCP/IP protocol suite results from a variety of high-level services supplied by application programs. The high-level protocols these programs use build on the basic transport services: unreliable datagram delivery and reliable stream transport. The applications usually follow the client-server model in which servers operate at known protocols ports so clients know how to contact them.

The highest level of protocols provides user services like Web browsing, remote login, and file and mail transfer. The chief advantages of having an internet on which to build such services are that it provides universal connectivity and simplifies the application protocols. In particular, when used by two machines that attach to an internet, end-to-end transport protocols can guarantee that a client program on the source machine communicates directly with a server on the destination machine. Because services like electronic mail use the end-to-end transport connection, they do not need to rely on intermediate machines to forward (whole) messages.

We have seen a variety of application level protocols and the complex dependencies among them. Although many application protocols have been defined, a few major applications such as Web browsing account for most packets on the Internet.

FOR FURTHER STUDY

One of the issues underlying protocol layering revolves around the optimal location of protocol functionality. Edge [1979] compares end-to-end protocols with the hop-by-hop approach. Saltzer, Reed, and Clark [1984] argues for having the highest level protocols perform end-to-end acknowledgement and error detection. A series of papers by Mills [RFCs 956, 957, and 958] proposes application protocols for clock synchronization, and report on experiments.

EXERCISES

31.1   It is possible to translate some application protocols into others. For example, it might be possible to build a program that accepts an FTP request, translates it to a TFTP request, passes the result to a TFTP server to obtain a file, and translates the reply back to FTP for transmission to the original source. What are the advantages and disadvantages of such protocol translation?

31.2   Consider the translation described in the previous question. Which pairs of protocols in
            Figure 31.1 are amenable to such translations?

31.3   Some application programs invoked by users may need access to IP without using TCP
            or UDP. Find examples of such programs. (Hint: think of ICMP.)

31.4   Where do multicast protocols fit into the diagram in Figure 31.1?

31.5   DNS allows access by both TCP and UDP. Find out whether your local operating sys-
            tem allows a single process to accept both TCP connections and UDP requests.

31.6   Choose a complex application like the *X window system*, and find out which protocols it
            uses.

31.7   Where does OSPF fit into the diagram in Figure 31.1?

31.8   The diagram in Figure 31.1 shows that FTP depends on TELNET. Does your local FTP
            client invoke the TELNET program, or does the FTP client contain a separate implemen-
            tation of the TELNET protocol?

31.9   Redraw Figure 31.1 for a Web browser. Which protocols does it use?

32

Internet Security And Firewall Design (IPsec)

32.1 Introduction

Like the locks used to help keep tangible property secure, computers and data networks need provisions that help keep information secure. Security in an internet environment is both important and difficult. It is important because information has significant value — information can be bought and sold directly or used indirectly to create new products and services that yield high profits. Security in an internet is difficult because security involves understanding when and how participating users, computers, services, and networks can trust one another as well as understanding the technical details of network hardware and protocols. Security is required on every computer and every protocol; a single weakness can compromise the security of an entire network. More important, because TCP/IP supports a wide diversity of users, services, and networks and because an internet can span many political and organizational boundaries, participating individuals and organizations may not agree on a level of trust or policies for handling data.

This chapter considers two fundamental techniques that form the basis for internet security: perimeter security and encryption. Perimeter security allows an organization to determine the services and networks it will make available to outsiders and the extent to which outsiders can use resources. Encryption handles most other aspects of security. We begin by reviewing a few basic concepts and terminology.

32.2 Protecting Resources

The terms *network security* and *information security* refer in a broad sense to confidence that information and services available on a network cannot be accessed by unauthorized users. Security implies safety, including assurance of data integrity, freedom from unauthorized access of computational resources, freedom from snooping or wiretapping, and freedom from disruption of service. Of course, just as no physical property is absolutely secure against crime, no network is completely secure. Organizations make an effort to secure networks for the same reason they make an effort to secure buildings and offices: basic security measures can discourage crime by making it significantly more difficult.

Providing security for information requires protecting both physical and abstract resources. Physical resources include passive storage devices such as disks and CD-ROMs as well as active devices such as users' computers. In a network environment, physical security extends to the cables, bridges, and routers that comprise the network infrastructure. Indeed, although physical security is seldom mentioned, it often plays an important role in an overall security plan. Obviously, physical security can prevent wiretapping. Good physical security can also eliminate sabotage (e.g., disabling a router to cause packets to be routed through an alternative, less secure path).

Protecting an abstract resource such as information is usually more difficult than providing physical security because information is elusive. Information security encompasses many aspects of protection:

- *Data integrity*. A secure system must protect information from unauthorized change.

- *Data availability* The system must guarantee that outsiders cannot prevent legitimate access to data (e.g., any outsider should not be able to block customers from accessing a Web site).

- *Privacy or confidentiality*. The system must prevent outsiders from making copies of data as it passes across a network or understanding the contents if copies are made.

- *Authorization*. Although physical security often classifies people and resources into broad categories, (e.g., all nonemployees are forbidden from using a particular hallway), security for information usually needs to be more restrictive (e.g., some parts of an employee's record are available only to the personnel office, others are available only to the employee's boss, and others are available to the payroll office).

- *Authentication*. The system must allow two communicating entities to validate each other's identity.

- *Replay avoidance*. To prevent outsiders from capturing copies of packets and using them later, the system must prevent a retransmitted copy of a packet from being accepted.

32.3 Information Policy

Before an organization can enforce network security, the organization must assess risks and develop a clear policy regarding information access and protection. The policy specifies who will be granted access to each piece of information, the rules an individual must follow in disseminating the information to others, and a statement of how the organization will react to violations.

An information policy begins with people because:

> *Humans are usually the most susceptible point in any security scheme. A worker who is malicious, careless, or unaware of an organization's information policy can compromise the best security.*

32.4 Internet Security

Internet security is difficult because datagrams traveling from source to destination often pass across many intermediate networks and through routers that are not owned or controlled by either the sender or the recipient. Thus, because datagrams can be intercepted or compromised, the contents cannot be trusted. As an example, consider a server that attempts to use *source authentication* to verify that requests originated from valid customers. Source authentication requires the server to examine the source IP address on each incoming datagram, and only accept requests from computers on an authorized list. Source authentication is *weak* because it can be broken easily. In particular, an intermediate router can watch traffic traveling to and from the server, and record the IP address of a valid customer. Later the intermediate router can manufacture a request that has the same source address (and intercept the reply). The point is:

> *An authorization scheme that uses a remote machine's IP address to authenticate its identity does not suffice in an unsecure internet. An imposter who gains control of an intermediate router can obtain access by impersonating an authorized client.*

Stronger authentication requires *encryption*. To encrypt a message, the sender applies a mathematical function that rearranges the bits according to a *key* which is known only to the sender. The receiver uses another mathematical function to decrypt the message. Careful choices of an encryption algorithm, a key, and the contents of messages can make it virtually impossible for intermediate machines to decode messages or manufacture messages that are valid.

32.5 IP Security (IPsec)

The IETF has devised a set of protocols that provide secure Internet communication. Collectively known as *IPsec* (short for *IP security*), the protocols offer authentication and privacy services at the IP layer, and can be used with both IPv4 and IPv6†. More important, instead of completely specifying the functionality or the encryption algorithm to be used, the IETF chose to make the system both flexible and extensible. For example, an application that employs IPsec can choose whether to use an authentication facility that validates the sender or to use an encryption facility that also ensures the payload will remain confidential; the choices can be asymmetric (e.g., authentication in one direction but not the other). Furthermore, IPsec does not restrict the user to a specific encryption or authentication algorithm. Instead, IPsec provides a general framework that allows each pair of communicating endpoints to choose algorithms and parameters (e.g., key size). To guarantee interoperability, IPsec does include a set of encryption algorithms that all implementations must recognize. The point is:

> *IPsec is not a single security protocol. Instead, IPsec provides a set of security algorithms plus a general framework that allows a pair of communicating entities to use whichever algorithms provide security appropriate for the communication.*

32.6 IPsec Authentication Header

Instead of changing the basic datagram header or creating an IP option, IPsec uses a separate *Authentication Header* (*AH*) to carry authentication information. Figure 32.1 illustrates the most straightforward use of an authentication header with IPv4.

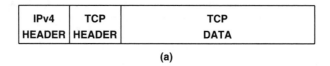

(a)

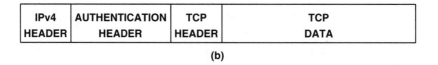

(b)

Figure 32.1 Illustration of (a) an IPv4 datagram, and (b) the same datagram after an IPsec authentication header has been added. The new header is inserted immediately after the IP header.

---

†The examples in this chapter focus on IPv4; Chapter 33 describes IPv6 in detail and illustrates how IPsec headers appear in IPv6 datagrams.

As the figure shows, IPsec inserts the authentication header immediately after the original IP header, but before the transport header. Furthermore, the *PROTOCOL* field in the IP header is changed to value *51* to indicate the presence of an authentication header.

If IPsec modifies the *PROTOCOL* field in the IP header, how does a receiver determine the type of information carried in the datagram? The authentication header has a *NEXT HEADER* field that specifies the type — IPsec records the original *PRO-TOCOL* value in the *NEXT HEADER* field. When a datagram arrives, the receiver uses security information from the authentication header to verify the sender, and uses the *NEXT HEADER* value to further demultiplex the datagram. Figure 32.2 illustrates the header format.

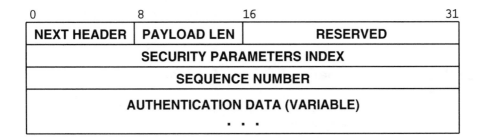

Figure 32.2 The IPsec authentication header format. The field labeled *NEXT HEADER* records the original value of the IP *PROTOCOL* field.

Interestingly, the *PAYLOAD LEN* field does not specify the size of the data area in the datagram. Instead, it specifies the length of the authentication header. Remaining fields are used to ensure security. Field *SEQUENCE NUMBER* contains a unique sequence number for each packet sent; the number starts at zero when a particular security algorithm is selected and increases monotonically. The *SECURITY PARAMETERS IN-DEX* field specifies the security scheme used, and the *AUTHENTICATION DATA* field contains data for the selected security scheme.

32.7 Security Association

To understand the reason for using a security parameters index, observe that a security scheme defines details that provide many possible variations. For example, the security scheme includes an authentication algorithm, a key (or keys) that the algorithm uses, a lifetime over which the key will remain valid, a lifetime over which the destination agrees to use the algorithm, and a list of source addresses that are authorized to use the scheme. Further observe that the information cannot fit into the header.

To save space in the header, IPsec arranges for each receiver to collect all the details about a security scheme into an abstraction known as a *security association (SA)*.

Each SA is given a number, known as a *security parameters index*, through which it is identified. Before a sender can use IPsec to communicate with a receiver, the sender must know the index value for a particular SA. The sender then places the value in the field *SECURITY PARAMETERS INDEX* of each outgoing datagram.

Index values are not globally specified. Instead, each destination creates as many SAs as it needs, and assigns an index value to each. The destination can specify a life-time for each SA, and can reuse index values once an SA becomes invalid. Conse-quently, the index cannot be interpreted without consulting the destination (e.g., the in-dex *1* can have entirely different meanings to two destinations). To summarize:

> *A destination uses the security parameters index to identify the securi-ty association for a packet. The values are not global; a combination of destination address and security parameters index is needed to identify an SA.*

32.8 IPsec Encapsulating Security Payload

To handle privacy as well as authentication, IPsec uses an *Encapsulating Security Payload* (*ESP*), which is more complex than an authentication header. A value *50* in the *PROTOCOL* field of the datagram informs a receiver that the datagram carries ESP. Figure 32.3 illustrates the conceptual organization.

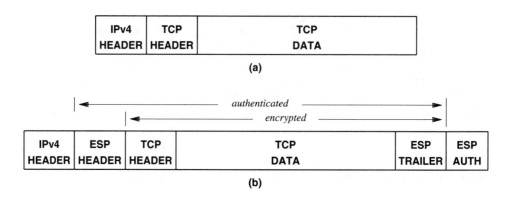

Figure 32.3 (a) A datagram, and (b) the same datagram using IPsec Encapsu-lating Security Payload. In practice, encryption means that fields are not easily identifiable.

As the figure shows, ESP adds three additional areas to the datagram. The *ESP HEADER* immediately follows the IP header and precedes the encrypted payload. The *ESP TRAILER* is encrypted along with the payload; a variable-size *ESP AUTH* field fol-lows the encrypted section.

ESP uses many of the same items found in the authentication header, but rearranges their order. For example, the *ESP HEADER* consists of 8 octets that identify the security parameters index and a sequence number.

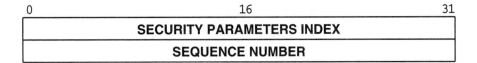

The *ESP TRAILER* consists of optional padding, a padding length field, *PAD LENGTH*, and a *NEXT HEADER* field that is followed by a variable amount of authentication data.

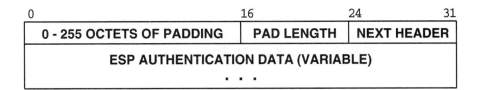

Padding is optional; it may be present for three reasons. First, some decryption algorithms require zeroes following an encrypted message. Second, note that the *NEXT HEADER* field is shown right-justified within a 4-octet field. The alignment is important because IPsec requires the authentication data that follows the trailer to be aligned at the start of a 4-octet boundary. Thus, padding may be needed to ensure alignment. Third, some sites may choose to add random amounts of padding to each datagram so eavesdroppers at intermediate points along the path cannot use the size of a datagram to guess its purpose.

32.9 Authentication And Mutable Header Fields

The IPsec authentication mechanism is designed to ensure that an arriving datagram is identical to the datagram sent by the source. However, such a guarantee is impossible to make. To understand why, recall that IP is a machine-to-machine layer, meaning that the layering principle only applies across one hop. In particular, each intermediate router decrements the time-to-live field and recomputes the checksum.

IPsec uses the term *mutable fields* to refer to IP header fields that are changed in transit. To prevent such changes causing authentication errors, IPsec specifically omits such fields from the authentication computation. Thus, when a datagram arrives, IPsec only authenticates immutable fields (e.g., the source address and protocol type).

32.10 IPsec Tunneling

Recall from Chapter 20 that VPN technology uses encryption along with IP-in-IP tunneling to keep inter-site transfers private. IPsec is specifically designed to accommodate an encrypted tunnel. In particular, the standard defines tunneled versions of both the authentication header and the encapsulating security payload. Figure 32.4 illustrates the layout of datagrams in tunneling mode.

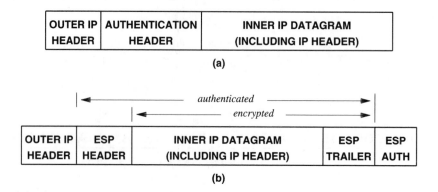

OUTER IP HEADER	AUTHENTICATION HEADER	INNER IP DATAGRAM (INCLUDING IP HEADER)

(a)

OUTER IP HEADER	ESP HEADER	INNER IP DATAGRAM (INCLUDING IP HEADER)	ESP TRAILER	ESP AUTH

(b)

Figure 32.4 Illustration of IPsec tunneling mode for (a) authentication and (b) encapsulating security payload. The entire inner datagram is protected.

32.11 Required Security Algorithms

IPsec defines a minimal set of algorithms that are mandatory (i.e., that all implementations must supply). In each case, the standard defines specific uses. Figure 32.5 lists the required algorithms.

Authentication	
HMAC with MD5	RFC 2403
HMAC with SHA-1	RFC 2404
Encapsulating Security Payload	
DES in CBC mode	RFC 2405
HMAC with MD5	RFC 2403
HMAC with SHA-1	RFC 2404
Null Authentication	
Null Encryption	

Figure 32.5 The security algorithms that are mandatory for IPsec.

32.12 Secure Sockets

By the mid 1990s when it became evident that security was important for Internet commerce, several groups proposed security mechanisms for use with the Web. Although not formally adopted by the IETF, one of the proposals has become a de facto standard.

Known as the *Secure Sockets Layer* (*SSL*), the technology was originally developed by Netscape, Inc. As the name implies, SSL resides at the same layer as the socket API. When a client uses SSL to contact a server, the SSL protocol allows each side to authenticate itself to the other. The two sides then negotiate to select an encryption algorithm that they both support. Finally, SSL allows the two sides to establish an encrypted connection (i.e., a connection that uses the chosen encryption algorithm to guarantee privacy).

32.13 Firewalls And Internet Access

Mechanisms that control *internet access* handle the problem of screening a particular network or an organization from unwanted communication. Such mechanisms can help prevent outsiders from: obtaining information, changing information, or disrupting communication on an organization's intranet. Successful access control requires a careful combination of restrictions on network topology, intermediate information staging, and packet filters.

A single technique known as an *internet firewall*†, has emerged as the basis for internet access control. An organization places a firewall at its connection to external networks (e.g., the global Internet). A firewall partitions an internet into two regions, referred to informally as the *inside* and *outside*.

32.14 Multiple Connections And Weakest Links

Although concept seems simple, details complicate firewall construction. First, an organization's intranet can have multiple external connections. The organization must form a *security perimeter* by installing a firewall at each external connection. To guarantee that the perimeter is effective, all firewalls must be configured to use exactly the same access restrictions. Otherwise, it may be possible to circumvent the restrictions imposed by one firewall by entering the organization's internet through another‡.

We can summarize:

> *An organization that has multiple external connections must install a firewall on each external connection and must coordinate all firewalls. Failure to restrict access identically on all firewalls can leave the organization vulnerable.*

---

†The term *firewall* is derived from building architecture in which a firewall is a thick, fireproof partition that makes a section of a building impenetrable to fire.

‡The well-known idea that security is only as strong as the weakest point has been termed the *weakest link axiom* in reference to the adage that a chain is only as strong as its weakest link.

32.15 Firewall Implementation

How should a firewall be implemented? In theory, a firewall simply blocks all unauthorized communication between computers in the organization and computers outside the organization. In practice, the details depend on the network technology, the capacity of the connection, the traffic load, and the organization's policies. Thus, no single solution works for all organizations; building an effective, customized firewall can be difficult.

To operate at network speeds, a firewall must have hardware and software optimized for the task. Fortunately, most commercial routers include a high-speed filtering mechanism that can be used to perform much of the necessary work. A manager can configure the filter in a router to request that the router block specified datagrams. As we discuss the details of filter mechanisms, we will see how filters form the basic building blocks of a firewall. Later we will see how filters can be used in conjunction with another mechanism to provide communication that is safe, but flexible.

32.16 Packet-Level Filters

Many commercial routers offer a mechanism that augments normal routing and permits a manager to further control packet processing. Informally called a *packet filter*, the mechanism requires the manager to specify how the router should dispose of each datagram. For example, the manager might choose to *filter* (i.e. block) all datagrams that come from a particular source or those used by a particular application, while choosing to route other datagrams to their destination.

The term *packet filter* arises because the filtering mechanism does not keep a record of interaction or a history of previous datagrams. Instead, the filter considers each datagram separately. When a datagram first arrives, the router passes the datagram through its packet filter before performing any other processing. If the filter rejects the datagram, the router drops it immediately.

Because TCP/IP does not dictate a standard for packet filters, each router vendor is free to choose the capabilities of their packet filter as well as the interface a manager uses to configure the filter. Some routers permit a manager to configure separate filter actions for each interface, while others have a single configuration for all interfaces. Usually, when specifying datagrams that the filter should block, a manager can list any combination of source IP address, destination IP address, protocol, source protocol port number, and destination protocol port number. For example, Figure 32.6 illustrates a filter specification.

In the example, the manager has chosen to block incoming datagrams destined for a few well-known services and to block one case of outgoing datagrams. The filter blocks all outgoing datagrams that originate from any host address matching the 16-bit prefix of *128.5.0.0* that are destined for a remote e-mail server (TCP port *25*). The filter also blocks incoming datagrams destined for FTP (TCP port *21*), TELNET (TCP port *23*), WHOIS (UDP port *43*), TFTP (UDP port *69*), or FINGER (TCP port *79*).

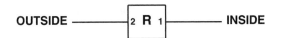

ARRIVES ON INTERFACE	IP SOURCE	IP DEST.	PROTOCOL	SOURCE PORT	DEST. PORT
2	*	*	TCP	*	21
2	*	*	TCP	*	23
1	128.5.0.0 / 16	*	TCP	*	25
2	*	*	UDP	*	43
2	*	*	UDP	*	69
2	*	*	TCP	*	79

Figure 32.6 A router with two interfaces and an example datagram filter specification. A router that includes a packet filter forms the basic building block of a firewall.

32.17 Security And Packet Filter Specification

Although the example filter configuration in Figure 32.6 specifies a small list of services that should be blocked, such an approach does not work well for an effective firewall. There are three reasons. First, the number of well-known ports is large and growing rapidly. Thus, listing each service requires a manager to update the list continually; an error of omission can leave the firewall vulnerable. Second, much of the traffic on an internet does not travel to or from a well-known port. In addition to programmers who can choose port numbers for their private client-server applications, services like *Remote Procedure Call (RPC)* assign ports dynamically. Third, listing ports of well-known services leaves the firewall vulnerable to *tunneling*. Tunneling can circumvent security if a host or router on the inside agrees to accept encapsulated datagrams from an outsider, remove one layer of encapsulation, and forward the datagram on to the service that would otherwise be restricted by the firewall.

How can a firewall use a packet filter effectively? The answer lies in reversing the idea of a filter: instead of specifying the datagrams that should be filtered, a firewall should be configured to block all datagrams except those destined for specific networks, hosts, and protocol ports for which external communication has been approved. Thus, a manager begins with the assumption that communication is not allowed, and then must examine the organization's information policy carefully before enabling any port. In fact, many packet filters allow a manager to specify a set of datagrams to admit instead of a set of datagrams to block. We can summarize:

To be effective, a firewall that uses datagram filtering should restrict access to all IP sources, IP destinations, protocols, and protocol ports except those computers, networks, and services the organization explicitly decides to make available externally. A packet filter that allows a manager to specify which datagrams to admit instead of which datagrams to block can make such restrictions easy to specify.

32.18 The Consequence Of Restricted Access For Clients

A blanket prohibition on datagrams arriving for an unknown protocol port seems to solve many potential security problems by preventing outsiders from accessing arbitrary servers in the organization. Such a firewall has an interesting consequence: it also prevents an arbitrary computer inside the firewall from becoming a client that accesses a service outside the firewall. To understand why, recall that although each server operates at a well-known port, a client does not. When a client program begins execution, it requests the operating system to select a protocol port number that is neither among the well-known ports nor currently in use on the client's computer. When it attempts to communicate with a server outside the organization, a client will generate one or more datagrams and send them to the server. Each outgoing datagram has the client's protocol port as the source port and the server's well-known protocol port as the destination port. The firewall will not block such datagrams as they leave. When it generates a response, the server reverses the protocol ports. The client's port becomes the destination port and the server's port becomes the source port. When the datagram carrying the response reaches the firewall, however, it will be blocked because the destination port is not approved. Thus, we can see an important idea:

If an organization's firewall restricts incoming datagrams except for ports that correspond to services the organization makes available externally, an arbitrary application inside the organization cannot become a client of a server outside the organization.

32.19 Proxy Access Through A Firewall

Of course, not all organizations configure their firewalls to block all datagrams destined for unknown protocol ports. In cases where a secure firewall is needed to prevent unwanted access, however, users on the inside need a safe mechanism that provides access to services outside. That mechanism forms the second major piece of firewall architecture.

In general, an organization can only provide safe access to outside services through a secure computer. Instead of trying to make all computer systems in the organization secure (a daunting task), an organization usually associates one secure computer with each firewall, and installs a set of application gateways on that computer. Because the computer must be strongly fortified to serve as a secure communication channel, it is often called a *bastion host*. Figure 32.7 illustrates the concept.

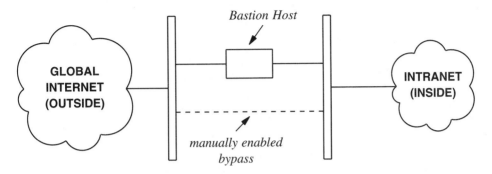

Figure 32.7 The conceptual organization of a bastion host embedded in a firewall. The bastion host provides secure access to outside services without requiring an organization to admit datagrams with arbitrary destinations.

As the figure shows, the firewall has two conceptual barriers. The outer barrier blocks all incoming traffic except (1) datagrams destined for services on the bastion host that the organization chooses to make available externally, and (2) datagrams destined for clients on the bastion host. The inner barrier blocks incoming traffic except datagrams that originate on the bastion host. Most firewalls also include a *manual bypass* that enables managers to temporarily pass some or all traffic between a host inside the organization and a host outside (e.g., for testing or debugging the network).

To understand how a bastion host operates, consider Web access. Because the firewall prevents the user's computer from receiving incoming datagrams, the user cannot use a browser for direct access. Instead, the organization arranges a proxy server on the bastion host. Inside the organization, each browser is configured to use the proxy. Whenever a user selects a link or enters a URL, their browser contacts the proxy. The proxy contacts the server, obtains the specified page, and then delivers it internally.

32.20 The Details Of Firewall Architecture

Now that we understand the basic firewall concept, the implementation should appear straightforward. Conceptually, each of the barriers shown in Figure 32.7 requires a router that has a packet filter†. Networks interconnect the routers and a bastion host. For example, an organization that connects to the global Internet might choose to implement a firewall as Figure 32.8 shows.

---

†Some organizations use a *one-armed firewall* configuration in which a single physical router implements all the functionality.

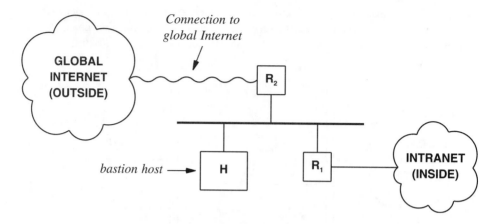

Figure 32.8 A firewall implemented with two routers and a bastion host. One of the routers has a connection to the rest of the Internet.

As the figure shows, router R_2 implements the outer barrier; it filters all traffic except datagrams destined for the bastion host, H. Router R_1 implements the inner barrier that isolates the rest of the corporate intranet from outsiders; it blocks all incoming datagrams except those that originate on the bastion host.

Of course, the safety of an entire firewall depends on the safety of the bastion host. If an intruder can gain access to the computer system running on the bastion host, they will gain access to the entire inside internet. Moreover, an intruder can exploit security flaws in either the operating system on the bastion host or the network applications it runs. Thus, managers must be particularly careful when choosing and configuring software for a bastion host. In summary:

> *Although a bastion host is essential for communication through a firewall, the security of the firewall depends on the safety of the bastion host. An intruder who exploits a security flaw in the bastion host operating system can gain access to hosts inside the firewall.*

32.21 Stub Network

It may seem that Figure 32.8 contains a superfluous network that connects the two routers and the bastion host. Such a network is often called a *stub network* because it is small (i.e., stubby). The question arises, "Is the stub network necessary or could a site place the bastion host on one of its production networks?" The answer depends on the traffic expected from the outside. The stub network isolates the organization from incoming datagram traffic. In particular, because router R_2 admits all datagrams destined for the bastion host, an outsider can send an arbitrary number of such datagrams across the stub network. If an external connection is slow relative to the capacity of a stub network, a separate physical wire may be unnecessary. However, a stub network is usually an inexpensive way for an organization to protect itself against disruption of service on an internal production network.

32.22 An Alternative Firewall Implementation

The firewall implementation in Figure 32.8 works well for an organization that has a single serial connection to the rest of the global Internet. Some sites have a different interconnection topology. For example, suppose a company has three or four large customers who each need to deposit or extract large volumes of information. The company wishes to have a single firewall, but allow connections to multiple sites†. Figure 32.9 illustrates one possible firewall architecture that accommodates multiple external connections.

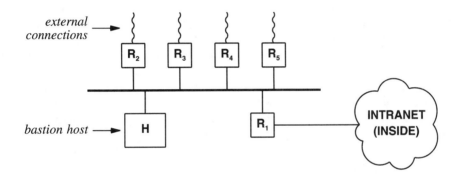

Figure 32.9 An alternative firewall architecture that permits multiple external connections through a single firewall. Using one firewall for multiple connections can reduce the cost.

As the figure shows, the alternative architecture extends a firewall by providing an outer network at which external connections terminate. Router R_1 acts as in Figure 32.8 to protect the site by restricting incoming datagrams to those sent from the bastion host. Routers R_2 through R_5 each connect one external site to the firewall.

To understand why firewalls with multiple connections often use a router per connection, recall that all sites mistrust one another. That is, the organization running the firewall does not trust any of the external organizations completely, and none of the external organizations trust one another completely. The packet filter in a router on a given external connection can be configured to restrict traffic on that particular connection. As a result, the owner of the firewall can guarantee that although all external connections share a single, common network, no datagram from one external connection will pass to another. Thus, the organization running the firewall can assure customers that it is safe to connect. To summarize:

---

†A single firewall can be less expensive and easier to administrate than a separate firewall per connection.

*When multiple external sites connect through a single firewall, an ar-
chitecture that has a router per external connection can prevent
unwanted packet flow from one external site to another.*

32.23 Monitoring And Logging

Monitoring is one of the most important aspects of a firewall design. The network
manager responsible for a firewall needs to be aware of attempts to bypass security.
Unless a firewall reports incidents, a manager may be unaware of problems.

Monitoring can be *active* or *passive*. In active monitoring, a firewall notifies a
manager whenever an incident occurs. The chief advantage of active monitoring is
speed — a manager finds out about a potential problem immediately. The chief disadvantage is that active monitors often produce so much information that a manager cannot comprehend it or notice problems. Thus, most managers prefer passive monitoring,
or a combination of passive monitoring with a few high-risk incidents also reported by
an active monitor.

In passive monitoring, a firewall logs a record of each incident in a file on disk. A
passive monitor usually records information about normal traffic (e.g., simple statistics)
as well as datagrams that are filtered. A manager can access the log at any time; most
managers use a computer program. The chief advantage of passive monitoring arises
from its record of events — a manager can consult the log to observe trends and when a
security problem does occur, review the history of events that led to the problem. More
important, a manager can analyze the log periodically (e.g., daily) to determine whether
attempts to access the organization increase or decrease over time.

32.24 Summary

Security problems arise because an internet can connect organizations that do not
have mutual trust. Several technologies are available to help ensure that information
remains secure when being sent across an internet. IPsec allows a user to choose
between two basic schemes: one that provides authentication of the datagram and one
that provides authentication plus privacy. IPsec modifies a datagram either by inserting
an Authentication Header or by using an Encapsulating Security Payload, which inserts
a header and trailer and encrypts the data being sent. IPsec provides a general framework that allows each pair of communicating entities to choose an encryption algorithm.
Because security is often used with tunneling (e.g., in a VPN), IPsec defines a secure
tunnel mode.

The firewall mechanism is used to control internet access. An organization places
a firewall at each external connection to guarantee that the organization's intranet
remains free from unauthorized traffic. A firewall consists of two barriers and a secure
computer called a bastion host. Each barrier uses a packet filter to restrict datagram
traffic. The bastion host offers externally-visible servers, and runs proxy servers that al-

low users to access outside servers. The filters are configured according to the organization's information policy. Usually, the firewall blocks all datagrams arriving from external sources except those datagrams destined for the bastion host.

A firewall can be implemented in one of several ways; the choice depends on details such as the number of external connections. In many cases, each barrier in a firewall is implemented with a router that contains a packet filter. A firewall can also use a stub network to keep external traffic off an organization's production networks.

FOR FURTHER STUDY

In the mid 1990s, the IETF announced a major emphasis on security, and required each working group to consider the security implications of its designs. Consequently, many RFCs address issues of internet security and propose policies, procedures, and mechanisms. Kent and Atkinson [RFC 2401] defines the IPsec architecture. Kent and Atkinson [RFC 2402] specifies the IPsec authentication header, and [RFC 2406] specifies the encapsulating security payload.

Many RFCs describe security for particular application protocols. For example, Wijnen et. al. [RFC 2575] presents the view-based security and Blumenthal and Wijnen [RFC 2574] presents a user-based security model, both are intended for use with SNMPv3.

Cheswick and Bellovin [1994] discusses firewalls and other topics related to the secure operation of TCP/IP internets. Kohl and Neuman [RFC 1510] describes the *kerberos* authentication service, and Borman [RFC 1411] discusses how *kerberos* can be used to authenticate TELNET.

EXERCISES

32.1   Many sites that use a bastion host arrange for software to scan all incoming files before admitting them to the organization. Why do organizations scan files?

32.2   Read the description of a packet filter for a commercially available router. What features does it offer?

32.3   Collect a log of all traffic entering your site. Analyze the log to determine the percentage of traffic that arrives from or is destined to a well-known protocol port. Do the results surprise you?

32.4   If encryption software is available on your computer, measure the time required to encrypt a 10 Mbyte file, transfer it to another computer, and decrypt it. Compare the result to the time required for the transfer if no encryption is used.

32.5   Survey users at your site to determine if they send sensitive information in e-mail. Are users aware that SMTP transfers messages in ASCII, and that anyone watching network traffic can see the contents of an e-mail message?

32.6   Survey employees at your site to find out how many use modems and personal computers to import or export information. Ask if they understand the organization's information policy.

32.7   Can a firewall be used with other protocol suites such as AppleTalk or Netware? Why or why not?

32.8   Can a firewall be combined with NAT? What are the consequences?

32.9   The military only releases information to those who "need to know." Will such a scheme work for all information in your organization? Why or why not?

32.10   Give two reasons why the group of people who administer an organization's security policies should be separate from the group of people who administer the organization's computer and network systems.

32.11   Some organizations use firewalls to isolate groups of users internally. Give examples of ways that internal firewalls can improve network performance and examples of ways internal firewalls can degrade network performance.

32.12   If your organization uses IPsec, find out which algorithms are being used. What is the key size?

33

The Future Of TCP/IP
(IPv6)

33.1 Introduction

Evolution of TCP/IP technology is intertwined with evolution of the global Internet for several reasons. First, the Internet is the largest installed TCP/IP internet, so many problems related to scale arise in the Internet before they surface in other TCP/IP internets. Second, funding for TCP/IP research and engineering comes from companies and government agencies that use the operational Internet, so they tend to fund projects that impact the Internet. Third, because most researchers use the global Internet daily, they have immediate motivation to solve problems that will improve service and extend functionality.

With millions of users at tens of thousands of sites around the world depending on the global Internet as part of their daily work environment, it might appear that the Internet is a completely stable production facility. We have passed the early stage of development in which every user was also an expert, and entered a stage in which few users understand the technology. Despite appearances, however, neither the Internet nor the TCP/IP protocol suite is static. Groups discover new ways to use the technology. Researchers solve new networking problems, and engineers improve the underlying mechanisms. In short, the technology continues to evolve.

The purpose of this chapter is to consider the ongoing evolutionary process and examine one of the most significant engineering efforts: a proposed revision of IP. When the proposal is adopted by vendors, it will have a major impact on TCP/IP and the global Internet.

33.2 Why Change?

The basic TCP/IP technology has worked well for over two decades. Why should it change? In a broad sense, the motivation revising the protocols arises from changes in underlying technologies and uses.

- *New Computer And Communication Technologies.* Computer and network hardware continues to evolve. As new technologies emerge, they are incorporated into the Internet.

- *New Applications.* As programmers invent new ways to use TCP/IP, additional protocol support is needed. For example, the emphasis on IP telephony has led to investigations of protocols for real-time data delivery.

- *Increases In Size And Load.* The global Internet has experienced many years of sustained exponential growth, doubling in size every nine months or faster. In 1999, on the average, a new host appeared on the Internet every two seconds. Traffic has also increased rapidly as animated graphics and video proliferate.

33.3 New Policies

As it expands into new countries, the Internet changes in a fundamental way: it gains new administrative authorities. Changes in authority produce changes in administrative policies, and mandate new mechanisms to enforce those policies. As we have seen, both the architecture of the connected Internet and the protocols it uses are evolving away from a centralized core model. Evolution continues as more national backbone networks attach, producing increasingly complex policies regulating interaction. When multiple corporations interconnect private TCP/IP internets, they face similar problems as they try to define policies for interaction and then develop mechanisms to enforce those policies. Thus, many of the research and engineering efforts surrounding TCP/IP continue to focus on finding ways to accommodate new administrative groups.

33.4 Motivation For Changing IPv4

Version *4* of the Internet Protocol (*IPv4*) provides the basic communication mechanism of the TCP/IP suite and the global Internet; it has remained almost unchanged since its inception in the late 1970s†. The longevity of version *4* shows that the design is flexible and powerful. Since the time IPv4 was designed, processor performance has increased over two orders of magnitude, typical memory sizes have increased by over a factor of 100, network bandwidth of the Internet backbone has risen by a factor of 7000, LAN technologies have emerged, and the number of hosts on the

---

†Versions *1* through *3* were never formally assigned, and version number *5* was assigned to the *ST* protocol.

Internet has risen from a handful to over 56 million. Furthermore, because the changes did not occur simultaneously, adapting to them has been a continual process.

Despite its sound design, IPv4 must be replaced soon. Chapter 10 describes the main motivation for updating IP: the imminent address space limitations. When IP was designed, a 32-bit address space was more than sufficient. Only a handful of organizations used a LAN; fewer had a corporate WAN. Now, however, most medium-sized corporations have multiple LANs, and most large corporations have a corporate WAN. Consequently, even with careful assignment and NAT technology, the current 32-bit IP address space cannot accommodate projected growth of the global Internet beyond the year 2020.

Although the need for a larger address space is the most immediate motivation, other factors contributed to the new design. In particular, to make IP better suited to real-time applications, thought was given to supporting systems that associate a datagram with a preassigned resource reservation. To make electronic commerce safer, the next version of IP is designed to include support for security features such as authentication.

33.5 The Road To A New Version Of IP

It took many years for the IETF to formulate a new version of IP. Because the IETF produces *open* standards, it invited the entire community to participate in the process. Computer manufacturers, hardware and software vendors, users, managers, programmers, telephone companies, and the cable television industry all specified their requirements for the next version of IP, and all commented on specific proposals.

Many designs were proposed to serve a particular purpose or a particular community. One of the major proposals would have made IP more sophisticated at the cost of increased complexity and processing overhead. Another design proposed using a modification of the OSI CLNS protocol. A third major design proposed retaining most of the ideas in IP, but making simple extensions to accommodate larger addresses. The design, known as *SIP*† (*Simple IP*), became the basis for an extended proposal that included ideas from other proposals. The extended version was named *Simple IP Plus* (*SIPP*), and eventually emerged as the design selected as a basis for the next IP.

Choosing a new version of IP was not easy. The popularity of the Internet means that the market for IP products around the world is staggering. Many groups see the economic opportunity, and hope that the new version of IP will help them gain an edge over the competition. In addition, personalities have been involved — some individuals hold strong technical opinions; others see active participation as a path to a promotion. Consequently, the discussions generated heated arguments.

---

†The acronym *SIP* now refers to the *Session Initiation Protocol* which is used for signaling (e.g., for IP telephony).

33.6 The Name Of The Next IP

The IETF decided to assign the revision of IP version number 6 and to name it *IPv6*† to distinguish it from the current *IPv4*. The choice to skip version number 5 arose after a series of mistakes and misunderstandings. In one mistake, the IAB caused widespread confusion by inadvertently publishing a policy statement that referred to the next version of IP as *IP version 7*. In a misunderstanding, an experimental protocol known as the *Stream Protocol (ST)* was assigned version number 5. The assignment led some to conclude that ST had been selected as the replacement for IP. In the end, the IETF chose 6 because doing so eliminated confusion.

33.7 Features Of IPv6

The proposed IPv6 protocol retains many of the features that contributed to the success of IPv4. In fact, the designers have characterized IPv6 as being basically the same as IPv4 with a few modifications. For example, IPv6 still supports connectionless delivery (i.e., each datagram is routed independently), allows the sender to choose the size of a datagram, and requires the sender to specify the maximum number of hops a datagram can make before being terminated. As we will see, IPv6 also retains most of the concepts provided by IPv4 options, including facilities for fragmentation and source routing.

Despite many conceptual similarities, IPv6 changes most of the protocol details. For example, IPv6 uses larger addresses, and adds a few new features. More important, IPv6 completely revises the datagram format by replacing IPv4's variable-length options field by a series of fixed-format headers. We will examine details after considering major changes and the underlying motivation for each.

The changes introduced by IPv6 can be grouped into seven categories:

- *Larger Addresses.* The new address size is the most noticeable change. IPv6 quadruples the size of an IPv4 address from 32 bits to 128 bits. The IPv6 address space is so large that it cannot be exhausted in the foreseeable future.

- *Extended Address Hierarchy.* IPv6 uses the larger address space to create additional levels of addressing hierarchy. In particular, IPv6 can define a hierarchy of ISPs as well as a hierarchical structure within a given site.

- *Flexible Header Format.* IPv6 uses an entirely new and incompatible datagram format. Unlike the IPv4 fixed-format header, IPv6 defines a set of optional headers.

- *Improved Options.* Like IPv4, IPv6 allows a datagram to include optional control information. IPv6 includes new options that provide additional facilities not available in IPv4.

---

†Some documents refer to the effort as "IP — The Next Generation," *IPng*.

- *Provision For Protocol Extension.* Perhaps the most significant change in IPv6 is a move away from a protocol that fully specifies all details to a protocol that can permit additional features. The extension capability has the potential to allow the IETF to adapt the protocol to changes in underlying network hardware or to new applications.

- *Support For Autoconfiguration And Renumbering.* IPv6 provides facilities that allow computers on an isolated network to assign themselves addresses and begin communicating without depending on a router or manual configuration. The protocol also includes a facility that permits a manager to renumber networks dynamically.

- *Support For Resource Allocation.* IPv6 has two facilities that permit preallocation of network resources: a flow abstraction and a differentiated service specification. The latter will use the same approach as IPv4's differentiated services.

33.8 General Form Of An IPv6 Datagram

IPv6 completely changes the datagram format. As Figure 33.1 shows, an IPv6 datagram has a fixed-size *base header* followed by zero or more *extension headers*, followed by data.

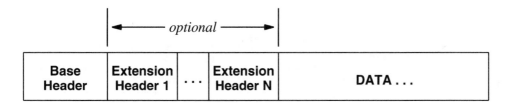

Figure 33.1 The general form of an IPv6 datagram with multiple headers. Only the base header is required; extension headers are optional.

33.9 IPv6 Base Header Format

Interestingly, although it must accommodate larger addresses, an IPv6 base header contains less information than an IPv4 datagram header. Options and some of the fixed fields that appear in an IPv4 datagram header have been moved to extension headers in IPv6. In general, the changes in the datagram header reflect changes in the protocol:

- Alignment has been changed from 32-bit to 64-bit multiples.

- The header length field has been eliminated, and the datagram length field has been replaced by a *PAYLOAD LENGTH* field.

- The size of source and destination address fields has been increased to 16 octets each.

- Fragmentation information has been moved out of fixed fields in the base header into an extension header.

- The *TIME-TO-LIVE* field has been replaced by a *HOP LIMIT* field.

- The *SERVICE TYPE* is renamed to be a *TRAFFIC CLASS* field, and extended with a *FLOW LABEL* field.

- The *PROTOCOL* field has been replaced by a field that specifies the type of the next header.

Figure 33.2 shows the contents and format of an IPv6 base header. Several fields in an IPv6 base header correspond directly to fields in an IPv4 header. As in IPv4, the initial 4-bit *VERS* field specifies the version of the protocol; *VERS* always contains 6 in an IPv6 datagram. As in IPv4, the *SOURCE ADDRESS* and *DESTINATION ADDRESS* fields specify the addresses of the sender and intended recipient. In IPv6, however, each address requires 16 octets. The *HOP LIMIT* field corresponds to the IPv4 *TIME-TO-LIVE* field. Unlike IPv4, which interprets a time-to-live as a combination of hop-count and maximum time, IPv6 interprets the value as giving a strict bound on the maximum number of hops a datagram can make before being discarded.

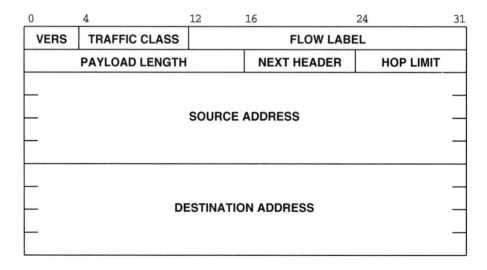

Figure 33.2 The format of the 40-octet IPv6 base header. Each IPv6 datagram begins with a base header.

IPv6 handles datagram length specifications in a new way. First, because the size of the base header is fixed at 40 octets, the base header does not include a field for the header length. Second, IPv6 replaces IPv4's datagram length field by a 16-bit *PAY-LOAD LENGTH* field that specifies the number of octets carried in the datagram excluding the header itself. Thus, an IPv6 datagram can contain 64K octets of data.

Two fields in the base header are used in making forwarding decisions. The IPv4 *SERVICE CLASS* field has been renamed *TRAFFIC CLASS*. In addition, a new mechanism in IPv6 supports resource reservation and allows a router to associate each datagram with a given resource allocation. The underlying abstraction, a *flow*, consists of a path through an internet along which intermediate routers guarantee a specific quality of service. Field *FLOW LABEL* in the base header contains information that routers use to associate a datagram with a specific flow and priority. For example, two applications that need to send video can establish a flow on which the delay and bandwidth is guaranteed. Alternatively, a network provider may require a subscriber to specify the quality of service desired, and then use a flow to limit the traffic a specific computer or a specific application sends. Note that flows can also be used within a given organization to manage network resources and ensure that all applications receive a fair share. A router uses the combination of datagram source address and flow identifier when associating a datagram with a specific flow. To summarize:

> *Each IPv6 datagram begins with a 40-octet base header that includes fields for the source and destination addresses, the maximum hop limit, the traffic class, the flow label, and the type of the next header. Thus, an IPv6 datagram must contain at least 40 octets in addition to the data.*

33.10 IPv6 Extension Headers

The paradigm of a fixed base header followed by a set of optional extension headers was chosen as a compromise between generality and efficiency. To be totally general, IPv6 needs to include mechanisms to support functions such as fragmentation, source routing, and authentication. However, choosing to allocate fixed fields in the datagram header for all mechanisms is inefficient because most datagrams do not use all mechanisms; the large IPv6 address size exacerbates the inefficiency. For example, when sending a datagram across a single local area network, a header that contains empty address fields can occupy a substantial fraction of each frame. More important, the designers realize that no one can predict which facilities will be needed.

The IPv6 extension header paradigm works similar to IPv4 options — a sender can choose which extension headers to include in a given datagram and which to omit. Thus, extension headers provide maximum flexibility. We can summarize:

IPv6 extension headers are similar to IPv4 options. Each datagram includes extension headers for only those facilities that the datagram uses.

33.11 Parsing An IPv6 Datagram

Each of the base and extension headers contains a *NEXT HEADER* field. Software on intermediate routers and at the final destination that process a datagram use the values in the *NEXT HEADER* fields to parse the datagram. Extracting all header information from an IPv6 datagram requires a sequential search through the headers. For example, Figure 33.3 shows the *NEXT HEADER* fields of three datagrams that contain zero, one, and two extension headers.

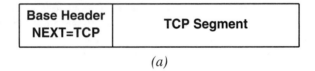

(a)

(b)

(c)

Figure 33.3 Three datagrams with (a) only a base header, (b) a base header and one extension, and (c) a base header plus two extensions. The *NEXT HEADER* field in each header specifies the type of the following header.

Of course, parsing an IPv6 datagram that only has a base header and data is as efficient as parsing an IPv4 datagram. Furthermore, intermediate routers only need to examine the *hop-by-hop* extension header; only endpoints process other extension headers.

33.12 IPv6 Fragmentation And Reassembly

As in IPv4, IPv6 arranges for the ultimate destination to perform datagram reassembly. However, the designers chose to make changes that avoid fragmentation by routers. Recall that IPv4 requires an intermediate router to fragment any datagram that is too large for the MTU of the network over which it must travel. In IPv6, fragmentation is end-to-end; no fragmentation needs to occur in intermediate routers. The source, which is responsible for fragmentation, has two choices: it can either use the *guaranteed minimum MTU* of *1280* octets or perform *Path MTU Discovery* to identify the minimum MTU along the path to the destination. In either case, the source fragments the datagram so that each fragment is less than the expected path MTU.

The IPv6 base header does not contain fields analogous to the fields used for fragmentation in an IPv4 header. Instead, when fragmentation is needed, the source inserts a small extension header after the base header in each fragment. Figure 33.4 shows the contents of a *Fragment Extension Header*.

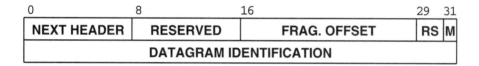

0	8	16	29	31
NEXT HEADER	RESERVED	FRAG. OFFSET	RS	M
DATAGRAM IDENTIFICATION				

Figure 33.4 The format of a Fragment Extension Header.

IPv6 retains the basic IPv4 fragmentation functionality. Each fragment must be a multiple of *8* octets, the single bit in the *M* field marks the last fragment like the IPv4 *MORE FRAGMENTS* bit, and the *DATAGRAM IDENTIFICATION* field carries a unique ID that the receiver uses to group fragments†. Finally, field *RS* is currently reserved; the two bits are set to zero on transmission and ignored by the receiver.

33.13 The Consequence Of End-To-End Fragmentation

The motivation for using end-to-end fragmentation lies in its ability to reduce overhead in routers and permit each router to handle more datagrams per unit time. Indeed, the CPU overhead required for IPv4 fragmentation can be significant — in a conventional router, the CPU can reach 100% utilization if the router fragments many or all of the datagrams it receives. However, end-to-end fragmentation has an important consequence: it alters the fundamental IPv4 assumption that routes change dynamically.

To understand the consequence of end-to-end fragmentation, recall that IPv4 is designed to permit routes to change at any time. For example, if a network or router fails, traffic can be routed along a different path. The chief advantage of such a system is flexibility — traffic can be routed along an alternate path without disrupting service and without informing the source or destination. In IPv6, however, routes cannot be

---

†IPv6 expands the IPv4 *IDENTIFICATION* field to 32 bits to accommodate higher speed networks.

changed as easily because a change in a route can also change the path MTU. If the path MTU along a new route is less than the path MTU along the original route, either an intermediate router must fragment the datagram or the original source must be informed. The problem can be summarized:

> *An internet protocol that uses end-to-end fragmentation requires a sender to discover the path MTU to each destination, and to fragment any outgoing datagram that is larger than the path MTU. End-to-end fragmentation does not accommodate route changes.*

To solve the problem of route changes that affect the path MTU, IPv6 includes a new ICMP error message. When a router discovers that fragmentation is needed, it sends the message back to the source. When it receives such a message, the source performs another path MTU discovery to determine the new minimum MTU, and then fragments datagrams according to the new value.

33.14 IPv6 Source Routing

IPv6 retains the ability for a sender to specify a loose source route. Unlike IPv4, in which source routing is provided by options, IPv6 uses a separate extension header. As Figure 33.5 shows, the first four fields of the Routing Header are fixed. Field *ROUTING TYPE* specifies the type of routing information; the only type that has been defined, type *0*, corresponds to loose source routing. The *TYPE-SPECIFIC DATA* field contains a list of addresses of routers through which the datagram must pass. Field *SEG LEFT* specifies the total number of addresses that remain in the list. Finally field *HDR EXT LEN* specifies the size of the Routing Header.

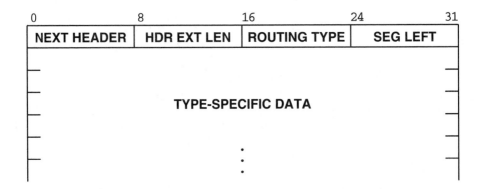

Figure 33.5 The format of an IPv6 Routing Header. Only type 0 (loose source route) is currently defined.

33.15 IPv6 Options

It may seem that IPv6 extension headers completely replace IPv4 options. However, the designers propose two additional extension headers to accommodate miscellaneous information not included in other extension headers. The additional headers are a *Hop By Hop Extension Header* and an *End To End Extension Header*. As the names imply, the two headers separate the set of options that should be examined at each hop from the set that are only interpreted at the destination.

Although each of the two option headers has a unique type code, both headers use the format illustrated in Figure 33.6.

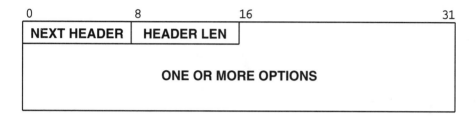

Figure 33.6 The format of an IPv6 option extension header. Both the *hop-by-hop* and *end-to-end* option headers use the same format; the *NEXT HEADER* field of the previous header distinguishes between the two types.

As usual, field *NEXT HEADER* gives the type of the header that follows. Because an option header does not have fixed size, the field labeled *HEADER LEN* specifies the total length of the header. The area labeled *ONE OR MORE OPTIONS* represents a sequence of individual options. Figure 33.7 illustrates how each individual option is encoded with a type, length, and value†; options are not aligned or padded.

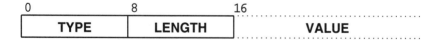

Figure 33.7 Encoding of an individual option in an IPv6 option extension header. Each option consists of a one-octet type and a one-octet length followed by zero or more octets of data for the option.

As the figure shows, IPv6 options follow the same form as IPv4 options. Each option begins with a one-octet *TYPE* field followed by a one-octet *LENGTH* field. If the option requires additional data, octets that comprise the *VALUE* follow the *LENGTH*.

---

†In the literature, an encoding of type, length, and value is sometimes called a *TLV encoding*.

The two high-order bits of each option *TYPE* field specify how a host or router should dispose of the datagram if it does not understand the option:

Bits In Type	Meaning
00	Skip this option
01	Discard datagram; do not send ICMP message
10	Discard datagram; send ICMP message to source
11	Discard datagram; send ICMP for non-multicast

In addition, the third bit in the *TYPE* field specifies whether the option can change in transit. Having such information is important for authentication — the contents of an option that can change in transit are treated as zeroes for purposes of authentication.

33.16 Size Of The IPv6 Address Space

In IPv6, each address occupies 16 octets, four times the size of an IPv4 address. The large address space guarantees that IPv6 can tolerate any reasonable address assignment scheme. In fact, if the designers decide to change the addressing scheme later, the address space is sufficiently large to accommodate a reassignment.

It is difficult to comprehend the size of the IPv6 address space. One way to look at it relates the magnitude to the size of the population: the address space is so large that every person on the planet can have sufficient addresses to have their own internet as large as the current Internet. A second way to think of IPv6 addressing relates it to the physical space available: the earth's surface has approximately 5.1×10^8 square kilometers, meaning that there are over 10^{24} addresses per square meter of the earth's surface. Another way to understand the size relates it to address exhaustion. For example, consider how long it would take to assign all possible addresses. A 16-octet integer can hold 2^{128} values. Thus, the address space is greater than 3.4×10^{38}. If addresses are assigned at the rate of one million addresses every microsecond, it would take over 10^{20} years to assign all possible addresses.

33.17 IPv6 Colon Hexadecimal Notation

Although it solves the problem of having insufficient capacity, the large address size poses an interesting new problem: humans who maintain internets must read, enter, and manipulate such addresses. Obviously, binary notation is untenable. However, the dotted decimal notation used for IPv4 does not make such addresses sufficiently compact either. To understand why, consider an example 128-bit number expressed in dotted decimal notation:

```
104.230.140.100.255.255.255.255.0.0.17.128.150.10.255.255
```

To help make address slightly more compact and easier to enter, the IPv6 designers propose using *colon hexadecimal notation* (abbreviated *colon hex*) in which the value of each 16-bit quantity is represented in hexadecimal separated by colons. For example, when the value shown above in dotted decimal notation has been translated to colon hex notation and printed using the same spacing, it becomes:

$$\mathtt{68E6:8C64:FFFF:FFFF:0:1180:96A:FFFF}$$

Colon hex notation has the obvious advantage of requiring fewer digits and fewer separator characters than dotted decimal. In addition, colon hex notation includes two techniques that make it extremely useful. First, colon hex notation allows *zero compression* in which a string of repeated zeros is replaced by a pair of colons. For example, the address:

$$\mathtt{FF05:0:0:0:0:0:0:B3}$$

can be written:

$$\mathtt{FF05::B3}$$

To ensure that zero compression produces an unambiguous interpretation, the proposal specifies that it can be applied only once in any address. Zero compression is especially useful when used with the proposed address assignment scheme because many addresses will contain contiguous strings of zeros. Second, colon hex notation incorporates dotted decimal suffixes; we will see that such combinations are intended to be used during the transition from IPv4 to IPv6. For example, the following string is valid colon hex notation:

$$\mathtt{0:0:0:0:0:0:128.10.2.1}$$

Note that although the numbers separated by colons each specify the value of a 16-bit quantity, numbers in the dotted decimal portion each specify the value of one octet. Of course, zero compression can be used with the number above to produce an equivalent colon hex string that looks quite similar to an IPv4 address:

$$\mathtt{::128.10.2.1}$$

Finally, IPv6 extends CIDR-like notation by allowing an address to be followed by a slash and an integer that specifies a number of bits. For example,

$$\mathtt{12AB::CD30:0:0:0:0\,/\,60}$$

specifies the first 60 bits of the address or $\mathtt{12AB00000000CD3}$ in hexadecimal.

33.18 Three Basic IPv6 Address Types

Like IPv4, IPv6 associates an address with a specific network connection, not with a specific computer. Thus, address assignments are similar to IPv4: an IPv6 router has two or more addresses, and an IPv6 host with one network connection needs only one address. IPv6 also retains (and extends) the IPv4 address hierarchy in which a physical network is assigned a prefix. However, to make address assignment and modification easier, IPv6 permits multiple prefixes to be assigned to a given network, and allows a computer to have multiple, simultaneous addresses assigned to a given interface.

In addition to permitting multiple, simultaneous addresses per network connection, IPv6 expands, and in some cases unifies, IPv4 special addresses. In general, a destination address on a datagram falls into one of three categories:

Unicast   The destination address specifies a single computer (host
            or router); the datagram should be routed to the destination
            along a shortest path.

Anycast   The destination is a set of computers, possibly at different
            locations, that all share a single address; the datagram
            should be routed along a shortest path and delivered to ex-
            actly one member of the group (i.e., the closest member)†.

Multicast   The destination is a set of computers, possibly at multiple
            locations. One copy of the datagram will be delivered to
            each member of the group using hardware multicast or
            broadcast if viable.

33.19 The Duality Of Broadcast And Multicast

IPv6 does not use the terms *broadcast* or *directed broadcast* to refer to delivery to all computers on a physical network or to a logical IP subnet. Instead, it uses the term *multicast*, and treats broadcast as a special form of multicast. The choice may seem odd to anyone who understands network hardware because more hardware technologies support broadcast than support multicast. In fact, a hardware engineer is likely to view multicasting as a restricted form of broadcasting — the hardware sends a multicast packet to all computers on the network exactly like a broadcast packet, and the interface hardware on each computer filters all multicast packets except those that software has instructed the interface hardware to accept.

In theory, the choice between multicast and limited forms of broadcast is irrelevant because one can be simulated with the other. That is, broadcasting and multicasting are duals of one another that provide the same functionality. To understand why, consider how to simulate one with the other. If broadcast is available, a packet can be delivered to a group by sending it to all machines and arranging for software on each computer to decide whether to accept or discard the incoming packet. If multicast is available, a

---

†Anycast addresses were formerly known as *cluster* addresses.

packet can be delivered to all machines by arranging for all machines to listen to one multicast group similar to the *all hosts* group discussed in Chapter 17.

33.20 An Engineering Choice And Simulated Broadcast

Knowing that broadcasting and multicasting are theoretical duals of one another does not help choose between them. To see why the designers of IPv6 chose multicasting as the central abstraction instead of broadcasting, consider applications instead of looking at the underlying hardware. An application either needs to communicate with a single application or with a group of applications. Direct communication is handled best via unicast; group communication is handled best by multicast or broadcast. To provide the most flexibility, group membership should not be determined by network connections, because group members can reside at arbitrary locations. Using broadcast for all group communication does not scale to handle an internet as large as the global Internet.

Not surprisingly, the designers pre-define some multicast addresses that can be used in place of an IPv4 network broadcast address. Thus, in addition to its own unicast address, each router is required to accept packets addressed to the *All Routers* multicast groups for its local environment.

33.21 Proposed IPv6 Address Space Assignment

The question of how to partition the IPv6 address space has generated much discussion. There are two central issues: how to manage address assignment and how to map an address to a route. The first issue focuses on the practical problem of devising a hierarchy of authority. Unlike the current Internet, which uses a two-level hierarchy of network prefix (assigned by the Internet authority) and host suffix (assigned by the organization), the large address space in IPv6 permits a multi-level hierarchy or multiple hierarchies. The second issue focuses on computational efficiency. Independent of the hierarchy of authority that assigns addresses, a router must examine each datagram and choose a path to the destination. To keep the cost of high-speed routers low, the processing time required to choose a path must be kept small.

As Figure 33.8 shows, the designers of IPv6 propose assigning address classes in a way similar to the scheme used for IPv4. Although the first 8 bits of an address are sufficient to identify its type, the address space is not partitioned into sections of equal size.

Binary Prefix	Type Of Address	Part Of Address Space
0000 0000	Reserved (IPv4 compatibility)	1/256
0000 0001	Unassigned	1/256
0000 001	NSAP Addresses	1/128
0000 010	IPX Addresses	1/128
0000 011	Unassigned	1/128
0000 1	Unassigned	1/32
0001	Unassigned	1/16
001	Aggregatable Global Unicast	1/8
010	Unassigned	1/8
011	Unassigned	1/8
100	Unassigned	1/8
101	Unassigned	1/8
110	Unassigned	1/8
1110	Unassigned	1/16
1111 0	Unassigned	1/32
1111 10	Unassigned	1/64
1111 110	Unassigned	1/128
1111 1110 0	Unassigned	1/512
1111 1110 10	Link-Local Unicast Addresses	1/1024
1111 1110 11	Site-Local Unicast Addresses	1/1024
1111 1111	Multicast Addresses	1/256

Figure 33.8 The proposed division of IPv6 addresses into types, which are analogous to IPv4 classes. As in IPv4, the prefix of an address determines its address type.

As the figure shows, only 15% of the address space has been assigned at present. The IETF will use the remaining portions as demand grows. Despite the sparse assignment, addresses have been chosen to make processing more efficient. For example, the high-order octet of an address distinguishes between multicast (all 1 bits) and unicast (a mixture of 0's and 1's).

33.22 Embedded IPv4 Addresses And Transition

Although the prefix *0000 0000* is labeled *Reserved* in the figure, the designers plan to use a small fraction of addresses in that section to encode IPv4 addresses. In particular, any address that begins with 80 zero bits followed by 16 bits of all ones or 16 bits of all zeros contains an IPv4 address in the low-order 32 bits. The value of the 16-bit field indicates whether the node also has a conventional IPv6 unicast address. Figure 33.9 illustrates the two forms.

80 zero bits	16 bits	32 bits
0000 0000	0000	**IPv4 Address**
0000 0000	FFFF	**IPv4 Address**

Figure 33.9 The encoding of an IPv4 address in an IPv6 address. The 16-bit
field contains *0000* if the node also has a conventional IPv6 address, and *FFFF* if it does not.

The encoding will be needed during a transition from IPv4 to IPv6 for two reasons.
First, a computer may choose to upgrade from IPv4 to IPv6 software before it has been
assigned a valid IPv6 address. Second, a computer running IPv6 software may need to
communicate with a computer that runs only IPv4 software.

Having a way to encode an IPv4 address in an IPv6 address does not solve the
problem of making the two version interoperate. In addition to address encoding, translation is needed. To use a translator, an IPv6 computer generates a datagram that contains the IPv6 encoding of the IPv4 destination address. The IPv6 computer sends the
datagram to a translator, which uses IPv4 to communicate with the destination. When
the translator receives a reply from the destination, it translates the IPv4 datagram to
IPv6 and sends it back to the IPv6 source.

It may seem that translating protocol addresses could fail because higher layer protocols verify address integrity. In particular, TCP and UDP, use a *pseudo header* in
their checksum computation. The pseudo header includes both the source and destination protocol addresses, so changing such addresses could affect the computation. However, the designers planned carefully to allow TCP or UDP on an IPv4 machine to communicate with the corresponding transport protocol on an IPv6 machine. To avoid
checksum mismatch, the IPv6 encoding of an IPv4 address has been chosen so that the
16-bit 1's complement checksum for both an IPv4 address and the IPv6 encoding of the
address are identical. The point is:

> *In addition to choosing technical details of a new Internet Protocol,
> the IETF work on IPv6 has focused on finding a way to transition
> from the current protocol to the new protocol. In particular, the
> current proposal for IPv6 allows one to encode an IPv4 address in-
> side an IPv6 address such that address translation does not change
> the pseudo header checksum.*

33.23 Unspecified And Loopback Addresses

As in IPv4, a few IPv6 addresses have been assigned special meaning. For example, the all 0's address:

$$0:0:0:0:0:0:0:0$$

is an *unspecified address* which cannot be assigned to any computer or used as a destination. It is only used as a source address during bootstrap by a computer that has not yet learned its address.

Like IPv4, IPv6 also has a *loopback address* that is used for testing software. The IPv6 loopback address is:

$$0:0:0:0:0:0:0:1$$

Any datagram sent to the loopback address will be delivered to the local machine; it must never be used as a destination address on an outgoing datagram.

33.24 Unicast Address Hierarchy

One of the most important changes between IPv4 and IPv6 arises from the allocation strategy used for unicast addresses and the resulting address hierarchy. Recall that the original IPv4 addressing scheme used a two-level hierarchy in which an address is divided into a globally unique prefix and a suffix. IPv6 extends the concept by adopting an address hierarchy with three conceptual levels as Figure 33.10 illustrates.

Level	Purpose
1	Globally-known public topology
2	Individual site
3	Individual network interface

Figure 33.10 The three conceptual levels of the IPv6 unicast address hierarchy. In practice, an address has additional structure.

The two lowest levels of the conceptual hierarchy are easiest to understand because they correspond to identifiable entities. The lowest level corresponds to a single attachment between a computer and a network. The middle level of the hierarchy corresponds to a set of computers and networks located at a *site*, which implies both contiguous physical connectivity and a single organization that owns and operates the equipment. We will see that the addressing scheme accommodates both large and small sites, and allows a site to have complex internal structure.

To provide flexibility, the top level of the hierarchy, which is labeled *public topology*, is not precisely defined. In general, one can think of the public topology as a "section" of the global Internet that is available for public access. Two types of public topology are envisioned. The first type corresponds to a major *Internet Service Provider (ISP)* that provides long-haul service to customers, which are known as *subscribers*. The second type, which is called an *exchange*, is a newly envisioned organization. According to the designers, exchanges will provide two functions. First, an exchange will operate like a NAP to interconnect major ISPs and pass traffic among them. Second, unlike current NAPs, exchanges will also service individual subscribers, which means that the exchange will assign the subscriber an address. The chief advantage of an address assigned by an exchange is that the address will not specify an ISP. Thus, a subscriber will be free to move from one ISP to another.

33.25 Aggregatable Global Unicast Address Structure

Authority for IPv6 address assignment flows down the hierarchy. Each top-level organization (e.g., an ISP or exchange) is assigned a unique prefix. When an organization becomes a subscriber of a top-level ISP, the organization is assigned a unique number for its site. Finally, a manager must assign a number to each network connection. To make routing efficient, successive sets of bits in the address are reserved for each assignment. Figure 33.11 illustrates the format, which is known as a *aggregatable global unicast address* format.

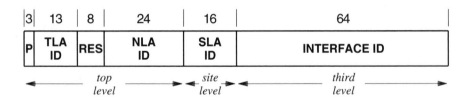

Figure 33.11 The division of an IPv6 aggregatable global unicast address into separate fields along with an indication of how those fields correspond to the three-level hierarchy.

The 3-bit field labeled *P* in the figure corresponds to the *format prefix*, which is 001 for an aggregatable global unicast address. The 8-bit *RES* field is reserved for the future and contains zeroes. Remaining fields in the address are arranged to make routing efficient. In particular, fields that correspond to the highest level of the hierarchy are grouped together to comprise the most significant bits of the address. Field *TLA ID* contains an identifier used for *Top-Level Aggregation* (i.e., a unique identifier assigned to the ISP or exchange that owns the address). The owner of the address uses field *NLA* to provide *Next-Level Aggregation* (e.g., to identify a particular subscriber).

The 16-bit field labeled *SLA ID* (*Site-Level Aggregation*) is available for a specific site to use. The designers envision it being used much like an IPv4 subnet field. Thus, a site with only a few networks can choose to treat the field as a network identifier, and a site that has many networks can use the field to partition networks into groups which can then be arranged in a hierarchy. To create a one-level hierarchy at the site, the organization must use a prefix to identify the group and a suffix to identify a particular network in the group. As with IPv4 subnetting, the division into groups improves routing efficiency because a routing table only contains routes to each of the other groups rather than to each individual network.

33.26 Interface Identifiers

As Figure 33.11 shows, the low-order 64 bits of an IPv6 aggregatable unicast address identifies a specific network interface. Unlike IPv4, however, the IPv6 suffix was chosen to be large enough to accommodate a direct encoding of the interface hardware address. Encoding a hardware address in an IP address has two consequences. First, IPv6 does not use ARP to resolve an IP address to a hardware address. Instead, IPv6 uses a *neighbor discovery protocol* available with a new version of ICMP (*ICMPv6*) to allow a node to determine which computers are its directly connected neighbors. Second, to guarantee interoperability, all computers must use the same encoding for a hardware address. Consequently, the IPv6 standards specify exactly how to encode various forms of hardware address. In the simplest case, the hardware address is placed directly in the IPv6 address; some formats use more complex transformations.

Two example encodings will help clarify the concept. For example, IEEE defines a standard 64-bit globally unique address format known as *EUI-64*. The only change needed when encoding an EUI-64 address in an IPv6 address consists of inverting bit 6 in the high-order octet of the address, which indicates whether the address is known to be globally unique.

A more complex change is required for a conventional 48-bit Ethernet address. Figure 33.12 illustrates the encoding. As the figure shows, bits from the original address are not contiguous in the encoded form. Instead, 16 bits with hexadecimal value 0xFFFE are inserted in the middle. In addition, bit 6, which indicates whether the address has global scope, is changed from 0 to 1. Remaining bits of the address, including the group bit (labeled g), the ID of the company that manufactured the interface (labeled c), and the manufacturer's extension are copied as shown.

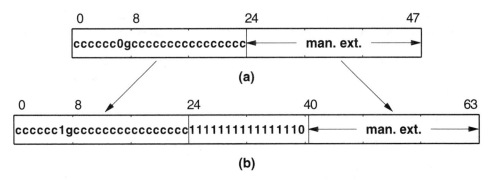

Figure 33.12 (a) The format of a 48-bit IEEE 802 address used with Ethernet, with bits labeled *c* specifying the company that manufactured the interface and bits in the *man. ext.* field specifying an extension the manufacturer chose to uniquely identify the unit, and (b) the encoding of the address in the low order 64 bits of an IPv6 unicast address.

33.27 Additional Hierarchy

Although the unicast address format in Figure 33.11 implies a strict hierarchy, many additional levels are possible. For example, bits of the *NLA ID* can be used to create a hierarchy of providers. Similarly, the 16-bit *SLA ID* can be divided to create a hierarchy within an organization. The large number of bits provides more flexibility than IPv4 subnetting. An organization can choose to divide into a two-level hierarchy of areas and assign subnets within each area. Alternatively, an organization can choose a three-level hierarchy of areas, subareas, and subnets within each subarea.

33.28 Local Addresses

In addition to the global unicast addresses described above, IPv6 includes prefixes for unicast addresses that have local scope. As Figure 33.8 shows, the standard defines two types: a *link-local address* is restricted to a single network, and a *site-local address* is restricted to a single site. Routers honor the scoping rules; they do not forward datagrams containing locally-scoped addresses outside the specified scope.

Local addresses solve two problems. Link-local addresses provide communication across a single physical network without danger of the datagram being forwarded across the internet. For example, when it performs neighbor discovery, an IPv6 node uses a link-local address. The scope rules specify that only computers on the same physical network as the sender will receive neighbor discovery messages. Similarly, computers connected to an *isolated network* (i.e., a network that does not have routers attached) can use link-local addresses to communicate.

Unlike a datagram containing link-local addresses, routers can forward datagrams containing site-local addresses throughout an entire organization. However, routers are prohibited from forwarding such datagrams to the global Internet. Thus, site-local addresses correspond to what IPv4 calls *private* or *nonroutable* addresses. An organization can assign and use site-local addresses throughout its private intranet without obtaining and assigning globally unique prefixes.

33.29 Autoconfiguration And Renumbering

IPv6 is designed to support *serverless autoconfiguration*† that allows computers to communicate without requiring a manager to specify an address. Two facilities discussed above make autoconfiguration possible and efficient: link-local addressing and embedded interface identifiers. To begin, a computer generates a link-local address by combining the link-local prefix:

$$1111\ 1110\ 10$$

with 54 zero bits and its 64-bit interface identifier.

Once it verifies that the link-local address is unique, a computer uses the address to send a *router solicitation* that requests additional information from a router. If a router is present on the network, the router responds by sending a *router advertisement* to inform the computer about prefixes that can be used for site-local or global addresses. When a router advertisement arrives, the computer makes the sender its default router. Finally, a flag in the advertisement tells the computer whether to rely on autoconfiguration or to use a conventional *managed configuration* (i.e., DHCP).

To facilitate network *renumbering*, IPv6 allows routers to limit the time a computer can retain a prefix. To do so, a router advertisement specifies two time values for each prefix: a valid lifetime and a preferred lifetime. A host must listen for additional router advertisements. When the preferred lifetime of a prefix expires, the prefix remains valid, but the host must use another prefix for all communication when possible. When the valid lifetime expires, the host must stop using the prefix, even if existing communication is in progress.

33.30 Summary

The IETF has defined a next generation of the Internet Protocol which is known as IPv6 because it has been assigned version number 6. IPv6 retains many of the basic concepts from the current protocol, IPv4, but changes most details. Like IPv4, IPv6 provides a connectionless, best-effort datagram delivery service. However, the IPv6 datagram format differs from the IPv4 format, and IPv6 provides new features such as authentication and support for flow-labeling.

IPv6 organizes each datagram as a series of headers followed by data. A datagram always begins with a 40-octet base header, which contains source and destination ad-

---

†Serverless autoconfiguration is also called *stateless autoconfiguration*.

dresses, a traffic class, and a flow identifier. The base header may be followed by zero or more extension headers, followed by data. Extension headers are optional — IPv6 uses them to hold much of the information IPv4 encodes in options.

An IPv6 address is 128 bits long, making the address space so large that the space cannot be exhausted in the foreseeable future. IPv6 uses address prefixes to determine the location and interpretation of remaining address fields. In addition to traditional unicast and multicast addresses, IPv6 also defines anycast addresses. A single anycast address can be assigned to a set of computers; a datagram sent to the address is delivered to exactly one computer in the set (i.e., the computer closest to the source).

IPv6 supports autoconfiguration and renumbering. Each host on an isolated network generates a unique link-local address which it uses for communication. The host also uses the link-local address to discover routers and obtain site-local and global prefix information. To facilitate renumbering, all prefixes are assigned a lifetime; a host must use a new prefix if the lifetime on an existing prefix expires.

FOR FURTHER STUDY

Many RFCs have appeared that contain information pertinent to IPv6. Deering and Hinden [RFC 2460] specifies the basic protocol. Thomson and Narten [RFC 2462] describes stateless address autoconfiguration. Narten, Nordmark, and Simpson [RFC 2461] discusses neighbor discovery. Conta and Deering [RFC 2463] specifies ICMPv6 as a companion to IPv6. Crawford [RFC 2464] describes encapsulation of IPv6 for transmission over Ethernet networks.

Many RFCs focus on IPv6 addressing. Hinden and Deering [RFC 2373] describes the basic addressing architecture including the meanings of prefixes. Hinden, O'Dell, and Deering [RFC 2374] considers the aggregatable global unicast address format. Hinden and Deering [RFC 2375] specifies multicast address assignments. Johnson and Deering [RFC 2526] describes reserved anycast addresses. Information about the 64-bit EUI format can be found in:

http://standards.ieee.org/regauth/oui/tutorials/EUI64.html

EXERCISES

33.1   The current standard for IPv6 has no header checksum. What are the advantages and disadvantages of this approach?

33.2   How should extension headers be ordered to minimize processing time?

33.3   Although IPv6 addresses are assigned hierarchically, a router does not need to parse an address completely to select a route. Devise an algorithm and data structure for efficient routing. (Hint: consider a longest-match approach.)

33.4   Argue that 128-bit addresses are larger than needed, and that 96 bits provides sufficient capacity.

33.5   Assume your organization intends to adopt IPv6. Devise an address scheme the organization will use to assign each host an address. Did you choose a hierarchical assignment within your organization? Why or why not?

33.6   What is the chief advantage of encoding an Ethernet address in an IPv6 address? The chief disadvantage?

33.7   Consider a host that forms a link-local address by encoding its 48-bit Ethernet address with the standard link-local prefix. Is the resulting address guaranteed to be unique on the network? Why or why not?

33.8   In the previous exercise, does the standard specify that the host must use the Neighbor Discovery Protocol to verify that the address is unique? Why or why not?

33.9   If you were asked to choose sizes for the top-level, next-level, and site ID fields of an IPv6 unicast address, how large would you make each? Why?

33.10 Read about the IPv6 authentication and security headers. Why are two headers proposed?

33.11 How does the IPv6 minimum MTU of 1280 affect its flexibility?

Appendix 1

A Guide To RFCs

Introduction

Most of the written information about TCP/IP and the connected Internet, including its architecture, protocols, and history, can be found in a series of reports known as *Request For Comments* or *RFCs*. An informal, loosely coordinated set of notes, RFCs are unusually rich in information and color. Before we consider the more serious aspects of RFCs, it is fitting that we take a few minutes to pay attention to the colorful side. A good place to begin is with Cerf's poem *'Twas the Night Before Start-up* (RFC 968), a humorous parody that describes some of the problems encountered when starting a new network. Knowing not to take itself too seriously has pervaded the Internet effort. Anyone who can remember both their first Internet meeting, filled with networking jargon, and Lewis Carroll's *Jabberwocky*, filled with strangely twisted English, will know exactly why D. L. Covill put them together in *ARPAWOCKY* (RFC 527).

Other RFCs seem equally frivolous. Interspersed amid the descriptions of ideas that would turn out to dramatically change networking, we find notes like RFC 416, written in early November, 1972: *The ARC System will be Unavailable for Use During Thanksgiving Week*. It says exactly what you think it says. Or consider Crispin's tongue-in-cheek humor found in RFC 748, which describes the *TELNET Randomly-Lose Option* (a proposed option for TELNET that makes it randomly drop characters). In fact, any RFC dated April 1 should be considered a joke. If such items do not seem insignificant, think about the seventy-five RFCs listed as *never issued*. All were assigned a number and had an author, but none ever saw the light of day. The holes in the numbering scheme remain, preserved as little reminders of ideas that vaporized or work that remains incomplete.

Even after the silly, lighthearted, and useless RFCs have been removed, the remaining documents do not conform to most standards for scientific writing. Unlike scholarly scientific journals that concentrate on identifying papers of important archival interest, screening them carefully, and filing them for posterity, RFCs provide a record of ongoing conversations among the principals involved in designing, building, measuring, and using the global Internet. The reader understands at once that RFCs include the thoughts of researchers on the leading edge of technological innovation, not the studied opinions of scholars who have completely mastered a subject. The authors are not always sure of the consequences of their proposals, or even of the contents, but they clearly realize the issues are too complex to understand without community discussion. For example, RFC 1173 purports to document the "oral traditions" (which is an oxymoron because it became part of the written tradition once the RFC was published).

Despite the inconsistencies in RFCs that sometimes make them difficult for beginners to understand, the RFC mechanism has evolved and now works extremely well. Because RFCs are available electronically, information is propagated to the community quickly. Because they span a broad range of interests, practitioners as well as designers contribute. Because they record informal conversations, RFCs capture discussions and not merely final conclusions. Even the disagreements and contradictory proposals are useful in showing what the designers considered before settling on a given protocol (and readers interested in the history of a particular idea or protocol can use RFCs to follow it from its inception to its current state).

Importance Of Host And Gateway Requirements Documents

Unlike most RFCs, which concentrate on a single idea or protocol, three special RFCs cover a broad range of protocols. The special documents are entitled *Requirements for Internet Routers* and *Requirements for Internet Hosts* (parts 1 and 2).

The requirements documents, published after many years of experience with the TCP/IP protocols, are considered a major revision to the protocol standards. In essence, requirement documents each review many protocols. They point out known weaknesses or ambiguities in the RFCs that define the protocols, state conventions that have been adopted by vendors, document problems that occur in practice, and list solutions to those problems that have been accumulated through experience. The RFCs for individual protocols have *not* been updated to include changes and updates from the requirements documents. Thus, readers must be careful to always consult the requirements documents when studying a particular protocol.

RFC Numerology

RFCs cover a surprisingly large range of sizes, with the average size being 47504.5 bytes. The largest, RFC 1166 (Internet numbers), contains 566778 bytes, while the smallest consists of a 27-byte text file:

This RFC was never issued.

A few interesting coincidences have occurred. For example, the ASCII text file for RFC 41 contains exactly 41 lines of text, and the ASCII text file for RFC 854, exactly 854 lines. RFC 1996 has a number that matches the year in which it was published. However, the number for no other RFC will match the year of publication.

The quantity of RFCs published per year varies widely. Figure A1.1 illustrates how the rate has changed over time. The surge of work in the 1970s represents an initial period of building; the high rate of publication in the 1990s has resulted from commercialization.

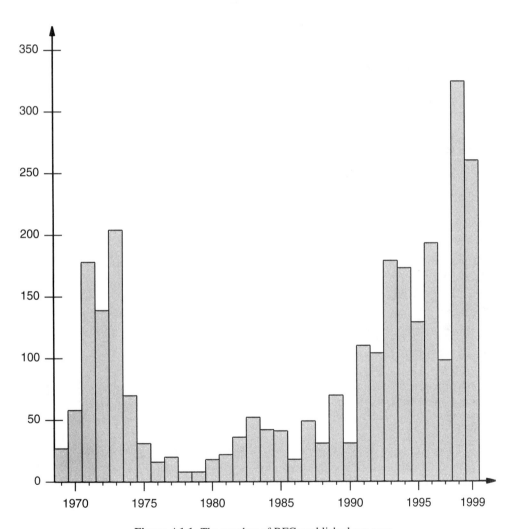

Figure A1.1 The number of RFCs published per year.

How To Obtain An RFC Over The Internet

RFCs are available electronically from many repositories around the world. Check with your local network administrator to find the site nearest you or begin with the following URL:

http://www.rfc-editor.org

Browsing Through RFCs

There are several indexes that can help one browse through RFCs. ISI publishes an index of all RFCs in chronological order. Readers often need to know which RFC contains the latest version of an official Internet protocol or which protocols are official and which are unofficial. To accommodate such needs, the IAB periodically publishes an RFC entitled *INTERNET OFFICIAL PROTOCOL STANDARDS*, which provides a list of all protocols that have been adopted as TCP/IP standards, along with the number of the most recent RFC or RFCs describing each protocol. RFC 1602, *The Internet Standards Process – Revision 2*, describes the Internet standardization process and defines the meaning of the terms *proposed standard*, *draft standard*, *Internet standard*, *required*, *recommended*, and *historic*.

Despite the available indexes, browsing through RFCs can be difficult, especially when the reader is searching for information pertinent to a given topic, which may be spread across RFCs published in many years. Browsing is particularly difficult because titles do not provide sufficient identification of the content. (How could one guess from the title *Leaving Well Enough Alone* that the RFC pertains to FTP?) Finally, having multiple RFCs with a single title (e.g., Internet Numbers) can be confusing because the reader cannot easily tell whether a document is out-of-date without checking the archive.

RFCs Arranged By Topic

The final section of this appendix provides help in finding information in RFCs because it contains a list of the first 2728 RFCs arranged by topic. Readers can find an earlier topical index in RFC 1000, which also includes an annotated chronological listing of the first 1000 RFCs. Although long, RFC 1000 is highly recommended as a source of authoritative and valuable critique – its introduction is especially fascinating. Recalling the origin of RFCs along with the origin of the ARPANET, the introduction captures the spirit of adventure and energy that still characterizes the Internet.

RFCs Organized By Major Category And Subtopic

1. Administrative

1a. Assigned Internet Numbers (official values used by protocols)

1700, 1340, 1166, 1117, 1062, 1060, 1020, 1010, 997, 990, 960, 943, 923, 900, 870, 820, 790, 776, 770, 762, 758, 755, 750, 739, 717, 604, 503, 433, 349, 322, 317, 204, 179, 175, 167

1b. Official IAB Standards and Other Lists of Protocols

2500, 2400, 2300, 2200, 2000, 1920, 1880, 1800, 1780, 1720, 1610, 1600, 1540, 1500, 1410, 1360, 1280, 1250, 1200, 1140, 1130, 1100, 1083, 1011, 991, 961, 944, 924, 901, 880, 840, 694, 661, 617, 582, 580, 552
774, 766

1c. Meeting Notes and Minutes

2316 –Report of the IAB Security Architecture Workshop
2130 –The Report of the IAB Character Set Workshop held 29 February - 1 March, 1996
1862 –Report of the IAB Workshop on Internet Information Infrastructure, October 12-14, 1994
1636 –Report of IAB Workshop on Security in the Internet Architecture - February 8-10, 1994
1588 –White Pages Meeting Report
1210 –Network and infrastructure user requirements for transatlantic research collaboration: Brussels, July 16-18, and Washington July 24-25, 1990
1152 –Workshop report: Internet research steering group workshop on very-high-speed networks
1077 –Critical issues in high bandwidth networking
1019 –Report of the Workshop on Environments for Computational Mathematics
1017 –Network requirements for scientific research: Internet task force on scientific computing
910, 807 - Multimedia mail meeting notes
898 – Gateway special interest group meeting notes
808, 805, 469 - Summary of computer mail services meeting held at BBN on 10 January 1979
585 – ARPANET users interest working group meeting
549, 396, 282, 253 - Minutes of Network Graphics Group meeting, 15-17 July 1973
371 – Demonstration at International Computer Communications Conference
327 – Data and File Transfer workshop notes
316 – ARPA Network Data Management Working Group
164, 131, 108, 101, 82, 77, 63, 37, 21 - Minutes of Network Working Group meeting, 5/16 through 5/19/71

1d. Meeting Announcements and Group Overviews

1160, 1120 - Internet Activities Board
828 – Data communications: IFIP's international "network" of experts
631 – International meeting on minicomputers and data communication: Call for papers
584 – Charter for ARPANET Users Interest Working Group
537 – Announcement of NGG meeting July 16-17
526 – Technical meeting: Digital image processing software systems
504 – Distributed resources workshop announcement
483 – Cancellation of the resource notebook framework meeting

474, 314, 246, 232, 134 - Announcement of NGWG meeting: Call for papers
471 – Workshop on multi-site executive programs
461 – Telnet Protocol meeting announcement
457 – TIPUG
456 – Memorandum: Date change of mail meeting
454 – File Transfer Protocol - meeting announcement and a new proposed
        document
453 – Meeting announcement to discuss a network mail system
374 – IMP System Announcement
359 – Status of the Release of the New IMP System (2600)
343, 331 - IMP System change notification
324 – RJE Protocol meeting
323 – Formation of Network Measurement Group (NMG)
320 – Workshop on Hard Copy Line Printers
309 – Data and File Transfer Workshop Announcement
299 – Information Management System
295 – Report of the Protocol Workshop, 12 October 1971
291, 188, 173 - Data Management Meeting Announcement
245, 234, 207, 140, 116, 99, 87, 85, 75, 43, 35 - Reservations for Network Group
        meeting
222 – Subject: System programmer's workshop
212 – NWG meeting on network usage
157 – Invitation to the Second Symposium on Problems in the Optimization of Data
        Communications Systems
149 – Best Laid Plans
130 – Response to RFC 111: Pressure from the chairman
111 – Pressure from the Chairman
48 –   Possible protocol plateau
46 –   ARPA Network protocol notes

1e. Distribution Lists

402, 363, 329, 303, 300, 211, 168, 155 - ARPA Network Mailing Lists
69 –   Distribution List Change for MIT
52 –   Updated distribution list

1f. Policies Documents

2717 –Registration Procedures for URL Scheme Names
2506 –Media Feature Tag Registration Procedure
2489 –Procedure for Defining New DHCP Options
2418, 1603 - IETF Working Group Guidelines and Procedures
2282, 2027 - IAB and IESG Selection, Confirmation, and Recall Process: Operation
        of the Nominating and Recall Committees
2278 –IANA Charset Registration Procedures
2277 –IETF Policy on Character Sets and Languages
2146, 1816, 1811 - US Government Internet Domain Names
2135 –Internet Society By-Laws
2050 –Internet Registry IP Allocation Guidelines
2042 –Registering New BGP Attribute Types
2014 –IRTF Research Group Guidelines and Procedures
1956 –Registration in the MIL Domain
1930 –Guidelines for creation, selection, and registration of an Autonomous System
        (AS)
1875 –UNINETT PCA Policy Statements
1371 –Choosing a Common IGP for the IP Internet

1g. Request for Comments Administrative

1h. Other

2. Requirements Documents and Major Protocol Revisions

2a. Host Requirements

2b. Gateway Requirements

3. Network Interface Level (Also see Section 8)

3a. Address Binding (ARP, RARP)

3b. Internet Protocol over another network (encapsulation)

3c. Nonbroadcast Multiple Access Networks (ATM, IP Switching, MPLS)

2702 –Requirements for Traffic Engineering Over MPLS
2684 –Multiprotocol Encapsulation over ATM Adaptation Layer 5
2682 –Performance Issues in VC-Merge Capable ATM LSRs
2643 –Cabletron's SecureFast VLAN Operational Model
2642 –Cabletron's VLS Protocol Specification
2641 –Cabletron's VlanHello Protocol Specification Version 4
2603 –ILMI-Based Server Discovery for NHRP
2602 –ILMI-Based Server Discovery for MARS
2601 –ILMI-Based Server Discovery for ATMARP
2583 –Guidelines for Next Hop Client (NHC) Developers
2520 –NHRP with Mobile NHCs
2443 –A Distributed MARS Service Using SCSP
2383 –ST2+ over ATM Protocol Specification - UNI 3.1 Version
2340 –Nortel's Virtual Network Switching (VNS) Overview
2337 –Intra-LIS IP multicast among routers over ATM using Sparse Mode PIM
2336 –Classical IP to NHRP Transition
2335 –A Distributed NHRP Service Using SCSP
2334 –Server Cache Synchronization Protocol (SCSP)
2333 –NHRP Protocol Applicability Statement
2332 –NBMA Next Hop Resolution Protocol (NHRP)
2331 –ATM Signalling Support for IP over ATM - UNI Signalling 4.0 Update
2297, 1987 - Ipsilon's General Switch Management Protocol Specification Version
      2.0
2269 –Using the MARS Model in non-ATM NBMA Networks
2226 –IP Broadcast over ATM Networks
2225, 1577 - Classical IP and ARP over ATM
2191 –VENUS - Very Extensive Non-Unicast Service
2170 –Application REQuested IP over ATM (AREQUIPA)
2149 –Multicast Server Architectures for MARS-based ATM multicasting
2129 –Toshiba's Flow Attribute Notification Protocol (FANP) Specification
2124 –Cabletron's Light-weight Flow Admission Protocol Specification Version 1.0
2121 –Issues affecting MARS Cluster Size
2105 –Cisco Systems' Tag Switching Architecture Overview
2098 –Toshiba's Router Architecture Extensions for ATM : Overview
2022 –Support for Multicast over UNI 3.0/3.1 based ATM Networks
1954 –Transmission of Flow Labelled IPv4 on ATM Data Links Ipsilon Version 1.0
1953 –Ipsilon Flow Management Protocol Specification for IPv4 Version 1.0
1932 –IP over ATM: A Framework Document
1755 –ATM Signaling Support for IP over ATM
1754 –IP over ATM Working Group's Recommendations for the ATM Forum's
      Multiprotocol BOF Version 1
1735 –NBMA Address Resolution Protocol (NARP)
1626 –Default IP MTU for use over ATM AAL5
1483 –Multiprotocol Encapsulation over ATM Adaptation Layer 5

3d. Other

2469 –A Caution On The Canonical Ordering Of Link-Layer Addresses
2427, 1490, 1294 - Multiprotocol Interconnect over Frame Relay
2341 –Cisco Layer Two Forwarding (Protocol) "L2F"
2175 –MAPOS 16 - Multiple Access Protocol over SONET/SDH with 16 Bit
      Addressing
2174 –A MAPOS version 1 Extension - Switch-Switch Protocol

2173 –A MAPOS version 1 Extension - Node Switch Protocol
2172 –MAPOS Version 1 Assigned Numbers
2171 –MAPOS - Multiple Access Protocol over SONET/SDH Version 1
1326 –Mutual Encapsulation Considered Dangerous

4. Internet Level

4a. Internet Protocol (IP)

2113 –IP Router Alert Option
1624, 1141 - Computation of the Internet Checksum via Incremental Update
1191, 1063 - Path MTU discovery
1071 –Computing the Internet checksum
1025 –TCP and IP bake off
815 – IP datagram reassembly algorithms
791, 760 - Internet Protocol
781 – Specification of the Internet Protocol (IP) timestamp option

4b. Internet Control Message Protocol (ICMP)

2521 –ICMP Security Failures Messages
1788 –ICMP Domain Name Messages
1256 –ICMP Router Discovery Messages
1018 –Some comments on SQuID
1016 –Something a host could do with source quench: The Source Quench
        Introduced Delay (SQuID)
792, 777 - Internet Control Message Protocol

4c. Multicast (IGMP)

2588 –IP Multicast and Firewalls
2502 –Limitations of Internet Protocol Suite for Distributed Simulation the Large
        Multicast Environment
2365 –Administratively Scoped IP Multicast
2357 –IETF Criteria for Evaluating Reliable Multicast Transport and Application
        Protocols
2236 –Internet Group Management Protocol, Version 2
1768 –Host Group Extensions for CLNP Multicasting
1469 –IP Multicast over Token-Ring Local Area Networks
1458 –Requirements for Multicast Protocols
1301 –Multicast Transport Protocol
1112, 1054, 988, 966 - Host extensions for IP multicasting

4d. Routing and Gateway Algorithms (BGP, GGP, RIP, OSPF)

2715 –Interoperability Rules for Multicast Routing Protocols
2676 –QoS Routing Mechanisms and OSPF Extensions
2650 –Using RPSL in Practice
2622, 2280 - Routing Policy Specification Language (RPSL
2519 –A Framework for Inter-Domain Route Aggregation
2453, 1723, 1388 - RIP Version 2
2439 –BGP Route Flap Damping
2385 –Protection of BGP Sessions via the TCP MD5 Signature Option
2370 –The OSPF Opaque LSA Option
2362, 2117 - Protocol Independent Multicast-Sparse Mode (PIM-SM): Protocol
        Specification
2338 –Virtual Router Redundancy Protocol
2329 –OSPF Standardization Report
2328, 2178, 1583, 1247, 1131 - OSPF Version 2

2283 –Multiprotocol Extensions for BGP-4
2281 –Cisco Hot Standby Router Protocol (HSRP)
2270 –Using a Dedicated AS for Sites Homed to a Single Provider
2260 –Scalable Support for Multi-homed Multi-provider Connectivity
2201, 2189 - Core Based Trees (CBT) Multicast Routing Architecture
2154 –OSPF with Digital Signatures
2103 –Mobility Support for Nimrod : Challenges and Solution Approaches
2102 –Multicast Support for Nimrod : Requirements and Solution Approaches
2092 –Protocol Analysis for Triggered RIP
2091 –Triggered Extensions to RIP to Support Demand Circuits
2082 –RIP-2 MD5 Authentication
2009 –GPS-Based Addressing and Routing
1998 –An Application of the BGP Community Attribute in Multi-home Routing
1997 –BGP Communities Attribute
1992 –The Nimrod Routing Architecture
1966 –BGP Route Reflection An alternative to full mesh IBGP
1965 –Autonomous System Confederations for BGP
1923 –RIPv1 Applicability Statement for Historic Status
1863 –A BGP/IDRP Route Server alternative to a full mesh routing
1817 –CIDR and Classful Routing
1793 –Extending OSPF to Support Demand Circuits
1787 –Routing in a Multi-provider Internet
1786 –Representation of IP Routing Policies in a Routing Registry (ripe-81++)
1774 –BGP-4 Protocol Analysis
1773, 1656 - Experience with the BGP-4 protocol
1772, 1655, 1268, 1164 - Application of the Border Gateway Protocol in the Internet
1771, 1654, 1267, 1163 - A Border Gateway Protocol 4 (BGP-4)
1765 –OSPF Database Overflow
1745 –BGP4/IDRP for IP---OSPF Interaction
1722 –RIP Version 2 Protocol Applicability Statement
1721, 1387 - RIP Version 2 Protocol Analysis
1702, 1701 - Generic Routing Encapsulation over IPv4 networks
1587 –The OSPF NSSA Option
1586 –Guidelines for Running OSPF Over Frame Relay Networks
1585 –MOSPF: Analysis and Experience
1584 –Multicast Extensions to OSPF
1582 –Extensions to RIP to Support Demand Circuits
1581 –Protocol Analysis for Extensions to RIP to Support Demand Circuits
1520 –Exchanging Routing Information Across Provider Boundaries in the CIDR
        Environment
1519, 1338 - Classless Inter-Domain Routing (CIDR): an Address Assignment and
        Aggregation Strategy
1517 –Applicability Statement for the Implementation of Classless Inter-Domain
        Routing (CIDR)
1504 –Appletalk Update-Based Routing Protocol: Enhanced Appletalk Routing
1482 –Aggregation Support in the NSFNET Policy-Based Routing Database
1479 –Inter-Domain Policy Routing Protocol Specification: Version 1
1478 –An Architecture for Inter-Domain Policy Routing
1477 –IDPR as a Proposed Standard
1465 –Routing Coordination for X.400 MHS Services Within a Multi Protocol /
        Multi Network Environment Table Format V3 for Static Routing
1403, 1364 - BGP OSPF Interaction
1397 –Default Route Advertisement In BGP2 and BGP3 Version of The Border
        Gateway Protocol

4e. IP: The Next Generation (IPng, IPv6)

4f. IP Address Allocation and Network Numbering

4g. Network Isolation (VPN, Firewall, NAT)

4h. Other

5. Host Level

5a. User Datagram Protocol (UDP)

5b. Transmission Control Protocol (TCP)

5c. Point-to-Point Protocols (PPP)

1979 –PPP Deflate Protocol
1978 –PPP Predictor Compression Protocol
1977 –PPP BSD Compression Protocol
1976 –PPP for Data Compression in Data Circuit-Terminating Equipment (DCE)
1975 –PPP Magnalink Variable Resource Compression
1974 –PPP Stac LZS Compression Protocol
1973 –PPP in Frame Relay
1968 –The PPP Encryption Control Protocol (ECP)
1967 –PPP LZS-DCP Compression Protocol (LZS-DCP)
1963 –PPP Serial Data Transport Protocol (SDTP)
1962 –The PPP Compression Control Protocol (CCP)
1934 –Ascend's Multilink Protocol Plus (MP+)
1915 –Variance for The PPP Connection Control Protocol and The PPP Encryption
        Control Protocol
1877 –PPP Internet Protocol Control Protocol Extensions for Name Server
        Addresses
1841 –PPP Network Control Protocol for LAN Extension
1764 –The PPP XNS IDP Control Protocol (XNSCP)
1763 –The PPP Banyan Vines Control Protocol (BVCP)
1762, 1376 - The PPP DECnet Phase IV Control Protocol (DNCP)
1663 –PPP Reliable Transmission
1662, 1549 - PPP in HDLC-like Framing
1661, 1548 - The Point-to-Point Protocol (PPP)
1638, 1220 - PPP Bridging Control Protocol (BCP)
1618 –PPP over ISDN
1598 –PPP in X.25
1570 –PPP LCP Extensions
1552 –The PPP Internetworking Packet Exchange Control Protocol (IPXCP)
1547 –Requirements for an Internet Standard Point-to-Point Protocol
1378 –The PPP AppleTalk Control Protocol (ATCP)
1377 –The PPP OSI Network Layer Control Protocol (OSINLCP)
1332, 1172 - The PPP Internet Protocol Control Protocol (IPCP)
1331, 1171, 1134 - The Point-to-Point Protocol (PPP) for the Transmission of
        Multi-protocol Datagrams over Point-to-Point Links

5e. Transaction Protocols and Distributed Operating Systems

2372 –Transaction Internet Protocol - Requirements and Supplemental Information
2371 –Transaction Internet Protocol Version 3.0
955 – Towards a transport service for transaction processing applications
938 – Internet Reliable Transaction Protocol functional and interface specification
722 – Thoughts on Interactions in Distributed Services
713 – MSDTP-Message Services Data Transmission Protocol
712 – Distributed Capability Computing System (DCCS)
708 – Elements of a Distributed Programming System
707 – High-level framework for network-based resource sharing
684 – Commentary on procedure calling as a network protocol
677 – Maintenance of duplicate databases
674 – Procedure call documents: Version 2
672 – Multi-site data collection facility
671 – Note on Reconnection Protocol
645 – Network Standard Data Specification syntax
615 – Proposed Network Standard Data Pathname syntax
610 – Further datalanguage design concepts
592 – Some thoughts on system design to facilitate resource sharing

5f. Protocols for Local Area Networks (NETBIOS)

5g. IP Mobility and Roaming

5h. Other

6. Application Level

6a. Telnet Protocol (TELNET)

6b. Telnet Options

6c. File Transfer and Access Protocols (FTP, TFTP, SFTP, NFS)

6d. Domain Name System (DNS)

1713 –Tools for DNS debugging
1712 –DNS Encoding of Geographical Location
1706, 1637, 1348 - DNS NSAP Resource Records
1591 –Domain Name System Structure and Delegation
1536 –Common DNS Implementation Errors and Suggested Fixes
1535 –A Security Problem and Proposed Correction With Widely Deployed DNS
       Software
1480, 1386 - The US Domain
1464 –Using the Domain Name System To Store Arbitrary String Attributes
1394 –Relationship of Telex Answerback Codes to Internet Domains
1183 –New DNS RR Definitions
1101 –DNS encoding of network names and other types
1035 –Domain names - implementation and specification
1034 –Domain names - concepts and facilities
1033 –Domain administrators operations guide
1032 –Domain administrators guide
1031 –MILNET name domain transition
973 – Domain system changes and observations
953, 811 - Hostname Server
921, 897 - Domain name system implementation schedule - revised
920 – Domain requirements
883 – Domain names: Implementation specification
882 – Domain names: Concepts and facilities
881 – Domain names plan and schedule
830 – Distributed system for Internet name service
819 – Domain naming convention for Internet user applications
799 – Internet name domains
756 – NIC name server - a datagram-based information utility
752 – Universal host table

6e. Mail and Message Systems (SMTP, MIME, POP, IMAP, X.400)

2683 –IMAP4 Implementation Recommendations
2646 –The Text/Plain Format Parameter
2645 –ON-DEMAND MAIL RELAY (ODMR) SMTP with Dynamic IP Addresses
2634 –Enhanced Security Services for S/MIME
2633 –S/MIME Version 3 Message Specification
2632 –S/MIME Version 3 Certificate Handling
2595 –Using TLS with IMAP, POP3 and ACAP
2586 –The Audio/L16 MIME content type
2557, 2110 - MIME Encapsulation of Aggregate Documents, such as HTML
       (MHTML)
2554 –SMTP Service Extension for Authentication
2530 –Indicating Supported Media Features Using Extensions to DSN and MDN
2524 –Neda's Efficient Mail Submission and Delivery (EMSD) Protocol
       Specification Version 1.3
2505 –Anti-Spam Recommendations for SMTP MTAs
2503 –MIME Types for Use with the ISO ILL Protocol
2487 –SMTP Service Extension for Secure SMTP over TLS
2480 –Gateways and MIME Security Multiparts
2476 –Message Submission
2449 –POP3 Extension Mechanism
2442 –The Batch SMTP Media Type
2426 –vCard MIME Directory Profile
2425 –A MIME Content-Type for Directory Information

1339 –Remote Mail Checking Protocol
1328 –X.400 1988 to 1984 downgrading
1211 –Problems with the maintenance of large mailing lists
1204 –Message Posting Protocol (MPP)
1203, 1176, 1064 - Interactive Mail Access Protocol: Version 3
1168 –Intermail and Commercial Mail Relay services
1153 –Digest message format
1137 –Mapping between full RFC 822 and RFC 822 with restricted encoding
1090 –SMTP on X.25
1056, 993, 984 - PCMAIL: A distributed mail system for personal computers
1049 –Content-type header field for Internet messages
1047 –Duplicate messages and SMTP
1026, 987 - Addendum to RFC 987: (Mapping between X.400 and RFC-822)
977 – Network News Transfer Protocol
976 – UUCP mail interchange format standard
974 – Mail routing and the domain system
937, 918 - Post Office Protocol: Version 2
934 – Proposed standard for message encapsulation
915 – Network mail path service
886 – Proposed standard for message header munging
841 – Specification for message format for Computer Based Message Systems
822 – Standard for the format of ARPA Internet text messages
821, 788 - Simple Mail Transfer Protocol
806 – Proposed Federal Information Processing Standard: Specification for message
        format for computer based message systems
786 – Mail Transfer Protocol: ISI TOPS20 MTP-NIMAIL interface
785 – Mail Transfer Protocol: ISI TOPS20 file definitions
784 – Mail Transfer Protocol: ISI TOPS20 implementation
780, 772 - Mail Transfer Protocol
771 – Mail transition plan
763 – Role mailboxes
757 – Suggested solution to the naming, addressing, and delivery problem for
        ARPANET message systems
754 – Out-of-net host addresses for mail
753 – Internet Message Protocol
751 – Survey of FTP mail and MLFL
744 – MARS - a Message Archiving and Retrieval Service
733 – Standard for the format of ARPA network text messages
724 – Proposed official standard for the format of ARPA Network messages
720 – Address Specification Syntax for Network Mail
706 – On the junk mail problem
680 – Message Transmission Protocol
644 – On the problem of signature authentication for network mail
577 – Mail priority
574 – Announcement of a mail facility at UCSB
561 – Standardizing Network Mail Headers
555 – Responses to critiques of the proposed mail protocol
539, 524 - Thoughts on the mail protocol proposed in RFC 524
498 – On mail service to CCN
491 – What is "Free"?
475 – FTP and network mail system
458 – Mail retrieval via FTP
333 – Proposed experiment with a Message Switching Protocol

278, 224, 221, 196 - Revision of the Mail Box Protocol

6f. Facsimile and Bitmaps

2639 –Internet Printing Protocol/1.0: Implementer's Guide
2569 –Mapping between LPD and IPP Protocols
2568 –Rationale for the Structure of the Model and Protocol for the Internet Printing
       Protocol
2567 –Design Goals for an Internet Printing Protocol
2566 –Internet Printing Protocol/1.0: Model and Semantics
2565 –Internet Printing Protocol/1.0: Encoding and Transport
2542 –Terminology and Goals for Internet Fax
2534 –Media Features for Display, Print, and Fax
2532 –Extended Facsimile Using Internet Mail
2531 –Content Feature Schema for Internet Fax
2306 –Tag Image File Format (TIFF) - F Profile for Facsimile
2305 –A Simple Mode of Facsimile Using Internet Mail
2304 –Minimal FAX address format in Internet Mail
2303 –Minimal PSTN address format in Internet Mail
2301 –File Format for Internet Fax
2159 –A MIME Body Part for FAX
2083 –PNG (Portable Network Graphics) Specification Version 1.0
1529, 1528, 1486 - Principles of Operation for the TPC.INT Subdomain: Remote
       Printing -- Administrative Policies
1314 –A File Format for the Exchange of Images in the Internet
809 – UCL facsimile system
804 – CCITT draft recommendation T.4
803 – Dacom 450/500 facsimile data transcoding
798 – Decoding facsimile data from the Rapicom 450
797 – Format for Bitmap files
769 – Rapicom 450 facsimile file format

6g. Graphics and Window Systems

1198 –FYI on the X window system
1013 –X Window System Protocol, version 11: Alpha update April 1987
965 – Format for a graphical communication protocol
553 – Draft design for a text/graphics protocol
493 – Graphics Protocol
401 – Conversion of NGP-0 Coordinates to Device Specific Coordinates
398 – ICP Sockets
387 – Some experiences in implementing Network Graphics Protocol Level 0
351 – Graphics information form for the ARPANET graphics resources notebook
336 – Level 0 Graphic Input Protocol
296 – DS-1 display system
292 – Graphics Protocol: Level 0 only
285 – Network graphics
268 – Graphics facilities information
199 – Suggestions for a network data-tablet graphics protocol
192 – Some factors which a Network Graphics Protocol must consider
191 – Graphics implementation and conceptualization at Augmentation Research
       Center
186 – Network graphics loader
184 – Proposed graphic display modes
181, 177 - Modifications to RFC 177
178 – Network graphic attention handling

125, 86 - Response to RFC 86: Proposal for Network Standard Format for a
     Graphics Data Stream
94 –   Some thoughts on Network Graphics

6h. Data Management

304 – Data management system proposal for the ARPA network
195 – Data computers-data descriptions and access language
194 – The Data Reconfiguration Service -- Compiler/Interpreter Implementation
     Notes
166 – Data Reconfiguration Service: An implementation specification
144 – Data sharing on computer networks
138 – Status report on proposed Data Reconfiguration Service
83 –   Language-machine for data reconfiguration

6i. Remote Job Entry (NETRJE, NETRJS)

740, 599, 589, 325, 189, 88 - NETRJS Protocol
725 – RJE protocol for a resource sharing network
499 – Harvard's network RJE
490 – Surrogate RJS for UCLA-CCN
477, 436 - Remote Job Service at UCSB
407 – Remote Job Entry Protocol
368 – Comments on "Proposed Remote Job Entry Protocol"
360 – Proposed Remote Job Entry Protocol
338 – EBCDIC/ASCII Mapping for Network RJE
307 – Using network Remote Job Entry
283 – NETRJT: Remote Job Service Protocol for TIPS
105 – Network Specifications for Remote Job Entry and Remote Job Output
     Retrieval at UCSB

6j. Remote Procedure Call (RPC)

2695 –Authentication Mechanisms for ONC RPC
2203 –RPCSEC_GSS Protocol Specification
1833 –Binding Protocols for ONC RPC Version 2
1831 –RPC: Remote Procedure Call Protocol Specification Version 2
1057 –RPC: Remote Procedure Call Protocol specification: Version 2
1050 –RPC: Remote Procedure Call Protocol specification

6k. Time and Date (NTP)

2030, 1769, 1361 - Simple Network Time Protocol (SNTP) Version 4 for IPv4, IPv6
     and OSI
1708 –NTP PICS PROFORMA - For the Network Time Protocol Version 3
1589 –A Kernel Model for Precision Timekeeping
1305, 1119, 1059 - Network Time Protocol (Version 3) Specification,
     Implementation
1165 –Network Time Protocol (NTP) over the OSI Remote Operations Service
1129 –Internet time synchronization: The Network Time Protocol
1128 –Measured performance of the Network Time Protocol in the Internet system
958, 957, 956 - Network Time Protocol (NTP)
868 – Time Protocol
867 – Daytime Protocol
778 – DCNET Internet Clock Service
738 – Time server
685 – Response time in cross network debugging
34 –   Some Brief Preliminary Notes on the Augmentation Research Center Clock
32 –   Connecting M.I.T

28 –   Time Standards

6l. Presentation and Representation (XDR, Character Encoding, HTML, XML)

2706 –ECML v1: Field Names for E-Commerce

2659 –Security Extensions For HTML

2482 –Language Tagging in Unicode Plain Text

2413 –Dublin Core Metadata for Resource Discovery

2376 –XML Media Types

2346 –Making Postscript and PDF International

2319 –Ukrainian Character Set KOI8-U

2279, 2044 - UTF-8, a transformation format of ISO 10646

2237 –Japanese Character Encoding for Internet Messages

2183 –Communicating Presentation Information in Internet Messages: The Content-Disposition Header Field

2070 –Internationalization of the Hypertext Markup Language

1980 –A Proposed Extension to HTML : Client-Side Image Maps

1952 –GZIP file format specification version 4.3

1951 –DEFLATE Compressed Data Format Specification version 1.3

1950 –ZLIB Compressed Data Format Specification version 3.3

1947 –Greek Character Encoding for Electronic Mail Messages

1942 –HTML Tables

1922 –Chinese Character Encoding for Internet Messages

1874 –SGML Media Types

1867 –Form-based File Upload in HTML

1866 –Hypertext Markup Language - 2.0

1843 –HZ - A Data Format for Exchanging Files of Arbitrarily Mixed Chinese and ASCII characters

1842 –ASCII Printable Characters-Based Chinese Character Encoding for Internet Messages

1832 –XDR: External Data Representation Standard

1815 –Character Sets ISO-10646 and ISO-10646-J-1

1766 –Tags for the Identification of Languages

1557 –Korean Character Encoding for Internet Messages

1555 –Hebrew Character Encoding for Internet Messages

1554 –ISO-2022-JP-2: Multilingual Extension of ISO-2022-JP

1489 –Registration of a Cyrillic Character Set

1468 –Japanese Character Encoding for Internet Messages

1456 –Conventions for Encoding the Vietnamese Language VISCII: VIetnamese Standard Code for Information Interchange VIQR: VIetnamese Quoted-Readable Specification

1278 –A string encoding of Presentation Address

1197 –Using ODA for translating multimedia information

1014 –XDR: External Data Representation standard

1003 –Issues in defining an equations representation standard

6m. Network Management (SNMP, CMOT, RMON)

2593 –Script MIB Extensibility Protocol Version 1.0

2580, 1904, 1444 - Conformance Statements for SMIv2

2579, 1903, 1443 - Textual Conventions for SMIv2

2578, 1902, 1442 - Structure of Management Information Version 2 (SMIv2)

2575, 2275, 2265 - View-based Access Control Model (VACM) for the Simple Network Management Protocol (SNMP)

2574, 2274, 2264 - User-based Security Model (USM) for version 3 of the Simple Network Management Protocol (SNMPv3)

2573, 2273, 2263 - SNMP Applications

2572, 2272, 2262 - Message Processing and Dispatching for the Simple Network Management Protocol (SNMP)

2571, 2271, 2261 - An Architecture for Describing SNMP Management Frameworks

2570 –Introduction to Version 3 of the Internet-standard Network Management Framework

2493 –Textual Conventions for MIB Modules Using Performance History Based on 15 Minute Intervals

2438 –Advancement of MIB specifications on the IETF Standards Track

2257 –Agent Extensibility (AgentX) Protocol Version 1

2107 –Ascend Tunnel Management Protocol - ATMP

2089 –V2ToV1 Mapping SNMPv2 onto SNMPv1 within a bi-lingual SNMP agent

2039 –Applicability of Standards Track MIBs to Management of World Wide Web Servers

1910 –User-based Security Model for SNMPv2

1909 –An Administrative Infrastructure for SNMPv2

1908, 1452 - Coexistence between Version 1 and Version 2 of the Internet-standard Network Management Framework

1906, 1449 - Transport Mappings for Version 2 of the Simple Network Management Protocol (SNMPv2)

1905, 1448 - Protocol Operations for Version 2 of the Simple Network Management Protocol (SNMPv2)

1901 –Introduction to Community-based SNMPv2

1856 –The Opstat Client-Server Model for Statistics Retrieval

1592, 1228 - Simple Network Management Protocol Distributed Protocol Interface Version 2.0

1503 –Algorithms for Automating Administration in SNMPv2 Managers

1446 –Security Protocols for version 2 of the Simple Network Management Protocol (SNMPv2)

1445 –Administrative Model for version 2 of the Simple Network Management Protocol (SNMPv2)

1441 –Introduction to version 2 of the Internet-standard Network Management Framework

1420, 1298 - SNMP over IPX

1419 –SNMP over AppleTalk

1418, 1283, 1161 - SNMP over OSI

1369 –Implementation Notes and Experience for the Internet Ethernet MIB

1352 –SNMP Security Protocols

1351 –SNMP Administrative Model

1346 –Resource Allocation, Control, and Accounting for the Use of Network Resources

1303 –A Convention for Describing SNMP-based Agents

1270 –SNMP Communications Services

1239 –Reassignment of experimental MIBs to standard MIBs

1224 –Techniques for managing asynchronously generated alerts

1215 –Convention for defining traps for use with the SNMP

1212 –Concise MIB definitions

1189, 1095 - Common Management Information Services and Protocols for the Internet (CMOT and CMIP)

1187 –Bulk Table Retrieval with the SNMP

1157, 1098, 1067 - Simple Network Management Protocol (SNMP)

1155, 1065 - Structure and identification of management information for TCP/IP-based internets

1109 –Report of the second Ad Hoc Network Management Review Group
1089 –SNMP over Ethernet
1076 –HEMS monitoring and control language
1028 –Simple Gateway Monitoring Protocol
1024 –HEMS variable definitions
1023 –HEMS monitoring and control language
1022 –High-level Entity Management Protocol (HEMP)
1021 –High-level Entity Management System (HEMS)

6n. Management Information Base Definitions (MIB)

2720, 2064 - Traffic Flow Measurement: Meter MIB
2677 –Definitions of Managed Objects for the NBMA Next Hop Resolution
      Protocol (NHRP)
2674 –Definitions of Managed Objects for Bridges with Traffic Classes, Multicast
      Filtering and Virtual LAN Extensions
2670 –Radio Frequency (RF) Interface Management Information Base for
      MCNS/DOCSIS compliant RF interfaces
2669 –DOCSIS Cable Device MIB Cable Device Management Information Base for
      DOCSIS compliant Cable Modems and Cable Modem Termination Systems
2668, 2239 - Definitions of Managed Objects for IEEE 802.3 Medium Attachment
      Units (MAUs)
2667 –IP Tunnel MIB
2666 –Definitions of Object Identifiers for Identifying Ethernet Chip Sets
2665, 2358, 1650 - Definitions of Managed Objects for the Ethernet-like Interface
      Types
2662 –Definitions of Managed Objects for the ADSL Lines
2621 –RADIUS Accounting Server MIB
2620 –RADIUS Accounting Client MIB
2619 –RADIUS Authentication Server MIB
2618 –RADIUS Authentication Client MIB
2613 –Remote Network Monitoring MIB Extensions for Switched Networks Version
      1.0
2605, 1567 - Directory Server Monitoring MIB
2594 –Definitions of Managed Objects for WWW Services
2592 –Definitions of Managed Objects for the Delegation of Management Script
2591 –Definitions of Managed Objects for Scheduling Management Operations
2584 –Definitions of Managed Objects for APPN/HPR in IP Networks
2564 –Application Management MIB
2562 –Definitions of Protocol and Managed Objects for TN3270E Response Time
      Collection Using SMIv2 (TN3270E-RT-MIB)
2561 –Base Definitions of Managed Objects for TN3270E Using SMIv2
2558, 1595 - Definitions of Managed Objects for the SONET/SDH Interface Type
2515, 1695 - Definitions of Managed Objects for ATM Management
2514 –Definitions of Textual Conventions and OBJECT-IDENTITIES for ATM
      Management
2513 –Managed Objects for Controlling the Collection and Storage of Accounting
      Information for Connection-Oriented Networks
2512 –Accounting Information for ATM Networks
2496, 1407, 1233 - Definitions of Managed Object for the DS3/E3 Interface Type
2495, 1406, 1232 - Definitions of Managed Objects for the DS1, E1, DS2 and E2
      Interface Types
2494 –Definitions of Managed Objects for the DS0 and DS0 Bundle Interface Type
2457 –Definitions of Managed Objects for Extended Border Node
2456 –Definitions of Managed Objects for APPN TRAPS

2455, 2155 - Definitions of Managed Objects for APPN
2417, 2366 - Definitions of Managed Objects for Multicast over UNI 3.0/3.1 based
    ATM Networks
2320 –Definitions of Managed Objects for Classical IP and ARP Over ATM Using
    SMIv2 (IPOA-MIB)
2287 –Definitions of System-Level Managed Objects for Applications
2266 –Definitions of Managed Objects for IEEE 802.12 Repeater Devices
2249, 1566 - Mail Monitoring MIB
2248, 1565 - Network Services Monitoring MIB
2238 –Definitions of Managed Objects for HPR using SMIv2
2233, 1573, 1229 - The Interfaces Group MIB using SMIv2
2232 –Definitions of Managed Objects for DLUR using SMIv2
2214 –Integrated Services Management Information Base Guaranteed Service
    Extensions using SMIv2
2213 –Integrated Services Management Information Base using SMIv2
2128 –Dial Control Management Information Base using SMIv2
2127 –ISDN Management Information Base using SMIv2
2115, 1315 - Management Information Base for Frame Relay DTEs Using SMIv2
2108, 1516, 1368 - Definitions of Managed Objects for IEEE 802.3 Repeater
    Devices using SMIv2
2096, 1354 - IP Forwarding Table MIB
2074 –Remote Network Monitoring MIB Protocol Identifiers
2063 –Traffic Flow Measurement: Architecture
2051 –Definitions of Managed Objects for APPC using SMIv2
2037 –Entity MIB using SMIv2
2024 –Definitions of Managed Objects for Data Link Switching using SMIv2
2021 –Remote Network Monitoring Management Information Base Version 2 using
    SMIv2
2020 –IEEE 802.12 Interface MIB
2013 –SNMPv2 Management Information Base for the User Datagram Protocol
    using SMIv2
2012 –SNMPv2 Management Information Base for the Transmission Control
    Protocol using SMIv2
2011 –SNMPv2 Management Information Base for the Internet Protocol using
    SMIv2
2006 –The Definitions of Managed Objects for IP Mobility Support using SMIv2
1907, 1450 - Management Information Base for Version 2 of the Simple Network
    Management Protocol (SNMPv2)
1850, 1253, 1252, 1248 - OSPF Version 2 Management Information Base
1792 –TCP/IPX Connection Mib Specification
1759 –Printer MIB
1757, 1271 - Remote Network Monitoring Management Information Base
1749 –IEEE 802.5 Station Source Routing MIB using SMIv2
1748, 1743, 1231 - IEEE 802.5 MIB using SMIv2
1747 –Definitions of Managed Objects for SNA Data Link Control (SDLC) using
    SMIv2
1742, 1243 - AppleTalk Management Information Base II
1724, 1389 - RIP Version 2 MIB Extension
1697 –Relational Database Management System (RDBMS) Management
    Information Base (MIB) using SMIv2
1696 –Modem Management Information Base (MIB) using SMIv2
1694, 1304 - Definitions of Managed Objects for SMDS Interfaces using SMIv2
1666 –Definitions of Managed Objects for SNA NAUs using SMIv2

1665 –Definitions of Managed Objects for SNA NAUs using SMIv2
1660, 1318 - Definitions of Managed Objects for Parallel-printer-like Hardware
     Devices using SMIv2
1659, 1317 - Definitions of Managed Objects for RS-232-like Hardware Devices
     using SMIv2
1658, 1316 - Definitions of Managed Objects for Character Stream Devices using
     SMIv2
1657 –Definitions of Managed Objects for the Fourth Version of the Border
     Gateway Protocol (BGP-4) using SMIv2
1643, 1623, 1398, 1284 - Definitions of Managed Objects for the Ethernet-like
     Interface Types
1628 –UPS Management Information Base
1612 –DNS Resolver MIB Extensions
1611 –DNS Server MIB Extensions
1604, 1596 - Definitions of Managed Objects for Frame Relay Service
1593 –SNA APPN Node MIB
1559, 1289 - DECnet Phase IV MIB Extensions
1525, 1493, 1286 - Definitions of Managed Objects for Source Routing Bridges
1515 –Definitions of Managed Objects for IEEE 802.3 Medium Attachment Units
     (MAUs)
1514 –Host Resources MIB
1513 –Token Ring Extensions to the Remote Network Monitoring MIB
1512, 1285 - FDDI Management Information Base
1474 –The Definitions of Managed Objects for the Bridge Network Control Protocol
     of the Point-to-Point Protocol
1473 –The Definitions of Managed Objects for the IP Network Control Protocol of
     the Point-to-Point Protocol
1472 –The Definitions of Managed Objects for the Security Protocols of the Point-
     to-Point Protocol
1471 –The Definitions of Managed Objects for the Link Control Protocol of the
     Point-to-Point Protocol
1461 –SNMP MIB extension for Multiprotocol Interconnect over X.25
1451 –Manager-to-Manager Management Information Base
1447 –Party MIB for version 2 of the Simple Network Management Protocol
     (SNMPv2)
1414 –Identification MIB
1382 –SNMP MIB Extension for the X.25 Packet Layer
1381 –SNMP MIB Extension for X.25 LAPB
1353 –Definitions of Managed Objects for Administration of SNMP Parties
1269 –Definitions of Managed Objects for the Border Gateway Protocol: Version 3
1230 –IEEE 802.4 Token Bus MIB
1227 –SNMP MUX protocol and MIB
1214 –OSI internet management: Management Information Base
1213, 1158, 1156, 1066 - Management Information Base for Network Management
     of TCP/IP-based internets:MIB-II

6o. Directory Services (X.500, LDAP, Whitepages)

2714 –Schema for Representing CORBA Object References in an LDAP Directory
2713 –Schema for Representing Java(tm) Objects in an LDAP Directory
2696 –LDAP Control Extension for Simple Paged Results Manipulation
2657 –LDAPv2 Client vs the Index Mesh
2649 –An LDAP Control and Schema for Holding Operation Signatures
2596 –Use of Language Codes in LDAP
2589 –Lightweight Directory Access Protocol (v3): Extensions for Dynamic
     Directory Services

6p. Information Services (HTTP, Gopher, WAIS)

6q. Bootstrap and Configuration Protocols (BOOTP, DHCP)

6r. Real-Time Multimedia and Quality of Service (RSVP, RTP)

2386 –A Framework for QoS-based Routing in the Internet
2382 –A Framework for Integrated Services and RSVP over ATM
2381 –Interoperation of Controlled-Load Service and Guaranteed Service with ATM
2380 –RSVP over ATM Implementation Requirements
2379 –RSVP over ATM Implementation Guidelines
2361 –WAVE and AVI Codec Registries
2354 –Options for Repair of Streaming Media
2343 –RTP Payload Format for Bundled MPEG
2327 –SDP: Session Description Protocol
2326 –Real Time Streaming Protocol (RTSP)
2250, 2038 - RTP Payload Format for MPEG1/MPEG2 Video
2216 –Network Element Service Specification Template
2215 –General Characterization Parameters for Integrated Service Network Elements
2212 –Specification of Guaranteed Quality of Service
2211 –Specification of the Controlled-Load Network Element Service
2210 –The Use of RSVP with IETF Integrated Services
2209 –Resource ReSerVation Protocol (RSVP) -- Version 1 Message Processing
        Rules
2208 –Resource ReSerVation Protocol (RSVP) -- Version 1 Applicability Statement
        Some Guidelines on Deployment
2207 –RSVP Extensions for IPSEC Data Flows
2206 –RSVP Management Information Base using SMIv2
2205 –Resource ReSerVation Protocol (RSVP) -- Version 1 Functional Specification
2198 –RTP Payload for Redundant Audio Data
2190 –RTP Payload Format for H.263 Video Streams
2032 –RTP Payload Format for H.261 Video Streams
2029 –RTP Payload Format of Sun's CellB Video Encoding
1890 –RTP Profile for Audio and Video Conferences with Minimal Control
1889 –RTP: A Transport Protocol for Real-Time Applications
1821 –Integration of Real-time Services in an IP-ATM Network Architecture
1789 –INETPhone: Telephone Services and Servers on Internet
1257 –Isochronous applications do not require jitter-controlled networks
1193 –Client requirements for real-time communication services
741 – Specifications for the Network Voice Protocol (NVP)

6s. Other

2703 –Protocol-independent Content Negotiation Framework
2614 –An API for Service Location
2610 –DHCP Options for Service Location Protocol
2609 –Service Templates and Service: Schemes
2608, 2165 - Service Location Protocol, Version 2
2552 –Architecture for the Information Brokerage in the ACTS Project GAIA
2533 –A Syntax for Describing Media Feature Sets
2447, 2446, 2445 - iCalendar Message-Based Interoperability Protocol (iMIP)
2244 –ACAP -- Application Configuration Access Protocol
2229 –A Dictionary Server Protocol
2188 –AT&T/Neda's Efficient Short Remote Operations (ESRO) Protocol
        Specification Version 1.2
2016 –Uniform Resource Agents (URAs)
1861, 1645, 1568 - Simple Network Paging Protocol - Version 3 -Two-Way
        Enhanced
1756 –Remote Write Protocol - Version 1.0
1703, 1569 - Principles of Operation for the TPC.INT Subdomain: Radio Paging --
        Technical Procedures

7. Program Documentation

120 – Network PL1 subprograms
119 – Network Fortran subprograms
74 –   Specifications for network use of the UCSB On-Line System

8. Network Specific (also see Section 3)

8a. ARPANET

1005, 878, 851, 802 - ARPANET AHIP-E Host Access Protocol (enhanced AHIP)
852 – ARPANET short blocking feature
789 – Vulnerabilities of network control protocols: An example
745 – JANUS interface specifications
716 – Interim Revision to Appendix F of BBN 1822
704 – IMP/Host and Host/IMP Protocol change
696 – Comments on the IMP/Host and Host/IMP Protocol changes
695 – Official change in Host-Host Protocol
692 – Comments on IMP/Host Protocol changes (RFCs 687 and 690)
690 – Comments on the proposed Host/IMP Protocol changes
687 – IMP/Host and Host/IMP Protocol changes
667 – BBN host ports
660 – Some changes to the IMP and the IMP/Host interface
642 – Ready line philosophy and implementation
638, 633 - IMP/TIP preventive maintenance schedule
632 – Throughput degradations for single packet messages
627 – ASCII text file of hostnames
626 – On a possible lockup condition in IMP subnet due to message sequencing
625 – On-line hostnames service
623 – Comments on on-line host name service
622 – Scheduling IMP/TIP down time
620 – Request for monitor host table updates
619 – Mean round-trip times in the ARPANET
613 – Network connectivity: A response to RFC 603
611 – Two changes to the IMP/Host Protocol to improve user/network
       communications
606 – Host names on-line
594 – Speedup of Host-IMP interface
591 – Addition to the Very Distant Host specifications
568, 567 - Response to RFC 567 - cross country network bandwidth
548 – Hosts using the IMP Going Down message
547 – Change to the Very Distant Host specification
533 – Message-ID numbers
528 – Software checksumming in the IMP and network reliability
521 – Restricted use of IMP DDT
508 – Real-time data transmission on the ARPANET
476, 434 - IMP/TIP memory retrofit schedule (rev 2)
449, 442 - Current flow-control scheme for IMPSYS
447, 445 - IMP/TIP memory retrofit schedule
417 – Link usage violation
410 – Removal of the 30-Second Delay When Hosts Come Up
406 – Scheduled IMP Software Releases
395 – Switch Settings on IMPs and TIPs
394 – Two Proposed Changes to the IMP-Host Protocol
369 – Evaluation of ARPANET services January-March, 1972
335 – New Interface - IMP/360
312 – Proposed Change in IMP-to-Host Protocol

8b. Host Front End Protocols

8c. ARPANET NCP (Obsolete Predecessor of TCP/IP)

8d. ARPANET Initial Connection Protocol

8e. USENET

8f. Other

9. Measurement

9a. General

9b. Surveys

9c. Statistics

10. Privacy, Security and Authentication

10a. General

10b. Encryption, Authentication and Key Exchange Algorithms

10c. IP Security Protocol (IPSec)

11. Network Experience and Demonstrations

12. Site Documentation

13. Protocol Standards By Other Groups Of Interest To The Internet

13a. ANSI

13b. NRC

13c. ISO

14. Interoperability With Other Applications And Protocols

14a. Protocol Translation and Bridges

14b. Tunneling and Layering

14c. Mapping of Names, Addresses, and Identifiers

1439 –The Uniqueness of Unique Identifiers
1236 –IP to X.121 address mapping for DDN
1069 –Guidelines for the use of Internet-IP addresses in the ISO Connectionless-
        Mode Network Protocol

15. Miscellaneous

15a. General

2664, 1594, 1325, 1206, 1177 - FYI on Questions and Answers - Answers to
        Commonly Asked "New Internet User" Questions
2636, 2604 - Wireless Device Configuration (OTASP/OTAPA) via ACAP
2635 –DON'T SPEW A Set of Guidelines for Mass Unsolicited Mailings and
        Postings (spam*)
2626 –The Internet and the Millennium Problem (Year 2000)
2555 –30 Years of RFCs
2468 –I REMEMBER IANA
2441 –Working with Jon, Tribute delivered at UCLA, October 30, 1998
2351 –Mapping of Airline Reservation, Ticketing, and Messaging Traffic over IP
2350 –Expectations for Computer Security Incident Response
2309 –Recommendations on Queue Management and Congestion Avoidance in the
        Internet
2235 –Hobbes' Internet Timeline
2234 –Augmented BNF for Syntax Specifications: ABNF
2151, 1739 - A Primer On Internet and TCP/IP Tools and Utilities
2150 –Humanities and Arts: Sharing Center Stage on the Internet
2057 –Source Directed Access Control on the Internet
1983, 1392 - Internet Users' Glossary
1958 –Architectural Principles of the Internet
1941, 1578 - Frequently Asked Questions for Schools
1935 –What is the Internet, Anyway?
1865 –EDI Meets the Internet Frequently Asked Questions about Electronic Data
        Interchange (EDI) on the Internet
1855 –Netiquette Guidelines
1775 –To Be "On" the Internet
1758, 1417, 1295 - NADF Standing Documents: A Brief Overview
1746 –Ways to Define User Expectations
1709 –K-12 Internetworking Guidelines
1691 –The Document Architecture for the Cornell Digital Library
1633 –Integrated Services in the Internet Architecture: an Overview
1580 –Guide to Network Resource Tools
1501 –OS/2 User Group
1498 –On the Naming and Binding of Network Destinations
1470, 1147 - FYI on a Network Management Tool Catalog: Tools for Monitoring
        and Debugging TCP/IP Internets and Interconnected Devices
1462 –FYI on "What is the Internet?"
1453 –A Comment on Packet Video Remote Conferencing and the
        Transport/Network Layers
1432 –Recent Internet Books
1402, 1290 - There's Gold in them thar Networks! or Searching for Treasure in all
        the Wrong Places
1400 –Transition and Modernization of the Internet Registration Service
1359 –Connecting to the Internet - What Connecting Institutions Should Anticipate
1345 –Character Mnemonics and Character Sets

1336, 1251 - Who's Who in the Internet: Biographies of IAB, IESG and IRSG
  Members
1324 –A Discussion on Computer Network Conferencing
1302 –Building a Network Information Services Infrastructure
1300 –Remembrances of Things Past
1296 –Internet Growth (1981-1991)
1291 –Mid-Level Networks Potential Technical Services
1259 –Building the open road: The NREN as test-bed for the national public
  network
1242 –Benchmarking terminology for network interconnection devices
1208 –Glossary of networking terms
1207 –FYI on Questions and Answers: Answers to commonly asked "experienced
  Internet user" questions
1199, 1099 - Request for Comments Summary Notes: 1100-1199
1192 –Commercialization of the Internet summary report
1181 –RIPE Terms of Reference
1180 –TCP/IP tutorial
1178 –Choosing a name for your computer
1173 –Responsibilities of host and network managers: A summary of the "oral
  tradition" of the Internet
1169 –Explaining the role of GOSIP
1167 –Thoughts on the National Research and Education Network
1118 –Hitchhikers guide to the Internet
1015 –Implementation plan for interagency research Internet
992 – On communication support for fault tolerant process groups
874 – Critique of X.25
531 – Feast or famine? A response to two recent RFC's about network information
473 – MIX and MIXAL?
472 – Illinois' reply to Maxwell's request for graphics information (NIC 14925)
429 – Character Generator Process
408 – NETBANK
361 – Deamon Processes on Host 106
313 – Computer based instruction
256 – IMPSYS change notification
225 – Rand/UCSB network graphics experiment
219 – User's view of the datacomputer
187 – Network/440 Protocol Concept
169 – Computer networks
146 – Views on issues relevant to data sharing on computer networks
13 –   Zero Text Length EOF Message

15b. Bibliographies

2007 –Catalogue of Network Training Materials
1463 –FYI on Introducing the Internet-- A Short Bibliography of Introductory
  Internetworking Readings
1175 –FYI on where to start: A bibliography of internetworking information
1012 –Bibliography of Request For Comments 1 through 999
829 – Packet satellite technology reference sources
290 – Computer networks and data sharing: A bibliography
243 – Network and data sharing bibliography

15c. Humorous RFCs

2551 –The Roman Standards Process -- Revision III
2550 –Y10K and Beyond

16. Unissued

2727, 2726, 2725, 2708, 2707, 2700, 2699, 2600, 2599, 2576, 1849, 1840, 1839,
1260, 1182, 1061, 853, 723, 715, 711, 710, 709, 693, 682, 676, 673, 670, 668, 665,
664, 650, 649, 648, 646, 641, 639, 605, 583, 575, 572, 564, 558, 554, 541, 540, 536,
517, 507, 502, 484, 481, 465, 444, 428, 427, 424, 397, 383, 380, 375, 358, 341, 337,
284, 279, 277, 275, 272, 262, 261, 260, 259, 258, 257, 248, 244, 220, 201, 159, 92,
26, 14

Appendix 2

Glossary Of Internetworking Terms And Abbreviations

TCP/IP Terminology

Like most large enterprises, TCP/IP has a language all its own. A curious blend of networking jargon, protocol names, and abbreviations, the language is both difficult to learn and difficult to remember. To outsiders, discussions among the cognoscenti sound like meaningless babble laced with acronyms at every possible opportunity. Even after a moderate amount of exposure, readers may find that specific terms are difficult to understand. The problem is compounded because some terminology is loosely defined and because the sheer volume is overwhelming.

This glossary helps solve the problem by providing short definitions for terms used throughout the Internet. It is not intended as a tutorial for beginners. Instead, we focus on providing a concise reference to make it easy for those who are generally knowledgeable about networking to look up the meaning of specific terms or acronyms quickly. Readers will find it substantially more useful as a reference after they have studied the text than before.

A Glossary of Terms and Abbreviations
In Alphabetical Order

10/100 hardware

Applied to any Ethernet hardware that can operate at either 10 Mbps or 100 Mbps.

10Base5

The technical name for the original thick Ethernet.

10Base2

The technical name for thin Ethernet.

10Base-T

The technical name for twisted pair Ethernet operating at 10 Mbps.

100Base-T

The technical name for twisted pair Ethernet operating at 100 Mbps. The term *100Base-TX* is more specific.

1000Base-T

The technical name for twisted pair Ethernet operating at 1000 Mbps (1 Gbps).

127.0.0.1

The IP *loopback* address used for testing. Packets sent to this address are processed by the local protocol software without ever being sent across a network.

2X Problem

An inefficient routing situation caused by mobile IP in which a datagram crosses the global Internet twice when traveling from a computer to a mobile that is visiting a nearby network.

576

The minimum datagram size all hosts and routers must handle.

802.3

The IEEE standard for Ethernet.

822

The TCP/IP standard format for electronic mail messages. Mail experts often refer to "822 messages." The name comes from RFC 822 that contains the specification. 822 format was previously known as 733 format.

9180

The default MTU size for sending IP datagrams over an ATM network.

AAL

(*ATM Adaptation Layer*) Part of the ATM protocols. Several adaptation layers exist; AAL5 is used for data.

ABR

Either *Available Bit Rate*, an ATM designation for service that does not guarantee a rate, or *Area Border Router*, an OSPF designation for a router that communicates with another area.

ACK

Abbreviation for *acknowledgement*.

ACK implosion

A reference to a problem that can occur with a reliable multicast protocol in which many acknowledgements (ACKs) go back to the source. Most reliable multicast schemes use designated routers to aggregate ACKs.

acknowledgement

A response sent by a receiver to indicate successful reception of information. Acknowledgements may be implemented at any level including the physical level (using voltage on one or more wires to coordinate transfer), at the link level (to indicate successful transmission across a single hardware link), or at higher levels (e.g., to allow an application program at the final destination to respond to an application program at the source).

acknowledgement aggregator

Used in a reliable multicast scheme to avoid the ACK implosion problem.

active open

The operation that a client performs to establish a TCP connection with a server at a known address.

adaptive retransmission

The scheme TCP uses to make the retransmission timer track the mean round-trip time.

address

An integer value used to identify a particular computer that must appear in each packet sent to the computer.

address binding

The translation of a higher-layer address into an equivalent lower-layer address (e.g., translation of a computer's IP address to the computer's Ethernet address).

address mask

A synonym for *subnet mask*.

address resolution

Conversion of a protocol address into a corresponding physical address (e.g., conversion of an IP address into an Ethernet address). Depending on the underlying network, resolution may require broadcasting on a local network. See ARP.

administrative scoping

A scheme for limiting the propagation of multicast datagrams. Some addresses are reserved for use within a site or within an organization.

ADSL
(*Asymmetric Digital Subscriber Line*) A popular DSL variant.

Advanced Networks and Services
The company that owned and operated the Internet backbone in 1995.

agent
In network management, an agent is the server software that runs on a host or router being managed.

AH
(*Authentication Header*) A header used by IPsec to guarantee the authenticity of a datagram's source.

all routers group
The well-known IP multicast group that includes all routers on the local network.

all systems group
The well-known IP multicast group that includes all hosts and routers on the local network.

anonymous FTP
An FTP session that uses login name *anonymous* to access public files. A server that permits anonymous FTP often allows the password *guest*.

anonymous network
A synonym for *unnumbered network*.

ANS
Abbreviation for *Advanced Networks and Services*.

ANSI
(*American National Standards Institute*) A group that defines U.S. standards for the information processing industry. ANSI participates in defining network protocol standards.

ANSNET
The Wide Area Network that formed the Internet backbone until 1995.

anycast
An address form introduced with IPv6 in which a datagram sent to the address can be routed to any of a set of computers. An *anycast address* is called a *cluster address*.

API
(*Application Program Interface*) The specification of the operations an application program must invoke to communicate over a network. The socket API is the most popular for internet communication.

application gateway
An application program that connects two or more heterogeneous systems and translates among them. E-mail gateways are especially popular.

application-server paradigm

A synonym for *client-server* paradigm.

area

In OSPF, a group of routers that exchange routing information.

area manager

A person in charge of an IETF area. The set of area managers form the IESG.

ARP

(*Address Resolution Protocol*) The TCP/IP protocol used to dynamically bind a high-level IP Address to a low-level physical hardware address. ARP is used across a single physical network and is limited to networks that support hardware broadcast.

ARPA

(*Advanced Research Projects Agency*) The government agency that funded the ARPANET, and later, the global Internet. The group within ARPA with responsibility for the ARPANET was IPTO (*Information Processing Techniques Office*), later called ISTO (*Information Systems Technology Office*). ARPA was named *DARPA* for many years.

ARPANET

A pioneering long haul network funded by ARPA (later DARPA) and built by BBN. It served from 1969 through 1990 as the basis for early networking research and as a central backbone during development of the Internet. The ARPANET consisted of individual packet switching nodes interconnected by leased lines.

ARQ

(*Automatic Repeat reQuest*) Any protocol that uses positive and negative acknowledgements with retransmission techniques to ensure reliability. The sender automatically repeats the request if it does not receive an answer.

AS

(*Autonomous System*) A collection of routers and networks that fall under one administrative entity and cooperate closely to propagate network reachability (and routing) information among themselves using an interior gateway protocol of their choice. Routers within an autonomous system have a high degree of trust. Before two autonomous systems can communicate, one router in each system sends reachability information to a router in the other.

ASN.1

(*Abstract Syntax Notation.1*) The ISO presentation standard protocol used by SNMP to represent messages.

Assigned Numbers

The RFC document that specifies (usually numeric) values used by TCP/IP protocols.

ATM

(*Asynchronous Transfer Mode*) A connection-oriented network technology that uses small, fixed-size cells at the lowest layer. ATM has the potential advantage of being able to support voice, video, and data with a single underlying technology.

ATM Adaptation Layer (AAL)

One of several protocols defined for ATM that specifies how an application sends and receives information over an ATM network. Data transmissions use AAL5.

ATMARP

The protocol a host uses for address resolution when sending IP over an ATM network.

AUI

(*Attachment Unit Interface*) The connector used for thick-wire Ethernet.

authority zone

A part of the domain name hierarchy in which a single name server is the authority.

backbone network

Any network that forms the central interconnect for an internet. A national backbone is a WAN; a corporate backbone can be a LAN.

base64

An encoding used with MIME to send non-textual data such as a binary file through e-mail.

base header

In the proposed IPng, the required header found at the beginning of each datagram.

baseband

Characteristic of any network technology like Ethernet that uses a single carrier frequency and requires all stations attached to the network to participate in every transmission. Compare to *broadband*.

bastion host

A secure computer that forms part of a security firewall and runs applications that communicate with computers outside an organization.

baud

Literally, the number of times per second the signal can change on a transmission line. Commonly, the transmission line uses only two signal states (e.g., two voltages), making the baud rate equal to the number of bits per second that can be transferred. The underlying transmission technique may use some of the bandwidth, so it may not be the case that users experience data transfers at the line's specified bit rate. For example, because asynchronous lines require 10 bit-times to send an 8-bit character, a 9600 baud asynchronous transmission line can only send 960 characters per second.

BCP

(*Best Current Practice*) A label given to a subset of RFCs that contain recommendations from the IETF about the use, configuration, or deployment of internet technologies.

Bellman-Ford

A synonym for *distance-vector*.

Berkeley broadcast

A reference to a nonstandard IP broadcast address that uses all zeros in the host portion instead of all ones. The name arises because the technique was introduced and propagated in Berkeley's BSD UNIX.

best-effort delivery

Characteristic of network technologies that do not provide reliability at link levels. IP works well over best-effort delivery hardware because IP does not assume that the underlying network provides reliability. The UDP protocol provides best-effort delivery service to application programs.

BGP

(*Border Gateway Protocol*) The major exterior gateway protocol used in the Internet. Four major versions of BGP have appeared, with BGP-4 being the current.

big endian

A format for storage or transmission of binary data in which the most-significant byte (bit) comes first. The TCP/IP standard network byte order is big endian. Compare to *little endian*.

binary exponential backoff

A technique used to control network contention or congestion quickly. A sender doubles the amount of time it waits between each successive attempt to use the network.

BISYNC

(*BInary SYNchronous Communication*) An early, low-level protocol developed by IBM and used to transmit data across a synchronous communication link. Unlike most modern link level protocols, BISYNC is byte-oriented, meaning that it uses special characters to mark the beginning and end of frames. BISYNC is often called BSC, especially in commercial products.

BNC

The style of connector used with thin-wire Ethernet.

BOOTP

Abbreviation for *BOOTstrap Protocol*, a protocol a host uses to obtain startup information, including its IP address, from a server.

bps

(*bits per second*) A measure of the rate of data transmission.

bridge

A computer that connects two or more networks and forwards packets among them. Bridges operate at the physical network level. For example, an Ethernet bridge connects two physical Ethernet cables, and forwards from one cable to the other exactly the packets that are not local. Bridges differs from repeaters because bridges store and forward complete packets, while repeaters forward all electrical signals. Bridges differ from routers because bridges use physical addresses, while routers use IP addresses.

broadband

Characteristic of any network technology that multiplexes multiple, independent network carriers onto a single cable (usually using frequency division multiplexing). For example, a single 50 Mbps broadband cable can be divided into five 10 Mbps carriers, with each treated as an independent Ethernet. The advantage of broadband is less cable; the disadvantage is higher cost for equipment at connections. Compare to *baseband*.

broadcast

A packet delivery system that delivers a copy of a given packet to all hosts that attach to it is said to broadcast the packet. Broadcast may be implemented with hardware (e.g., as in Ethernet) or with software (e.g., IP broadcasting in the presence of subnets).

broadcast and prune

A technique used in data-driven multicast forwarding in which routers forward each datagram to each network until they learn that the network has no group members.

brouter

(*Bridging ROUTER*) A device that operates as a bridge for some protocols and as a router for others (e.g., a brouter can bridge DECNET protocols and route IP).

BSC

(*Binary Synchronous Communication*) See BISYNC.

BSD UNIX

(*Berkeley Software Distribution UNIX*) The version of UNIX released by U.C. Berkeley or one of the commercial systems derived from it. BSD UNIX was the first to include TCP/IP protocols.

care-of address

A temporary IP address used by a mobile while visiting a foreign network.

category 5 cable

A standard for wiring that is used with twisted pair Ethernet.

CBT

(*Core Based Trees*) A demand-driven multicast routing protocol that builds shared forwarding trees.

CCIRN

(*Coordinating Committee for Intercontinental Research Networking*) An international group that helps coordinate international cooperation on internetworking research and development.

CCITT

(*Consultative Committee on International Telephony and Telegraphy*) The former name of International Telecommunications Union.

CDDI

(*Copper Distributed Data Interface*) An adaptation of the FDDI network technology for use over copper wires.

cell

A small, fixed-size packet. The fixed size makes hardware optimization possible. Cells are often associated with ATM networks in which a cell contains 48 octets of data and 5 octets of header.

cell tax

A reference to the 10% header overhead imposed by ATM.

CGI

(*Common Gateway Interface*) A technology a server uses to create a Web page dynamically when the request arrives.

checksum

A small, integer value computed from a sequence of octets by treating them as integers and computing the sum. A checksum is used to detect errors that result when the sequence of octets is transmitted from one machine to another. Typically, protocol software computes a checksum and appends it to a packet when transmitting. Upon reception, the protocol software verifies the contents of the packet by recomputing the checksum and comparing to the value sent. Many TCP/IP protocols use a 16-bit checksum computed with one's complement arithmetic, with all integer fields in the packet stored in network byte order.

CIDR

(*Classless Inter-Domain Routing*) The standard that specifies the details of both classless addressing and an associated routing scheme.

CL

See *connectionless service*.

class of address

The category of an IP address. The class of an address determines the location of the boundary between network prefix and host suffix.

classful addressing

The original IPv4 addressing scheme in which host addresses were divided into three classes: A, B, and C.

classless addressing

An extension of the original IPv4 addressing scheme that ignores the original class boundaries. Classless addressing was motivated by the problem of address space exhaustion.

client-server

The model of interaction in a distributed system in which a program at one site sends a request to a program at another site and awaits a response. The requesting program is called a client; the program satisfying the request is called the server. It is usually easier to build client software than server software.

closed window

A situation in TCP where a receiver has sent a window advertisement of zero because no additional buffer space is available. The sending TCP cannot transmit additional data until the receiver opens the window.

cluster address

The term originally used for *anycast* address.

CO

See *connection-oriented service*.

codec

(*coder/decoder*) A hardware device used to convert between an analog audio signal and a stream of digital values.

congestion

A situation in which traffic (temporarily) exceeds the capacity of networks or routers. TCP includes a congestion control mechanism that allows it to back off when the internet becomes congested.

connection

An abstraction provided by protocol software. TCP provides a connection from an application on one computer to an application on another.

connection-oriented service

Characteristic of the service offered by any technology that requires communicating entities to establish a connection before sending data. TCP provides connection-oriented service as does ATM hardware.

connectionless service

Characteristic of any packet delivery service that treats each packet or datagram as a separate entity and allows communicating entities to transmit data before establishing communication. Each packet carries a destination address to identify the intended recipient. Most network hardware, the Internet Protocol (IP), and the User Datagram Protocol (UDP) provide connectionless service.

COPS

(*Common Open Policy Service*) A protocol used with RSVP to verify whether a request meets policy constraints.

core architecture

Characteristic of an internet architecture that has a central routing system surrounded by local routing systems. The original Internet had a single backbone network, and used a core architecture. As ISPs developed backbone systems, the Internet moved away from a single core.

count to infinity

A popular synonym for the *slow convergence* problem.

CRC

(*Cyclic Redundancy Code*) A small, integer value computed from a sequence of octets used to detect errors that result when the sequence of octets is transmitted from one machine to another. Typically, packet switching network hardware computes a CRC and appends it to a packet when transmitting. Upon reception, the hardware verifies the contents of the packet by recomputing the CRC and comparing it to the value sent. Although more expensive to compute, a CRC detects more errors than a checksum that uses additive methods.

CR-LF

(*Carriage Return - Line Feed*) A two-character sequence used to terminate text lines in application-layer protocols such as TELNET and SMTP.

CSMA/CD

(*Carrier Sense Multiple Access with Collision Detection*) A characteristic of network hardware that operates by allowing multiple stations to contend for access to a transmission medium by listening to see if the medium is idle, and a mechanism that allows the hardware to detect when two stations simultaneously attempt transmission. Ethernet uses CSMA/CD.

CSU/DSU

(*Channel Service Unit / Data Service Unit*) An electronic device that connects a computer or router to a digital circuit leased by the telephone company. Although the device fills two rolls, it usually consists of a single physical piece of hardware.

cumulative acknowledgement

An alternative to the selective acknowledgements used by TCP. A cumulative acknowledgement reports all data that has been received successfully rather than each piece of data that arrives.

DARPA

(*Defense Advanced Research Projects Agency*) Former name of ARPA.

data-driven multicast

A scheme for multicast forwarding that uses the broadcast and prune approach. See *demand-driven multicast*.

datagram

See *IP datagram*.

DCE

(*Data Communications Equipment*) Term ITU protocol standards apply to switching equipment that forms a packet switched network to distinguish it from the computers or terminals that connect to the network. Also see *DTE*.

DDCMP

(*Digital Data Communication Message Protocol*) The link level protocol used in the original NSFNET backbone.

DDN

(*Defense Data Network*) The part of the Internet associated with U.S. military sites.

default route

A single entry in a list of routes that covers all destinations which are not included explicitly. The routing tables in most routers and hosts contain an entry for a default route.

delay

One of the two primary measures of a network. Delay refers to the difference between the time a bit of data is injected into a network and the time the bit exits.

delayed acknowledgement

A heuristic employed by a receiving TCP to avoid silly window syndrome.

demand-driven multicast

A scheme for multicast forwarding that requires a router to join a shared forwarding tree before deliverying packets. See *data-driven multicast*.

demultiplex

To separate from a common input into several outputs. Demultiplexing occurs at many levels. Hardware demultiplexes signals from a transmission line based on time or carrier frequency to allow multiple, simultaneous transmissions across a single physical cable. IP software demultiplexes incoming datagrams, sending each to the appropriate high-level protocol module or application program. See *multiplex*.

DHCP

(*Dynamic Host Configuration Protocol*) A protocol that a host uses to obtain all necessary configuration information including an IP address. DHCP is popular with ISPs because it allows a host to obtain a temporary IP address.

DiffServe

(*Differentiated Services*) A scheme adopted to replace the original IP type of service. DiffServe provides up to 64 possible types of service (e.g., priorities); each datagram carries a field in the header that specifies the type of service it desires.

directed broadcast address

An IP address that specifies "all hosts" on a specific network. A single copy of a directed broadcast is routed to the specified network where it is broadcast to all machines on that network.

distance-vector

A class of routing update protocols that use a distributed shortest path algorithm (SPF) in which each participating router sends its neighbors a list of networks it can reach and the distance to each network.

DNS

(*Domain Name System*) The on-line distributed database system used to map human-readable machine names into IP addresses. DNS servers throughout the connected Internet implement a hierarchical namespace that allows sites freedom in assigning machine names and addresses. DNS also supports separate mappings between mail destinations and IP addresses.

domain

A part of the DNS naming hierarchy. Syntactically, a domain name consists of a sequence of names (labels) separated by periods (dots).

dotted decimal notation

A syntactic form used to represent 32-bit binary integers that consists of four 8-bit numbers written in base 10 with periods (dots) separating them. Many TCP/IP application programs accept dotted decimal notation in place of destination machine names.

dotted hex notation

A syntactic form used to represent binary values that consists of hexadecimal values for each 8-bit quantity with dots separating them.

dotted quad notation

A syntactic form used to represent binary values that consists of hexadecimal values for each 16-bit quantity with dots separating them.

DS3

A telephony classification of speed for leased lines equivalent to approximately 45 Mbps.

DSL

(*Digital Subscriber Line*) A set of technologies used to provide high-speed data service over the copper wires that connect between telephone offices, local residences or businesses.

DTE

(*Data Terminal Equipment*) Term ITU protocol standards apply to computers and/or terminals to distinguish them from the packet switching network to which they connect. Also see *DCE*.

DVMRP

(*Distance Vector Multicast Routing Protocol*) A protocol used to propagate multicast routes.

E.164

An address format specified by ITU and used with ATM.

EACK

(*Extended ACKnowledgement*) Synonym for *SACK*.

echo request and reply

A type of message that is used to test network connectivity. The ping program uses ICMP echo request and reply messages.

EGP

(*Exterior Gateway Protocol*) A term applied to any protocol used by a router in one autonomous system to advertise network reachability to a router in another autonomous system. BGP-4 is currently the most widely used exterior gateway protocol.

EIA

(*Electronics Industry Association*) A standards organization for the electronics industry. Known for RS232C and RS422 standards that specify the electrical characteristics of interconnections between terminals and computers or between two computers.

encapsulation

The technique used by layered protocols in which a lower level protocol accepts a message from a higher level protocol and places it in the data portion of the low-level frame. Encapsulation means that datagrams traveling across a physical network have a sequence of headers in which the first header comes from the physical network frame, the next from the Internet Protocol (IP), the next from the transport protocol, and so on.

end-to-end

Characteristic of any mechanism that operates only on the original source and final destination. Applications and transport protocols like TCP are classified as end-to-end.

epoch date

A point in history chosen as the date from which time is measured. TCP/IP uses January 1, 1900, Universal Time (formerly called Greenwich Mean Time) as its epoch date. When TCP/IP programs exchange date or time of day they express time as the number of seconds past the epoch date.

ESP

(*Encapsulating Security Payload*) A packet format used by IPsec to send encrypted information.

Ethernet

A popular local area network technology invented at the Xerox Corporation Palo Alto Research Center. An Ethernet is a passive coaxial cable; the interconnections contain all active components. Ethernet is a best-effort delivery system that uses CSMA/CD technology. Xerox Corporation, Digital Equipment Corporation, and Intel Corporation developed and published the standard for 10 Mbps Ethernet. Originally, Ethernet used a coaxial cable. Later versions use a smaller coaxial cable (*thinnet*) or twisted pair cable (10Base-T).

Ethernet meltdown

An event that causes saturation or near saturation on an Ethernet. It usually results from illegal or misrouted packets, and typically lasts only a short time.

EUI-64

A 64-bit IEEE layer-2 addressing standard.

exponential backoff

See *binary exponential backoff*.

extension header

Any of the optional IPv6 headers that follows the base header.

eXternal Data Representation

See *XDR*.

extra hop problem

A routing problem in which a datagram takes an extra, unnecessary trip across a network. The problem can be difficult to detect because communication appears to work.

fair queueing

A well-known technique for controlling congestion in routers. Called "fair" because it restricts every host to an equal share of router bandwidth. Fair queueing is not completely satisfactory because it does not distinguish between small and large hosts or between hosts with a few active connections and those with many.

Fast Ethernet

A popular term for 100Base-T Ethernet.

FCCSET

(*Federal Coordinating Council for Science, Engineering, and Technology*) A government group noted for its report that called for high-speed computing and high-speed networking research.

FDDI

(*Fiber Distribution Data Interface*) A token ring network technology based on fiber optics. FDDI specifies a 100 Mbps data rate using 1300 nanometer light wavelength, and limits networks to approximately 200 km in length, with repeaters every 2 km or less.

FDM

(*Frequency Division Multiplexing*) The method of passing multiple, independent signals across a single medium by assigning each a unique carrier frequency. Hardware to combine signals is called a multiplexor; hardware to separate them is called a demultiplexor. Also see *TDM*.

file server

A process running on a computer that provides access to files on that computer to programs running on remote machines. The term is often applied loosely to computers that run file server programs.

FIN

A special TCP segment used to close a connection. Each side must send a FIN.

firewall

A configuration of routers and networks placed between an organization's internal internet and a connection to an external internet to provide security.

five-layer reference model

The protocol layering model used by TCP/IP. Although originally controversial, the success of TCP/IP has led to wide acceptance.

fixed-length subnetting

A subnet address assignment scheme in which all physical nets in an organization use the same mask. The alternative is *variable-length subnetting*.

flat namespace

Characteristic of any naming in which object names are selected from a single set of strings (e.g., street names in a typical city). Flat naming contrasts with hierarchical naming in which names are divided into subsections that correspond to the hierarchy of authority that administers them.

flow

A general term used to characterize a sequence of packets sent from a source to a destination. Some technologies define a separate flow for each pair of communicating applications, while others define a single flow to include all packets between a pair of hosts.

flow control

Control of the rate at which hosts or routers inject packets into a network or internet, usually to avoid congestion.

Ford-Fulkerson algorithm

A synonym for the distance-vector algorithm that refers to the researchers who discovered it.

forwarding

The process of accepting an incoming packet, looking up a next hop in a routing table, and sending the packet on to the next hop. IP routers perform datagram forwarding.

fragment extension header

An optional header used by IPv6 to mark a datagram as a fragment.

fragmentation

The process of dividing an IP datagram into smaller pieces when they must travel across a network that cannot handle the original datagram size. Each fragment has the same format as a datagram; fields in the IP header specify whether a datagram is a fragment, and if so, the offset of the fragment in the original datagram. IP software at the receiving end must reassemble fragments to produce the original datagram.

frame

Literally, a packet as it is transmitted across a serial line. The term derives from character oriented protocols that added special start-of-frame and end-of-frame characters when transmitting packets. We use the term throughout this book to refer to the objects that physical networks transmit.

Frame Relay

The name of a connection-oriented network technology that is offered by telephone companies.

FTP

(*File Transfer Protocol*) The TCP/IP standard, high-level protocol for transferring files from one machine to another. FTP uses TCP.

full duplex

Characteristic of a technology that allows simultaneous transfer of data in two directions. TCP provides full duplex connections.

FYI

(*For Your Information*) A subset of the RFCs that contain tutorials or general information about topics related to TCP/IP or the connected Internet.

gated

(*GATEway Daemon*) A program run on a router that uses an IGP to collect routing information from within one autonomous system and EGP to advertise the information to another autonomous system.

gateway

Any mechanism that connects two or more heterogeneous systems and translates among them. Originally, researchers used the term *IP gateway* for dedicated computers that route IP datagrams; vendors have adopted the term *IP router*.

gateway requirements

See *router requirements*.

Gbps

(*Giga Bits Per Second*) A measure of the rate of data transmission equal to 2^{30} bits per second. Also see *Kbps*, *Mbps*, and *baud*.

GGP

(*Gateway to Gateway Protocol*) The protocol originally used by core gateways to exchange routing information. GGP is now obsolete.

gopher

An early menu-driven information service used in the Internet.

GOSIP

(*Government Open Systems Interconnection Profile*) A U.S. government procurement document that specified agencies may use OSI protocols in new networks after August 1991. Although GOSIP was originally thought to eliminate the use of TCP/IP on government internets, clarifications have specified that government agencies can continue to use TCP/IP.

graceful shutdown

A protocol mechanism that allows two communicating parties to agree to terminate communication without confusion even if underlying packets are lost, delayed, or duplicated. TCP uses a 3-way handshake to guarantee graceful termination.

graft

An operation in which a multicast router joins a shared forwarding tree; the opposite of *prune*.

GRE

(*Generic Routing Encapsulation*) A scheme for encapsulating information in IP that includes IP-in-IP as one possibility.

H.323

An ITU recommendation for a suite of protocols used for IP telephony.

half duplex

Characteristic of a technology that only permits data transmission in one direction at a time. Compare to *full duplex*.

hardware address

The low-level addresses used by physical networks. Synonyms include *physical address* and *MAC address*. Each type of network hardware has its own addressing scheme (e.g., an Ethernet address is 48 bits).

header

Information at the beginning of a packet or message that describes the contents and specifies a destination.

HELLO

A protocol used on the original NSFNET backbone. Although obsolete, Hello is interesting because it uses delay as the routing metric and chooses a path with minimum delay.

HELO

The command on the initial exchange of the SMTP protocol.

hierarchical addressing

An addressing scheme in which an address can be subdivided into parts that each identify successively finer granularity. IP addresses use a two-level hierarchy in which the first part of the address identifies a network and the second part identifies a particular host on that network. Routers use the network portion to forward a datagram until the datagram reaches a router that can deliver it directly. Subnetting introduces additional levels of hierarchical routing.

historic

An IETF classification used to discourage the use of a protocol. In essence, a program that is declared historic is obsolete.

hold down

A short fixed time period following a change to a routing table during which no further changes are accepted. Hold down helps avoid routing loops.

hop count

A measure of distance between two points in an internet. A hop count of *n* means that *n* routers separate the source and destination.

hop limit

The IPv6 name for the datagram header field that IPv4 calls *time to live*. The hop limit, which prevents datagrams from following a routing loop forever, is decremented by each router along the path.

host

Any end-user computer system that connects to a network. Hosts include devices such as printers, small notebook computers, as well as large supercomputers. Compare to *router*.

host requirements

A long document that contains revisions and updates of many TCP/IP protocols. The host requirements document is published in a pair of RFCs. See *router requirements*.

host-specific route

An entry in a routing table that refers to a single host computer as opposed to routes that refer to a network, an IP subnet, or a default.

HTML

(*HyperText Markup Language*) The standard document format used for Web pages.

HTTP

(*Hypertext Transfer Protocol*) The protocol used to transfer Web documents from a server to a browser.

hub

An inexpensive electronic device to which multiple computers attach, usually using twisted pair wiring, to send and receive packets. A hub operates at layer 2 by replicating signals. Ethernet hubs are especially popular.

IAB

(*Internet Architecture Board*) A small group of people who set policy and direction for TCP/IP and the global Internet. The IAB was formerly known as the *Internet Activities Board*. See *IETF*.

IAC

(*Interpret As Command*) An escape used by TELNET to distinguish commands from normal data.

IANA

(*Internet Assigned Number Authority*) Essentially one individual (Jon Postel), IANA was originally responsible for assigning IP addresses and the constants used in TCP/IP protocols. Replaced by ICANN in 1999.

ICANN

(*Internet Corporation For Assigned Names and Numbers*) The organization that took over the IANA duties after Postel's death.

ICCB

(*Internet Control and Configuration Board*) A predecessor to the IAB.

ICMP

(*Internet Control Message Protocol*) An integral part of the Internet Protocol (IP) that handles error and control messages. Specifically, routers and hosts use ICMP to send reports of problems about datagrams back to the original source that sent the datagram. ICMP also includes an echo request/reply used to test whether a destination is reachable and responding.

ICMPv6

(*Internet Control Message Protocol version 6*) The version of ICMP that has been defined for use with IPv6.

IEN

(*Internet Engineering Notes*) A series of notes developed in parallel to RFCs. Although the series is obsolete, some IENs contain early discussion of TCP/IP and the Internet not found in RFCs.

IESG

(*Internet Engineering Steering Group*) A committee consisting of the IETF chairperson and the area managers. The IESG coordinates activities among the IETF working groups.

IETF

(*Internet Engineering Task Force*) A group of people under the IAB who work on the design and engineering of TCP/IP and the global Internet. The IETF is divided into areas, which each has an independent manager. Areas are further divided into working groups.

IGMP

(*Internet Group Management Protocol*) A protocol that hosts use to keep local routers apprised of their membership in multicast groups. When all hosts leave a group, routers no longer forward datagrams that arrive for the group.

IGP

(*Interior Gateway Protocol*) The generic term applied to any protocol used to propagate network reachability and routing information within an autonomous system. Although there is no single standard IGP, RIP is among the most popular.

IMP

(*Interface Message Processor*) The original term for packet switches in the ARPANET; now loosely applied to a switch in any packet network.

InATMARP

(*Inverse ATM ARP*) Part of the address resolution protocol needed for non-broadcast multiple access networks such as ATM.

indirect delivery

Delivery of a datagram through a router as opposed to a direct transmission from the source host to the destination host.

INOC

(*Internet Network Operations Center*) Originally, a group of people at BBN that monitored and controlled the Internet core gateway system. Now applied to any group that monitors an internet.

inter-autonomous system routing

Also known as exterior routing. BGP-4 is currently the most popular protocol for exterior routing.

International Organization for Standardization

See *ISO*.

International Telecommunications Union (ITU)

An international organization that sets standards for interconnection of telephone equipment. It defined the standards for X.25 network protocols. (Note: in Europe, *PTT*s offer both voice telephone services and X.25 network services).

internet

Physically, a collection of packet switching networks interconnected by routers along with TCP/IP protocols that allow them to function logically as a single, large, virtual network. When written in upper case, Internet refers specifically to the global Internet.

Internet

The collection of networks and routers that spans over 200 countries, and uses TCP/IP protocols to form a single, cooperative virtual network.

Internet address

See *IP address*.

Internet Draft

A draft document generated by the IETF; if approved, the document will become an RFC.

Internet Protocol

See IP.

Internet Society

The non-profit organization established to foster interest in the Internet. The Internet Society is the host organization of the IAB.

Internet worm

A program designed to travel across the Internet and replicate itself endlessly. When a student released the Internet worm, it made the Internet and many attached computers useless for hours.

interoperability

The ability of software and hardware on multiple machines from multiple vendors to communicate meaningfully. This term best describes the goal of internetworking, namely, to define an abstract, hardware independent networking environment that makes it possible to build distributed computations that interact at the network transport level without knowing the details of underlying technologies.

Intranet

A private corporate network consisting of hosts, routers, and networks that use TCP/IP technology. An intranet may or may not connect to the global Internet.

IP

(*Internet Protocol*) The TCP/IP standard protocol that defines the IP datagram as the unit of information passed across an internet and provides the basis for connection-less, best-effort packet delivery service. IP includes the ICMP control and error message protocol as an integral part. The entire protocol suite is often referred to as TCP/IP because TCP and IP are the two fundamental protocols.

IP address

A 32-bit address assigned to each host that participates in a TCP/IP internet. IP addresses are the abstraction of physical hardware addresses just as an internet is an abstraction of physical networks. To make routing efficient, each IP address is divided into a network portion and a host portion.

IP datagram

The basic unit of information passed across a TCP/IP internet. An IP datagram is to an internet as a hardware packet is to a physical network — each datagram contains a source and destination address along with data.

IP gateway

A synonym for *IP router*.

IP-in-IP

The encapsulation of one IP datagram inside another for transmission through a tunnel. IP in IP is often used to send multicast datagrams across the Internet.

IP multicast

An addressing and forwarding scheme that allows transmission of IP datagrams to a subset of hosts. The Internet currently does not have extensive facilities for routing IP multicast.

IP router

A device that connects two or more (possibly heterogeneous) networks and passes IP traffic between them. As the name implies, a router looks up the datagram's destination address in a routing table to choose a next hop.

IP switching

Originally a high-speed IP forwarding technology developed by Ipsilon Corporation, now generally used in reference to any of several similar technologies.

IP telephony

A telephone system that uses IP to transport digitized voice.

IPng

(*Internet Protocol — the Next Generation*) A term applied to all the activities surrounding the specification and standardization of the next version of IP. Also see *IPv6*.

IPsec

(*IP SECurity*) A security standard that allows the sender to choose to authenticate or encrypt a datagram. IPsec can be used with either IPv4 or IPv6.

IPv4

(*Internet Protocol version 4*). The official name of the current version of IP.

IPv6

(*Internet Protocol version 6*). The name of the next version of IP. Also see *IPng*.

IRSG

(*Internet Research Steering Group*) The group of people who head the IRTF.

IRTF

(*Internet Research Task Force*) A group of people working on research problems related to TCP/IP and the connected Internet. The IRTF is not as active as the IETF.

ISDN

(*Integrated Services Digital Network*) The name of the digital network service that telephone carriers provide.

ISO

(*International Organization for Standardization*) An international body that drafts, discusses, proposes, and specifies standards for network protocols. ISO is best know for its 7-layer reference model that describes the conceptual organization of protocols. Although it has proposed a suite of protocols for Open System Interconnection, the OSI protocols have not been widely accepted in the commercial market.

ISOC

Abbreviation for *Internet SOCiety*.

isochronous

Characteristic of a network system that does not introduce jitter. The conventional telephone system is isochronous.

ISODE

(*ISO Development Environment*) Software that provides an ISO transport level protocol interface on top of TCP/IP. ISODE was designed to allow researchers to experiment with ISO's higher-level OSI protocols without requiring an internet that supports the lower levels of the OSI suite.

ISP

(*Internet Service Provider*) Any organization that sells Internet access, either permanent connectivity or dialup access.

ITU

Abbreviation for the *International Telecommunication Union*, a standards organization.

jitter

A technical term used to describe unwanted variance in delay caused when one packet in a sequence must be delayed more than another. The typical cause of jitter is other traffic on a network.

Karn's Algorithm

An algorithm that allows transport protocols to distinguish between valid and invalid round-trip time samples, and thus improve round-trip estimations.

Kbps

(*Kilo Bits Per Second*) A measure of the rate of data transmission equal to 2^{10} bits per second. Also see *Gbps*, *Mbps*, and *baud*.

keepalive

A small message sent periodically between two communicating entities to ensure that network connectivity remains intact and that both sides are still responding. BGP uses keepalives.

LAN

(*Local Area Network*) Any physical network technology designed to span short distances (up to a few thousand meters). Usually, LANs operate at tens of megabits per second through several gigabits per second. Examples include Ethernet and FDDI. See *MAN* and *WAN*.

layer 1

A reference to the hardware interface layer of communication. The name is derived from the ISO 7-layer reference model. Layer 1 specifications refer to physical connections, including connector configuration and voltages on wires. (Sometimes called *level 1*.)

layer 2

In the ISO 7-layer model, a reference to link level communication (e.g., frame format). In the TCP/IP 5-layer model, layer 2 refers to physical frame format and addressing. Thus, a layer 2 address is a MAC address (e.g., an Ethernet address).

layer 3

In the ISO 7-layer model, a reference to the network layer. In the TCP/IP 5-layer model, a reference to the internet layer (IP and the IP datagram format). Thus, an IP address is a layer 3 address.

leaf

A graph-theoretic term for a router or a network at the ''edge'' of an internet.

link-local address

An address used with IPv6 that has significance only on a single network.

link state routing

One of two approaches used by routing protocols in which routers broadcast status messages and use Dijkstra's SPF algorithm to compute shortest paths. See *distance vector routing*.

link status routing

A synonym for *link state routing*.

LIS

(*Logical IP Subnet*) A group of computers connected via ATM that use ATM as an isolated local network. A computer in one LIS cannot send a datagram directly to a computer in another LIS.

little endian

A format for storage or transmission of binary data in which the least-significant byte (bit) comes first. See *big endian*.

LLC

(*Logical Link Control*) One of the fields in an NSAP header.

logical subnet

An abbreviation of *Logical IP Subnet* (*LIS*).

long haul network

Older term for *wide area network* (*WAN*).

longest-prefix matching

The technique used by IP routers when searching a routing table. Among all entries that match the destination address, a router picks the one that has the longest subnet mask.

loopback address

A network address used for testing which causes outgoing data to be processed by the local protocol software without sending packets. IP uses 127.0.0.0 as the loop-back prefix.

LSR

(*Loose Source Route*) An IP option that contains a list of router addresses that the datagram must visit in order. Unlike a strict source route, a loose source route allows the datagram to pass through additional routers not on the list. See *SSR*.

MABR

(*Multicast Area Border Router*) The MOSPF term for a multicast router that exchanges routing information with another area.

MAC

(*Media Access Control*) A general reference to the low-level hardware protocols used to access a particular network. The term *MAC address* is often used as a synonym for *physical address*.

mail bridge

Informal term used as a synonym for a *mail gateway*.

mail exchanger

A computer that accepts e-mail; some mail exchangers forward the mail to other computers. DNS has a separate address type for mail exchangers.

mail exploder

Part of an electronic mail system that accepts a piece of mail and a list of addresses as input and sends a copy of the message to each address on the list. Most electronic mail systems incorporate a mail exploder to allow users to define mailing lists locally.

mail gateway

A machine that connects to two or more electronic mail systems (especially dissimilar mail systems on two different networks) and transfers mail messages among them. Mail gateways usually capture an entire mail message, reformat it according to the rules of the destination mail system, and then forward the message.

MAN

(*Metropolitan Area Network*) Any physical network technology that operates at high speeds (usually hundreds of megabits per second through several gigabits per second) over distances sufficient for a metropolitan area. See *LAN* and *WAN*.

Management Information Base

See *MIB*.

martians

Humorous term applied to packets that turn up unexpectedly on the wrong network, often because of incorrect routing tables.

mask

See *subnet mask*.

maximum transfer unit

See *MTU*.

MBONE

(*Multicast BackBONE*). A cooperative agreement among sites to forward multicast datagrams across the Internet by use of IP tunneling.

Mbps

(*Millions of Bits Per Second*) A measure of the rate of data transmission equal to 2^{20} bits per second. Also see *Gbps*, *Kbps*, and *baud*.

MIB

(*Management Information Base*) The set of variables (database) that a system running an SNMP agent maintains. Managers can fetch or store into these variables.

MILNET

(*MILitary NETwork*) Originally part of the ARPANET, MILNET was partitioned in 1984.

MIME

(*Multipurpose Internet Mail Extensions*) A standard used to encode data such as images as printable ASCII text for transmission through e-mail.

mobile IP

A technology developed by the IETF to permit a computer to travel to a new site while retaining its original IP address. The computer contacts a server to obtain a second, temporary address, and then arranges for all datagrams to be forwarded to it.

Mosaic

An early Web browser program.

MOSPF

(*Multicast Open Shortest Path First*) Multicast Extensions to the OSPF routing protocol.

MPLS

(*Multi-Protocol Label Switching*) A technology that uses high speed switching hardware to carry IP datagrams. MPLS is descended from IP switching and label switching.

mrouted

(*Multicast ROUTE Daemon*) A program used with a protocol stack that supports IP multicast to establish multicast routing.

MSL

(*Maximum Segment Lifetime*) The longest time a datagram can survive in the Internet. Protocols use the MSL to guarantee a bound on the time duplicate packets can survive.

MSS

(*Maximum Segment Size*) A term used with TCP. The MSS is the largest amount of data that can be transmitted in one segment. Sender and receiver negotiate maximum segment size at connection startup.

MTU

(*Maximum Transfer Unit* or *Maximum Transmission Unit*) The largest amount of data that can be transferred across a given physical network. The MTU is determined by the network hardware.

multi-homed host

A host using TCP/IP that has connections to two or more physical networks.

multicast

A technique that allows copies of a single packet to be passed to a selected subset of all possible destinations. Some hardware (e.g., Ethernet) supports multicast by allowing a network interface to belong to one or more multicast groups. IP supports an internet multicast facility.

multiplex

To combine data from several sources into a single stream in such a way that it can be separated again later. Multiplexing occurs at many levels. See *demultiplex*.

multiplicative decrease

A technique used by TCP to reduce transmission when congestion occurs. TCP decreases the size of the effective window by half each time a segment is lost.

NACK

(*Negative Acknowledgement*) A response from the recipient of data to the sender of that data to indicate that the transmission was unsuccessful (e.g., that the data was corrupted by transmission errors). Usually, a NACK triggers retransmission of the lost data.

Nagle algorithm

A self-clocking heuristic that clumps outgoing data to improve throughput and avoid silly window syndrome.

NAK

Synonym for *NACK*.

name resolution

The process of mapping a name into a corresponding address. The domain name system provides a mechanism for naming computers in which programs use remote name servers to resolve a machine name into an IP address.

NAP

(*Network Access Point*) One of several physical locations where ISPs interconnect their networks. A NAP also includes a route server that supplies each ISP with reachability information from the routing arbiter system. In addition to NAPs, many ISPs now have private peering arrangements.

NAT

(*Network Address Translation*) A technology that allows hosts with private addresses to communicate with an outside network such as the global Internet.

NBMA

(*Non-Broadcast Multi-Access*). A characteristic of a network that connects multiple computers but does not supply hardware-level broadcast. ATM is the prime example of a NBMA network.

Net 10 address

A general reference to a nonroutable address (i.e., one that is reserved for use in an intranet and not used on the global Internet). The prefix 10.0.0.0 was formerly assigned to ARPANET; it was designated as a nonroutable address when the ARPANET ceased operation.

NetBIOS

(*Network Basic Input Output System*) NetBIOS is the standard interface to networks on IBM PC and compatible personal computers. TCP/IP includes guidelines that describe how to map NetBIOS operations into equivalent TCP/IP operations.

network byte order

The TCP/IP standard for transmission of integers that specifies the most significant byte appears first (big endian). Sending machines are required to translate from the local integer representation to network byte order, and receiving machines are required to translate from network byte order to the local machine representation.

network management

See *MIB* and *SNMP*.

Next Header

A field used in IPv6 to specify the type of the item that follows.

NFS

(*Network File System*) A protocol originally developed by SUN Microsystems, Incorporated that uses IP to allow a set of cooperating computers to access each other's file systems as if they were local.

NIC

(*Network Interface Card*) A hardware device that plugs into the bus on a computer and connects the computer to a network.

NIST

(*National Institute of Standards and Technology*) Formerly, the National Bureau of Standards. NIST is one standards organization within the US that establishes standards for network protocols.

NLA

(*Next Level Aggregation*) In IPv6 addressing, the third most significant set of bits in a unicast address. Also see *TLA*.

NOC

(*Network Operations Center*) Originally, the organization at BBN that monitored and controlled several networks that formed part of the global Internet. Now, used for any organization that manages a network.

nonroutable address

Any address that uses one of the network prefixes which are reserved for use in intranets. Routers in the global Internet will report an error if a datagram containing a nonroutable address accidentally reaches them. See *net-10 address*.

NSAP

(*Network Service Access Point*) An address format that can be encoded in 20 octets. The ATM Forum recommends using NSAP addresses.

NSF

(*National Science Foundation*) A U.S. government agency that funded some of the research and development of the Internet.

NSFNET

(*National Science Foundation NETwork*) Used to describe the Internet backbone in the U.S., which is supported by NSF.

NVT

(*Network Virtual Terminal*) The character-oriented protocol used by TELNET.

OC series standards

A series of standards for the transmission of data over optical fiber. For example, the popular OC3 standard has a bit rate of approximately 155 million bits per second.

octet

An 8-bit unit of data. Although engineers frequently use the term *byte* as a synonym for octet, a byte can be smaller or larger than 8 bits.

one-armed router

An IP router that understands two addressing domains, but only has one physical network connection. One-armed routers are typically used to add security or address translation rather than to forward packets between networks. Also called a *one-armed firewall*.

OSI

(*Open Systems Interconnection*) A reference to protocols developed by ISO as a competitor for TCP/IP. They are not widely deployed or supported.

OSPF

(*Open Shortest Path First*) A link state routing protocol design by the IETF.

OUI

(*Organizationally Unique Identifier*) Part of an address assigned to an organization that manufactures network hardware; the organization assigns a unique address to each device by using its OUI plus a suffix number.

out of band data

Data sent outside the normal delivery path, often used to carry abnormal or error indicators. TCP has an *urgent data* facility for sending out-of-band data.

packet

Used loosely to refer to any small block of data sent across a packet switching network.

packet filter

A mechanism in a router that can be configured to reject some types of packets and admit others. Packet filters are used to create a security firewall.

path MTU

The minimum MTU along a path from the source to destination, which specifies the largest datagram that can be sent along the path without fragmentation. The standard recommends that IP use Path MTU Discovery.

PCM

(*Pulse Code Modulation*) A standard for voice encoding used in digital telephony that produces 8000 8-bit samples per second.

PDN

(*Public Data Network*) A network service offered by a common carrier.

PDU

(*Packet Data Unit*) An ISO term used for either packet or message.

peering arrangement

An cooperative agreement between two ISPs to exchange both reachability information and data packets. In addition to peering at NAPs, large ISPs often have private peering arrangements.

PEM

(*Privacy Enchanced Mail*) A protocol for encrypting e-mail to prevent others from reading messages as they travel across an internet.

perimeter security

A network security mechanism that places a firewall at each connection between a site and outside networks.

physical address

A synonym for *MAC address* or *hardware address*.

PIM-DM

(*Protocol Independent Multicast Dense Mode*) A data-driven multicast routing protocol similar to DVMRP.

PIM-SM

(*Protocol Independent Multicast Sparse Mode*) A demand-driven multicast routing protocol that extends the ideas in CBT.

PING

(*Packet InterNet Groper*) The name of a program used with TCP/IP internets to test reachability of destinations by sending them an ICMP echo request and waiting for a reply. The term is now used like a verb as in, "please ping host *A* to see if it is alive."

playback point

The minimum amount of data required in a jitter buffer before playback can begin.

point-to-point network

Any network technology such as a serial line that connects exactly two machines. Point-to-point networks do not require attached computers to have a hardware address.

poison reverse

A heuristic used by distance-vector protocols such as RIP to avoid routing loops. When a route disappears, instead of simply removing the route from its advertisement, a router advertises that the destination is no longer reachable.

POP

(*Post Office Protocol*) The protocol used to access and extract e-mail from a mailbox.

port

See *protocol port*.

positive acknowledgement

Synonym for *acknowledgement*.

POTS

(*Plain Old Telephone Service*) A reference to the standard voice telephone system.

PPP

(*Point to Point Protocol*) A protocol for framing IP when sending across a serial line. Also see *SLIP*.

promiscuous ARP

See *proxy ARP*.

promiscuous mode

A feature of network interface hardware that allows a computer to receive all packets on the network.

protocol

A formal description of message formats and the rules two or more machines must follow to exchange those messages. Protocols can describe low-level details of machine to machine interfaces (e.g., the order in which the bits from a byte are sent across a wire), or high-level exchanges between application programs (e.g., the way in which two programs transfer a file across an internet). Most protocols include both intuitive descriptions of the expected interactions as well as more formal specifications using finite state machine models.

protocol port

The abstraction that TCP/IP transport protocols use to distinguish among multiple destinations within a given host computer. TCP/IP protocols identify ports using small positive integers. Usually, the operating system allows an application program to specify which port it wants to use. Some ports are reserved for standard services (e.g., electronic mail).

provider prefix

An addressing scheme in which an ISP owns a prefix of an address and assigns each customer addresses that begin with the prefix. IPv6 offers provider prefix addressing.

provisioned service

A service that is configured manually.

proxy

Any device or system that acts in place of another (e.g., a proxy Web server acts in place of another Web server).

proxy ARP

The technique in which one machine, usually a router, answers ARP requests intended for another by supplying its own physical address. By pretending to be another machine, the router accepts responsibility for forwarding packets. The purpose of proxy ARP is to allow a site to use a single IP network address with multiple physical networks.

prune

An operation in which a multicast router removes itself from a shared forwarding tree; the opposite of *graft*.

pseudo header

Source and destination IP address information sent in the IP header, but included in a TCP or UDP checksum.

PSN

(*Packet Switching Node*) The formal name of ARPANET packet switches that replaced the original term *IMP*.

PSTN

(*Public Switched Telephone Network*) The standard voice telephone system.

public key encryption

An encryption technique that generates encryption keys in pairs. One of the pair must be kept secret, and one is published.

PUP

(*Parc Universal Packet*) In the internet system developed by Xerox Corporation, a PUP is the fundamental unit of transfer, like an IP datagram is in a TCP/IP internet. The name was derived from the name of the laboratory at which the Xerox internet was developed, the Palo Alto Research Center (PARC).

push

The operation an application performs on a TCP connection to force data to be sent immediately. A bit in the segment header marks pushed data.

PVC

(*Permanent Virtual Circuit*) The type of virtual circuit established by an administrator rather than by software in a computer. Unlike an SVC, a PVC lasts a long time (e.g., weeks or months).

QoS

(*Quality of Service*) Bounds on the loss, delay, jitter, and minimum throughput that a network guarantees to deliver. Some proponents argue that QoS is necessary for real-time traffic.

RA

See *routing arbiter*.

RARP

(*Reverse Address Resolution Protocol*) A protocol that can be used at startup to find an IP address. Although once popular, most computers now use *BOOTP* or *DHCP* instead.

RDP

(*Reliable Datagram Protocol*) A protocol that provides reliable datagram service on top of the standard unreliable datagram service that IP provides. RDP is not among the most widely implemented TCP/IP protocols.

reachability

A network is "reachable" from a given host if a datagram can be sent from the host to a destination on the network. Exterior routing protocols exchange reachability information.

reassembly

The process of collecting all the fragments of an IP datagram and using them to create a copy of the original datagram. The ultimate destination performs reassembly.

RED

(*Random Early Discard*) A technique routers use instead of tail-drop when their queue overflows to improve TCP performance. As the queue fills, the router begins discarding datagrams at random.

redirect

An ICMP message sent from a router to a host on a local network to instruct the host to change a route.

reference model

A description of how layered protocols fit together. TCP/IP uses a 5-layer reference model; earlier protocols used the ISO 7-layer reference model.

regional network

A network that covers a medium-size geographical area such as a few cities or a state.

reliable multicast

A multicast delivery system that guarantees reliable transfer to every member.

reliable transfer

Characteristic of a mechanism that guarantees to deliver data without loss, without corruption, without duplication, and in the same order as it was sent, or to inform the sender that delivery is impossible.

repeater

A hardware device that extends a LAN. A repeater copies electrical signals from one physical network to another. No longer popular.

replay

An error situation in which packets from a previous session are erroneously accepted as part of a later session. Protocols that do not prevent replay are not secure.

reserved address

A synonym for *nonroutable address*.

reset

A segment sent by TCP to report an error.

resolution

See *address resolution*

RFC

(*Request For Comments*) The name of a series of notes that contain surveys, measurements, ideas, techniques, and observations, as well as proposed and accepted TCP/IP protocol standards. RFCs are available on-line.

RIP

(*Routing Information Protocol*) A protocol used to propagate routing information inside an autonomous system. RIP derives from an earlier protocol of the same name developed at Xerox.

RJE

(*Remote Job Entry*) A service that allows submission of a (batch) job from a remote site.

rlogin

(*Remote LOGIN*) The remote login protocol developed for UNIX by Berkeley. Rlogin offers essentially the same service as TELNET.

ROADS

(*Running Out of ADdress Space*) A reference to the possible exhaustion of the IPv4 address space.

round trip time

The total time required to traverse a network from a source computer to a destination and back to the source. TCP uses round trip times to compute a retransmission timer.

route

In general, a route is the path that network traffic takes from its source to its destination. In a TCP/IP internet, each IP datagram is routed independently; routes can change dynamically.

route aggregation

The technique used by routing protocols to combine multiple destinations that have the same next hop into a single entry. A default route provides the highest degree of aggregation.

route server

A server that operates at a NAP and uses BGP to communicate reachability information from the routing arbiter database.

routed

(*Route Daemon*) A program devised for UNIX that implements the RIP protocol. Pronounced "route-d."

router

A special purpose, dedicated computer that attaches to two or more networks and forwards packets from one to the other. In particular, an IP router forwards IP datagrams among the networks to which it connects. A router uses the destination address on a datagram to choose a next-hop to which it forwards the datagram. Researchers originally used the term *gateway*.

router alert

An IP option that causes each intermediate router to examine a datagram even if the datagram is not destined to the router.

router requirements

A document that contains updates to TCP/IP protocols used in routers. See *host requirements*.

routing arbiter

A replicated, authenticated database that contains all possible routes in the Internet. Each ISP that connects to a NAP uses BGP to communicate with a route server to obtain information.

routing loop

An error condition in which a cycle of routers each has the next router in the cycle as the shortest path to a given destination.

RP

(*Rendezvous Point*) The router used as a target for a join request in a demand-driven multicast scheme.

RPB

(*Reverse Path Broadcast*) A synonym for *RPF*.

RPC

(*Remote Procedure Call*) A technology in which a program invokes services across a network by making modified procedure calls. The NFS protocol uses a specific type of RPC.

RPF

(*Reverse Path Forwarding*) A technique used to propagate broadcast packets that ensures there are no routing loops. IP uses reverse path forwarding to propagate subnet broadcast and multicast datagrams.

RPM

(*Reverse Path Multicast*) A general approach to multicasting that uses the TRPB algorithm.

RS

See *route server*.

RS232

A standard by EIA that specifies the electrical characteristics of slow speed interconnections between terminals and computers or between two computers. Although the standard commonly used is RS232C, most people refer to it as RS232.

RST

(*ReSeT*) A common abbreviation for a TCP *reset* segment.

RSVP

(*Resource ReserVation Protocol*) The protocol that allows an endpoint to request a flow with specific QoS; routers along the path to the destination must agree before they approve the request.

RTCP

(*RTP Control Protocol*) The companion protocol to RTP used to control a session.

RTO

(*Round trip Time-Out*) The delay used before retransmission. TCP computes RTO as a function of the current round trip time and variance.

RTP

(*Real-time Transport Protocol*) The primary protocol used to transfer real-time data such as voice and video over IP.

RTT

(*Round Trip Time*) A measure of delay between two hosts. The round trip time consists of the total time taken for a single packet or datagram to leave one machine, reach the other, and return. In most packet switching networks, delays vary as a result of congestion. Thus, a measure of round trip time is an average, which can have high standard deviation.

SA

(*Security Association*) Used with IPsec to denote a binding between a set of security parameters and an identifier carried in a datagram header. A host chooses SA bindings; they are not globally standardized. See *SPI*.

SACK

(*Selective ACKnowledgement*) An acknowledgement mechanism used with sliding window protocols that allows the receiver to acknowledge packets received out of order, but within the current sliding window. Also called extended acknowledgement. Compare to the *cumulative acknowledgement* scheme used by TCP.

SAR

(*Segmentation And Reassembly*) The process of dividing a message into cells, sending them across an ATM network, and reforming the original message. AAL5 performs SAR when sending IP across an ATM network.

segment

The unit of transfer sent from TCP on one machine to TCP on another. Each segment contains part of a stream of bytes being sent between the machines as well as additional fields that identify the current position in the stream and a checksum to ensure validity of received data.

selective acknowledgement

See SACK.

self clocking

Characteristic of any system that operates periodically without requiring an external clock (e.g., uses the arrival of a packet to trigger an action).

self-healing

Characteristic of a mechanism that overcomes failure automatically. A dual FDDI ring is self-healing because it can accommodate failure of a station or a link.

self-identifying frame

Any network frame or packet that includes a field to identify the type of the data being carried. Ethernet uses self-identifying frames, but ATM does not.

server

A running program that supplies service to clients over a network. Examples include providing access to files or to World Wide Web pages.

seven-layer reference model

See *ISO*.

SGMP

(*Simple Gateway Monitoring Protocol*) A predecessor of SNMP.

shared tree

A forwarding scheme used by demand-driven multicast routing protocols. A shared tree is an alternative to a shortest path tree.

shortest path routing

Routing in which datagrams are directed over the shortest path; all routing protocols try to compute shortest paths. Also see *SPF*.

shortest path tree

The multicast forwarding tree that is optimal from a given source to all members of the group. A shortest path trees is an alternative to a shared tree.

signaling

A telephony term that refers to protocols which establish a circuit.

silly window syndrome

A condition that can arise in TCP in which the receiver repeatedly advertises a small window and the sender repeatedly sends a small segment to fill it. The resulting transmission of small segments makes inefficient use of network bandwidth.

SIP

(*Session Initiation Protocol*) A protocol devised by the IEFT for signaling in IP telephony. (Note: SIP was formerly used to refer to *Simple IP*, a protocol that served as the basis for IPv6.)

SIPP

(*SIP Plus*) An extension of *Simple IP* that was proposed for IPv6. See *IPv6*.

site-local address

An address used with IPv6 that has significance only at a single site.

sliding window

Characteristic of protocols that allow a sender to transmit more than one packet of data before receiving an acknowledgement. After receiving an acknowledgement for the first packet sent, the sender ''slides'' the packet window and sends another. The number of outstanding packets or bytes is known as the window size; increasing the window size improves throughput.

SLIP

(*Serial Line IP*) A framing protocol used to send IP across a serial line. SLIP is popular when sending IP over dialup phone lines. See *PPP*.

slow convergence

A problem in distance-vector protocols in which two or more routers form a routing loop that persists until the routing protocols increment the distance to infinity.

slow-start

A congestion avoidance scheme in TCP in which TCP increases its window size as ACKs arrive. The term is a slight misnomer because slow-start achieves high throughput by using exponential increases.

SMDS

(*Switched Multimegabit Data Service*) A connectionless packet service developed by regional telephone companies.

SMI

(*Structure of Management Information*) Rules that describe the form of MIB variables.

SMTP

(*Simple Mail Transfer Protocol*) The TCP/IP standard protocol for transferring electronic mail messages from one machine to another. SMTP specifies how two mail systems interact and the format of control messages they exchange to transfer mail.

SNA

(*System Network Architecture*) The name applied to an architecture and a class of network products offered by IBM Corporation. SNA does not interoperate with TCP/IP.

SNAP

(*SubNetwork Attachment Point*) An IEEE standard for a small header that is added to data when sending across a network that does not have self-identifying frames. The SNAP header specifies the type of the data.

SNMP

(*Simple Network Management Protocol*) A protocol used to manage devices such as hosts, routers, and printers. A specific version is denoted with a suffix (e.g., SNMPv3). Also see *MIB*.

SOA

(*Start Of Authority*) A keyword used with DNS to denote the beginning of the records for which a particular server is the authority. Other records in the server are reported as non-authoritative answers.

socket API

The set of procedures an application uses to communicate over a TCP/IP network. The name is derived from an abstraction offered by the Unix operating system.

soft state

A technique in which a receiver times out information rather than depending on the sender to maintain it. Soft state works well when the sender and receiver become disconnected.

source quench

A congestion control technique in which a machine experiencing congestion sends a message back to the source of the packets requesting that the source stop transmitting. In a TCP/IP internet, routers send an ICMP source quench message when a datagram overruns the input queue.

source route

A route that is determined by the source. In IP, a source route consists of a list of routers a datagram should visit; the route is specified as an IP option. Source routing is most often used for debugging. See *LSR* and *SSR*.

source tree

A synonym for *shortest path tree*.

SPF

(*Shortest Path First*) A class of routing update protocols that uses Dijkstra's algorithm to compute shortest paths. See *link state routing*.

SPI

(*Security Parameters Index*) The identifier IPsec uses to specify the Security Association that should be used to process a datagram.

split horizon update

A heuristic used by distance-vector protocols such as RIP to avoid routing loops. Routes are not advertised over the interface from which they were learned.

SS7

(*Signaling System 7*) The conventional telephone system standard used for signaling.

SSL

(*Secure Sockets Layer*) A de facto standard for secure communication created by Netscape, Inc. SSL was an Internet Draft, but did not become an RFC.

SSR

(*Strict Source Route*) An IP option that contains a list of router addresses that the datagram must visit in order. See *LSR*.

standard byte order

See *network byte order*.

STD

(*STanDard*) The designation used to classify a particular RFC as describing a standard protocol.

store-and-forward

The paradigm used by IP routers in which an incoming datagram is stored in memory until it can be forwarded on toward its destination.

subnet addressing

An extension of the IP addressing scheme that allows a site to use a single IP network address for multiple physical networks. Outside of the site using subnet addressing, routing continues as usual by dividing the destination address into a network portion and a local portion. Routers and hosts inside a site using subnet addressing interpret the local portion of the address by dividing it into a physical network portion and a host portion.

subnet mask

A bit mask used to select the bits from an IP address that correspond to the subnet. Each mask is 32 bits long, with one bits in the portion that identifies a network and zero bits in the portion that identifies a host.

SubNetwork Attachment Point

See *SNAP*.

supernet addressing

Another name for *CIDR*.

SVC

(*Switched Virtual Circuit*) The type of virtual circuit established dynamically and terminated when no longer needed; usually software in a computer requests an SVC. Unlike a PVC, an SVC can have a short duration.

SWS

See *silly window syndrome*.

SYN

(*SYNchronizing segment*) The first segment sent by the TCP protocol, it is used to synchronize the two ends of a connection in preparation for opening a connection.

T3

The telephony designation for a protocol used over DS3-speed lines. The term is often used (incorrectly) as a synonym for DS3.

tail drop

A policy routers use to manage queue overflow which simply discards all datagrams that arrive after the queue is full. More harmful to TCP throughput than RED.

TCP

(*Transmission Control Protocol*) The TCP/IP standard transport level protocol that provides the reliable, full duplex, stream service on which many application protocols depend. TCP allows a process on one machine to send a stream of data to a process on another. TCP is connection-oriented in the sense that before transmitting data, participants must establish a connection. All data travels in TCP segments, which each travel across the Internet in an IP datagram. The entire protocol suite is often referred to as TCP/IP because TCP and IP are the two fundamental protocols.

TCP/IP Internet Protocol Suite

The official name of the TCP/IP protocols.

TDM

(*Time Division Multiplexing*) A technique used to multiplex multiple signals onto a single hardware transmission channel by allowing each signal to use the channel for a short time before going on to the next one. Also see *FDM*.

TDMA

(*Time Division Multiple Access*) A method of network access in which time is divided into slots and each node on the network is assigned one of the slots. Because all nodes using TDMA must synchronize exactly (even though the network introduces propagation delays between them), TDMA technologies are difficult to design and the equipment is expensive.

TELNET

The TCP/IP standard protocol for remote terminal service. TELNET allows a user at one site to interact with a remote timesharing system at another site as if the user's keyboard and display connected directly to the remote machine.

TFTP

(*Trivial File Transfer Protocol*) The TCP/IP standard protocol for file transfer with minimal capability and minimal overhead. TFTP depends only on the unreliable, connectionless datagram delivery service (UDP), so it is designed for use on a local network.

thicknet

Used to refer to the original thick coaxial cable used with 10Base5 Ethernet. See *thinnet*, *10Base2*, and *10Base-T*.

thinnet

Used to refer to the thinner, more flexible coaxial cable used with 10Base2 Ethernet. See *thicknet*, *10Base5*, and *10Base-T*.

three-way handshake

The 3-segment exchange TCP uses to reliably start or gracefully terminate a connection.

TLA

(*Top Level Aggregation*) In IPv6 addressing, the second most significant set of bits in a unicast address. Also see *NLA*.

TLI

(*Transport Layer Interface*) An alternative to the socket interface defined for System V UNIX.

TLV encoding

Any representation format that encodes each item with three fields: a type, a length, and a value. IP options often use TLV encoding.

tn3270

A version of TELNET for use with IBM 3270 terminals.

token ring

When used in the generic sense, a type of network technology that controls media access by passing a distinguished packet, called a token, from machine to machine. A computer can only transmit a packet when holding the token. When used in a specific sense, it refers to the token ring network hardware produced by IBM.

TOS

(*Type Of Service*) A reference to the original interpretation of the field in an IPv4 header that allows the sender to specify the type of service desired. Now replaced by *DiffServe*.

TP-4

A protocol designed by ISO to be similar to TCP.

traceroute

A program that prints the path to a destination. Traceroute sends a sequence of datagrams with the Time-To-Live set to 1, 2, etc., and uses the ICMP TIME EX-CEEDED messages that are returned to determine routers along the path.

traffic class

A reference to a set of services available in the *DiffServe* interpretation.

traffic policing

A reference to mechanisms used with systems that guarantee QoS. Incoming traffic is measured, and any traffic that exceeds the agreed bounds is discarded.

traffic shaping

A reference to mechanisms used with systems that guarantee QoS. Incoming traffic is placed in a buffer and clocked out at a fixed rate.

trailer encapsulation

A nonconventional method of encapsulating IP datagrams for transmission in which the "header" information is placed at the end of the packet. Trailers have been used with Ethernet to aid in aligning data on page boundaries. ATM's AAL5 uses trailers.

transceiver

A device that connects a host interface to a local area network (e.g., Ethernet). Ethernet transceivers contain analog electronics that apply signals to the cable and sense collisions.

triggered updates

A heuristic used with distance-vector protocols such as RIP. When a routing table changes, the router sends updates immediately without waiting for the next cycle.

TRPB

(*Truncated Reverse Path Broadcast*) A technique used in data-driven multicasting to forward multicast datagrams. See *broadcast* and *prune*.

TRPF

(*Truncated Reverse Path Forwarding*) A synonym for *TRPB*.

TTL

(*Time To Live*) A technique used in best-effort delivery systems to avoid endlessly looping packets. For example, each IP datagram is assigned an integer time to live when it is created. Each router decrements the time to live field when the datagram arrives, and a router discards any datagram if the time to live counter reaches zero.

tunneling

A technique in which a packet is encapsulated in a high-level protocol and passed across a transport system. The MBONE tunnels each IP multicast datagram inside a conventional IP datagram; a VPN uses tunneling to pass encrypted datagrams between sites. See *IP-in-IP*.

twisted pair Ethernet

The 10Base-T Ethernet wiring scheme that uses twisted pair wires from each computer to a hub. See *thicknet* and *thinnet*.

type of service routing

A routing scheme in which the choice of path depends on the characteristics of the underlying network technology as well as the shortest path to the destination.

UART

(*Universal Asynchronous Receiver and Transmitter*) An electronic device consisting of a single chip that can send or receive characters on asynchronous serial communication lines that use RS232. UARTs are flexible because they have control lines that allow the designer to select parameters like transmission speed, parity, number of stop bits, and modem control. UARTs appear in terminals, modems, and on the I/O boards in computers that connect the computer to terminal(s).

UCBCAST

See *Berkeley broadcast*.

UDP

(*User Datagram Protocol*) The protocol that allows an application program on one machine to send a datagram to an application program on another. UDP uses the Internet Protocol (IP) to deliver datagrams. Conceptually, the important difference between UDP datagrams and IP datagrams is that UDP includes a protocol port number, allowing the sender to distinguish among multiple application programs on a given remote machine.

unicast

A method of addressing and routing in which a packet is delivered to a single destination. Most IP datagrams are sent via unicast. See *multicast*.

universal time

The international standard time reference that was formerly called Greenwich Mean Time. It is also called universal coordinated time.

unnumbered network

A technique for conserving IP network prefixes that leaves a point to point connection between two routers unnumbered.

unreliable delivery

Characteristic of a mechanism that does not guarantee to deliver data without loss, corruption, duplication, or in the same order as it was sent. IP is unreliable.

urgent data

The method used in TCP to send data out of band. A receiver processes urgent data immediately upon receipt.

URI

(*Uniform Resource Identifier*) A generic term used to refer to a URN or a URL.

URL

(*Uniform Resource Locator*) A string that gives the location of a piece of information. The string begins with a protocol type (e.g., FTP) followed by the identification of specific information (e.g., the domain name of a server and the path name to a file on that server).

URN

(*Uniform Resource Name*) A string that gives the location of a piece of information. Unlike a URL, a URN is guaranteed to persist over long periods of time.

UUCP

(*Unix to Unix Copy Program*) An application program developed in the mid 1970s for version 7 UNIX that allows one UNIX timesharing system to copy files to or from another UNIX timesharing system over a single (usually dialup) link. Because UUCP is the basis for electronic mail transfer in UNIX, the term is often used loosely to refer to UNIX mail transfer.

variable-length subnetting

A subnet address assignment scheme in which each physical net in an organization can have a different mask. The alternative is *fixed-length subnetting*.

vBNS

(*very high speed Backbone Network Service*) The 155 Mbps backbone network that was deployed in 1995 and is now used for networking research.

VC

(*Virtual Circuit*) A path through a network from one application to another that is used to send data. The VC, established either by protocol software or manually, provides the illusion of a ''connection''. Although the concept is the same, ATM expands the term to *Virtual Channel*.

vector-distance

Now called *distance-vector*.

very high speed Backbone Network Service

See vBNS.

virtual circuit

The basic abstraction provided by a connection-oriented protocol like TCP. Once a virtual circuit has been created, it stays in effect until explicitly shut down.

VLSM

(*Variable Length Subnet Mask*) A subnet mask used with variable length subnetting.

VPI/VCI

(*Virtual Path Identifier* plus *Virtual Circuit Identifier*) A connection identifier used by ATM; each connection a host opens is assigned a unique VPI/VCI.

VPN

(*Virtual Private Network*) A technology that connects two or more separate sites over the Internet, but allows them to function as if they were a single, private network. VPN software guarantees that although packets travel across the Internet, the contents remains private.

WAN

(*Wide Area Network*) Any physical network technology that spans large geographic distances. Also called long-haul networks, WANs have significantly higher delays and higher costs than networks that operate over shorter distances. See *LAN* and *MAN*.

well-known port

Any of a set of protocol port numbers preassigned for specific uses by transport level protocols (i.e., TCP and UDP). Each server listens at a well-known port, so clients can locate it.

window

See *sliding window*.

window advertisement

A value used by TCP to allow a receiver to tell a sender the size of an available buffer.

Windows Sockets Interface

A variant of the socket API developed by Microsoft. Often called *WINSOCK*.

working group

A group of people in the IETF working on a particular protocol or design issue.

World Wide Web

The large hypermedia service available on the Internet that allows a user to browse information.

WWW

See *World Wide Web*.

X

See *X-Window System*.

X.25

An older protocol standardized by the ITU which was popular in Europe before TCP/IP.

X25NET

(*X.25 NETwork*) A service offered by CSNET that passed IP traffic between a subscriber site and the Internet using X.25.

X.400

The ITU protocol for electronic mail.

XDR

(*eXternal Data Representation*) The standard for a machine-independent data representation. To use XDR, a sender translates from the local machine representation to the standard external representation and a receiver translates from the external representation to the local machine representation.

X-Window System

A software system developed at MIT for presenting and managing output on bit-mapped displays. Each window consists of a rectangular region of the display that contains textual or graphical output from one remote program. A special program called a window manager allows the user to create, move, overlap, and destroy windows.

zero window

See *closed window*.

zone of authority

Term used in the domain name system to refer to the group of names for which a given name server is an authority. Each zone must be supplied by two name servers that have no common point of failure.

Bibliography

ABRAMSON, N. [1970], The ALOHA System – Another Alternative for Computer Communications, *Proceedings of the Fall Joint Computer Conference.*

ANDREWS, D. W., and G. D. SHULTZ [1982], A Token-Ring Architecture for Local Area Networks: An Update, *Proceedings of Fall 82 COMPCON,* IEEE.

ATALLAH, M., and D. E. COMER [June 1998], Algorithms for Variable Length Subnet Address Assignment, *IEEE Transactions on Computers,* vol. 47:6, 693-699.

BBN [1981], A History of the ARPANET: The First Decade, *Technical Report* Bolt, Beranek, and Newman, Inc.

BBN [December 1981], Specification for the Interconnection of a Host and an IMP (revised), *Technical Report 1822,* Bolt, Beranek, and Newman, Inc.

BERTSEKAS D., and R. GALLAGER [1991], *Data Networks,* 2nd edition, Prentice-Hall, Upper Saddle River, New Jersey.

BIAGIONI E., E. COOPER, and R. SANSOM [March 1993], Designing a Practical ATM LAN, *IEEE Network,* 32-39.

BIRRELL, A., and B. NELSON [February 1984], Implementing Remote Procedure Calls, *ACM Transactions on Computer Systems,* 2(1), 39-59.

BLACK, U., [1995], *ATM: Foundation for Broadband Networks,* Prentice-Hall, Upper Saddle River, New Jersey.

BOGGS, D., J. SHOCH, E. TAFT, and R. METCALFE [April 1980], Pup: An Internetwork Architecture, *IEEE Transactions on Communications.*

BORMAN, D., [April 1989], Implementing TCP/IP on a Cray Computer, *Computer Communication Review,* 19(2), 11-15.

BROWNBRIDGE, D., L. MARSHALL, and B. RANDELL [December 1982], The Newcastle Connections or UNIXes of the World Unite!, *Software – Practice and Experience,* 12(12), 1147-1162.

CASNER, S., and S. DEERING [July 1992], First IETF Internet Audiocast, *Computer Communications Review,* 22(3), 92-97.

CERF, V., and E. CAIN [October 1983], The DOD Internet Architecture Model, *Computer Networks.*

CERF, V., and R. KAHN [May 1974], A Protocol for Packet Network Interconnection, *IEEE Transactions of Communications,* Com-22(5).

CERF, V. [October 1989], A History of the ARPANET, *ConneXions, The Interoperability Report,* 480 San Antonio Rd, Suite 100, Mountain View, California.

CHERITON, D. R. [1983], Local Networking and Internetworking in the V-System, *Proceedings of the Eighth Data Communications Symposium.*

CHERITON, D. [August 1986], VMTP: A Transport Protocol for the Next Generation of Communication Systems, *Proceedings of ACM SIGCOMM '86,* 406-415.

CHESSON, G. [June 1987], Protocol Engine Design, *Proceedings of the 1987 Summer USENIX Conference,* Phoenix, AZ.

CHESWICK, W., and S. BELLOVIN [1998], *Firewalls And Internet Security: Repelling the Wiley Hacker,* 2nd edition, Addison-Wesley, Reading, Massachusetts.

CLARK, D., and W. FANG [August 1998], Explicit Allocation Of Best-Effort Packet Delivery Service, *IEEE/ACM Transactions On Networking,* 6(4).

CLARK, D., M. LAMBERT, and L. ZHANG [August 1987], NETBLT: A High Throughput Transport Protocol, *Proceedings of ACM SIGCOMM '87.*

CLARK, D., V. JACOBSON, J. ROMKEY, and H. SALWEN [June 1989], An Analysis of TCP Processing Overhead, *IEEE Communications,* 23-29.

COHEN, D., [1981], On Holy Wars and a Plea for Peace, *IEEE Computer,* 48-54.

COMER, D. E., [1999], *Computer Networks And Internets,* 2nd edition, Prentice-Hall, Upper Saddle River, New Jersey.

COMER, D. E. and J. T. KORB [1983], CSNET Protocol Software: The IP-to-X25 Interface, *Computer Communications Review,* 13(2).

COMER, D. E., T. NARTEN, and R. YAVATKAR [April 1987], The Cypress Network: A Low-Cost Internet Connection Technology, *Technical Report TR-653,* Purdue University, West Lafayette, IN.

COMER, D. E., T. NARTEN, and R. YAVATKAR [1987], The Cypress Coaxial Packet Switch, *Computer Networks and ISDN Systems,* vol. 14:2-5, 383-388.

COMER, D. E. and D. L. STEVENS [1999], *Internetworking With TCP/IP: Volume II: Design, Implementation, and Internals,* 3rd edition, Prentice-Hall, Upper Saddle River, New Jersey.

COMER, D. E. and D. L. STEVENS [1996], *Internetworking With TCP/IP Volume III – Client-Server Programming And Applications, BSD socket version,* 2nd edition, Prentice-Hall, Upper Saddle River, New Jersey.

COMER, D. E. and D. L. STEVENS [1994], *Internetworking With TCP/IP Volume III – Client-Server Programming And Applications, AT&T TLI version,* Prentice-Hall, Upper Saddle River, New Jersey.

COMER, D. E. and D. L. STEVENS [1997], *Internetworking With TCP/IP Volume III – Client-Server Programming And Applications, Windows Sockets version,* Prentice-Hall, Upper Saddle River, New Jersey.

COTTON, I. [1979], Technologies for Local Area Computer Networks, *Proceedings of the Local Area Communications Network Symposium.*

DALAL Y. K., and R. S. PRINTIS [1981], 48-Bit Absolute Internet and Ethernet Host Numbers, *Proceedings of the Seventh Data Communications Symposium.*

DEERING S. E., and D. R. CHERITON [May 1990], Multicast Routing in Datagram Internetworks and Extended LANs, *ACM Transactions on Computer Systems,* 8(2), 85-110.

DEERING, S., D. ESTRIN, D. FARINACCI, V. JACOBSON, C-G LIU, and L. WEI [August 1994], An Architecture for Wide-Area Multicasting Routing, *Proceedings of ACM SIGCOMM '94,* 126-135.

DENNING P. J., [September-October 1989], *The Science of Computing: Worldnet,* in American Scientist, 432-434.

DENNING P. J., [November-December 1989], *The Science of Computing: The ARPANET After Twenty Years,* in American Scientist, 530-534.

DE PRYCKER, M. [1995], *Asynchronous Transfer Mode Solution for Broadband ISDN,* 3rd edition, Prentice-Hall, Upper Saddle River, New Jersey.

DIGITAL EQUIPMENT CORPORATION., INTEL CORPORATION, and XEROX CORPORATION [September 1980], *The Ethernet: A Local Area Network Data Link Layer and Physical Layer Specification.*

DION, J. [Oct. 1980], The Cambridge File Server, *Operating Systems Review,* 14(4), 26-35.

DRIVER, H., H. HOPEWELL, and J. IAQUINTO [September 1979], How the Gateway Regulates Information Control, *Data Communications.*

EDGE, S. W. [1979], Comparison of the Hop-by-Hop and Endpoint Approaches to Network Interconnection, in *Flow Control in Computer Networks,* J-L. GRANGE and M. GIEN (EDS.), North-Holland, Amsterdam, 359-373.

EDGE, S. [1983], An Adaptive Timeout Algorithm for Retransmission Across a Packet Switching Network, *Proceedings of ACM SIGCOMM '83.*

ERIKSSON, H. [August 1994], MBONE: The Multicast Backbone, *Communications of the ACM,* 37(8), 54-60.

FALK, G. [1983], The Structure and Function of Network Protocols, in *Computer Communications, Volume I: Principles,* CHOU, W. (ED.), Prentice-Hall, Upper Saddle River, New Jersey.

FARMER, W. D., and E. E. NEWHALL [1969], An Experimental Distributed Switching System to Handle Bursty Computer Traffic, *Proceedings of the ACM Symposium on Probabilistic Optimization of Data Communication Systems,* 1-33.

FEDOR, M. [June 1988], GATED: A Multi-Routing Protocol Daemon for UNIX, *Proceedings of the 1988 Summer USENIX conference,* San Francisco, California.

FLOYD, S. and V. JACOBSON [August 1993], Random Early Detection Gateways for Congestion Avoidance, *IEEE/ACM Transactions on Networking,* 1(4).

FRANK, H., and W. CHOU [1971], Routing in Computer Networks, *Networks,* 1(1), 99-112.

FULTZ, G. L., and L. KLEINROCK, [June 14-16, 1971], Adaptive Routing Techniques for Store-and-Forward Computer Communication Networks, presented at *IEEE International Conference on Communications,* Montreal, Canada.

GERLA, M., and L. KLEINROCK [April 1980], Flow Control: A Comparative Survey, *IEEE Transactions on Communications.*

HINDEN, R., J. HAVERTY, and A. SHELTZER [September 1983], The DARPA Internet: Interconnecting Heterogeneous Computer Networks with Gateways, *Computer.*

INTERNATIONAL ORGANIZATION FOR STANDARDIZATION [June 1986a], Information processing systems — Open Systems Interconnection — *Transport Service Definition,* International Standard number 8072, ISO, Switzerland.

INTERNATIONAL ORGANIZATION FOR STANDARDIZATION [July 1986b], Information processing systems — Open Systems Interconnection — *Connection Oriented Transport Protocol Specification,* International Standard number 8073, ISO, Switzerland.

INTERNATIONAL ORGANIZATION FOR STANDARDIZATION [May 1987a], Information processing systems — Open Systems Interconnection — *Specification of Basic Specification of Abstract Syntax Notation One (ASN.1),* International Standard number 8824, ISO, Switzerland.

INTERNATIONAL ORGANIZATION FOR STANDARDIZATION [May 1987b], Information processing systems — Open Systems Interconnection — *Specification of Basic Encoding Rules for Abstract Syntax Notation One (ASN.1),* International Standard number 8825, ISO, Switzerland.

INTERNATIONAL ORGANIZATION FOR STANDARDIZATION [May 1988a], Information processing systems — Open Systems Interconnection — *Management Information Service Definition, Part 2: Common Management Information Service,* Draft International Standard number 9595-2, ISO, Switzerland.

INTERNATIONAL ORGANIZATION FOR STANDARDIZATION [May 1988a], Information processing systems — Open Systems Interconnection — *Management Information Protocol Definition, Part 2: Common Management Information Protocol,* Draft International Standard number 9596-2.

JACOBSON, V. [August 1988], Congestion Avoidance and Control, *Proceedings ACM SIGCOMM '88.*

JAIN, R. [January 1985], On Caching Out-of-Order Packets in Window Flow Controlled Networks, *Technical Report,* DEC-TR-342, Digital Equipment Corporation.

JAIN, R. [March 1986], Divergence of Timeout Algorithms for Packet Retransmissions, *Proceedings Fifth Annual International Phoenix Conference on Computers and Communications,* Scottsdale, AZ.

JAIN, R. [October 1986], A Timeout-Based Congestion Control Scheme for Window Flow-Controlled Networks, *IEEE Journal on Selected Areas in Communications,* Vol. SAC-4, no. 7.

JAIN, R., K. RAMAKRISHNAN, and D-M. CHIU [August 1987], Congestion Avoidance in Computer Networks With a Connectionless Network Layer. *Technical Report,* DEC-TR-506, Digital Equipment Corporation.

JAIN, R. [1991], *The Art of Computer Systems Performance Analysis,* John Wiley & Sons, New York.

JAIN, R. [May 1992], Myths About Congestion Management in High-speed Networks, *Internetworking: Research and Experience,* 3(3), 101-113.

JAIN, R. [1994], *FDDI Handbook; High-Speed Networking Using Fiber and Other Media,* Addison Wesley, Reading, Massachusetts.

JENNINGS, D. M., L. H. LANDWEBER, and I. H. FUCHS [February 28, 1986], Computer Networking for Scientists and Engineers, *Science* vol 231, 941-950.

JUBIN, J. and J. TORNOW [January 1987], The DARPA Packet Radio Network Protocols, *IEEE Proceedings.*

KAHN, R. [November 1972], Resource-Sharing Computer Communications Networks, *Proceedings of the IEEE,* 60(11), 1397-1407.

KARN, P., H. PRICE, and R. DIERSING [May 1985], Packet Radio in the Amateur Service, *IEEE Journal on Selected Areas in Communications,*

KARN, P., and C. PARTRIDGE [August 1987], Improving Round-Trip Time Estimates in Reliable Transport Protocols, *Proceedings of ACM SIGCOMM '87.*

KAUFMAN, C., PERLMAN, R., and SPECINER, M. [1995], *Network Security: Private Communication in a Public World,* Prentice-Hall, Upper Saddle River, New Jersey.

KENT, C., and J. MOGUL [August 1987], Fragmentation Considered Harmful, *Proceedings of ACM SIGCOMM '87.*

LAMPSON, B. W., M. PAUL, and H. J. SIEGERT (EDS.) [1981], *Distributed Systems - Architecture and Implementation (An Advanced Course),* Springer-Verlag, Berlin.

LAMPSON, B. W., V. SRINIVASAN, and G. VARGHESE [June 1999], IP Lookups Using Multiway and Multicolumn Search, *IEEE/ACM Transactions on Networking,* vol 7, 324-334.

LANZILLO, A. L., and C. PARTRIDGE [January 1989], Implementation of Dial-up IP for UNIX Systems, *Proceedings 1989 Winter USENIX Technical Conference,* San Diego, CA.

LEFFLER, S., M. McKUSICK, M. KARELS, and J. QUARTERMAN [1996], *The Design and Implementation of the 4.4BSD UNIX Operating System,* Addison Wesley, Reading, Massachusetts.

MCNAMARA, J. [1998], *Technical Aspects of Data Communications,* 2nd edition, Digital Press, Digital Equipment Corporation, Bedford, Massachusetts.

MCQUILLAN, J. M., I. RICHER, and E. ROSEN [May 1980], The New Routing Algorithm for the ARPANET, *IEEE Transactions on Communications,* (COM-28), 711-719.

METCALFE, R. M., and D. R. BOGGS [July 1976], Ethernet: Distributed Packet Switching for Local Computer Networks, *Communications of the ACM,* 19(7), 395-404.

MILLS, D., and H-W. BRAUN [August 1987], The NSFNET Backbone Network, *Proceedings of ACM SIGCOMM '87.*

MORRIS, R. [1979], Fixing Timeout Intervals for Lost Packet Detection in Computer Communication Networks, *Proceedings AFIPS National Computer Conference,* AFIPS Press, Montvale, New Jersey.

NAGLE, J. [April 1987], On Packet Switches With Infinite Storage, *IEEE Transactions on Communications,* Vol. COM-35:4.

NARTEN, T. [Sept. 1989], Internet Routing, *Proceedings ACM SIGCOMM '89.*

NEEDHAM, R. M. [1979], System Aspects of the Cambridge Ring, *Proceedings of the ACM Seventh Symposium on Operating System Principles,* 82-85.

NEWMAN, P., G. MINSHALL, and T. L. LYON [April 1998], IP Switching — ATM Under IP, *IEEE Transactions on Networking,* Vol. 6:2, 117-129.

OPPEN, D., and Y. DALAL [October 1981], The Clearinghouse: A Decentralized Agent for Locating Named Objects, Office Products Division, XEROX Corporation.

PARTRIDGE, C. [June 1986], Mail Routing Using Domain Names: An Informal Tour, *Proceedings of the 1986 Summer USENIX Conference,* Atlanta, GA.

PARTRIDGE, C. [June 1987], Implementing the Reliable Data Protocol (RDP), *Proceedings of the 1987 Summer USENIX Conference,* Phoenix, Arizona.

PARTRIDGE, C. [1994], *Gigabit Networking,* Addison-Wesley, Reading, Massachusetts.

PELTON, J. [1995], *Wireless and Satellite Telecommunications,* Prentice-Hall, Upper Saddle River, New Jersey.

PERLMAN, R. [2000], *Interconnections: Bridges and Routers,* 2nd edition, Addison-Wesley, Reading, Massachusetts.

PETERSON, L. [1985], *Defining and Naming the Fundamental Objects in a Distributed Message System,* Ph.D. Dissertation, Purdue University, West Lafayette, Indiana.

PETERSON, L., and B. DAVIE, [1999], *Computer Networks: A Systems Approach,* 2nd edition, Morgan Kaufmann, San Francisco, CA.

PIERCE, J. R. [1972], Networks for Block Switching of Data, *Bell System Technical Journal,* 51.

POSTEL, J. B. [April 1980], Internetwork Protocol Approaches, *IEEE Transactions on Communications,* COM-28, 604-611.

POSTEL, J. B., C. A. SUNSHINE, and D. CHEN [1981], The ARPA Internet Protocol, *Computer Networks.*

QUARTERMAN, J. S., and J. C. HOSKINS [October 1986], Notable Computer Networks, *Communications of the ACM,* 29(10).

RAMAKRISHNAN, K. and R. JAIN [May 1990], A Binary Feedback Scheme For Congestion Avoidance In Computer Networks, *ACM Transactions on Computer Systems,* 8(2), 158-181.

REYNOLDS, J., J. POSTEL, A. R. KATZ, G. G. FINN, and A. L. DESCHON [October 1985], The DARPA Experimental Multimedia Mail System, *IEEE Computer.*

RITCHIE, D. M. [October 1984], A Stream Input-Output System, *AT&T Bell Laboratories Technical Journal,* 63(8), 1987-1910.

RITCHIE, D. M., and K. THOMPSON [July 1974], The UNIX Time-Sharing System, *Communications of the ACM,* 17(7), 365-375; revised and reprinted in *Bell System Technical Journal,* 57(6), [July-August 1978], 1905-1929.

ROSE, M. [1993], *The Internet Message: Closing The Book with Electronic Mail,* Prentice-Hall, Upper Saddle River, New Jersey.

SALTZER, J. [1978], Naming and Binding of Objects, *Operating Systems, An Advanced Course,* Springer-Verlag, 99-208.

SALTZER, J. [April 1982], Naming and Binding of Network Destinations, *International Symposium on Local Computer Networks,* IFIP/T.C.6, 311-317.

SALTZER, J., D. REED, and D. CLARK [November 1984], End-to-End Arguments in System Design, *ACM Transactions on Computer Systems,* 2(4), 277-288.

SHOCH, J. F. [1978], Internetwork Naming, Addressing, and Routing, *Proceedings of COMPCON.*

SHOCH, J. F., Y. DALAL, and D. REDELL [August 1982], Evolution of the Ethernet Local Computer Network, *Computer.*

SOLOMON, J. [1997], *Mobile IP: The Internet Unplugged,* Prentice-Hall, Upper Saddle River, New Jersey.

SOLOMON, M., L. LANDWEBER, and D. NEUHEGEN [1982], The CSNET Name Server, *Computer Networks* (6), 161-172.

SRINIVASAN, V., and G. VARGHESE [February 1999], Fast Address Lookups Using Controlled Prefix Expansion, *ACM Transactions on Computer Systems*, vol. 17, 1-40.

STALLINGS, W. [1997], *Local and Metropolitan Area Networks,* Prentice-Hall, Upper Saddle River, New Jersey.

STALLINGS, W. [1998], *High-Speed Networks: TCP/IP and ATM Design Principles,* Prentice-Hall, Upper Saddle River, New Jersey.

STEVENS, W. R. [1998], *UNIX Network Programming,* 2nd edition, Prentice-Hall, Upper Saddle River, New Jersey.

SWINEHART, D., G. MCDANIEL, and D. R. BOGGS [December 1979], WFS: A Simple Shared File System for a Distributed Environment, *Proceedings of the Seventh Symposium on Operating System Principles,* 9-17.

TICHY, W., and Z. RUAN [June 1984], Towards a Distributed File System, *Proceedings of Summer 84 USENIX Conference,* Salt Lake City, Utah, 87-97.

TOMLINSON. R. S. [1975], Selecting Sequence Numbers, *Proceedings ACM SIGOPS/SIGCOMM Interprocess Communication Workshop,* 11-23, 1975.

WATSON, R. [1981], Timer-Based Mechanisms in Reliable Transport Protocol Connection Management, *Computer Networks*, North-Holland Publishing Company.

WEINBERGER, P. J. [1985], The UNIX Eighth Edition Network File System, *Proceedings 1985 ACM Computer Science Conference,* 299-301.

WELCH, B., and J. OSTERHAUT [May 1986], Prefix Tables: A Simple Mechanism for Locating Files in a Distributed System, *Proceedings IEEE Sixth International Conference on Distributed Computing Systems,* 1845-189.

WILKES, M. V., and D. J. WHEELER [May 1979], The Cambridge Digital Communication Ring, *Proceedings Local Area Computer Network Symposium.*

XEROX [1981], Internet Transport Protocols, *Report XSIS 028112,* Xerox Corporation, Office Products Division, Network Systems Administration Office, 3333 Coyote Hill Road, Palo Alto, California.

ZHANG, L. [August 1986], Why TCP Timers Don't Work Well, *Proceedings of ACM SIGCOMM '86.*

Index